THE LAW, PRINCIPLES, AND PRACTICE OF LEGAL ETHICS

FIRST EDITION

THE LAW, PRINCIPLES, AND PRACTICE OF LEGAL ETHICS

FIRST EDITION

VICTORIA VULETICH &

NELSON P. MILLER

VANDEPLAS PUBLISHING LLC

UNITED STATES OF AMERICA

The Law, Principles, and Practice of Legal Ethics

Vuletich, Victoria, and Nelson P. Miller

Published by:

Vandeplas Publishing LLC – July 2011

801 International Parkway, 5th Floor
Lake Mary, FL. 32746
USA

www.vandeplaspublishing.com

ISBN: 978-1-60042-142-6

[I]t is apparent, that the framers of the constitution contemplated [the Constitution] as a rule for the government of courts, as well as of the legislature.

Why otherwise does it direct the judges to take an oath to support it? This oath certainly applies, in an especial manner, to their conduct in their official character. How immoral to impose it on them, if they were to be used as the instruments, and the knowing instruments, for violating what they swear to support?

The oath of office, too, imposed by the legislature, is completely demonstrative of the legislative opinion on this subject. It is in these words, "I do solemnly swear that I will administer justice without respect to persons, and do equal right to the poor and to the rich; and that I will faithfully and impartially discharge all the duties incumbent on me as according to the best of my abilities and understanding, agreeably to the constitution, and laws of the United States."

Why does a judge swear to discharge his duties agreeably to the constitution of the United States, if that constitution forms no rule for his government? if it is closed upon him, and cannot be inspected by him?

If such be the real state of things, this is worse than solemn mockery. To prescribe, or to take this oath, becomes equally a crime.

> — *Chief Justice John Marshall in Marbury v. Madison, 5 U.S. 137, 180 (1803)*

PREFACE

There was a time when farmers on the Great Plains, at the first sign of a blizzard, would run a rope from the back door out to the barn. They all knew stories of people who had wandered off and been frozen to death, having lost sight of home in a whiteout while still in their own backyards.

Today we live in a blizzard of another sort.... We all know stories of people who have wandered off ... and been separated from their own souls, losing their moral bearings.... They make headlines because they take so many innocents down with them. [PARKER J. PALMER, A HIDDEN WHOLENESS—A JOURNEY TOWARD AN UNDIVIDED LIFE (Jossey-Bass 2009).]

Law remains a highly engaging and valuable profession. Yet many would also say that lawyers and law students are in crisis. A recent president of the Association of American Law Schools noted in her address "pervasive discontent with legal practive both within and outside the bar."[1] Lawyers suffer from the highest rates of depression after adjusting for socio-demographic factors. Lawyers are three to four times more likely to suffer from major depressive disorder and are at a greater risk of alcoholism and drug use than the general population.[2] Study indicates that as many as 44 percent of law students meet the criteria for clinically significant levels of psychological distress.[3] Law students also report significantly higher levels of alcohol and drug use than college and high school graduates

---

[1] Deborah L. Rhode, *The Professional Responsibility of Professional Schools,* ASSN. AMER. L. SCHOOLS NEWSLETTER (Feb. 1998).

[2] Peterson, *Stemming the Tide of Law Student Depression: What Law Schools Need to Learn From the Science of Positive Psychology,* 9 YALE J. HEALTH POLICY L. & ETHICS 357 (2009), *citing* MARTIN E.P. SELIGMAN, AUTHENTIC HAPPINESS 117 (2002), and Eaton, *Occupations and the Prevalence of Major Depressive Disorder,* 32 J. OCCUPATIONAL MED. 1079, 1083 (1990).

[3] Peterson, *supra* note 1,, *citing* Lynda L. Murdoch, *Psychological Distress and Substance Abuse in Law Students: The Role of Moral Orientation and Interpersonal Style* 87 (unpublished Ph.D dissertation, Simon Fraser University).

of the same age do, while their alcohol use increases between their second and third year of law school.[4]

The cause of the crisis in lawyer and law student mental health is complicated and multi-faceted, the subject of much research and commentary. Study and commentary often cite as one cause, the constant moral and ethical challenges that lawyers face. In law practice, the opportunity for shortcuts abounds, as do the incentives to take them.

The culture of the law profession would have lawyers bifurcate morality into one set of standards governing law practice and a second set of personal standards. Professional culture encourages lawyers to believe that ethics consists of technical rules one must follow even when contrary to personal morality, not to mention counterintuitive to generally accepted moral standards. Professional culture does not help law students and lawyers reconcile these conflicting expectations, though reconciliation of professional with personal standards is something that lawyers must do every day throughout a law career. Empirical study indicates that personal values, particularly honesty and equal treatment, predict lawyer response to ethics issues.[5]

Many commentators have already observed that approaching legal ethics in such a hypertechnical, academic, and "objective" process, devoid of and even contrary to personal and societal morals, threatens lawyers' professional and personal integrity, career and life satisfaction, and mental and physical health. It also undermines the respect and credibility of the law profession in the eyes of the public.[6] Studies suggest that in contrast to other professional programs, law school tends to arrest the natural development of a law student's morality and that lawyers do not resume that development once in law practice.[7]

This text attempts to bridge this cultural divide—to provide a framework for law students to digest and adopt the profession's

---

[4] Peterson, *supra* note 1, citing, Hess, *Heads and Hearts: The Teaching and Learning Environment in Law School*, 52 J. LEGAL EDUC. 75 (2002).

[5] Josephine Palermo & Adrian Evans, *Relationships Between Personal Values and Reported Behavior on Ethical Scenarios for Law Students*, 25 BEHAV. SCI. & THE LAW 121-136 (2007).

[6] Elkins, *The Moral Labyrinth of Zealous Advocacy*, 21 CAP. U. L. REV. 735 (1992)

[7] *See* WILLIAM M. SULLIVAN, ANNE COLBY, JUDITH WELCH WEGNER, LLOYD BOND, & LEE S. SHULMAN, EDUCATING LAWYERS: PREPARATION FOR THE PROFESSION OF LAW 133 (Jossey-Bass 2007); *see also* RICHARD A. POSNER, THE PROBLEMATICS OF MORAL AND LEGAL THEORY vii-viii (1999) (law school associated with a decline in interest in public-interest law).

conduct rules while continuing to develop and adhere to their personal moral standards. One way in which we pursue this goal is to organize the subject of professional responsibility by the attributes that the law and rules represent. We want you to explore, organize, recall, practice, and evaluate the law and rules of professional responsibility by how well their moral fields serve the attributes you want to preserve and develop.

There is a connection between the professional and personal, between the rules and morality. We hope to make it more evident for you. Professional responsibility is a matter of taking on a professional identity, of becoming someone, not merely a matter of keeping one's conduct barely within the law and rules. We hope to highlight for you critical intersections where you can choose whom you want to become as a lawyer and person, the two roles, professional and personal, working together. There should be no better way to learn and apply the rules than by connecting them with your personal moral and ethical ambition. This book goes beyond the usual *rules* approach to professional responsibility, or even the *skills* approach, favoring *judgment* and *identity* approaches that those who study legal education more and more advocate.[8]

We did not choose the moral field and attributes, by the way. We asked you, Professional Responsibility students, to let us know what personal, professional, and ethical ambition you were bringing to law school, by writing your own personal codes. We then collected and studied those codes, discovering that law students bring to law school remarkably rich and varied, but also uniformly appropriate, moral and ethical ambition.[9] Although you gave us dozens of other wonderful moral and ethical commitments, we chose some of your most popular ones including obedience, citizenship, respect, mastery, reputation, relationship, loyalty, honesty, candor, access, provision, responsibility, and authority.

This book has some other distinctive features. It offers learning objectives to help you focus and concentrate on what you should hope to achieve in each section, indeed what law-firm managing partners

---

[8] *See, e.g.,* Michael Robertson, *Challenges in the Design of Legal Ethics Learning Systems: An Educational Perspective,* 8 Legal Ethics 222. 226-229 (2005).
[9] *See* Nelson P. Miller, *Meta-Ethical Competence as a Lawyer Skill: Variant Ethics Affecting Lawyer and Client Decision-Making,* 9 COOLEY J. PRAC. & CLIN. L. 91, 93-96 (2007).

hope that you learn in this course.[10]   It also offers practitioner biographies to give you models of how lawyers develop ethical identity. We also help you analyze the rules of professional conduct into memorable statements. Our analysis shows that the rules are literally off the charts in their reading difficulty, meaning in the length and complexity of their sentences and terms. Finally, the book offers several practice vignettes to help you place your learning in its practice context.

So, welcome to this journey of career-long moral reconciliation. We hope that you find within these pages, useful and meaningful tools to help you in this most important of journeys. We hope you appreciate this book's design, even as we welcome your comments, evaluation, and encouragement.

---

[10] *See* Nelson Miller and Victoria Vuletich, *Who Is the Customer and What Are We Selling? Employer-Based Objectives for the Ethical Competence of Law School Graduates*, 33 J. LEGAL PROF. 223 (2009).

ACKNOWLEDGMENTS

We wish to thank and acknowledge the work of many professors at the Thomas M. Cooley Law School. Particular thanks go to Associate Dean of Students and Professionalism Amy Timmer, Associate Dean of the Ann Arbor Campus Joan Vestrand, Assistant Dean Martha Moore, Professional Responsibility Department Chair Nancy Wonch, and Professional Responsibility Department members Peter Kempl and Florise Neville-Ewell.

The authors also wish to thank Cooley's founder, Justice Thomas Brennan, and its visionary president and dean, Don LeDuc. Justice Brennan conceived Cooley's distinctive mission. President and Dean LeDuc brought it to unparalleled success as the nation's largest law school. There would not have been the opportunity for this work if it were not for their vision and leadership.

The authors also wish to thank and acknowledge the work of Cooley's Associate Dean of Libraries Duane Strojney and Faculty Center Director Vickie Eggers. Cooley Law School brings extraordinary staff expertise to the study and development of its educational program. Cooley's instructional-support services are the best within the legal academy.

The authors also wish to thank and acknowledge the work of Cooley librarians Aletha Honsowitz, John Michaud, Julianne Claydon, and Amy Ash. The authors also owe a considerable debt of gratitude to research assistants Samantha Darrow, Kaitlyn Trizna, and Joseph Hogue for work on this book.

SUMMARY OF CONTENTS

Preface vii
Acknowledgments xi
Table of Cases xxvii
Table of Rules xl

Chapter I. Obedience 1
    A.   Perspectives on Responsibility 2
    B.   Sources of Professional Responsibility 10
    C.   Lawyer Discipline 22
    D.   Professionalism 35
    E.   Reporting Misconduct 37

Chapter II. Citizenship 47
    A.   Organization of the Bar 48
    B.   Bar Admission 50
           1.   Character. 52
           2.   Fitness 67
    C.   Unauthorized Practice 74

Chapter III. Relationship 93
    A.   Representation 94
    B.   Scope and Allocation 100
    C.   Competence 114
    D.   Diligence 131

Chapter IV. Authenticity 141
    A.   Communication 142
    B.   Advice and Counsel 149
    C.   Organization as Client 161
    D.   Confidentiality 168

Chapter V. Productivity 189

A. Fees 190
B. Client Property 214
C. Lawyer Supervision 219
D. Supervision of Nonlawyer Assistants 228
E. Sale of a Law Practice 232

Chapter VI. Respect 235

A. Toward Others 236
B. For Opposing Parties and Counsel 243
C. As Prosecutor 264
D. For Judges 273

Chapter VII. Honesty 279

A. Statements to Others 280
B. Unrepresented Persons 286
C. Represented Persons 291
D. Statements in Tribunals 300

Chapter VIII. Integrity 325

A. Meritorious Contentions 326
B. Expediting Litigation 340
C. The Tribunal's Decorum 343
D. Role Consistency 361

Chapter IX. Loyalty 371

A. Conflicts Framework 371
B. Current-Client Conflicts 374
C. Former-Client Conflicts 400
D. Prospective-Client Conflicts 407

Chapter X. Transparency 413

A. Imputed Conflicts 414
B. Conflicts of Government Lawyers 422
C. Conflicts of Third-Party Neutrals 432
D. Evaluations for Third Persons 446

Chapter XI. Reputation 453

A. Communication 454
B. Soliciting 459
C. Marketing 470
D. Specializing 491

Chapter XII. Access 497
    A.   Pro Bono Service...498
    B.   Appointments...505
    C.   Legal-Services Organization...............................510
    D.   Inclusive Representation.......................................518

Chapter XIII. Authority.. 533
    A.   Regulating Judges...534
    B.   Promoting Independence.......................................541
    C.   Upholding Law..542
    D.   Personal Conduct...561
    E.   Judicial Campaigns..568

Conclusion 577

Appendices 581
    I.   CALIFORNIA RULES OF PROFESSIONAL CONDUCT 581
    II. DELAWARE RULES OF PROFESSIONAL CONDUCT.............................602
    III. MICHIGAN RULES OF PROFESSIONAL CONDUCT 643

Index 675

TABLE OF CONTENTS

Preface vii

Acknowledgments xi

Table of Cases xxvii

Table of Rules xl

Chapter I. Obedience 1
   A. Perspectives on Responsibility 2
        Significance 2
        Necessity 2
        Complexity 3
        Misconduct 3
        Reflexivity 4
        Legacy 4
        Identity 5
        Reputation 5
        Guidance 5
        Worldviews 6
        Choices 6
        Pragmatism 6
        Instrumentalism 7
        Morality 7
        Realism 8
        Humanism 9
        Faith 9
   B. Sources of Professional Responsibility 10
        Lawyer Independence 10
        Financing Practice 11
        In re Guirard 12
        Model Rules 17
        Conduct Rules 18
        Types of Rules 19
        Reading Rules 19
        Ethics Opinions 20
        Statutes 21
        Regulations 21

C. Lawyer Discipline...22
  Disciplinary Authority..22
  Goals of Discipline..23
  Levels of Discipline...23
  In re James H. Himmel..24
  Procedures..27
  Initial Review..28
  Request for Investigation...28
  State ex rel. Oklahoma Bar Assn. v. Kinsey...30
  Disclosure...33
  Representation...33
  Charges..33
  Hearing..34
  Other Enforcement...34
  Mixed Legal Services...35
D. Professionalism...35
  Significance..35
  Style...36
  Beyond the Minimum...36
E. Reporting Misconduct...37
  The Privilege of Self-Regulation..37
  Duty to Report...37
  In re Riehlmann...38
  Question of Fitness...43
  Inferring Knowledge..43
  Privileged Information..44
  Time and Place for Reporting...44
  Terminology...45

Chapter II. Citizenship...47
A. Organization of the Bar...48
  Bar Associations..48
  American Bar Association...48
  Local Bar Associations...49
  Affinity Bar Associations...49
  State Bar Associations..49
B. Bar Admission..50
  Licensure..50
  Multistate Professional Responsibility Exam...51
  Timing..51
  Reciprocity...51
  1. Character...52
     Law School Admission..52
     Bar Application...52
     Definition of Good Character..53
     Crimes...54
     In re Hamm...54
     Representations...60
     Finances..60
     Personal Behavior...61
     In re Application of Converse...61

2. Fitness...67
   Disability 67
   Substance Abuse 68
   In the Matter of the Reinstatement Petition of Feinberg.............68
   Substance Abuse and Mental Health 72
   Compensating Tools 72
   Service to Others..74

C. Unauthorized Practice...74
   Non-lawyers 74
   Defining Practice...75
   The Florida Bar v. We The People Forms and Service Ctr. 76
   Administrative Representation 80
   Self-Representation..81
   Shenkman v. Bragman 81
   Licensed Practitioners 83
   Birbrower, Montalbano, Condon & Frank, P.C. v. Superior Ct.......83
   Temporary Admission 88
   Multijurisdictional Practice 89
   Federal and Foreign Lawyers 90
   Restrictions on Practice 90

Chapter III. Relationship...93
A. Representation..94
   Accepting Representation..96
   Declining Representation...96
   Grounds for Declining 97
   Completing Representation..97
   Terminating Representation...98
   Withdrawing from Litigation...98
   Grounds for Withdrawal..99
   Retaining Liens...99
   Law Firm Departures 100

B. Scope and Allocation...100
   Distinguishing Scope from Allocation.......................................100
   Allocation of Authority 101
   Decisions to Settle 102
   Luethke v. Suhr...102
   Endorsement...106
   Limited-Scope Representation..107
   Unbundling Services 107
   Opinion 05-06 108
   Appeals...112
   Withdrawal from Litigation 113
   Declining Cases 113

C. Competence..114
   Conduct Rule 114
   Multiple Dimensions 115
   Acquiring Proficiency 116
   Incompetence's Consequences 116
   Excusable Neglect...117
   Martinelli v. Farm-Rite, Inc...117

In re Harris.. 120
Malpractice.. 122
Archuleta v. Hughes... 123
Errors in Judgment 124
Non-Client Liability... 125
Malpractice Causation... 126
Jones Motor Co. v. Holtkamp, Liese, Beckemeier & Childress, P.C....... 127
Malpractice Challenges.. 129
Malpractice Defenses... 130
Malpractice Insurance.. 130
Malpractice Policies... 130
D. Diligence..131
Amco Builders & Developers, Inc. v. Team Ace Joint Venture............ 132
Extraordinary Circumstances... 134
Limiting Liability.. 135
Settling Liability... 135
Ineffective Assistance of Counsel.. 135
Rompilla v. Beard.. 136

Chapter IV. Authenticity **141**
A. Communication..142
Informed Consent.. 143
In re Harris.. 143
B. Advice and Counsel 149
Independent Professional Judgment 149
In re Coffey's Case 150
Insurance Counsel.. 154
In re Rules of Prof. Conduct and Insurer Imposed Billing 155
Candid Advice... 158
In re Harrison.. 159
Broader Advice.. 160
C. Organization as Client..161
Authorized Constituents... 162
Reporting Up... 163
Reporting Out.. 163
Dual Representation 165
Divided Representation 166
Resolution Submitted by Council Members Jones and Kenyatta 166
D. Confidentiality...168
People v. Meredith 169
Implied Authorization... 173
Preventing Bodily Harm 174
In re Goebel.. 174
Mitigating Crime.. 177
McClure v. Thompson... 178
Preventing Crime or Fraud 182
In re Lane's Case... 183
Self-Protective Measures.. 186
Organization Clients.. 187
Attorney-Client Privilege.. 187

Chapter V. Productivity 189
A. Fees 190
Type of Fees 190
Sheresky Aronson & Mayefsky, LLP v. Whitmore 191
Attitude Toward Fees 193
Regulation of Fees 194
Reasonableness of Fees 195
In the Matter of Green 196
Determining Reasonableness 200
Billing Practices 200
Documenting Fees 201
Reasonable Expenses 201
Retainer Fees 202
Non-Refundable Fees 202
Charging Liens 203
Retaining Liens 203
Engagement Fees 203
Contingency Fees 204
Culpepper & Carroll, PLLC v. Cole 206
Reasonableness of Contingency Fees 208
In re Calahan 209
Quantum Meruit 211
Keys v. Mercy Hospital 212
Fee Divisions 213
Money Laundering 214
B. Client Property 214
Fiduciary Practice 214
In the Matter of Disciplinary Proceedings Against Strnad 216
Rule Against Commingling 217
Lawyer Trust Accounts 218
Interest on Lawyer Trust Accounts 218
Client-Protection Funds 219
C. Lawyer Supervision 219
Managerial Authority 219
In re Cohen 220
Subordinate Lawyers 223
In re Lightfoot 224
Mitigating Factors 228
D. Supervising Nonlawyer Assistants 228
Delegating Responsibility 228
In re Meltzer 229
Conduct Compatible with Lawyer Obligations 231
Supervising Trust Accounts 232
E. Sale of a Law Practice 232
Client Autonomy 232
Conditions of Sale 233

Chapter VI. Respect 235
A. Toward Others 236
The Public 236

Limitations 237
In re Campbell 238
Obtaining Evidence 241
Inadvertent Document Disclosures 241
Metadata 242
Waiver 242
B. For Opposing Parties and Counsel 243
Respect for Adversaries 243
Jayhawk Capital Mgt., LLC v. LSB Indus., Inc. ... 244
Zealous Advocacy 245
Traxler v. Ford Motor Co 246
Discovery Abuses 251
Threatening Opposing Counsel 252
Economics of Unfairness 252
Lee v. American Eagle Airlines, Inc 253
Discipline for Unfairness 259
Matter of Geisler 259
Interfering with Witnesses 262
Advising Agents 263
Violating Court Rules 263
Trial Procedures 264
C. As Prosecutor 264
Special Duties 264
Suppressing Evidence 265
The North Carolina State Bar v. Nifong 266
Public Statements 270
Exoneration 270
Cross-Examination 271
Plea Negotiation 272
Federal Prosecutors 272
D. For Judges 273
Knowing False Statements 273
Dayton Bar Assn. v. O'Brien 273
Criticizing Judges 276
Judicial Campaigns 276

Chapter VII. Honesty 279
A. Statements to Others 280
Course of the Representation 280
Matter of Apt. 281
Knowledge of Falsity 283
Participating in or Authorizing Ruses 284
In the Matter of Leyh 284
Immaterial Falsehoods 285
Disclosure to Prevent Crime or Fraud 285
B. Unrepresented Persons 286
Disclosing Interests 286
In re Pautler 287
Advising the Unrepresented 290
C. Represented Persons 291
Preventing Overreaching 291

Communication Authorized by Law 292
Communication Between Clients.. 292
Inducing Others 293
Obtaining Consent of Counsel.. 294
State ex rel. Oklahoma Bar Assn. v. Harper 295
Second Opinions.. 298
Management Employees of Represented Corporations 298
Other Employees of Represented Corporations 299

D. Statements in Tribunals...300
Candor Toward Tribunals 300
False Statements 301
In re Discipline of Wilka 301
Misleading Silence.. 305
Temptation Abounds.. 305
Defining Tribunals 306
Beyond Representation... 306
In re Barker 307
Correcting False Statements... 309
Disclosing Legal Authority... 310
Massey v. Prince George's County 310
Offering False Evidence.. 313
In re Bailey 314
In re Page 316
Knowledge of Falsity.. 318
Refusing to Offer False Evidence 319
Constitutional Rights to Testify 319
Criminal or Fraudulent.. 320
Ex-Parte Proceedings 320
Ndreko v. Ridge 321

Chapter VIII. Integrity...325
A. Meritorious Contentions 326
Bringing and Defending Proceedings... 326
Parallel Sanctions 327
In re Caranchini.. 327
Determining Frivolousness... 331
Reasonable Investigation 332
Lawyer Disciplinary Bd. v. Neely 332
Extending, Modifying, or Reversing Law... 336
Smith v. Commonwealth... 336
Client Directives 339
Defending Criminal Cases 340
B. Expediting Litigation..340
Dilatory Actions to Impede 340
Columbus Bar Assn. v. Finneran 341
Causes and Motives for Delay.. 342
Types of Delay 343
C. The Tribunal's Decorum..343
Improper Influence and Communications 343
United States v. Thoreen 344
In the Matter of Abbott.. 348

Interviewing Jurors.. 351
Cook v. American Steamship 352
Means Prohibited by Law... 355
Ex Parte Communications.. 356
Trial Publicity... 356
Prejudicing a Proceeding... 357
In re Duncan 358
Timing Is Everything... 360
Gag Orders 360
Permitted Extrajudicial Statements 361

D. Role Consistency...361
Advocate as Witness 361
In re Atwater 362
Permissible Dual Roles 364
Disqualification as Substantial Hardship 364
D.J. Inv. Group, L.L.C. v. DAE/Westbrook, L.L.C. 365
Tactical Abuse 368
Advocacy in Nonadjudicative Proceedings 368

Chapter IX. Loyalty 371
A. Conflicts Framework 371
Loyalty's Value 371
Specificity of Conflicts Rules.. 372
Difficulty of Conflicts Rules.. 372
Conflict-Recognition Techniques... 372
Client Consent to Conflicts... 373
Client Relations and Expense.. 373

B. Current-Client Conflicts...374
Concurrent Conflicts of Interest.. 374
State ex rel. Nebraska State Bar v. Frank.. 375
Haley v. Boles 377
Positional Conflicts 378
Attorney General v. Michigan Public Service Commn. 379
Nonconsentable Concurrent Conflicts 382
Multiple Adverse Representations 382
Informed Consent.. 383
Holloway v. Arkansas 383
Transactional Conflicts.. 387
Specific Conflicts... 388
Passante v. McWilliam 390
Business Transactions with a Client 392
Substantial Gifts from Clients 393
In re Lupo 394
Financial Assistance 397
Collateral Compensation 398
Aggregate Settlements 398
Limiting and Settling Malpractice Claims 399
Sexual Relations... 399

C. Former-Client Conflicts 400
Persistent Loyalty.. 400
Distinguishing Current from Former Clients 401

Substantially Related Matters 401
Haagen-Dazs Co. v. Perche No! Gelato, Inc. 402
Imputed Disqualification 406
Lawyers Changing Firms 406
D. Prospective-Client Conflicts 407
Loyalty to Prospective Clients 407
Sturdivant v. Sturdivant 408
Intake Procedures 411
Imputed Disqualification 411

Chapter X. Transparency 413
A. Imputed Conflicts 414
Imputed Disqualification in Firms 414
Associated in a Firm 415
Considering Screening 415
Amendment to Permit Screening 416
Adequacy of Screening 416
Hitachi, Ltd. v. Tatung 417
Lawyers Leaving a Firm 421
Lawyers Joining a Firm 422
B. Conflicts of Government Lawyers 422
Government Service of Lawyers 422
Former Government Lawyers 424
Park-N-Shop, Ltd. v. City of Highwood 424
Imputed Disqualification 426
Negotiating for Private Employment 426
In re Sofaer 426
Confidential Government Information 429
In re White 429
Current Government Lawyers 432
C. Conflicts of Third-Party Neutrals 432
Former Third-Party Neutrals 432
James v. Mississippi 433
Negotiating for Employment 438
Imputed Disqualification and Screening 438
Cho v. Superior Court 439
Current Third-Party Neutrals 442
La Serena Properties, L.L.C. v. Weisbach 443
D. Evaluations for Third Persons 446
Opinion Letters 446
Mehaffy, Rider, Windholz & Wilson v. Central Bank Denver, N.A. 447
Loss of Confidentiality and Privilege 450
Sarbanes-Oxley Act 450

Chapter XI. Reputation 453
A. Communication 454
False or Misleading Communications 454
Unjustified Expectations 455
A Historic Example 455
Unsubstantiated Comparisons 456

Another Historic Example... 456
Law-Firm Names... 457
Disclosing Licensure 457
Karlena Zachery 458
B. Soliciting...459
Prohibition Against Solicitation.. 459
Ohralik v. State Bar Association 460
Real-Time Communications... 465
Ambulance Chasing 465
The Florida Bar v. Barrett 466
Group Legal Services.. 469
Access to Legal Services 469
Educational Information... 470
C. Marketing..470
Lawyer Advertising 470
Lawyer Referral Services... 471
Paying Others for Referrals... 471
Lawyer-to-Lawyer Referrals 472
First Amendment Protection... 472
Shapero v. Kentucky Bar Association 473
Florida Bar v. Went For It, Inc. 477
Specific Advertisements.. 482
Florida Bar v. Pape 483
Law-Firm Websites.. 486
Interactive Websites 486
Lawyer Websites 487
Political Contributions 490
D. Specializing..491
Advertising Certification... 491
Walker v. Board of Professional Responsibility 492

Chapter XII. Access 497
A. Pro Bono Service...498
Social Imperatives... 498
Value of Pro Bono 498
Business Imperatives 499
Aspirational Goal.. 500
In re Fischer 500
Low Bono.. 504
Defining Pro Bono 504
Distinguishing Pro Bono 505
Quality of Representation 505
B. Appointments..505
Accepting Appointments 505
Appointments in Criminal Cases... 506
Appointment Lists... 507
The Florida Bar v. Rubin 507
Declining for Good Cause 509
C. Legal-Services Organization..510
Legal Aid 510
Conflicts of Interest.. 511

E.E.O.C. v. Luby's 512
Legal Services Programs 516
Ask-a-Lawyer Programs 516
Turning a Blind Eye 517
Law-Reform Activities 517
D. Inclusive Representation 518
Diminished-Capacity Clients 518
In the Matter of Disciplinary Action Against Kuhn 519
Practical and Strategic Issues 522
In re S.H. 522
Representing Children 525
Protective Actions 525
In re Guardianship of Henderson 526
Cross-Cultural Representation 528
Communication Registers 529
Sound Inter-Cultural Practices 529
Access to the Profession 530
Lawyers of Color 530
Increasing Access 530

Chapter XIII. Authority 533
A. Regulating Judges 534
History of Regulation 534
ABA Code of Judicial Conduct 535
Organization of the ABA Code 535
Scope 536
Civil and Criminal Liability 537
Terminology 537
Application 539
B. Promoting Independence 541
Canon 1 541
Evident Partiality 541
C. Upholding Law 542
Canon 2 542
Caperton v. A.T. Massey Coal Co. 547
In re Blake 553
Financial Influences 560
D. Personal Conduct 561
Canon 3 561
In re Mosley 566
E. Judicial Campaigns 568
Canon 4 568
Republican Party of Minnesota v. White 570

Conclusion 577

Appendices 581
I. CALIFORNIA RULES OF PROFESSIONAL CONDUCT 581
II. DELAWARE RULES OF PROFESSIONAL CONDUCT 602

III. MICHIGAN RULES OF PROFESSIONAL CONDUCT 643

Index...675

TABLE OF CASES AND OPINIONS

ABA Comm. on Ethics & Prof. Resp. Formal Opin. No. 94-383, 252

ABA Formal Ethics Opin. 00-418 (2000), 150

ABA Formal Ethics Opin. 01-421 (2001), 154

ABA Formal Ethics Opin. 04-433 (2004), 44

ABA Formal Ethics Opin. 09-454 (2009), 266

ABA Formal Ethics Opin. 10-457 (2010), 487

ABA Formal Ethics Opin. 87-353 (1987), 320

ABA Formal Ethics Opin. 95-396 (1995), 297-298

ABA Formal Ethics Opin. 96-404 (1996), 113

Alexander v. Turtur & Assocs., Inc., 146 S.W.3d 113 (Tex. 2004), 130

Alken-Ziegler, Inc. v. Waterbury Headers Corp., 600 N.W.2d 638 (Mich. 1999), 133

Allen v. International Truck & Engine, 2006 WL 2578896 (S.D. Ind. Sept. 6, 2006), 294

Amco Builders & Developers, Inc. v. Team Ace Joint Venture, 666 N.W.2d 623 (Mich. 2003), 132

American Canoe Assn., Inc. v. City of St.

Alaska Ethics Opin. 2005-1 (2005), 526

Albans, 18 F. Supp2d 620 (S.D. W. Va. 1998), 292

Anders v. California, 386 U.S. 738 (1967), 338

Andrew Corp. v. Beverly Mfg. Co., 415 F. Supp.2d 919 (N.D. Ill. 2006), 388

Andrews v. Kentucky Bar Assn., 169 S.W.3d 862 (Ky. 2005), 306

Andrews v. Saylor, 80 P.3d 482 (N.M. Ct. App. 2003), 126

Ankerman v. Mancuso, 860 A.2d 244 (Conn. 2004), 393

Application of Feingold, 296 A.2d 492 (Me. 1972), 66

Archuleta v. Hughes, 969 P.2d 409 (Utah 1998), 123

Arizona Ethics Op. 05-05 (2005), 309

Arnold v. Kemp, 813 S.W.2d 770 (Ark. 1991), 507

Atlanta-Journal Constitution v. State, 596 S.E.2d 694 (Ga. Ct. App. 2004), 360

Attorney General v. Michigan Public Service Commn., 625 N.W.2d 16 (Mich. Ct. App. 2001), 379

Attorney Grievance Commn. v. Alsafty, 838 A.2d 1213 (Md. 2003), 458

Attorney Grievance Commn. v. Childress, 770 A.2d 685 (Md. 2001), 60

Attorney Grievance Commn. v. Culver, 849 A.2d 423 (Md. 2004), 332

Attorney Grievance Commn. v. DeMaio, 842 A.2d 802 (Md. 2004), 306

Attorney Grievance Commn. v. Ficker, 706 A.2d 1045 (Md. 1998), 232

Attorney Grievance Commn. v. Mooney, 753 A.2d 17 (Md. 2000), 228

Attorney Grievance Commn. v. Rose, 892 A.2d 469 (Md. 2006), 343

Attorney Grievance Commn. v. Wallace, 793 A.2d 535 (Md. 2002), 343

Attorney Grievance Commn. v. Zdravkovich, 762 A.2d 950 (Md. 2000), 332

Attorney Q. v. Mississippi State bar, 587 So.2d 228 (Miss. 1991), 291

Attorney U. v. Mississippi, 678 So.2d 963 (Miss. 1996), 44

Augustine v. Dept. of Veteran Affairs, 429 F.3d 1334 (Fed. Cir. 2005), 90

Bailey v. Algonquin Gas Transm. Co., 788 A.3d 478 (R.I. 2002), 117

Baird v. State Bar of Arizona, 401 U.S. 1 (1971), 65

Barnard v. Thompson, 489 U.S. 546 (1989), 50

Barr v. MacGugan, 78 P.3d 660 (Wash. Ct. App. 2003), 134

Barrett v. Virginia State Bar, 611 S.E.2d 375 (Va. 2005), 291

Bates v. State Bar of Arizona, 433 U.S. 350 (1977), 462,472,474,477-478,492

Berger v. United States, 295 U.S. 78 (1935), 264

Bernier v. DuPont, 715 N.E.2d 442 (Mass. Ct. App. 1999), 364

Biomet, Inc. v Barnes & Thornburg, 791 N.E.2d 760 (Ind. Ct. App. 2003), 130

Birbrower, Montalbano, Condon & Frank, P.C., 949 P.2d 1 (Cal. 1998), 83

Blum v. Stenson, 465 U.S. 886 (1984), 208

Boranian v. Clark, 20 Cal. Rptr.3d 405 (2004), 125

Bordenkircher v. Hayes, 434 U.S. 357 (1978), 272

Bothwell v. Republic Tobacco Co., 912 F. Supp. 1221 (D. Neb. 1995), 506

Bracy v. Gramley, 520 U.S. 899 (1997), 560

Brady v. United States, 373 U.S. 83 (1963), 265

Britton and Gray, P.C. v. Shelton, 69 P.3d 1210 (Okla. Ct. Civ. App. 2003), 99

Bronson v. Pennsylvania Bd. of Probation and Parole, 421 A.2d 1021 (Pa. 1980), 338

Brown v. Hartlage, 456 U.S. 45 (1982), 573

Brown v. Legal Fdn., 538 U.S. 216 (2003), 218

Burden-Meeks v. Welch, 319 F.3d 897 (7th Cir. 2003), 450

Burke v. Lewis, 122 P.3d 533 (Utah 2005), 510

California Formal Ethics Opin. 2005-168 (2005), 487

Cammer v. United States, 350 U.S. 399 (1956), 347

Campellone v. Cragan, 910 So.2d 363 (Fla. Ct. App. 2005), 166

Caperton v. A.T. Massey Coal Co., 129 S. Ct. 2252 (2009), 547

Caplin & Drysdale v. United States, 109 S.Ct. 2667 (1989), 214

Carbis Walker, LLP v. Hill, Barth and King, LLC, 930 A.2d 573 (Pa. Super. Ct. 2007), 242

Carbone v. Tierney, 864 A.2d 308 (N.H. 2004), 126

Carter v. Mississippi Bar, 654 So.2d 505 (Miss. 1995), 343

Central Hudson Gas & Elec. Corp. v. Public Service Commn., 447 U.S. 557 (1980), 474,479-481,493

Chambers v. Kay, 56 P.3d 645 (Cal. 2002), 213

Chapman v. California, 386 U.S. 18 (1967), 386

Chapman v. Pacific Tel. & Tel., 613 F.2d 193 (9th Cir 1979), 346

Cho v. Superior Ct., 45 Cal. Rptr.2d 863 (Cal. Ct. App. 1995), 439

Christianburg Garment Co. v. EEOC, 434 U.S. 412 (1978), 257

Cincinnati Bar Assn. v. Haas, 699 N.E.2d 919 (Ohio 1998), 472

Clark v. Rowe, 701 N.E.2d 624 (Mass. 1998), 130

Cleveland Bar Assn. v. CompManagement, 818 N.E.2d 1181 (Ohio 2004), 80

Cohen v. Hurley, 366 U.S. 117 (1961), 463,479

Cole v. Appalchian Power Co., 903 F. Supp. 975 (S.D. W.Va. 1995), 299

Collins v. CSX Transp., 441 S.E.2d 150 (N.C. 1994), 343

Colorado v. Carpenter, 893 P.2d 777 (Colo. 1997), 472

Columbus Bar Assn. v. Battisti, 739 N.E.2d 344 (Ohio 2000), 280

Columbus Bar Assn. v. Finneran, 687 N.E.2d 405 (1997), 341

Commonwealth v. Greer, 314 A.2d 513 (Pa. 1974), 337

Commonwealth v. Maricle, 10 S.W.3d 117 (Ky. 1999), 426

Commonwealth v. McCullum, 602 A.2d 313 (Pa. 1992), 360

Community Dental Services v. Tani, 282 F.3d 1164 (9th Cir. 2002), 134

Conn. Bar Assn. Comm. on Prof. Ethics Op. 98-5 (1998), 108

Constand v. Cosby, 229 F.R.D. 472 (E.D. Pa. 2005), 360

Cook v. American Steamship, 134 F.3d 771 (6th Cir. 1998), 351

Corcoran v. Northeast Illinois Reg. Commuter R.R. Co., 803 N.E.2d 807 (Ill. Ct. App. 2003), 472

Cotton v. Kronenberg, 44 P.3d 878 (Wash. Ct. App. 2002), 393

Countrywide Home Loans, Inc. v. Kentucky Bar Assn. 113 S.W.3d 105 (Ky. 2003), 76

County of L.A. v. United States Dist. Ct., 223 F.3d 990 (9th Cir. 2000), 402

Cowan Liebowitz & Larman, P.C. v. Kaplan, 902 So.2d 755 (Fla. 2005), 126

Culpepper & Carroll, PLLC v. Cole, 929 So.2d 1224 (La. 2006), 206

Cunningham v. Sams, 588 S.E.2d 484 (N.C. Ct. App. 2003), 364

Cunningham v. Sommerville, 388 S.E.2d 301 (W. Va. 1989), 510

Curtis v. Kentucky Bar Assn., 959 S.W.2d 94 (Ky. 1998), 232

D.J. Inv. Group, L.L.C. v. DAE/Westbrook, L.L.C., 147 P.3d 414 (Utah 2006), 365

Daniels v. Alander, 844 A.2d 182 (Conn. 2004), 305, 309

Davis v. Alabama State Bar, 676 So.2d 306 (Ala. 1996), 228

Dayton Bar Assn. v. O'Brien, 812 N.E.2d 1263 (Ohio 2004), 273

Disciplinary Action Against Dvorak, 554 N.W.2d 399 (Minn. 1996), 503

Disciplinary Counsel v. Alexicole, Inc., 822 N.E.2d 348 (Ohio 2004), 80

Disciplinary Counsel v. Firth, 754 N.E.2d 219 (Ohio 2001), 457

Disciplinary Counsel v. Rich, 633 N.E.2d 1114 (Ohio 1994), 286

Doe v. McMaster, 585 S.E.2d 773 (S.C. 2003), 76

Dodrill v. Executive Director, 842 S.W.2d 383 (Ark. 1992), 327

Dondi Props. Corp. v. Commerce Sav. & Loan Assn., 121 F.R.D. 284 (N.D. Tex. 1988), 237

Duran v. Carris, 238 F.3d 1268 (10th Cir. 2001), 107

Duvall v. Bledsoe, 617 S.E.2d 601 (Ga. 2005), 402

Dweck Law Firm, LLP v. Mann, 340 F. Supp.2d 353 (S.D. N.Y. 2004), 211

E.E.O.C. v. Luby's Inc., 347 F. Supp.2d 743 (D. Ariz. 2004), 512

Ellis v. Maine, 448 F.2d 1325 (1st Cir. 1971), 110

Ellis v. United States, 356 U.S. 674 (1958), 339

EU v. San Francisco County Democratic Central Comm., 489 U.S. 214 (1989), 573

FMC Techs., Inc. v. Edwards, 420 F. Supp.2d 1153 (W.D. Wash. 2006), 382

Fang v. Bock, 28 P.3d 456 (Mont. 2001), 126

FTC v. Cement Institute, 333 U.S. 683 (1948), 549

Farrin v. Thigpen, 173 F. Supp.2d 427 (M.D. N.C. 2001), 482

Featherstone v. Schaerrer, 34 P.3d 194 (Utah 2001), 299

Fedl's Case, 815 A.2d 383 (N.H. 2002), 252

Fidelity National Title Ins. Co. v. Intercounty National Title Ins. Co., 310 F.3d 537 (7th Cir. 2002), 99

Fire Ins. Exchange v. Bell, 643 N.E.2d 310 (Ind. 1994), 285

Fletcher v. Comission on Judicial Perf., 968 P.2d 958 (Cal. 1998), 542

Florida Bar Ethics Opin. 07-3 (Jan. 16, 2009), 487

Florida Bar v. Barrett, 897 So.2d 1269 (Fla. 2005), 466

Florida Bar v. Barthof, 775 So.2d 957 (Fla. 2000), 53

Florida Bar v. Becerra, 661 So.2d 299 (Fla. 1995), 79

Florida Bar v. Brumbaugh, 355 So.3d 1186 (Fla. 1978), 78-79

Florida Bar v. Catarcio, 709 So.2d 96 (Fla. 1998), 79

Florida Bar v. Consolidated Bus. & Legal Forms, Inc., 386 So.2d 797 (Fla. 1980), 79

Florida Bar v. Dancu, 490 So.2d 40 (Fla. 1986), 218

Florida Bar v. Frederick, 756 So.2d 79 (Fla. 2000), 252

Florida Bar v. Grasso, 760 So.2d 940 (Fla. 2000), 214

Florida Bar v. Lange, 711 So.2d 518 (Fla. 1998), 484

Florida Bar v. Pape, 918 So.2d 240 (Fla. 2005), 483

Florida Bar v. Rotstein, 835 So.3d 241 (Fla. 2002), 306

Florida Bar v. Rubin, 549 So.2d 1000 (1989), 507

Florida Bar v. Taylor, 648 So.2d 1190 (Fla. 1994), 398

Florida Bar v. We the People Forms and Service Center of Sarasota, Inc., 883 So.2d 1280 (Fla. 2004), 76

Florida Bar v. Went for It, Inc., 515 U.S. 618 (1995), 477,494

Florida Bd. Bar Examiners ex rel. Barry University School of Law, 821 So.2d 1050 (Fla. 2002), 50

Florida Sup. Ct Adv. Opin. 2009-20, 355

Former Employees of Chevron Prods. Co. v. U.S. Secy. Of Labor, 245 F. Supp.2d 1312 (Ct. Intl. Trade 2002), 310

Francis v. Piper, 597 N.W.2d 922 (Minn. Ct. App. 1999), 125

Freeman v. Vicchiarelli, 827 F. Supp. 300 (D. N.J. 1993), 364

Friedman v. Rogers, 440 U.S. 1 (1979), 457

Frisby v. Schultz, 487 U.S. 474 (1988), 480

Froom v. Perel, 872 A.2d 1067 (N.J. Superior Ct. 2005), 126

Garrison v. State of Louisiana, 379 U.S. 64 (1964), 277

Gentile v. State Bar, 501 U.S. 1030 (1991), 357-358

Giboney v. Empire Storage & Ice. Co. 336 U.S. 490 (1949), 462

Gibson v. Berryhill, 411 U.S. 564 (1973), 551

Gilles v. Wiley, Malehorn & Sirota, 783 A.2d 756 (N.J. Superior Ct. 2001), 98

Glasser v. United States, 315 U.S. 60 (1941), 378

Goldfarb v. Virginia State Bar, 421 U.S. 773 (1975), 21,463,479,494

Gray v. Memorial Med. Ctr., Inc., 855 F. Supp. 377 (S.D. Ga. 1994), 415

Grievance Admin. v. August, 475 N.W.2d 256 (1991), 69

Haagen-Dazs Co. v. Perche No! Gelato, Inc., 639 F. Supp. 282 (N.D. Cal. 1986), 402

Haley v. Boles, 824 S.W.2d 796 (Tex. Ct. App. 1992), 377

Hardy v. San Fernando Valley C. of C., 222 P.2d 314 (Cal. Ct. App. 1950), 85

Hatfield v. Seville Centrifugal Bronze, 732 N.E.2d 1077 (Ohio C.P. 2000), 401

Hawkins v. Commission for Lawyer Disc., 988 S.W.2d 927 (Tex. Ct. App. 1999), 509

Hayes v. Commonwealth, 25 S.W.3d 463 (Ky. 2000), 294

Healthnet, Inc. v. Health Net, Inc., 289 F. Supp.2d 755 (S.D. W. Va. 2003), 406-407

Heard v. Foxshire Assocs., LLC, 806 A.2d 348 (Md. Ct. Spec. App. 2002), 364

Heintz v. Jenkins, 514 U.S. 291 (1995), 21

Hempstead Video, Inc. v. Incorporated Village of Valley Stream, 409 F.3d 127 (2d Cir. 2005), 416

Hewlett-Packard Co. v. Bausch & Lomb, Inc., 115 F.R.D. 308 (N.D. Cal. 1987), 450

Hitachi, Ltd. v. Tatung Co., 419 F. Supp.2d 1158 (N.D. Cal. 2006), 417

Holdren v. General Motors Corp., 13 F. Supp.2d 1192 (D. Kan 1998), 293

Holland v. The Gordy Co., 2003 WL 19858000 (Mich. Ct. App. April 29, 2003), 224

Hollaway v. Arkansas, 435 U.S. 475 (1978), 383

Home Care Indus. Inc. v. Murray, 154 F. Supp.2d 861 (D. N.J. 2001), 166

Hopkins v. Troutner, 4 P.3d 557 (Idaho 2000), 291

Idaho State Bar v. Frazier, 28 P.3d 363 (Idaho 2001), 214

Idaho State Bar v. Hawkley, 92 P.3d 1069 (Idaho 2002), 331

Idaho State Bar v. Warrick, 44 P.3d 1141 (Idaho 2002), 314

In re Adkins, 596 S.E.2d 1, (2004), 203

In re Admonition Issued In Panel File No. 99-42, 621 N.W.2d 240 (Minn. 2001), 20

In re Air Crash Disaster, 909 F. Supp. 1116 (N.D. Ill. 1995), 286

In re Albin, 982 P.2d 385 (Kan. 1999), 280

In re Alcorn, 41 P.3d 600 (Ariz. 2002), 305

In re Anonymous, 637 N.E.2d 171 (Ind. 1994), 456

In re Anonymous, 698 N.E.2d 808 (Ind. 1998), 217

In re Anonymous, 783 N.E.2d 1130 (Ind. 2003), 491

In re Appeal of Lane, 544 N.W.2d 367 (1996), 65-66

In re Appert, 315 N.W.2d 204 (Minn. 1981), 465

In re Application of Converse, 602 N.W.2d 500 (Neb. 1999), 61

In re Arrotta, 96 P.3d 213 (Ariz. 2004), 57

In re Asher, 772 A.2d 1161 (D.C. 2001), 217

In re Atwater, 586 S.E.2d 589 (S.C. 2003), 362

In re Bahn, 13 S.W.3d 865 (Tex. Ct. App. 2000), 368

In re Barr, 13 S.W.2d 525 (Tex. Rev. Trib. 1998), 542

In re Bailey, 821 A.2d 851 (Del. 2003), 220

In re Bailey, 848 So.2d 530 (La. 2003), 314

In re Barker, 572 S.E.2d 460 (S.C. 2002), 307

In re Baxter, 940 P.2d 37 (Kan. 1997), 217

In re Bell-South Corp., 334 F.3d 941 (11th Cir 2003), 560

In re Berg, 955 P.2d 1240 (Kan. 1998), 399

In re Betancourt, 661 N.Y.S.2d 208 (N.Y. App. Div. 1997), 217

In re Blackmon, 629 S.E.2d 369 (S.C. 2006), 214

In re Blake, 539 S.E.2d 710 (S.C. 2000), 309

In re Blake, 912 So.2d 907 (Miss. 2005), 553

In re Blaylock, 978 P.2d 381 (Or. 1999), 465

In re Boone, 7 P.3d 270 (Kan. 2000), 343

In re Boone, 66 P.3d 896 (Kan. 2003), 327

In re Boulger, 637 N.W.2d 710 (N.D. 2001), 394

In re Braun, 734 N.E.2d 535 (Ind. 2000), 399

In re Cater, 887 A.2d 1 (D.C. 2005), 232

In re Calahan, 930 So.2d 916 (La. 2006), 209

In re Caldwell, 809 N.Y.S.2d 59 (2006), 60

In re Campbell, 199 P.3d 776 (Kan. 2009), 238

In re Capper, 757 N.E.2d 138 (Ind. 2001), 298

In re Caranchini, 956 S.W.2d 910 (Mo. 1997), 327

In re Cardwell, 50 P.3d 897 (Colo. 2002), 305

In re Cherry, 715 N.E.2d 382 (Ind. 1999), 343

In re Cleaver-Bascombe, 892 A.2d 396 (D.C. 2006), 301

In re Cline, 756 So.2d 284 (La. 2000), 231

In re Coale, 775 N.E.2d 1079 (Ind. 2002), 455

In re Coffey's Case, 880 A.2d 403 (N.H. 2005), 150

In re Cohen, 612 S.E.2d 294 (Ga. 2005), 306

In re Cohen, 847 A.2d 1162 (D.C. Ct. App. 2004), 220

In re Cole, 738 N.E.2d 1035 (Ind. 2000), 482

In re Cooperman, 633 N.E.2d 1069 (N.Y. Ct. App. 1994), 204

In re County of L.A., 223 F.3d 990 (9th Cir. 2000), 438

In re Crisel, 461 N.E.2d 994 (Ill. 1984), 26

In re D'Amico, 668 So.2d 730 (La. 1996), 465

In re Davis, 740 N.E.2d 855 (Ind. 2001), 392

In re DeBartolo, 488 N.E.2d 947 (Ill. 1986), 60

In re Deddish, 557 S.E.2d 655 (S.C. 2001), 83

In re Desilets, 291 F.3d 925 (6th Cir. 2002), 90

In re Diggs, 544 S.E.2d 628 (S.C. 2001), 306,309

In re Disciplinary Action Against Bunch, 784 N.W.2d 64 (Minn. 2010), 237

In re Disciplinary Proceedings Against Bolte, 699 N.W.2d 914 (2005), 83

In re Disciplinary Proceedings Against Winter, 522 N.W.2d 504 (Wis. 1994), 131

In re Discipline of Eicher, 661 N.W.2d 354 (S.D. 2003), 252

In re Discipline of Wilka, 638 N.W.2d 245 (S.D. 2001), 301

In re Duncan, 533 S.E.2d 94 (S.C. 2000), 357,358

In re Eadie, 36 P.3d 468 (Or. 2001), 280

In re Eicher, 661 N.W.2d 354 (S.D. 2003), 305

In re Eliasen, 913 P.2d 1163 (Idaho 1996), 283

In re Ellender, 889 So.2d 225 (La. 2004), 561

In re Envtl. Ins. Dec. Judgment Actions, 600 A.2d 165 (N.J. Super. Ct. Law Div. 1991), 299

In re Farmer, 950 P.2d 713 (Kan. 1997), 232

In re Fischer, 89 P.3d 817 (Colo. 2004), 500

In re Flack, 33 P.3d 1281 (Kan. 2001), 518

In re Fong, 762 N.Y.S.2d 367 (N.Y. Sup. Ct. 2003), 503

In re Foos, 770 N.E.2d 335 (Ind. 2002), 470

In re Franco, 66 P.3d 805 (Kan. 2003), 457-458

In re Freimark, 702 A.2d 1286 (N.J. 1997), 218

In re Gallo, 835 A.2d 682 (N.J. 2003), 147

In re Glorioso, 819 So.2d 320 (La. 2002), 217

In re Goebel, 735 N.E.2d 1178 (Ind. 2000), 394

In re Goff, 837 So.2d 1201 (La. 2003), 472

In re Graham, 503 N.W.2d 476 (minn. 1993), 343

In re Gross, 759 N.E.2d 288 (Mass. 2001), 280

In re Guardianship of Henderson, 838 A.2d 1277 (N.H. 2003), 526

In re Guirard, 11 So.3d 1017 (La. 2009), 12

In re Hagedorn, 904 N.E.2d 659 (Ind. 2009), 241

In re Hamm, 123 P.3d 652 (Ariz. 2005), 54

In re Hampton, 919 So.2d 949 (Miss. 2006), 327

In re Harper, 571 S.E.2d 292 (S.C. 2002), 149-150

In re Harris, 180 P.3d 558 (Kan. 2008), 120

In re Harris, 618 A.2d 852 (N.J. 1993), 147

In re Harris, 847 So.2d 1185 (La. 2003), 307

In re Harris, 868 A.2d 1011 (N.J. 2005), 143

In re Harrison, 587 S.E.2d 105 (S.C. 2003), 159

In re Hermina, 907 A.2d 790 (D.C. 2006), 306

In re Hoffman, 670 N.W.2d 500 (N.D. 2003), 433

In re Hoffman, 883 So.2d 425 (La. 2004), 398

In re Howes, 940 P.2d 159 (N.M. 1997), 226

In re James H. Himmel, 533 N.E.2d 790 (Ill. 1988), 24

In re Huelskamp, 740 N.E.2d 846 (Ind. 2000), 456

In re Hughes, & Coleman, 60 S.W.2d 540 (Ky. 2001), 491

In re Jones, 581 N.W.2d 876 (Neb. 1998), 561

In re Kaszynski, 620 N.W.2d 708 (Minn. 2001), 232

In re Keller, 729 N.E.2d 865 (Ind. 2003), 470

In re Kendall, 804 N.E.2d 1152 (Ind. 2004), 202

In re Kight, 685 N.E.2d 472 (Ind. 1997), 343

In re Kleinsmith, 124 P.3d 579 (N.M. Ct. App. 2005), 509

In re LaPinska, 381 N.E.2d 700 (Ill. 1978), 26

In re Levin, 514 N.E.2d 174 (Ill. 1987), 26

In re Levine, 847 P.2d 1093 (Ariz. 1993), 327

In re Lewis, 86 S.W.3d 419 (Ky. 2002), 50

In re Lightfoot, 217 F.3d 914 (7th Cir 2000), 224

In re Litz, 721 N.E.2d 258 (Ind. 1999), 357

In re Lowery, 999 S.W.2d 639 (Tex. Rev. Trib. 1998), 561

In re Lund, 19 P.3d 110 (Kan. 2001), 217

In re Lupo, 851 N.E.2d 404 (Mass. 2006), 394

In re Luzzo, 756 So.2d 76 (Fla. 2000), 561

In re M.R., 638 A.2d 1274 (N.J. 1994), 518

In re Matthews, 462 A.2d 165 (N.J. 1983), 57

In re McAlevy, 354 A.2d 289 (1976), 66

In re Meltzer, 741 N.Y.S.2d 240 (N.Y. Supreme Ct. App. Div. 2002), 229

In re Merkel, 138 P.3d 847 (Or. 2006), 285

In re Mitchell, 946 P.2d 999 (Kan. 1997), 343

In re Moore, 704 A.2d 1187 (D.C. 1997), 232

In re Mosley, 102 P.3d 555 (Nev. 2004), 566

In re Mozingo, 497 S.E.2d 729 (S.C. 1998), 343

In re Mullins, 649 N.E.2d 1024 (Ind. 1995), 320,526

In re Murphy, 519 S.E.2d 791 (S.C. 1999), 309

In re Myers, 584 S.E.2d 357 (S.C. 2003), 219

In re Nelson, 681 N.W.2d 352 (Minn. 2004), 392

In re O'Meara, 834 A.2d 235 (N.H. 2003), 307

In re Ortner, 699 N.W.2d 865 (S.D. 2005), 305

In re Page, 774 N.E.2d 49 (Ind. 2002), 316

In re Pautler, 47 P.3d 1175 (Colo. 2002), 287

In re Pinkins, 213 B.R. 818 (Bankr. E.D. Mich. 1997), 74

In re Porter, 930 So.2d 875 (La. 2006), 306

In re Primus, 436 U.S. 412 (1978), 469

In re Pyle, 91 P.3d 1222 (Kan. 2004), 293

In re O'Connor, 553 N.E.2d 481 (Ind. 1990), 158

In re R.M.J., 455 U.S. 191 (1982), 474-477,479

In re Richard, 986 P.2d 1117 (N.M. 1999), 332

In re Riehlmann, 891 So.2d 1239 (La. 2005), 38

In re Rigolosi, 526 A.2d 670 (N.J. 1987), 147

In re Rinella, 677 N.E.2d 909 (Ill. 1997), 399

In re Ring, 692 N.E.2d 35 (Mass. 1998), 343

In re Rivers, 331 S.E.2d 332 (S.C. 1984), 228

In re Romero, 690 N.E.2d 707 (Ind. 1998), 343

In re Roose, 69 P.3d 43 (Colo. 2003), 306

In re Ruffin, 610 S.E.2d 803 (S.C. 2005), 332

In re Rules of Prof. Conduct and Insurer Imposed Billing Rules and Procedures, 2 P.3d 806 (Mont. 2000), 155

In re S.H., 987 P.2d 735 (Ala. 1999), 522,526

In re Schapiro, 845 So.2d 170 (Fla. 2003), 542

In re Scott, 657 N.W.2d 567 (Minn. 2003), 307

In re Seelig, 850 A.2d 477 (N.J. 2004), 305

In re Segall, 638 N.Y.S.2d 444 (N.Y. App. Div. 1996), 228

In re Sledge, 859 So.2d 671 (La. 2003), 17

In re Sofaer, 728 A.2d 625 (D.C. Ct. App. 1999), 426

In re Spagnoli, 559 A.2d 1352 (N.J. 1989), 147

In re Summer, 105 P.3d 848 (Or. 2005), 284

In re Steele, 868 A.2d 146 (D.C. 2005), 314

In re Stolar, 401 U.S. 23 (1971), 65

In re Struthers, 877 P.2d 789 (Ariz. 1994), 232

In re Tocco, 984 P.2d 539 (Ariz. 1999), 283

In re Toups, 773 So.2d 709 (La. 2000), 383

In re Trewin, 684 N.W.2d 121 (Wis. 2004), 392-393

In re Tsoutsouris, 748 N.E.2d 856 (Ind. 2001), 400

In re Tweedly, 20 P.3d 1245 (Kan. 2001), 343

In re Vincenti, 704 A.2d 927 (N.J. 1998), 457

In re Von Wiegen, 470 N.E.2d 838 (N.Y. Sup. Ct. 1984), 477

In re Walmsley, 725 N.E.2d 25 (Ind. 2000), 456

In re White, 11 A.3d 1226 (D.C. Ct. App. 2011), 429

In re White, 699 So.2d 375 (La. 1997), 343

In re Whitney, 120 P.3d 550 (Wash. 2005), 306-307

In re Winthrop, 848 N.E.2d 961 (Ill. 2006), 285,320

In re Yao, 661 N.Y.S.2d 199 (N.Y. App. Div. 1997), 332

In re Yavacino, 494 A.2d 801 (N.J. 1985), 219

In re Zang, 741 P.2d 267 (Ariz. 1987), 454

In re Zeitler, 866 A.2d 171 (N.J. 2005), 147,343

In re Zohdy, 892 So.2d 1277 (La. 2005), 332

In the Matter of Abbott, 925 A.3d 482 (Del. 2007), 348

In the Matter of Disc. Action Against Kuhn, 785 N.W.2d 195 (N.D. 2010), 519

In the Matter of Disc. Proceedings Against Strnad, 505 N.W.2d 134 (Wisc. 1993), 216

In the Matter of Disciplinary Proceedings Against Marine, 264 N.W.2d 285 (Wisc. 1978), 216

In the Matter of Green, 11 P.3d 1078 (Colo. 2000), 196

In the Matter of Leyh, Ariz. Sup. Ct. Disc. Commn. Rpt. 06-0600 (2006), 284

In the Matter of the Reinstatement Petition of David S. Feinberg, State of Mich. Atty. Disc. Bd. No. 08-70-RP (Mar. 25, 2010), 68

Iowa Sup. Ct. Atty. Disc. Bd. v. Box, 715 N.W.2d 758 (Iowa 2006), 298

Iowa Sup. Ct. Atty. Disc. Bd. v. Howe, 706 N.W.2d 360 (Iowa 2005), 264

Iowa Sup. Ct. Bd. of Prof. Ethics & Conduct v. Visser, 629 N.W.2d 376 (Iowa 2001), 360

Jayhawk Capital Mgt., LLC v. LSB Indus., Inc., No. 2:08-cv-02561-EFM (D. Kan. April 12, 2011), 244

James v. Mississippi, 962 So.2d 528 (Miss. 2007), 433

Jewell v. Maynard, 383 S.E.2d 536 (Va. 1989), 506

Johnson v. Carleton, 765 A.2d 571 (Me. 2001), 130

Jones v. Beverly Health & Rehab. Services, 68 F. Supp.2d 1304 (N.D. Fla. 1999), 415

Jones's Case, 628 A.2d 254 (N.H. 1993), 252

Jones Motor Co. v. Holtkamp Liese Beckmeier & Childress, P.C., 197 F.3d 119 (7th Cir. 1999), 127

Kaempe v. Myers, 367 F.3d 958 (D.C. Cir. 2004), 130

Kala v. Aluminum Smelting & Refining Co., 688 N.E.2d 258 (1998), 416

Karlnea Zachery, Mass. Bd. Bar Overseers Pub. Reprimand No. 2007-3 (Jan. 26, 2007), 458

Kaye Scholer LLP v. Zalis, 878 So.2d 447 (Fla. Ct. App. 2004), 242

Keller v. State Bar of California, 496 U.S. 1 (1990), 50

Keys v. Mercy Hosp., 537 So.2d 1223 (La. 1989), 212

Kittler v. Eckberg, Lammers, Briggs, Wolff & Vierling, 535 N.W.2d 653 (Minn. Ct. Ap. 1995), 470

Klupt v. Krongard, 728 A.2d 727 (Md. Ct. Spec. App. 1999), 368

Konigsberg v. State Bar, 353 U.S. 252 (1957), 59

Kopf v. Wing, 942 F.2d 265 (4th Cir 1991), 312

Kramer v. Tribe, 156 F.R.D. 96 (D. N.J. 1994), 357

Kyles v. Whitley, 514 U.S. 419 (1995), 266

L.A. County Ethics Opin. 504 (2000), 525

La Serena Properties, L.L.C. v. Weisbach, 112 Cal. Rptr.3d 597 (Cal. Ct. App. 2010), 443

Laird v. Tatum, 409 U.S. 824 (1972), 574

Laremont-Lopez v. Southeastern Tidewater Opportunity Ctr., 968 F. Supp. 1075 (E.D. Va. 1997), 110

Lathrop v. Donohue, 367 U.S. 820 (1961), 50

Law Students Research Council v. Wadmond, 401 U.S. 154 (1971), 65

Lawyer Disc. Bd. v. Neely, 528 S.E.2d 468 (W.Va. 1998), 331, 332

Lawyer Disc. Bd. v. Sims, 574 S.E.2d 795 (W. Va. 2002), 360

Leak-Gilbert v. Fahle 55 P.3d 1054 (Okla. 2002), 125

Lee v. American Eagle Airlines, Inc., 93 F. Supp.2d 1322 (S.D. Fla. 2000), 253

Leis v. Flynt, 439 U.S. 438 (1979), 88

Lerner v. Laufer, 819 A.2d 471 (N.J. Superior Ct. 2003), 107

Liljeberg v. Health Services Acquisition Corp., 486 U.S. 847 (1988), 560,568

Logue v. Dore, 103 F.3d 1040 (1st Cir. 1997), 542

Lowe v. Experian, 328 F. Supp.2d 1122 (D. Kan. 2004), 368

Lucas v. State, 572 S.E.2d 274 (S.C. 2002), 319

Luethke v. Suhr, 650 N.W.2d 220 (Neb. 2002), 102

Maine Ethics Opin. 178 (2002), 234

Makins v. District of Columbia, 861 A.2d 590 (D.C. 2004), 102

Mallard v. United States Dist. Ct., 490 U.S. 296 (1989), 506

Malonis v. Harrington, 816 N.E.2d 115 (Mass. 2004), 211

Manion v. Nagin, 394 F.3d 1062 (8th Cir. 2005), 165

Martinelli v. Farm Rite, Inc., 785 A.2d 33 (N.J. Superior Ct. 2001), 117

Maryland Ethics Opin. 2005-15 (2005), 310

Maryland State Bar Ethics Opin. 2004-29 (2004), 470

Mason v. Florida bar, 208 F.3d 952 (11th Cir. 2000), 482

Massey v. Prince George's County, 907 F. Supp. 138 (D. Md. 1995), 310

Matter of Apt, 946 P.2d 1002 (Kan. 1997), 281

Matter of Geisler, 614 N.E.2d 939 (Ind. 1993), 259

Mays v. Neal, 928 S.W.2d 830 (Ark. 1997), 228

McCallum v. CSX Transp., Inc., 149 F.R.D. 104 (M.D. N.C. 1993), 299

McClure v. Thompson, 323 F.3d 1233 (9th Cir. 2003), 168

McCoy v. Court of Appeals, 486 U.S. 429 (1988), 337

McIntyre v. Ohio Elections Commn., 514 U.S. 334 (1995), 575

Medina County Bar Assn. v. Grieselhuber, 678 N.E.2d 535 (Ohio 1997), 457

Mehaffy, Rider ,Windholz & Wilson v. Central Bank Denver, N.A., 892 P.2d 230 (Colo. 1995), 447

Merrill Lynch Bus. Fin. Services, Inc. v. Nudell, 239 F. Supp.2d 1170 (D. Colo. 2003), 368

Merritt v. Hopkins Goldenberg, P.C. 841 N.E.2d 1003 (Ill. Ct. App. 2005), 126

Mezrano v. Alabama State Bar, 434 SO.2d 732 (Ala. 1983), 457

Mich. Ethics Opin. RI-203, 203

Missouri v. Jenkins, 491 U.S. 274 (1989), 228

Monroe v. City of Topeka, 988 P.2d 228 (Kan. 1999), 415,422

Monsanto Co. v. Aetna Cas. & Sur. Co., 593 A.2d 1013 (Del. Super Ct. 1990), 299

Montana Ethics Opin. 011115 (2001), 286

Moore v. Judicial Inquiry Commn., 891 So.2d 848 (Ala. 2004), 535

Morse v. Clark, 890 So.2d 496 (Fla. Dist. Ct. App. 2004), 382

N.Y. City Bar Assn. Ethics Opin. 2001-1 (March 2, 2001), 487

NAACP v. Florida Dept. of Corr., 122 F. Supp.3d 1335 (M.D. Fla. 2000), 299

Navellier v. Sletten, 262 F.3d 923 (9th Cir. 2001), 542

Nevada Yellow Cab Corp. v. Eighth Jud. Dist. Ct., 152 P.3d 737 (Nev. 2007), 398

New York Times v. Sullivan, 376 U.S. 254 (1964), 277

Nix v. Whiteside, 475 U.S. 157 (1986), 320

North Carolina State Bar Ethics Commn. 2003 Formal Opin. No. 1 (2003), 343

North Carolina State Bar Ethics Commn. 2005 Formal Opin. No. 9 (2006), 163

North Carolina State Bar Ethics Commn. Formal Opin. No. 98-18 (1999), 525

North Carolina State Bar v. Culverson, 627 S.E.2d 644 (N.C. 2006), 454

North Carolina State Bar v. Nifong, Disc. Hrg. Commn. 06-DHC-35 (June 16, 2007), 266

Nrdeko v. Ridge, 351 F. Supp.2d 904 (D. Minn. 2004), 321

Obert v. Republic Western Ins. Co., 264 F. Supp.2d 106 (D. R.I. 2003), 327

Office of Disc. Counsel v. Wrona, 908 A.2d 1281 (Pa. 2006), 306

Ohralik v. Ohio State Bar Assn., 436 U.S. 447 (1978), 460,474-475,479

Oregon Ethics Opin. 2005-59 (2005), 332

Oxford Sys., Inc. v. Cellpro, Inc., 45 F. Supp.2d 1055 (W.D. Wash. 1999), 401

Palmer v. Pioneer Inn Assocs., Ltd., 257 F.3d 999 ((th Cir. 2001), 299

Panzino v. City of Phoenix, 999 P.2d 198 (Ariz. 2000), 117

Pappas v. Waggoner's Heating & Air, Inc., 108 P.3d 9 (Okla. Ct. Civ. App. 2004), 433

Park-N-Shop, Ltd. V. City of Highwood, 864 F. Supp. 82 (N.D. Ill. 1994), 424

Parker v. Pepsi-Cola Gen. Bottlers, Inc., 249 F. Supp.2d 1006 (N.D. Ill. 2003), 292

Parklane Hosiery Co. v. Shore, 439 U.S. 322 (1979), 328

Passante v. McWilliam, 62 Cal. Rptr.2d 298 (Cal. Ct. App. 1997), 390

Patterson v. Balsamico, 440 F.3d 104 (2d Cir. 2006), 383

Patterson v. New York, 432 U.S. 197 (1977), 340

Peel v. Attorney Regis. & Disc. Commn. of Illinois, 496 U.S. 91 (1990), 491

Pennsylvania Ethics Op. 98-83 (1998), 113

People ex rel. Lawyers Inst. of San Diego v. Merchants Protective Corp., 209 P. 363 (Cal. 1922), 85

People v. Albright, 91 P.3d 1063 (Colo. O.P.D.J. 2003), 307

People v. Casey, 948 P.2d 1014 (Colo, 1997), 226,228

People v. DePallo, 754 N.E.2d 751 (N.Y. 2001), 320

People v. Donaldson, 113 Cal. Rptr. 538 (Ct. App. 2001), 362

People v. Finley, 141 P.3d 911 (Colo. Ct. App. 2006), 362

People v. Hohertz, 102 P.3d 1019 (Colo. Office Presiding Disc. Judge 2004), 168

People v. Jennings, 83 Cal. Rptr.2d 33 (Cal. Ct. App. 1999), 320

People v. Mason, 938 P.2d 133 (Colo. 1997), 393

People v. Milner, 35 P.3d 670 (Colo. O.P.D.J. 2001), 232

People v. Zimmerman, 938 P.2d 131 (Colo. 1997), 471

Perkins v. General Motors Corp., 129 F.R.D. 655 (W.D. Mo. 1990), 330

Pincay v. Andrews, 389 F.3d 853 (9th Cir. 2004), 117

Pioneer Investm. Services Co. v. Brunswick Assocs. Ltd. Partnership, 507 U.S. 380 (1993), 117

Piper v. Portnoff Law Assocs., Ltd., 396 F.3d 227 (3d Cir. 2005), 21

Platt v. Jack Cooper Transp. Co., 959 F.2d 91 (8th Cir 1992), 331

Pope v. Federal Express Corp., 138 F.R.D. 675 (W.D. Mo. 1990), 329-330

Pope v. Federal Express Corp., 49 F.3d 1327 (8th Cir. 1995), 330

Pro-Hand Services Trust v. Monthei, 49 P.3d 56 (Mont. 2002), 411

Prudential Ins. Co. v. Dewey, Ballantine, Bushby, Palmer & Wood, 605 N.E.2d 318 (N.Y. Ct. App. 1992), 126

Puder v. Buechel, 874 A.2d 534 (N.J. 2005), 102

Raymark Indus., Inc. v. Butera, Beausang, Cohen & Brennan, 193 F.3d 210 (3d Cir. 1999), 204

Reese v. Owens-Corning Fiberglass, 962 F. Supp. 1418 (D. Kan. 1997), 510

Reetz v. Kinsman Marine Trans. Co., 330 N.W.2d 638 (Mich. 1982), 264

Reilly v. Computer Assocs. Long_term Disability Plan, 423 F. Supp.2d 5 (E.D. N.Y. 2006), 422

Republican Party of Minnesota v. White, 536 U.S. 765 (2002), 570

Resolution Submitted by Council Members Brenda Jones and Kwame Kenyatta (Feb. 2008), 166

Robinette v. Barnes, 854 F.2d 909 (6th Cir. 1988), 311

Rompilla v. Beard, 545 U.S. 374 (2005), 136

Rus, Miliband & Smith v. Conkle & Olesten, 6 Cal. Rptr.3d 612 (Cal. Ct. App. 2003), 211

S.D. Warren Co. v. Duff-Norton, 302 F. Supp.2d 762 (W.D. Mich. 2004), 402

Samuels v. Mix, 989 P.2d 701 (Cal. 1999), 130

San Diego County Bar Assn. Ethics Opin. 2006-1 (2006), 487

Santacroce v. Neff, 134 F. Supp.2d 366 (D. N.J. 2001), 401

Scheehle v. Justice of Sup. Ct. of Arizona, 120 P.3d 1092 (Ariz. 2005), 506

Schultz v. Schultz, 783 So.2d 329 (Fla. Dist. Ct. App. 2001), 433

Schware v. Board of Examiners, 353 U.S. 232 (1957), 60,65

Schwartz v. Kogan, 132 F.3d 1387 (11th Cir. 1998), 500

Semler v. Oregon State Bd. of Dental Examiners, 294 U.S. 608 (1935), 463

Shapero v. Kentucky Bar Assn., 486 U.S. 466 (1988), 473,479-481

Shenkman v. Bragman, 682 N.W.2d 516 (Mich. Ct. App. 2004), 81

Sherman v. Almeida, 747 A.2d 470 (R.I. 2000), 537

Simko v. Blake, 532 N.W.2d 842 (Mich. 1995), 125

Simpson Perf. Prods. v. Horn, 92 P.3d 283 (Wyo. 2004), 379

Smith & Nephew, Inc. v. Ethicon, Inc., 98 F. Supp.2d 106 (D. Mass. 2000), 415

Smith v. Commonwealth, 574 A.2d 558 (Pa. 1990), 336

Smith v. Haden, 868 F. Supp. 1 (D. D.C. 1994), 126

Smith v. Kalamazoo Ophthalmology, 322 F. Supp.2d 883 (W.D. Mich. 2004), 299

Smith v. Robbins, 528 U.S. 259 (2000), 340

South Carolina Adv. Comm. on Stds. of Jud. Conduct Opin. 17-2009, 356

South Carolina Ethics Opin. 2003-06 (2003), 234

Spratley v. State Farm Mut. Ins. Co., 78 P.3d 603 (Utah 2003), 168

St. Amant v. Thompson, 390 U.S. 727 (1968), 277

State Bar of Arizona Commn. on Rules of Prof. Conduct Op. 05-06 (2005), 107,108

State Bar of Arizona v. Arizona Land Title & Trust Co., 366 P.2d 1 (Ariz. 1961), 75

State Bar of Georgia Formal Adv. Opin. 05-10 (Ga. Sup. Ct. April 25, 2006), 252

State ex rel. Cosenza v. Hill, 607 S.E.2d 811 (W. Va. 2004), 422

State ex rel. Oklahoma Bar Assn. v. Bedford, 956 P.2d 148 (Okla. 1997), 332

State ex rel. Oklahoma Bar Assn. v. Bolusky, 23 P.2d 268 (Okla. 2001), 285

State ex rel. Oklahoma Bar Assn. v. Butner, 976 P.2d 542 (Okla. 1998), 298

State ex rel. Oklahoma Bar Assn. v. Cox, 48 P.3d 780 (Okla. 2002), 262

State ex rel. Oklahoma Bar Assn. v. Dobbs, 94 P.3d 31 (Okla. 2004), 307

State ex rel. Oklahoma Bar Assn. v. Downes, 121 P.3d 1058 (Okla. 2005), 364

State ex rel. Oklahoma Bar Assn. v Harper, 995 P.2d 1143 (Okla. 2000), 295

State ex rel. Oklahoma Bar Assn. v. Hawkley, 92 P.3d 1069 (Idaho 2002), 331

State ex rel. Oklahoma Bar Assn. v. Kinsey, 205 P.3d 866 (Okla. 2008), 30

State ex rel. Oklahoma Bar Assn. v. Giger, 72 P.3d 27 (Okla. 2003), 32

State ex rel. Oklahoma Bar Assn. v. Patmon, 939 P.2d 1155 (Okla. 1997), 232

State ex rel. NSBA v. Frederiksen, 635 N.W.2d 427 (Neb. 2001), 218

State ex rel. Nebraska State Bar Assn. v. Frank, 631 N.W.2d 485 (Neb. 2001), 375

State ex rel. Ogden Newspapers, Inc. v. Wilkes, 566 S.E.2d 560 (W. Va. 2002), 402

State ex rel. Tyler v. MacQueen, 447 S.E.2d 289 (W. Va. 1994), 432

State v. Downes, 121 P.3d 1058 (Okla. 2005), 400

State v. Gilliam, 748 So.2d 622 (La. Ct. App. 1999), 292

State v. Goltz, 111 S.W.3d 1 (Tenn. Crim. App. 2003), 264

State v. Grossberg, 705 A.2d 608 (Del. Super. Ct. 1997), 360

State v. McDowell, 669 N.W.2d 204 (Wis. Ct. App. 2003), 318

State v. P.Z., 703 A.2d 901 (N.J. 1997), 294

State v. Smolen, 17 P.3d 456 (Okla. 2000), 397-398

State v. Stockert, 684 N.W.2d 605 (N.D. 2004), 542

Stengart v. Loving Care Agency, Inc., 990 A.2d 650 (N.J. 2010), 241

Stern v. Grand, 773 P.2d 1074 (Colo. 1989), 510

Stewart v. Bee-Dee Neon & Signs, Inc., 751 So.2d 196 (Fla. Dist. Ct. App. 2000), 231

Storey v. Cello Holdings, L.L.C., 347 F.3d 370 (2d Cir 2003), 326

Sturdivant v. Sturdivant, 241 S.W.3d 740 (Ark. 2006), 408

Straubinger v. Schmitt,792 A.2d 481 (N.J. Sup. Ct. App. Div. 2002), 398-399

Stricklan v. Koella, 546 S.W.2d 810 (Tenn. Ct. App. 1976), 125

Strickland v. Washington, 466 US. 668 (1984), 137

Supreme Court of New Hampshire v. Piper, 470 U.S. 274 (1985), 50

Supreme Court of Virginia v. Friedman, 487 U.S. 59 (1988), 50

Swiss Reinsurance America Corp. V. Roetzel & Andress, 837 N.E.2d 1215 (2005), 154

Synergy Assocs., Inc. v. Sun Biotechnologies, Inc., 350 F.3d 681 (7th Cir. 2003), 510

TIG Ins. Co. v. Giffin Winning Cohen & Bodewes, P.C., 444 P.3d 587 (7th Cir. 2006), 126

Tennessee Formal Ethics Opin. 95-F-137, 493

Tischler v. Watts, 827 A.2d 1036 (N.J. 2003), 134

Traxler v. Ford Motor Co., 576 N.W.2d 398 (Mich. Ct. App. 1998), 246

Trone v. Smith, 621 F.2d 994 (9th Cir. 1980), 403

Trumbull County Bar Assn. v. Makridis, 671 N.E.2d 31 (Ohio 1996), 293

Twohig v. Blackmer, 918 P.2d 332 (N.M. 1996), 360

United States v. Bingham, 769F. Supp. 1039 (N.D. Ill. 1991), 360

United States v. Brown, 356 F. Supp.2d 470 (M.D. Pa. 2005), 292

United States v. Cantor, 897 F.Supp. 110 (S.D. N.Y. 1995), 44

United States v. Cirami, 563 F.2d 26 (2d Cir. 1977), 135

United States v. Edwards, 39 F. Supp.2d 716 (M.D. La. 1999), 165

United States v. Edwards, 777 F.2d 364 (7th Cir 1985), 338

United States v. Godwin, 272 F.3d 659 (4th Cir. 2001), 542

United States v. Gonzalez-Lopez, 548 U.S. 140 (2006), 100

United States v. Goot, 894 F.2d 231 (7th Cir. 1990), 432

United States v. Hefferon, 314 F.3d 211 (5th Cir. 2002), 542

United States v. Joseph Binder Schweizer Empl. Co., 167 F. Supp.2d 862 (E.D. N.C. 2001), 292

United States v. Ketner, 370 F. Supp.2d 1045 (C.D. Cal. 2005), 422

United States v. McVeigh, 964 F. Supp. 313 (D. Colo. 1997), 360

United States v. Midgett, 342 F.3d 321 (4th Cir. 2003), 318

United States v. Ryan-Webster, 353 F.3d 353 (4th Cir. 2003), 35

United States v. Schwarz, 283 F.3d 76 (2d Cir. 2002), 398

United States v. Singleton, 165 F.3d 1297 (10th Cir 1999), 272

United States v. Thoreen, 653 F.2d 1332 (9th Cir. 1981), 344
United States v. W.R. Grace, 401 F. Supp.2d 1065 (D. Mont. 2005), 299
United Transp. Union v. Michigan State Bar, 401 U.S. 576 (1971), 469
Utah State Bar Ethics Advisory Opin. 114-15, 124

Valley/50th Avenue, L.L.C. v. Stewart, 153 P.3d 186 (Wash. 2007), 393
Vermont Ethics Op. 2000-3 (2000), 113
Viner v. Sweet, 70 P.3d 1046 (Cal. 2003), 126
Vinson v. Vinson, 588 S.E.2d 392 (Va. Ct. App. 2003), 383
Virginia Ethics Opin. 1530 (1993), 339
Virginia Legal Ethics Opin. 1842 (Sept. 30, 2008), 487
Virginia Pharmacy Bd. v. Virginia Citizens Consumer Council, 425 U.S. 748 (1976), 462, 478

Walker v. Board of Prof. Resp., 38 S.W.3d 540 (Tenn. 2001), 492
Walker v. State Dept. of Transp. & Dev. 817 So.2d 57 (La. 2002), 429
Weigel v. Farmers Ins. Co., 158 S.W.3d 147 (Ark. 2004), 365
White v. General Motors Corp., 126 F.R.D. 563 (D. Kan. 1989), 328

White v. General Motors Corp., 139 F.R.D.178 (D. Kan. 1991), 329
White v. General Motors Corp., 699 F. Supp. 1485 (D. Kan. 1988), 328
White v. General Motors Corp., 908 F.2d 675 (10th Cir. 1990), 329
White v. General Motors Corp., 977 F.2d 499 (10th Cir. 1992), 329
White v. Jungbauer, 128 P.3d 263 (Colo. Ct. App. 2005), 126
Whiting v. Lacara, 187 F.3d 317 (2d Cir. 1999), 98
Wilkerson v. Brown, 995 P.2d 393 (Kan. Ct. App. 1999), 292
Williams v. State, 805 A.2d 880 (Del. 2002), 379
Williamson v. Lee Optical Co., 348 U.S. 483 (1955), 463
Withrow v. Larkin, 421 U.S. 35 (1975), 547
Wood v. McGrath, North, Mullin & Kratz, P.C. 589N.W.2d 103 (Neb. 1999), 125
Woodruff v. Tomlin, 616 F.2d 924 (6th Cir. 1980), 125

Zarabia v. Bradshaw, 912 P.2d 5 (Ariz. 1996), 507
Zauderer v. Office of Disciplinary Counsel, 471 U.S. 626 (1985), 473-476, 479, 493
Zok v. Collins, 18 P.3d 39 (Alaska 2001), 130

TABLE OF RULES AND STATUTES

5 C.F.R. 2637.201, 424
17 C.F.R. 205.1-205.7, 450
17 C.F.R. 205.2, 21
17 C.F.R. 205.3, 163
31 C.F.R. Part 10, 22
31 C.F.R. 10.3 et seq., 80

5 U.S.C. 555, 80
8 U.S.C. 1252, 322
17 U.S.C. 205.3, 164
18 U.S.C. 207, 424
18 U.S.C. 401, 348
18 U.S.C. 401-402, 327
18 U.S.C. 1503, 344
18 U.S.C. 1504, 344
18 U.S.C. 1623, 359
18 U.S.C. 3006A, 327
28 U.S.C. 144, 535
28 U.S.C. 455, 535
28 U.S.C. 1912, 327
28 U.S.C. 1927, 327,352,354-355
28 U.S.C. 2254, 137
42 U.S.C. 1983, 311
42 U.S.C. 1988, 208,253
42 U.S.C. 2000e, 253

ABA CJC Canon 1, 541
ABA CJC Canon 2, 542
ABA CJC Canon 3, 561
ABA CJC Canon 4, 568-569
ABA CJC Canon 5, 575
ABA CJC Canon 7, 571
ABA CJC R. 2.4, 560
ABA Defense Function Std. 3-5.7, 272
ABA Defense Function Std. 4-7.6, 272
ABA Model Ct. R. on Ins. Disclosure, 130
ABA MRPC Preamble, 10,21,122
ABA MRPC 1.0, 45,143,318

ABA MRPC 1.1, 18,19-20,114-115,122
ABA MRPC 1.2, 97,101-102,107-108, 113-114,339,374
ABA MRPC 1.3, 113,131,245
ABA MRPC 1.4, 101-102,141-143,149, 168,201,374
ABA MRPC 1.5, 195-196,200-201,203-204,208,212-213,472
ABA MRPC 1.6, 142,169,286
ABA MRPC 1.7, 97,154,165,374,378-379, 383,387-388,398,400-401,424,511,517
ABA MRPC 1.8, 135,203-204,388,393-394,397-400,414
ABA MRPC 1.9, 400-401,406,414,422, 424,517
ABA MRPC 1.10, 406,414-417,421,517
ABA MRPC 1.11, 97,423-426,429,432, 438
ABA MRPC 1.12, 433,438,441-442
ABA MRPC 1.13, 142,161-163,165,298
ABA MRPC 1.14, 518,525
ABA MRPC 1.15, 215,217-218
ABA MRPC 1.16, 95,97-100,132,203,339
ABA MRPC 1.17, 233-234
ABA MRPC 1.18, 95,407,411,487,489
ABA MRPC 2.1, 141,149-150,154,158, 160,168
ABA MRPC 2.3, 446-447
ABA MRPC 2.4, 442
ABA MRPC 3.1, 252,326-327,331-332, 336,339-340
ABA MRPC 3.2, 340-341,343
ABA MRPC 3.3, 300-301,305-307,309-310,313-314,319-320,326,343
ABA MRPC 3.4, 243,245,251-252,262-264
ABA MRPC 3.5, 343-344,351,355-356
ABA MRPC 3.6, 356-358,361

ABA MRPC 3.7, 362,364-365,368
ABA MRPC 3.8, 264-266,270-272
ABA MRPC 3.9, 306,368
ABA MRPC 4.1, 252,280,283-286,326, 487
ABA MRPC 4.2, 291-294,298
ABA MRPC 4.3, 286-287,290-293,299
ABA MRPC 4.4, 236-237,241-242,252
ABA MRPC 5.1, 219-220
ABA MRPC 5.2, 223-224,226
ABA MRPC 5.3, 228-229,231
ABA MRPC 5.4, 10,11,154
ABA MRPC 5.5, 88-90
ABA MRPC 5.6, 90
ABA MRPC 5.7, 35
ABA MRPC 6.1, 498-500,504
ABA MRPC 6.2, 506-507,509-510
ABA MRPC 6.3, 511
ABA MRPC 6.4, 517
ABA MRPC 6.5, 516-517
ABA MRPC 7.1, 454-455,457,482,487, 504
ABA MRPC 7.2, 470-472
ABA MRPC 7.3, 459,464-465,469,473
ABA MRPC 7.4, 491
ABA MRPC 7.5, 457-458
ABA MRPC 7.6, 490
ABA MRPC 8.1, 306
ABA MRPC 8.2, 273,276-277
ABA MRPC 8.3, 37,43-44
ABA MRPC 8.4, 3,252,280,487,571
ABA MRPC 8.5, 22
ABA Prosecution Function Std. 3-4.1, 272
ABA Prosecution Function Std. 3-4.2, 272
ABA Standards for Imposing Lawyer Sanctions 2.2, 23
ABA Standards for Imposing Lawyer Sanctions 3.0, 23
ABA Standards for Imposing Lawyer Sanctions 4.21, 23
ABA Standards for Imposing Lawyer Sanctions 4.23, 23
ABA Standards for Imposing Lawyer Sanctions, 7.3, 199
ABA Standards for Imposing Lawyer Sanctions 9.32, 503
Alaska RPC 1.14, 524
Ariz. RPC 1.0, 45
Ariz. RPC 1.6, 112
Ariz. RPC 1.7, 514

Ariz. RPC 1.9, 514-515
Ariz. RPC 1.13, 161
Ariz. RPC 3.3, 111
Ariz. RPC 4.4, 237
Ariz. RPC 6.3, 514-515
Ariz. RPC 8.2, 273
Ariz. RPC 8.4, 111
Ark. RPC 1.9, 409-410
Ark. RPC 1.18, 408-410
Ark. RPC 3.1, 326
Ark. RPC 3.3, 300
Ark. RPC 4.1, 281
Ark. RPC 4.3, 287

Cal. Bus. & Prof. Code 6126, 74
Cal. Bus. & Prof. Code 6146, 204
Cal. Code Civ. P. 340.6, 130
Cal. Code Civ. P. 1281.9, 445
Cal. Prof. Conduct R. 3-110, 18
Cal. Prof. Conduct R. 3-300,391
Cal. Prof. Conduct R. 3-310, 417,419
Cal. R. Ct. 5.70, 107
Citizens Protection Act, 28 U.S.C. 530, 21, 272
Colo. RPC 1.5, 198
Colo. RPC 4.3, 289

D.C. RPC 1.1, 221
D.C. RPC 1.2, 222
D.C. RPC 1.11, 426,428-431
D.C. RPC 5.1, 222-223
D.C. RPC 5.3, 222-223
D.C. RPC 5.5, 222
D.C. RPC 8.4, 431
Del. RPC 1.14, 518
Del. RPC 1.16, 95
Del. RPC 1.17, 233
Del. RPC 2.1, 149
Del. RPC 3.5, 349-350
Del. RPC 5.1, 220
Del. RPC 5.2, 224
Del. RPC 5.3, 229
Del. RPC 5.5, 88
Del. RPC 5.6, 90
Del. RPC 5.7, 35
Del. RPC 7.3, 459
Del. RPC 7.6, 490
Del. RPC 8.4, 349

Fair Debt Collection Practices Act, 15 U.S.C. 1692, 21
Fed. R. App. P. 38, 327

Fed. R. Civ. P. 11, 327
Fed. R. Civ. P. 60, 117
Fla. Bar R. 4-6.1, 500
Fla. Bar R. 4-7.1, 484
Fla. Bar R. 4-7.2, 483-486
Fla. Bar R. 4-7.4, 468,478
Fla. Bar R. 4-7.8, 478
Fla. Stat. Ann. 120.62, 80
Fla. Stat. Ann. 454.23, 74
Fla. Stat. Ann. Bar R. 4-1.1, 18

Ga. Code 15-19-50, 75
Ga. Bar R. 5.5, 90
Ga. RPC 5.4, 11

Ill. RPC 1.5, 472
Ind. CJC Canon 3, 561
Ind. Code Prof. Resp. 7-102, 259
Ind. RPC 1.3, 159
Ind. RPC 1.4, 159
Ind. RPC 1.6, 317
Ind. RPC 2.1, 160
Ind. RPC 3.3, 316-318
Ind. RPC 3.4, 259
Ind. RPC 8.4, 160,259

Kan. RPC 1.1, 120-121
Kan. RPC 1.5, 472
Kan. RPC 4.1, 281,283
Kan. RPC 4.4, 238-240
Kan. RPC 8.4, 238-240
Kan. Stat. Ann. 38-2310, 240
Kan. Sup. Ct. R. 203, 240
Kan. Sup. Ct. R. 219, 241

La. Disc. R. 2-106, 212
La. RPC 1.2, 208
La. RPC 1.5, 210
La. RPC 1.7, 14
La. RPC 1.10, 414
La. RPC 5.3, 14
La. RPC 5.4, 13,14
La. RPC 5.5, 14
La. RPC 8.3, 39-41
La. RPC 8.4, 13,14,39-40,210

Mass. RPC 1.7, 396
Mass. RPC 1.8, 396
Mass. RPC 7.1, 459
Mass. RPC 7.5, 459
Mass. RPC 8.3, 45
Md. Code State Govt., 9-1607.1, 80

Md. RPC 6.4, 518
Md. RPC 6.5, 516
Mich. Comp. L. 55.300a, 74
Mich. Comp. L. 338.3467, 74
Mich. Comp. L. 438.31, 202
Mich. Comp. L. 600.916, 74,82
Mich. Comp. L. 600.2922, 82
Mich. Comp. L. 600.5838
Mich. Comp. L. 700.3703, 82
Mich. Ct. R. 2.003, 535
Mich. Ct. R. 2.114, 327
Mich. Ct. R. 2.201, 82
Mich. Ct. R. 8.121, 204
Mich. Ct. R. 9.112, 29
Mich. Ct. R. 9.113, 29
Mich. Ct. R. 9.123, 69,71-72
Mich. RPC 1.1, 115
Mich. RPC 1.7, 380-382
Mich. RPC, 3.4, 243
Mich. RPC 8.4, 4
Minn. CJC Canon 2, 543
Minn. CJC Canon 5, 571
Minn. RPC 6.1, 499
Minn. RPC 7.1, 454-455
Minn. RPC 7.5, 458
Minn. RPC 8.2, 571
Minn. R. Lawyer Prof. Resp. 8-14, 571
Miss. CJC Canon 1, 557
Miss. CJC Canon 3, 559
Miss. RPC 3.2, 341
Mo. RPC 4-3.1, 329-331
Mo. RPC 4-3.2, 329-331
Mo. RPC 4-8.4, 329-331
Money Laundering Act of 1986, 18 U.S.C. 1957, 214

N.C. CJC Canon 2, 567-568
N.C. Rev. RPC 8.1, 53
N.C. Rev. RPC 8.5, 22
N.D. RPC 1.14, 520-522
N.H. RPC 1.5, 152
N.H. RPC 1.14, 526
N.H. RPC 2.1, 153
N.J. RPC 3.7, 362
N.Y. Disc. R. 1-102, 229-230
N.Y. Disc. R. 1-104, 230
N.Y. Disc. R. 3-101, 230
N.Y. Disc. R. 3-102, 230
N.Y. Disc. R. 3-103, 230
N.Y. Disc. R. 6-101, 230
Neb. DR 5-105, 376-377

Ohio Disc. R. 1-102, 275,342
Ohio Disc. R. 7-102, 342
Ohio Disc. R. 9-101, 275
Ohio Gov. Bar R. III §4, 130
Okla RPC 4.2, 296-297
Okla. RPC 8.1. 57
Oregon Rev. Stat. 752.035, 88

Pa. Post Conviction Relief Act, 42 Pa. Cons. Stat. 9541 et seq., 137
Pa. RPC 1.11, 423,436-437
Pa. RPC 1.12, 433-437
Pa. RPC 3.9, 369

Real Estate Settlement Procedures Act, 12 U.S.C. 2601 et seq., 21

S.C. RPC 1.1, 308
S.C. RPC 1.7, 308
S.C. RPC 3.1, 308
S.C. RPC 3.3, 308
S.C. RPC 3.4, 308
S.C. RPC 3.6, 359
S.C. RPC 4.1, 308
S.C. RPC 4.4, 237
S.C. RPC 8.4, 308
S.D. RPC 1.7, 375
S.D. RPC 1.8, 388
S.D. RPC 1.9, 400
S.D. RPC 1.18, 407
S.D. RPC 3.3, 303
S.D. RPC 3.4, 303
S.D. RPC 4.1, 303
S.D. RPC 8.4, 303

Sarbanes-Oxley Act, 15 U.S.C. 7245, 21,163,450
State Bar of Mich. R. 16

Tenn. Disc. R. 2-101, 492-495
Tenn. RPC 4.2, 292
Tenn. Sup. Ct. R. 43, 218
Tex. Govt. Code 81.101, 75

Utah RPC 1.5, 123
Utah RPC 1.4, 142
Utah RPC 1.15, 215
Utah RPC 3.7, 365-366
Utah RPC 7.4, 491
Utah RPC 8.3, 37-38

Wash. Disc. R. 1-102, 346
Wash. Disc. R. 7-102, 346
Wash. Disc. R. 7-106, 346
Wash. RPC 1.2, 101
Wash. RPC 2.3, 447
Wash. RPC 2.4, 443
Wash. RPC 3.5, 344
Wash. RPC 3.6, 357
Wash. RPC 3.8, 265
Wash. RPC 7.2, 471
W. Va. RPC 3.1, 334-335
W. Va. RPC 6.2, 506
W. Va. RPC 6.3, 511
Wy. CJC Application, 539
Wy. CJC Preamble, 536
Wy. CJC Scope, 536
Wy. CJC Terminology, 538
Wy. CJC Canon 1, 541
Wy. CJC Canon 4, 569

CHAPTER I

OBEDIENCE

Perspectives, Sources of Law, Professionalism

*"If I want to be great I have to win the
victory over myself—self discipline."*
— *Harry Truman*

[W]hen a righteous act is represented as being done with a steadfast soul and sundered from all view to any advantage... , it far surpasses and eclipses any similar action that was in the least affected by any extraneous incentives; it elevates the soul and inspires the wish to be able to act in this way. Even moderately young children feel this impression, and duties should never be represented to them in any other way.
— *Immanuel Kant*

OBJECTIVE: Given conduct issues implicating a lawyer's professional responsibility, articulate the significance that a lawyer's willingness to obey the law of professional responsibility has for the lawyer and public, varying perspectives lawyers and non-lawyers hold on responsibility, and the sources of law and discipline procedures likely to govern that conduct issue.

Applicable Rules

1.0 Terminology

5.4 Professional Independence of Lawyer

5.7 Responsibilities Regarding Law-Related Services

8.3 Reporting Professional Misconduct

8.4 Misconduct

8.5 Disciplinary Authority – Choice of Law

Your entry into the profession and practice of law depends on your willingness to obey constitutions, laws, rules, and regulations governing lawyers. This chapter articulates how important personal and professional responsibility is to a practicing lawyer. It also shows how law practice depends on the lawyer's willingness to obey the law of professional responsibility. The whole text is really an argument for personal and professional responsibility, but we thought that taking a few minutes to consider that question directly would be worthwhile. Unless you believe that the subject of responsibility is significant, you will not give it the time and attention that it deserves. After an introduction to the subject of responsibility, this chapter then asks you to examine briefly some perspectives on responsibility. Lawyers tend properly toward practicality and pragmatism. This course is not one in philosophy. Yet lawyers also learn how to recognize and draw on the varying perspectives of their clients and others with whom they deal. We felt that you might appreciate a little instruction in those perspectives, so that you understand how differently other lawyers, clients, and persons may think and operate. The chapter then describes the conventional sources for regulation of professional responsibility, introducing you to the conduct rules. The chapter continues with a description of the forms of and procedures for lawyer discipline. The chapter ends with a discussion of professionalism.

A. Perspectives on Responsibility

Significance. The first objective of any course on the professional conduct of lawyers is that you grasp the subject's significance. Most of us believe that we have a sound sense of responsibility, even while we believe that many others do not. Human nature is to think more of ourselves and less of others than we ought. A myth prevails among new law students that professional responsibility is simply common sense with which you are born and that professors cannot teach you. This inaccurate mindset leads law students and lawyers into peril. If your mindset and attitude are that ethics is simple common sense, then you will see only the simple and common sense, when to the contrary the rules are often complex and technical. You will fail ethics examinations and later suffer grievance and discipline in practice. This course helps you recalibrate your mindset to understand and adopt the profession's conduct rules to guide your law practice.

Necessity. You need a professional responsibility course, whether you recognize it yet or not. Pragmatically, you need this course just to become a lawyer. To qualify for a law license, you must pass three tests on professional responsibility including the examination in this course, the Multistate Professional Responsibility exam, and the bar exam—more tests than other law subjects. Whether you agree with them yet or not, bar leaders who govern the profession think that you need this course. Accreditation standards require that your law school offer instruction in professional responsibilities. You cannot become a lawyer without knowing enough of this subject to pass examinations on it.

Complexity. You also need this course for law practice. Law practice and the professional conduct it requires are more complex than you may think. There are situations common to the practice of law that, without this course, you would not recognize as involving important responsibilities. No matter what type of law you practice, you will use professional responsibility every day of your law career, whether your actions involve setting a fee, responding to discovery requests, talking to a witness, advising your corporate client, or a hundred other daily routines of law practice. If it were even possible for you to gain a law license without knowing the subject of professional responsibility, which it is not, then you would quickly lose that license if you did not know your professional responsibilities. The profession has conduct rules, and it enforces them. Many lawyers' favorite page of the monthly state-bar magazine is the notice of discipline, where they read the names and bad actions of disbarred or disciplined professional acquaintances. In the worst of cases, if you do not know your professional responsibility, then a client might also sue you, a prosecutor charge you with a crime, and a court sanction you. Your bad decisions can affect not only you but also innocent others.

Misconduct. For lawyers, responsibility is both a foundational and broad subject. Notice how broadly ABA MODEL RULE OF PROF. CONDUCT 8.4, a state version of which the text reproduces below, defines lawyer misconduct. Rule 8.4 is a "catch all" rule. Violating any other conduct rule implicates Rule 8.4. Rule 8.4 also defines as misconduct several kinds of behavior like dishonesty, fraud, and crimes implicating unfitness, that other rules do not necessarily address. Rule 8.4 also defines as misconduct attempting to violate a rule or inducing another to do so. Can you see why the conduct rules would prohibit attempts and inducing rule violations? Whom might lawyers commonly induce to violate conduct rules? Misconduct even includes a lawyer's implying that the lawyer has an undue influence on a judge or other government official. Read Rule 8.4 for these and related proscriptions. As you do so, consider what scienter Rule 8.4 requires as to each form of violation. If a lawyer does not know that the lawyer is breaking a conduct rule, is it still professional misconduct?

MICH. R. PROF. CONDUCT 8.4: Misconduct.
It is professional misconduct for a lawyer to:
(a) violate or attempt to violate the Rules of Professional Conduct, knowingly assist or induce another to do so, or do so through the acts of another;
(b) engage in conduct involving dishonesty, fraud, deceit, misrepresentation, or violation of the criminal law, where such conduct reflects adversely on the lawyer's honesty, trustworthiness, or fitness as a lawyer;
(c) engage in conduct that is prejudicial to the administration of justice;
(d) state or imply an ability to influence improperly a government agency or official; or
(e) knowingly assist a judge or judicial officer in conduct that is a violation of the Code of Judicial Conduct or other law.

INQUIRY

Reflexivity. Although you will learn your responsibilities by intense study in this course, you must soon know your responsibilities automatically, instinctively, as a matter of course. You will take many actions "in the heat of the moment," without time to read rules, consult experts, and research and reflect on the right course. You must build the cognitive frameworks and performance habits now to keep your conduct within the rules later, even if you forget the specific rules governing that conduct. That is the nature of law knowledge, that your consistent performance of it is more important than how you acquire or retain it. Masterful lawyers may forget the chapter and verse of the conduct rules, but they are sure to follow every rule from the knowledge they learned in law school and the habits and practices that they acquired in law school clinical programs and early in law practice. You must study the rules until you can discern, quickly and consistently, what they require in every practice circumstance that you are likely to encounter. This course and its subject of responsibility are important.

Legacy. There are other, more-positive and internal reasons why you should attend to your personal and professional responsibilities in law practice. Responsibility goes far deeper than ethics rules. It goes to who we are and who we become as lawyers. When 80-year-old Jerold Solovy, superlative trial lawyer and long-time chair of one of the nation's largest and most respected law firms Jenner & Block, died on January 19, 2011, his Chicago Tribune obituary haled not his Supreme Court victories but his legendary commitment to pro-bono service and improvement of the judicial system. The obituary quoted Mr. Solovy as crediting his career and success to his upbringing in a conservative Jewish synagogue where the charitable principles he learned became the core of who he was as a professional. Lawyer-conduct rules alone would not have led Mr. Solovy to his achievements. Given their technical and occasionally obscure nature, rules alone might have led Mr. Solovy away from greatness. His heirs, partners, and associates might have been appalled, not proud, if he had solely followed the rules. Responsibility can and should rest on broader grounds.

Identity. Mr. Solovy and this book's authors are not the only ones to have appreciated the power of personal responsibility to shape a professional career and ethic. The profession gives you the same message. Section 9 of the Preamble to the ABA MODEL RULES OF PROFESSIONAL CONDUCT states that "difficult issues of professional discretion ... must be resolved through the exercise of sensitive professional and moral judgment guided by basic principles underlying the rules." Section 16 reiterates that the rules do not "exhaust the moral and ethical considerations that should inform a lawyer...." "The Rules simply provide a framework for the ethical practice of law," section 16 concludes. With conduct rules providing only a framework, it is up to you to discern, develop, and commit yourself to maintaining the framework's foundations, walls, and rooms. You choose how sound to make your construction as a lawyer. Your identity as a lawyer is not the product solely of the conduct rules. Your identity may begin there but goes much deeper.

Reputation. Think of a famous lawyer whose law license the state bar has revoked (President Clinton may come to mind) or who tarnished a career with personal scandal (Governor Spitzer may come to mind). These lawyers did not fail because they did not know the conduct rules. They were once just like you, sitting in a law school class with great dreams for their future and no thought of personal and professional scandal. Law students and lawyers are just as likely as non-lawyers are to adopt that perilous not-my-problem attitude when it comes to self-evaluation. Lawyers who fall from professional and public grace have the same training and licensure, and similar intellect and commitments, as you will. What was wrong with them could just as easily be wrong with us. The uncomfortable and even unnerving truth is that given the wrong set of circumstances, we are each just one bad decision away from professional and personal disgrace.

Guidance. To help you avoid ending up with a similar fate, this book helps you build more than the conduct rules' minimal framework. The rules' drafters admit that the rules are not enough to guide you. How do you develop more sensitive, aware, and moral personal and professional judgment? You must consider subjects that non-lawyers would readily recognize as responsibility issues but that law schools too rarely have. Those subjects include personality, character, faith, emotion, discernment, self-awareness, interpersonal dynamics, intercultural skills, addictions, worldviews, attitudes, and mindsets. Expect some personal discomfort while exploring these topics. Constructing or reconstructing personal and professional identity can require changing old thoughts, patterns, and habits, saving and amplifying valuable commitments, qualities, and attributes while jettisoning the rest. We believe it is an important process for your professional development, even as we continue to believe that it remains important for us. We would disserve you by simply focusing on conduct rules while ignoring their unavoidable intersection with their related informing subjects.

Worldviews. Lawyers, like non-lawyers, draw on a wide range of worldviews, perspectives, and ethics when shaping and confirming their own professional responsibility. What is different about lawyers is that they develop the capacity to recognize the ethics of others and then to help those others, particularly clients, draw on, modify, and remediate those ethics. Personal and professional success lies in meta-ethical competence, in which you develop the capacity to recognize what ethics you and others are following and the benefits and hazards that following those ethics produce. Clients will ensure that your professional circumstances vary so widely that you will need to be able to move back and forth among variant ethics, from pragmatism to ideals, and from morality to instrumentalism. What follows here is a survey of a few of those ethics that you will encounter, draw upon, and remediate, and help others do so, in law practice. Think of these worldviews or ethics as you study lawyer conduct rules and cases. Which of these ethics do you think the lawyers whom you see disciplined in the cases in this book were following?

Choices. Imagine that you must make a simple choice, say, whether to join a local bar association. You are already a member of the state bar from which you earned a law license. You have started your sole practice, served a few clients, and met some of the local lawyers. One of those lawyers, an officer of the local bar association, urged you to join the local bar and, when you hedged, sent you a follow-up letter with an application form. Now you must choose whether to pay the $200 annual fee to join the local bar association, which is a voluntary association whose 1,300 members practice in or near the county where you reside and have your law office. How do you go about making that simple decision? What ethic will you follow, and how does it reveal your worldview and meta-ethical competence? The following text describes some of the common worldviews or ethics that lawyers, clients, and others employ when making choices.

Pragmatism. You might decide whether to join the local bar by determining whether you have $200 in your office checking account. You have just encountered your first worldview or ethic known as *pragmatism*, to make choices based primarily on what is immediately possible. Let us be pragmatic: there is no sense in speculating about the value of joining the local bar when you do not have the money. All of us think pragmatically from time to time. Lawyers value pragmatic thinking. So do clients. There is little sense in having your thoughts in the rarified air when what you propose to a client is practically impossible. Identifying the possible is a large part of sound counsel. On the other hand, pragmatic thinking can be shortsighted. Just because something appears presently impossible does not mean that one should not pursue it. Some new lawyers would wisely charge the $200 annual fee to a credit card and join the local bar even when they did not have the money in the checking account. On the other hand, just because something is possible does not mean that one should do it. Some new lawyers would wisely save the $200 for some other purpose. Lawyers recognize pragmatism's limitations and counsel clients accordingly. Most significantly, just because it is occasionally possible for a lawyer to break a conduct rule undiscovered and to gain something from it does not mean that a lawyer should do it.

Instrumentalism. You might decide whether to join the local bar by determining what you will gain from it. You have just encountered a second worldview or ethic known as instrumentalism, to make choices based on the predicted results of actions. Instrumental reasoning depends on if-then judgments: if I take this course, then I will realize that result. If you join a local bar association, then you may have access to newsletters, library resources, section meetings, and other career and professional-development resources. You may also receive client referrals from the professional network you develop. Some new lawyers would judge those and other benefits to be worthwhile. Other new lawyers would not. Lawyers reason instrumentally, just as clients do. Lawyers help clients make greater use of instrumental reasoning because of its power and appropriateness. Yet lawyers also recognize instrumentalism's limitations. Not every if becomes a then. Predictions can be unreliable, especially when we have incomplete information or there are too many other variables than the one considered. Instrumental reasoning can in the worst case become like gambling on results the probabilities for which may not be particularly attractive. Gamble often enough, and you are sure to come up a loser, when in some instances for lawyer and client losing is simply not an option. Would you break a conduct rule risking the loss of your law license simply because your action looked sure to produce a good result? We hope not, but some lawyers have taken that gamble and lost.

Morality. You might decide whether to join the local bar by evaluating what you understand to be fitting to the role of a new lawyer in a professional community. You have just encountered a third worldview or ethic known as *morality*, to make choices on how well your actions fit with the circumstances then existing. A moral judgment might impel a new lawyer to join the local bar whether or not the money to do so was immediately available (pragmatism) and it looked like it would benefit the new lawyer (instrumentalism). New lawyers have specific roles and responsibilities in a community of professionals. Their roles include providing the energy, initiative, and innovation to preserve and promote the community's wellbeing and the wellbeing of those whom the community serves. Their responsibilities include accepting the guidance of master lawyers whose conduct establishes and preserves the community's norms. It is fitting that new lawyers assume these duties toward the profession. Morality is the repository of accumulated experience and wisdom. Lawyers recognize morality's power to guide their own conduct and the conduct of their clients, especially when pragmatic thinking seems shortsighted and instrumental thinking seems uncertain. They also recognize when morality becomes inflexible formalism, not suited to peculiar circumstances. Lawyers recognize morality's admonition not to break conduct rules but also remain sensitive to each rule's purpose and specific application.

Figure

Jon Muth, a partner in the litigation division of the 90-lawyer firm Miller Johnson, is a lawyer whose career almost any lawyer might hope to emulate. Mr. Muth stressed legal services to the poor. when president of the 33,000-plus member State Bar of Michigan, While practicing law full-time as a bet-the-company litigator, he founded the Legal Assistance Center, a lawyer-funded courthouse-based nonprofit organization that has served 80,000 unrepresented patrons, providing legal forms and information. Mr. Muth, who has received his state bar's highest award for service to the profession, now makes a practice specialty out of mediating high-stakes cases. Long a mentor to new and experienced lawyers, Mr. Muth still finds the time to help lawyers and judges with disciplinary matters. Some lawyers make far more than their expected contribution to the profession. Mr. Muth is one of those rare lawyers.

Realism. You might decide whether to join the local bar by determining whether judges and other decision-makers who may hold your future and the future of your clients populate it. You have just encountered a fourth worldview or ethic known as *realism*, to make choices based on the power structures and relationships that exist anywhere persons gather. A realist's judgment might be that if you remain an outsider to those whose accommodations can make a difference in your law practice, then you will receive those accommodations less often than an insider would. You might decide to join the local bar to meet judges and other bar leaders so that they develop confidence in you. New lawyers can operate in certain circles at a slight disadvantage simply because they do not share history and relationship with decision-makers. Then again, new lawyers may have an advantage for that same reason, that they have no negative history or relationship with those same decision-makers. Lawyers are realists. They recognize that membership within certain groups can have its advantages and disadvantages. Lawyers help clients think in a realist's terms, even while they discourage over-reliance on a realist's thinking. We are a nation under law, not despots. There are times when it is critical that a client trust a judge even when the client has a realist's view not to do so. Although realism has its place, a realist's arguments have no place whatsoever in certain settings. For instance, you seldom (if ever) would make a realist's argument to a judge because to do so would be to disrespect the judge's role and risk sanction.

Humanism. You might decide whether to join the local bar based on whether it would affirm and elevate the dignity that you see for yourself as a new lawyer. You have just encountered a fifth worldview or ethic known as *humanism,* to make choices based on the degree to which actions respect and augment what you discern it means for you and others to be fully engaged as human. A humanist's judgment might be that if you join the local bar, then you will experience the fullness of professional life, as you interact with other lawyers whose equal commitment to the profession elevates you all to a level none of you would reach without the other. You would support bar social and professional events that call members to respect through civility and professionalism the reputation, dignity, and commitment of each member. You would celebrate what it means to be a lawyer, as an intrinsically valued calling peculiarly fitted to preserving and increasing the dignity of both lawyer and client. Lawyers draw on humanistic arguments at times, perhaps most often when called in public performance to defend liberties most basic to human flourishing. Lawyers also help clients temper their humanistic yearnings with pragmatic, instrumental, and moral advice. One cannot always do what exalts the self (what feels good), especially when it involves rule-breaking misconduct.

Faith. You might decide to join the local bar based on a providential view of the circumstance through which the opportunity to do so arose. You have just encountered a sixth worldview or ethic known as a faith or spiritual ethic, to make choices trusting that circumstances work for the good of those who believe in their significance. A new lawyer of faith might take the invitation of an experienced lawyer to join the local bar as a singular event to treat with due respect for its potential significance to the new lawyer's calling. The experienced lawyer did not reach out to just anyone but to you. To ignore that invitation might be to close the door to an even more significant opportunity that was contingent on trusting and accepting the invitation. When a new lawyer discerns how events connect with one another for the new lawyer's benefit, the new lawyer engages those events with greater hope and commitment. Consciousness of faith's possibilities leads to commitment to faithful action, elevating the new lawyer even as the new lawyer elevates the faith that spurred the consciousness and action. Lawyers draw on faith, just as they help their clients do so. These perspectives are just a few of those that you will encounter in law practice, particularly when discerning your own personal and professional responsibility, while discerning the personal and professional responsibility of others.

B. Sources for Professional Responsibility

Lawyer Independence. Paragraph [11] of the Preamble of the ABA MODEL RULES OF PROFESSIONAL CONDUCT asserts that an "independent legal profession" preserves "government under law" while paragraph [13] echoes that lawyers "play a vital role in the preservation of society." Magna Carta in 1215 labeled our commitment to the *law of the land*, while the 5th and 14th Amendments called it *due process of law*, and today we speak of the *rule of law*. No matter the lexicon, both the public and lawyers have long recognized the value of both a commitment to law and to an educated profession sufficiently independent and well trained to administer it. Historically, government has left regulation of lawyer conduct to the states. States have in turn left regulation of lawyer conduct to the judicial branch and law profession, preserving a substantial degree of professional independence. Other professions, like the medical and nursing professions, are subject to state administrative regulations as a primary source for professional regulation, but not lawyers. Recognize this commitment to professional independence in the various sources of law regulating lawyer conduct. Consider the following state version of ABA MODEL RULE OF PROF. CONDUCT 5.4 titled "Professional Independence of a Lawyer." Can you articulate why Rule 5.4 might be necessary or appropriate?

GEORGIA RULE OF PROF. CONDUCT 5.4: Professional Independence of a Lawyer

(a) A lawyer or law firm shall not share legal fees with a nonlawyer, except that:

(1) an agreement by a lawyer with the lawyer's firm, partner, or associate may provide for the payment of money, over a reasonable period of time after the lawyer's death, to the lawyer's estate or to one or more specified persons;

(2) a lawyer or law firm who purchases the practice of a deceased, disabled, or disappeared lawyer may, pursuant to the provisions of Rule 1.17, pay to the estate or other representative of that lawyer the agreed-upon purchase price; and

(3) a lawyer or law firm may include nonlawyer employees in a compensation or retirement plan, even though the plan is based in whole or in part on a profit-sharing arrangement; and

(4) a lawyer who undertakes to complete unfinished business of a deceased lawyer may pay to the estate of the deceased lawyer that proportion of the total compensation which fairly represents the services rendered by the deceased lawyer.

(5) A lawyer may pay a referral fee to a bar-operated non-profit lawyer referral service where such fee is calculated as a percentage of legal fees earned by the lawyer to whom the service has referred a matter pursuant to Rule 7.3. Direct Contact with Prospective Clients.

(b) A lawyer shall not form a partnership with a nonlawyer if any of the activities of the partnership consist of the practice of law.

(c) A lawyer shall not permit a person who recommends, employs, or pays the lawyer to render legal services for another to direct or regulate the lawyer's professional judgment in rendering such legal services.

(d) A lawyer shall not practice with or in the form of a professional corporation or association authorized to practice law for a profit, if:

(1) a nonlawyer owns any interest therein, except that a fiduciary representative of the estate of a lawyer may hold the stock or interest of the lawyer for a reasonable time during administration;

(2) a nonlawyer is a corporate director or officer thereof; or

(3) a nonlawyer has the right to direct or control the professional judgment of a lawyer.

The maximum penalty for a violation of this Rule is disbarment.

_____

INQUIRY

Financing Practice. You might have discerned that several of the above Rule 5.4's prohibitions have as much to do with financing law practice as they do with ensuring the independence of lawyers. The two, finance and control, go hand in hand. If non-lawyers own law firms, then the lawyers who work for those non-lawyers just may shape their services as much to satisfy the non-lawyer owners as their own professional responsibilities. Law practice can be lucrative. So far, the law profession has resisted the efforts of accounting firms and other corporate entities not controlled by lawyers, to finance and take over the provision of legal services. So long as lawyers control legal services, the services are likely to conform to the law profession's norms and standards. If accountants or others control legal services, then the services are likely to change in important ways. In a similar way, if non-lawyer employees of a law firm share directly in fees a lawyer earns from legal work, then those non-lawyer employees may conduct themselves in a manner inconsistent with a lawyer's professional responsibility. For instance, they might solicit in-person new clients, advertise in a misleading manner, or do other things that a lawyer must not do under lawyer rules of conduct. These rules against non-lawyers controlling and sharing in fees from legal services may look to non-lawyers like protectionism, but they serve important functions in ensuring the integrity of legal services. Consider the following case.

In re Guirard,
Louisiana Supreme Court
11 So.3d 1017 (2009)

PER CURIAM.[fn]

This disciplinary matter arises from formal charges filed by the Office of Disciplinary Counsel ("ODC") against respondents, E. Eric Guirard and Thomas R. Pittenger, attorneys licensed to practice law in Louisiana.

UNDERLYING FACTS

Respondents are partners in a law practice operating under the name of E. Eric Guirard and Associates, P.L.C. (the "law firm" or the "firm"). The law firm, which has offices in Baton Rouge and New Orleans, has operated since July 1994 and handles primarily plaintiff's personal injury cases.[fn] In 2000, the ODC began investigating respondents' employment of five "case managers," all nonlawyers, who assisted in the processing of the personal injury claims being handled by the firm prior to litigation. One of the primary issues under investigation concerned the compensation of the case managers. These employees were paid their compensation by regular bi-monthly payroll from the firm's general operating account as a commission computed as a percentage of the firm's gross legal fees collected on the individual settled cases that the individual case manager worked on and settled during the payroll period.[fn] ...

The ODC also investigated the activities of the case managers and the law firm's investigators with regard to the unauthorized practice of law. Specifically, the ODC sought to determine whether these nonlawyer employees were properly supervised by respondents or whether the nonlawyers were actually performing the duties of an attorney in violation of the Rules of Professional Conduct.

At respondents' firm, the receptionist typically transferred telephone calls from new prospective clients to the case manager on duty to receive such calls. If the phone call came in after business hours, an answering service paged the duty case manager. The duty case manager spoke to the new prospective client, and decided if the case was one that the firm would be interested in handling. The duty case manager gathered certain information and gave it to one of the law firm's investigators, who in turn met with the prospective client at his or her home and had the prospective client sign an attorney-client contingency fee contract. The investigator also obtained other signed forms from the client, including releases for medical records and employment and wage information, and took photographs, if needed. The investigator returned the signed contract and other information to the law firm's office, and was thereupon paid $50 for the visit.[fn] The investigator also received additional compensation if he obtained signed contracts for additional clients while visiting the initial client.[fn]

After the signed contract and other information was returned to the law firm, the material was reviewed by either Mr. Guirard or Mr. Pittenger. In most cases the file was then assigned to a case manager, who processed the file pursuant to instructions contained in the law firm's Case Manager Manual.[fn] After the client completed medical treatment, the case manager prepared an evaluation of the case on a form used by the firm. The completed form and the case file were forwarded to either Mr. Guirard or Mr. Pittenger, who would approve a high dollar value and a low dollar value on the case for purposes of making a settlement demand.[fn] The file was then returned to the case manager, who would send a demand letter signed by a lawyer. The case manager was responsible for contacting the insurance adjuster and negotiating a settlement. When a settlement was reached, the case manager notified the client, arranged for the client to come to the office to pick up the settlement check, and prepared the settlement disbursement statement. Mr. Guirard typically met with the client to disburse the settlement funds. ...

DISCIPLINARY PROCEEDINGS

In February 2004, the ODC filed two counts of formal charges against respondents jointly. In Count I, the ODC alleged that respondents paid their case managers percentage commissions on gross legal fees, and thereby improperly shared legal fees with nonlawyers, in violation of Rules 5.4(a) and 8.4(a) of the Rules of Professional Conduct. ... In Count II, the ODC alleged that respondents have employed a "business first" model in operating their law firm,[fn] resulting in a situation in which their nonlawyer employees have

engaged in the unauthorized practice of law, either by design, or by respondents' failure to supervise, or by some combination of the two.
...

Hearing Committee Report [fn]

After considering the evidence and testimony presented at the 2004 and 2007 hearings, the hearing committee ... adopted the joint stipulation of facts. ...   As stipulated, a commission was paid to nonlawyer employees that was computed as a percentage of the firm's gross legal fees collected on specific individual settled cases. The testimony of respondents also makes it clear that, for the most part, if the case managers did not settle cases within a particular amount of time, the cases would be transferred to litigation, and the case managers would receive zero compensation for the work they had put into the case, unless a special bonus was assigned. The committee noted that the case managers were compensated on a percentage of the gross fees for each individual file; they were not compensated on a percentage of net profits of the firm.

Based on these factual findings, the committee found that respondents violated Rules 1.7(b), 5.4(a), and 8.4(a) of the Rules of Professional Conduct. The committee specifically rejected respondents' assertion that the percentage compensation paid to the case managers is a form of profit sharing and therefore ethically permissible... . The committee commented that this is not a situation in which the case managers are paid a percentage of net profits at the end of the year on the general business of the law firm; rather, "each nonlawyer receives a piece of the action if the case is [settled] by them. This is fee splitting and always has been." ...   Under these circumstances, the committee found the case manager has an "overwhelming motive to settle a claim at any price" before losing control over the file.

In Count II, the committee found that during the year 2000, the case managers negotiated directly with insurance adjusters, reached settlement agreements during telephone conversations when negotiations took place, and dealt directly with clients concerning settlement offers. The committee also found that an attorney in the firm established parameters of a high and a low within which to settle a case, and that the case managers were then allowed to negotiate a settlement between these two figures, independently of any supervision by an attorney.

Based on these factual findings, the committee found that respondents violated Rules 1.7(b), 5.3(a), 5.5(a) and (b), 8.4(a), 8.4(b), 8.4(c), and 8.4(d). Nonlawyers would initiate the attorney-client relationship and the case managers would advise clients whether they had a viable claim. They also advised prospective clients regarding the execution of legal documents, the attorney-client contract, medical releases, and other documents. In addition, the case managers were given leeway in settling individual cases using their own judgment without supervision from an attorney. The committee acknowledged that an attorney established the highs and lows for settlement purposes, but concluded it was the case manager who utilized the professional judgment in settlement.[fn] The case managers also had great leeway in managing the file, including obtaining settlement authority from the client, determining liability, determining probable insurance coverage, and determining an applicable prescription date. ...

The committee determined that respondents violated duties owed to their clients, the public, and the legal profession. The committee found respondents acted intentionally but they "were of the sincere belief that they were following professional guidelines and were not in violation of the Rules of Professional Conduct. In this regard, their actions were more negligent than they were intentional." The committee found no evidence of any harm to respondents' clients (but noted that "it would be almost impossible to determine that at this stage in the proceedings"), and concluded that the applicable baseline sanction in this matter is suspension. ...

Based on this reasoning, the committee recommended that respondents be suspended from the practice of law for one year and one day. ...

Rejecting the hearing committee's finding that respondents confected the law firm's procedures and compensation plan in a "negligent" fashion, the [attorney-discipline] board determined that respondents' conduct was intentional. The board found that the law firm's office procedures were carefully crafted and documented in forms and in a Case Manager Manual, and that respondents expected their employees to follow these procedures, notwithstanding any suggestion by Mr. Guirard to the contrary.[fn] The board determined that although no actual harm was proven as to any specific client, the potential for harm to clients, the public, the legal system, and the profession was immeasurable. By allowing nonlawyers to practice law, respondents ran the risk of having cases settled improperly and proceedings later being declared nullities. By implementing the compensation plan at issue, the potential for conflict between the client's interests and the case managers' interests was also great.[fn] Further, by improperly paying their case managers and investigators bonuses for "signing up" clients, the reputation of the legal profession and the legal system has undoubtedly been marred. The board found the applicable baseline sanction is disbarment.

In aggravation, the board found a pattern of misconduct, multiple offenses, substantial experience in the practice of law, and illegal conduct. The mitigating factors found by the board are the following: absence of a prior disciplinary record, timely good faith effort to rectify the consequences of the misconduct, full and free disclosure to the disciplinary board and a cooperative attitude toward the proceedings, and good character and reputation.[fn]

As to the Rule 5.4 violation, ... respondents in the instant matter have engaged in improper fee splitting with nonlawyers in violation of Rule 5.4. ... [R]espondents' compensation arrangement with their case managers and office staff had the potential to harm their clients. Once the nonlawyers were given a financial interest in respondents' legal fees, there was the obvious possibility that the interests of the nonlawyers could interfere with respondents' independent judgment in the case. ...

Respondents filed an objection to the disciplinary board's recommendation. Accordingly, the case was docketed for oral argument pursuant to Supreme Court Rule XIX, §11(G)(1)(b).

DISCUSSION

... Respondents do not contest that they have violated the Rules of Professional Conduct as alleged in the formal charges. Their misconduct involves conflicts of interest, failure to supervise their nonlawyer staff, impermissible fee sharing with nonlawyers, and facilitation of the unauthorized practice of law. Thus, the only issue before us is the appropriate sanction to be imposed.

In considering that issue, we are mindful that disciplinary proceedings are designed to maintain high standards of conduct, protect the public, preserve the integrity of the profession, and deter future misconduct. [C] The discipline to be imposed depends upon the facts of each case and the seriousness of the offenses involved considered in light of any aggravating and mitigating circumstances. [C] ...

Our prior decisions ... establish that the baseline sanction for the facilitation of the unauthorized practice of law by a nonlawyer is disbarment. In cases involving fee sharing with a nonlawyer, we have imposed a suspension of one year and one day. [C] For respondents' misconduct involving both facilitation of the unauthorized practice of law and fee sharing, the overall baseline sanction is disbarment.

As aggravating factors, we recognize a dishonest or selfish motive, a pattern of misconduct, and substantial experience in the practice of law... .

Having considered these factors in light of the record in its entirety, we decline to deviate from the baseline sanction of disbarment. Respondents delegated the handling of their clients' cases to their nonlawyer staff.   This was a systematic practice as part of the "business first" model knowingly employed by respondents.   By structuring their law firm in the manner in which they did, respondents harmed their clients, who, as we noted in [In re Sledge, 859 So.2d 671 (La. 2003)], "were deprived of the benefit of a thoughtful, individualized and professional legal analysis of their cases."   Respondents then motivated the nonlawyers to settle the clients' claims as quickly as possible in order to collect a paycheck.   Of course, these egregious practices profited respondents as well.

We conclude we would be remiss in our constitutional duty to regulate the practice of law if we were to impose any sanction in this case less than disbarment.   Therefore, respondents are hereby disbarred. ...

"What Were They Thinking?"
In *In re Guirard,* the grievance committee, board, and justices all saw in the respondent lawyers' case-manager system a "business first" model that violated multiple conduct rules. If the system was that obvious of a violation of the rules, not to mention the conventions of law practice, how do you think the lawyers justified it? The full opinion, reciting the substantial fee-shared and bonus amounts earned by the several case managers, indicates that it was a lucrative system. The system was certainly practical and efficient, and certainly benefited the lawyers and case managers.   Can you see how substantially the system may have hurt the clients? Why did the lawyers not see the harm to the clients? Or did they see the harm but just not care about it?

I N Q U I R Y

Model Rules. So, where does the law of professional responsibility reside? The answer to this question is not neat and tidy. In this text, you will study the American Bar Association's MODEL RULES OF PROFESSIONAL CONDUCT because the Multistate Professional Responsibility Exam will test you on those rules, and you will very likely have to pass that test for licensure. Yet the ABA Model Rules do not regulate lawyer conduct in any jurisdiction. They are *model* rules, meaning that the American Bar Association encourages state bars to adopt them. The American Bar Association is the largest voluntary professional association in the world, with more than 400,000 members—about one half of all American lawyers. The American Bar Association accredits law school, offers continuing legal education and information about the law, provides programs to assist lawyers and judges in their work, and supports member initiatives to improve the legal system. It does not regulate lawyer conduct. Paralleling a change in the profession that gradually made it more open but also more transactional, the American Bar Association first adopted moral Canons of Ethics in 1908, a more specific MODEL CODE OF PROFESSIONAL RESPONSIBILITY in 1969 that was still largely aspirational, and then finally the MODEL RULES OF PROFESSIONAL CONDUCT in 1983 containing detailed specific requirements and prohibitions.

Conduct Rules. State bars or state supreme courts, or both working in coordination, regulate most lawyer conduct, meaning that law is a self-regulating or at least a judicially regulated profession, with lawyers comprising the judiciary. State-bar committees review and recommend conduct rules, which state supreme courts adopt. The conduct rules are most often modified versions of the ABA MODEL RULES OF PROFESSIONAL CONDUCT. Some states have made very few changes to the Model Rules when adopting their own rules. Other states have made extensive changes to the Model Rules, while still others rely on conduct rules drawn from the earlier ABA MODEL CODE OF PROFESSIONAL RESPONSIBILITY. Thus, although the Multistate Professional Responsibility Exam will test you on a single set of Model Rules, you will practice under conduct rules that are likely to be at least slightly different. Your studies for your state's bar exam should alert you to those state-specific differences. Compare and contrast the following ABA Model Rule to similar and dissimilar state rules on the same subject.

> **ABA MODEL R. PROF. CONDUCT 1.1: Competence.** A lawyer shall provide competent representation to a client. Competent representation requires the legal knowledge, skill, thoroughness and preparation reasonably necessary for the representation.

> **FLORIDA STATUTES ANN. BAR R. 4-1.1: Competence.** A lawyer shall provide competent representation to a client. Competent representation requires the legal knowledge, skill, thoroughness, and preparation reasonably necessary for the representation.

> **CALIFORNIA PROF. CONDUCT R. 3-110: Failing to Act Competently.**
> (A) A member shall not intentionally, recklessly, or repeatedly fail to perform legal services with competence.
> (B) For purposes of this rule, "competence" in any legal service shall mean to apply the 1) diligence, 2) learning and skill, and 3) mental, emotional, and physical ability reasonably necessary for the performance of such service.
> (C) If a member does not have sufficient learning and skill when the legal service is undertaken, the member may nonetheless perform such services competently by 1) associating with or, where appropriate, professionally consulting another lawyer reasonably believed to be competent, or 2) by acquiring sufficient learning and skill before performance is required.

Types of Rules. Notice the (archaic) use of the word "shall" in the above ABA MODEL RULE OF PROF. CONDUCT 1.1. Paragraph 14 of the Model Rule's Scope provision defines categories of conduct rules. The first category, known as *imperative* or *mandatory* rules, prescribes conduct in which a lawyer must or must not engage. Mandatory rules sometimes use "shall" and other times use "must" to prescribe the required conduct. A lawyer's violation of a mandatory rule subjects the lawyer to discipline. The second category of rules, known as *permissive* rules, defines conduct in which a lawyer may engage if the lawyer so wishes depending on the lawyer's own judgment. Permissive rules often use "may" to define permissive conduct. A lawyer cannot be disciplined for violating a permissive rule. No discipline attaches to doing or not doing what the rule permits. A third category merely describes a lawyer's role without specifying conduct. Why did the American Bar Association adopt descriptive statements among its conduct rules? Paragraphs 14 and 21 of the Model Rule's Scope provision also state the difference between a conduct rule and the Comment following it, calling the rule "authoritative" but the Comment merely illustrative. The Comments introduce another category of "shoulds" that we can call *aspirational.* Lawyers should aspire to conduct that recognizes the spirit of the conduct rules, not merely their letter.

Reading Rules. Readability tests show that the ABA MODEL RULES OF PROFESSIONAL CONDUCT and equivalent state versions are very difficult to read. The sentences are on average very long and complex. Rules often state multiple conditions to their application. A single rule may actually contain multiple prescriptions and prohibitions—mandatory *do's* and prohibitive *don'ts* that a lawyer must parse from the rule and then follow. Many law students are unfamiliar with the practice conventions to which the rules refer and contexts in which lawyers apply them, making learning the rules even harder. Law students must learn both the rule and its law-practice context. One way to ensure a working knowledge of the rules is to reduce each rule to its several conditions and, for each condition, the rule's proscriptive and prohibitive statements. For example, Rule 1.1 above proscribes that when representing a client (the condition), a lawyer must serve competently (the proscription). Rule 1.1 also proscribes that when representing a client (the condition), a lawyer must have the required law knowledge (the proscription). Do you see other proscriptions in Rule 1.1? Do not underestimate the complexity of these conduct rules or the challenge of your rule studies. Some students underestimate the rules' subtlety. To ensure that you see the detail and breadth of each new rule, develop the habit of generating rule statements like the following longer list for Rule 1.1:

- when representing a client, serve competently;
- determine what is reasonably necessary to each representation;
- have the knowledge necessary to each representation;
- use the skill necessary to each representation;
- be as thorough as necessary in each representation;
- prepare as necessary for each representation;
- if you lack the requisite knowledge, either acquire it or decline the representation;
- if you lack the requisite skill, either acquire it or decline the representation;
- if anything will prevent you from being thorough, then decline the representation;
- if anything will prevent you from being prepared, then decline the representation.

Ethics Opinions. Another way in which the law profession self-regulates is through ethics opinions promulgated by the American Bar Association's Standing Committee on Ethics and Professional Responsibility or state ethics committees. By ethics opinions, we do not mean appellate-court decisions affirming, modifying, or reversing actual decisions on lawyer discipline. Those court decisions have their own influence. By ethics opinions, we mean the formal and informal statements of ethics committees that address common situations without identifying specific events, names, or places. Ethics opinions are only advisory, not binding. *See* In re Admonition Issued in Panel File No 99-42, 621 N.W.2d 240 (Minn. 2001) (no discipline under ethics opinion not addressed by conduct rules). Still, ethics opinions do help practitioners discern what the conduct rules require in instances where there might be two or more rule interpretations. In addition to researching ethics opinions, lawyers may also request an ethics opinion on a specific subject, although it may take longer for the ethics committee to issue the opinion than the lawyer has to act on the matter. Lawyers also take frequent resort to ethics hotlines maintained by state bars, keeping records of their call. Help interpreting conduct rules is often no more than a toll-free telephone call away. The American Bar Association also offers an ETHICSearch web-based ethics-opinion research service. The American Law Institute has also published the RESTATEMENT OF THE LAW (THIRD), THE LAW GOVERNING LAWYERS (2000). The RESTATEMENT both summarizes existing conduct rules and projects what those rules should be, although it does not yet generally receive the notoriety and respect earned by earlier Restatements.

Statutes. Law is increasingly complex. Vast quantities of new federal and state statutes govern the conduct of many industries, trades, and professions. Lawyers have not been immune to those statutes and regulations. Paragraph [10] of the Preamble to the ABA MODEL RULES OF PROFESSIONAL CONDUCT notes that the profession is only "largely" self-governing while paragraph [12] admits only "relative" professional autonomy. The profession appropriately resists legislative control to ensure individual rights and limited government. Still, federal and state statutes governing specific events, fields, or transactions may also regulate lawyer conduct. For example, federal antitrust provisions prohibit lawyers and local bars from price-fixing. *See* Goldfarb v. Virginia State Bar, 421 U.S. 773 (1975). Lawyers must also comply with the Fair Debt Collection Practices Act, 15 U.S.C. §1692(a), *see* Heintz v. Jenkins, 514 U.S. 291 (1995); Piper v. Portnoff Law Assocs., Ltd., 396 F.3d 227 (3d Cir. 2005), and the Real Estate Settlement Procedures Act, 12, U.S.C. §2601 et seq. Also, the Citizens Proection Act, 28 U.S.C. §530(b), holds federal-government lawyers responsible to comply with state laws and rules governing lawyers in the state in which the federal-government lawyer practices, settling a dispute that began with federal prosecutors interviewing represented persons without consent of their lawyers in violation of state ethics rules. For two other examples, federal statutes also dictate certain conduct of lawyers representing debtors in bankruptcy and limit the fees that lawyers may charge in representing Federal Tort Claims Act claimants. These are just a few of the many statutes governing lawyer conduct in specific situations. The trends that gave rise to these statutes have not abated. You can expect greater legislative control of lawyers in the future, both state and federal, and potentially international.

Regulations. Federal and state administrative regulations also regulate lawyer conduct. For example, the Sarbanes-Oxley Act, 15 U.S.C. §7245, authorized the Securities Exchange Commission to regulate the conduct of lawyers "appearing and practicing before the Commission." The Commision then construed "appearing and practicing before the Commission" very broadly to include providing advice on federal securities laws relating to a corporate client's preparation of any document that the client incorporates into a Commission submission. 17 C.F.R. §205.2(a). The Act's substantive provisions require lawyers to report securities-law violations to a corporate client's chief executive or legal counsel and then, if necessary, to the corporate board or audit committee. For another example, Internal Revenue Service regulations dictate certain conduct expected of lawyers advising clients on tax-sheltered investments. 31 C.F.R. Part 10. Federal regulations also prohibit lawyers from soliciting victims and families of victims of airplane crashes for a certain period after the crash. Other federal regulations prohibit lawyers from sending junk facsimile transmissions.

C. Lawyer Discipline

Disciplinary Authority. Obtaining a law license is a necessary first step toward law practice. Keeping your license is a necessary second step. The law profession has determined that conduct rules require enforcement. Violating conduct rules does not subject a lawyer to criminal-like penalties. Lawyers do not go to jail or pay fines for breaking conduct rules, although criminal charges may certainly arise out of the same set of circumstances (say, embezzlement of client funds) that gives rise to conduct-rule enforcement. So, too, may a civil action for malpractice. Instead, enforcement is against a lawyer's license. The strongest enforcement action is license revocation, also known as *disbarment*. License suspension for long or short periods is the second most-serious enforcement action. License suspension generally requires that the lawyer contact every client with a pending matter and every court in which the lawyer has a pending matter, notifying of the suspension. Private admonition or public reprimand are lesser sanctions. Costs and limited restitution may also be part of enforcement. Bars publish discipline in bar journals, making loss of reputation another and often most-severe enforcement action. Notice how the following similar state version of ABA MODEL RULE OF PROF. CONDUCT 8.5 treats the relationship of admission to discipline.

NORTH CAROLINA REV. RULE OF PROF. CONDUCT 8.5: **Disciplinary Authority; Choice of Law.**
    (a) Disciplinary Authority. A lawyer admitted to practice in North Carolina is subject to the disciplinary authority of North Carolina, regardless of where the lawyer's conduct occurs. A lawyer not admitted in North Carolina is also subject to the disciplinary authority of North Carolina if the lawyer provides or offers to provide any legal services in North Carolina. A lawyer may be subject to the disciplinary authority of both North Carolina and another jurisdiction for the same conduct.
    (b) Choice of Law. In any exercise of the disciplinary authority of North Carolina, the rules of professional conduct to be applied shall be as follows:
    (1) for conduct in connection with a matter pending before a tribunal, the rules of the jurisdiction in which the tribunal sits, unless the rules of the tribunal provide otherwise; and
    (2) for any other conduct, the rules of the jurisdiction in which the lawyer's conduct occurred, or, if the predominant effect of the conduct is in a different jurisdiction, the rules of that jurisdiction shall be applied to the conduct. A lawyer is not subject to discipline if the lawyer's conduct

conforms to the rules of a jurisdiction in which the lawyer reasonably believes the predominant effect of the lawyer's conduct will occur.

INQUIRY

Goals of Discipline. As you explore first the substance (level) of discipline and then the procedure for discipline through the next few sections of this chapter, keep in mind the several goals of lawyer discipline. The conduct rules help lawyers identify and serve the interests of clients, opposing counsel, opposing parties, judges, witnesses, members of the public, and the profession. Discipline begins with the same general educational purpose but also serves additional purposes to end misconduct, punish and rehabilitate wrongdoers, deter others from future misconduct, provide relief from harm, and improve public trust in the justice system and profession. *See* Fred C. Zacharias, *The Purposes of Lawyer Discipline*, 45 WM. & MARY L.REV. 675 (2003).

Level of Discipline. Much of this book addresses how to conform your conduct so as to avoid any discipline. Consider, though, the question of what level of discipline the profession should impose for certain misconduct. For example, you saw in the above *In re Guirard* case disagreement between the grievance committee and discipline board whether the respondent lawyers should be suspended for one year or disbarred. If discipline can be anything from as little as a private reprimand to as much as disbarment, then how should an attorney-discipline board decide? The American Bar Association's Standards for Imposing Lawyer Sanctions, Standards 2.2 to 2.8, rank levels of discipline. The standards, which several states follow or accept as influential, and discipline cases give some hints as to how to evaluate the level of discipline. The respondent lawyer's intent can be important, as can the degree of harm to the client or others, and the harm to the reputation of lawyers generally and public confidence in the justice system. *See* ABA STANDARDS FOR IMPOSING LAWYER SANCTIONS, STANDARDS 2.2, 3.0, 4.21, 4.23. The incidence of prior misconduct by the same respondent lawyer and the duration of the lawyer's present misconduct can also be factors, as can the lawyer's cooperation with grievance officials. Often, the cases will consider aggravating and mitigating circumstances. As you read the following case addressing the level of discipline, consider whether you agree or disagree with, or are surprised at, its outcome.

In re James H. Himmel,
Illinois Supreme Court
533 N.E.2d 790 (1988)

Justice STAMOS delivered the opinion of the court:

... We will briefly review the facts, which essentially involve three individuals: respondent, James H. Himmel, licensed to practice law in Illinois... ; his client, Tammy Forsberg... ; and her former attorney, John R. Casey.

The complaint alleges that respondent had knowledge of John Casey's conversion of Forsberg's funds and respondent failed to inform the Commission of this misconduct. The facts are as follows.

In October 1978, Tammy Forsberg was injured in a motorcycle accident. In June 1980, she retained John R. Casey to represent her in a personal injury or property damage claim resulting from the accident. Sometime in 1981, Casey negotiated a settlement of $35,000 on Forsberg's behalf. Pursuant to an agreement between Forsberg and Casey, one-third of any monies received would be paid to Casey as his attorney fee.

In March 1981, Casey received the $35,000 settlement check, endorsed it, and deposited the check into his client trust fund account. Subsequently, Casey converted the funds.

Between 1981 and 1983, Forsberg unsuccessfully attempted to collect her $23,233.34 share of the settlement proceeds. In March 1983, Forsberg retained respondent to collect her money and agreed to pay him one-third of any funds recovered above $23,233.34.

Respondent investigated the matter and discovered that Casey had misappropriated the settlement funds. In April 1983, respondent drafted an agreement in which Casey would pay Forsberg $75,000 in settlement of any claim she might have against him for the misappropriated funds. By the terms of the agreement, Forsberg agreed not to initiate any criminal, civil, or attorney disciplinary action against Casey. ... Respondent stood to gain $17,000 or more if Casey honored the agreement. In February 1985, respondent filed suit against Casey for breaching the agreement, and a $100,000 judgment was entered against Casey. If Casey had satisfied the judgment, respondent's share would have been approximately $25,588.

The complaint stated that at no time did respondent inform the Commission of Casey's misconduct. According to the Administrator, respondent's first contact with the Commission was in response to the Commission's inquiry regarding the lawsuit against Casey.

... Casey was subsequently disbarred on consent on November 5, 1985.

A hearing on the complaint against the present respondent was held before the Hearing Board of the Commission on June 3, 1986. In its report, the Hearing Board noted that the evidence was not in dispute. The evidence supported the allegations in the complaint and provided additional facts as follows.

... After being retained, respondent made inquiries regarding Casey's conversion... . Forsberg told respondent that she simply wanted her money back and specifically instructed respondent to take no other action. Because of respondent's efforts, Forsberg collected another $10,400 from Casey. Respondent received no fee in this case.

The Hearing Board found that respondent received unprivileged information that Casey converted Forsberg's funds, and that respondent failed to relate the information to the Commission in violation of Rule 1-103(a) of the Code. The Hearing Board noted, however, that respondent had been practicing law for 11 years, had no prior record of any complaints, obtained as good a result as could be expected in the case, and requested no fee for recovering the $23,233.34. Accordingly, the Hearing Board recommended a private reprimand.

Upon the Administrator's exceptions to the Hearing Board's recommendation, the Review Board reviewed the matter. The Review Board's report stated that the client had contacted the Commission prior to retaining respondent and, therefore, the Commission did have knowledge of the alleged misconduct. Further, the Review Board noted that respondent respected the client's wishes regarding not pursuing a claim with the Commission. Accordingly, the Review Board recommended that the complaint be dismissed. ...

We begin our analysis by examining whether a client's complaint of attorney misconduct to the Commission can be a defense to an attorney's failure to report the same misconduct. Respondent offers no authority for such a defense and our research has disclosed none. Common sense would dictate that if a lawyer has a duty under the Code, the actions of a client would not relieve the attorney of his own duty. ...

As to respondent's argument that he did not report Casey's misconduct because his client directed him not to do so, we again note respondent's failure to suggest any legal support for such a defense. ... A lawyer may not choose to circumvent the rules by simply asserting that his client asked him to do so. ...

Though respondent repeatedly asserts that his failure to report was motivated not by financial gain but by the request of his client, we do not deem such an argument relevant in this case. This court has stated that discipline may be appropriate even if no dishonest motive for the misconduct exists. [Cc] ...

... We conclude, then, that respondent possessed unprivileged knowledge of Casey's conversion of client funds, which is illegal conduct involving moral turpitude, and that respondent failed in his duty to report such misconduct to the Commission. Because no defense exists, we agree with the Hearing Board's finding that respondent has violated Rule 1-103(a) and must be disciplined.

The third issue concerns the appropriate quantum of discipline to be imposed in this case. The Administrator contends that respondent's misconduct warrants at least a censure, although the Hearing Board recommended a private reprimand and the Review Board recommended dismissal of the matter entirely. In support of the request for a greater quantum of discipline, the Administrator cites to the purposes of attorney discipline, which include maintaining the integrity of the legal profession and safeguarding the administration of justice. The Administrator argues that these purposes will not be served unless respondent is publicly disciplined so that the profession will be on notice that a violation of Rule 1-103(a) will not be tolerated. The Administrator argues that a more severe sanction is necessary because respondent deprived the Commission of evidence of another attorney's conversion and thereby interfered with the Commission's investigative function... . [T]he Administrator notes that Casey converted many clients' funds after respondent's duty to report Casey arose. The Administrator also argues that both respondent and his client behaved in contravention of the Criminal Code's prohibition against compounding a crime by agreeing with Casey not to report him, in exchange for settlement funds.

In his defense, respondent reiterates his arguments that he was not motivated by desire for financial gain. He also states that Forsberg was pleased with his performance on her behalf. According to respondent, his failure to report was a "judgment call" which resulted positively in Forsberg's regaining some of her funds from Casey.

In evaluating the proper quantum of discipline to impose, ... [w]e reiterate our statement that "'[w]hen determining the nature and extent of discipline to be imposed, the respondent's actions must be viewed in relationship "to the underlying purposes of our disciplinary process, which purposes are to maintain the integrity of the legal profession, to protect the administration of justice from reproach, and to safeguard the public." (*In re LaPinska* (1978), [381 N.E.2d 700].)'" *In re Levin* (1987), [] 514 N.E.2d 174, quoting *In re Crisel* (1984), [] 461 N.E.2d 994.

Bearing these principles in mind, we agree with the Administrator that public discipline is necessary in this case to carry out the purposes of attorney discipline. While we have considered the Boards' recommendations in this matter, we cannot agree with the

Review Board that respondent's conduct served to rectify a wrong and did not injure the bar, the public, or the administration of justice. Though we agree with the Hearing Board's assessment that respondent violated Rule 1-103 of the Code, we do not agree that the facts warrant only a private reprimand. As previously stated, the evidence proved that respondent possessed unprivileged knowledge of Casey's conversion of client funds, yet respondent did not report Casey's misconduct.

This failure to report resulted in interference with the Commission's investigation of Casey, and thus with the administration of justice. Perhaps some members of the public would have been spared from Casey's misconduct had respondent reported the information as soon as he knew of Casey's conversions of client funds. We are particularly disturbed by the fact that respondent chose to draft a settlement agreement with Casey rather than report his misconduct. As the Administrator has stated, by this conduct, both respondent and his client ran afoul of the Criminal Code's prohibition against compounding a crime.... Both respondent and his client stood to gain financially by agreeing not to prosecute or report Casey for conversion. According to the settlement agreement, respondent would have received $17,000 or more as his fee. If Casey had satisfied the judgment entered against him for failure to honor the settlement agreement, respondent would have collected approximately $25,588.

We have held that fairness dictates consideration of mitigating factors in disciplinary cases. [Cc] Therefore, we do consider the fact that Forsberg recovered $10,400 through respondent's services, that respondent has practiced law for 11 years with no record of complaints, and that he requested no fee for minimum collection of Forsberg's funds. However, these considerations do not outweigh the serious nature of respondent's failure to report Casey, the resulting interference with the Commission's investigation of Casey, and respondent's ill-advised choice to settle with Casey rather than report his misconduct.

Accordingly, it is ordered that respondent be suspended from the practice of law for one year.

Respondent suspended.

INQUIRY

Procedures. The procedures for discipline are important, particularly as they reflect policies vital to the administration of a justice system. Any system of discipline must offer due process to the involved lawyer. Other considerations include public confidence in the accountability of lawyers, victim protection, deterring lawyer misconduct, rehabilitating lawyers who are found to have violated conduct rules, and helping lawyers access other resources, for example when violations involve substance abuse or other non-professional behavior. The American Bar Association developed MODEL RULES FOR LAWYER DISCIPLINARY ENFORCEMENT that account for these interests. State bars and supreme courts adopt discipline procedures consistent with those rules and similar to administrative-enforcement practices within other professions. Administrative agencies and tribunals that separately recognize lawyers for practice before them will follow similar procedures to address misconduct allegations. A summary of common procedures follows.

Initial Review. Toward these ends, states employ discipline procedures that generally begin by empowering an independent counsel to investigate and prosecute lawyer misconduct through an attorney grievance commission. A grievance commission is the rough equivalent of a special prosecutor's office. Depending on the bar's size, lawyers may serve full-time as disciplinary counsel, often joining the National Organization of Bar Counsel. Grievance officials have authority to establish and publicize simple procedures so that lawyers, clients, and members of the public may complain to the grievance commission of suspected lawyer misconduct. Grievance commissions tend to establish initial procedures to review public complaints for facial merit. Lawyers do not make every client happy. Clients may complain of conduct that does not implicate a rule and would not establish misconduct if proven. Initial review rejects those meritless complaints. A lawyer against whom a person has lodged a complaint that has no merit on its face may never hear of the complaint. Commissions may also keep confidential those facially meritless complaints to protect a rule-abiding lawyer's reputation.

Request for Investigation. Grievance officials will notify a respondent lawyer when a complaint asserts probable cause to pursue disciplinary charges. Procedural rules may require the lawyer to respond promptly to the request for investigation. Lawyers must follow those rules when contesting misconduct allegations. In other words, the procedural rules may not only help resolve grievances against lawyers based on allegations of misconduct. The procedural rules may also impose specific duties on lawyers, the failure in which may result in further discipline beyond the underlying allegations. The grievance commission, state supreme court, and state bar may deem the failure to follow a procedural rule to be independent ground for discipline. Rules of procedure are thus a second source of law regulating lawyer conduct. Consider the following examples of procedures enabling persons to allege lawyer misconduct. Then consider an opinion illustrating that a lawyer must respect those procedures even when illness and other personal issues distract and challenge the lawyer.

MICH. CT. R. 9.112: Requests for Investigation.

(A) Availability to Public. The administrator shall furnish a form for a request for investigation to a person who alleges misconduct against an attorney. Forms must be available to the public through each state bar office and county clerk's office. Use of the form is not required for filing a request for investigation.

(B) Form of Request. A request for investigation of alleged misconduct must

(1) be in writing;

(2) describe the alleged misconduct, including the approximate time and place of it;

(3) be signed by the complainant; and

(4) be filed with the administrator.

(C) Handling by Administrator.

(1) *Request for Investigation of Attorney.* After making a preliminary investigation, the administrator shall either

(a) notify the complainant and the respondent that the allegations of the request for investigation are inadequate, incomplete, or insufficient to warrant the further attention of the commission; or

(b) serve a copy of the request for investigation on the respondent by ordinary mail at the respondent's address on file with the State Bar as required by Rule 2 of the Supreme Court Rules Concerning the State Bar of Michigan. Service is effective at the time of mailing, and nondelivery does not affect the validity of service. If a respondent has not filed an answer, no formal complaint shall be filed with the board unless the administrator has served the request for investigation by registered or certified mail return receipt requested.
* * *

MICH. CT. R. 9.113: Answer by Respondent.

(A) Answer. Within 21 days after being served with a request for investigation under MCR 9.112(C)(1)(b), the respondent shall file with the administrator a signed, written answer in duplicate fully and fairly disclosing all the facts and circumstances pertaining to the alleged misconduct. The administrator may allow further time to answer. Misrepresentation in the answer is grounds for discipline. ...

(B) Refusal or Failure to Answer.

(1) A respondent may refuse to answer a request for investigation on expressed constitutional or professional grounds.

(2) The failure of a respondent to answer within the time permitted is misconduct. See MCR 9.104(A)(7).

(3) If a respondent refuses to answer under ubrule (B)(1), the refusal may be submitted to a hearing panel for adjudication.

(C) Attorney-Client Privilege. A person who files a request for investigation of an attorney waives any attorney-client privilege that he or she may have as to matters relating to the request for the purposes of the commission's investigation.

———————

State ex rel. Oklahoma Bar Assn. v. Kinsey,
Oklahoma Supreme Court
205 P.3d 866 (2008)

COLBERT, J.

¶1 This Rule 6 proceeding for lawyer discipline presents an extreme example of a lawyer's repeated failure to respond to client grievances and her failure to comply with requests of the General Counsel for information regarding the grievances. It also involves the lawyer's repeated failure to participate in the disciplinary process and her failure to respond to this Court when directed to do so. Under the uncontested facts related in this opinion, this Court is left with no choice but to order this lawyer's disbarment.

¶2 Respondent, Letitia Denise Kinsey, was admitted to the Oklahoma Bar Association in 2000. She has practiced mainly in the areas of criminal and family law.

¶3 Respondent's prior and current disciplinary actions were based on her failure to file a written response within twenty days to two separate sets of client grievances. The first six client grievances were received by the General Counsel between March and October of 2006. They contained allegations of client neglect, failure to communicate with clients, and failure to account for attorney fees paid to Respondent. In addition, the General Counsel filed a grievance alleging that Respondent or her staff made misrepresentations to the Office of General Counsel.

¶4 In each of these matters, Respondent failed to respond in writing to the grievances as required by Rule 8.1(b) of the Oklahoma Rules of Professional Conduct (ORPC), [c] ("a lawyer in connection ... with a disciplinary matter, shall not ... knowingly fail to respond to a lawful demand for information from ... [a] disciplinary authority"), and Rule 5.2 of the Rules Governing Disciplinary Proceedings (RGDP), [c] ("The failure of a lawyer to answer within twenty (20) days after service of the grievance ... or such further time as may be granted by the General Counsel, shall be grounds for discipline."). The General Counsel was forced to obtain a subpoena duces tecum from the Professional Responsibility Commission (PRC) and Respondent's deposition was held on January 19, 2007.

¶5 Respondent was unprepared to respond to the allegations in the grievances. Instead, she offered a number of excuses for her failure to respond. These included her "extreme medical problems" along with the medical issues surrounding her mother and grandmother, her difficulty in receiving her mail, and her divorce. She claimed that the client files that she needed to respond to the grievances were locked in the trunk of her car and the trunk would not open. ...

¶6 On February 23, 2007, Respondent and the Office of General Counsel entered into a Diversion Program Agreement pursuant to Rule 5.1 of the RGDP and Respondent was given a private PRC reprimand. ... The private reprimand was given "in exchange for the Commission foregoing the filing of a formal complaint with the Oklahoma Supreme Court."

¶7 The Diversion Program Agreement made the private reprimand "conditioned upon her participation pursuant to [the] Agreement." The Agreement required Respondent to make contact with the Ethics Counsel within twenty days to schedule periodic meetings with Respondent's medical doctor, the Ethics Counsel, and other monitors who may be designated to oversee the Agreement. Respondent failed to carry out the terms of the Agreement, although she did continue to see her medical doctor periodically.

¶8 During the one-year term of the Agreement, the General Counsel opened seven new client grievances for formal investigation. The substance of the allegations was much the same as the earlier grievances, namely, client neglect, failure to communicate, and failure to account for attorney fees paid. As before, responses to the grievances were not forthcoming. ... Once again, the General Counsel was forced to depose Respondent in order to obtain verbal responses to the grievances.

¶9 At the October 23, 2007, deposition, Respondent acknowledged that she had failed to comply with the terms of the February 23, 2007, Diversion Program Agreement. She attributed her failure to a variety of factors ranging from her ill mother, an abusive ex-husband, a burglary at her office, a break-in of her car, and other general distractions. ...

¶10 The complaint in this matter was filed on December 28, 2007. It is based solely on Respondent's failures in responding to the second set of client grievances and it alleges seven counts of violations of Rule 8.1(b) ORPC and Rule 5.2 RGDP. ...

¶11 A Professional Responsibility Tribunal (PRT) panel was convened and a hearing was set for February 26, 2008. Although Respondent had been personally served with notice of the hearing, she did not appear. ... The PRT panel ... chose to reset the hearing to March 17, 2008... . Respondent failed ... to appear at the March 17, 2008, hearing. ...

¶13 The PRT panel determined that none of the litany of excuses offered by Respondent justified her failure to respond in writing to the grievances. It concluded that a violation of Rule 8.1(b) ORPC and Rule 5.2 RGDP had been demonstrated as to each of the seven counts by clear and convincing evidence. It recommended unanimously a *suspension for a period of no less than two years and one day,* and probably longer." That recommendation and the record were forwarded to this Court.

¶14 ... Respondent failed to enter an appearance in this matter or to file a brief. By an order dated June 19, 2008, this Court ordered Respondent to show cause why the discipline recommended by the PRT panel or another disciplinary sanction should not be imposed. Still, no response was received. This Court suspended Respondent *sua sponte* from the practice of law on July 10, 2008, pending this opinion by which final discipline is now imposed. ...

ANALYSIS

... ¶16 There is no doubt that Respondent has failed repeatedly and knowingly to respond to lawful demands of a disciplinary authority in violation of Rule 8.1(b) ORPC. ...

¶17 Respondent's recalcitrant conduct demonstrates a pattern of neglect that extends far beyond her failure to respond to the grievances or the complaint. She failed to comply with the terms of her Diversion Program Agreement. Respondent failed twice to attend her hearing before the PRT. She offered to resign and an affidavit of resignation was prepared and forwarded to her. Yet, true to her pattern of neglect, she did not follow through. Respondent has entered no appearance before this Court, nor has she filed a brief. When *ordered* by this Court to show cause concerning the final discipline to be imposed, Respondent did not respond. ...

¶19 This Court "take[s] a particularly dim view of disobedience to court orders. The integrity of the judicial system demands that lawyers, who are officers of the court, respect its authority.... Public confidence in the judicial system demands that the court hold lawyers accountable for disobedience to its orders." *State ex rel. Okla. Bar Ass'n v. Giger,* 2003 OK 61, ¶34, 72 P.3d 27, 38. A lawyer whose pattern of neglect extends to disobeying an order from this Court in her disciplinary action cannot be allowed to hold responsibility for the legal affairs of others.

¶20 Respondent's continuing wilful disobedience to the disciplinary authorities in this matter together with clear and convincing evidence of repeated violations of the ORPC and RGDP require this Court to order Respondent's disbarment. In view of her expressed but unfulfilled desire to resign her membership in the Oklahoma Bar Association, this Court must conclude that Respondent anticipated this outcome.

¶21 Respondent's name is ordered stricken from the Roll of Attorneys. Costs are assessed in the amount of $1,262.52.

RESPONDENT DISBARRED; COSTS ASSESSED.

> *Practice*
>
> The lawyer's heart skipped a beat when he noticed the unopened envelope's return address: the Attorney Grievance Commission. The lawyer had helped several other lawyers answer grievances, a common and wise practice among practitioners to get the help of another lawyer when addressing one's own conduct before a regulatory body. The unrepresented lawyer has a fool for a client, or so the saying goes. Yet the lawyer had never received a request for investigation of his own conduct. He looked again at the envelope from the Grievance Commission with his name as addressee, gulped, and opened it. "We are pleased to respond to your request for statistics... ," the letter began. The lawyer breathed a huge sigh of relief and then laughed at himself. He had forgotten that he had asked the Commission for some information a month earlier to give a talk on ethics to a local bar.

INQUIRY

Disclosure.   As the above *Oklahoma Bar Assn.* case indicates, a lawyer must answer a grievance official's request for investigation. In that respect, lawyer-misconduct proceedings are quite different from criminal proceedings in which the defendant has a constitutional privilege against self-incrimination. Why the difference? Bar officials assert that the practice of law is a privilege, not a right. What makes law practice a privilege? How is law practice different from a right to work? Complete disclosure is clearly the rule. A lawyer who tells only half of the story may suffer discipline for failing to state the whole truth. Lawyers do occasionally rely in misconduct proceedings on their Fifth Amendment privilege against self-incrimination, but they do so to protect against criminal charges, not to save their law license. In a criminal proceeding, there is no penalty for invoking the privilege. In a misconduct proceeding, the decisionmakers will construe the respondent lawyer's refusal to disclose information as if the information would have been adverse and will further construe the refusal as misconduct in itself, whether or not the lawyer bases the refusal on a privilege against self-incrimination. Grievance officials use the lawyer's answer to determine whether to issue a formal charge of misconduct. A substantial percentage of grievances result in dismissal after answer and before charge.

Representation.   The lawyer who receives a request for investigation and certainly a misconduct charge should seek legal counsel. Most do, although a few lawyers rely on self-representation in grievance matters.   Their reasons, all bad reasons, include cost, embarrassment, and confidence in one's own skills. The saying goes that the lawyer who represents him- or herself has a fool for a client. Misconduct proceedings can be frightening and emotional, distorting the respondent lawyer's assessment of the lawyer's own interests and best tactics. Sound and experienced counsel removes those risks of self-representation. Lawyers specialize in representing other lawyers in misconduct proceedings, often joining the Association of Professional Responsibility Lawyers.   A misconduct charge is an excellent time for the respondent lawyer to retain a lawyer representative who is experienced in misconduct proceedings and to rely on that lawyer's wise counsel. It is also a good time for the respondent lawyer to find a mentor lawyer outside of the respondent lawyer's own law firm.

Charges. Grievance officials use the respondent lawyer's answer to determine whether to bring formal charges. As the above *Oklahoma Bar Assn.* case suggests, when grievance officials determine to move forward with misconduct charges, the grievance system resolves disputed charges by hearing before an independent panel. Yet as is the case for parties to civil litigation of private disputes, a respondent lawyer can often resolve misconduct charges without the uncertainty, risk, and publicity of a trial-like hearing. Not all charges result in hearing. Charges may lead to information or negotiation resulting in dismissal or voluntary sanctions. Like prosecutors, grievance officials have multiple constituents including the state supreme court, bar staff and leaders, the profession generally, the public, and the misconduct's victims. Voluntary sanctions may satisfy those constituents more than involuntarily imposed discipline. Respondent lawyers may also have more to gain from settlement than hearing, in compensating victims, removing uncertainty, and preserving reputation.

Hearing. When the parties cannot resolve charges voluntarily, the charges proceed to hearing. The grievance officials who bring the misconduct charges and the respondent lawyer play no role in constituting the panel, which the state supreme court or its delegated attorney-discipline board will typically appoint. Lawyers will be on the hearing panel. Non-lawyer citizens may also be on panels, depending on the public participation required by the procedural rules. Why do you think many state supreme courts permit public participation on lawyer-misconduct hearing panels? There is often some discovery before the hearing so that the hearing is fair and efficient. The panel's chair will conduct the hearing under rules of evidence and procedure like those for civil litigation. Those rules may elevate the grievance official's proof burden above the usual preponderance-of-the-evidence burden for civil cases to a clear-and-convincing-evidence standard. Can you articulate why the higher burden before discipline? Hearings result in orders of dismissal or discipline including the sanction. Grievance officials or respondent lawyer may appeal, typically directly to the state supreme court. That direct appeal is why you see discipline opinions in court reports, not because the lower courts hear misconduct charges. The lower courts do not. Misconduct proceedings are administrative in nature.

Other Enforcement. A license proceeding is not the only deterrent to lawyer misconduct. Like non-lawyers, lawyers engaged in misconduct may also face criminal charge, court sanctions administrative penalty, and civil liability. Lawyers certainly owe clients duties to comply with professional standards of care, the violation of which may be malpractice when it results in a client's damage. Conduct rules do not necessarily establish a lawyer's standard of care for civil-liability purposes. Conduct rules have a slightly different purpose. Yet lawyers do face malpractice liability. They can also face criminal charge when their actions violate criminal codes against such activities as forgery and suborning (procuring) perjury. *See* United States v. Ryan-Webster, 353 F.3d 353 (4th Cir. 2003) (forgery conviction arising out of law practice). When a lawyer's misconduct occurs in a pending case, the court may also sanction the lawyer under court rules, imposing a fine or other penalty related to the case.

Mixed Legal Services. Consider one final issue regarding the discipline of lawyers for professional misconduct, having to do with the scope of the disciplinary rules. There is no question that lawyers are subject to the rules when practicing law. Yet drawing on their other education, skills, and experience, some lawyers provide tax, accounting, business-consulting, financial-advising, or other professional services that may not in themselves constitute legal services but nonetheless relate to legal services. A lawyer who combines legal service with other non-legal professional services is subject to lawyer conduct rules when providing those law-related services. So, too, is a lawyer whose client is unaware that the law-related services are not legal services. Read the following identical state version of ABA MODEL RULE OF PROF. CONDUCT 5.7 for these provisions on law-related services. Which lawyer conduct rules do you think might be most important to a client in those law-related-service settings? Rules against conflicts of interest and promising confidentiality may be two good examples.

> **DELAWARE R. PROF. CONDUCT 5.7: Responsibilities Regarding Law-Related Services.**
>
> (a) A lawyer shall be subject to the Rules of Professional Conduct with respect to the provision of law-related services, as defined in paragraph (b), if the law-related services are provided:
>
> (1) by the lawyer in circumstances that are not distinct from the lawyer's provision of legal services to clients; or
>
> (2) in other circumstances by an entity controlled by the lawyer individually or with others if the lawyer fails to take reasonable measures to assure that a person obtaining the law-related services knows that the services are not legal services and that the protections of the client-lawyer relationship do not exist.
>
> (b) The term "law-related services" denotes services that might reasonably be performed in conjunction with and in substance are related to the provision of legal services, and that are not prohibited as unauthorized practice of law when provided by a nonlawyer.

D. Professionalism

Significance. Ask any lawyer today about the importance of lawyer professionalism and you will get no disagreement: the professionalism of lawyers is critical to public respect for and productive functioning of the legal system. The justice system is only as good as its lawyers. Ask the same lawyers what professionalism is and you will receive varying answers. Variety in personal styles and professional approaches can be a good thing. There are, on the other hand some central principles of professionalism. The American Bar Association's Section on Legal Education and Admission to the Bar published a 1996 report *Teaching and Learning Professionalism* identifying the hallmarks of professionalism as expertise, learning, client service, public good, common calling, and promotion of justice. The American Bar Association's well-known 1992 MacCrate Report identified client service, competence, access to and quality of justice, self-governance, anti-bias, and professional development. *See* ABA Section on Legal Education & Admission to the Bar, *Legal Education and Professional Development—An Educational Continuum, Report of the Task Force on Law Schools and the Profession: Narrowing the Gap* (ABA 1992).

Style. If ethics law tells lawyers *what* they may and must not do, then we can best describe professionalism as *how* lawyers choose to go about what they do. Unlike ethics rules, there are no mandatory professionalism rules. Professionalism is the unwritten code of behavior in the legal culture. It can be the source of friction because there are different schools of thought as to what should be this unwritten code. Lawyers choose what it means to be professional. Professionalism involves style, but style leads quickly to substance. Your professionalism forms your professional identity, which then translates into professional relationships, commitments, and opportunities. Do not underestimate the significance of professionalism. It is a powerful concept, shaping the careers and legacies of lawyers.

Beyond the Minimum. In a sense, professionalism challenges you to do more than the minimum. Conduct rules represent the absolute minimum standards of professional behavior. The profession adopts rules through a quasi-legislative process. The profession adopts only those rules the vast majority of lawyers would accept. Controversial rules or rules susceptible to disagreement among respectable lawyers do not pass the process. You may hear that the conduct rules are the "floor, not the ceiling." Yet just because the conduct rules allow you to do something, does not always mean it is a good idea for you to do so. Lawyers whom others regard as highly professional for the way they go about their work, understand this concept. They have developed the "sensitive professional and moral judgment" to which the Model Rules' Preamble refers and which is necessary to the standard of success to which most of us aspire. This text highlights instances where the conduct rules stop and professionalism begins. We want you to have the choice and opportunity to reap the greater benefits that professionalism brings.

E. Reporting Misconduct

The Privilege of Self-Regulation. Membership in the community of lawyers entails one specific responsibility that not all law students appreciate. To ensure the integrity of the profession and protect clients and the public, lawyers in most states must report misconduct by other members of the bar about which they know, unless their information is within a privilege. Lawyers enjoy a privilege of self-regulation that other professionals do not. Administrative boards or agencies regulate physicians, nurses, beauticians, morticians, real estate agents, and other service professionals. While lawyers tend to staff and govern all aspects of the lawyer-discipline system, the boards and agencies regulating other professionals may include non-professional members and may depend on non-professional staff. While lawyers and judges draft and adopt lawyer conduct rules, statutes enacted by non-professional legislators and regulations promulgated by non-professional administrators govern other professions. Lawyers comprise the panels that hear and decide allegations of lawyer misconduct. Non-professional administrative boards tend to hear and decide misconduct allegations against other professionals. Lawyers have it good in those and other respects.

Duty to Report. The duty under ABA MODEL RULE OF PROFESSIONAL CONDUCT 8.3 to report misconduct goes hand in hand with those privileges. Self-regulation is a great privilege, but as do all privileges, it comes with great responsibility. Some lawyers may take an extreme approach to the duty either by using it as a figurative weapon to report other lawyers for the slightest perceived transgression or by abdicating their responsibility to the profession by overlooking serious misconduct. Think again of the *In re Himmel* case above. While reporting a fellow professional can seem callous toward the professional relationship, in some cases one lawyer's failure to report another can result in substantial harm to members of the public. Read the following identical state version of ABA MODEL RULE OF PROFESSIONAL CONDUCT 8.3, referred to as the snitch rule by those who are ignorant and disrespectful of the critical self-regulatory system it protects. Then, consider a case where the failure to report nearly had the worst of all possible negative consequences.

UTAH R. PROF. CONDUCT 8.3: **Reporting Professional Misconduct.**
(a) A lawyer who knows that another lawyer has committed a violation of the Rules of Professional Conduct that raises a substantial question as to

that lawyer's honesty, trustworthiness or fitness as a lawyer in other respects shall inform the appropriate professional authority.

(b) A lawyer who knows that a judge has committed a violation of applicable Rules of Judicial Conduct that raises a substantial question as to the judge's fitness for office shall inform the appropriate authority.

(c) This Rule does not require disclosure of information otherwise protected by Rule 1.6 or information gained by a lawyer or judge while participating in an approved lawyers assistance program.

In re Riehlmann,
Louisiana Supreme Court
891 So.2d 1239 (2005)

...UNDERLYING FACTS

Respondent is a criminal defense attorney who was formerly employed as an Assistant District Attorney in the Orleans Parish District Attorney's Office. One evening in April 1994, respondent met his close friend and law school classmate, Gerry Deegan, at a bar near the Orleans Parish Criminal District Court. Like respondent, Mr. Deegan had been a prosecutor in the Orleans Parish District Attorney's Office before he "switched sides" in 1987. During their conversation in the bar, Mr. Deegan told respondent that he had that day learned he was dying of colon cancer. In the same conversation, Mr. Deegan confided to respondent that he had suppressed exculpatory blood evidence in a criminal case he prosecuted while at the District Attorney's Office. Respondent recalls that he was "surprised" and "shocked" by his friend's revelation, and that he urged Mr. Deegan to "remedy" the situation. It is undisputed that respondent did not report Mr. Deegan's disclosure to anyone at the time it was made. Mr. Deegan died in July 1994, having done nothing to "remedy" the situation of which he had spoken in the bar.

Nearly five years after Mr. Deegan's death, one of the defendants whom he had prosecuted in a 1985 armed robbery case was set to be executed by lethal injection on May 20, 1999. In April 1999, the lawyers for the defendant, John Thompson, discovered a crime lab report which contained the results of tests performed on a piece of pants leg and a tennis shoe that were stained with the perpetrator's blood during a scuffle with the victim of the robbery attempt. The crime lab report concluded that the robber had Type "B" blood. Because Mr. Thompson has Type "O" blood, the crime lab report proved he could not have committed the robbery; nevertheless, neither the crime lab report nor the blood-stained physical evidence had been disclosed to Mr. Thompson's defense counsel prior to or during trial. Respondent claims that when he heard about the inquiry of Mr. Thompson's lawyers, he immediately realized that this was the case to which Mr. Deegan had referred in their April 1994 conversation in the bar. On April 27, 1999, respondent executed an affidavit for Mr. Thompson in which he attested that during the 1994 conversation, "the late Gerry Deegan said to me that he had intentionally suppressed blood evidence in the armed robbery trial of John Thompson that in some way exculpated the defendant."

In May 1999, respondent reported Mr. Deegan's misconduct to the [Office of Disciplinary Counsel]. In June 1999, respondent testified in a hearing on a motion for new trial in Mr. Thompson's armed robbery case. During the hearing, respondent testified that Mr. Deegan had told him that he "suppressed exculpatory evidence that was blood evidence, that seemed to have excluded Mr. Thompson as the perpetrator of an armed robbery." Respondent also admitted that he "should have reported" Mr. Deegan's misconduct, and that while he ultimately did so, "I should have reported it sooner, I guess."

On September 30, 1999, respondent gave a sworn statement to the ODC in which he was asked why he did not report Mr. Deegan's disclosure to anyone at the time it was made. Respondent replied:

> I think that under ordinary circumstances, I would have. I really honestly think I'm a very good person. And I think I do the right thing whenever I'm given the opportunity to choose. This was unquestionably the most difficult time of my life. Gerry, who was like a brother to me, was dying. And that was, to say distracting would be quite an understatement. I'd also left my wife just a few months before, with three kids, and was under the care of a psychiatrist, taking antidepressants. My youngest son was then about two and had just recently undergone open-heart surgery. I had a lot on my plate at the time. A great deal of it of my own making; there's no question about it. But, nonetheless, I was very, very distracted, and I simply did not give it the important consideration that it deserved. But it was a very trying time for me. And that's the only explanation I have, because, otherwise, I would have reported it immediately had I been in a better frame of mind.

DISCIPLINARY PROCEEDINGS

Formal Charges

On January 4, 2001, the ODC filed one count of formal charges against respondent, alleging that his failure to report his unprivileged knowledge of Mr. Deegan's prosecutorial misconduct violated Rules 8.3(a) (reporting professional misconduct), [and] 8.4(c) (engaging in conduct involving dishonesty, fraud, deceit, or misrepresentation)....

Formal Hearing

When this matter proceeded to a formal hearing before the committee, ... when asked whether he recognized during the barroom conversation that Mr. Deegan had violated his ethical duties, respondent replied, "Well, certainly." Respondent admitted that he gave the conversation no further thought after he left the bar because he was "distracted" by his own personal problems. ...

Disciplinary Board Recommendation

... The [disciplinary] board found respondent must have understood from his 1994 conversation with Mr. Deegan that Mr. Deegan had suppressed Brady evidence.... . The board concluded that a reasonable lawyer under the circumstances would have formed a firm opinion that Mr. Deegan had wrongfully failed to disclose the blood evidence, and that respondent did in fact form such an opinion because he advised Mr. Deegan that what he (Deegan) did was "not right" and that he (Deegan) had to "rectify" the situation. Accordingly, the board found respondent had sufficient knowledge of misconduct by Mr. Deegan to trigger a duty to report the misconduct to the disciplinary authorities.

The board then turned to a discussion of whether respondent's failure to report Mr. Deegan's misconduct for more than five years after learning of it constituted a failure to report under Rule 8.3(a). The board acknowledged that Rule 8.3(a) does not provide any specific time limit or period within which the misconduct must be reported. Nevertheless, the board reasoned that Rule 8.3(a) serves no useful purpose unless it is read to require reporting to an appropriate authority within a reasonable time under the circumstances. [Cc] ... Applying these principles to the instant case, the board determined respondent's disclosure in 1999 of misconduct he discovered in 1994 was not timely and did not satisfy the requirements of Rule 8.3(a).

The board also found that respondent's conduct violated Rule 8.4(d) because his inactivity following Mr. Deegan's disclosure was prejudicial to the administration of justice.

The board found respondent knowingly violated a duty owed to the profession, and that his actions resulted in both actual and potential injury to Mr. Thompson. The board noted that if respondent had taken further action in 1994, when Mr. Deegan made his confession, Mr. Thompson's innocence in connection with the armed robbery charge may have been established sooner. The board also observed that negative publicity attached to respondent's actions, thereby causing harm to the legal profession. The board determined the baseline sanction for respondent's conduct is a suspension from the practice of law.[fn]

... Considering the prior jurisprudence,[fn] the board determined that some period of suspension is appropriate for respondent's conduct. In light of the significant mitigating factors in this matter, the board recommended that respondent be suspended from the practice of law for six months. One board member dissented and would recommend a suspension of at least one year and one day.

DISCUSSION

... The American legal profession has long recognized the necessity of reporting lawyers' ethical misconduct. When the American Bar Association adopted its first code of ethics in 1908, Canon 29 of the Canons of Professional Ethics, entitled "Upholding the Honor of the Profession," encouraged lawyers to "expose without fear or favor before the proper tribunals corrupt or dishonest conduct in the profession, ..." [C] More than sixty years later, the ABA enacted Disciplinary Rule 1-103(A) of the Model Code of Professional Responsibility, the predecessor of the current Rule 8.3(a) of the Model Rules of Professional Conduct. Both the 1969 Code, in DR 1-103(A), and the 1983 Model Rules, in Rule 8.3(a), make it clear that the duty to report is not merely an aspiration but is mandatory, the violation of which subjects the lawyer to discipline.[fn] [C]

... Louisiana's rule is based on ABA Model Rule 8.3; however, there are several differences between the Model Rule and the Louisiana Rule that was in effect in 2001, at the time the formal charges were filed in this case.[fn] Most significantly, Model Rule 8.3 requires a lawyer to report the misconduct of another lawyer only when the conduct in question "raises a substantial question" as to that lawyer's fitness to practice. Louisiana's version of Rule 8.3 imposed a substantially more expansive reporting requirement, in that our rule required a lawyer to report all unprivileged knowledge of any ethical violation by a lawyer, whether the violation was, in the reporting lawyer's view, flagrant and substantial or minor and technical. ...

DETERMINATION OF RESPONDENT'S MISCONDUCT AND APPROPRIATE DISCIPLINE

... [W]e find the ODC proved by clear and convincing evidence that respondent violated Rule 8.3(a). First, we find that respondent should have known that a reportable event occurred at the time of his 1994 barroom conversation with Mr. Deegan. Stated another way, respondent's conversation with Mr. Deegan at that time gave him sufficient information that a reasonable lawyer under the circumstances would have formed a firm opinion that the conduct in question more likely than not occurred. Regardless of the actual words Mr. Deegan said that night, and whether they were or were not "equivocal," respondent understood from the conversation that Mr. Deegan had done something wrong. ... The circumstances under which the conversation took place lend further support to this finding. On the same day that he learned he was dying of cancer, Mr. Deegan felt compelled to tell his best friend about something he had done in a trial that took place nine years earlier. It simply defies logic that respondent would now argue that he could not be sure that Mr. Deegan actually withheld Brady evidence because his statements were vague and non-specific.

We also find that respondent failed to promptly report Mr. Deegan's misconduct to the disciplinary authorities. As respondent himself acknowledged, he should have reported Mr. Deegan's statements sooner than he did. There was no reason for respondent to have waited five years to tell the ODC about what his friend had done. ...

Having found professional misconduct, we now turn to a discussion of an appropriate sanction. In considering that issue, we are mindful that the purpose of disciplinary proceedings is not primarily to punish the lawyer, but rather to maintain the appropriate standards of professional conduct, to preserve the integrity of the legal profession, and to deter other lawyers from engaging in violations of the standards of the profession. [Cc]

Respondent's actions violated the general duty imposed upon attorneys to maintain and preserve the integrity of the bar. [Cc] While we adhere to our observation in *Brigandi* that an attorney's failure to comply with the reporting requirement is a "serious offense," in the instant case, we find that respondent's conduct was merely negligent. Accordingly, Standard 7.3 of the ABA's *Standards for Imposing Lawyer Sanctions* provides that the appropriate baseline sanction is a reprimand.[fn]

The only aggravating factor present in this case is respondent's substantial experience in the practice of law. As for mitigating factors, we adopt those recognized by the disciplinary board, placing particular emphasis on the absence of any dishonest or selfish motive on respondent's part. ... Under all of the circumstances presented, we conclude that a public reprimand is the appropriate sanction.

Accordingly, we will reprimand respondent for his actions.

Conclusion

Reporting another lawyer's misconduct to disciplinary authorities is an important duty of every lawyer. Lawyers are in the best position to observe professional misconduct and to assist the profession in sanctioning it. While a Louisiana lawyer is subject to discipline for not reporting misconduct, it is our hope that lawyers will comply with their reporting obligation primarily because they are ethical people who want to serve their clients and the public well. Moreover, the lawyer's duty to report professional misconduct is the foundation for the claim that we can be trusted to regulate ourselves as a profession.

If we fail in our duty, we forfeit that trust and have no right to enjoy the privilege of self-regulation or the confidence and respect of the public. ...

"What Were They Thinking?"

We do not have to ask what the respondent in the above *In re Riehlman* case was thinking because he explained it. Did what he was thinking—that he had left his wife, he was depressed, his friend was dying—justify his not reporting the prosecutor's misconduct? The wrongly convicted person spent five years languishing in jail anticipating his execution between the time that the respondent learned of the prosecutor's misconduct and eventually reported it, and then was nearly executed. Does your unhappiness justify that you make others unhappy? Is our poor mental health an excuse not to consider the mental health (not to mention the legal rights) of others? How do you think the wrongly incarcerated person felt that the respondent received only a public reprimand, when the person may have spent an additional five years in prison because of the respondent's violation? What if the state had executed the person without the respondent coming forward?

INQUIRY

Question of Fitness. When must a lawyer report another lawyer's misconduct? ABA Model Rule 8.3 requires knowledge of a violation through a non-privileged source and that the violation "raises a substantial question as to that lawyer's honesty, trustworthiness or fitness as a lawyer... ." The *In re Riehlman* opinion points out that the ABA Model Rule 8.3 includes a condition that the Louisiana Rule 8.3 did not. The former Louisiana Rule 8.3 did not include the substantial-question-of-fitness condition, meaning that Louisiana-licensed lawyers owed a duty to report *all* misconduct whether it raised a substantial question of fitness or was instead only minor or even technical. Which version do you prefer, the ABA Model Rule 8.3 with the extra condition or the old Louisiana version without it? On one hand, you might prefer the discretion that the ABA Model Rule 8.3 seems to imply to make subjective judgments about questions of fitness. In close cases, that condition could easily become your safe harbor not to report. On the other hand, you might not want that discretion because the counsel whom you decide to report might question your subjective judgment and motives. What is your opinion as to whether the ABA Model Rule 8.3 goes far enough?

Inferring Knowledge.   While ABA Model Rule 8.3 requires reporting when a lawyer "*knows* that another lawyer has committed a violation" (emphasis added), grievance officials may have to infer knowledge. Can you see why? How often do individuals admit a state of mind that will implicate their professional license? Proof of state of mind is always problematic and usually circumstantial. ABA MODEL RULE OF PROF. CONDUCT 1.0 "Terminology" provides in its subrule (f) that while to "know" means to have "actual knowledge," "A person's knowledge may be inferred from circumstances." ABA Formal Ethics Opinion 04-433 acknowledges that ABA Model Rule 8.3's knowledge condition but asserts that cases and ethics opinions "conclude that 'knowledge' is determined by an objective standard." *See also* Attorney U v. Mississippi Bar, 678 So.2d 963, 972 (Miss. 1996) (standard must be objective, "not tied to the subjective beliefs of the lawyer in question"). Do the Ethics Opinion and case just cited go too far? Or, should we indeed hold lawyers to knowing the conduct rules and, thus, knowing when other lawyers have violated them?

Privileged Information. When would a lawyer learn about another lawyer's misconduct in a setting when that knowledge would be privileged and thus prevent the lawyer from reporting it? Lawyers who violate misconduct rules sometimes consult other lawyers about those violations to obtain their advice and representation. The lawyer who has another lawyer as a client owes that other lawyer the duty not to disclose confidential information. *See* ABA MODEL RULE OF PROF. CONDUCT 1.6. A lawyer who learns of another lawyer's conduct-rule violation through a consultation in which the other lawyer is seeking the first lawyer's advice must not disclose that information. Do you think that the respondent's prosecutor friend in *In re Riehlman* was seeking advice and counsel from the respondent about the conduct-rule violation?

Time and Place for Reporting. Notice that the ABA Model Rule 8.3 requires a report to "the appropriate professional authority." Who do you think that authority might be? The respondent in *In re Riehlman* argued that the prosecutor to whom he initially reported his dead friend's misconduct was the appropriate professional authority. 891 So.2d at 1248. The Louisiana Supreme Court disagreed, holding that the state bar's Office of Disciplinary Counsel was the appropriate professional authority. *Id.* at 1247, 1248. Can you see why the report of lawyer misconduct should be to the misconduct officials? Some states modify ABA Model Rule 8.3 to substitute the specific grievance officials for the Model Rule 8.3's non-specific language. *See* MICH. R. PROF. CONDUCT 8.3(a) ("shall inform the Attorney Grievance Commission"). As the *In re Riehlman* case illustrates, the timing of the report can also be important. *See* United States v. Cantor, 897 F.Supp. 110 (S.D. N.Y. 1995) (report within a reasonable time). Where delay in reporting will harm no one, there is some authority for waiting until a matter concludes, although harm from delay compels immediate reporting. *See* MASS. R. PROF. CONDUCT 8.3 comment 3A. Can you foresee other examples in addition to *In re Riehlman* where delay in reporting could lead to harm to others?

Terminology. You can now see from your study of the first few conduct rules that professional responsibility has a language of its own, as do other law fields. Rule 1.0 of the ABA MODEL RULES OF PROFESSIONAL CONDUCT, an identical state version of which we reproduce below, defines specific words and phrases as terms of art within the field of lawyer misconduct. Keep in mind that your use of language on the subject of lawyer misconduct must be as precise as it is in other law fields. Precision with language is a key lawyer skill. Apply it here as you would elsewhere.

ARIZONA RULE OF PROF. CONDUCT 1.0: Terminology

(a) "Belief" or "believes" denotes that the person involved actually supposed the fact in question to be true. A person's belief may be inferred from circumstances.

(b) "Confirmed in writing," when used in reference to the informed consent of a person, denotes informed consent that is given in writing by the person or a writing that a lawyer promptly transmits to the person confirming an oral informed consent. See paragraph (e) for the definition of "informed consent." If it is not feasible to obtain or transmit the writing at the time the person gives informed consent, then the lawyer must obtain or transmit it within a reasonable time thereafter.

(c) "Firm" or "law firm" denotes a lawyer or lawyers in a law partnership, professional corporation, sole proprietorship or other association; or lawyers employed in a legal services organization or the legal department of a corporation or other organization. Whether government lawyers should be treated as a firm depends on the particular Rule involved and the specific facts of the situation.

(d) "Fraud" or "fraudulent" denotes conduct that is fraudulent under the substantive or procedural law of the applicable jurisdiction and has a purpose to deceive.

(e) "Informed consent" denotes the agreement by a person to a proposed course of conduct after the lawyer has communicated adequate information and explanation about the material risks of and reasonably available alternatives to the proposed course of conduct.

(f) "Knowingly," "known," or "knows" denotes actual knowledge of the fact in question. A person's knowledge may be inferred from circumstances.

(g) "Partner" denotes a member of a partnership, a shareholder in a law firm organized as a professional corporation, or a member of an association authorized to practice law.

(h) "Reasonable" or "reasonably" when used in relation to conduct by a lawyer denotes the conduct of a reasonably prudent and competent lawyer.

(i) "Reasonable belief" or "reasonably believes" when used in reference to a lawyer denotes that the lawyer believes the matter in question and that the circumstances are such that the belief is reasonable.

(j) "Reasonably should know" when used in reference to a lawyer denotes that a lawyer of reasonable prudence and competence would ascertain the matter in question.

(k) "Screened" denotes the isolation of a lawyer from any participation in a matter through the timely imposition of procedures within a firm that are reasonably adequate under the circumstances to protect information that the isolated lawyer is obligated to protect under these Rules or other law.

(*l*) "Substantial" when used in reference to degree or extent denotes a material matter of clear and weighty importance.

(m) "Tribunal" denotes a court, an arbitrator in an arbitration proceeding or a legislative body, administrative agency or other body acting in an adjudicative capacity. A legislative body, administrative agency or other body acts in an adjudicative capacity when a neutral official, after the presentation of evidence or legal argument by a party or parties, will render a legal judgment directly affecting a party's interests in a particular matter.

(n) "Writing" or "written" denotes a tangible or electronic record of a communication or representation, including handwriting, typewriting, printing, photostating, photography, audio or video recording and e-mail. A "signed" writing includes an electronic sound, symbol or process attached to or logically associated with a writing and executed or adopted by a person with the intent to sign the writing.

Career and Professional Development

Law firms and other organizations that employ lawyers each have their own professional culture. Within the lawyer conduct rules, what serves as professional dress, address, demeanor, and conduct varies widely. What passes for confidence in one organization may come off as arrogance in another. What passes for camaraderie in one organization may come off as insult in another. Knowing the conduct rules is simply a beginning to recognizing the subtle ways in which organizations develop professional community and maintain commitment and unity. You should recognize your ability and willingness to adapt to the professional culture of organizations with which you consider employment. Your personality and preferences may influence an organization's culture but are unlikely to change it. The organization's culture may be more likely to change you. Choose that influence wisely.

CHAPTER II

CITIZENSHIP

Organization of the Bar, Admission to Practice, Unauthorized Practice, Professional Discipline

Our government is emphatically a government of the people. ... Its whole security and efficiency depend upon the intelligence, virtue, independence, and moderation of the people.
—Justice Joseph Story

No organization of lawyers can long survive which has not for its primary object the protection of the public.
—Roberts P. Hudson

OBJECTIVE: Given a person who is interested in becoming a lawyer, articulate for that person the role that bar admission, licensure and unauthorized-practice rules play in regulating law practice, including character and fitness requirements, and describe the means by which the law profession disciplines lawyers.

Applicable Rules

1.0 Terminology

5.5 Unauthorized Practice; Multijurisdictional Practice

5.6 Restrictions on Right to Practice

6.4 Law Reform Activities Affecting Client Interests

8.1 Bar Admission and Disciplinary Matters

Your willingness to obey constitutions, laws, rules, and regulations governing lawyers helps you gain citizenship in a nation and membership in a profession. The welfare of a society depends on a broad and diverse citizenship well educated in the forms and conventions of law. To earn a law degree and practice law is to become a citizen in the fullest sense of that word. A nation and community are not strong unless there is broad private access to legal education and legal services. To engage in law practice is to join and embrace two communities, first that of the general citizenry and then the professional community of lawyers. Your commitment to legal education demonstrates your willingness to engage your civic duties at the highest level. Do not overlook your public role as a highly educated and qualified citizen, even as you prepare to join the professional community of lawyers. We begin this course book with that broadest sense of citizenship in communities formed around the rule of law. Preserve your sense of citizenship, even as you study to become a lawyer. The chapter addresses organization of the bar, admission to the bar, and unauthorized practice of law, demonstrating how the profession and public ensure responsible legal services.

A. Organization of the Bar

Bar Associations. The professional community of lawyers forms around membership in national, state, local, and affinity bar associations. The use of the word *bar* may seem curious at first, especially given its association with that other place where one may become intoxicated in several ways.. Yet its usage is highly appropriate when thinking of the word's other common meaning, to stop or prevent one's passage. In a courtroom, the bar was the railing and gate beyond which the court permitted only qualified members of the legal profession. To be a member of the bar is to have fulfilled all of the requirements to gain access to that special place where trained advocates argue the cause of justice before authorities empowered to provide it. There are several kinds of bar associations. You may already have joined a bar association as a student member. Often, bar associations recruit and welcome law-student members. You may some day be a member of several bar associations. Consider the following descriptions.

American Bar Association. The American Bar Association is the world's largest voluntary professional organization with about 400,000 members comprising about one third of the country's lawyers. Its sheer size warrants influence. The United States Department of Education recognizes the American Bar Association as the accrediting body for law schools. The American Bar Association also makes influential reviews of national legislation affecting the law profession and justice system, and on the qualifications of federal judges. Although the American Bar Association's size gives its initiatives national scope and influence, its many specific law-field sections help focus its activities at a level meaningful to the practitioner. Practitioners find helpful its section journals, newsletters, conferences, and other activities and services, even if the organization does not regularly address state-specific issues. You need not join the American Bar Association to practice law, but many, particularly those who get involved in the organization's activities, are better lawyers for having done so. As you will see throughout this course, the American Bar Association also promulgates highly influential MODEL RULES OF PROFESSIONAL CONDUCT.

Local Bar Associations. At the opposite end of the geographic spectrum are local bar associations, often organized at the county level or by metropolitan area. Like the American Bar Association, local bar associations are voluntary organizations. You need not join your local bar, although many lawyers do so, especially in those locales where the local bar offers meaningful programs and benefits. Some of those benefits may include orientation programs for new lawyers, bench-bar committees addressing the fair and efficient administration of the local courts, continuing legal education programs, networking events and lawyer-referral systems, social events like golf outings, pro-bono and charitable activities, newsletters, and annual dinners and meetings. Depending on the locale and the culture and administration of the local bar, local bars may offer practitioners more meaningful interaction with other lawyers than national or state bars.

Affinity Bar Associations. Lawyers also join national, state, and local bar associations based on culture, national origin, ethnicity, field of interest, and other affinities. For example, the National Bar Association is an organization of primarily African-American lawyers and judges, while the Hispanic National Bar Association represents the interests of thousands of Hispanic-American lawyers and judges. The American Association for Justice supports plaintiff's trial lawyers, while the Defense Research Institute supports attorneys who defend individuals and businesses in civil litigation. The National Association of Criminal Defense Lawyers and American Corporate Counsel Association are other active national organizations centered on specific lawyer affinities or roles. Each of these organizations promotes the continuing education and professional development of its members, while also offering services, professional networking, and social support. These are just a few of hundreds of national, state, and local affinity bars. Affinity bars can make a significant difference in a lawyer's career.

State Bar Associations. The most important bar association, though, of which most lawyers will be a member is at the state level, not the national or local level. In most states, you must gain admission to the state's bar in order to practice law regularly in that state. The

Supreme Court has held it constitutional for a state to require licensure through a state bar to engage in law practice in that state. *See* Lathrop v. Donohue, 367 U.S. 820 (1961);   *cf.* Barnard v. Thompson, 489 U.S. 546 (1989) (striking down one-year residency requirement for Virgin Islands bar);   Supreme Court of Virginia v. Friedman, 487 U.S. 59 (1988) (striking down preference that would have permitted residents to waive in but required non-residents to take bar exam);   Supreme Court of New Hampshire v. Piper, 470 U.S. 274 (1985) (striking down residency requirement).   Most states maintain a *unified* or *integrated* bars requiring licensing.   Only a few maintain a *voluntary* bar not requiring licensure.   There are limits on what a unified or integrated bar may require of you or any other licensee.   The First and Fourteenth Amendments' free-speech and freedom of-association rights prohibit an integrated state bar from requiring that you pay dues supporting political or ideological causes unrelated to the bar's core activities involving law reform and professional regulation.   *See* Keller v. State Bar of California, 496 U.S. 1 (1990).   An integrated state bar may require you to pay dues that will help discipline members, reimburse clients defrauded by unscrupulous lawyers, and revise ethics rules.   It may not require you to pay dues to support gun control, a nuclear-weapons freeze, or other political and ideological issues.   Integrated bars examine their actions to ensure that they are *Keller*-permissible in between these two ends of the spectrum.

B. Bar Admission

Licensure.   If state bars license lawyers, then how do lawyers gain bar admission?   There are two principal ways of gaining admission to the bar of a particular state.   Both ways begin with earning a law degree from an ABA-accredited law school, as is true in most states, *see* Florida Bd. Bar Examiners ex rel. Barry University School of Law, 821 So.2d 1050 (Fla. 2002), or an unaccredited law school recognized specially by the state supreme court, *see* In re Lewis, 86 S.W.3d 419 (Ky. 2002).   In the traditional method of admission, an applicant must then submit a detailed application proving that the applicant has the "character and fitness" to handle the legal matters of others.   The applicant has the burden of proving character and fitness.   The applicant must also pass the state's bar-examination requirements. For admission to practice, an applicant must pass both the character-and-fitness part of the application process and all bar-exam requirements.

Multistate Professional Responsibility Exam. Nearly all state bars require that you pass the Multistate Professional Responsibility Exam (MPRE) in addition to the state bar examination. Check the National Conference of Bar Examiners website for the few jurisdictions that do not require it. Your law school's Professional Responsibility course should prepare you to take and pass the Multistate Professional Responsibility Exam. The 125-minute Multistate Professional Responsibility Exam has 60 multiple-choice questions testing your knowledge and application of the ABA MODEL RULES OF PROFESSIONAL CONDUCT and ABA MODEL CODE OF JUDICIAL CONDUCT. State bars require different scores, some states higher than others. The National Conference of Bar Examiners administers the exam in early March, August, and November each year at many sites throughout the country including many law schools. You must register approximately one month before the exam. Do not rely on word from others for your state bar's Multistate Professional Responsibility Exam requirements. State bars change their exam requirements from time to time, making unreliable the experience of others. Check with the National Conference of Bar Examiners and your state bar.

Timing. As to your timing for taking the Multistate Professional Responsibility Exam, many states permit you to take the exam while in law school. You may want to take the exam shortly after your Professional Responsibility course in law school, well before you graduate and focus on the bar exam. Research your state bar's requirements. Some state bars require that you take the exam within a certain time of when you take that state's bar exam, meaning that your Multistate Professional Responsibility Exam score will not count and you will have to retake it if you took it too early. Find out your state bar's exam-timing requirements now. Register now for the exam date that makes the most sense. Find out what Multistate Professional Responsibility Exam score your state requires. Plan to study for the exam before taking it. Some commercial bar-review courses offer special classes for the Multistate Professional Responsibility Exam as part of your fee for bar-exam review. You may retake the Multistate Professional Responsibility Exam if you fail to achieve your state bar's required score, but retaking the exam may delay your bar licensure if you waited too long to take the Multistate Professional Responsibility Exam. Take the Multistate Professional Responsibility Exam early enough to allow for a retake, if necessary. The National Conference of Bar Examiners does not release the names of individuals who fail the Multistate Professional Responsibility Exam. You can take it as many times as required for you to pass.

Reciprocity. A second method of gaining admission is reciprocal admission (also known as *reciprocity*). About one half of all state bars offer reciprocal admission. Reciprocal admission allows attorneys who have practiced a certain number of years and who are in good standing in one state bar to gain admission to another state's bar by application and fee, without retaking a bar exam and once again proving character and fitness. Both states must permit reciprocal admission. A state that offers reciprocal admission to another reciprocity state will not license a lawyer from a non-reciprocity state. Some of the larger state bars in warmer states, Florida, California, and Georgia among them, do not allow reciprocal admission. Can you imagine why? An experienced, licensed lawyer seeking admission to or from a non-reciprocity state must sit for the bar examination, no matter how long or where the lawyer has practiced. Following sections address character and fitness issues and temporary admission.

1.   Character

Law School Admission. Your proof to a state bar of your good character to practice law begins with the application you completed to enter law school. Standard 501(b) of the American Bar Association Section of Legal Education and Admissions to the Bar's *Standards and Rules of Procedure for Approval of Law Schools* permits an accredited law school to admit only those students who "appear capable of satisfactorily completing its educational program and being admitted to the bar." Standard 501 requires law schools to consider your character, not just your academic abilities, because law schools must not admit students who lack the character for admission to the bar. You made character representations on your law-school application. Those representations must have been accurate when you made them. You must also update your law-school application if anything happened during law school to make your application information inaccurate or misleading.

Bar Application. You must then make character representations when you apply for admission to a state bar. The applicant has the burden of proving sufficient moral and ethical fitness to enjoy the sacred privilege of representing another person's interests. In many states, the applicant must meet this burden with clear and convincing evidence. State bars compare your law-school application to your bar application to ensure that both are accurate, consistent with one another, and complete. Check your law school application now, correcting and updating it as necessary. Every representation you make on your bar application must be complete and accurate. Notice how the following identical state version of ABA MODEL RULE OF PROF. CONDUCT 8.1 treats the representations that an applicant makes for licensure. A knowing false statement of material fact or knowing omission creating a misapprehension is professional misconduct.

> NORTH CAROLINA REV. RULE OF PROF. CONDUCT 8.1: **Bar Admission and Disciplinary Matters.**
> An applicant for admission to the bar, or a lawyer in connection with a bar admission application or in connection with a disciplinary matter, shall not:
> (a) knowingly make a false statement of material fact; or
> (b) fail to disclose a fact necessary to correct a misapprehension known by the person to have arisen in the matter, or knowingly fail to respond to a lawful demand for information from an admissions or disciplinary authority, except that this Rule does not require disclosure of information otherwise protected by Rule 1.6.

INQUIRY

Definition of Good Character. In general, proof of character involves comparing your attributes to standards that the public and the professional community accept. State bars use various verbal formulations to define the requisite character for admission. *Good moral character* is a common phrase. *Morality* refers to the fitness of one's conduct in any particular situation when judged by all attendant circumstances. Because character implicates the complete professional, not simpy single discrete acts, the standards for good character, though well known, are not fixed. Character issues tend to arise around categories including criminal conviction, financial mismanagement, and personal behaviors that suggest that the applicant would not be trustworthy as a lawyer. Consider each of those categories. Notice as you explore these categories that the conduct in question need not relate directly to law practice. *See* The Florida Bar v. Barthof, 775 So.2d 957 (Fla. 2000) (probation for golf-course dispute involving threat of violence).

> *Figure*
> John Berry, at different times the Executive Director of two of the bars Florida and Michigan and deputy Executive Director for Arizona's bar, is a preeminent example of a lawyer committed to the profession. Berry is presently the nation's top expert on lawyer professonalism, having served on the American Bar Association's Commission on Evaluation of Disciplinary Enforcement (the McKay Commission) and Standing Committee on Professional Discipline. Berry's recent work for the Florida Bar helped win a national award for lawyer professionalism. Berry also led the Florida Bar's legal division for 15 years, during which he saw the worst of lawyers but also

grew in his respect for them, attributing their downfalls most often to stress and poor management. Berry rooted his bar leadership in 20 years of law practice and in his personal faith. Appreciate the contribution to the profession that one lawyer can make with the right commitment and grounding. Consider John Berry to be a lawyer's lawyer.

Crimes. Criminal history is obviously important. Lawyers must first be willing to abide by the law, especially the criminal laws that represent the outer bounds of accepted conduct. Conviction for serious crimes of violence (murder, criminal sexual misconduct, assault and battery) demonstrates disrespect for the law, not to mention for the victims of that violence. Conviction for crimes of dishonesty (embezzlement, retail fraud) demonstrates disrespect for truth and law. Other crimes, like drunk driving, that are not violent and do not involve dishonesty may yet demonstrate callousness or carelessness toward the rights and for the welfare of others. There are no fixed rules disqualifying an applicant for licensure for any of these crimes. Even applicants responsible for serious crimes could theoretically qualify for licensure when able to demonstrate rehabilitation and current good character, although admissions officials will look more closely at those applicants. Consider the following case.

In re Hamm,
Arizona Supreme Court
123 P.3d 652 (2005)

McGREGOR, Chief Justice.

¶1 James Hamm petitioned this Court ... to review the recommendation of the Committee on Character and Fitness (the Committee) that his application for admission to the State Bar of Arizona (the Bar) be denied. Having reviewed the record and the Committee's report, we conclude that James Hamm has failed to establish the good moral character necessary to be admitted to the practice of law in Arizona and deny his application.

I.

¶2 In September 1974, James Hamm was twenty-six years old and living on the streets of Tucson. Although he previously had attended divinity school and worked as a part-time pastor, Hamm describes his life in 1974 as reflecting a series of personal and social failures. In 1973, he had separated from his wife, with whom he had a son. Although he had no criminal record, he supported himself by selling small quantities of marijuana and, again according to Hamm, he used marijuana and other drugs and abused alcohol.

¶3 On September 6, 1974, Hamm met two young men who identified themselves as college students from Missouri. The two, Willard Morley and Zane Staples, came to Tucson to buy twenty pounds of marijuana. Hamm agreed to sell it to them, but apparently was unable to acquire that quantity of marijuana. Rather than call off the transaction, Hamm and two accomplices, Garland Wells and Bill Reeser, agreed to rob Staples and Morley of the money intended for the purchase. ... Hamm shot Morley in the back of the head, killing him. At the same time, Wells shot Staples. Hamm then shot Staples in the back as he tried to escape and shot Morley once again. Wells also shot Morley, then pursued Staples, whom he ultimately killed outside of the car. Hamm and Wells took $1400.00 from the glove compartment, fled the scene in the van driven by Reeser, and left the bodies of Morley and Staples lying in the desert.

¶4 ... Initially charged with two counts of first-degree murder and two counts of armed robbery, Hamm pled guilty to one count of first-degree murder and was sentenced to life in prison, with no possibility of parole for twenty-five years.

¶5 Once in prison, Hamm began taking steps toward rehabilitation and became a model prisoner. After spending one year in maximum security, he applied for and received a job in a computer training program that allowed him to be transferred to medium security. Once in medium security, Hamm apparently took advantage of any and every educational opportunity the prison system had to offer. He completed certificates in yoga and meditation and, on his own, studied Jungian psychology. He helped fellow inmates learn to read and write and to take responsibility for their actions. He obtained a bachelor's degree in applied sociology, *summa cum laude,* from Northern Arizona University through a prison study program.

¶6 After Hamm completed six years in medium security, prison officials transferred him to minimum security, where he worked on paint and construction crews. He received a significant degree of freedom, which allowed him to live in a dormitory rather than in a cell and occasionally to drive unaccompanied to nearby towns. He testified that he was the only inmate permitted to head a work crew. Hamm reported to the Committee that he played an instrumental role on various prison committees, particularly the committee that developed a new grievance procedure within the Department of Corrections. In addition, he wrote grant proposals for libraries, for handicapped prisoners, and for obtaining greater legal assistance for prisoners.

¶7 While in prison, he met and married Donna Leone. She and Hamm founded Middle Ground Prison Reform (Middle Ground), a prisoner and prisoner family advocacy organization involved in lobbying for laws related to the criminal justice system and prisons. Middle Ground also provides public education about those topics.

¶8 In 1989, the Governor, acting on the recommendation of the Arizona Board of Pardons and Parole (the Board), commuted Hamm's sentence. When he had served nearly seventeen years, in July 1992, the Board released Hamm on parole.... In December 2001, the Arizona Board of Executive Clemency[fn] granted Hamm's third application for absolute discharge.

¶9 Between his release in August 1992 and his absolute discharge in December 2001, Hamm performed thousands of hours of community service. He advocated for prisoners' rights in various forums by writing position papers, appearing on radio programs, testifying in legislative hearings, and speaking at churches, schools, and civic organizations. He also appeared in a public service video encouraging children not to do drugs or join gangs. Hamm now works as the Director of Advocacy Services at Middle Ground Prison Reform.

¶10 While on parole, Hamm graduated from the Arizona State University College of Law. In July 1999, Hamm passed the Arizona bar examination and, in 2004, filed his Character and Fitness Report with the Committee.

II.

... ¶16 The ultimate question in cases such as this is whether the applicant has established good moral character....

¶17 We ... agree with Hamm that, under the Rule applicable to Hamm's application, our concern must be with the applicant's present moral character. ... Past misconduct, however, is not irrelevant. Rather, this Court must determine what past bad acts reveal about an applicant's current character.

III.

¶18 ... [T]he Committee conducted a formal hearing to consider Hamm's application. ... Hamm, representing himself, and his wife presented extensive testimony. In addition, the Committee heard from three licensed attorneys who had worked with Hamm and who recommended his admission and also considered letters from those opposed to and in support of Hamm's application. ... In its report, the Committee stated that, in reaching its conclusions, it considered the following:

1) Hamm's unlawful conduct, which included the commission of two violent "execution style" murders and his testimony as to the facts surrounding the murders.

2) Hamm's omissions on his Application and his testimony in explaining his failure to disclose all required information.

3) Hamm's neglect of his financial responsibilities and/or violation of a longstanding child support court order and his testimony as to his failure to comply with the court order.

4) Hamm's mental or emotional instability impairing his ability to perform the functions of an attorney including his testimony as to any diagnosis and treatment.[fn]

¶19 After reviewing all these factors, the Committee concluded that Hamm had not met his burden of establishing that he possesses the requisite character and fitness for admission to the Bar and accordingly recommended that his application be denied. We now consider the Committee's findings, together with pertinent facts.

A.

¶20 The serious nature of Hamm's past criminal conduct is beyond dispute. Hamm acknowledges that no more serious criminal conduct exists than committing first-degree murder. ...

¶21 Hamm's past criminal conduct and the serious nature of that conduct affect the burden he must meet to establish good moral character. He must first establish rehabilitation from prior criminal conduct, a requirement that adds to his burden of showing current good moral character. [C]

¶22 The added burden becomes greater as past unlawful conduct becomes more serious. In *In re Arrotta,* we considered an application for reinstatement from an attorney who, eight years earlier, pled guilty to mail fraud and bribery. 208 Ariz. 509, 96 P.3d 213 (2004). We noted there that "the more serious the misconduct that led to disbarment, the more difficult is the applicant's task in showing rehabilitation." *Id.* at 512 ¶ 12, 96 P.3d at 216. An applicant for initial admission to the Bar who is attempting to overcome the negative implications of a serious felony on his current moral character likewise must overcome a greater burden for more serious crimes. We agree with the New Jersey Supreme Court, which recognized that "in the case of extremely damning past misconduct, a showing of rehabilitation may be virtually impossible to make." *In re Matthews,* 94 N.J. 59, 462 A.2d 165, 176 (1983). Indeed, we are aware of no instance in which a person convicted of first-degree murder has been admitted to the practice of law.

¶23 To show rehabilitation, Hamm must show that he has accepted responsibility for his criminal conduct. ... Hamm *says* he has done so, repeatedly and strongly, but some of his other statements indicate to the contrary. ...

¶24 ... Hamm was not completely forthright in his testimony about the murders.[fn] Hamm has insisted in his filings with this Court that he did not intend to kill, but only to rob, his victims. The agreed facts, however, lead directly to the inference that Hamm intended to kill. ...

[H]e shot Morley without ever attempting a robbery and shot him a second time to make certain he was dead; and he also shot Staples to prevent his escape. ...   His failure to confront the fact that these murders were intentional undermines his statements that he fully accepts responsibility for his actions.

¶25 ... We are impressed with the sincerity and fervor of those who testified or submitted letters on Hamm's behalf. Were rehabilitation the only showing Hamm must make to establish good moral character, we would weigh those factors tending to show rehabilitation against those tending to show a lack thereof. ...

¶26 ... Even assuming that Hamm has established rehabilitation, showing rehabilitation from criminal conduct does not, in itself, establish good moral character. Rehabilitation is a necessary, but not sufficient, ingredient of good moral character. An applicant must establish his current good moral character, independent of and in addition to, evidence of rehabilitation. We conclude that Hamm failed to make that showing.

B.

¶27 We share the Committee's deep concern about Hamm's longstanding failure to fulfill, or even address, his child support obligation to his son, born in 1969, four years before Hamm and his first wife separated. Not until he prepared his application for admission to the Bar in 2004 did Hamm make any effort to meet his responsibility to provide support for his son. ...

¶28 ... A few months after he and his wife separated in 1973, Hamm was arrested on a misdemeanor charge of failing to pay child support. On May 6, 1974, James and Karen Hamm's divorce decree set Hamm's child support payments at $75.00 a month. Hamm made no effort to learn the extent of his financial obligation to his son from 1974, when Hamm was twenty-six years old, until 2004, when he was fifty-five. During those nearly thirty years, he gained sophistication and attended law school. He must have known, and certainly should have known, that he had long avoided a basic parental obligation.[fn6] [FN6. Hamm also cannot attribute his failure to pay child support to the absence of funds. Even while in prison, Hamm earned "somewhere around a hundred dollars a month probably," but used no portion of those earnings to discharge his obligation.] ...

¶32 We also agree with the Committee that Hamm did not display honesty and candor in discussing his failure to pay child support with the Committee. Hamm testified both that his son told him personally that he had been adopted and that his son "adamantly refused" to accept interest payments on the unpaid child support.

¶33 Hamm's son testified, however, that he had never been adopted, that prior to his contact with Hamm he had changed his name himself, and that he had not told Hamm he had been adopted. Hamm's son also did not report adamantly refusing interest payments. ...

C.

¶35 We further conclude that Hamm did not adequately explain his failure to disclose an incident involving him and his current wife, Donna, when he submitted his application to the Committee.

¶36 In 1996, Hamm and Donna engaged in a physical altercation outside a convenience store. Donna "yelled the word 'kidnap' out of the window" of the vehicle Hamm was driving, causing him to pull over and leave the vehicle. During their tussle, Donna tore Hamm's shirt. Both called the police, who arrested neither Hamm nor Donna. The incident and what Donna describes as her "embellishments" caused such great concern to the Hamms, particularly because Hamm was on parole, that Donna submitted to a polygraph administered by a private company to demonstrate that Hamm had not kidnapped her. The two also underwent marital counseling.

¶37 Nonetheless, when filling out his Character and Fitness Report, Hamm failed to disclose the incident to the Committee. Question 25 on the report asks specifically whether the applicant, among other things, has been "questioned" concerning any felony or misdemeanor.[fn] Hamm told the Committee that, in reading the application, he missed the word "questioned" in the list of encounters with law enforcement that Question 25 directs an applicant to report. ...

D.

¶39 Hamm's actions during these proceedings also raise questions about his fitness to practice law. The introduction to Hamm's petition before this Court begins: "The consequences of this case for Petitioner take it out of the ordinary realm of civil cases. If the Committee's recommendation is followed, it will prevent him from earning a living through practicing law. This deprivation has consequences of the greatest import for Petitioner, who has invested years of study and a great deal of financial resources in preparing to be a lawyer...." This language repeats nearly verbatim the language of the United States Supreme Court in *Konigsberg v. State Bar,* 353 U.S. 252, 77 S.Ct. 722, 1 L.Ed.2d 810 (1957), in which the Court wrote: "While this is not a criminal case, its consequences for Konigsberg take it out of the ordinary run of civil cases. The Committee's action prevents him from earning a living by practicing law. This deprivation has grave consequences for a man who has spent years of study and a great deal of money in preparing to be a lawyer." *Id.* at 257-58[]. If an attorney submits work to a court that is not his own, his actions may violate the rules of professional conduct. [Cc] We are concerned about Hamm's decision to quote from the Supreme Court's opinion without attribution and are equally troubled by his failure to acknowledge his error. ...   Hamm apparently either does not regard his actions as improper or simply refuses to take responsibility. In either case, his actions here do not assist him in making the requisite showing of good moral character.[fn] ...

V.

¶43 Because James Hamm has failed to meet his burden of proving that he is of good moral character, we deny his application for admission to the State Bar of Arizona.

INQUIRY

Representations.   *Hamm,* an extreme case, nonetheless illustrates two important principles: (1) it is not criminal or other negative history that determines the outcome but the applicant's ability to demonstrate current good character; and (2) the integrity of the applicant's application can be just as important to showing good character as proving rehabilitation from the negative history. Other cases suggest that even applicants responsible for crimes as non-serious as parking tickets may fail to qualify when the number and recency of the convictions, or the applicant's inadequate disclosure or treatment of them in the application process, demonstrates a lack of character. *See* In re Caldwell, 27 A.D.3d 154, 809 N.Y.S.2d 59 (2006) (suspension for unpaid parking tickets); In re DeBartolo, 488 N.E.2d 947 (Ill. 1986) (denial of admission). Arrest followed by dismissal of the charges or acquittal may nonetheless implicate bad character. *See* Attorney Grievance Commn. v. Childress, 770 A.2d 685 (Md. 2001) (suspension upheld despite felony conviction's reversal). It is a fine line between placing history in its context on one hand and failing to accept responsibility for it on the other hand. With the right sensitivity and respect, and under the right circumstances, an applicant may successfully explain arrests, aliases, and other circumstances that bar-admission officials might otherwise misconstrue as disqualifying for lack of good character. *See, e.g.,* Schware v Board of Examrs., 353 U.S. 232 (1957) (former communist demonstrates fitness for law practice through military service and other exemplary conduct).

Finances.   Personal finances can also be important to demonstrating the good character necessary for bar admission. The practice of law often involves holding money or other intangible assets in trust for clients. Lawyers have regular access to financial and personal information that an unscrupulous person could misuse for personal gain to the detriment of others. Lawyers must be trustworthy around finances. Bad personal or professional finances can demonstrate a person's inability or unwillingness to manage finances properly. They can also create an excuse or fuel the temptation to misuse others' finances. Would you entrust your million-dollar settlement to a lawyer who was in desperate straits owing creditors hundreds of thousands of dollars? Debt is not bad in itself. Character-and-fitness officials recognize that the costs of higher education, medical emergencies, family support, and other necessities can result in an accumulation of substantial debt. The great majority of bar applicants have some debt and many of them substantial debt. What is more important is an applicant's ability to prove that the applicant is acting responsibly toward that debt.

Personal Behavior. Good character does not end with avoiding crimes and maintaining decent finances. Personal misbehavior can also demonstrate poor character and affect bar admission and licensure. It is hard in this area to define specific categories of misconduct calling into question an applicant's character, although the cases often involve such actions as bullying, incivility, personal attacks, misuse of procedures, public attacks, and similar conduct that has the effect of reducing public trust in lawyers, the law, and the justice system. Lawyers must show appropriate restraint even when confronting injustice, if the justice system is to be the arbiter and not the individual lawyer. See how these principles operate in the following case.

In re Application of Converse,
Nebraska Supreme Court
602 N.W.2d 500 (1999)

PER CURIAM.

Paul Raymond Converse appeals a decision of the Nebraska State Bar Commission (Commission) denying his request to take the July 1998 Nebraska bar examination. Converse claims that the decision of the Commission should be reversed because the Commission rested its denial of Converse's application, at least in part, upon conduct protected by the First Amendment to the U.S. Constitution and, in the alternative, that Converse's conduct did not constitute sufficient cause under Nebraska law for denying his application on the ground of deficient moral character. For the reasons that follow, we affirm the decision of the Commission.

FACTUAL BACKGROUND

... After the completion of his first semester at the University of South Dakota (USD) Law School, Converse sent a letter to then assistant dean Diane May regarding certain issues—not relevant to this appeal—that he had had with the law school during fall classes, closing that letter with the phrase, "Hope you get a full body tan in

Costa Rica." Subsequent to that note, Converse had several more encounters with May, beginning with his writing letters to May about receiving grades lower than what he believed he had earned in an appellate advocacy class.

After he received a grade he believed to be unjustified by his performance in the appellate advocacy course, Converse wrote letters to May and to the USD law school dean, Barry Vickrey, requesting assistance with an appeal of that grade. In addition to writing letters to Vickrey and May, Converse also sent a letter to the South Dakota Supreme Court regarding the appellate advocacy course professor's characterization of his arguments, with indications that carbon copies of the letter were sent to two well-known federal court of appeals judges. The letter was written to suggest the professor believed her stance on certain issues was more enlightened than that of the judges. Converse sent numerous correspondence to various people regarding the grade appeal against the specific professor. Despite all such correspondence, Converse testified at the hearing that no formal appeal of the grievance was ever filed. Converse's grade was never adjusted.

The evidence showed that following the grade "appeal," Converse prepared a memorandum and submitted it to his classmates, urging them to recall an "incident" in which yet another professor lashed out at him in class, and to be cognizant of the image that incident casts "on [that professor's] core professionalism" prior to completing class evaluations. Converse also wrote a letter to a newspaper in South Dakota, the Sioux Falls Argus Leader, regarding a proposed fee increase at the USD law school. Converse immediately began investigating the salaries of USD law professors and posted a list of selected professors' salaries on the student bulletin board, as well as writing a letter that accused Vickrey of trying to pull a "fast one."

Converse's next altercation at the USD law school involved a photograph of a nude female's backside that he displayed in his study carrel in the USD law library. The picture was removed by a law librarian. In response to the removal of this photograph, Converse contacted the American Civil Liberties Union (ACLU) and received a letter indicating that his photograph might be a protected expression under the First Amendment. Once again, Converse went to the student newspaper to alert the student body of the actions of the law school authorities, accusing them of unconstitutional censorship.

Converse redisplayed the photograph once it was returned by the law librarians. Vickrey received several complaints about the photograph from other students, classifying Converse's behavior as "unprofessional and inappropriate." Upon Converse's redisplay of the photograph, Vickrey sent him a memorandum explaining that the picture would not be removed only because Vickrey did not want to involve the school in controversy during final examinations. Converse testified that he redisplayed the photograph in order to force the alleged constitutional issue.

The evidence also revealed that Converse filed an ethics complaint with the North Dakota Bar Association regarding certain correspondence between Vickrey and a retired justice of the North Dakota Supreme Court. The complaint was dismissed. Converse went to the USD student newspaper, claiming that a letter from a retired North Dakota justice to the ACLU, in response to questions from Vickrey, was a violation of professional ethics... . In addition to going to the press, Converse also contacted the president of USD, referring to Vickrey as an "incompetent" and requesting that Vickrey be fired. In addition to this incident, Converse reported his suspicions about USD's student health insurance policy to the student newspaper under the title of "Law Student Suspects Health Insurance Fraud," as well as in a separate article alleging that USD had suppressed an investigation of its insurance carrier.

The Commission also heard testimony regarding Converse's attempt to obtain an internship with the U.S. Attorney's office in South Dakota. Converse arranged for the internship on his own, only to have his request subsequently rejected by the law school. Upon receiving his denial, Converse sent a complaint to all of USD's law school faculty members. Vickrey testified that Converse's internship was rejected because he failed to comply with the law school's procedures regarding internships. Converse then contacted the chairperson of the law school committee of the South Dakota State Bar Association with his complaint, expressly referring to Vickrey as being "arrogant." There is no indication of a response from the chairperson in the record.

The issue next considered by the Commission was that of various litigation threatened by Converse. Converse indicated that he would "likely" be filing a lawsuit against Vickrey for violations of his First Amendment rights. Converse was also involved in a dispute with other law students, in which he threatened to file a lawsuit and warned the students that all lawsuits in which they were involved would need to be reported to proper authorities when they applied to take a bar examination. Further, Converse posted signs on the bulletin board at the law school denouncing a professor, in response to the way in which Converse's parking appeal was handled, and then went to the student newspaper to criticize the process and those involved in that appeal.

One of the final issues addressed by the Commission in its hearing was that of a T-shirt Converse produced and marketed on which a nude caricature of Vickrey is shown sitting astride what appears to be a large hot dog. The cartoon on the shirt also contains the phrase "Astride the Peter Principle," which Converse claims connotes the principle that Vickrey had been promoted past his level of competence; however, Converse admits that the T-shirt could be construed to have certain sexual overtones. Converse admitted that the creation of this T-shirt would not be acceptable behavior for a lawyer.

In response to not being allowed to post signs and fliers at the law school, Converse sent a memo to all law students in which he noted to his fellow students that his "Deanie on a Weanie" T-shirts were in stock. In that same memo, Converse included a note to his schoolmates: "So far 4 causes of action have arisen, courtesy Tricky Vickrey. [He then listed what he believed the causes of action to be.] When you pass the SD Bar, if you want to earn some atty [sic] fees, get hold of me and we can go for one of these. I've kept evidence, of course." Vickrey asked Converse not to wear his T-shirt to his graduation ceremony, and Converse decided that "it would be a better choice in [his] life not to go to that commencement." Converse acknowledges that Vickrey's request was made in a civil manner.

The evidence also revealed that prior to law school, Converse, in his capacity as a landlord, sued a tenant for nonpayment of rent and referred to the tenant as a "fucking welfare bitch." At the hearing, in response to questioning from the Commission, Converse testified at great length as to how he tends to personally attack individuals when he finds himself embroiled in a controversy. ...

ANALYSIS

... [T]he threshold question we must answer is whether conduct arguably protected by the First Amendment can be considered by the Commission during an investigation into an applicant's moral character and fitness to practice law. We answer this question in the affirmative.

There are four U.S. Supreme Court cases that provide particular guidance with respect to this issue. In *Konigsberg v. State Bar,* 366 U.S. 36[] (1961), the bar applicant argued that when the California bar commission forced him to either answer questions about his affiliation with the Communist Party or to face the repercussions of not being certified as possessing the required moral character to sit for the bar, the commission violated his First Amendment rights. The Supreme Court disagreed, pointing out that "regulatory statutes, not intended to control the content of speech but incidentally limiting its unfettered exercise, have not been regarded as the type of law the First or Fourteenth Amendment [forbids] ... when they have been found justified by subordinating valid governmental interests." 366 U.S. at 50-51[]. In the context of a character inquiry, "it is difficult, indeed, to imagine a view of the constitutional protections of speech and association which would automatically ... exclude all reference to prior speech or association on such issues as character, purpose, credibility, or intent." 366 U.S. at 51[]. ...

In 1971, the Court was once again confronted with the issue and decided a trilogy of cases concerning the bar admissions procedures of various states. See, *Baird v. State Bar of Arizona,* 401 U.S. 1[] (1971); *In re Stolar,* 401 U.S. 23[] (1971); *Law Students Research Council v. Wadmond,* 401 U.S. 154[] (1971). It was the final case in this trilogy, *Law Students Research Council v. Wadmond,* that clarified the law as to the appropriate depth of a state bar commission's inquiry on an applicant's moral character. The Court declined to uphold a First Amendment attack against the admission procedure of the New York bar association. The Court upheld the statute, which required that the admitting authority be "'satisfied that [the applicant] possesses the character and general fitness requisite for an attorney and ounselor-at-law.'" 401 U.S. at 156[]. ...

Were we to adopt the position asserted by Converse in this case, the Commission would be limited to conducting only cursory investigations of an applicant's moral character and past conduct. Justice Potter Stewart, writing for the majority in *Law Students Research Council v. Wadmond, supra,* noted that the implications of such an attack on a bar screening process are that no screening process would be constitutionally permissible beyond academic examination and an extremely minimal check for serious, concrete character deficiencies. ... Assuming but not deciding that Converse's conduct may have been protected by the First Amendment to the U.S. Constitution, *Law Students Research Council v. Wadmond, supra,* makes clear that a bar commission is allowed to consider speech and conduct in making determinations of an applicant's character, and that is precisely what has occurred in the instant case. ...

There is no question that "[a] state can require high standards of qualification, such as good moral character or proficiency in its law, before it admits an applicant to the bar...." *Schware v. Board of Bar Examiners,* 353 U.S. 232, 239[] (1957). ... Therefore, the burden is upon Converse to adequately prove his fitness to practice law in Nebraska, and the evidence will be viewed in this light. ...

We considered an appeal of a similarly situated bar applicant in *In re Appeal of Lane,* 249 Neb. 499, 544 N.W.2d 367 (1996). *In re Appeal of Lane* involved an individual seeking readmission to the Nebraska bar whose past included confrontations with law school faculty, the use of strong and profane language with fellow students at his bar review course, the use of intimidating and rude conduct directed at a security guard at the place where he was taking his bar review course, and some controversial interactions with females. We held that, taken together, "these incidents show that Lane is prone to turbulence, intemperance, and irresponsibility, characteristics which are not acceptable in one who would be a counselor and advocate in the legal system," and we upheld the denial of his application. *Id.* at 510, 544 N.W.2d at 374.

We explained in *In re Appeal of Lane,* 249 Neb. At 511, 544 N.W.2d at 375, that the "requisite restraint in dealing with others is *obligatory conduct for attorneys* because '[t]he efficient and orderly administration of justice cannot be successfully carried on if we allow attorneys to engage in unwarranted attacks on the court [or] opposing counsel.... Such tactics seriously lower the public respect for ... the Bar.'" (Emphasis supplied.) (Quoting *Application of Feingold,* 296 A.2d 492 (Me.1972)). Furthermore, "'[a]n attorney who exhibits [a] lack of civility, good manners and common courtesy ... tarnishes the ... image of ... the bar....'" *Id.* (Quoting *In re McAlevy,* 69 N.J. 349, 354 A.2d 289 (1976)). We held in *In re Appeal of Lane,* 249 Neb. At 512, 544 N.W.2d at 375, that "abusive, disruptive, hostile, intemperate, intimidating, irresponsible, threatening, or turbulent behavior is a proper basis for the denial of admission to the bar." *Id.* Expanding on this holding, we stated:

> Care with words and respect for courts and one's adversaries is a necessity, not because lawyers and judges are without fault, but because trial by combat long ago proved unsatisfactory. ...
>
> The profession's insistence that counsel show restraint, self-discipline and a sense of reality in dealing with courts, other counsel, witnesses and adversaries is more than insistence on good manners. It is based on the knowledge that civilized, rational behavior is essential if the judicial system is to perform its function. Absent this, any judicial proceeding is likely to degenerate into [a] verbal free-for-all .... [H]abitual unreasonable reaction to adverse rulings ... is conduct of a type not to be permitted of a lawyer when acting as a lawyer. *What cannot be permitted in lawyers, cannot be tolerated in those applying for admission as lawyers."* (Emphasis supplied.) 249 Neb. At 513, 544 N.W.2d at 376. ...

The evidence in this case shows that Converse's numerous disputes and personal attacks indicate a "pattern and a way of life which appear to be [Converse's] normal reaction to opposition and disappointment." See *In re Appeal of Lane,* 249 Neb. 499, 512, 544 N.W.2d 367, 376 (1996). The totality of the evidence clearly establishes that Converse possesses an inclination to personally attack those with whom he has disputes. ...

In addition to Converse's tendency to personally attack those individuals with whom he has disputes, his pattern of behavior indicates an additional tendency to do so in arenas other than those specifically established within the legal system. This tendency is best exemplified by observing Converse's conduct in situations where there were avenues through which Converse could have and should have handled his disputes, but instead chose to mount personal attacks on those with whom he had disputes through letters and barrages in the media.

One such incident occurred when Converse received the below average grade in the appellate advocacy course, and he wrote letters to various individuals regarding his arguments. Converse testified that he wrote letters to members of the South Dakota Supreme Court, Judge Richard Posner, Judge Alex Kozinski, and others, but filed no formal appeal. Moreover, upon return of the nude photograph, Converse testified that he redisplayed the photograph to force the issue with the university, but chose not to pursue any action regarding the alleged violation of his rights. There was also the incident regarding Converse's internship with the U.S. Attorney's office, where Converse went outside established procedures, arranged for the internship on his own, and then complained to all faculty and to members of the South Dakota bar when his request was denied for not complying with established procedures. Finally, there was Converse's production and marketing of the T-shirt containing a nude depiction of Vickrey on a hot dog as a result of the ongoing tension between Vickrey and himself. Converse is 48 years old, and his actions cannot be excused as isolated instances of youthful indiscretions. ...

CONCLUSION

The Commission correctly determined that Converse possessed insufficient moral character and was unfit to practice law in the State of Nebraska. ...

AFFIRMED; APPLICATION DENIED.

_____

2.   Fitness

Disability. Although "character and fitness" is the common phrase one reads when bars evaluate candidates for admission, fitness has a distinct meaning when it comes to a lawyer's continuing physical and mental ability to serve clients. Certainly, law firms and other employers of lawyers owe the same duty as employers of non-lawyers to accommodate the disabilities of lawyers so that they can continue in their work. Yet some physical or mental conditions—death is the most obvious one—make it impossible for a lawyer to fulfill ordinary duties of diligence and competence. Hospitalization and other invasive or restrictive treatment for any number of illnesses or other conditions can make it impossible for a lawyer to conduct meetings, make court appearances, draft documents, and do the other routine tasks law practice requires. Even solely or primarily mental conditions like schizophrenia, paranoia, or depression in severe cases can make law practice impossible or imprudent. Sometimes, the restrictions that a physical or mental condition imposes are obvious and uncontested. Other times, the advance of a condition may be slow and uncertain, leaving contested the lawyer's ability to practice. Most bars offer disability proceedings different and apart from misconduct proceedings, the result of which may be a non-disciplinary license suspension until the interfering condition abates, with reinstatement possible.

Substance Abuse. Many bars also offer substance-abuse programs known as Lawyer and Judges Assistance Programs. These programs can help a lawyer recover from alcohol use, illicit drug use, and related habits that interfere with law practice and jeopardize a lawyer's license. There is a high correlation between misconduct charges and substance abuse. Grievance officials know much about that correlation. They are often willing to support a respondent lawyer's participation in an Assistance Program, much like a criminal-charge diversion program. Lawyers share the responsibility to care for one another within the profession. Know the programs and resources available to lawyers even if you do not need that help. You should be sensitive to the mental and physical health and general welfare of other lawyers. Your timely intervention on behalf of another lawyer could save that lawyer's license and career. Be responsible in this area, as you are in other areas. Consider one illustrative case.

In the Matter of the Reinstatement
Petition of David S. Feinberg,
State of Michigan Attorney Discipline Board
No. 08-70-RP (March 25, 2010)

Petitioner's license to practice law was suspended for two years in two separate orders effective March 31, 2005, arising from four consolidated cases involving his 2002 representation of a law student in a school disciplinary hearing while under the influence of drugs; two 2005 convictions, one for possession of cocaine and another for violation of his probation; and various other misconduct, including neglect of client matters. Petitioner was licensed to practice law in Michigan in 1989. According to his testimony, respondent's addiction to cocaine commenced in 1992. He participated in in-patient treatment for his addiction to substances several times over the years. After a relapse and treatment in 2002, he maintained sobriety for 2 and 1/2 years, but relapsed in 2004 when he was arrested for possession of cocaine.

Petitioner initially sought reinstatement in February 2007, and that petition was denied in July 2007, by Ingham County Hearing Panel #3. The petition for reinstatement in this case was filed on May 8, 2008, and was denied by Livingston County Hearing Panel #1 on April 2, 2009. Petitioner has filed a petition for review of the second order denying reinstatement. We affirm the order denying reinstatement.

Livingston County Hearing Panel #1 found that petitioner failed to prove by clear and convincing evidence that he met the following requirements of MCR 9.123(B):

> (4) he or she has complied fully with the order of discipline;
> (5) his or her conduct since the order of discipline has been exemplary and above reproach;
> * * *
> (7) taking into account all of the attorney's past conduct, including
> the nature of the misconduct which led to the revocation or suspension, he or she nevertheless can safely be recommended to the public, the courts, and the legal profession as a person fit to be consulted by others and to represent them and otherwise act in matters of trust and confidence, and in general to aid in the administration of justice as a member ofthe bar and as an officer of the court[.]

The panel in this matter made it clear that while several specific things troubled them, they were making their decision based upon "all of the attorney's past conduct." [C] As we have explained:

> Subrule 7 requires the clear conclusion that the petitioner can safely be recommended as a person fit to be consulted in matters oftrust and confidence. MCR 9.103(A) defines the license to practice law as "a continuing proclamation by the Supreme Court that the holder is fit to be entrusted with professional and judicial matters and to aid in the administration of justice." To affix such a proclamation of safety, or "stamp of approval," [*Grievance Administrator v August,* 438 Mich 296,311; 475 NW2d256 (1991)], upon someone who has committed serious misconduct would seem to require a searching inquiry into the causes for the conduct resulting in discipline and the most convincing showing that a genuine transformation has occurred. [*In Re Reinstatement of Arthur R. Porter, Jr.,* 97-302-RP (1999).]

... [T]he questions presented on review in reinstatement matters are sometimes not factual, and are rarely truly legal, but often call for the exercise of the panel's considered judgment. ...

Petitioner's brief cites cases for the proposition that there is an implicit assumption that a suspended lawyer will be reinstated, and that the running of the time period in a suspension order establishes a *prima facie* case of eligibility for reinstatement. This is not the law.... .

Petitioner also argues for more consistency in reinstatement decisions. Again, this is not the reinstatement scheme set forth in the court rules or caselaw. ...

We conclude that there is proper evidentiary support for the panel's decision to deny the petition for reinstatement. The misconduct for which petitioner was suspended involved appearing under the influence of substances at a hearing, neglect of client matters, and criminal convictions for possession of cocaine (which was in violation of a criminal court's probation order). Thus, respondent's recovery and rehabilitation from his addiction to substances was one key area of inquiry at the hearing below. However, the panel also noted other conduct that had not been the subject of a formal complaint and may not be related to substance abuse, such as the failure to fully recompense the estate of a former client who deposited with petitioner a substantial sum of money (the Wittenberg estate), and petitioner's "apparent misrepresentation to a magistrate in the 54A District Court."

Petitioner was a party to a matter pending in the 54A District Court. A hearing in that court was scheduled to take place on the same day a hearing in this reinstatement matter had been noticed. The hearing in these discipline proceedings was adjourned, but petitioner never informed the magistrate of this. Instead, he appeared before the magistrate, who had requested that he put his request for adjournment in the district court matter on the record, and tendered the notice of hearing in these proceedings as evidence of conflicting hearing dates. He did this even though the reinstatement hearing had been adjourned. Petitioner testified below that he had other things to do on the day of the 54A hearing and had already requested time off of work. Asked why he did not file a motion to adjourn the district court hearing that recited the actual basis for the request instead of relying on a superseded notice of hearing in these proceedings, petitioner testified:

> Because I only had two weeks and I had been speaking to her on the phone. Filing a motion, I mean it's the same thing as me appearing at the time of the hearing. She already told me she was going to grant it, *because of the fact that there was a conflict.* She said, just come in and we'll put it on the record .... [C]

Clearly, this conduct provides evidentiary support for the panel's conclusion that petitioner has not met his burden of establishing compliance with MCR 9.123(B)(5) and (7) by clear and convincing evidence.

The hearing panel also made reference to petitioner's unpaid obligations to the Wittenberg estate. As the July 30, 2007 panel report denying petitioner's first petition for reinstatement explains, Donald B. Wittenberg, now deceased, filed a civil action against petitioner in 2007 alleging breach of contract, fraudulent misrepresentation, legal malpractice and breach of fiduciary duty. ...

The hearing panel in petitioner's first reinstatement case found, among other things, that petitioner "took some of Mr. Wittenberg's money to purchase a house that petitioner titled in his name and paid himself a fee. Neither of those acts were disclosed to Mr. Wittenberg." The panel concluded that various aspects of the transaction and subsequent events were inconsistent with the requirements of MCR 9.123(B), and the panel further found "petitioner's belated agreement to pay $20,000 over time to Mr. Wittenberg'S estate ... insignificant in light of his other conduct." In this proceeding, petitioner has acknowledged that he did not display the proper attitude toward the Wittenberg matter before the initial reinstatement panel. However, we are not convinced from this record that petitioner fully appreciates his responsibilities to clients similarly situated to Mr. Wittenberg. ... [T]he record needs more elaboration to enable a hearing panel and this Board to assess (1) the nature of the improper conduct, and (2) whether petitioner has undergone a "genuine transformation"[fn] such that he can be safely held out to members of the public as a Michigan lawyer.

Although we have commented on some of the bases for the panel's decision, and we agree with the panel that petitioner may yet establish his fitness before a hearing panel, we reiterate that neither the court rules nor this opinion provide a formula for reinstatement.

Finally, the hearing panel below opined that "the protection of the public demands that certain conditions be met prior to the petitioner's next appearance before a reinstatement panel." Among the seven conditions set forth were continued abstinence, participation LJAP, and participation in a support group to prevent relapse with respect to substance abuse as well as to detect and prevent ethical lapses. Although the conditions precedent suggested by the panel are quite sensible and will doubtless be important factors in a subsequent proceeding, given the deliberately indeterminate nature of MCR 9.123(B)'s requirements, we are not prepared to say that these conditions are either necessary or sufficient for reinstatement in a subsequent proceeding.   For example, a hearing panel might be persuaded that petitioner has met the requirements of MCR 9.123(B) even if he remains employed as a car salesperson, or if he can show clearly and convincingly that he has maintained sobriety through participation in programs or methods other than the Lawyers and Judges Assistance Program.[fn] However, the burden remains heavy and petitioner would be well advised to heed the areas of concern identified by each tribunal that has considered discipline or reinstatement matters involving him. He should, of course, also be prepared to establish that his conduct has been exemplary and reflects an understanding of, and willingness to abide by, the obligations of an attorney.

For all of the foregoing reasons, the order of the hearing panel denying reinstatement is affirmed.

INQUIRY

Substance Abuse and Mental Health.   Unfortunately, mental health within the law profession is often not good. A 1990 John Hopkins study concluded that lawyers lead the business world in the incidence of depression, after adjusting for socio-economic factors, leaving the law profession with the highest suicide rate. The ABA estimates that 15% to 20% of lawyers within the United States suffer from alcoholism or substance abuse. Problems can begin in law school. Researchers studying law-student mental health found in one study that by the end of their first year, 32% of the students were depressed—and the depression rate rose to 40% by the end of the third year. The same study subjects reported that two years after law school, 17% of them were still depressed. Compare those figures to the 6.7% rate of major depressive order in the general adult American population. *See Depression Statistics in General and in Lawyers,* LawyersWithDepression.com.

Compensating Tools. We cite these statistics not to scare you but rather to equip you. Forewarned is forearmed. Law practice is stressful. Stress endangers those who are not equipped, as these statistics show. Yet the practice of law can also be a richly rewarding endeavor, especially if you have the psychological and spiritual tools to manage its challenges properly. Integrating your psychological awareness and moral beliefs with your professional practice can help you compensate. Here are some other tools:

- Avoid perfectionism. As lawyers, we tend to be precise, analytical, logical, and rational, which is good to a point. Yet judges, other lawyers, and clients are often imperfect. So are we. Do not be overly hard on yourself when you are not perfect. Do not be overly hard on others, either.

- Embrace ambiguity. Lawyers often engage in binary yes-no, all-or-nothing thinking. Yet the law is often necessarily ambiguous, as are the circumstances in which we apply it. Do not expect everything to be clear. Appreciate nuance, flexibility, compromise, and ambiguity.

- Confront your fears. Lawyers often avoid or are uncomfortable recognizing and addressing emotions, whether our own or those of others. Yet emotions are important. They affect decisions, health, and relationships. Do not be governed by your fears, but do not ignore them, either. Admit and deal with them.

- Learn how to manage failure. Lawyers tend to fear failure. We judge ourselves by external measures. Yet everyone fails. Those who seldom fail seldom risk and consequently succeed less often than they could have. See occasional failure as necessary to more-frequent success.

- Practice insight. Lawyers are often skilled at recognizing the motivation and character of others, but we may have more than the usual difficulty in recognizing our own motivation and character. Sometimes the most difficult person to get to know is one's self. Yet knowing one's self (without blaming and projection) may be the quickest path to improvement. Acknowledging a weakness is often the only way to begin managing it. Know thyself.

- Balance work with the rest of life. Lawyers are properly ambitious. There is so much good to do. Yet working beyond reasonable hours can destroy one's perspective and health. Take time for yourself, friends, and family—always. Do it now, not later when you have made partner, paid off school loans, or accomplished some other career or financial goal.

- Practice healthy habits. Lawyers sometimes allow work to interfere with basic needs. Eating a healthy diet, getting sufficient sleep, and exercising consistently in pleasurable ways are keys to mental and physical health.

- Practice contentment. Society bombards professionals with messages that we should be thinner or stronger, have more or less hair, live in a bigger or better house, drive a faster or fancier car, and be number one in everything, keeping us in constant discontentment. Appreciate who you are and what you have—every day. Remember that whatever you may lack, you have much more than others. There is always someone who would happily trade places with you.

Service to Others.   It is often said that the best route to contentment is to help someone else.   Human nature is naturally self centered.   We focus on our own wants and needs, making it easy to view the glass as half empty.   John Maxwell, an internationally recognized expert on leadership, warns in his book *Becoming a Person of Influence*, "We always think of ourselves first, we never think of what is good for others."   He urges, "To understand others we must apply this quote in our priorities: The least important word: I.   The most important word: We.   The two most important words: Thank you.   The three most important words: All is forgiven.   The four most important words: What is your opinion?   The five most important word: You did a good job.   The six most important words: I want to understand you better."

C. Unauthorized Practice

Non-Lawyers.   The subject of the unauthorized practice of law begins with a prohibition against legal services provided by non-lawyers.   A majority of states use an unauthorized-practice-of-law statute to bar non-lawyers from law practice.   Some of those statutes make unauthorized practice a criminal misdemeanor, *see, e.g.,* CAL. BUS. & PROF. CODE §6126;   42 PA. C.S.A. §2524(a), while others make it a felony, *see, e.g.,* FLA. STAT. ANN. §454.23, crimes punishable by imprisonment or fine.   Some states make unauthorized practice punishable by contempt while also offering injunctions, fines, and restitution. *See, e.g.,* MICH. COMP. L. §600.916.   You can also find specific provisions against the unauthorized practice of law by certain trades or professions where unauthorized practice is a particular temptation. *See, e.g.,* MICH. COMP. L. §55.300a(2)(j) (prohibiting notary publics from engaging in the unauthorized practice of law);   MICH. COMP. L. §338.3467(1)(b) (prohibiting immigration clerical assistant from engaging in the unauthorized practice of law); *see also* In re Pinkins, 213 B.R. 818 (Bankr. E.D. Mich. 1997) (law firm's legal assistants engaged in unauthorized practice of law by explaining legal options and giving legal advice to clients, and using legal judgment).   State-bar rules may authorize an unauthorized-practice committee of the bar to institute civil actions to prosecute unauthorized practice by non-lawyers. *See* STATE BAR OF MICH. RULE 16.   Consider one such unauthorized-practice statute.

> MICH. COMP. L. §600.916. Unauthorized practice of law
> (1) A person shall not practice law or engage in the law business, shall not in any manner whatsoever lead others to believe that he or she is authorized to practice law or to engage in the law business, and shall not in any manner whatsoever represent or designate himself or herself as an

attorney and counselor, attorney at law, or lawyer, unless the person is regularly licensed and authorized to practice law in this state. A person who violates this section is guilty of contempt of the supreme court and of the circuit court of the county in which the violation occurred, and upon conviction is punishable as provided by law. This section does not apply to a person who is duly licensed and authorized to practice law in another state while temporarily in this state and engaged in a particular matter. (2) A domestic violence victim advocate's assistance that is provided in accordance with section 2950c does not violate this section.

Practice

The picture on the law firm website spoke a thousand words: the smiling face of the eager law student excited to be working at a busy downtown law firm, and the proud faces of the lawyers who had hired her. Yet the title that the firm gave the student—"lawyer"—spelled a huge problem. The firm held the law student out as a lawyer, allowed her to counsel clients and sign retainer agreements on behalf of the firm. The state bar was puzzled when it began receiving complaints about the "lawyer" and could not find any lawyer by that name in its database. When the state bar contacted the firm and student, the responses were indifference and even contempt. Only when the ensuing complaint sought a court order prohibiting the student from engaging in the unauthorized practice of law did the light bulb go off. Yet by then it was too late. The law student had just bought herself a significant character and fitness issue that would delay her admission to the bar, when she and her firm might have avoided it by respectfully responding to the bar and ceasing the unauthorized activity.

INQUIRY

Defining Practice. It may not be obvious exactly what constitutes law practice when it comes to applying these unauthorized-practice provisions. Certainly, appearing on behalf of a party in litigation would be law practice. *See* GA. CODE 15-19-50(1). So, too, would a person's drafting a will from scratch to meet the estate-planning objectives of a client. Yet what of offering standard contract, real-estate, and will forms? Would a non-lawyer's selling forms that a lawyer drafted constitute law practice? *See* TEX. GOVT. CODE §81.101 (authorizing non-lawyer sale of legal software products that state that they are not a substitute for a lawyer's advice). Would it be law practice for a non-lawyer to help a client fill in a form that a lawyer had drafted? Does it help to define the practice of law as that which lawyers customarily do and non-lawyers do not do? *See* State Bar of Arizona v. Arizona Land Title & Trust Co., 366 P.2d 1 (Ariz. 1961). Title companies, financial advisors, real-estate agents, notary publics, accountants, tax preparers, and legal assistants are some of the usual unauthorized-practice suspects. *See* Countrywide Home Loans, Inc. v.

Kentucky Bar Assn., 113 S.W.3d 105 (Ky. 2003) (non-lawyer loan officers may close real-estate transactions but not give legal advice); Doe v. McMaster, 585 S.E.2d 773 (S.C. 2003) (non-lawyer's unsupervised title search and note drafting is unauthorized law practice). Consider a case against a popular unauthorized-practice target to discern from its lengthy injunction the broader contours of just what other actions may constitute law practice.

The Florida Bar v. We the People Forms and Service Center of Sarasota, Inc.,

Florida Supreme Court
883 So.2d 1280 (2004)

PER CURIAM.

We review a referee's report recommending that respondents, We The People Forms and Service Center of Sarasota, Inc., ("WTP/Sarasota") and Danielle Kingsley be enjoined from engaging in the unlicensed practice of law (UPL). ... We approve the referee's findings of fact and conclusion of law that respondents have engaged in UPL in Florida, and we enjoin such practice in the future. We further approve the referee's recommendation that respondents be jointly and severally assessed a monetary penalty of $9000.

FACTS

On July 26, 2002, The Florida Bar filed a Petition Against the Unlicensed Practice of Law against respondents. The petition alleged that respondents had engaged in nine counts of UPL. The nine counts involved numerous separate incidents. The Bar sought an injunction as well as $9000 in monetary penalties against respondents.

The referee granted the Bar's motion for judicial notice and its motion to deem matters admitted. Respondents also agreed to the entry of summary judgment in the proceedings before the referee. After holding a hearing on costs and penalties, the referee issued a report finding that there was no dispute of fact as to the following:

1. Respondent Kingsley and Respondent WTP/Sarasota were not and are not members of The Florida Bar and ... they were not and are not licensed to practice law in Florida.

2. Respondents advertise legal form preparation services beyond the business activities of typing legal forms and notary services, and selling legal forms and general printed information.

3. Respondents offered legal services directly to their customers by employing a licensed Florida attorney, Robert A. Norgard, to give legal advice to Respondents' customers. ...

[The opinion recited the separate cases in federal bankruptcy court and Florida state circuit court, and one out-of-court matter, in which respondents provided legal services.]

12. Respondent Kingsley contacted opposing parties and the attorneys for opposing parties on behalf of customers in reference to legal matters.

Based on the foregoing, the referee concluded that respondents had engaged in the unlicensed practice of law in Florida in violation of the decisions of this Court by (1) providing customers with legal assistance in the selection, preparation, and completion of legal forms; (2) correcting customers' errors or omissions; (3) preparing or assisting in the preparation of pleadings and other legal documents for their customers; (4) corresponding with opposing parties or the attorneys of opposing parties as the representative of a customer in a legal matter; (5) hiring a licensed Florida attorney to provide legal advice to respondents' customers; (6) holding a licensed Florida attorney out to their customers as respondents' supervising attorney; and (7) advertising their services in such a way that led the public to believe that respondents were capable of providing legal services.

In light of these conclusions, the referee recommended:

A. That We The People Forms and Service Center of Sarasota, Inc. and Danielle Kingsley be found to have engaged in the unlicensed practice of law in the State of Florida.

B. That We The People Forms and Service Center of Sarasota, Inc. and Danielle Kingsley be restrained and enjoined from engaging in the following activities:

1. Holding themselves out to the public in such a manner that the public places some reliance on [Respondents] to properly prepare legal documents;

2. Representing to the public, either personally or by use of advertisement, that We The People Forms and Service Center of Sarasota, Inc. and/or Danielle Kingsley, or any persons that [are] either employed by or who act in concert with Respondents, that they are capable of advising and handling matters requiring legal skills;

3. Advertising any legal form preparation services beyond the business activities of typing legal forms and notary services, and selling legal forms and general printed information;

4. Advertising in a manner which suggests to the public that the services offered by We The People Forms and Service Center of Sarasota, Inc. and/or Danielle Kingsley are the equivalent of or a substitute for the services of an attorney;

5. Advertising in any fashion which may lead a reasonable lay person to believe that We The People Forms and Service Center of Sarasota,

Inc. and/or Danielle Kingsley offer to the public legal service, legal advice or personal legal assistance regarding any legal matter;

6. Completing forms or assisting in the completion of forms that are not simplified forms approved by the Supreme Court of Florida, except to the extent permitted by *The Florida Bar v. Brumbaugh*, 355 So.2d 1186 (Fla.1978);

7. Providing personal services in the preparation of legal documents that goes beyond selling forms, typing forms, providing written information or providing secretarial or notary services;

8. Preparing or assisting in the preparation of any pleadings, motions, legal memoranda, arguments, briefs, notices, or any other legal documents or pleadings for another person;

9. Using the title paralegal or legal assistant unless Respondent Kingsley is working for and under the supervision of a member of The Florida Bar and performs specifically delegated substantive legal work for which a member of The Florida Bar is responsible;

10. Offering legal services directly to the public by employing a member of The Florida Bar to provide the lawyer supervision required by Rule 10-2.1(b) of the Rules Regulating The Florida Bar;

11. Giving advice and making decisions on behalf of another person that requires legal skill and a knowledge of the law greater than that possessed by the average citizen;

12. Giving legal advice to another person concerning the application, preparation, advisability, or quality of any legal instrument or document or forms thereof in connection with any legal proceeding or procedure;

13. Construing or interpreting the legal effect of Florida or Federal laws and statutes for another person, as those laws relate to any legal matter including probate, dissolution of marriage and bankruptcy matters;

14. Giving advice and/or explaining legal remedies and options to another person that affects their procedural and substantive legal rights, duties and privileges;

15. Having direct contact with another person in the nature of consultation, explanation, recommendation, advice and assistance in the provision, selection and completion of preprinted legal forms;

16. Initiating and controlling a lawyer-client relationship, setting fees and paying an attorney to do work for a third party;

17. Engaging in any personal legal assistance in the preparation of legal forms including correcting customer's errors or omissions or providing customers with any assistance in preparing the forms other than mere typing;

18. Advising another person as to the need for a will or living trust and related documents and/or identifying the type of will or living trust and related documents most appropriate for another person;

19. Assembling and/or drafting a will, living trust, deed, durable power of attorney or related documents for another person;

20. Executing and/or advising on the execution of a will, living trust, deed, durable power of attorney or related documents for another person;

21. Funding and/or advising on the funding of a living trust for another person;

22. Otherwise directly or indirectly through other persons engaging in the practice of law in the State of Florida until licensed to do so.

C. That the costs of this proceeding be taxed against Respondents jointly and severally.

D.That Respondents should be jointly and severally assessed a monetary penalty of $9000.00, payable to the Supreme Court of Florida.

On September 24, 2003, respondents filed with this Court objections to the referee's report.

ANALYSIS

Having reviewed the record, we conclude that competent, substantial evidence exists to support the referee's factual findings. We further conclude that under our case law, respondents' actions constitute the unlicensed practice of law. *See, e.g., Florida Bar v. Catarcio,* 709 So.2d 96 (Fla.1998) (holding that a nonlawyer who has direct contact with individuals in the nature of consultation, explanation, recommendations, advice, and assistance in the provision, selection, and completion of legal forms engages in the unlicensed practice of law); *Florida Bar v. Becerra,* 661 So.2d 299 (Fla.1995) (enjoining a nonlawyer from advertising in any fashion that may lead a reasonable lay person to believe that the nonlawyer may offer to the public legal services, legal advice, or personal legal assistance); *Florida Bar v. Consol. Bus. & Legal Forms, Inc.,* 386 So.2d 797 (Fla.1980) (holding that a corporation engaged in the unlicensed practice of law where its officers and stockholders were nonlawyers with no legal training who supervised and maintained a degree of control over the legal services it furnished through its lawyer employees and noting the inherent conflict of interest between the legal needs of the client and the monetary policy of the corporation and how such a business structure permits unlicensed and unregulated persons to profit from the providing of services which by law they are prohibited from providing); *Florida Bar v. Brumbaugh,* 355 So.2d 1186, 1194 (Fla.1978) (holding that while a nonlawyer may sell certain legal forms and type up instruments completed by clients, a nonlawyer "must not engage in personal legal assistance in conjunction with her business activities, including the correction of errors and omissions").[fn] We conclude that respondents may be enjoined from engaging in such behavior.

We now turn to the issue of the recommended $9000 penalty against respondents. In 2000, Rule Regulating the Florida Bar 10-7.1 was amended to permit a referee in a UPL proceeding to recommend "the imposition of a civil penalty not to exceed $1000 per incident." [C] In this case, after holding a hearing and finding that respondents engaged in the unlicensed practice of law, the referee recommended the assessment of nine $1000 fines, one for each count of UPL set forth in the Bar's petition.

We conclude that the facts of the instant proceeding justify imposition of the penalty. The record clearly shows that respondents engaged in numerous acts of UPL. Further, at the hearing on costs and penalties, the Bar stated that WTP/Sarasota is "operating as usual." Thus, it seems that WTP/Sarasota has been unfazed by the possibility that penalties may be imposed upon it in the instant proceeding. In light of the foregoing, we approve the referee's recommendation that respondents We The People Forms and Service Center of Sarasota, Inc., and Danielle Kingsley be jointly and severally assessed a monetary penalty of $9000. ...

It is so ordered.

INQUIRY

Administrative Representation. Some federal and state statutes permit non-lawyers to represent parties in administrative proceedings. Some of the provisions are general as to any administrative proceeding, see, e.g., 5 U.S.C. §555(B); FLA. STAT. ANN. §120.62, while others specify the administrative proceedings in which non-lawyers may represent parties, see, e.g., 31 C.F.R. §10.3 et seq. (IRS proceedings); 37 C.F.R. §1.31 (patent applications); MD. CODE, STATE GOVT. §9-1607.1(a) (healthcare, prison, insurance, and business administrative disputes). In the absence of an authorizing statute or regulation, a non-lawyer's representation in an administrative proceeding is unauthorized practice. See Disciplinary Counsel v. Alexicole, Inc., 822 N.E.2d 348 (Ohio 2004). Given a statute or regulation authorizing a non-lawyers representation in an administrative proceeding, a non-lawyer's doing so would not be the unauthorized practice of law. See Cleveland bar Assn. v. CompManagement, 818 N.E.2d 1181 (Ohio 2004). Can you articulate the policies for and against these provisions? Do these provisions implicate separation-of-powers issues, given that they are legislative or administrative, while it is the judicial branch that plays the greater role and has the greater interest in regulating lawyers?

Self-Representation.   While they may appear to some to represent economic protectionism and employment guarantees for lawyers, unauthorized-practice statutes do not prohibit an individual from self-representation.   A litigant can always represent him- or herself in civil litigation.   Self-representation can actually be quite common in certain courts involving certain matters like landlord-tenant actions and uncontested, no-asset, no-children divorces. Problems arise, though, when an individual litigant's interests overlap with the interests of an unrepresented spouse, estate, corporation, or other person or entity.   Just because an unrepresented non-lawyer has a cause of action to prosecute or defend does not mean that the non-lawyer may simultaneously represent the interests of other similarly aligned parties.   Estates and corporations must ordinarily have lawyers represent them.   As you read one such case, notice the relief that the court grants to forestall unauthorized practice.   Notice also the ground on which the court recognizes the right of self-representation.

Shenkman v. Bragman,
Michigan Court of Appeals
682 N.W.2d 516 (2004)

BANDSTRA, J.

... Plaintiff is the personal representative of his grandfather's estate and brought this wrongful death action against defendant without employing an attorney to do so.   The lower court concluded that plaintiff was thus engaged in the unauthorized practice of law and, as a result, dismissed the complaint without prejudice.   The sole issue before us is, therefore, whether plaintiff was engaged in the unauthorized practice of law under these facts. We conclude that he was and affirm the lower court order dismissing his complaint.

This case involves the construction of a statute, the wrongful death act, MCL 600.2922. ...

Plaintiff relies heavily on language from the statute indicating that a wrongful death action "shall be brought by, and in the name of, the personal representative" of the decedent's estate.   MCL 600.2922(2). This language has never been construed in any precedent considering the question or facts at issue here.   Further, we find totally inapposite the few cases that the litigants claim are analogous or otherwise helpful.

Instead, we find some guidance in the statutory scheme into which this language fits.... .

Under these provisions, a person or corporation who would otherwise be liable for a death remains so even though the "party injured" is no longer able to "maintain an action," being deceased. MCL 600.2922(1). That person or corporation is liable to the heirs of the decedent's estate who suffer damages as a result of the death. MCL 600.2922(3). However, subsection 2922(3) does not authorize those heirs to themselves bring an action. Instead, subsection 2922(2) says that the action "shall be brought by, and in the name of, the personal representative of the estate...."

Viewed in this context, the subsection 2922(2) language appellant relies on is best understood as merely establishing the process by which liability for damages, preserved notwithstanding the death that gives rise to the operation of the statute, must be pursued. The estate, not the heirs, may bring an action and, as with other matters involving the estate, the duly appointed personal representative acts for, or represents, the estate. See, e.g., MCL 700.3703(1) (a personal representative is a fiduciary who must act to advance the best interests of the estate). It is in that sense that the estate's action is "brought by, and in the name of," the personal representative. That the estate's cause of action is "brought by, and in the name of," the personal representative does not mean, however, that the cause of action transfers over to, or becomes the right of, the personal representative.

We note that this analysis comports with MCR 2.201. Although actions must generally be "prosecuted in the name of the real party in interest," MCR 2.201(B), a "personal representative ... may sue in his or her own name without joining the party for whose benefit the action is brought," MCR 2.201(B)(1). ... [A] personal representative is a separate entity from the estate served and that the estate, not the personal representative, remains "the real party in interest ... for whose benefit the action is brought." MCR 2.201(B), MCR 2.201(B)(1).

And this presents the fatal flaw in appellant's argument. That argument is premised on his constitutional right as a nonlawyer to represent himself "in his own proper person...." Const. 1963, art. 1, § 13. We acknowledge that right. However, under the statute as we analyze it, appellant is not the true plaintiff here; the estate is. Appellant is not, in other words, representing himself in this litigation. Instead, he is representing a client, the estate. Thus, he is engaged in the unauthorized practice of law. MCL 600.916. The trial court did not err in so concluding.

We affirm.

INQUIRY

Licensed Practitioners. It is not only non-lawyers who must avoid unauthorized practice of law. Lawyers who hold a law license can also run afoul of unauthorized-practice provisions when they practice in a jurisdiction in which they do not hold a license or when they assist a non-lawyer in unauthorized practice. Often, lawyers rely on legal assistants and secretaries to perform research, review files, communicate with clients, and prepare court papers. When doing so, they must ensure that non-lawyer staff members are not giving legal advice or performing unsupervised legal services, or the lawyer will be responsible for that unauthorized practice. *See* In re Deddish, 557 S.E.2d 655 (S.C. 2001) (lawyer responsible for assisting unauthorized practice by assistant who gave clients advice at lawyer's seminar). Lawyers who retire and allow their license to lapse or convert to inactive status must cease practice, for to continue would constitute unauthorized practice. *See* In re Disciplinary Proceedings Against Bolte, 699 N.W.2d 914 (2005). State bars disagree on whether a licensed lawyer may retain a suspended or disbarred lawyer as a legal assistant. The case that follows illustrates another one of the unauthorized-practice challenges that lawyers face, when they have a client with business in another state.

Birbrower, Montalbano, Condon & Frank, P.C. v. Superior Court,
California Supreme Court
949 P.2d 1 (1998)

CHIN, Justice.

Business and Professions Code section 6125 states: "No person shall practice law in California unless the person is an active member of the State Bar."[fn] We must decide whether an out-of-state law firm, not licensed to practice law in this state, violated section 6125 when it performed legal services in California for a California-based client under a fee agreement stipulating that California law would govern all matters in the representation.

Although we are aware of the interstate nature of modern law practice and mindful of the reality that large firms often conduct activities and serve clients in several states, we do not believe these facts excuse law firms from complying with section 6125. ... We therefore conclude that, to the extent defendant law firm Birbrower, Montalbano, Condon & Frank, P.C. (Birbrower), practiced law in California without a license, it engaged in the unauthorized practice of law in this state. [C] We also conclude that Birbrower's fee agreement with real party in interest ESQ Business Services, Inc. (ESQ), is invalid to the extent it authorizes payment for the substantial legal services Birbrower performed in California. If, however, Birbrower can show it generated fees under its agreement for limited services it performed in New York, and it earned those fees under the otherwise invalid fee agreement, it may, on remand, present to the trial court evidence justifying its recovery of fees for those New York services. ...

I. BACKGROUND

... Birbrower is a professional law corporation incorporated in New York, with its principal place of business in New York. During 1992 and 1993, Birbrower attorneys, defendants Kevin F. Hobbs and Thomas A. Condon (Hobbs and Condon), performed substantial work in California relating to the law firm's representation of ESQ. Neither Hobbs nor Condon has ever been licensed to practice law in California. None of Birbrower's attorneys were licensed to practice law in California during Birbrower's ESQ representation.

ESQ is a California corporation with its principal place of business in Santa Clara County. In July 1992, the parties negotiated and executed the fee agreement in New York, providing that Birbrower would perform legal services for ESQ, including "All matters pertaining to the investigation of and prosecution of all claims and causes of action against TANDEM COMPUTERS INCORPORATED [Tandem]." The "claims and causes of action" against Tandem, a Delaware corporation with its principal place of business in Santa Clara County, California, related to a software development and marketing contract between Tandem and ESQ dated March 16, 1990 (Tandem Agreement). The Tandem Agreement stated that "The internal laws of the State of California (irrespective of its choice of law principles) shall govern the validity of this Agreement, the construction of its terms, and the interpretation and enforcement of the rights and duties of the parties hereto." ...

ESQ eventually settled the Tandem dispute, and the matter never went to arbitration. But before the settlement, ESQ and Birbrower modified the contingency fee agreement.[fn] The modification changed the fee arrangement from contingency to fixed fee, providing that ESQ would pay Birbrower over $1 million. ...

In January 1994, ESQ sued Birbrower for legal malpractice and related claims in Santa Clara County Superior Court. Birbrower ... filed a counterclaim, which included a claim for attorney fees for the work it performed in both California and New York. ... ESQ moved for summary judgment... [arguing] that by practicing law without a license in California and by failing to associate legal counsel while doing so, Birbrower violated section 6125, rendering the fee agreement unenforceable.   Based on these undisputed facts, the Santa Clara Superior Court granted ESQ's motion for summary adjudication....

II. DISCUSSION

A. The Unauthorized Practice of Law

The California Legislature enacted section 6125 in 1927 as part of the State Bar Act (the Act), a comprehensive scheme regulating the practice of law in the state. [C] Since the Act's passage, the general rule has been that, although persons may represent themselves and their own interests regardless of State Bar membership, no one but an active member of the State Bar may practice law for another person in California. [C] The prohibition against unauthorized law practice is within the state's police power and is designed to ensure that those performing legal services do so competently. [C]

A violation of section 6125 is a misdemeanor. (§6126.) Moreover, "No one may recover compensation for services as an attorney at law in this state unless [the person] was at the time the services were performed a member of The State Bar." (*Hardy v. San Fernando Valley C. of C.* (1950) 99 Cal.App.2d 572, 576, 222 P.2d 314 [].)

Although the Act did not define the term "practice law," case law explained it as " 'the doing and performing services in a court of justice in any matter depending therein throughout its various stages and in conformity with the adopted rules of procedure.'" (*People ex rel. Lawyers' Institute of San Diego v. Merchants' Protective Corp.* (1922) 189 Cal. 531, 535, 209 P. 363 [].) *Merchants* included in its definition legal advice and legal instrument and contract preparation, whether or not these subjects were rendered in the course of litigation. ...

In addition to not defining the term "practice law," the Act also did not define the meaning of "in California." ...

... In our view, the practice of law "in California" entails sufficient contact with the California client to render the nature of the legal service a clear legal representation. In addition to a quantitative analysis, we must consider the nature of the unlicensed lawyer's activities in the state. Mere fortuitous or attenuated contacts will not sustain a finding that the unlicensed lawyer practiced law "in California." The primary inquiry is whether the unlicensed lawyer engaged in sufficient activities in the state, or created a continuing relationship with the California client that included legal duties and obligations.

Our definition does not necessarily depend on or require the unlicensed lawyer's physical presence in the state. Physical presence here is one factor we may consider in deciding whether the unlicensed lawyer has violated section 6125, but it is by no means exclusive. ... We must decide each case on its individual facts.

This interpretation acknowledges the tension that exists between interjurisdictional practice and the need to have a state-regulated bar. ...

B. The Present Case

The undisputed facts here show that ... Birbrower engaged in unauthorized law practice *in California* on more than a limited basis, and no firm attorney engaged in that practice was an active member of the California State Bar. ... [I]n 1992 and 1993, Birbrower attorneys traveled to California to discuss with ESQ and others various matters pertaining to the dispute between ESQ and Tandem. Hobbs and Condon discussed strategy for resolving the dispute and advised ESQ on this strategy. Furthermore, during California meetings with Tandem representatives in August 1992, Hobbs demanded Tandem pay $15 million, and Condon told Tandem he believed damages in the matter would exceed that amount if the parties proceeded to litigation. Also in California, Hobbs met with ESQ for the stated purpose of helping to reach a settlement agreement and to discuss the agreement that was eventually proposed. Birbrower attorneys also traveled to California to initiate arbitration proceedings before the matter was settled. As the Court of Appeal concluded, "... the Birbrower firm's in-state activities clearly constituted the [unauthorized] practice of law" *in California*. ...

... Whether an attorney is duly admitted in another state and is, in fact, competent to practice in California is irrelevant in the face of section 6125's language and purpose. ...

... Birbrower alternatively asks us to create an exception to section 6125 for work incidental to private arbitration or other alternative dispute resolution proceedings. Birbrower points to fundamental differences between private arbitration and legal proceedings, including procedural differences relating to discovery, rules of evidence, compulsory process, cross-examination of witnesses, and other areas. ...

We decline Birbrower's invitation to craft an arbitration exception to section 6125's prohibition of the unlicensed practice of law in this state. Any exception for arbitration is best left to the Legislature, which has the authority to determine qualifications for admission to the State Bar and to decide what constitutes the practice of law. ...

C. Compensation for Legal Services

Because Birbrower violated section 6125 when it engaged in the unlawful practice of law in California, the Court of Appeal found its fee agreement with ESQ unenforceable in its entirety. Without crediting Birbrower for some services performed in New York, for which fees were generated under the fee agreement, the court reasoned that the agreement was void and unenforceable because it included payment for services rendered to a California client in the state by an unlicensed out-of-state lawyer. ...

It is a general rule that an attorney is barred from recovering compensation for services rendered in another state where the attorney was not admitted to the bar. ...

Birbrower asserts that even if we agree with the Court of Appeal and find that none of the above exceptions allowing fees for unauthorized California services apply to the firm, it should be permitted to recover fees for those limited services it performed exclusively *in New York* under the agreement. In short, Birbrower seeks to recover under its contract for those services it performed for ESQ in New York that did not involve the practice of law in California, including fee contract negotiations and some corporate case research. ...

We agree with Birbrower that it may be able to recover fees under the fee agreement for the limited legal services it performed for ESQ in New York to the extent they did not constitute practicing law in California, even though those services were performed for a California client.   Because section 6125 applies to the practice of law in California, it does not, in general, regulate law practice in other states. ...

III. DISPOSITION

We conclude that Birbrower violated section 6125 by practicing law in California. To the extent the fee agreement allows payment for those illegal local services, it is void, and Birbrower is not entitled to recover fees under the agreement for those services. The fee agreement is enforceable, however, to the extent it is possible to sever the portions of the consideration attributable to Birbrower's services illegally rendered in California from those attributable to Birbrower's New York services. Accordingly, we affirm the Court of Appeal judgment to the extent it concluded that Birbrower's representation of ESQ in California violated section 6125, and that Birbrower is not entitled to recover fees under the fee agreement for its local services. We reverse the judgment to the extent the court did not allow Birbrower to argue in favor of a severance of the illegal portion of the consideration (for the California fees) from the rest of the fee agreement, and remand for further proceedings consistent with this decision.

GEORGE, C.J., and MOSK, BAXTER, WERDEGAR and BROWN, JJ., concur.

KENNARD, Justice, dissenting[, omitted].

––––––––––––––––––––––

"What Were They Thinking?"

Not only did the client in the above case not have to pay the lawyers for most of their work (work that the lawyers valued at a minimum of one million dollars), but the client also sued for malpractice. So much of law practice is local—the rules, parties, disputes, customs, jury pools, judges, culture, and conventions. Practice in an unfamiliar jurisdiction can be hazardous. Probably, if the lawyers had associated with licensed local counsel, they would have earned their fee and avoided malpractice allegations memorialized and publicized in an appellate opinion. The lawyers' renegotiation of their fee agreement suggests that economics played a role in their actions. Were they more concerned with their fee than with their client's welfare? In other words, was it greed? Or did the client simply find a convenient way to beat their lawyers out of a fee? Either way, consider carefully how others can construe your actions. What seemed at the time like a good idea to earn a larger fee can look later like something quite different.

INQUIRY

Temporary Admission or "pro hac vice." . The *Birbrower* lawyers also argued (unsuccessfully) for several exceptions to the unauthorized practice rules. Under certain circumstances, conduct rules permit a lawyer whom another jurisdiction has licensed to provide services on a temporary basis in a jurisdiction in which the lawyer is not licensed. ABA MODEL RULE OF PROF. CONDUCT 5.5 contains model provisions for temporary admission. Under Rule 5.5(c)(2), a lawyer who does not hold a license in the state may request a local court to permit the lawyer to appear in that one case only, if the state's rules and local customs permit such *pro hac vice* ("one turn only") admission. *See* Leis v. Flynt, 439 U.S. 438 (1979) (no right to appear *pro hac vice*). Rule 5.5(c)(1) authorizes another favored means of temporary service, which is to hire licensed local counsel. Can you articulate advantages to doing so? Some lawyers would not appear in a foreign jurisdiction, even *pro hac vice*, without retaining and consulting a respected local lawyer. Read carefully an identical state version of ABA MODEL RULE OF PROFESSIONAL CONDUCT 5.5 first for its central provision limiting law practice to lawyers licensed in the jurisdiction and then for these exceptions.

DELAWARE R. PROF. CONDUCT 5.5.   **Unauthorized Practice of Law; Multijurisdictional Practice of Law**

(a) A lawyer shall not practice law in a jurisdiction in violation of the regulation of the legal profession in that jurisdiction, or assist another in doing so.

(b) A lawyer who is not admitted to practice in this jurisdiction shall not:

(1) except as authorized by these Rules or other law, establish an office or other systematic and continuous presence in this jurisdiction for the practice of law; or

(2) hold out to the public or otherwise represent that the lawyer is admitted to practice law in this jurisdiction.

(c) A lawyer admitted in another United States jurisdiction or in a foreign jurisdiction, and not disbarred or suspended from practice in any jurisdiction, may provide legal services on a temporary basis in this jurisdiction that:

(1) are undertaken in association with a lawyer who is admitted to practice in this jurisdiction and who actively participates in the matter;

(2) are in or reasonably related to a pending or potential proceeding before a tribunal in this or another jurisdiction, if the lawyer, or a person the lawyer is assisting, is authorized by law or order to appear in such proceeding or reasonably expects to be so authorized;

(3) are in or reasonably related to a pending or potential arbitration, mediation, or other alternative dispute resolution proceeding in this or another jurisdiction, if the services arise out of or are reasonably related to the lawyer's practice in a jurisdiction in which the lawyer is admitted to practice and are not services for which the forum requires pro hac vice admission; or

(4) are not within paragraphs (c)(2) or (c)(3) and arise out of or are reasonably related to the lawyer's practice in a jurisdiction in which the lawyer is admitted to practice.

(d) A lawyer admitted in another United States jurisdiction, or in a foreign jurisdiction, and not disbarred or suspended from practice in any jurisdiction, may provide legal services in this jurisdiction that:

(1) are provided to the lawyer's employer or its organizational affiliates after compliance with Supreme Court Rule 55.1(a)(1) and are not services for which the forum requires pro hac vice admission; or

(2) are services that the lawyer is authorized to provide by federal law or other law of this jurisdiction.

INQUIRY

Multijurisdictional Practice. Notice that Rule 5.5's title indicates that it also addresses multijurisdictional practice. As you can see from the *Birbrower* case, it makes sense to connect the subjects of unauthorized practice and multijurisdictional practice. Can you find the multijurisdictional-practice rules in Rule 5.5? Rule 5.5(c)(2), (3), and (4) anticipate that lawyers will represent clients in matters that cross state lines. Under Rule 5.5(c)(2), a lawyer may generally travel to another state in which the lawyer is not licensed, to take the deposition of a witness in an action filed in the lawyer's home state in which the lawyer is licensed. The lawyer must simply be licensed in one or more of the jurisdictions to which the matter is reasonably related. Similarly, Rule 5.5(c)(3) authorizes temporary alternative-dispute-resolution services across state lines, so long as the lawyer is licensed in at least one jurisdiction to which the matter is reasonably related. After *Birbrower*, the California legislature amended its statute to include a similar exception. Notice, too, that Rule 5.5(d) permits in-house counsel (corporate counsel) to practice across state lines for their employer so long as they are licensed in at least one jurisdiction. Can you see why state bars and the public would have less of a concern over unauthorized practice by in-house counsel?

Federal and Foreign Lawyers. Rule 5.5(d)(2) authorizes lawyers licensed in at least one jurisdiction to practice in federal tribunals that permit it, even if the subordinate state law would not. *See* Augustine v. Dept. of Veteran Affairs, 429 F.3d 1334 (Fed. Cir. 2005); In re Desilets, 291 F.3d 925 (6th Cir. 2002). To comply with World Trade Organization international trade agreement, some states have added a provision permitting foreign lawyers limited domestic-practice rights. *See, e.g.,* GA. BAR RULE 5.5(e). These provisions tend to limit the practice of foreign lawyers to matters involving foreign law and the interests of their foreign clients. The expectation is that lawyers licensed in the United States will have reciprocal foreign-practice rights.

Restrictions on Practice. Let us end our studies on the privilege to practice law as a citizen of the nation and member of the professional community, with a rule prohibiting restrictions on the right to practice. Although we typically call law practice a privilege, in some instances the profession recognizes it to be a right. There is a policy that once licensed, a lawyer should retain the right to practice so long as the lawyer remains in good standing. There are some circumstances where others may have an interest in preventing a lawyer from practicing, not because the lawyer has engaged in any misconduct but for economic or other reasons. ABA MODEL RULE OF PROF. CONDUCT 5.6 and equivalent state versions like the one reproduced below prohibit lawyers from restricting practice through employment agreements (covenants not to compete) or settlements of malpractice allegations. What policy supports Rule 5.6's prohibition on restrictions on the right to practice?

> DELAWARE R. PROF. CONDUCT 5.6: **Restrictions on Right to Practice.**
> A lawyer shall not participate in offering or making:
> (a) a partnership, shareholders, operating, employment, or other similar type of agreement that restricts the rights of a lawyer to practice after termination of the relationship, except an agreement concerning benefits upon retirement; or
> (b) an agreement in which a restriction on the lawyer's right to practice is part of the settlement of a client controversy.
> _____

Career and Professional Development

Choosing the bar to which to apply is an important career decision. It is not easy for lawyers to move from state to state, applying for multiple bar licenses and taking multiple bar exams. How do law students and law graduates decide in which state to start? A job offer in a specific location is a very good reason to seek licensure from that state, if the job involves law practice in that state. Yet for some law students and graduates, the choice of state license precedes the job offer. Although many law firms employ law graduates while they are preparing to take a bar exam or waiting for bar results, some employers require job candidates to pass the bar and obtain the license before the job is available. Law students and graduates often consider seeking a license from the state where they attended law school, they most anticipate a job offer to arise, their strongest professional network exists, economic indicators are most favorable, their practice-area interest are most prevalent, reciprocity between states makes multiple-licensure possible, their social network exists, they most prefer to live, and their family members reside. Can you think of other criteria? How will you decide?

CHAPTER III

RELATIONSHIP

Representation, Scope, Allocation, Diligence, Competence

"Whenever you are in conflict with someone, there is one factor that can make the difference between damaging your relationship and deepening it. That factor is attitude."
— William James

I believe that a sense of calling is essential for law ... students. The search for truth... is a central commitment of the legal scholar. Is there not also a commitment... for the law ... student to search for the good? A renewed understanding of what it means to be a professional should include a commitment to something other than acquisition and success.
— Dean Roger Cramton

OBJECTIVE: Given a client to represent, discern and articulate the standards of competence one must meet for the representation to be adequate, the standards of diligence one must meet for the representation to be timely and effective, and the standards that will determine the scope of authority for the representation.

Applicable Rules

1.1 Competence

1.2 Scope of Representation and Allocation of Authority

1.3 Diligence

1.16 Declining or Terminating Relationship

We have seen now that personal and professional responsibility begins with recognizing the need to obey authority (constitutions, laws, rules, and regulations) governing lawyers. Your willingness to obey helps you acquire citizenship in a polity and community, and membership within the law profession. This chapter next helps you locate responsibility in its core of competent and diligent service to those with whom you have a client relationship. Every lawyer should want to be masterful in the work that the lawyer does. Competence (the basic ability to do the legal work at hand) and diligence (the exercise of one's will to do it) are two legs of mastery's stool. An equally important third leg has to do with the scope of the client's work and allocation of authority between client and lawyer. Who decides exactly what it is that the lawyer is to do? Without a client to represent in a specific matter and the client's authority to act in that matter, a lawyer can have all of the competence and diligence to get things done but nothing to do. The concept of relationship draws together these three central attributes of representation, competence, and diligence. Without any one of those attributes, legal service will be ineffective, and the lawyer will break the conduct rules. Consider how the conduct rules treat each of these three attributes.

A. Representation

The concept of representation is central to the practice of law and the rules that govern that practice. Many of the conduct rules apply to lawyers when they deal with non-clients. Examples include the rules on truthfulness, respect, and advertising. In the course of a representation, lawyers must not lie to or disrespect non-client members of the public, or break advertising rules when attempting to attract clients. Lawyers also owe duties to tribunals, to opposing parties and counsel, within law firms, and to the profession and public. Yet many more of the rules apply only or primarily to a lawyer's representation of a client. The rules on competence and diligence are the central examples. Lawyers owe no duty to non-clients to act competently or diligently. Those duties arise only when there is a lawyer-client representation. Lawyers owe the duties of competence and diligence to clients, not to strangers, opposing parties, opposing counsel, and others. The same is true as to rules on communication, fees, confidentiality, and conflicts of interest. It makes a difference to the lawyer whether a person is the lawyer's client, meaning whether the lawyer represents the person, and there is a representation relationship. A lawyer must know whom the lawyer represents including when the representation begins and ends. Chapter IV on communication, confidentiality, and advising addresses ABA Model Rule 1.13's special issues around organization clients. It is especially important to distinguish an organization client from its managers.

The ABA MODEL RULES OF PROFESSIONAL CONDUCT do not define in direct fashion what constitutes a representation. Two rules instead do so by implication. ABA Model Rule 1.18 "Duties to Prospective Client" defines a *prospective* client as one "who discusses with a lawyer the possibility of forming a client-lawyer relationship with respect to a matter... ." By implication then, a representation relationship forms when lawyer and client discuss a specific matter and agree that the lawyer will represent the client in that specific matter. Prospective-client status is important only because the lawyer must treat as confidential information that the prospective client shares, and the information may disqualify the lawyer from other representations. We will discuss those rules further in Chapter IV on confidentiality and Chapter VI on conflicts of interest. The other rule that implies a definition for a representation is ABA Model Rule 1.16 "Declining or Terminating Representation." Model Rule 1.16 details when an attorney must decline to take a client and, in stituatons where representation has begun, when the attorney must terminated the representation. As you will see below, Model Rule 1.16 has abundant detail on whom not to represent, summarized in its Comment [1] that "[a] lawyer should not accept representation in a matter unless it can be performed competently, promptly, without improper conflict of interest and to completion." Thus by implication, a representation involves an agreement between lawyer and client for the lawyer to provide competent and diligent representation in a specific matter to its conclusion. Consider a similar state version of Model Rule 1.16.

> **DELAWARE R. PROF. CONDUCT 1.16:**   **Declining or Terminating Representation.**
> (a) Except as stated in paragraph (c), a lawyer shall not represent a client or, where representation has commenced, shall withdraw from the representation of a client if:
> (1) the representation will result in violation of the rules of professional conduct or other law;
> (2) the lawyer's physical or mental condition materially impairs the lawyer's ability to represent the client; or
> (3) the lawyer is discharged.
> (b) Except as stated in paragraph (c), a lawyer may withdraw from representing a client if:
> (1) withdrawal can be accomplished without material adverse effect on the interests of the client;
> (2) the client persists in a course of action involving the lawyer's services that the lawyer reasonably believes is criminal or fraudulent;
> (3) the client has used the lawyer's service to perpetrate a crime or fraud;
> (4) a client insists upon taking action that the lawyer considers repugnant or with which the lawyer has a fundamental disagreement;

(5) the client fails substantially to fulfill an obligation to the lawyer regarding the lawyer's services and has been given reasonable warning that the lawyer will withdraw unless the obligation is fulfilled;

(6) the representation will result in an unreasonable financial burden on the lawyer or has been rendered unreasonably difficult by the client; or

(7) other good cause for withdrawal exists.

(c) A lawyer must comply with applicable law requiring notice to or permission of a tribunal when terminating a representation. When ordered to do so by a tribunal, a lawyer shall continue representation notwithstanding good cause for terminating the representation.

(d) Upon termination of representation, a lawyer shall take steps to the extent reasonably practicable to protect a client's interests, such as giving reasonable notice to the client, allowing time for employment of other counsel, surrendering papers and property to which the client is entitled and refunding any advance payment of fee or expense that has not been earned or incurred. The lawyer may retain papers relating to the client to the extent permitted by other law.

INQUIRY

Accepting Representation. A key step to protect yourself against misconduct charges and malpractice claims is to state in a clear writing whether you have a lawyer-client relationship with any person, whom you believe may have that expectation. You do that by using retention, non-retention, termination, and closing letters. A retention agreement details the scope and nature of the attorney-client relationship. Important fields to include are the subject matter of the representation, limitations on the representation (what it does *not* include), the fee including how you will calculate it, expenses, and billing, payment, and interest. Retention agreements may also describe the lawyer's duties to the client such as to keep the client reasonably informed and communicate all settlement offers, and the client's duties to the lawyer such as to cooperate with the lawyer and keep the lawyer apprised of a current telephone number and address. The retention letter or agreement should also state what will trigger the lawyer to withdraw and how the lawyer will calculate the fee on withdrawal. The lawyer should give the client the retention letter when retained or immediately after retention. Chapter V on fees has further discussion and examples. Remember that it can be much easier to enter a representation than to leave it. Choose clients carefully.

Declining Representation. Lawyers should send a non-retention (decline) letter to prospective clients who have consulted with the lawyer and who may anticipate or expect representation. Lawyers send non-retention letters immediately after an initial consultation in which the lawyer decides not to represent the prospective client, or as soon thereafter as the lawyer makes that decision. Non-retention letters tell the prospective client that the consultation formed no lawyer-client relationship, that the attorney does not represent the prospective client in the matter, and any time limitations on the client's matter, urging them to see another attorney as soon as possible. Non-retention letters are critical to protect a lawyer from a client who mistakenly believes the lawyer represents the client after the consultation. The law judges the question of whether a consultation forms a lawyer-client relationship from the perspective of the *client*, not the lawyer. Prospective clients who reasonably believed that a lawyer represented them have successfully sued for malpractice in a matter where the statue of limitations expired soon after the consultation.

Grounds for Declining. The above ABA Model Rule 1.16 lists grounds for declining representation. One of the listed grounds is obvious: Model Rule 1.16(a)(2)'s caution that when the lawyer lacks the physical or mental health to undertake the representation. Other grounds are not obvious, like Model Rule 1.16(a)(1)'s caution to decline a representation when it will result in a rule violation. The reference incorporates the conflict-of-interest rules, ABA Model Rules 1.7 to 1.11, that lawyers must not undertake representations that create prohibited conflicts, and other rules like ABA Model Rule 1.2(d)'s prohibition against assiting a client with criminal or fraudulent conduct. Model Rule 1.16 leaves unstated other grounds on which to decline. Keep in mind that lawyers may generally choose whether to undertake a representation. It is generally permissible and may be wise to decline a matter in order to maintain a balance in one's life or practice, or because the representation's lawful goal is not good for the community, or for similar personal, professional, moral, and social reasons.

Completing Representation. It is also a prudent practice for a lawyer to notify the client when the representation concludes. Even in cases where the representation's conclusion seems obvious, such as on the acquittal of a client charged with a crime, a closing letter is often appropriate. There may be lingering issues such as the release of impounded property or lingering risks such as the possibility of new charges that make either the lawyer or client expect the representation to continue. The lawyer who is mistaken in believing that the representation has concluded may be surprised at not being paid fees. The client on the other hand may justifiably show that the lawyer has unreasonably neglected or abandoned the matter. A closing letter summarizes the representation, clarifies the matter's final status, instructs the client as to the return or safekeeping of client materials, addresses any fee issues, and notifies the client that the representation has concluded. It will also likely trigger the running of the limitations period on malpractice. *See, e.g.,* MICH. COMP. L. §600.5838 (malpractice claims accrue when the professional discontinues service). As is true of decline letters, lawyers can also use closing letters to thank the client, notify the client of other available legal services about which the client may not be aware, and otherwise market the practice. Many lawyers draw a substantial part of their practice from former clients.

Terminating Representation. ABA Model Rule 1.16 also requires lawyers to terminate representation for any of the reasons that the same rule requires a lawyer to decline representation. Those reasons would include poor health, avoiding conflicts of interest, and avoiding assisting a client in criminal or fraudulent conduct. The prudent lawyer confirms in writing the lawyer's termination of representation. A letter terminating the representation should include a balanced and accurate statement documenting the reason for termination. Denigrating the terminated client is not helpful. Preserving the former client's respect can be important both for the client in learning from the event and for the lawyer in preserving reputation and avoiding unmerited grievances. A termination letter should state the steps that the lawyer will take to protect the former client's property or interests, the lawyer's expectation regarding the bill, and the lawyer's instructions regarding return or safekeeping of the client's file and materials. Termination letters, like decline letters, help ensure that there is no confusion over the date and terms of the representation's conclusion, and that the limitations period begins to run.

Withdrawing from Litigation. If the lawyer has appeared in pending litigation, then the lawyer must have the court's permission to withdraw. Obtaining permission to withdraw will ordinarily depend on filing a motion that notifies the client, appearing in court on the hearing of that motion, stating grounds for withdrawal without violating the attorney-client privilege, and obtaining the order for withdrawal from the court and serving it on the client and other parties or their counsel. Courts hesitate permitting a lawyer to withdraw from complex litigation or when trial is near. *See, e.g.,* Whiting v. Lacara, 187 F.3d 317 (2d. Cir. 1999) (reversing trial court's refusal to permit withdrawal on eve of trial). Doing so can burden the court and other parties, and prejudice the client. *See, e.g.,* Gilles v. Wiley, Malehorn & Sirota, 783 A.2d 756 (N.J. Superior Ct. 2001) (fact issue in malpractice case whether lawyer's withdrawal inadequately protected client). Keep in mind the rule that it is easy to get in and hard to get out when it comes to litigation. A good practice is to ensure at the litigation's outset that you are prepared to complete the representation on the payment made and terms established at the litigation's outset.   A retainer (money up front) is customary and appropriate in some fields, where clients are less likely to pay and courts more likely to refuse withdrawal. *Cf.* Fidelity National Title Ins. Co. v. Intercounty National Title Ins. Co., 310 F.3d 537 (7th Cir. 2002) (reversing denial of motion to withdraw for nonpayment of more than $470,000 in fees).

Grounds for Withdrawal.   ABA Model Rule 1.16(b) lists several grounds for withdrawing like those for declining or terminating representation.   Notice the generosity of the first ground, stated in Model Rule 1.16(b)(1), that a lawyer may withdraw when "withdrawal can be accomplished without material adverse effect on the interests of the client... ."   Representation is not conscription.   Lawyers have no obligation to continue if they can withdraw without harm to the client. Given the generosity of the first ground, do we need a list of other grounds?   Other grounds are sufficiently subjective that the lawyer probably has other ways out of distasteful and disagreeable representations, although the first ground just listed makes other grounds superfluous.   For example, Model Rule 1.16(b)(4) permits withdrawal when "a client insists upon taking action that the lawyer considers repugnant or with which the lawyer has a fundamental disagreement... ."   The list also ends with a catch-all "good cause" provision.   While Model Rule 1.16(b) grants withdrawal in permissive terms, that the lawyer *may* withdraw, there are clearly times when withdrawal is mandatory, that the lawyer *must* withdraw.   For example, while Model Rule 1.16(b)(3) permits a lawyer to withdraw for client having used the lawyer's services for crime or fraud, Model Rule 1.2(d) turns that permission into a mandate if the client is currently using the lawyer's services to commit the crime or perpetrate the fraud.

Retaining Liens.   ABA Model Rule 1.16(d) requires lawyers to take reasonable steps to protect client interests when the representation concludes.   Those steps can include giving the client time to find other counsel.   Lawyers commonly grant clients 30 days to find another lawyer, and courts grant similar time on a lawyer's withdrawal. During that period, circumstances may require the lawyer to continue the lawyer's services, such as by filing a critical witness list, motion, or claim of appeal, even in the event of non-payment. Model Rule 1.16(d) requires a lawyer to surrender papers to which the law entitles the client but permits a lawyer to retain papers as permitted by other law. These provisions are an oblique reference to state lien laws.   Most states allow a lawyer to assert a *retaining lien* against the client's file to leverage payment of fees, if retaining the file does not jeopardize the client's matter. *See, e.g.,* Britton and Gray, P.C. v. Shelton, 69 P.3d 1210 (Okla. Ct. Civ. App. 2003).   The client's file is critical to many litigated and other matters, meaning that in many cases the lawyer must return the file even if owed fees. Moreover, if retaining the file does not jeopardize the client's matter, then the lawyer gains little if anything in the way of leverage by holding it, making the concept of a retaining lien in most instances an empty remedy.

Law Firm Departures. ABA Model Rule 1.16(a)(3) requires lawyers to terminate representation when the client discharges the lawyer. The rule should be obvious. In criminal cases, clients even have a Sixth Amendment right to the *choice* of counsel, not merely to having counsel. *See* United States v. Gonzalez-Lopez, 548 U.S. 140 (2006). Instead, though, some lawyers find it hard to accept firing. The client may terminate the representation. The most difficult representation questions can arise when a lawyer departs a law firm. In those instances, the departing lawyer and the remaining law firm may each have competing interests in retaining the client. The client gets to choose whether to depart with the lawyer or remain with the law firm. The relationship between the lawyer and law firm complicates these situations. Agency law and contract law govern that lawyer-law firm relationship. Lawyers owe fiduciary duties and duties of loyalty to their law partners and firm. Lawyers who solicit law firm clients while still owing those duties may violate those duties. The prudent course in those situations is for the lawyer and law firm to negotiate a joint letter to clients whose matters the departing lawyer has handled, notifying those clients of the lawyer's departure and stating an orderly process and date certain by which clients should notify the lawyer and firm of their intention with respect to continued representation. Clients are not property. They do not belong to lawyer or law firm.

B. Scope and Allocation

Distinguishing Scope from Allocation. Now that you have a basic understanding of the concept of representation, consider two related concepts: (1) the scope of a representation; and (2) the allocation of authority between lawyer and client within the representation. The scope of a representation has to do with the subjects that it will cover, meaning what legal issues the client expects the lawyer to address within the representation. Clients may have multiple legal issues. Lawyer and client should define just which issues the client has retained the lawyer to address. The scope of representation is important because if the lawyer has one sense of the scope while the client has another, the lawyer may address legal issues on which the lawyer lacks the client's authority or may neglect issues that the client expects the lawyer to address. The allocation of authority between lawyer and client is a slightly different but overlapping issue. Allocation of authority answers the question of who (lawyer or client) gets to decide what actions to take to further the representation. Some things only the client should decide, while other things that a lawyer should get to decide. The ABA MODEL RULES OF PROFESSIONAL CONDUCT give lawyers specific guidance on these important concepts of the scope of a lawyer's representation and the allocation of authority between lawyer and client. Consider an identical state version of ABA Model Rule 1.2.

> **WASH. R. OF PROF. CONDUCT 1.2:   Scope of Representation and Allocation of Authority Between Client and Lawyer.**
> (a) Subject to paragraphs (c) and (d), a lawyer shall abide by a client's decisions concerning the objectives of representation and, as required by Rule 1.4, shall consult with the client as to the means by which they are to be pursued. A lawyer may take such action on behalf of the client as is impliedly authorized to carry out the representation. A lawyer shall abide by a client's decision whether to settle a matter. In a criminal case, the lawyer shall abide by the client's decision, after consultation with the lawyer, as to a plea to be entered, whether to waive jury trial and whether the client will testify.
> (b) A lawyer's representation of a client, including representation by appointment, does not constitute an endorsement of the client's political, economic, social or moral views or activities.
> (c) A lawyer may limit the scope of the representation if the limitation is reasonable under the circumstances and the client gives informed consent.
> (d) A lawyer shall not counsel a client to engage, or assist a client, in conduct that the lawyer knows is criminal or fraudulent, but a lawyer may discuss the legal consequences of any proposed course of conduct with a client and may counsel or assist a client to make a good faith effort to determine the validity, scope, meaning or application of the law.

INQUIRY

Allocation of Authority. ABA Model Rule 1.2 begins by reserving for the client the authority to determine the objectives of the lawyer's representation. In doing so, the client also necessarily sets the scope of the representation. If the client's objective is to sell a home while complying with all law, rule, and regulation, then the lawyer will address the legal services to the lawful sale of the home, not the filing of a divorce action or the preparation of a will. Yet the provision also reminds the lawyer that it is not the lawyer's role to tell the client what the client should pursue. The client determines the ends. Lawyers can help clients recognize what ends are achievable, lawful, wise, and prudent, but the client still sets the ends, not the lawyer. The lawyer must respect the client's autonomy. By referring to ABA Model Rule

1.4, Model Rule 1.2 requires the lawyer to "reasonably consult" with the client regarding the means that the lawyer will use to achieve the client's ends. For instance, that duty to consult might require the lawyer to communicate the cost, burden, and disruption of filing a lawsuit, even though it would then be up to the lawyer to determine how to file the lawsuit. The lawyer need not communicate the minutiae. ABA Model Rule 1.2(a) authorizes the lawyer to do what "is impliedly authorized" to achieve the client's ends.

Decisions to Settle. While there can be questions over what constitutes means and what constitutes ends, ABA Model Rule 1.2(a) is clear that the client decides whether to settle including, in a criminal case, whether to enter a plea. Rule 1.2(a) similarly reserves the questions of whether to demand a jury and testify to the criminal-case defendant. What happens when the lawyer decides to settle without the client's authority and communicates that decision to the other side? As the second of the following cases makes clear, the general rule, contrary to the agency principles discussed above in this chapter, is that the lawyer's unauthorized settlement does not bind the client. This rule is an exception to the broader rule that clients do generally suffer the consequences of their lawyers' incompetence—only not when it comes to accepting a settlement. The rule is not uniform. A very few jurisdictions do allow the lawyer to bind a client to an unauthorized settlement. *See* Makins v. District of Columbia, 861 A.2d 590 (D.C. 2004). There are also other instances when the lawyer's unauthorized settlement will bind the client, such as when the client accepts openly and thereby ratifies the settlement. *See* Puder v. Buechel, 874 A.2d 534 (N.J. 2005).

Luethke v. Suhr,
Nebraska Supreme Court
650 N.W.2d 220 (2002)

GERRARD, J. ...

FACTUAL BACKGROUND

On June 27, 1995, Luethke was injured in an automobile accident. Attorney Mary Wickenkamp filed suit on Luethke's behalf... . The appellants retained attorney Alan Plessman to represent them in the suit filed by Luethke.

... [T]he day before a scheduled pretrial conference, Plessman faxed the following letter, in pertinent part, to Wickenkamp:

> I hereby offer to pay to you and your clients and any subrogees or lienholders we have notice of, that sum of $16,000.00, in exchange for a complete release of liability for our insureds and Continental

Western Insurance Company; and a dismissal with prejudice of the pending suit, with all parties to bear their own costs and fees.

[The insurance company] gave me that authority to be accepted by you before 5:00 p.m. today. Thereafter it is withdrawn. So, if this is a deal, fax me back a note to that effect.

Later that same day, Wickenkamp responded in a faxed letter, in pertinent part:

I have not been able to make contact with my client by 5:00 to get positive authority to accept your offer of $16,000. I am willing to recommend your offer to my client, but I need to meet with Jon to discuss it. As we have discussed before, this young man has a developmental disability and I need to make certain his decision in this matter is informed.

That same day, Plessman responded to Wickenkamp and extended the offer until 9 a.m. the following morning.

On July 21, 1998, Wickenkamp accepted Plessman's offer via faxed letter: "My client will accept the offer.... Thanks for your cooperation in getting this done. I will assume that we are not meeting today with the Judge [for pretrial conference] and will call his office this morning." The district court judge's docket notes for July 21, 1998, read: "'Case settled. Paperwork coming.'"

Plessman sent settlement documents to Wickenkamp on July 21, 1998, with a letter stating: "Enclosed are settlement papers, I need back after they're signed, along with directions on how to cut checks for payment of the $16,000.00. Once I know that, I can get the drafts in a day or so." In a letter dated July 29, 1998, Wickenkamp responded:

Thank you for getting me the settlement documents so promptly. I've sent them on to my client. His uncle wants to review them with me and Jon as well. I'm on my way out of town and have a meeting with them set after I come back. Please understand it is not a problem. The uncle has been involved throughout this and just wants to make sure my client, who is somewhat disabled, understands everything. I do not anticipate any problem with the settlement, it's just a matter of logistics. I will be in touch when I return.

The record provides no further correspondence between Plessman and Wickenkamp, and Plessman testified that the next thing he received was Wickenkamp's motion to withdraw as counsel. Plessman never received executed settlement or dismissal documents.

... Wickenkamp[...] withdrew as counsel in October 1998 after having her professional employment terminated by Luethke. ...

[At a hearing to enforce the settlement agreement,] Plessman testified regarding the correspondence between himself and Wickenkamp about the settlement agreement. The court received and admitted into evidence, without objection, Plessman's and Wickenkamp's correspondence and the settlement documents drafted by Plessman. ... Wickenkamp verified that Luethke retained her as his attorney in this litigation, that she notified Plessman by letter that "My client will accept the offer," and that she withdrew as counsel in October 1998 after Luethke terminated her employment. Wickenkamp did not testify as to the content of her conversations with Luethke, invoking attorney-client privilege, but stated that she and Luethke had spoken during the timeframe of the letters between herself and Plessman regarding settlement negotiations.

... Luethke testified that although Wickenkamp originally anticipated receiving $84,000 or $64,000 for Luethke's case, she urged him to accept a settlement of $16,500 because they were not making headway with the other numbers. Luethke stated that the only time he authorized Wickenkamp to settle the case for him was when she presented him with a $64,000 offer; she, however, urged him to refuse the offer because she felt he could get more. Luethke testified that he never agreed to settle the case for $16,000—not during a meeting alone with Wickenkamp and not during a subsequent meeting at his mother's house with Wickenkamp, his mother, himself, and his uncle Norman Schmitt present.

... Schmitt testified that at no time during Wickenkamp's representation of Luethke did Schmitt understand her to have the authority to settle Luethke's case for $16,000.

The district court's "Judgment on Defense of Settlement Agreement" concluded: "Upon consideration, I find in favor of plaintiff [Luethke]. ... I wish I could reach the opposite conclusion, but I believe the wiser public policy and the law requires the ruling I make in this particular instance."

The appellants then filed an appeal of the judgment of the district court... .

ANALYSIS

... Nebraska law is clear that the decision to settle a lawsuit belongs to the client; because the client bears the risk when settling or refusing to settle a dispute, it is the client, not the lawyer, who should assess whether the risk is acceptable. [C] ...

Thus, as a general rule, in this state and in a vast majority of other jurisdictions, lawyers may enter settlement agreements only when the client expressly authorizes the lawyer to do so. The ordinary employment or retainer of a lawyer to represent a client with respect to litigation does not of itself give the lawyer the implied or apparent authority to bind the client by a settlement or compromise of the claim; and, in the absence of express authority, knowledge, or consent, the lawyer cannot do so.   A lawyer's execution of a settlement agreement without a client's knowledge or consent constitutes a breach of duty to the client; and it may constitute a fraud upon the court. [Cc]

The appellants argue, however, that under Nebraska agency law, Wickenkamp can bind Luethke to a settlement because she acted with apparent authority in her correspondence with Plessman.   The appellants cite Nebraska cases where a lawyer acted with apparent authority and, under agency law, bound the client to the lawyer's action.   None of these cases, however, involved a lawyer's binding a client to a settlement agreement without that client's express authority.   From the nature of the attorney-client relationship itself, a lawyer derives authority to manage the conduct of litigation on behalf of a client, including the authority to make certain procedural or tactical decisions.   [Cc].   That authority, however, is hardly absolute. Equally rooted in the law is the principle that without a grant of authority from the client, a lawyer cannot compromise or settle a claim ([c]), and settlements negotiated by lawyers without authority from their clients are generally not binding.   A narrow exception to this rule occurs when a lawyer settles a claim in excess of actual authority, but *in the presence of his or her client,* generally in open court, and the client remains silent regarding the terms of the settlement. [Cc]   No such circumstance is present in the instant case.

We hold, therefore, that although lawyers retain apparent authority to make procedural and tactical decisions through the existence of the attorney-client relationship, a lawyer cannot settle a client's claim without express authority from the client.   In other words, ... if the lawyer seeks to enter a settlement, the opposing party should ascertain whether the lawyer has received actual authority from the client to take such action.   A party who enters a settlement agreement without verifying the opposing counsel's actual authority to settle does so at his or her peril.

The appellants argue that preventing lawyers from binding clients to settlement agreements without express authority would create problems in agency law and, in general, disrupt the practice of law. ... Deciding that lawyers need express authority in the limited situation of *out-of-court* settlements will not, as the appellants argue, eviscerate the apparent authority of attorneys and agency law principles.   In fact, several district courts already have rules which specifically require that in order to be recognized or considered by the court, agreements between parties to a suit, other than those made in open court or otherwise recorded by a court reporter, must be reduced to writing and signed by the parties. [Cc] ...

After reviewing the record, we conclude that the district court did not clearly err in determining that Luethke did not grant express authority to Wickenkamp to compromise or settle his personal injury claim for the sum of $16,000. ...

CONCLUSION

... The judgment of the district court is, therefore, affirmed, and this cause is remanded to the district court for a trial on the merits of the personal injury cause of action.

AFFIRMED, AND CAUSE REMANDED WITH DIRECTIONS.

"What Were They Thinking?"

Plaintiff's counsel in the above case may in fact have had the client's authority to settle for the lower figure. The client's testimony to the contrary may have been untruthful. Buyer's remorse is common in settlements. Documenting a client's authority can help avoid these situations. Another possibility is that the lawyer and client misunderstood one another. The lawyer may have thought that the lawyer had the client's authority when the client did not intend it. Again, documentation can prevent misunderstanding before it has consequences. What would have made the lawyer want to think that the lawyer had authority? Given their greater experience and legal training, lawyers routinely have better judgment about settlements than clients have. They also can face costs (both trial time and expense) that clients may not face. In other words, in some cases lawyers are under more pressure to settle than clients are. Courage, loyalty, willingness to accept risk, and respect for the client's autonomy are key lawyer attributes in such instances.

INQUIRY

Endorsement. Notice the statement in ABA Model Rule 1.2(b) to the effect that, "A lawyer's representation of a client, including representation by appointment, does not constitute an endorsement of the client's political, economic, social or moral views or activities." Can you articulate the reason for this provision? Lawyers do often represent unpopular clients, particularly by appointment in defense of indigent clients charged with serious crimes. Chapter X addresses ABA Model Rule 6.2 on the duty to accept appointments. Do you think the public appreciates that lawyers have a duty to accept those assignments even when they involve representing an infamous client who has allegedly committed a heinous crime? Rule 1.2(b) gives a lawyer some protection, although one can question its benefit. One should understand the limited scope of the duty to accept court assignments. For the most part, lawyers may select clients and choose to associate only with reputable clients and clients whose views the lawyer would endorse. It may even be important to the mental health and moral and professional development of a lawyer to make deliberate choices at least from time to time.

Limited-Scope Representation. ABA Model Rule 1.2(c) permits a lawyer to limit the scope of a representation "if the limitation is reasonable under the circumstances and the client gives informed consent." An example is Lerner v. Laufer, 819 A.2d 471 (N.J. Superior Ct. 2003), in which the court dismissed a malpractice claim against a lawyer whom a client maintained had not investigated the merits of a divorce settlement. The lawyer showed that the client had retained the lawyer solely to review the proposed judgment and not to conduct discovery or other investigation in the case. You may wonder about Rule 1.2(c)'s qualification that the limited scope of the work must be reasonable. Why should a lawyer not be able to select what to do or not to do for a client? The problem is that some client matters are so integrated that a little help might be worse than none. One example is the lawyer who helps a client prepare and file a complaint in pro per (ghostwritten as if the client is unrepresented) in a complex matter in which the client lacks the knowledge and skill to conduct the litigation unrepresented. The filing may do nothing more than lead to a dismissal that bars the client from later pursuing the claim with effective representation. The filing may also mislead the court into treating the client as an unrepresented party due greater deference, when the client had the lawyer's limited-scope representation in ghostwriting the complaint. *See* Duran v. Carris, 238 F.3d 1268 (10th Cir. 2001) (disapproving of practice). Courts and bars continue to disagree on the ethics of ghostwriting.

Unbundling Services. Model Rule 1.2(c) permits a lawyer to limit the scope of representation so long as the client consents and the limitation is reasonable. Some bars recognize that limited-scope representation, including providing ghostwritten pleadings, can be an important means of providing access to justice for parties who can only afford limited representation. *See* State Bar of Ariz. Comm. on Rules of Prof. Conduct Op. 05-06 (2005); Cal. Rule of Court 5.70 (2003). The so-called unbundling of legal services from the traditional manner of a lawyer handling everything from start to finish may provide important stopgap legal service at critical junctures. Better, some help than no help at all. Other bars stress the problems that an unrepresented party can create for the party, opposing party, and court, and the misrepresentation a lawyer makes when not disclosing that the lawyer drafted the pleading, court paper, or other document.

See Conn. Bar Assn. Comm. on Prof. Ethics Op. 98-5 (1998). What Rule 1.2(c) requires is that the lawyer knows the client's situation, ensures that any limitation is reasonable, informs the client to gain the client's consent, and knows how the court will treat the ghostwritten pleading or court paper. Consider the following ethics opinion on limited representation and ghostwriting, while recognizing that other bars and courts, especially the federal courts, disagree with its approval of the ghostwriting practice.

Opinion 05-06
State Bar of Arizona Committee on
Rules of Professional Conduct
(July 2005)

An attorney representing a client may enter into an agreement limiting the scope of services to a specific and discrete task. An attorney is required to have sufficient knowledge and skill to provide reliable counsel to the limited scope client as to the advisability of the action requested by the client. The attorney providing limited scope representation is not required to disclose to the court or other tribunal that the attorney is providing assistance to a client proceeding *in propria persona.*

FACTS[fn]

The inquiring attorneys are affiliated with an agency providing legal services to low- and moderate-income individuals. One of the two attorneys also practices in the area of family law. The inquiring attorneys contend that legal service programs can provide assistance to a larger number of low-income clients if an attorney is permitted to limit the scope of the representation of these clients. According to the inquiring attorneys, limited scope representation permits an attorney to assist a client with a discrete task and then proceed to help another client once that specific task is completed. The inquiring attorneys have submitted various questions relating to limited scope representation. ...

OPINION

The inquiring attorneys identify an increasingly real side effect of our adversarial legal system, that is, the proliferation of parties representing themselves in court. In Arizona, this practice is especially prevalent in the domestic relations arena. ... While the reasons vary, often the decision to proceed *in propria persona* is influenced by the high cost of retaining an attorney.

Parties in both divorce and non-divorce actions are representing themselves more frequently on issues that will have long-term consequences in their lives. Private practitioners and public interest attorneys have responded to the needs of these clients by limiting their representation to certain identifiable and discrete tasks. Though long a practice in the representation of clients in transactional matters, limited scope representation[fn] has only more recently become commonplace and studied within the litigation context.

Supporters of limited scope representation justify it as a point of entry for clients who may not be able to afford the full services of a lawyer. Under such an arrangement, a client and a lawyer agree prior to any work being done that the lawyer will limit the lawyer's efforts to the completion of one or more particular tasks. Usually this entails representation of the client's interests only through a portion of a lawsuit or transaction. The lawyer thus satisfies their agreement when the tasks are completed. By limiting the representation, a lawyer and client can agree that the client will pay less than if the lawyer were retained for full representation. If the client requires additional services after the completion of the tasks, the lawyer and client can continue the representation under the auspices of a separate agreement.

In addition to addressing the costs of retaining a lawyer, limiting representation is also of value to public interest and *pro bono* attorneys looking to maximize the number of low- and moderate-income clients they are able to serve. Public interest resources and a *pro bono* attorney's time may preclude the long-term representation of a client in a large transaction or complex lawsuit. An attorney faced with representing a client under such circumstances may choose to forsake the representation given the demands that would be placed on the attorney. By limiting the scope of representation, clients expected to require a significant amount of attorney time may get the representation they need at a certain stage in their transaction or proceedings without committing the attorney to a long-term representation. Similarly, these attorneys can address the issues of more low- and moderate-income clients by containing the work they do for a particular client before proceeding to address the issues of another client. ...

... Limited scope representation is ... permitted as long as the client provides informed consent[fn] to the limited representation, the scope of the representation is not so limited as to violate the Rules of Professional Conduct or other law, the attorney does not advise the client to do something that the attorney would be prohibited from doing personally, and the limited scope representation is reasonable under the circumstances. ...

... While an attorney providing limited scope representation has a duty to provide competent representation as to the task that the attorney has been asked to do, it is not enough to be competent only in the performance of that task. Rather, an attorney providing limited scope representation must know enough to counsel the client regarding the advisability of the action contemplated. [Cc] Just like most other representations, the required skill and knowledge is that of a general practitioner. [C] An attorney offering limited scope representation thus should gather enough information from the client to get a general practitioner's understanding of how the case or transaction will be affected by the task that the lawyer has been asked to do.[fn] [C] Because the representation is expressly limited, however, the attorney is not expected to have the same thoroughness of knowledge or understanding about those matters outside the limited services agreement as would be expected in a full representation. [Cc] In all instances, an attorney should consider consulting with or referring a potential client to another attorney if he or she does not have the requisite level of skill and knowledge.

... If the attorney cannot provide reliable counsel on the advisability of the action, the limitation on the representation is not reasonable under the circumstances, and the representation will violate both ER 1.1 and ER 1.2(c). [C] ...

... Courts in other jurisdictions have determined that Rule 11 prohibits an attorney from preparing court filings for a *pro per* litigant without signing them, or have cited Rule 11 in disapproval of such practice. *See, e.g., Ellis v. Maine*, 448 F.2d 1325, 1328 (1st Cir. 1971); *Laremont-Lopez v. Southeastern Tidewater Opportunity Ctr.*, 968 F. Supp. 1075, 1078-79 (E.D. Va. 1997), *aff'd*, 172 F.3d 44 (4th Cir. 1999); [c]. No Arizona court has yet published a decision concluding that Rule 11 requires an attorney to inform the court when the attorney is providing limited scope representation to a *pro per* client. ...

If an attorney does no more than provide limited advice to a *pro per* client without assisting in the drafting of documents to be submitted to the court or attending court proceedings, the Committee does not believe that this type of limited scope representation needs to be disclosed to the court. Similarly, where an attorney providing limited scope representation actually enters an appearance in the client's case as part of the limited scope agreement, the appearance can be made without disclosing to the court or tribunal that the attorney and client have agreed to a limited scope representation. An attorney choosing to enter a formal appearance in a dispute assumes the risk that a court or tribunal will not permit the attorney's withdrawal upon the termination of the agreed-upon task. *See* ER 1.16(c) (requiring an attorney to continue representation when ordered by a tribunal notwithstanding good cause for termination).

An attorney limiting the scope of representation may in some cases, however, choose to go beyond merely providing advice to the client and will draft pleadings or other submissions that the attorney knows will be presented to a court without that attorney actually entering a formal appearance. ... For this reason, documents which a lawyer assisted in preparing for a *pro per* client are usually submitted to the court in the name of the *pro per* client, a practice also known as "ghostwriting." The ghostwriting of pleadings and other court submissions is a frequent way for an attorney providing limited scope representation to assist a *pro per* litigant without committing to the entire litigation. The question this raises is whether the ghostwriting of pleadings or other court-submitted documents by a lawyer violates Ethical Rules 3.3(a)(1) and 8.4(c), which require attorneys to be truthful and avoid false representations in their dealings with a court or tribunal, and 8.4(a), which prohibits an attorney from violating the ethical rules or doing so through the acts of another.

Other ethics committees and courts have addressed similar questions with mixed results. On the one hand are opinions stating that there is no ethical prohibition on ghostwriting, and that the practice is freely permitted without ever needing to advise the court that it is occurring. [Cc] On the other are opinions that find that ghostwriting is unethical *per se* as a fraud upon the court that can only be remedied by advising the court that the submitted document was prepared by or with the assistance of an attorney. [Cc]

Still others have landed somewhere in the middle of the fray. The majority of bar associations that have reviewed this issue have supported the notion that an attorney drafting documents for a *pro per* client for court submission must provide some form of disclosure to the court when the attorney provides "substantial," "significant," or "extensive" assistance to the client. [Cc] This view has been repeated in various courts as well. [Cc] Some courts and ethics committees from other jurisdictions go so far as requiring disclosure of an attorney's involvement in the preparation of court documents on the filed document.[fn]   [Cc]   Imposing this type of disclosure rule, however, exceeds the scope of our authority.

While acknowledging the existence of the above opinions, the Committee finds that disclosure to the court or tribunal of an attorney's assistance with a court filing is not necessary when the *pro per* client submits the document for filing. The Committee concludes that the submission of ghostwritten documents without informing the court or tribunal does not violate ER 3.3(a)(1) and ER 8.4(c) because the practice is not inherently misleading to the court or tribunal. When presented with a document prepared with the assistance of counsel, the Committee believes that a court or tribunal can generally determine whether that document was written with a lawyer's help. ER 3.3(a)(1) proscribes against an attorney making or failing to correct a false statement of fact or law to the court or tribunal. We do not believe that the omission of an attorney's name from a filed document is a false statement of fact or law that is either made or needs to be corrected. Because the disclosure of an attorney's assistance with court filings is not obligatory under the ethical rules, by deduction, the submission of ghostwritten materials by a *pro per* client does not contravene ER 8.4(a)'s prohibition against violating the ethical rules through the acts of another, such as the attorney's client.

Some courts and ethics committees have evidenced disfavor with lawyers ghostwriting court documents because they believe the practice provides an unfair advantage in that courts are willing to afford more leeway to *pro per* clients. [Cc] The authorities argue that a *pro per* party who is actually receiving the services of a lawyer thus receives the benefits of legal assistance and special treatment by the court at the same time. Another view is that it interferes with a court's ability to superintend the conduct of counsel and parties during litigation.   [C]   Notwithstanding these arguments,[fn] courts are usually able to correctly assess when to afford *pro per* litigants appropriate latitude and when these litigants are being given the benefit of assistance of counsel. For case management purposes, a court can confirm the existence of assisting counsel by directly asking the *pro per* litigant if the issue becomes important to the resolution of the case. ...

As to whether an attorney may disclose the existence of a limited scope representation to the court when not required, this issue turns on whether the client's confidential information relating to the representation may be disclosed in accordance with ER 1.6. The rule lists several circumstances in which the attorney is permitted to disclose the client's confidential information related to the representation as well as others in which the attorney is prohibited from making such a disclosure. ER 1.6 also specifically allows for the disclosure of a client's confidential information as long as the client consents after consultation. *See* ER 1.6(a). An attorney wanting to disclose the attorney's role in the limited scope representation to the court when not obligated to do so should ensure that at least one of these circumstances applies.

INQUIRY

Appeals.   One area where limited representation is ordinarily reasonable is with respect to appeals. Trial lawyers often have one set of skills, and appellate lawyers have another set. In much of civil litigation, appeals are rare. A lawyer who represents a client in litigation at the trial-court level may have no interest in representing the client in the event of the necessity of an appeal, and no expectation that the lawyer will do so.   In those cases, the lawyer should communicate to the client, preferably at the outset of the representation, that the representation does not include appeals. Comment [4] to ABA Model Rule 1.3 provides that a lawyer whose client suffers an adverse result at the trial-court level "must keep the client reasonably informed about the status of the representation by advising the client of the possibility of an appeal before relinquishing responsibility for the matter."   Comment [4] then continues, "Whether the lawyer is obligated to prosecute the appeal for the client depends on the scope of the representation the lawyer has agreed to provide to the client."   In the event of the necessity of an appeal and the lawyer's interest in pursuing it, the lawyer and client may then discuss new terms for appellate representation.   A standard form of agreement for lawyers working on a contingency-fee arrangement is to provide in the initial fee agreement that the lawyer's services do not include services on appeal.   Notwithstanding that limitation, can you imagine why lawyers who help a contingency-fee client prevail at the trial-court level may nonetheless offer to represent the client on appeal?

Withdrawal from Litigation.   A lawyer must have the court's permission to withdraw from representation in pending litigation. Under the right circumstances, lawyers may properly seek to withdraw from litigation when a client indicates intent to terminate the representation, *see* VT. ETHICS OP. 2000-3 (2000) (mental-health commitment), or insists on making poor decisions affecting the lawyer's ability to conduct the litigation, *see* PA. ETHICS OP. 98-83 (1998) (approving withdrawal for client's irrational refusal to allow lawyer to retain necessary experts).   Courts hesitate to allow counsel to withdraw from pending litigation when withdrawal will leave the client unrepresented or substantially delay the proceeding while the client retains and informs new counsel.   Courts may be especially hesitant when the client has a mental impairment. *See* ABA ETHICS OP. 96-404 (1996) (take protective action rather than withdraw leaving unrepresented impaired client).   Wise lawyers make sensitive, informed, and insightful judgments before commencing litigation with clients who exhibit mental and emotional impairments.

Declining Cases.   You have just seen above that a lawyer may decline some representations and should probably decline other representations.   A lawyer must decline other representations.   ABA Model Rule 1.2(d) prohibits a lawyer from helping a client commit a crime or fraud.   In cases in which the client's planned crime or fraud is evident from the beginning, that prohibition means declining the prospective client's matter at the outset.   In other cases in which the client's planned crime or fraud becomes evident only later, that prohibition means ensuring that the client ends the plan or, if the client will not, then withdrawing from the representation and ensuring that the client does not use the lawyer's services to continue the planned crime or fraud. Notice that Rule 1.2(d)'s prohibition is not against representing a client who has already committed a crime or fraud. The justice system often calls on lawyers to represent the guilty. Rather, Rule 1.2(d)'s prohibition is against allowing a client to use a lawyer's services to commit a crime or fraud. Importantly, Rule 1.2(d) permits a lawyer to discuss with a client why the law would deem a certain course of action to be criminal or fraudulent, so that the client may desist. Such is an essential nature of a lawyer's advice.

C. Competence

A lawyer's relationship with a client depends not just on the fact of representation but also on its basic competence. One cannot maintain a client relationship without competent legal service. The lawyer's representation, scope of representation, and allocated authority define the lawyer's competence. When the client establishes the goal of the work and its parameters, the client also defines what constitutes diligence and competence.

Conduct Rule. ABA Model Rule 1.1 states in full, "A lawyer shall provide competent representation to a client. Competent representation requires the legal knowledge, skill, thoroughness, and preparation reasonably necessary for the representation." When the ABA Model Rules made the rule on competence the first substantive rule, the rules highlighted competence's centrality to law practice. A lawyer is nothing if not competent. In that respect, you may have already regarded competence as given, thinking that of course a lawyer must be competent. The concept of competence, though, is a little more complex than you might imagine and the attribute a little more elusive. What is obvious in theory is not always easy in practice. Notice for example how Model Rule 1.1 defines competence along the dimensions of knowledge, skill, thoroughness, and preparation. Think about the distinctions between these dimensions. Do they each implicate different behaviors and involve different qualities? How much do knowledge and skill relate to experience? If competence depends on experience, then does that make incompetent every new lawyer and every experienced lawyer who enters a new field? How does the rule help you answer the latter question? This section explores these questions.

Multiple Dimensions. Competence's first dimension, knowledge, reflects the need of lawyers to possess an adequate doctrinal base on which to draw in formulating their advice and taking action. Lawyers should know the law before they advise clients and provide other legal services. The second dimension, skill, calls our attention to the need to apply that knowledge base in ways that meaningfully address the client's objectives. It is not enough to be smart about the law. A lawyer must also be skilled in using it. Legal analysis involves action logic, applying legal concepts to specific situations in strategic manner. The third dimension, thoroughness and preparation, calls our attention to the lawyer's work ethic, that the lawyer must care enough about the client's matter to devote the lawyer's knowledge and skill to pursuing the client's objectives. These three dimensions, knowledge, skills, and ethics, work together in complex ways to form the competent professional. Consider the Official Comment to a similar state version of ABA Model Rule 1.1.

> MICH. RULE PROF. CONDUCT 1.1: **Competence.**
>
> A lawyer shall provide competent representation to a client. A lawyer shall not:
>
> (a) handle a legal matter which the lawyer knows or should know that the lawyer is not competent to handle, without associating with a lawyer who is competent to handle it;
>
> (b) handle a legal matter without preparation adequate in the circumstances; or
>
> (c) neglect a legal matter entrusted to the lawyer.
>
> COMMENTS
>
> **Legal Knowledge and Skill.** In determining whether a lawyer is able to provide competent representation in a particular matter, relevant factors include the relative complexity and specialized nature of the matter, the lawyer's general experience, the lawyer's training and experience in the field in question, the preparation and study the lawyer is able to give the matter, and whether it is feasible to refer the matter to, or associate or consult with, a lawyer of established competence in the field in question. In many instances, the required proficiency is that of a general practitioner. Expertise in a particular field of law may be required in some circumstances.
>
> A lawyer need not necessarily have special training or prior experience to handle legal problems of a type with which the lawyer is unfamiliar. A newly admitted lawyer can be as competent as a practitioner with long experience. Some important legal skills, such as the analysis of precedent, the evaluation of evidence and legal drafting, are required in all legal problems. Perhaps the most fundamental legal skill consists of determining what kind of legal problems a situation may involve, a skill that necessarily transcends any particular specialized knowledge. A lawyer can provide adequate representation in a wholly novel field through necessary study. Competent representation can also be provided through the association of a lawyer of established competence in the field in question.

In an emergency, a lawyer may give advice or assistance in a matter in which the lawyer does not have the skill ordinarily required where referral to or consultation or association with another lawyer would be impractical. Even in an emergency, however, assistance should be limited to that reasonably necessary in the circumstances, for ill-considered action under emergency conditions can jeopardize the client's interest.

A lawyer may offer representation where the requisite level of competence can be achieved by reasonable preparation. This applies as well to a lawyer who is appointed as counsel for an unrepresented person. See also Rule 6.2.

Thoroughness and Preparation. Competent handling of a particular matter includes inquiry into and analysis of the factual and legal elements of the problem, and use of methods and procedures meeting the standards of competent practitioners. It also includes adequate preparation. The required attention and preparation are determined in part by what is at stake; major litigation and complex transactions ordinarily require more elaborate treatment than matters of lesser consequence.

Maintaining Competence. To maintain the requisite knowledge and skill, a lawyer should engage in continuing study and education. If a system of peer review has been established, the lawyer should consider making use of it in appropriate circumstances.

Acquiring Proficiency. Notice the above Comment's encouragement that a lawyer can provide competent representation in a novel field. Lawyers are lifelong learners. Just because you practice in one law field does not mean that you cannot provide competent service in another law field. As a lawyer, you have transferable skills. Studying the law in a new field through articles, books, seminars, workshops, conferences, and other means can qualify you for work in a new field. So, too, can working with experienced counsel. Co-counseling a case, meaning enlisting the services of a lawyer who is already experienced and skilled in the field, can be a great way not only to learn through observing and interacting but also to strengthen your professional network. Lawyers commonly enter new fields by first co-counseling with experienced counsel until they find that they have mastered the relevant knowledge and skills.

Incompetence's Consequences. One might think that when a lawyer acts incompetently, the justice system would simply allow the client to get another lawyer to fix whatever irregularity the incompetent lawyer caused. Unfortunately, the justice system often cannot operate that way. In some instances, swift action by the client to retain new counsel and by new counsel to remediate the situation, together with the generous exercise of the court's discretion, may avoid harm to the client. Yet in many other instances, the justice system will consider it too late to undo the untoward consequences of the incompetent lawyer's actions. The general rule of agency, equally applicable to lawyers and clients, is that the agent's mistake binds the principal, meaning that the lawyer's mistake binds the client. *See* Panzino v. City of Phoenix, 999 P.2d 198 (Ariz. 2000). In most instances, clients suffer the consequences of their lawyers' mistakes. The client need not also be at fault. A lawyer's incompetence may bind the client even if the client did not neglect the matter. *See* Bailey v. Algonquin Gas Transmission Co., 788 A.2d 478 (R.I. 2002).

Excusable Neglect. Courts are often reluctant or unable to help lawyers whose incompetence has prejudiced a client, notwithstanding rules of procedure like FED. R. CIV. P. 60(b) that permit courts to grant relief from orders and judgments based on excusable neglect. When considering the nature of lawyer competence, it is important to realize that the law holds lawyers to firm high standards. The justice system does not generally grant mulligans or do-overs, nor does it allow lawyers to plead ignorance of the law and rules as an excuse for a second try. Although FED. R. CIV. P. 60(b) and like state rules offer relief from orders and judgments for excusable neglect, the Supreme Court has interpreted Rule 60(b) not to excuse "inadvertence, ignorance of the rules, or mistakes construing the rules" even when that incompetence harms an otherwise innocent party. *See* Pioneer Investment Services Co. v. Brunswick Assocs. Ltd. Partnership, 507 U.S. 380 (1993). *Pioneer Investment Services* held a key factor to be whether the lawyer had reasonable control of the circumstances. If circumstances were beyond the lawyer's control, then relief is likely. *See, e.g.,* Pincay v. Andrews, 389 F.3d 853 (9th Cir. 2004) (en banc) (paralegal's error recording filing due date warrants discretionary extension of time to file). If on the other hand the lawyer could have avoided the problem by competent action, then relief is unlikely. The Supreme Court's Rule 60(b) standard gives incompetent lawyers no substantial protection. You might be surprised at what events and circumstances courts will decline to excuse. Consider the following two cases each involving matters of relative routine to which lawyers must nonetheless give due attention. As you read the cases, note the different issues at stake, in the first case whether the client should have relief from the lawyer's mistake, and in the second case whether the lawyer should suffer discipline for it.

Martinelli v. Farm-Rite, Inc.,
Superior Court of New Jersey
785 A.2d 33 (2001)

WINKELSTEIN, J.A.D.

The question presented is whether the failure of defense counsel's computer diary system to pick up the date to appeal an arbitrators' award constitutes an extraordinary circumstance allowing relaxation

of the thirty-day time frame within which to demand a trial *de novo.*
[C] The motion judge, in an oral decision, concluded that a computer
failure did not constitute an "extraordinary circumstance" under the
rule. We agree and affirm.

I

Plaintiff, who operates a farm in Hammonton, New Jersey, claims
defendant supplied him with a defective water pump resulting in the
loss of his blueberry crop in 1993. Suit was filed on October 30, 1998,
and the case was referred to arbitration on May 19, 2000. [C] ...

Upon completion of the arbitration proceeding, the arbitrators
assessed liability at eighty percent upon defendant and twenty percent
upon plaintiff; they awarded plaintiff damages of $150,000. ... On June
20, 2000 plaintiff filed a motion to confirm the arbitration award, [c],
which defense counsel received on June 22, 2000. Upon receipt of the
motion defense counsel reviewed his file. He discovered that due to an
apparent system failure, his computerized diary had not alerted him to
file a demand for a trial *de novo* within the thirty-day time period as
required by *R.* 4:21A-6(b)(1).

Defense counsel's office was in the end stage of converting from an
Alpha-Micro Mainframe Computer System to a local area network
(LAN) PC Service System. Counsel relied on the computer "markup"
system to diary statutes of limitations and other deadlines, including a
diary notation to alert him when to file a demand for a trial *de novo.*
Counsel had no backup diary system. Without dispute, counsel had no
reason to suspect, in advance of the incident, that the system would
not operate correctly. Not until counsel received the motion to
confirm the arbitrators' award did the system failure become known
and was the loss of the diary notation discovered.

At oral argument defense counsel acknowledged that he was
unaware of any other circumstance in which the system failed.
Although the reason for the system failure has not been conclusively
determined, counsel suspects it was a malfunction of the system's
software.

II

The thirty-day period to file a notice of rejection of an arbitrators'
award and demand for a trial *de novo* may be extended upon a showing
of extraordinary circumstances. ...

... [A] computer malfunction is not sufficient justification for late
submission of documents to the court, whether required by statute,
court rule or court order. One does not need to be an expert to
recognize that computers do not always work. It is not uncommon for
previously accessible data to suddenly disappear. There can be any
number of reasons why a computer system fails. There can be human
errors inputting and accessing the data, electrical failures, power

surges, and computer viruses. Not all programs are as dependable as others. Quite simply, systems fail regularly and do not always perform to their specifications. Such an occurrence is neither exceptional, unusual, nor without precedent. ...

Counsel had control over what type of diary or markup system to use. He had a choice to rely on one or more electronic systems, a manual system, or a combination of systems. As Judge Higbee stated in denying defendant's motion, it becomes a question of how an attorney manages an office, what systems to set up and how they are monitored. She said: "[w]hether you're relying on a[n] associate, a secretary or a computer, it's your job to make sure whatever you rely on is working and functioning well. And if it's not, you have [to] bear the risk...."

... [S]ystem failures are common occurrences in a modern office environment. For most practitioners, computers have revolutionized their practice. They generally result in substantial savings of time and money. But they come with a cost—they are technologically complex and do not always work.

Computer failures, not unlike human failures, must be anticipated. Just as with a manual diary system, where it is commonplace to have at least one backup system available in anticipation of mistakes which are bound to be made by attorneys and other office staff, the same should hold true when a diary system is computerized. In today's environment a computer failure, which results in the late filing of a demand for trial *de novo,* must be treated the same as a wrong date marked on a calendar or the failure of an attorney to properly supervise staff. It is an occurrence that can be anticipated and guarded against. ...

... [P]ermitting a computer failure to justify a late submission would open the proverbial floodgates for violations of deadlines imposed by statutes, court rules and court orders. ...

... An attorney is compelled to determine the appropriate method to assure compliance with the thirty-day rule. To permit a computer failure to constitute an excuse to file late is contrary to the underlying goals of the arbitration process—to bring about an inexpensive, expeditious adjudication of disputes and to help ease the caseload of the courts. [C] ...

Affirmed.

————————————

In re Harris,
Superior Court of Kansas
180 P.3d 558 (2008)

PER CURIAM:

This is an uncontested, original proceeding in discipline filed by the office of the Disciplinary Administrator against Stephen D. Harris, an attorney licensed to practice law in the state of Kansas since April 1993. ...

On June 12, 2007, a hearing on the formal complaint was held before a hearing panel of the Kansas Board for Discipline of Attorneys. Respondent appeared pro se. ... At the outset of the hearing, Respondent stipulated to the facts and rule violations alleged in the formal complaint.

Based upon its findings of fact, the hearing panel concluded as a matter of law that Respondent violated six rules of professional conduct[including] KRPC 1.1... . The panel recommended that Respondent be suspended for a period of 3 months from the practice of law in the State of Kansas. Respondent filed no exceptions to the panel's final hearing report.

The hearing panel made ... findings of fact, by clear and convincing evidence, which are reproduced in narrative form, as follows: ...

> Beginning September 1, 2004, pursuant to a rule change, the United States Bankruptcy Court required that all pleadings be filed electronically. In order to file electronic pleadings with the bankruptcy court, an attorney must have a login name and password.

> In January 2005, Respondent attempted to file a bankruptcy case, in behalf of another client, using paper pleadings rather than electronic pleadings. The bankruptcy court sent Respondent an order and in the order advised Respondent that petitions and other pleadings must be filed electronically. The court ordered Respondent to attend the required training, pass the examination, and obtain a login name and password within 30 days. Respondent failed to obtain a login name and password within 30 days.

> On March 31, 2005, Respondent attempted to file a bankruptcy case in behalf of another client. On April 11, 2005, a bankruptcy judge advised Respondent in writing that he was not permitted to file a bankruptcy case using paper pleadings and that all pleadings must be filed electronically.

> In July 2005, C.G. retained Respondent to prepare and file a bankruptcy case in his behalf prior to the change in bankruptcy laws scheduled for October 2005. Respondent informed C.G. that it would take 6 to 8 weeks to file the bankruptcy. C.G. paid

Respondent an advanced fee of $800. Despite the fact that Respondent knew that he did not have a login name and password to enable him to file bankruptcy cases, Respondent agreed to represent C.G.

On September 12, 2005, Respondent spoke with C.G. by telephone. At that time, C.G. informed Respondent that he needed the bankruptcy case to be filed immediately because his two vehicles had been repossessed. During the conversation, C.G. asked Respondent whether Respondent had a login name and password to enable him to file bankruptcy pleadings. Respondent informed C.G. that he had a login name and password. Later, in the same telephone conversation, Respondent informed C.G. that he did not have a login name and password but that he would get one by the end of the week. Still later in the telephone conversation, Respondent assured C.G. that he would obtain a login name and password with sufficient time to file the bankruptcy before the laws changed.

Because Respondent had not filed his bankruptcy, because Respondent did not have a login name and password, and because C.G. believed that Respondent misrepresented his ability to file the bankruptcy case, C.G. terminated Respondent's representation. C.G. requested that Respondent refund the $800 advanced fee paid to Respondent. Respondent never refunded any of the advanced fee. (Subsequently, C.G. retained new counsel, who was able to prepare and file the bankruptcy case prior to the change in the bankruptcy laws.)

On September 18, 2005, C.G. filed a complaint with the Disciplinary Administrator's office. ...

Based upon the findings of fact, the hearing panel concluded as a matter of law that Respondent violated KRPC 1.1... . The panel's conclusions are summarized, as follows:

KRPC 1.1 requires attorneys to provide competent representation to their clients. The rule states that competent representation requires the legal knowledge, skill, thoroughness and preparation reasonably necessary for the representation. Respondent failed to competently represent C.G. when he failed to prepare and electronically file the bankruptcy petition. ...

The hearing panel considered ... Standard 4.62: "Suspension is generally appropriate when a lawyer knowingly deceives a client, and causes injury or potential injury to the client." ...

We adopt the hearing panel's findings of fact and its conclusions of law. Further, we agree with the panel's recommended discipline of suspension for a period of 3 months from the practice of law in the state of Kansas, although a minority of the court would impose a longer suspension. ...

Figure

    E. Norman Veasey is the 2005 winner of the American Bar Association's Michael Franck Professional Responsibility Award. Mr. Veasey is senior partner at Weil Gotshal advising global corporate clients on corporate governance issues. Mr. Veasey's main contribution to the profession was as chief judge of the Delaware Supreme Court for 12 years up until 2004. Mr. Veasey led nationwide programs in professionalism and efficient operation of the courts, while there, and as the President of the Conference of Chief Justices. Mr. Veasey has also chaired the American Bar Association Business Law Section and its Special Committee on Evaluation of the Rules of Professional Conduct. It is the hallmark of a special professional to serve the profession while also fulfilling one's obligations to one's employer and clients. By doing so, Mr. Veasey turned what might have been an ordinary business-law practice into leading the nation's state courts in professionalism and access reforms.

INQUIRY

Malpractice. The above cases might have reminded you that even if conduct rules like ABA Model Rule 1.1 did not mandate competence, then the common law of professional negligence would in any case provide its own deterrent to incompetence. That is, the common law will hold liable the lawyer whose breach of the lawyer's standard of care causes client harm. Malpractice liability acts as a deterrent whether or not conduct rules provide their own deterrent. In a sense, then, there is a natural intersection between conduct rules and malpractice claims. Conduct rules should establish a standard of care. If a client suffers loss from the breach of that standard, then one might assume that the client would have a malpractice claim. Perhaps surprisingly, though, the conduct rules provide otherwise. The law treats conduct issues apart from malpractice issues because the two systems, professional discipline and tort liability, differ in their goals. The ABA MODEL RULES OF PROFESSIONAL CONDUCT in Section [20] of their Preamble and Scope provision state explicitly, "Violation of a Rule should not itself give rise to a cause of action against a lawyer nor should it create any presumption in such a case that a legal duty has been breached." The standard of care comes from expert testimony as to custom and practice, not conduct rules. Can you articulate why misconduct should be apart from malpractice? Consider the following case decided under an adopted state version of the same Preamble and Scope provision.

Archuleta v. Hughes,
Utah Supreme Court
969 P.2d 409 (1998)

DURHAM, Associate Chief Justice:

... Archuleta was injured in an automobile accident and was subsequently represented by Donald Hughes in an action for personal injuries. Hughes settled with the other driver's insurance company for $9,286, which included $2,400 for unpaid medical expenses allegedly related to injuries sustained in the accident. Hughes took one third of the settlement-including $800 representing one third of the $2,400 recovered for unpaid medical expenses. Archuleta claimed that, because those expenses could have been submitted under the Personal Injury Protection ("PIP") portion of her insurance policy, it was malpractice for Hughes to submit them to the tortfeasor's insurer and then to take a portion of them as fees. After Archuleta received the settlement proceeds, she dismissed Hughes as her attorney.

In 1994, Archuleta filed a complaint against Hughes alleging malpractice and negligence. ...

... The jury returned a verdict of nonsuit on the malpractice and negligence claims. Archuleta filed an appeal... . [T]he Utah Court of Appeals subsequently affirmed the trial court's decision. We granted Archuleta's Petition for Writ of Certiorari. ...

II. LEGAL MALPRACTICE

Archuleta contends that Hughes should not have charged a fee on a portion of her medical bills that could have been submitted to PIP. She asserts that Hughes committed malpractice and fraud by collecting a percentage of that amount properly part of a PIP settlement, arguing the fee was excessive and unreasonable in violation of the Utah Rules of Professional Conduct. Archuleta thus premised her constructive fraud and malpractice claims on a violation of the Utah Rules of Professional Conduct.

Before today, this court has not resolved the underlying question of whether a violation of the Utah Rules of Professional Conduct establishes a cause of action. Archuleta asserts that Hughes collected an unreasonable fee in violation of rule 1.5. *See* Utah Rules of Professional Conduct Rule 1.5. She further argues that the fee was unreasonable and its collection unethical according to Utah State Bar Ethics Advisory Opinion No. 114.[Fn3. The advisory opinion explains: "[I]t would be unethical, in virtually all cases, for a lawyer to charge a contingent fee for collecting a claim against his client's own insurer under the PIP coverage when the attorney has been engaged on a contingent fee basis to handle a personal injury claim against a third party...." Utah State Bar Ethics Advisory Opinion No. 114-15.] Archuleta claims that because Hughes' fee was unreasonable and his actions unethical, Hughes is liable for negligence, fraud and malpractice.

However, the Rules of Professional Conduct provide that a "[v]iolation of a rule should not give rise to a cause of action, nor should it create any legal presumption that a legal duty has been breached." Utah Rules of Professional Conduct, Scope. ...

We agree with the court of appeals, and conclude that the Utah Rules of Professional Conduct are not designed to create a basis for civil liability. Other jurisdictions addressing this issue agree. [Cc] The legal standards applicable to malpractice claims are entirely adequate to protect clients as plaintiffs, and Archuleta's claims here were tried to and rejected by the jury.

We do note, however, that the conduct of Hughes in this case may have been unethical.[fn] PIP benefits are often a source of confusion, especially when an attorney is attempting to settle medical bills that are the result of different accidents. To avoid cumbersome litigation and confusion over these issues, we observe that a retainer agreement should specifically state and explicitly disclose that an insured can submit PIP claims directly to his insurance company without a lawyer's assistance. It should also disclose that the attorney will take a fee from all recoveries including items that could have been submitted under an insured's PIP coverage but were not. This practice gives the insured client an option to either submit his own bills to his PIP or allow the attorney to take care of all of the bills, with the knowledge that the attorney will take a fee calculated on recoveries including PIP payments. ...

Affirmed.

———————

INQUIRY

Errors in Judgment. Lawyers can and do disagree about tactics, without implicating their competence. The standard of care requires lawyers to exercise that degree of skill, knowledge, and diligence possessed by lawyers of ordinary competence, but it does not define every decision. Law practice leaves substantial room for judgment especially around the number and identity of witnesses to call at contested trials and hearings, and the probability and likely value of various outcomes in litigated and transactional matters. Malpractice law uses an error-in-judgment rule to protect those decisions that a competent lawyer might make even if they turn out badly later, as some decisions inevitably do. *See, e.g.,* Simko v. Blake, 532 N.W.2d 842 (Mich. 1995) (no malpractice claim for failure to call witness at trial); Stricklan v. Koella, 546 S.W.2d 810 (Tenn. Ct. App. 1976) (no malpractice claim for lawyer's good-faith choices in preparing for trial); *but see* Woodruff v. Tomlin, 616 F.2d 924 (6th Cir. 1980) (remanding for trial of malpractice claim for failure to contact potential witnesses and rely on applicable statutes). Unsettled law can increase the room for a lawyer's exercise of judgment, although it may also require the lawyer to advise the client about the potential effect of that unsettled law. *See* Wood v. McGrath, North, Mullin & Kratz, P.C., 589 N.W.2d 103 (Neb. 1999) (standard of care may require lawyer to advise client of unsettled treatment of unvested stock options as part of a marital estate in divorce action) (remanding malpractice claim for trial).   What practices might you adopt to minimize malpractice liability for judgment calls? Some lawyers keep clients informed in writing of tactical options and decisions, giving clients greater opportunity to review, approve, and participate.

Non-Client Liability.   The above *Archuleta* case explores the standard of care that a lawyer owes a client, confirming that its source is in the ordinary customs and practices of other minimally competent lawyers rather than in the conduct rules. To whom does a lawyer owe these duties? In the usual case, the client is the one whom a lawyer's malpractice harms. In some cases, though, a non-client third party suffers from the lawyer's malpractice. The classic example involves the lawyer who commits malpractice while drafting or arranging for the execution of a will, resulting in the will being void or leaving out intended beneficiaries. The intended beneficiaries suffer the harm, not (strictly speaking) the client who executes the will and then dies. Malpractice law uses the concept of legal duty to patrol the boundary of lawyer malpractice liability. In most cases, that boundary stops at clients. Non-clients have no malpractice action for harm. A common exception is for intended beneficiaries of a will, where the law in some states accepts that the lawyer was acting for the benefit of those beneficiaries. *See, e.g.,* Leak-Gilbert v. Fahle, 55 P.3d 1054 (Okla. 2002). Yet courts will look closely to ensure that the testator actually intended the malpractice claimant to be a beneficiary. *See* Boranian v. Clark, 20 Cal.Rptr.3d 405 (2004) (lawyer has no duty to potential will beneficiary to clarify testator's ambiguous intent); *see also* Francis v. Piper, 597 N.W.2d 922 (Minn. Ct. App. 1999) (no duty to testator's sister where sister was not an intended beneficiary and testator simply lacked capacity).   A few states extend the duty beyond will beneficiaries to instances where the lawyer provided services knowing that a third party would rely on those services and acting toward them, in a relationship approaching privity. *See, e.g.,* Cowan Liebowitz & Latman, P.C. v. Kaplan, 902 So.2d 755 (Fla. 2005); Prudential Ins. Co. v. Dewey, Ballantine, Bushby, Palmer & Wood, 605 N.E2d 318 (N.Y. Ct. App. 1992).

Malpractice Causation. Fortunately, not every breach of the standard of care (and not every violation of a conduct rule) causes client harm. The causation question in malpractice cases is like causation in other tort cases, that it depends on the client claimant showing that but for the lawyer's breach of the standard of care, the client would not have suffered the loss that the client is claiming. This proof can be more difficult than you might think. *See, e.g.,* White v. Jungbauer, 128 P.3d 263 (Colo. Ct. App. 2005) (jury issue whether $350,000 settlement amount was reasonable or better-prepared lawyer could have obtained more); *see also* Merritt v. Hopkins Goldenberg, P.C., 84 1 N.E.2d 1003 (Ill. Ct. App. 2005) (client fails to prove that lawyer's incompetence resulted in a lower settlement). Just because the client could have obtained a higher award does not mean that the higher award would have been collectible. *See* Smith v. Haden, 868 F.Supp. 1 (D. D.C. 1994) (client must show collectibility of higher award); *cf.* Carbone v. Tierney, 864 A.2d 308 (N.H. 2004) (lawyer must show uncollectibility of higher award). In other instances, the client would have suffered harm anyway such as when subject to criminal or administrative charges. *See, e.g.,* Fang v. Bock, 28 P.3d 456 (Mont. 2001) (no malpractice where deportation ordered notwithstanding lawyer's breach of standard of care in advising guilty plea). In transactional rather than litigation matters, the client may be unable to prove that the lawyer's breach of the standard of care resulted in any worse of a deal than the client would have obtained without the breach. *See* Froom v. Perel, 872 A.2d 1067 (N.J. Superior Ct. 2005) (no causation where client failed to prove better real estate deal but for lawyer's breach); Viner v. Sweet, 70 P.3d. 1046 (Cal. 2003) (same regarding securities deal). Proximate cause can also be an issue when the incompetent lawyer could not have reasonably foreseen the loss that the client suffers. *See, e.g.,* TIG Insurance Co. v. Giffin Winning Cohen & Bodewes, P.C., 444 F.3d 587 (7th Cir. 2006) (affirming dismissal of malpractice case for lack of proximate cause, where incompetent lawyer's failure to produce documents led to a million-dollar attorney fee expense); *but see* Andrews v. Saylor, 80 P.3d 482 (N.M. Ct. App. 2003) (incompetence by lawyer hired to remediate malpracticing lawyer's incompetence was foreseeable). Consider one case confirming the complexity of the causation issue.

Jones Motor Co. v. Holtkamp, Liese
Beckemeier & Childress, P.C.,
United States Court of Appeals for the Seventh Circuit
197 F.3d 119 (1999)

POSNER, Chief Judge.

The plaintiffs in this legal malpractice suit appeal from its dismissal on the defendants' motion for summary judgment, raising a novel issue concerning the law of legal malpractice. The issue, which arises when as in this case the plaintiff is complaining that his lawyer booted a procedural entitlement, such as the right to a jury trial, is whether the plaintiff must show that his lawyer's negligence not only caused him to lose but brought about an unjust result—the wrong party won. The plaintiffs are the Jones Motor Company, a trucker, and its insurer. The defendants are lawyers who represented Jones in a personal injury lawsuit brought against it by Elston Cannon. ...

The underlying suit had been filed in a state court in St. Clair County and assigned to a judge who we are told, and accept for purposes of deciding this appeal, has the reputation of favoring plaintiffs in personal injury suits. Jones's lawyers negligently failed to make a timely *effective* request for a jury because they failed to accompany the request with payment of the fee for a jury trial. As a result the case was tried to the judge, who entered a judgment of $2.8 million for the plaintiff; the suit was then settled for $2.5 million. In the present case, the malpractice case, Jones tendered the opinion of an experienced lawyer in St. Clair County that had the case been tried to a jury, the verdict would have been in the neighborhood of $500,000. Jones and its insurer, which paid a part of the $2.5 million settlement, are suing for the $2 million difference. ...

... Through the defendants' negligence Jones and its insurer lost their right to a jury trial and were forced to submit to a bench trial—which means they got a trial before an authorized tribunal. They allege no error in the conduct of the trial by the judge whom they did not want to try the case, and they did not appeal from the judgment that he rendered, large as it was. The plaintiffs thus got a fair trial and there is no basis for supposing that the judgment was excessive, albeit it may have been higher than it would have been had Jones's lawyers not thrown away their client's right to a jury trial. Some Illinois cases say or imply that you cannot get a judgment for malpractice against a lawyer unless you can show that you had a meritorious claim... [cc], and Jones's lawyers argue correctly that their client had no entitlement not to be mulcted by a judgment of $2.8 million. ...

... Although the judge who tried the case against Jones may have a reputation of being more liberal in personal-injury suits than the average jury in his county, it is impossible to infer from this that the $2.8 million judgment that he rendered against Jones was too high; the average jury verdict in such a case might be too low. Of course if this judge were *prejudiced* against motor carriers, or litigants named Jones, or defendants in personal injury cases, there would be a basis for inferring that the negligence of Jones's lawyer had cost Jones a shot *to which Jones was entitled* at a lower damages award, albeit an entitlement not certain to be enforced even by a jury; but of this there is no evidence.

Yet this analysis is not satisfactory either. We must ask why Illinois allows a defendant in a civil suit to elect to be tried by a jury even though the plaintiff would prefer a bench trial. The answer must be that *each* party is deemed entitled to seek the "protection" of the jury against being tried by a judge. [C]   That entitlement, a real legal entitlement and not just a tactical opportunity to obtain a more favorable tribunal, was worth something to Jones, and it was kicked away by the defendants' negligence. The only reason for treating it differently from other entitlements, such as the entitlement to introduce evidence or to enforce a substantive right, is practical; it is the difficulty of valuing its loss. [C]   The difficulty becomes impossibility in a case (which is not this case, however) in which, at the time the right to a jury trial is forfeited, the identity of the judge who will try the case in lieu of the jury is not known. There is variance among judges as well as among juries, and it is very hard to say that the average jury is likely to be more favorable to a defendant than the average judge. Hence the foreseeable loss in such a case would be extremely hard to estimate.

What is true, but not helpful to Jones, is that a defendant who has a very *weak* case—a case he deserves to lose—will prefer a jury trial. [C]   The reason is that there is greater variance (implying less accuracy) in jury verdicts and therefore a greater chance that a weak case will convince a jury than that it will convince a judge. The fact that Jones wanted a jury instead of a judge would ordinarily signal a weak rather than a strong case, but the inference is countered here by the argument that even with a strong case a defendant might prefer a jury to a judge known to favor plaintiffs in personal-injury suits.

... [G]iven the uncertainty of harm we think the plaintiff in such a case must do more than the plaintiffs have done here to show that they can prove damages to a reasonable certainty. Some degree of speculation is permissible in computing damages, [cc], because reasonable doubts as to remedy ought to be resolved against the wrongdoer; but there are limits. Although there is plenty of evidence that the defendant in any personal-injury case assigned to the judge who presided at *Cannon v. Jones Motor Group, Inc.* would want a jury rather than this judge to determine damages, there is no credible evidence of what a jury might have awarded. The principal evidence is the opinion of the lawyer who thought Cannon's case worth to a jury in the range of $500,000, but this was offered as a bare conclusion without data of actual verdicts in St. Clair County in comparable cases from which some reasonable confidence interval, some range in which any jury verdict would be quite likely to lie, might have been computed. No reasonable trier of fact could have been allowed to award damages to Jones and its insurer on the basis of such unsubstantiated expert testimony. [Cc]

The plaintiffs argue that the way to compute damages in this case is simply to try the malpractice claim to a jury. That is a bad suggestion quite apart from the fact that a jury in a federal district court is not drawn from the same pool as the jury in a state court. The suggestion overlooks the fact that given the variance among juries, it would be necessary to try the malpractice claim a number of times in order to get a sense of the *average* performance of a jury in this case, and it is the difference between the judge's judgment and the judgment that Jones could have *expected* from a jury, which would be an average jury performance, that is the measure of what Jones lost as a result of its lawyers' negligence. So the suit was rightly dismissed after all.

AFFIRMED.

I N Q U I R Y

Malpractice Challenges. The above case illustrates the challenge that causation can present for a client suing a lawyer for malpractice. There are other challenges. Malpractice actions generally require expert testimony from other lawyers regarding the standard of care and causation. *See, e.g.,* Kaempe v. Myers, 367 F.3d 958 (D.C. Cir. 2004) (dismissal for lack of expert testimony on standard); Johnson v. Carleton, 765 A.2d 571 (Me. 2001) (same); *see also* Alexander v. Turtur & Assocs., Inc., 146 S.W.3d 113 (Tex. 2004) (requiring expert testimony on causation). Courts do not require experts only where the sta4ndard, its breach, and causation are obvious enough for jurors to appreciate without that testimony. *See, e.g.,* Zok v. Collins, 18 P.3d 39 (Alaska 2001) (failure to oppose motions at trial). Expert testimony can be expensive. The high cost of preparing and pursuing a malpractice case means that smaller claims may go uncompensated. Some lawyers specialize in handling legal-malpractice claims for clients who have suffered harm, but those lawyers face the same challenges that other lawyers working on contingency fees face to select cases whose return will enable continued practice.

Malpractice Defenses. In addition to the above challenges, clients maintaining a malpractice action also face the usual defense of contributory or comparative negligence, if the client has failed to act with reasonable care as to the client's own matter. *See, e.g.,* Clark v. Rowe, 701 N.E.2d 624 (Mass. 1998) (plaintiff client 70% comparatively negligent in legal malpractice claim over loan refinancing). The *in pari delicto* or unclean hands doctrines may also bar the claim of a client who is involved with the lawyer in dishonest conduct.   Statutes of limitations also bar untimely filed legal malpractice claims, although the law may toll the period until the representation's conclusion, *see, e.g.,* CAL. CODE CIV. PROC. §340.6(a)(2); Biomet, Inc. v. Barnes & Thornburg, 791 N.E.2d 760 (Ind. Ct. App. 2003), or until the client should have discovered the malpractice. *See, e.g.,* CAL. CODE CIV. PROC. §340.6; Samuels v. Mix, 989 P.2d 701 (Cal. 1999).

Malpractice Insurance.   Most lawyers maintain malpractice insurance. Many lawyers would say that it is foolishness not to do so. Many lawyers will also refuse to refer cases to a lawyer who does not maintain malpractice insurance and refuse to co-counsel cases with them.   If one considers vicarious liability and negligent-referral theories, then dealing with an uninsured lawyer can make an insured lawyer the uninsured lawyer's insurer. For that reason, some lawyers will require other lawyers with whom they deal to provide proof of current malpractice insurance. A client has an equal or greater interest in having a lawyer who insures against malpractice. One state requires lawyers to maintain malpractice insurance, *see* OREGON REV. STAT. §752.035, while another state requires law firm partnerships and professional corporations to do so, OHIO GOV. BAR R. III §4. Several states require lawyers to notify the state bar whether they maintain malpractice insurance, and a few require lawyers to notify their clients. *See* ABA MODEL CT. R. ON INSURANCE DISCLOSURE (2004) (notify state high court of malpractice insurance and any lapse of insurance). Responsible lawyers will not only maintain malpractice insurance but will also reassure their clients that if the lawyer breaches a professional standard in a way that causes the client harm, then the client should seek recompense out of that insurance. The insurance is there to protect both lawyer and client.

Malpractice Policies. Malpractice insurance policies are the same in some respects and different in other respects. They tend to be claims-made policies, meaning that they cover claims made while the lawyer has the policy in effect. The lawyer who allows the policy to lapse loses coverage. For that reason, lawyers who take a break from law practice or who retire should maintain coverage. Insurers will write less expensive prior-acts or tail coverage for lawyers who are not in active practice. The policies cover only those whom they identify as insureds. A lawyer should take care that the policy names all those whom the lawyer intends to insure including, if applicable, non-lawyer employees of the firm. The policies have limits often written in two figures such as $300,000/$500,000 with the first figure a per-occurrence limit and the second figure a per-policy-period limit. Deductibles vary with the premium lower as the deductible increases. The policies typically promise not just indemnity but also defense, the cost of which can be significant. The insurers typically get to choose the defense lawyer, although some policies permit the insured lawyer to participate in or approve the choice. Some policies permit the insurer to settle without the insured lawyer's consent, while others require the insured lawyer's consent. Can you articulate why a lawyer might want to ensure no settlement without consent? The policies also exclude coverage for intentional acts involving fraudulent and criminal conduct. Malpractice insurance will not help a client whose lawyer absconds with the client's funds.

D. Diligence

Students tend to conflate the concepts of competence and diligence, but the drafters of the ABA MODEL RULES OF PROFESSIONAL CONDUCT made separate rules on competence and diligence for a reason. Dictionary.com defines diligence as "constant and earnest effort to accomplish what is undertaken; persistent exertion of body or mind." Competence implicates the ability to perform. Diligence implicates the willingness. It is one thing to have the education, skill, and ability. It is another thing to choose to exercise it. Some lawyers who have abundant skill simply fail to apply it. The reasons may be many, such as distraction, overwork, or dislike for a particular client or matter, or there may be no reason. One thing is sure, that procrastination for any reason is the enemy of the diligent. When Comment [3] to ABA Model Rule 1.3 states in passive language, "Perhaps no professional shortcoming is more widely resented than procrastination," Comment [3] means to describe *client* resentment. Clients hate a lawyer's procrastination, and not only because (as Comment [3] continues), "A client's interests often can be adversely affected by the passage of time or the change in conditions; in extreme instances, as when a lawyer overlooks a statute of limitations, the client's legal position may be destroyed." A lawyer's refusal to return a client's telephone call can display a basic lack of respect and civility. *See, e.g.,* In re Disciplinary Proceedings Against Winter, 522 N.W.2d 504 (Wis. 1994) (suspension for not returning 50 client calls). There are sometimes good reasons to bide one's time about a certain matter, as facts come to light, judgment forms, and wisdom discerns the best course of action. On the other hand, many times a situation calls for nothing more than prompt and straightforward action, a simple exercise of will moving a client's matter forward. Comment [4] cautions a lawyer, "Unless the relationship is terminated as provided in Rule 1.16, a lawyer should carry through to conclusion all matters undertaken for a client." Consider the following case.

Amco Builders & Developers, Inc. v. Team Ace Joint Venture,
Michigan Supreme Court
666 N.W.2d 623 (2003)

MICHAEL F. CAVANAGH, J.

This case requires us to decide whether the trial court's refusal to set aside a default judgment was an abuse of discretion. Because we find that the trial judge did not abuse his discretion in refusing to set aside the default judgment, we reverse the judgment of the Court of Appeals.

I

This case involves claims for breach of contract and tortious interference with a contractual relationship.... .

On November 23, 1998, the circuit court directed defendants ... to produce Clarence Carson, the principal of [defendant] Intervale, for deposition within thirty days. This order was entered only after the trial judge "bent over backwards" for defendants, even providing defense counsel an opportunity to contact Mr. Carson to ensure that he could appear within thirty days. The order provided that "[f]ailure to produce Clarence Carson in conformity with this Order shall subject Defendant to a motion for default judgment."

When defendants Intervale and Acme/Intervale Joint Venture failed to comply with the order, plaintiff filed a motion for default judgment against defendants. At the January 15, 1999, hearing on the motion, defense counsel stated that he had been unable to reach Mr. Carson because of the holidays and the illness of defense counsel's son. He acknowledged that he had "not participated" in discovery and admitted "not having been available to properly represent" defendants. However, he assured the court that communications with his clients had been restored. The court granted the motion for default and the order of default was entered against both defendants.... .

Both defendants moved to set aside the default on February 12, 1999. Although defendants' attorney assumed responsibility for the delay, the motion was denied on March 12, 1999, because the court found that neither defendant demonstrated good cause to set aside the default.

Default judgment in the amount of $595,606.15 was entered against only Intervale when defense counsel did not appear for the March 18, 1999, hearing on the issue of damages.[fn]

New counsel for defendant moved to set aside the default entry against both Intervale and Acme/Intervale Joint Venture, as well as the default judgment against Intervale, claiming that Mr. Carson was not aware that the court had ordered his production for deposition. The court denied the motion ... because it had "bent over backwards ... making sure that ... [prior defense counsel] had the okay from his clients that they would be produced for deposition within the period of time." The circuit court was not satisfied that good cause for setting aside the default and the default judgment was presented. ...

Defendant appealed.... . The Court of Appeals reversed ... [f]inding that the actions of defense counsel constituted abandonment.... .

II

... This Court historically has cautioned appellate courts not to substitute their judgment in matters falling within the discretion of the trial court, and has insisted upon deference to the trial court in such matters. ...

III

The setting aside of a default or default judgment is governed by MCR 2.603(D)(1), which provides: "A motion to set aside a default or a default judgment, except when grounded on lack of jurisdiction over the defendant, shall be granted only if good cause is shown and an affidavit of facts showing a meritorious defense is filed." ...

... To show "good cause," a party may establish "'(1) a substantial defect or irregularity in the proceeding upon which the default was based,'" or " '(2) a reasonable excuse for failure to comply with the requirements which created the default....' " *Alken-Ziegler[, Inc. v. Waterbury Headers Corp.*, 461 Mich. 219, 230, 600 N.W.2d 638 (1999)] (citation omitted).

Defendant asserts that there is good cause for setting aside the default and the default judgment because the actions of prior defense counsel constituted abandonment. While, generally, an attorney's negligence is attributable to that attorney's client, abandonment by counsel has been held to constitute good cause for setting aside a default or default judgment. ...

There is significant evidence in the record from which the trial judge could conclude that defendant was not abandoned by prior counsel. At the April 30, 1999, hearing, the trial judge stated that despite prior counsel's son's medical problems, prior counsel continued to represent defendants and "was here most of the time with regard to this case." The trial judge also stated that he "bent over backwards" to assure that prior counsel "had the okay from his clients that they would be produced for deposition within the period of time." Before entering the order compelling production of Mr. Carson, the trial judge apparently provided prior counsel with an opportunity to contact Mr. Carson to ensure that he could appear for a deposition within thirty days. Prior counsel assured the court that the order was "okay."

... Moreover, in response to defendants' argument below that Mr. Carson lacked knowledge of significant aspects of the case, the trial court stated that it recalled being told by prior counsel that he was in communication with his clients.

The trial judge examined all the evidence regarding prior counsel's representation and determined that prior counsel did not abandon the representation; therefore, defendant had not presented good cause for setting aside the default and the default judgment. In light of the evidence in the record and the trial judge's reasoned decision based on that evidence we cannot conclude that the trial court's refusal to set aside the default judgment was an abuse of discretion.

IV

We agree with plaintiff and the dissenting Court of Appeals judge that the Court of Appeals majority failed to accord the circuit court's ruling the deference it was due and, thus, we reverse the ruling of the Court of Appeals.

INQUIRY

Extraordinary Circumstances. One would think that some circumstances might excuse a party for a lawyer's lack of diligence. There are such cases granting a party an excuse where the party's lawyer faced a sudden onset of cancer with delibilitating effects of aggressive radiation and chemotherapy treatments, *see* Tischler v. Watts, 827 A.2d 1036 (N.J. 2003), or suffered severe clinical depression, *see* Barr v. MacGugan, 78 P.3d 660 (Wash. Ct. App. 2003). One wonders whether the onset of debilitating illness and the beginning of treatment would ordinarily be so sudden as to excuse a lawyer from referring pending cases to other counsel. The line that the courts appear to draw here has not to do with counsel's incompetence, which would be clear enough, but with protecting a party who acts diligently but whose lawyer has abandoned the representation. *See, e.g.,* Community Dental Services v. Tani, 282 F.3d 1164 (9th Cir. 2002) (abandonment of representation ends agency relationship, relieving party of consequences of abandonment); United States v. Cirami, 563

F.2d 26 (2d Cir. 1977) (mental illness causing attorney to abandon case warrants vacating default judgment). The above *Amco Builders* case shows that abandonment must be complete for the exception to apply.

Limiting Liability. Lawyers are experts at helping others manage liability. Why not manage and limit their own liability through contractual agreements with clients? ABA Model Rule 1.8(h)(1) prohibits a lawyer from "mak[ing] an agreement prospectively limiting the lawyer's liability to a client for malpractice unless the client is independently represented in making the agreement... ." Subrule 1.8(h)(1) effectively prohibits limiting liability in nearly all representations because very few clients will have a lawyer negotiate a fee agreement with their lawyer (Subrule 1.8(h)(1)'s condition for limiting liability). Can you appreciate the reason for Rule 1.8(h)(1)'s prohibition? Lawyers have a tremendous advantage over most clients in appreciating the risk of liability and the value of its limitation. They also have a conflict of interest when advising a client about their own liability. The rare instance when a client may obtain independent representation to negotiate a liability waiver with the client's own counsel tends to involve a sophisticated corporate client with a high-risk representation in which it makes sense to shift some of that risk from counsel to client.

Settling Liability. ABA Model Rule 1.8(h)(2) places a similar condition on a lawyer settling a malpractice claim with a client, for the same reason that the lawyer will ordinarily have far greater expertise regarding the value of the settlement and a conflict of interest in advising the client about it. In this instance, though, Subrule 1.8(h)(2) does not require independent representation. Instead, it requires that the lawyer advise the client or former client "in writing of the desireability of seeking" independent counsel and to give the client or former client "a reasonable opportunity to seek the advice of" that independent counsel. A malpracticing lawyer can make no rush settlement with the aggrieved client. The lawyer must advise the client in writing to get independent counsel and give the client time to do so.

Ineffective Assistance of Counsel. To this point, we have focused the discussion on the incompetence and lack of diligence of lawyers involved in transactional and civil proceedings. Lawyers who fail to pursue diligently their clients' defense in criminal proceedings face create other, in some cases far more serious, problems for their clients. Implicit in the discussion to this point has been the sense that the greater the significance to the client of the matter the client entrusts to the lawyer, the greater the obligation the lawyer has to ensure its diligent treatment. Lawyers should act diligently with even the smallest of matters. Yet what constitutes diligence often depends on how significant is the client's matter. When criminal proceedings threaten long-term incarceration or even the death penalty, lawyer diligence increases inevitably. Indeed, constitutional due process guarantees the effective assistance of counsel. As you consider the following case defining the contours of effective assistance, appreciate how it at the same time defines reasonable diligence.

Rompilla v. Beard,
United States Supreme Court
545 U.S. 374 (2005)

Justice SOUTER delivered the opinion of the Court.

This case calls for specific application of the standard of reasonable competence required on the part of defense counsel by the Sixth Amendment. We hold that even when a capital defendant's family members and the defendant himself have suggested that no mitigating evidence is available, his lawyer is bound to make reasonable efforts to obtain and review material that counsel knows the prosecution will probably rely on as evidence of aggravation at the sentencing phase of trial.

I

On the morning of January 14, 1988, James Scanlon was discovered dead in a bar he ran in Allentown, Pennsylvania, his body having been stabbed repeatedly and set on fire. Ronald Rompilla was indicted for the murder and related offenses, and the Commonwealth gave notice of intent to ask for the death penalty. Two public defenders were assigned to the case.

The jury at the guilt phase of trial found Rompilla guilty on all counts, and during the ensuing penalty phase, the prosecutor sought to prove three aggravating factors to justify a death sentence: that the murder was committed in the course of another felony; that the murder was committed by torture; and that Rompilla had a significant history of felony convictions indicating the use or threat of violence. [C] The Commonwealth presented evidence on all three aggravators, and the jury found all proven. Rompilla's evidence in mitigation consisted of relatively brief testimony: five of his family members argued in effect for residual doubt, and beseeched the jury for mercy, saying that they believed Rompilla was innocent and a good man. Rompilla's 14-year-old son testified that he loved his father and would visit him in prison. The jury acknowledged this evidence to the point of finding, as two factors in mitigation, that Rompilla's son had testified on his behalf and that rehabilitation was possible. But the jurors assigned the greater weight to the aggravating factors, and sentenced

Rompilla to death. The Supreme Court of Pennsylvania affirmed both conviction and sentence. [C]

In December 1995, with new lawyers, Rompilla filed claims under the Pennsylvania Post Conviction Relief Act, 42 Pa. Cons.Stat. §9541 *et seq.* (2004), including ineffective assistance by trial counsel in failing to present significant mitigating evidence about Rompilla's childhood, mental capacity and health, and alcoholism. The postconviction court found that trial counsel had done enough to investigate the possibilities of a mitigation case, and the Supreme Court of Pennsylvania affirmed the denial of relief. [C]

Rompilla then petitioned for a writ of habeas corpus under 28 U.S.C. §2254 in Federal District Court, raising claims that included inadequate representation. The District Court found that the State Supreme Court had unreasonably applied *Strickland v. Washington,* 466 U.S. 668[] (1984), as to the penalty phase of the trial, and granted relief for ineffective assistance of counsel. ...

A divided Third Circuit panel reversed. ...

We granted certiorari, [c], and now reverse.[fn]

II

... Ineffective assistance under *Strickland* is deficient performance by counsel resulting in prejudice, 466 U.S., at 687[], with performance being measured against an "objective standard of reasonableness," *id.,* at 688[], "under prevailing professional norms," *ibid.;* [c]. ...

A

A standard of reasonableness applied as if one stood in counsel's shoes spawns few hard-edged rules, and the merits of a number of counsel's choices in this case are subject to fair debate. This is not a case in which defense counsel simply ignored their obligation to find mitigating evidence, and their workload as busy public defenders did not keep them from making a number of efforts, including interviews with Rompilla and some members of his family, and examinations of reports by three mental health experts who gave opinions at the guilt phase. None of the sources proved particularly helpful.

Rompilla's own contributions to any mitigation case were minimal. Counsel found him uninterested in helping, as on their visit to his prison to go over a proposed mitigation strategy, when Rompilla told them he was "bored being here listening" and returned to his cell. [C] To questions about childhood and schooling, his answers indicated they had been normal, [c], save for quitting school in the ninth grade, [c]. There were times when Rompilla was even actively obstructive by sending counsel off on false leads. [C]

The lawyers also spoke with five members of Rompilla's family (his former wife, two brothers, a sister-in-law, and his son), [c], and counsel testified that they developed a good relationship with the family in the course of their representation, [c]. ...

The third and final source tapped for mitigating material was the cadre of three mental health witnesses who were asked to look into Rompilla's mental state as of the time of the offense and his competency to stand trial. [C] But their reports revealed "nothing useful" to Rompilla's case, [c], and the lawyers consequently did not go to any other historical source that might have cast light on Rompilla's mental condition.

When new counsel entered the case to raise Rompilla's postconviction claims, however, they identified a number of likely avenues the trial lawyers could fruitfully have followed in building a mitigation case. School records are one example, which trial counsel never examined in spite of the professed unfamiliarity of the several family members with Rompilla's childhood, and despite counsel's knowledge that Rompilla left school after the ninth grade. [C] Other examples are records of Rompilla's juvenile and adult incarcerations, which counsel did not consult, although they were aware of their client's criminal record. And while counsel knew from police reports provided in pretrial discovery that Rompilla had been drinking heavily at the time of his offense, [c], and although one of the mental health experts reported that Rompilla's troubles with alcohol merited further investigation, [c], counsel did not look for evidence of a history of dependence on alcohol that might have extenuating significance. ...

B

There is an obvious reason that the failure to examine Rompilla's prior conviction file fell below the level of reasonable performance. Counsel knew that the Commonwealth intended to seek the death penalty by proving Rompilla had a significant history of felony convictions indicating the use or threat of violence, an aggravator under state law. Counsel further knew that the Commonwealth would attempt to establish this history by proving Rompilla's prior conviction for rape and assault, and would emphasize his violent character by introducing a transcript of the rape victim's testimony given in that earlier trial. [C] ... It is also undisputed that the prior conviction file was a public document, readily available for the asking at the very courthouse where Rompilla was to be tried.

It is clear, however, that defense counsel did not look at any part of that file, including the transcript, until warned by the prosecution a second time. ...

... Without making reasonable efforts to review the file, defense counsel could have had no hope of knowing whether the prosecution was quoting selectively from the transcript, or whether there were circumstances extenuating the behavior described by the victim. The obligation to get the file was particularly pressing here owing to the similarity of the violent prior offense to the crime charged and Rompilla's sentencing strategy stressing residual doubt. ...

The notion that defense counsel must obtain information that the State has and will use against the defendant is not simply a matter of common sense. As the District Court points out, the American Bar Association Standards for Criminal Justice in circulation at the time of Rompilla's trial describes the obligation in terms no one could misunderstand in the circumstances of a case like this one: "... The investigation should always include efforts to secure information in the possession of the prosecution and law enforcement authorities. ..."

... It flouts prudence to deny that a defense lawyer should try to look at a file he knows the prosecution will cull for aggravating evidence, let alone when the file is sitting in the trial courthouse, open for the asking. ...

C

Since counsel's failure to look at the file fell below the line of reasonable practice, there is a further question about prejudice, that is, whether "there is a reasonable probability that, but for counsel's unprofessional errors, the result of the proceeding would have been different." 466 U.S. at 694[]. ... We think Rompilla has shown beyond any doubt that counsel's lapse was prejudicial; Pennsylvania, indeed, does not even contest the claim of prejudice.

If the defense lawyers had looked in the file on Rompilla's prior conviction, it is uncontested they would have found a range of mitigation leads that no other source had opened up. ... The same file discloses test results that the defense's mental health experts would have viewed as pointing to schizophrenia and other disorders, and test scores showing a third grade level of cognition after nine years of schooling. [C][fn]

... The jury never heard any of this and neither did the mental health experts who examined Rompilla before trial. ...

This evidence adds up to a mitigation case that bears no relation to the few naked pleas for mercy actually put before the jury, and although we suppose it is possible that a jury could have heard it all and still have decided on the death penalty, that is not the test. ...

The judgment of the Third Circuit is reversed, and Pennsylvania must either retry the case on penalty or stipulate to a life sentence.

It is so ordered.

Career and Professional Development

Survey shows that the number one skill that law firms want their new associates to exhibit is the ability to convey to clients confidence in their law knowledge and skills. New lawyers may have more current knowledge of law than the lawyers who hire them. They may also have more current technology skills. Law firms depend on new associates to keep the firm's knowledge and skills current. Develop confidence in what you bring to your new law practice. Find activities in law school that build your confidence. Organize study groups, participate in competitions, serve as a student ambassador, and lead a student organization. Find activities in the professional community outside of school. Support pro-bono service, attend local bar events, and clerk in a law office. Be aware about how effectively you communicate your mastery of your work to the people around you.

CHAPTER IV

AUTHENTICITY

Advice, Counsel, Communication, Transparency

> *The true student of [law] is thought to have studied virtue above all things; for he wishes to make his fellow citizens good and obedient to the law…. By human virtue we mean not that of the body but that of the soul…. But if this is so, clearly the student of [law] must know somehow the facts about soul, as the man who is to heal the eyes or the body as a whole must know about the eyes or the body; and all the more since [law] is more prized and better than medicine…. The student of [law], then, must study the soul….*
> — Aristotle

OBJECTIVE: Given the need to advise, counsel, or otherwise communicate with a client and with others about the client's matter, articulate the conduct rules one must meet in those communications to ensure one's authentic and rule-abiding representation.

Applicable Rules

1.4 Communication

1.6 Confidentiality

1.13 Organization as Client

2.1 Advisor

The first three chapters have shown us that the willingness to accept authority qualifies a lawyer for citizenship in a nation and membership in a profession, which then leads to relationship with and representation of clients. The next important objective is that you see that the quality of that representation and relationship depends on your authenticity in communicating with clients. There are four conduct rules that in one respect or another govern lawyer-client communications. The first rule, ABA Model Rule 1.4 titled "Communication," helps lawyers appreciate that they must keep clients informed. The second rule, ABA Model Rule 2.1 titled "Advisor," helps lawyers appreciate that they should exercise broad and sensitive judgment in advising and counseling their clients. The third rule, ABA Model Rule 1.13 titled "Organization as Client," reminds lawyers that when giving advice and counsel, they must be aware of just who precisely their client is. The fourth rule, ABA Model Rule 1.6 titled "Confidentiality," helps lawyers appreciate that they must safeguard their client's information, keeping their clients informed without unduly informing others. This chapter treats those four subjects in the following four sections.

A. Communication

The first rule of authentic representation is to keep a client informed. ABA Model Rule 1.4 governs a lawyer's communications with a client. Do not underestimate Model Rule 1.4's significance. Its critical provision in Subrule 1.4(a)(1) requires that a lawyer tell the client promptly about decisions requiring the client's informed consent. Subrules 1.4(a)(3) and 1.4(b) second and broaden Rule 1.4(a)(1) into a more general mandate to keep the client reasonably informed of the matter's status and explain matters relating to the representation so that the client can make informed decisions. Together, these three subrules remind lawyers that to represent a client is not to usurp the client's authority but to communicate with the client to allow the client to make informed decisions. Subrules 1.4(a)(2), (4), and (5) provide other helpful detail. Subrule 1.4(a)(2) provides that although a lawyer may generally choose the means for pursuing the client's objective, the lawyer must reasonably consult with the client about those means. Subrule 1.4(a)(4) requires a lawyer to comply promptly with a client's reasonable information requests. Subrule 1.4(a)(5) requires a lawyer to tell the client when the conduct rules prohibit the lawyer from doing what the client asks. Read a similar state version of ABA Model Rule 1.4 below before considering some issues that it raises.

UTAH R. PROF. CONDUCT 1.4: **Communication.**
 (a) A lawyer shall:
(1) promptly inform the client of any decision or circumstance with respect to which the client's informed consent, as defined in Rule 1.0(e), is required by these Rules;
(2) reasonably consult with the client about the means by which the client's objectives are to be accomplished;
(3) keep the client reasonably informed about the status of the matter;
(4) promptly comply with reasonable requests for information; and

(5) consult with the client about any relevant limitation on the lawyer's conduct when the lawyer knows that the client expects assistance not permitted by the Rules of Professional Conduct or other law.

(b) A lawyer shall explain a matter to the extent reasonably necessary to permit the client to make informed decisions regarding the representation.

INQUIRY

Informed Consent. ABA Model Rule 1.4(a)(1) requiring a lawyer to tell a client about those matters that require the client's informed consent refers to the definition of informed consent in ABA Model Rule 1.0(e), reproduced at the end of Chapter 1. The definition stresses the lawyer's need to communicate "adequate information and explanation about the material risks of and reasonably available alternatives to the proposed course of conduct." It is foremost the client's matter, not the lawyer's matter. The lawyer's obligation is to inform the client about the matter, not to decide it for the client. You may not yet appreciate the challenges that lawyers face in providing good communication. Clients do not always listen. They do not always want to listen. Even when they do appear to listen and understand a lawyer's counsel, they sometimes make choices that to the lawyer can seem wrong, even perverse. The temptation may be to make "better" decisions for the client without consulting the client. Lawyers must resist that temptation. We do not lead our clients' lives, nor do we dictate to them how they should choose their commitments and construct their relationships. The question for the lawyer is not the quality of the client's decision. The question is whether the lawyer has fulfilled the duty to communicate, a duty that just as surely reveals flaws in a lawyer's character as it does the quality of a client's life and decisions. The case that follows Rule 1.4 suggests that a lawyer's failure to keep a client informed tends to be a symptom of deeper issues. Although the court labels it inexplicable, can you tell what the lawyer's problem was in the following case?

In re Harris,
New Jersey Supreme Court
868 A.2d 1011 (2005)

Justice ALBIN delivered the opinion of the Court.

Respondent is a persistent violator of the Rules of Professional Conduct. Since becoming a lawyer, the number and nature of her transgressions have struck at the core values that define a lawyer's responsibility to clients, the court, and the profession. Basic honesty and a minimal level of competence are indispensable qualifications to practice law in this State. The pattern of respondent's conduct over a course of years makes clear that she does not possess those essential qualifications. When a lawyer's derelictions are so many and so grave, our paramount concern must be to protect the public and maintain the public's confidence in the integrity of the profession. Based on the record before us, we are constrained to enter an Order disbarring respondent.

I.

Respondent E. Lorraine Harris was admitted to the New Jersey Bar in 1994. Since that time, she has amassed an extensive ethics record. In 1999, she received a temporary suspension lasting one month for potential misappropriation of escrow monies. [C] In 2000, she received a temporary suspension lasting nine days for failing to comply with a fee arbitration determination. [C] That same year, in an unpublished order respondent was admonished and in a published order reprimanded for failing to provide clients with a written basis for her fee and failing to provide a written contingency fee agreement. [C]

In 2001, with respect to respondent's representation of three separate clients, we suspended respondent for six months for lack of diligence, gross neglect, failure to safeguard client property, charging an unreasonable fee, failure to promptly deliver funds to a third party, record-keeping violations, false statements of material fact to a tribunal, failure to cooperate with disciplinary authorities, and misrepresentation. [C] That same year, in an unpublished order, we suspended respondent for an additional three months for lack of diligence, failure to expedite litigation, knowingly making a false statement of material fact to a tribunal, failure to cooperate with disciplinary authorities, and misrepresentation. In that last matter, respondent asked for and obtained several last-minute adjournments of a municipal court case. After failing to appear in court on the scheduled trial date, respondent then faxed a letter to the municipal court thanking it for granting her adjournment request when, in truth, she had neither requested nor received another adjournment. The manipulative dishonesty exhibited in that case is a leitmotif running through the current matters before this Court. ...

II.

The current disciplinary violations before this Court arise out of respondent's derelictions in representing numerous clients.... .

Brittingham Matter

Between 1995 and 1997, respondent represented Thomas J. Brittingham in a breach of contract suit filed in federal court. In that matter, respondent failed to inform the client about filed motions and court orders; failed to return telephone calls and to communicate with the client; failed to return parts of the file to the client after her termination as counsel, despite a magistrate's order to do so; and generally mishandled the case. ...

Lisa Matter

Between 1995 and 1999, respondent represented Joseph Lisa in a wrongful termination claim against his employer.... . Respondent was retained to file a claim with the federal Equal Employment Opportunity Commission (EEOC) on the client's behalf. Although respondent had 300 days in which to file the claim, she missed the deadline date and filed a late claim. As a result, the claim was dismissed as out of time and the client was denied a hearing before the EEOC. In addition, during a twenty-month period between 1995 and 1997 and a twenty-two month period between 1997 and 1999, respondent did not communicate in writing with her client. The client "resorted to certified mail in his dealings with respondent, because of his difficulty in reaching her." ...

Rochester Matter

Respondent represented Lewis Rochester in a divorce matter in 1997. Respondent failed to deliver $2,500 in settlement funds to Rochester and to explain that she was keeping those funds as payment for her services. Respondent also did not send her client a final bill or a copy of the divorce decree. ...

Cassidy Matter

Respondent represented Deborah Cassidy in municipal court in August and September of 1999 on a charge of driving while under the influence of alcohol. Respondent engaged in a "pattern of procrastination" in a "straightforward municipal court matter." She failed to resolve the case timely, made multiple "last-minute requests for adjournment," repeatedly failed to give the municipal court sufficient advance notice of her inability to attend hearings, and misrepresented that she had received no discovery, when, in fact, she had received at least a portion of it. Respondent also "failed to act responsibly in representing her client's interests," which resulted in the issuance of a warrant for her client's arrest. ...

Eckrich Matter

Respondent represented her husband, Joseph C. Eckrich, on a traffic summons in a municipal court matter. ...

... In this case, for no sound reason, a "simple traffic ticket" was "not resolved for almost a year." ...

Rodriguez Matter

In early 1996, respondent began representing Juan Rodriguez in a worker's compensation case as a result of a work-related injury to Rodriguez's hand. "Little happened in the case until December 1997," at which time Rodriguez received from his employer's insurance carrier a check for $6,212, "representing forty-nine weeks' pay reduced for a 20% permanent partial disability." Respondent had Rodriguez pay to her from those proceeds $1,578, an unearned fee that she was prohibited by statute from taking without court approval. For the next twenty-three months, respondent took little or no action, which resulted in the dismissal of the worker's compensation case in November 1999 for lack of prosecution.

A fee arbitration committee later entered an order that respondent was not entitled to any portion of the $1,578 paid to her by Rodriguez. Nevertheless, respondent "steadfastly refused to abide by that committee's determination" and did not return the unearned fee. ...

Hillenbrand Matter

In November 1997, respondent began representing Richard Hillenbrand on a disorderly persons offense in municipal court. After he was found guilty, Hillenbrand retained respondent to file an appeal *de novo* in the Superior Court. Hillenbrand gave respondent $500 in payment for the cost of the trial transcript. The municipal court warned respondent on four separate occasions that the transcript payment was due; nonetheless, respondent failed to remit payment. As a result of respondent's inexplicable conduct, the appeal was dismissed. After reinstatement of the appeal, respondent was given an extension of time in which to file a brief, and yet she still failed to do so in a timely fashion, resulting in a second dismissal. ...

Comer Matter

In January 2001, Mary Ann Comer paid respondent a $1,420 retainer to represent Elliot Milton Valentine in a criminal matter. Comer later filed a request for arbitration in connection with that fee. Respondent did not file an answer. ...

Clement Matter

In November 1999, respondent filed on behalf of Mark Clement a federal civil rights and employment discrimination action against Public Service Electric and Gas Company, Inc. (PSE & G). ...

PSE & G's counsel moved to dismiss Clement's complaint because respondent failed to allege a necessary jurisdictional component for a Title VII claim[fn] and because PSE & G was not a state actor for purposes of a Section 1983 claim.[fn] The court ordered respondent to show cause why the complaint should not be dismissed and sanctions imposed for filing a frivolous action. ... The court dismissed the complaint for failure to state a claim and imposed sanctions. ...

III.

Based on the DRB's findings of ethical violations in eleven separate matters... , the DRB found that respondent lacked diligence in seven matters; engaged in dishonest conduct, lacked candor, or engaged in conduct prejudicial to the administration of justice in seven matters;

failed to properly communicate with her clients in three matters; was grossly negligent in two matters; did not take proper steps on termination of representation in two matters; did not take required actions by a suspended attorney in two matters; knowingly disobeyed the rules of a tribunal in two matters; used a misleading professional designation in one matter; failed in safekeeping property in one matter; and brought a frivolous case in one matter. ... In the past, respondent has been admonished, reprimanded, suspended for six months, and suspended for three months for violating the Rules of Professional Conduct, in six prior matters.

... Respondent replies that she has not had a sufficient opportunity to show that she can comply with the ethical norms expected of a lawyer. She points out that in her solo practice days she did not have the guidance of a seasoned member of the bar and that she has been suspended since 2001. ...

... "[T]he purpose of the disciplinary review process is to protect the public from unfit lawyers and promote public confidence in our legal system." *In re Gallo,* 178 N.J. 115, 122, 835 A.2d 682 (2003); *see also In re Rigolosi,* 107 N.J. 192, 206, 526 A.2d 670 (1987) ("The purpose of a disciplinary proceeding, as distinguished from a criminal prosecution, is not so much to punish a wrongdoer as it is to protect the public from an untrustworthy lawyer." [(citation omitted)]). Another goal of the process is to spur a disciplined attorney, who is redeemable, to comply with the high standards that our profession demands.

The public will soon lose confidence in our legal system if those who practice law in our courts are not honest and competent. ...

Misconduct that breaches a fundamental and solemn trust, such as the knowing misappropriation of a client's funds, is itself sufficient to trigger automatic disbarment. ... However, a string of lesser, yet serious, professional improprieties within a fixed time period compounded by a long, unrepentant ethical history will also demand severe discipline. *See, e.g., In re Zeitler,* 182 N.J. 389, 392-94, 400, 866 A.2d 171 (2005) (holding that disbarment was warranted based on misconduct in three separate disciplinary matters evidencing pattern of neglect when combined with lengthy history of ethical violations dating back almost thirty years); *In re Harris,* 131 N.J. 117, 117-18, 618 A.2d 852 (1993) (ordering disbarment of attorney for conduct in ten matters involving lack of diligence, gross neglect, failure to communicate, conduct involving dishonesty, deceit, or misrepresentation, failure to safeguard client or third party property, abandonment of clients, and failure to cooperate with ethics authorities); *In re Spagnoli,* 115 N.J. 504, 505, 520, 559 A.2d 1352 (1989) (disbarring attorney for "'ethical violations spree'" that included pattern of neglect, gross negligence, lack of due diligence, failure to communicate with clients, failure to cooperate in disciplinary hearings, and failure to return files).

... We agree with the three dissenting members of the DRB who believe that respondent has crossed a line. In their dissent, they summarized the sad and hapless professional life of respondent, who "in a relatively short, ten-year career, has proven to be a completely dysfunctional attorney who has no regard for the truth. Every aspect of respondent's law practice suffers from her delinquent conduct. Innumerable clients have complained to the ethics authorities about her actions; she has repeatedly taken retainers and performed little or no work, grossly neglected legitimate claims, and lied to the clients about their cases. ..." The dissenting DRB members concluded that respondent was "beyond redemption" and recommended that she be disbarred. ... Respondent's tenure as an attorney has been marked by incompetence, deceit, and disloyalty to clients, a number of whom have been victimized by respondent. Although we take note that she has made contributions to her community and church, we cannot chance another run by respondent as an attorney. The risk to the public is too great.

The record does not allow us to find that respondent is professionally salvageable. Ultimately, we are invested with the duty of protecting the public and preserving the integrity of the legal profession. For those reasons, we must disbar respondent. ...

"What Were They Thinking?"

It may be hard to tell in any one case why a lawyer fails or refuses to communicate with a client and instead neglects the communication and maybe even the matter. Surely, in some cases the neglect involves the lawyer's distraction with other matters, perhaps other clients and cases, or personal health, family problems, or financial issues. Distraction does not excuse a failure to communicate but may help explain it. Yet an obstinate refusal to respond to client communications as in the above case, requiring clients to resort to certified mailings, begs for some deeper explanation. The lawyer in the above case was contributing to her community and church while simultaneously ignoring her clients' welfare. The power that lawyers hold over their clients' matters gives law practice an allure. For some lawyers, the allure of power translates into disregarding and disrespecting the client's authority and autonomy. In the end, though, the licensing authority does not have to explain it. It will disbar a completely dysfunctional attorney.

B. Advice and Counsel

Communication alone, though, is not enough for authentic representation. Clients look for more from their lawyers than simply the status of a matter, its material risks, and available options. Model Rule 1.4's mandate, that a lawyer communicate enough information for the client to decide, needs a counterbalance. Clients retain lawyers for candid advice based on a range of considerations, not just mechanical information about status and options. Lawyers exercise professional wisdom based on their education augmented by their experience. They have a unique ability to see all at once for their clients a range of important moral, relational, familial, economic, social, and political considerations. That ability and role of lawyers to act as genuine advisors rather than merely ciphers is what makes ABA Model Rule 2.1 one of the most important conduct rules. Model Rule 2.1 may receive short shrift in the law school classroom. It can be difficult to devise law school-exam scenarios testing the subtle but powerful principles of Model Rule 2.1 that lawyers should do more than communicate. Read an identical state version of ABA Model Rule 2.1 before considering a case addressing the extent of the duty it imposes. Consider which of lawyers' several roles the rule most reflects.

> **DELAWARE R. PROF. CONDUCT 2.1: Advisor.**
> In representing a client, a lawyer shall exercise independent professional judgment and render candid advice. In rendering advice, a lawyer may refer not only to law but to other considerations, such as moral, economic, social and political factors, that may be relevant to the client's situation.

INQUIRY

Independent Professional Judgment. Model Rule 2.1 mandates that lawyers both exercise independent judgment and render candid advice. How do these two mandates relate? Is one of these two mandates more important than the other is? Model Rule 2.1's spirit that lawyers have more to do than share information—that they are also effective advisors—finds its specific expression in the rule's first provision that lawyers must exercise independent professional judgment. To be independent, a lawyer's judgment must be free from other influences. Cases suggest that those influences can include the interest of organizations with which the lawyer works, other non-clients with whom the lawyer has a relationship, and even the lawyer's own interest. A lawyer's personal interest could affect unduly the lawyer's professional judgment. *See* In re Harper, 571 S.E.2d 292 (S.C.

2002) (nine-month suspension for advising client to invest in lawyer's development business); ABA Formal Ethics Op. 00-418 (2000) (lawyer owning stock in client's business must ensure independent judgment). The concept of independence introduces conflict-of-interest rules that we will study later in the text. For now, consider the following case showing what can happen when a lawyer fails to comply with the letter and spirit of Model Rule 2.1, by maintaining other interests.

In re Coffey's Case,
New Hampshire Supreme Court
880 A.2d 403 (2005)

DUGGAN, J.

On December 29, 2003, the Supreme Court Committee on Professional Conduct (committee) filed a petition to suspend the respondent, John J. Coffey, from the practice of law for two years. ... We adopt the referee's findings, but we conclude that the respondent's conduct warrants disbarment.

The referee found, and the record supports, the following facts. On July 9, 1998, the respondent's client, Natalie Hopkins, signed a deed conveying to the respondent property located on Ocean Boulevard in Rye. The conveyance was for a stated consideration of $50,000, which was based in part upon the respondent's estimated fee of $30,000 for handling an appeal to this court. The property had been assessed at over $200,000.

The events leading up to this conveyance began in June 1970, when Hopkins and her friends, John and Caroline Canty, purchased the Rye property as joint tenants with the right of survivorship. The property passed to Hopkins after Caroline Canty died in 1986 and John Canty died in 1991.

From 1992 to 1996, the Cantys' son, John Canty, Jr., made various claims in probate court concerning his father's estate. The respondent represented Hopkins in these proceedings and drafted her will, which bequeathed the property to John Canty, Sr.'s grandchildren. The probate court ruled in Hopkins' favor and, on appeal, we summarily affirmed the probate court's decision. [C]

Nonetheless, John Canty, Jr. continued to press his claims and sued Hopkins in 1997, claiming to have a remainder interest in the Rye property. The respondent, on Hopkins' behalf, moved to dismiss the suit on res judicata grounds. The trial court granted the motion and Canty appealed to this court. [C] ...

In May 1998, the respondent discussed the cost of the appeal with Hopkins and told her that the appeal could cost more than $30,000.

Hopkins told the respondent that she did not want to dip into her liquid assets and he proposed to take a mortgage on the Rye property as payment for her legal fees. ...

... After Hopkins indicated that she was not interested in mortgaging the property, the respondent proposed that he purchase the property.

The respondent recommended three law firms in the Portsmouth area with real estate practices to draft a deed conveying the property to the respondent. Hopkins selected Attorney Bernard Pelech, whom the respondent contacted to prepare a warranty deed conveying the property to him "largely [as] a gift, and partly for fees," subject to a life estate for Hopkins. The respondent paid Attorney Pelech for this service.

Hopkins signed the deed on July 9, 1998, in Attorney Pelech's office. The respondent was also present. Attorney Pelech testified that his understanding was that Hopkins owed the respondent $40,000 in past legal bills and that the conveyance would be in consideration for past and future legal services. The respondent's billing records indicate that Hopkins actually owed $5,305 for the work that had been done on the appeal through May 27, 1998. Attorney Pelech also was unaware that the property being conveyed was the subject matter of the pending appeal.

At the time Hopkins deeded the Rye property to the respondent, she was eighty-one years old and her mental condition was deteriorating. The referee found "overwhelming evidence" that she was "at best, mentally impaired, and at worst, suffering from dementia because of Alzheimer's [disease]." The referee also found "by clear and convincing evidence that [Ms.] Hopkins lacked the mental capacity to make an informed decision about conveying the Rye property to the respondent on July 9, 1998." In reaching this conclusion, the referee relied upon medical evidence as well as the testimony of friends, neighbors, police and nurses who had contact with Hopkins in late 1997 and the first half of 1998. ...

... Based upon these factual findings, and others set forth below, the referee found that the respondent had violated multiple Rules of Professional Conduct. The referee found that the respondent violated these rules "knowingly, as opposed to negligently and that his conduct caused injury or potential injury to [Ms.] Hopkins."

The referee found as aggravating factors Hopkins' vulnerability, the respondent's selfish motive and his substantial experience in the practice of law. As mitigating factors, the referee found the respondent's unblemished disciplinary record, his cooperation with the committee's investigation and his character and reputation. The referee recommends that the respondent be suspended from the practice of law for two years. ...

The respondent first challenges the referee's findings concerning Hopkins' mental condition. He points to evidence suggesting that any mental impairment was at an early stage... . Although there is some evidence to support the respondent's contention, there is also substantial evidence to support the referee's conclusion that Hopkins lacked the mental capacity to make an informed decision about conveying the Rye property to the respondent. We thus defer to the referee's finding on this issue. [C]

The respondent also argues that there was "substantial evidence" that Hopkins intended to convey the Rye property to him as a gift. He argues that Hopkins had the mental capacity to make this gift based upon the testimony of Donna Williams, an elderly protection worker at the New Hampshire Department of Health and Human Services, and Attorney Pelech's assessment that Hopkins understood the nature of the transaction.

Although the respondent testified that Hopkins proposed to convey the property to him as a gift, the referee found this testimony "not credible" for two reasons. First, unlike many other conversations with Hopkins, the respondent had no handwritten notes concerning their discussions of the cost of the appeal and alternative methods for payment. Second, [Hopkins' neighbor Mary Lou] Lannon testified that Hopkins told her the respondent wanted to buy her home. Lannon's testimony was corroborated by an entry in her personal journal on May 12, 1998, noting that Hopkins told her that the respondent wanted to purchase the Rye property. Thus, the respondent's claim that Hopkins intended to convey the Rye property to him as a gift is not compelled by the record. ...

To the extent that the respondent asserts that he was "absolutely unaware" of Hopkins' deteriorating mental condition, the referee found by clear and convincing evidence that this was by choice and that the respondent turned a "blind eye" towards Hopkins' mental condition. ...

The third issue raised by the respondent is whether there was sufficient evidence to support the referee's finding that his estimated and actual fee for handling the appeal was "clearly excessive" under Rule 1.5(a). ...

The referee relied upon the testimony of the committee's expert, Attorney Elizabeth Cazden, who has handled numerous appeals, including fifty-four reported decisions. Attorney Cazden testified that a reasonable fee for the Canty appeal would be in the "five to ten thousand dollar range" but could be as much as $12,000. ...

Review of the respondent's billing records showed that he billed 225 hours to write the brief, including "day after day after day of anywhere from ten to eighteen hours," and eighty-five hours to prepare for the oral argument. During his two-week vacation in July 1998, the respondent billed forty-nine hours reviewing twenty-four cases cited in the appellant's brief while he was out of town without access to research facilities. The respondent admitted that his billing records reflect a combination of his hours and his paralegal's and secretary's time and that all of the time was billed at the rate of $175 per hour. Attorney Cazden concluded that both the estimated fee of $30,000 and the actual fee of $64,242.89 charged for the appeal were clearly excessive. ...

We thus reject the respondent's contention that Hopkins had the mental capacity to deed the Rye property to him as a gift and that he did not know that her mental condition had deteriorated at the time of the conveyance. We adopt the referee's findings that the respondent violated the following Rules of Professional Conduct: ... Rule 2.1 by failing to exercise independent professional judgment in rendering advice to his client... .

We agree with the referee that there are two mitigating factors present in this case; however, we do not ascribe them significant weight. ...

With regard to aggravating factors, we agree that the respondent acted selfishly by charging excessive fees and entering into a transaction with his client, the terms of which were unreasonable to her. The respondent's conduct was particularly egregious in light of Hopkins' vulnerability due to her declining mental health. We agree with the referee that substantial experience in the practice of law is an additional aggravating factor. [Cc] Furthermore, the respondent has not accepted responsibility for his ethical violations, but has instead maintained that he followed the proper procedure in arranging for Hopkins to deed the Rye property to him as a gift. [C] We find that these important aggravating factors justify an increase in the level of sanction recommended.

In light of the serious injury suffered by Hopkins and the significant aggravating factors present in this case, we disagree with the referee that a two-year suspension is an adequate sanction. Rather, we conclude that disbarment is necessary for the protection of the public and the preservation of the integrity of the legal profession. [C] The conduct of a lawyer who selfishly takes advantage of an elderly, mentally ill client by charging an exorbitant fee and then relies upon less than forthright testimony to defend his conduct requires disbarment. Accordingly, the respondent is hereby disbarred and is

ordered to reimburse the committee for all of its expenses, including legal fees, incurred in investigating and prosecuting this matter. [C]
   So Ordered.

INQUIRY

Insurance Counsel. Another area (beyond self-interest) where lawyers find problems offering their clients independent judgment is in representing insured clients at the request and cost of insurers. Insurance policies tend to give liability insurers the right to choose counsel. Because insurers owe insureds obligations to defend and indemnify, insurers have the greater financial interest in selecting lawyers whose skill set and fee structure meets the insurer's requirements. Those lawyers will often have a long-term professional relationship with the insurer but no prior or anticipated future relationship with the insured client. The insurance policies also often give the insurer sole right to determine settlement. The insurer's settlement authority means that although the lawyer's client is the insured, the insurer often decides the litigation's outcome. If the lawyer takes instructions from the insurer on settlement decisions, then the lawyer may also listen to the insurer on how to conduct the defense. Problems arise in that in most cases, the insured, not the insurer, is the defendant with the liability, and insurance policies have limits. The insurer may pressure defense counsel to limit defense costs because the insurer has low policy limits to risk or for other reasons. If limited representation results in a verdict in excess of the policy limits, then the insured client has lost because of the lawyer's failure to exercise the independent judgment ABA Model Rule 2.1 on advice, ABA Model Rule 1.7(a) on conflicts of interest, and ABA Model Rule 5.4(c) on lawyer independence (rules we study later) all require. Problems can also arise when there are coverage issues, in which event the lawyer retained by the insurer to represent the insured must not advise the insurer regarding whether there is coverage. *See* Swiss Reinsurance America Corp. v. Roetzel & Andress, 837 N.E.2d 1215 (2005) (insurer has no standing to sue retained counsel following disputed representation). Consider the following opinion holding, like ABA FORMAL ETHICS OP. 01-421 (2001), that lawyers not impair their independent judgment because of an insurer's influence.

In re Rules of Prof. Conduct and Insurer Imposed Billing Rules and Procedures,

Montana Supreme Court
2 P.3d 806 (2000)

Justice W. WILLIAM LEAPHART delivered the Opinion of the Court.

¶1 In an original application for declaratory judgment, Petitioners assert that insurer-imposed billing rules and procedures violate the Rules of Professional Conduct. ...

Discussion ...

¶15 Rule 2.1 provides in part: "**Advisor.** In representing a client, a lawyer shall exercise independent professional judgment and render candid advice." ...

¶16 In the present case, the parties do not dispute that insurers' billing and practice rules typically "impose conditions [upon an attorney appointed by an insurer to represent an insured] limiting or directing the scope and extent of the representation of his or her client." ...

¶17 As a representative set of litigation guidelines, we briefly consider the guidelines submitted by the St. Paul Companies (hereafter, St. Paul)[... under] St. Paul's Litigation Management Plan (hereafter, the Plan).... .

¶18 St. Paul promotes a "team" approach to litigation in which each member has distinct responsibilities. The claim professional is "responsible for disposition of claims, whether in suit or not. We expect the St. Paul claim professional to take the lead in initiating settlement negotiations... . We also expect the claim professional to have significant input into development of the litigation strategy (i.e., settle or try)." The Plan also "recognizes that defense counsel's primary responsibility and obligation are to protect and further the interests of the insured in the conduct of the litigation. Our goal is to cooperate with the insured and defense counsel to achieve the best result possible."

¶19 However, the Plan states that "[m]otion practice, discovery and research are items that have historically caused us some concern and which we plan to monitor closely. While we foresee very few differences of opinion, *we require that defense counsel secure the consent of the claim professional prior to scheduling depositions, undertaking research, employing experts or preparing motions*" (emphasis added).

¶20 Thus, the Plan expressly requires prior approval before a defense attorney may undertake to schedule depositions, conduct research, employ experts, or prepare motions. The Plan concludes that "[w]e understand that any conflicts between the St. Paul Litigation Management Plan and the exercise of your independent judgment to protect the interests of the insured must be resolved in favor of the insured. We expect, however, to be given an opportunity to resolve any such conflicts with you before you take any action that is in substantial contravention of the Plan." ...

¶37 Respondents argue vigorously that the interests of an insurer and an insured usually coincide and that most litigation is settled within an insured's coverage limits. These arguments gloss over the stark reality that the relationship between an insurer and insured is permeated with potential conflicts. [Cc] In cases where an insured's exposure exceeds his insurance coverage, where the insurer provides a defense subject to a reservation of rights, and where an insurer's obligation to indemnify its insured may be excused because of a policy defense, there are potential conflicts of interest.

¶38 We reject Respondents' implicit premise that the Rules of Professional Conduct need not apply when the interests of insurers and insureds coincide. The Rules of Professional Conduct have application in all cases involving attorneys and clients. Moreover, whether the interests of insurers and insureds coincide can best be determined with the perfect clarity of hindsight. Before the final resolution of any claim against an insured, there clearly exists the potential for conflicts of interest to arise. Further, we reject the suggestion that the contractual relationship between insurer and insured supersedes or waives defense counsels' obligations under the Rules of Professional Conduct. We decline to recognize a vast exception to the Rules of Professional Conduct that would sanction relationships colored with the appearance of impropriety in order to accommodate the asserted economic exigencies of the insurance market. [C] We hold that under the Rules of Professional Conduct, the insured is the *sole* client of defense counsel.

¶39 We caution, however, that this holding should not be construed to mean that defense counsel have a "blank check" to escalate litigation costs nor that defense counsel need not ever consult with insurers. ... Nor, finally, should our holding be taken to signal that defense counsel cannot be held accountable for their work.

¶40 Respondents argue further, however, that even if an insurer is not a co-client of defense counsel, an insurer's control of litigation is necessary and appropriate. Respondents argue that the insurer must control the litigation in order to meet its duties to the insured to indemnify and to provide a defense. Further, Respondents argue that the insured has a good faith duty to cooperate with the insurer in defense of a claim that warrants an insurer's control of litigation, and that in any event insureds agree to insurers' control of litigation.

Respondents also argue that insureds typically contract for a limited defense that does not protect their reputational interests and that they are not entitled to unlimited expenditures on their behalf. Further, Respondents assert that insurers and insureds have "aligned" interests in minimizing litigation costs and settlements.

¶41 None of these arguments is persuasive. Animating them is the deeply flawed premise that by contract insurers and insureds may dispense with the Rules of Professional Conduct. ...

¶43 Respondents also suggest that the billing and practice rules' requirement of prior approval is not as strict as it appears, that insurers employ it to ensure that they are consulted, and that they "rarely" withhold approval. They contend that preapproval is permissible because the insurer "is entitled not to pay for services that are overpriced or unnecessary to the case."

¶44 We conclude that whether the requirement of prior approval seldom results in denials of authorization for defense counsel to perform legal services begs the question whether the requirement of prior approval violates the Rules of Professional Conduct. Without reaching the issue here, moreover, we caution further that a mere *requirement* of consultation may be indistinguishable, in its interference with a defense counsel's exercise of independent judgment and ability to provide competent representation, from a requirement of prior approval. Further, the entitlement of insurers not to pay for overpriced or unnecessary services, which Petitioners do not dispute, also begs the question whether the requirement of prior approval violates the Rules of Professional Conduct.

¶45 Finally, Respondents argue that their billing and practice rules do not interfere with defense counsels' freedom of action. As previously discussed, they suggest that when an insurer denies approval for particular actions that defense counsel propose, nothing prevents defense counsel from exercising their independent judgment and doing the very thing for which the insurer has denied approval. We reject Respondents' underlying dubious premise that the threat of withholding payment does not interfere with the independent judgment of defense counsel. The very action taken by Petitioners in seeking declaratory relief in the present case is a blunt repudiation of that speculative premise. Further, if the threat of withholding payment were quite as toothless as Respondents suggest, we doubt that they would make such a threat, let alone that they would expressly incorporate it in their billing and practice rules. ...

¶47 We conclude that the requirement of prior approval fundamentally interferes with defense counsels' exercise of their *independent* judgment.... Further, prior approval creates a substantial appearance of impropriety in its suggestion that it is insurers rather than defense counsel who control the day to day details of a defense. ...

¶51 We hold that defense counsel in Montana who submit to the requirement of prior approval violate their duties under the Rules of Professional Conduct to exercise their independent judgment and to give their undivided loyalty to insureds. [Cc] ...

¶78 We [further] hold that disclosure by defense counsel of detailed descriptions of professional services to third-party auditors without first obtaining the contemporaneous fully informed consent of insureds violates client confidentiality under the Rules of Professional Conduct.

———————

INQUIRY

Candid Advice. ABA Model Rule 2.1's other mandate, in addition to giving independent advice, is to give candid advice. To be candid is to be open, to the point, and even blunt. One can be sensitive to the client's situation, but one should not sugar coat or gloss advice. Clients need to hear truth from their lawyer because they may not be hearing it from anyone else. Comment [1] to Model Rule 2.1 puts it plainly:

> A client is entitled to straightforward advice expressing the lawyer's honest assessment. Legal advice often involves unpleasant facts and alternatives that a client may be disinclined to confront. In presenting advice, a lawyer endeavors to sustain the client's morale and may put advice in as acceptable a form as honesty permits. However, a lawyer should not be deterred from giving candid advice by the prospect that the advice will be unpalatable to the client.

The problem that some lawyers have in giving candid advice is that lawyers want to help and get paid to help clients, but some clients a lawyer cannot help in some situations. Consider for example the discipline case of In re O'Connor, 553 N.E.2d 481 (Ind. 1990), in which the court approved disbarment of a lawyer who over-promised that he would gain the release from prison of the client's son who was simply not eligible for release. As you read the following case, consider the role of discipline in these candid-advice cases.

In re Harrison
South Carolina Supreme Court
587 S.E.2d 105 (2003)

PER CURIAM:

In this attorney disciplinary matter, respondent and the Office of Disciplinary Counsel have entered into an Agreement for Discipline by Consent... .   In the agreement, respondent admits misconduct and consents to the imposition of a thirty day suspension from the practice of law. We accept the agreement and suspend respondent from the practice of law for thirty days.[fn]   The facts, as set forth in the agreement, are as follows.

Facts

Respondent was retained to represent a client and her children with regard to injuries sustained in an automobile accident. Respondent failed to reduce the contingency fee agreement to writing.

Over a period of four years, respondent never communicated in writing with the client and only had three meetings with the client. The client initiated all contact with respondent regarding her case.

Within three months of agreeing to represent the client, respondent learned that the client's physicians did not support the contention that the client's injuries were caused by the car accident. However, respondent failed to render candid advice to the client regarding the merits of her case.   When the client contacted respondent to inquire about the status of her case, respondent repeatedly told her he was working on the case and, on one occasion, told her the case was "on the docket." Respondent failed to inform the client of the applicable statute of limitations. When the client finally confronted respondent about the lack of progress with her case, respondent informed her that he had never filed the lawsuit because he and the client "would be laughed out of court."

Respondent's deceit and misrepresentation prevented the client from seeking competent legal advice and making an informed decision regarding the merits of her case. As a result of respondent's inaction and failure to render timely legal advice, the client has been barred from any recovery for herself or her children due to the expiration of the statute of limitations.

Law

Respondent admits that by his conduct he has violated ... : Rule 1.3 (a lawyer shall act with reasonable diligence and promptness in representing a client); Rule 1.4 (a lawyer shall explain a matter to the extent reasonably necessary to permit the client to make informed decisions regarding the representation, keep the client reasonably informed about the status of the matter, and promptly comply with reasonable requests for information); ... Rule 2.1 (in representing a client, a lawyer shall exercise independent professional judgment and render candid advice); ... and Rule 8.4(a) (it is professional misconduct for a lawyer to violate the Rules of Professional Conduct). ...

Conclusion

We hereby accept the Agreement for Discipline by Consent and suspend respondent from the practice of law in this state for thirty days. ...

DEFINITE SUSPENSION.

INQUIRY

Broader Advice. Recall Model Rule 2.1's admonition to include moral, economic, social, political, and other advice as appropriate. Giving broader advice than simply what the law requires, permits, or prohibits depends on the broader perspective that we gain from studying human and organizational behavior in the rich context of our law practices. It can also require fortitude and courage. An example is the *Linares* case in which the lawyer for Rush-Presbyterian St. Luke's Hospital in Chicago advised physicians not to remove life support for a young child in a permanet long-term non-recoverable vegetative state, even though the parents authorized it, physicians supported it, law likely authorized it, and there was no genuine risk. *See* David A. Hyman, *When and Why Lawyers Are Problems*, 57 DEPAUL L.REV. 267, 277-278 (2008). Mounting medical and legal costs led the child's father to enter the hospital unit with a gun, disconnect the child's respirator, allow the child to die in his arms, and then surrender his gun—all likely occasioned by the hospital lawyer's hesitation to consider anything other than potential legal risks. The prosecutor then sought first-degree-murder charges against the grieving father, again likely considering only what the law might permit, while missing the larger social and political context. The jury refused understandably to indict the father, and citizens later voted the prosecutor out of office, ending an imbroglio begun by the hospital lawyer's hesitation. Comment [2] to Model Rule 2.1 gives the moral to this sad story, that "[a]dvice couched in narrow legal terms may be of little value to a client, especially where practical considerations, such as cost or effects on other people, are predominant."

C. Organization as Client

When studying how a lawyer must communicate with a client and do so giving independent and candid advice drawing on a range of factors, one other consideration arises. When an organization is the client, the lawyer must distinguish the client from the communication. Lawyers communicate with organization clients through organization representatives including company presidents, board members, department heads, and managers. The representatives, though, are not the lawyer's client. The lawyer must ensure in those situations that the representatives know that the lawyer's client is the organization. The lawyer must keep the organization's interests ahead of the individual interests of its representatives, particularly where those interests begin to conflict. If you have not taken a business-organizations course, then you may not fully appreciate that the law considers a corporation to be a legal person. The law considers the organization as distinct from the individuals who operate it. That concept of the organization as a distinct legal person holds as true for the professional conduct rules as it does in other areas. Consider a similar state version of ABA Model Rule 1.13, Subrule (a) of which addresses that fundamental concept.

> **ARIZONA R. PROF. CONDUCT 1.13: Organization as Client.**
> (a) A lawyer employed or retained by an organization represents the organization acting through its duly authorized constituents.
> (b) If a lawyer for an organization knows that an officer, employee or other person associated with the organization is engaged in action, intends to act or refuses to act in a matter related to the representation that is a violation of a legal obligation to the organization, or a violation of law that reasonably might be imputed to the organization, and that is likely to result in substantial injury to the organization, the lawyer shall proceed as is reasonably necessary in the best interest of the organization. Unless the lawyer reasonably believes that it is not necessary in the best interest of the organization to do so, the lawyer shall refer the matter to higher authority in the organization, including, if warranted by the circumstances, to the highest authority that can act on behalf of the organization as determined by applicable law.
> (c) Except as provided in paragraph (d), if
> (1) despite the lawyer's efforts in accordance with paragraph (b) the highest authority that can act on behalf of the organization insists upon or fails to address in a timely and appropriate manner an action or refusal to act, that is clearly a violation of law, and
> (2) the lawyer reasonably believes that the violation is reasonably certain to result in substantial injury to the organization,
> then the lawyer may reveal information relating to the representation whether or not Rule 1.6 permits such disclosure, but only if and to the extent the lawyer reasonably believes necessary to prevent substantial injury to the organization.

(d) Paragraph (c) shall not apply with respect to information relating to a lawyer's representation of an organization to investigate an alleged violation of law, or to defend the organization or an officer, employee or other constituent associated with the organization against a claim arising out of an alleged violation of law.

(e) A lawyer who reasonably believes that he or she has been discharged because of the lawyer's actions taken pursuant to paragraphs (b) or (c), or who withdraws under circumstances that require or permit the lawyer to take action under either of those paragraphs, shall proceed as the lawyer reasonably believes necessary to assure that the organization's highest authority is informed of the lawyer's discharge or withdrawal.

(f) In dealing with an organization's directors, officers, employees, members, shareholders or other constituents, a lawyer shall explain the identity of the client when the lawyer knows or reasonably should know that the organization's interests are adverse to those of the constituents with whom the lawyer is dealing.

(g) A lawyer representing an organization may also represent any of its directors, officers, employees, members, shareholders or other constituents, subject to the provisions of ER 1.7. If the organization's consent to the dual representation is required by ER 1.7, the consent shall be given by an appropriate official of the organization other than the individual who is to be represented, or by the shareholders.

INQUIRY

Authorized Constituents. Model Rule 1.13(a)'s phrase that a lawyer represents the organization as it acts through "duly authorized constituents" is key. Lawyers must have some individual or group of individuals with whom to communicate when representing an organization, particularly on the terms and scope of the lawyer's retention but also to make decisions for the organization based on the lawyer's information. Neither Model Rule 1.13 nor its official Comments identify those constituents with whom a lawyer may communicate and on whom a lawyer may rely. State agency law and the laws that govern corporations, partnerships, and other organizational forms determine who is an authorized constituent. Depending on that law, those persons may be only the company president or general counsel, or they may be subordinate employees whom the organization designates to handle the assigned matter. The important points are to be sure that you communicate with the authorized representative, communicate confidential information only to the authorized representative, and accept instructions only from the authorized representative. Another important point reflected in Model Rule 1.13(f) is that you ensure that those persons know that you represent the company, not them. For instance, your duty of confidentiality addressed in the next section runs to the client organization, not its representative. You may have to share the representative's information with other organization constituents for the good of the organization, even if the representative would prefer that you keep it confidential with them.

Reporting Up. Following the Enron and Worldcom collapses, Congress enacted the Sarbanes-Oxley Act legislation that, among other things, requires professionals to report certain wrongdoing within a publicly traded corporation up through the corporate hierarchy to responsible corporate managers. This legislation in effect federalized Model Rule 1.13's similar duties. In fact, the American Bar Association patterned Model Rule 1.13's amendments after the Sarbanes-Oxley Act. Compare the Sarbanes-Oxley Act's lawyer provisions below with Model Rule 1.13 above.

> **15 U.S.C. §7245: Rules of professional responsibility for attorneys.**
> Not later than 180 days after July 30, 2002, the Commission shall issue rules, in the public interest and for the protection of investors, setting forth minimum standards of professional conduct for attorneys appearing and practicing before the Commission in any way in the representation of issuers, including a rule—
> **(1)** requiring an attorney to report evidence of a material violation of securities law or breach of fiduciary duty or similar violation by the company or any agent thereof, to the chief legal counsel or the chief executive officer of the company (or the equivalent thereof); and
> **(2)** if the counsel or officer does not appropriately respond to the evidence (adopting, as necessary, appropriate remedial measures or sanctions with respect to the violation), requiring the attorney to report the evidence to the audit committee of the board of directors of the issuer or to another committee of the board of directors comprised solely of directors not employed directly or indirectly by the issuer, or to the board of directors.

Reporting Out. When the Securities Exchange Commission issued rules as Congress directed, it added the provision reflected in Model Rule 1.13(c) permitting a lawyer to report out an unaddressed material violation within a publicly traded corporation. *See* 17 C.F.R. §205.3(d). Both Model Rule 1.13 and the Commission's regulations under Sarbanes-Oxley permit lawyers to report unaddressed corporate wrongdoing to regulators if necessary. Neither the model rule nor the regulations *require* lawyers to do so. Can you articulate why a lawyer must report up but only may (rather than must) report out? Interestingly, while some states accept that the federal law and regulations preempt state licensing laws, *see* N.C. STATE BAR ETHICS COMMN. 2005 FORMAL OPIN. NO. 9 (2006), other states disagree and would hold lawyers to the state's duty of confidentiality, *see* WASH. FORMAL ETHICS OPIN. RE: EFFECT OF SEC'S SARBANES-OXLEY REGLNS. (2003). As you consider the breadth and detail of the Commission's regulations, excerpts of which are below, see if you can discern why the Commission felt that each of its many twists and turns was necessary. Regulations tend to be experiential, not abstract. Can you imagine corporate scenarios that warranted each provision?

17 U.S.C. §205.3 Issuer as client.

(a) Representing an issuer. An attorney appearing and practicing before the Commission in the representation of an issuer owes his or her professional and ethical duties to the issuer as an organization. That the attorney may work with and advise the issuer's officers, directors, or employees in the course of representing the issuer does not make such individuals the attorney's clients.

(b) Duty to report evidence of a material violation.

(1) If an attorney, appearing and practicing before the Commission in the representation of an issuer, becomes aware of evidence of a material violation by the issuer or by any officer, director, employee, or agent of the issuer, the attorney shall report such evidence to the issuer's chief legal officer (or the equivalent thereof) or to both the issuer's chief legal officer and its chief executive officer (or the equivalents thereof) forthwith. By communicating such information to the issuer's officers or directors, an attorney does not reveal client confidences or secrets or privileged or otherwise protected information related to the attorney's representation of an issuer.

(2) The chief legal officer (or the equivalent thereof) shall cause such inquiry into the evidence of a material violation as he or she reasonably believes is appropriate to determine whether the material violation described in the report has occurred, is ongoing, or is about to occur. If the chief legal officer (or the equivalent thereof) determines no material violation has occurred, is ongoing, or is about to occur, he or she shall notify the reporting attorney and advise the reporting attorney of the basis for such determination. Unless the chief legal officer (or the equivalent thereof) reasonably believes that no material violation has occurred, is ongoing, or is about to occur, he or she shall take all reasonable steps to cause the issuer to adopt an appropriate response, and shall advise the reporting attorney thereof. ...

(3) Unless an attorney who has made a report under paragraph (b)(1) of this section reasonably believes that the chief legal officer or the chief executive officer of the issuer (or the equivalent thereof) has provided an appropriate response within a reasonable time, the attorney shall report the evidence of a material violation to:

(i) The audit committee of the issuer's board of directors;

(ii) Another committee of the issuer's board of directors consisting solely of directors who are not employed, directly or indirectly, by the issuer and are not, in the case of a registered investment company, "interested persons" as defined in section 2(a)(19) of the Investment Company Act of 1940 (15 U.S.C. 80a-2(a)(19)) (if the issuer's board of directors has no audit committee); or

(iii) The issuer's board of directors (if the issuer's board of directors has no committee consisting solely of directors who are not employed, directly or indirectly, by the issuer and are not, in the case of a registered investment company, "interested persons" as defined in section 2(a)(19) of the Investment Company Act of 1940 (15 U.S.C. 80a-2(a)(19))).

(4) If an attorney reasonably believes that it would be futile to report evidence of a material violation to the issuer's chief legal officer and chief executive officer (or the equivalents thereof) under paragraph (b)(1) of this section, the attorney may report such evidence as provided under paragraph (b)(3) of this section.

(5) An attorney retained or directed by an issuer to investigate evidence of a material violation reported under paragraph (b)(1), (b)(3), or (b)(4) of this section shall be deemed to be appearing and practicing before the Commission. ...

(d) Issuer confidences.

(1) Any report under this section (or the contemporaneous record thereof) or any response thereto (or the contemporaneous record thereof) may be used by an attorney in connection with any investigation, proceeding, or litigation in which the attorney's compliance with this part is in issue.

(2) An attorney appearing and practicing before the Commission in the representation of an issuer may reveal to the Commission, without the issuer's consent, confidential information related to the representation to the extent the attorney reasonably believes necessary:

(i) To prevent the issuer from committing a material violation that is likely to cause substantial injury to the financial interest or property of the issuer or investors;

(ii) To prevent the issuer, in a Commission investigation or administrative proceeding from committing perjury, proscribed in 18 U.S.C. 1621; suborning perjury, proscribed in 18 U.S.C. 1622; or committing any act proscribed in 18 U.S.C. 1001 that is likely to perpetrate a fraud upon the Commission; or

(iii) To rectify the consequences of a material violation by the issuer that caused, or may cause, substantial injury to the financial interest or property of the issuer or investors in the furtherance of which the attorney's services were used.

Dual Representation. Model Rule 1.13(g) permits a lawyer to represent simultaneously an organization and one or more of its directors, officers, employees, members, shareholders or other constituents, but subject to the conflicts-of-interest rule, Model Rule 1.7. *See, e.g.*, Manion v. Nagin, 394 F.3d 1062 (8th Cir. 2005) (dual representation of corporation and its executive director). Again, we will study conflicts of interest later. For now, appreciate that in some instances, the organization and its constituent will have similar interests, particularly in disputes with someone from outside of the organization. For example, when a person injured by an employee's negligent driving sues both the employee and the organization, a defense lawyer would ordinarily have no conflict in defending both the organization and the employee. A lawyer may also find no conflict in representing a corporation and its sole shareholder in a dispute with an outside entity. *See, e.g.,* United States v. Edwards, 39 F.Supp.2d 716 (M.D. La. 1999).

Divided Representation. If, on the other hand, a dispute turns inward between the organization and employee over indemnity for litigation awards and costs or other employment rights, then a single lawyer could ordinarily not represent both the organization and the employee. *See, e.g.,* Home Care Indus. Inc. v. Murray, 154 F.Supp.2d 861 (D. N.J. 2001) (law firm disqualified from representing corporation in severance dispute with former CEO after advising former CEO); *see also* Campellone v. Cragan, 910 So.2d 363 (Fla. Ct. App. 2005) (lawyer disqualified from representing both corporation and majority shareholder in dispute with minority shareholder). Even experienced and sophisticated attorneys can have trouble determining whom they represent, discerning dual and divided allegiance, and making sound judgments regarding duly authorized constituents. Consider that Detroit City Council members submitted the following resolution on the way to Mayor Kwame Kilpatrick's resignation and imprisonment on state and federal convictions. The courts eventually ordered public disclosure of the materials the City's Law Department withheld from the City Council when obtaining Council approval of an $8.5 million settlement of an appeal in the trial in which Kilpatrick had committed perjury.

Resolution submitted by Council Members
Brenda Jones and Kwame Kenyatta
(February 2008)

WHEREAS Recent events have transpired that resulted in serious allegations that the Mayor and members of his administration have engaged in conduct which may include a breach of the public trust and misuse of public funds; and

WHEREAS The Detroit City Council is the legislative branch of the City charged with fiscal oversight and a fiduciary obligation to the citizens of Detroit; and

WHEREAS The City of Detroit Law Department is headed by the Corporation Counsel and is mandated by the Detroit City Charter, Section 6-403, to defend all actions or proceedings against the City and to obtain the consent of the City Council to settle all civil litigation; and

WHEREAS Rule 1.13 of the Michigan Rules of Professional Conduct (MRPC) requires that a lawyer employed to represent an entity represents the entity as distinct from its individual officials, directors, or employees; therefore the Corporation Counsel's obligation of representation is to the City as the entity, including both the executive and legislative branches of government; and

WHEREAS On September 11, 2007, a unanimous jury determined that Mayor Kilpatrick and the City violated the Whistleblower's

Protection Act and awarded plaintiffs Gary Brown and Harold Nelthrope $6.5 million (six million, five hundred thousand dollars); and

WHEREAS The Mayor adamantly vowed to appeal the verdict but abruptly changed course following facilitation on October 17, 2007, and requested City Council's approval to pay $8,400,000.00 (eight million, four hundred thousand dollars) in settlement of the plaintiffs' claims (including $400,000.00 to Walter Harris for a related claim yet to come to trial); and

WHEREAS In reliance upon information provided by the Corporation Counsel, City Council accepted the recommendation as being in the best interest of the citizens, and voted to approve the settlement on October 23, 2007; and

WHEREAS City Council has subsequently learned that critical information/documents relative to the recommendation for settlement was not disclosed at the time of the request for City Council approval; and

WHEREAS The withheld information/documents are vital to the fulfillment of City Council's Charter mandated obligations generally, and its role pursuant to section 6-403, specifically, mandating that no civil litigation of the City may be settled without the consent of the Council, and impacts upon ongoing related issues of serious import to the City; and

WHEREAS This information was known and available to the corporation counsel at the time of settlement and thereafter, and as revealed in the recent Freedom of Information Act (FOIA) litigation, [c], some of it has been obtained by the local press but has yet to be published or provided to the City Council; and

WHEREAS Pursuant to a ruling by the Wayne County Circuit Court on February 5, 2008[,] ordering disclosure of the information/documents, the subject information/documents are being held under seal of the court pending the termination of any appeal(s) and/or the lifting of a court-ordered stay; and

WHEREAS The City's decision to pursue appeal of the Wayne County Circuit Court's ruling will likely result in the information/documents remaining under seal for an indefinite period of time and further delay in disclosing the subject information/documents to City Council will seriously undermine the Council's ability to make informed decisions with respect to pending and potential legal matters; and

WHEREAS City Council, as the legislative branch of the City with fiscal responsibility and authority to settle litigation, and as an indivisible part of the City which is the defendant in the aforementioned litigation, has an absolute right to receive and review the subject information/documents; NOW THEREFORE BE IT

RESOLVED That the Corporation Counsel, including any and all outside legal counsel retained by the City or the Mayor in defense of [the civil lawsuit against the City and mayor] shall immediately disclose to the Detroit City Council all information/documents identified by the Wayne County Circuit Court in its February 5, 2008 decision in [the FOIA litigation] as well as reproductions of electronic communications between the Mayor and/or members of his administration transmitted utilizing City of Detroit communication devices as referenced in pleadings in the above-referenced matter; and **BE IT FURTHER**

RESOLVED That consistent with the powers and duties prescribed to Detroit City Council in ... the Charter, Corporation Counsel and all outside legal counsel retained by the City or the Mayor in defense of [the lawsuit] are requested to appear for a closed session of Detroit City Council... and to produce **all** documents at issue... .

D. Confidentiality

As the foregoing example suggests, lawyers could neither communicate with clients nor give candid advice as the above Model Rules 1.4 and 2.1 require, unless conduct rules simultaneously bound lawyers to confidentiality regarding their clients' matters. McClure v. Thompson, 323 F.3d 1233 (9th Cir. 2003) (confidentiality is "critical component of reasonable representation). A lawyer's duty of confidentiality differs from the attorney-client privilege. The attorney-client privilege protects confidential attorney-client communications from compelled disclosure in litigation. The attorney-client privilege is a rule of evidence connected to litigation. The lawyer's duty of confidentiality is far broader. It is a conduct rule regarding all communications, whether or not confidential, and whether or not litigation-related. See Spratley v. State Farm Mut. Ins. Co., 78 P.3d 603n.2 (Utah 2003) (confidentiality remains after client waives privilege). For example, the duty of confidentiality prevents a lawyer from chatting with a client's roommate about a client's matter, when the roommate instead of the client answers the client's telephone. See People v. Hohertz, 102 P.3d 1019 (Colo. Office Presiding Disc. Judge 2004) (attorney disbarred for violations including disclosure of confidences to client's roommate). The duty of confidentiality bars disclosure even when the disclosures are already public information. See, e.g., State ex rel. Okla. Bar Assn. v. Chappell, 93 P.3d 25 (Okla.

2004) (violation of confidentiality to disclose prior criminal charge). The duty of confidentiality binds a lawyer not to speak about a client's matter unless authorized by client or rule to do so, even after the client relationship has ended. Read a similar state version of ABA Model Rule 1.6, followed by a case illustrating that a lawyer must not deprive others of evidence that the lawyer holds confidential.

INDIANA R. PROF. CONDUCT 1.6: Confidentiality of Information.
(a) A lawyer shall not reveal information relating to representation of a client unless the client gives informed consent, the disclosure is impliedly authorized in order to carry out the representation or the disclosure is permitted by paragraph (b).

(b) A lawyer may reveal information relating to the representation of a client to the extent the lawyer reasonably believes necessary:

(1) to prevent reasonably certain death or substantial bodily harm;

(2) to prevent the client from committing a crime or from committing fraud that is reasonably certain to result in substantial injury to the financial interests or property of another and in furtherance of which the client has used or is using the lawyer's services;

(3) to prevent, mitigate or rectify substantial injury to the financial interests or property of another that is reasonably certain to result or has resulted from the client's commission of a crime or fraud in furtherance of which the client has used the lawyer's services;

(4) to secure legal advice about the lawyer's compliance with these Rules;

(5) to establish a claim or defense on behalf of the lawyer in a controversy between the lawyer and the client, to establish a defense to a criminal charge or civil claim against the lawyer based upon conduct in which the client was involved, or to respond to allegations in any proceeding concerning the lawyer's representation of the client; or

(6) to comply with other law or a court order.

(c) In the event of a lawyer's physical or mental disability or the appointment of a guardian or conservator of an attorney's client files, disclosure of a client's names and files is authorized to the extent necessary to carry out the duties of the person managing the lawyer's files.

People v. Meredith,
California Supreme Court
631 P.2d 46 (1981)

TOBRINER, Justice.

Defendants Frank Earl Scott and Michael Meredith appeal from convictions for the first degree murder and first degree robbery of David Wade. Meredith's conviction rests on eyewitness testimony that he shot and killed Wade. Scott's conviction, however, depends on the theory that Scott conspired with Meredith and a third defendant, Jacqueline Otis, to bring about the killing and robbery. To support the theory of conspiracy the prosecution sought to show the place where the victim's wallet was found, and, in the course of the case this piece of evidence became crucial. The admissibility of that evidence comprises the principal issue on this appeal.

At trial the prosecution called Steven Frick, who testified that he observed the victim's partially burnt wallet in a trash can behind Scott's residence. Scott's trial counsel then adduced that Frick served as a defense investigator. Scott himself had told his former counsel that he had taken the victim's wallet, divided the money with Meredith, attempted to burn the wallet, and finally put it in the trash can. At counsel's request, Frick then retrieved the wallet from the trash can. Counsel examined the wallet and then turned it over to the police.

The defense acknowledges that the wallet itself was properly admitted into evidence. The prosecution in turn acknowledges that the attorney-client privilege protected the conversations between Scott, his former counsel, and counsel's investigator. ... The issue before us, consequently, focuses upon a narrow point: whether under the circumstances of this case Frick's observation of the location of the wallet, the product of a privileged communication, finds protection under the attorney-client privilege.

This issue, one of first impression in California, presents the court with competing policy considerations. On the one hand, to deny protection to observations arising from confidential communications might chill free and open communication between attorney and client and might also inhibit counsel's investigation of his client's case. On the other hand, we cannot extend the attorney-client privilege so far that it renders evidence immune from discovery and admission merely because the defense seizes it first.

Balancing these considerations, we conclude that an observation by defense counsel or his investigator, which is the product of a privileged communication, may not be admitted unless the defense by altering or removing physical evidence has precluded the prosecution from making that same observation. In the present case the defense investigator, by removing the wallet, frustrated any possibility that the police might later discover it in the trash can. The conduct of the defense thus precluded the prosecution from ascertaining the crucial fact of the location of the wallet. Under these circumstances, the prosecution was entitled to present evidence to show the location of the wallet in the trash can; the trial court did not err in admitting the investigator's testimony. ...

On the night of April 3, 1976, Wade (the victim) and Jacqueline Otis, a friend of the defendants, entered a club known as Rich Jimmy's. Defendant Scott remained outside by a shoeshine stand. A few minutes later codefendant Meredith arrived outside the club. He told Scott he planned to rob Wade, and asked Scott to go into the club, find

Jacqueline Otis, and ask her to get Wade to go out to Wade's car parked outside the club.

In the meantime, Wade and Otis had left the club and walked to a liquor store to get some beer. Returning from the store, they left the beer in a bag by Wade's car and reentered the club. Scott then entered the club also and, according to the testimony of Laurie Ann Sam (a friend of Scott's who was already in the club), Scott asked Otis to get Wade to go back out to his car so Meredith could "knock him in the head."

When Wade and Otis did go out to the car, Meredith attacked Wade from behind. After a brief struggle, two shots were fired; Wade fell, and Meredith, witnessed by Scott and Sam, ran from the scene.

Scott went over to the body and, assuming Wade was dead, picked up the bag containing the beer and hid it behind a fence. Scott later returned, retrieved the bag, and took it home where Otis and Meredith joined him.[fn]

... James Schenk, Scott's first appointed attorney[,] ... visited Scott in jail more than a month after the crime occurred and solicited information about the murder, stressing that he had to be fully acquainted with the facts to avoid being "sandbagged" by the prosecution during the trial. In response, Scott gave Schenk the same information that he had related earlier to the police. In addition, however, Scott told Schenk something Scott had not revealed to the police: that he had seen a wallet, as well as the paper bag, on the ground near Wade. Scott said that he picked up the wallet, put it in the paper bag, and placed both behind a parking lot fence. He also said that he later retrieved the bag, took it home, found $100 in the wallet and divided it with Meredith, and then tried to burn the wallet in his kitchen sink. He took the partially burned wallet, Scott told Schenk, placed it in a plastic bag, and threw it in a burn barrel behind his house.

Schenk, without further consulting Scott, retained Investigator Stephen Frick and sent Frick to find the wallet. Frick found it in the location described by Scott and brought it to Schenk. After examining the wallet and determining that it contained credit cards with Wade's name, Schenk turned the wallet and its contents over to Detective Payne, investigating officer in the case. Schenk told Payne only that, to the best of his knowledge, the wallet had belonged to Wade. ...

Prior to trial, a third attorney, Hamilton Hintz, was appointed for Scott. Hintz unsuccessfully sought an in limine ruling that the wallet of the murder victim was inadmissible and that the attorney-client privilege precluded the admission of testimony concerning the wallet by Schenk or Frick.

At trial Frick, called by the prosecution, identified the wallet and testified that he found it in a garbage can behind Scott's residence. On cross-examination by Hintz, Scott's counsel, Frick further testified that he was an investigator hired by Scott's first attorney, Schenk, and that he had searched the garbage can at Schenk's request. Hintz later called Schenk as a witness: Schenk testified that he told Frick to search for the wallet immediately after Schenk finished talking to Scott. Schenk also stated that Frick brought him the wallet on the following day; after examining its contents Schenk delivered the wallet to the police. Scott then took the stand and testified to the information about the wallet that he had disclosed to Schenk.

The jury found both Scott and Meredith guilty of first degree murder and first degree robbery. It further found that Meredith, but not Scott, was armed with a deadly weapon. Both defendants appeal from their convictions. ...

The fundamental purpose of the attorney-client privilege is, of course, to encourage full and open communication between client and attorney. ...

In the criminal context, as we have recently observed, these policies assume particular significance.... .

Judicial decisions have recognized that the implementation of these important policies may require that the privilege extend not only to the initial communication between client and attorney but also to any information which the attorney or his investigator may subsequently acquire as a direct result of that communication. ...

... [T]he attorney-client privilege is not strictly limited to communications, but extends to protect observations made as a consequence of protected communications.[fn] We turn therefore to the question whether that privilege encompasses a case in which the defense, by removing or altering evidence, interferes with the prosecution's opportunity to discover that evidence.[fn] ...

When defense counsel alters or removes physical evidence, he necessarily deprives the prosecution of the opportunity to observe that evidence in its original condition or location. ... To extend the attorney-client privilege to a case in which the defense removed evidence might encourage defense counsel to race the police to seize critical evidence. [C] ...

We therefore conclude that whenever defense counsel removes or alters evidence, the statutory privilege does not bar revelation of the original location or condition of the evidence in question.[fn] We thus view the defense decision to remove evidence as a tactical choice. If defense counsel leaves the evidence where he discovers it, his observations derived from privileged communications are insulated from revelation. If, however, counsel chooses to remove evidence to examine or test it, the original location and condition of that evidence loses the protection of the privilege. Applying this analysis to the present case, we hold that the trial court did not err in admitting the investigator's testimony concerning the location of the wallet. ...

In other circumstances, when it is not possible to elicit such testimony without identifying the witness as the defendant's attorney or investigator, the defendant may be willing to enter a stipulation which will simply inform the jury as to the relevant location or condition of the evidence in question. When such a stipulation is proffered, the prosecution should not be permitted to reject the stipulation in the hope that by requiring defense counsel personally to testify to such facts, the jury might infer that counsel learned those facts from defendant. [C] ...

The judgment, as so modified[regarding terms of sentence], is affirmed.

BIRD, C. J., and MOSK and NEWMAN, JJ., concur.
RICHARDSON, J., concurs in the result.

INQUIRY

Implied Authorization. Obviously, lawyers do speak quite regularly about their clients' matters. For example, lawyers talk to opposing counsel and parties, judges and court staff, and expert and lay witnesses. Much of that speaking is without a client's express authorization. Model Rule 1.6(a) recognizes that a lawyer has implied authorization in those circumstances where a reasonable client would expect the lawyer to disclose client information in order to advance the client's matter. May a lawyer speak to other lawyers in the same law firm about a client's matter? Informal in-office discussion about client matters can give lawyers important review, input, evaluation, background, and context. Lawyers are wise to depend on their law partners to ensure that they maintain an objective view of a client's matter. Sharing client matters within a law firm may also be important to the management of the firm. Comment [5] to Model Rule 1.6 confirms, "Lawyers in a firm may, in the course of the firm's practice, disclose to each other information relating to a client of the firm, unless the client has instructed that particular information be confined to specified lawyers." A lawyer must generally not speak to lawyers from other firms about a client's matter without client consent. *See* Commonwealth v. Downey, 842 N.E.2d 955 (Mass. Ct. App. 2006) (violation of confidentiality for criminal-defense lawyers to wear television-production concealed microphones during trial without client's informed consent); In re Mandelman, 514 N.W.2d 11 (Wis.

1994) (discipline for sharing client files with other lawyers without client consent when seeking to transfer files to new counsel). As we will see again when studying ABA Model Rule 5.3 on lawyer supervision of non-lawyer staff, lawyers must also ensure that their non-lawyer staff do not disclose client confidences. *See* State ex rel. Okla. Bar Assn. v. McGee, 48 P.3d 787 (Okla. 2002) (discipline of lawyer for secretary revealing client information).

Preventing Bodily Harm. Model Rule 1.6(b) lists six circumstances when a lawyer may disclose information without the client's authorization. All or several of those circumstances involve disclosures that may affect the client adversely. For example, Model Rule 1.6(b)(1) permits a lawyer to reveal information necessary to prevent death or substantial bodily harm. The implication is that the client may have injured someone who needs rescue or may be about to do so. The lawyer's disclosure may lead directly to the client's arrest, yet Model Rule 1.6(b)(1) permits the disclosure. The lawyer's disclosure would presumably be to the potential victim or law-enforcement authorities. Consider one horrific case in which the lawyer instead disclosed the confidential information of one client of the firm to another client of the firm, purportedly to dissuade the latter client from harming the former client. The case also establishes that *any* information relating to the representation, even false information, is confidential.

In re Goebel,
Indiana Supreme Court
703 N.E.2d 1045 (1998)

... The facts are essentially undisputed. The respondent was a partner in a Crawfordsville law firm. During relevant periods, another partner ... represented a client of the firm ... in a guardianship matter. The partner sent correspondence about the guardianship proceeding to the client at 3813 East 300 South [Street] in a specified Indiana city. The mail was returned marked "No Such Street—NSS."

While the partner was representing the guardianship client, the respondent represented a client ... against criminal charges. The guardianship client's husband was a witness for the prosecution in the criminal proceeding pending against the criminal client. The criminal client informed the respondent of his intent to locate and kill the guardianship client and her husband, being aware that the respondent's firm represented her. The respondent attempted to dissuade the criminal client from doing so.

On December 16, 1993, the criminal client appeared in the respondent's law office and demanded the respondent reveal the location or address of the guardianship client. The respondent showed the envelope which had been mailed by the partner to the guardianship client at 3813 East 300 South and which had been returned with the notation "No Such Street-NSS." The criminal client copied the address. The respondent did not report the criminal client's actions to police or the guardianship client. Two days later, the criminal client murdered the guardianship client's husband at her home at the actual address of 3813 South 300 East. The criminal client was convicted of the murder and sentenced to life in prison without the possibility of parole. ...

In its petition for review, the Commission challenges the hearing officer's finding that the respondent revealed the guardianship client's returned envelope bearing the wrong address to dissuade the criminal client from committing a criminal act. ... [T]he respondent contends that the information he gave the criminal client was false and, therefore, not within the scope of Prof. Cond. R. 1.6(a). "[I]nformation relating to representation of a client," as stated in Prof. Cond. R. 1.6(a), is a broad definition and has been construed to include all information relating to the representation regardless of the source." ABA Comm. on Ethics and Professional Responsibility, Formal Op. 94-380 (1994). Thus, "information" may include the identity or whereabouts of a client. Comment, *American Bar Association Annotated Model Rules of Professional Conduct,* p. 87. The respondent provided information gained during the course of the representation—an address that not only expressly indicated where the guardianship client could *not* be located, but which also contained a very strong suggestion of where the guardianship client *could* be located-to another person without the guardianship client's consent. As such, he wrongfully disclosed information contrary to the dictates of Prof. Cond. R. 1.6(a). Therefore, the next and more difficult issue is whether his disclosure was excepted from the duty of confidentiality imposed by the rule. The Commission argues that it was not.

The evidence reveals that the criminal client had been searching for the guardianship client's home for months and had even traveled to Bowling Green, Kentucky, in search of it. The criminal client had told the respondent he wanted to kill the guardianship client, her husband, and the two police investigators handling the criminal client's case. During a police interview after the murder, the respondent expressed his fear of the criminal client and revealed that the criminal client had threatened both the respondent and his family.

Professional Conduct Rule 1.6(b) provides that a lawyer may reveal information relating to the representation of a client to the extent the lawyer believes is reasonably necessary to prevent the client from committing any criminal act. The respondent's counsel claimed during final arguments before the hearing officer, and the hearing officer found, that the respondent revealed the address on the envelope to "dissuade" his client from committing murder. However, the colloquy between the respondent and police during the respondent's interview after the murder does not support that conclusion:

> ...
> Police: ... [D]id [the criminal client] come to your office and was shown A. [sic] an address where uh [the guardianship client] was reportedly living at [...]?
> Respondent: I believe, I think so. I'm almost positive. I think what the conversation was. Was he pressing me to find out the address and uh I ask [the partner] about it and she said every piece of mail that she had sent to the address given to her by [the guardianship client] had been returned and I believe I showed him an envelope to substantiate that I didn't know her address by showing him an envelope with whatever address it was.
> Police: Did he write that address down?
> Respondent: I think he did. Yes. ... Pretty sure he did.
> Police: All the information that he was trying to gather from you and other sources was for what purpose?
> Respondent: To track down [the guardianship client's husband], it appeared.
> Police: To do what?
> Respondent: To get rid of him. I assume.
> Police: To kill him?
> Respondent: Yes. I think so.
> **Commission's Exhibit 1, at pp. 8-9.**

After giving the information to the criminal client, the respondent did not notify local police, the sheriff, or the guardianship client.[fn] Both the content of the respondent's interview with police and his lack of action after showing the envelope to the criminal client to prevent him from locating the guardianship client demonstrate that the respondent did not display the envelope to prevent commission of a criminal act, but rather that he did so based on the criminal client's forceful demand.[fn]   Accordingly, we find that the respondent's divulging of the information relating to his firm's representation of the guardianship client was not excepted from Rule 1.6's confidentiality requirements. We conclude that the respondent violated the rule.

Now that we have found misconduct, we must determine the appropriate sanction. ...

The respondent violated one of the foundations of the attorney-client relationship-confidentiality. A client must be able to trust her attorney to keep confidential information gained in the course of representation. ... The observance of the ethical obligation of a lawyer to hold inviolate confidential information of the client not only facilitates the full development of facts essential to proper representation of the client but also encourages individuals to seek early legal assistance. We are aware, of course, that the respondent faced very difficult circumstances when his threatening client confronted him as to the whereabouts of the guardianship client. While the respondent's fear for his own safety is understandable under the circumstances, such fear did not justify his revelation of confidential information. ... That the respondent revealed the information in this instance under conditions of severe duress is a strong and compelling mitigating factor, but does not change the fact that he violated the rule. ...

... [T]he respondent was motivated by self interest in revealing the information, albeit understandably so for his own interest of self-preservation. Moreover, the information which the respondent conveyed to the criminal client could not be obtained from other sources outside that law office. ... However, we are fully aware of the very difficult situation leading to the respondent's disclosure of the confidential information and therefore conclude that a public reprimand adequately addresses the misconduct.

Accordingly, the respondent, William A. Goebel, is hereby reprimanded and admonished for the misconduct set forth in this opinion. ...

Costs of this proceeding are assessed against the respondent.

"What Were They Thinking"

The horrible outcome of the above case makes one wonder what the criminal-defense lawyer was thinking when he decided to show the returned envelope to the criminal-case client who had threatened to murder the witness client. Was it simply awful judgment combined with fear of the criminal-case client's forceful demands? Lawyers must have courage and composure, never letting a client bully the lawyer for advantage or information. Does the fact that the lawyer let the criminal-case client copy the slightly incorrect address leave a reasonable inference that the criminal-defense lawyer intended to help the client murder the witness? What should happen to the lawyer—discipline, criminal conviction, etc.—if it was the latter instead of the former? Do you think that the guardianship client was satisfied with the lawyer's reprimand after the lawyer's rule violation led directly to the murder of her husband?

INQUIRY

Mitigating Crime. Rule 1.6(b) does not *require* that a lawyer disclose client information to prevent death or substantial bodily harm. Should it? Some states do require a lawyer to disclose information necessary to prevent death or substantial bodily harm. *See, e.g.,* ILLINOIS R. PROF. CONDUCT 1.6(c). Which do you think is the better rule? Can you think of any circumstance when you would not make a disclosure to prevent a crime or the worsening of the results of a crime, relating to your legal services? If so, then consider the potential effect on your liberty, finances, career, and reputation if you did not make such a disclosure. Also, appreciate the challenges that some lawyers, especially criminal-defense lawyers, can face in these situations where the victim of the client's crime may need rescue and where the client may be trying to use the lawyer to hide the crime. A lawyer's action may in that circumstance be both to save life and to prevent a death that would worsen the client's crime. Consider the following extraordinary case.

McClure v. Thompson,
United States Court of Appeals for the Ninth Circuit
323 F.3d 1233 (2003)

WILLIAM W. FLETCHER, Circuit Judge:

Oregon state prisoner Robert A. McClure appeals the district court's denial of his 28 U.S.C. §2254 habeas corpus petition challenging his jury trial conviction for three aggravated murders. McClure's original defense attorney, Christopher Mecca, placed an anonymous telephone call to law enforcement officials directing them to the locations of what turned out to be the bodies of two children whom McClure was ultimately convicted of killing. The district court rejected McClure's arguments that the disclosure constituted ineffective assistance of counsel, holding there was no breach of the duty of confidentiality and no actual conflict of interest. We affirm.

I. Background

A. Offense, Arrest and Conviction

On Tuesday, April 24, 1984, the body of Carol Jones was found in her home in Grants Pass, Oregon. She had been struck numerous times on the head, arms and hands with a blunt object. A gun cabinet in the home had been forced open and a .44 caliber revolver was missing. Two of Jones' children—Michael, age 14, and Tanya, age 10—were also missing. The fingerprints of Robert McClure, a friend of Jones, were found in the blood in the home. On Saturday, April 28, McClure was arrested in connection with the death of Carol Jones and the disappearance of the children.

That same day, McClure's mother contacted attorney Christopher Mecca and asked him to represent her son. ... McClure revealed to Mecca the separate remote locations where the children could be found. On Tuesday, May 1, Mecca, armed with a map produced during his conversations with McClure, arranged for his secretary to place an anonymous phone call to a sheriff's department... .

Later that day and the following day, sheriff's deputies located the children's bodies... . The children had each died from a single gunshot wound to the head. Mecca then withdrew from representation. ...

B. Disclosure of the Children's Whereabouts

The parties agree that Mecca and McClure met at the jail and spoke on the telephone on a number of occasions between April 28 and May 1. ...

... In his notes, Mecca wrote that McClure had initially claimed that he was "being framed" for the murder, but that he was nervous about his fingerprints being in the house. He had asked Mecca to help him remove some other potential evidence, which Mecca declined to do. ...

According to his notes, when Mecca next spoke with McClure on Monday, McClure was less adamant in his denial. ... "It was at that time," Mecca wrote, "when I realized in my own mind that he had committed the crime and the problem regarding the children intensified." Mecca wrote that he "was extremely agitated over the fact that these children might still be alive."

After a Monday night visit to the crime scene, Mecca returned to the jail to speak with McClure again, at which time he "peeled off most of the outer layers of McClure and realized that there was no doubt in my mind that he had ... killed Carol Jones." ... "[E]ach time as I would try to leave," Mecca recalled in his notes, "[McClure] would spew out other information, bits about the children, and he would do it in the form of a fantasy." Mecca wrote that he "wanted to learn from him what happened to those children." ... He told McClure "that we all have hiding places, that we all know when we go hiking or driving or something, we all remember certain back roads and remote places," and that McClure "related to me ... one place where a body might be" and then "described [where] the other body would be located." Mecca wrote that he "wasn't going to push him for anything more," but "when I tried to leave, he said, and he said it tentatively, 'would you like me to draw you a map and just give you an idea?' and I said 'Yes' and he did[.]" Mecca recorded that "at that time, I felt in my own mind the children were dead, but, of course, I wasn't sure."

Very late on Monday evening, McClure telephoned Mecca at home and said, "I know who did it." Mecca recorded in his notes that the next morning he went to meet with McClure, and asked him about this statement. McClure told Mecca that "Satan killed Carol." When Mecca asked, "What about the kids?" McClure replied, "Jesus saved the kids." Mecca wrote in his notes that this statement "hit me so abruptly, I immediately assumed that if Jesus saved the kids, that the kids are alive[.]" ...

Mecca then returned to the jail Tuesday afternoon and, according to his notes, "advised McClure that if there was any possibility that these children were alive, we were obligated to disclose that information in order to prevent, if possible, the occurrence of what could be [the elevation of] an assault to a murder, for instance. I further indicated that if he really requested psychiatric help, to help him deal with his problem, that this perhaps was the first step." "In any event," Mecca recorded in his notes, "he consented." "I arranged to have the information released anonymously to the Sheriff's Department with directions to the bodies." He noted that there was "no provable way to connect" McClure to the information, "but I think it's rather obvious from those in the know, who the information came from." ...

Mecca testified in his deposition that he thought that if the children were alive, it might relieve McClure of additional murder charges, but that the children were his main concern. ...

McClure disagreed with Mecca's account of the events leading up to the anonymous call. In testimony in both the state and federal district court proceedings, he repeatedly insisted that he did not give Mecca permission to disclose any information and that he was reassured that everything he told Mecca would remain confidential. He said Mecca pressured him into disclosing information.... .

The district court denied McClure's federal habeas petition. The court indicated that it found Mecca "highly credible" and that it disbelieved McClure. ...

McClure timely appealed. ...

McClure contends that Mecca's disclosure of McClure's confidential statements about the location of the children violated McClure's Sixth Amendment right to effective assistance of counsel. ABA Model Rule of Professional Conduct 1.6 sets forth a widely recognized duty of confidentiality: "A lawyer shall not reveal information relating to representation of a client[.]" Our legal system is premised on the strict adherence to this principle of confidentiality, and "[t]he Supreme Court has long held attorneys to stringent standards of loyalty and fairness with respect to their clients." *Damron v. Herzog*, 67 F.3d 211, 214 (9th Cir.1995). There are few professional relationships "involving a higher trust and confidence than that of attorney and client," and "few more anxiously guarded by the law, or governed by sterner principles of morality and justice." *Id.* (quoting *Stockton v. Ford*, 52 U.S. (11 How.) 232[] (1850)).

As critical as this confidential relationship is to our system of justice, the duty to refrain from disclosing information relating to the representation of a client is not absolute. ... First, a lawyer may reveal confidential information if "the client consents after consultation."

Second, "[a] lawyer may reveal such information to the extent the lawyer reasonably believes necessary to prevent the client from committing a criminal act that the lawyer believes is likely to result in imminent death or substantial bodily harm[.]" ABA Model Rule of Professional Conduct 1.6(b)(1) (1983). The relevant provisions of the Oregon Code of Professional Responsibility echo both the general principle of confidentiality and these particular exceptions. [Cc][fn] ...

McClure argues that Mecca rendered constitutionally ineffective assistance because he breached his duty of confidentiality by not obtaining McClure's informed consent before disclosure. ...

... [T]he mere fact of consent is not sufficient to excuse what would otherwise be a breach of the duty of confidentiality. Consent must also be informed. That is, the client can provide valid consent only if there has been appropriate "consultation" with his or her attorney. Mecca's consultation with McClure regarding his consent to disclosure was addressed in the state court and district court findings. Both courts found that Mecca did not advise McClure about the potential harmful consequences of disclosure. ...

... It is not enough, as the district court suggests, that McClure "did not dissuade Mecca from his intentions" to share the map with authorities. The onus is not on the client to perceive the legal risks himself and then to dissuade his attorney from a particular course of action. ... We disagree with the district court's conclusion that this case was so exceptional that the attorney's basic consultation duties did not apply. It is precisely because the stakes were so high that Mecca had an obligation to consult carefully with his client. ...

... Nonetheless, we believe that where an attorney's or a client's omission to act could result in "imminent death or substantial bodily harm" constituting a separate and more severe crime from the one already committed, the exception to the duty of confidentiality may be triggered. ABA Model Rule 1.6(b)(1). ...

McClure argues that the statement Mecca says abruptly changed his mind about the status of the children—McClure's comment that "Jesus saved the kids"—was so vague and ambiguous that it was not a sufficient basis for a "reasonable belief" that disclosure was necessary. ...

Given the implicit factual findings of the state court, and the explicit factual findings of the district court, which are at least plausible in light of the record viewed in its entirety, [c], we disagree. ...

The district court made a number of specific findings regarding the factual basis for Mecca's belief that the children were alive. It found that only McClure knew the true facts and that he deliberately withheld them, leading Mecca to believe the children were alive. It found that McClure controlled the flow of information, and that when

Mecca informed McClure that he had an obligation to disclose the children's whereabouts if there were a chance they were alive, McClure did not tell him they were dead. ...

The district court also made specific factual findings regarding the nature of Mecca's investigation and inquiry. It found that "Mecca attempted to discern whether the children were alive" and "that Mecca investigated to the best of his ability under extremely difficult circumstances." ...

This is a close case, even after we give the required deference to the state and district courts. The choices made by McClure's counsel give us significant pause, and, were we deciding this case as an original matter, we might decide it differently. But we take as true the district court's specific factual findings as to what transpired... , and we conclude that Mecca made the disclosure "reasonably believ[ing] [it was] necessary to prevent the client from committing a criminal act that [Mecca] believe[d] [was] likely to result in imminent death or substantial bodily harm[.]" ABA Model Rule 1.6(b)(1). Mecca therefore did not violate the duty of confidentiality in a manner that rendered his assistance constitutionally ineffective. ...

For the foregoing reasons, we conclude that McClure did not receive constitutionally ineffective assistance of counsel. Accordingly, the district court's denial of McClure's petition for writ of habeas corpus is

AFFIRMED.

INQUIRY

Preventing Crime or Fraud. Model Rule 1.6(b)(2) permits a lawyer to disclose confidential client information in order to prevent a client from using the lawyer's services to commit a crime or fraud resulting in substantial loss to another. Model Rule 1.6(b)(2) does not require disclosure of past crimes or frauds. The lawyer whose client confesses in confidence does not then have a duty to disclose the confession. Model Rule 1.6(b)(3) does permit a lawyer to disclose a past client crime or fraud using the lawyer's services, to mitigate or rectify another's substantial loss. The key limitation to both Subrule 1.6(b)(2) and (3) is that the client must have used the lawyer's services to further the crime or fraud. Lawyers, in other words, need not stand mute while clients use their services to perpetrate or continue harmful crimes and frauds. Consider the following illustrative case.

In re Lane's Case,
New Hampshire Supreme Court
889 A.2d 3 (2005)

GALWAY, J.

... The record reflects the following facts. ...

... Lane & Bentley represented the estate of Robert Bennett. Dick Bennett served as the executor of the estate. The final accounting of the estate was filed in November 1993, showing a total value of $5,497, but a net balance of $0 because of expenditures. ...

Jane Bennett[, Robert Bennett's wife,] retained an attorney to prepare a will and trust agreement, which she executed in June 1993, appointing herself and [her son] Dick Bennett as co-trustees. She also provided Dick Bennett with a durable power of attorney. In June 1994, Jane Bennett moved from her residence in Keene to the Woodard Home, an assisted living facility in Keene. Around the same time, Lane became romantically involved with (Jane's daughter) Molly. In 1995, Molly and Ann Kunz Bennett became concerned about their mother's health and financial situation. They requested to meet with their brother, Dick Bennett, their mother, Jane Bennett, and her attorney, and all of them met twice in the summer of 1995. At the second meeting, Dick Bennett produced ... an analysis of funds, indicating that the trust then had a balance of $308,762, not including Jane Bennett's home in Keene and a cottage in Swanzey, which were worth a combined $440,000. ...

Jane Bennett's mental condition continued to deteriorate and, by the end of 1995, it became apparent that she had to be placed in a nursing home. Molly and Ann Kunz Bennett contended that she should be placed in a nursing home in Keene, where she had lived her entire life. Dick Bennett wanted to place her in a home in Manchester, citing a potential lack of funds, despite the fact that only a few months earlier he had assured his sisters that trust assets would provide for their mother for eighteen years. Concerned about their mother's placement and Dick Bennett's conflicting statements, the sisters retained attorney Silas Little who, in January 1996, brought a petition against Dick Bennett in probate court seeking the appointment of a new guardian for their mother. Dick Bennett hired attorney David Wolowitz to contest the petition.

The guardianship proceedings were terminated when, in March 1996, Jane Bennett became very ill and the parties agreed, out of necessity, to place her in a Keene nursing home. Additionally, Dick Bennett agreed to provide his sisters an accounting of the trust assets. The accounting indicated that, as of April 30, 1996, the fund balance was merely $65,917, compared with the almost $309,000 balance reported a half-year earlier. The sisters were suspicious and asked Attorney Little to investigate. ...

... Lane obtained, from storage, the file concerning Robert Bennett's estate. In the file, Lane discovered an accounting that had been prepared by Dick Bennett, as executor of the estate, on August 20, 1993, and submitted to Lane & Bentley. The accounting showed insurance proceeds from two policies, "National Grange Mutual" and "Merchants Insurance," totaling approximately $126,000. The accounting also showed that there was a value of $121,000 remaining. Lane, without contacting Dick Bennett or Attorney Wolowitz, gave Attorney Little a copy of that accounting. ...

In July 1996, Lane married Molly. On or around August 1, 1996, Ann Kunz Bennett, now Lane's sister-in-law, discovered, in her mother's home in Keene, an invoice for a life insurance policy underwritten by John Hancock Mutual Life Insurance Company (John Hancock). She also found a cancelled check showing payment of the premium for the policy through the end of 1990, less than two years before her father's death. Because Ann Kunz Bennett was leaving the country the next day, she turned these items over to Lane and Molly, and asked Lane if he could obtain further information about the policy referenced on the invoice.

Lane contacted John Hancock by telephone to discover whether there had been a policy in effect at the time of Robert Bennett's death. He was advised that the policy had been in effect, that a claim had been made on the policy and that there was no named beneficiary on the policy. He later received a letter advising him that any further information relating to the claim would require a written request. During his testimony, Lane expressed concern that if the policy had a value of $200,000, it might have an impact upon the estate's tax reporting obligations. On August 30, 1996, Lane wrote a letter to John Hancock, on Lane & Bentley letterhead, requesting further information.... .

John Hancock sent the requested materials to Lane, including a copy of a cancelled check in the amount of $100,000 paid to the order of Jane Bennett. A stamp on the back of the check indicated that it had been deposited at the First New Hampshire Bank in Hooksett. Additionally, John Hancock sent Lane a "facility of payment" form which provided that, in the event of Robert Bennett's death without a designated beneficiary, the proceeds were to be paid to the surviving spouse. Lane took the cancelled check to the First New Hampshire Bank branch in Keene, and asked a customer service representative if the stamp on the back indicated where the check had been deposited. A few days later, the customer service representative not only told

Lane where the check had been deposited, but also gave him a copy of the deposit slip indicating that the check had been deposited in a joint account of Jane Bennett and Dick Bennett.

Without consulting Dick Bennett or Attorney Wolowitz, Lane turned these materials over to Attorney Little. Several months later, in 1997, Attorney Little initiated litigation seeking to remove Dick Bennett as trustee of his mother's trust. That litigation was settled in 2001.

In September 2001, Attorney Wolowitz notified the committee of possible ethical transgressions by Lane. On December 15, 2003, the committee found that Lane had violated the New Hampshire Rules of Professional Conduct ... when he disclosed information to a third party relating to his representation of the estate. ...

The committee argues that Lane turned confidential information relating to his representation of his former client, Dick Bennett, over to the attorney representing Lane's wife, Molly Bennett Lane, who was engaged in an ongoing dispute with her brother [Dick Bennett] over the accounting of funds in their mother's trust. Such information indicated, among other things, that Dick Bennett may have been lying about the existence of a life insurance policy. Thus, the committee argues that Lane used information to the disadvantage of his former client. ... [W]e agree with the committee that such information was used to Dick Bennett's disadvantage. ...

Lane ... argues that his actions were permitted by Rule 1.6(b)... . Lane contends that, at the time he turned the documents over to Attorney Little, he was doing so to prevent Dick Bennett from committing the criminal acts of general theft... . The referee found that Lane reasonably believed that his disclosure was necessary to prevent future criminal activity by Dick Bennett which would cause substantial injury to Jane Bennett. We conclude that the record reasonably supports this finding. [C]

... The evidence indicates that Lane knew that Dick Bennett, along with Jane Bennett, was a co-trustee of the trust created after Robert Bennett's death. Lane knew that in August 1995, Dick Bennett provided an accounting showing that the trust had over $300,000 exclusive of certain real estate. ... In May 1996, Lane learned of another accounting showing a balance of $65,917. In August 1996, Lane learned that Ann Kunz Bennett had discovered an invoice and a cancelled check indicating the existence of a John Hancock policy. Lane corroborated the existence of the policy by contacting John Hancock. Lane also learned that the $100,000 proceeds from the policy had been paid into a joint account in the names of Jane and Dick Bennett. Neither the existence of the policy nor the deposit into the account had been disclosed by Dick Bennett in any of the accountings for the estate or the trust. In addition, Lane knew that Dick Bennett had denied the existence of the insurance policy.

At the time of the disclosure, Lane knew that there had been a large, sudden and mysterious diminution of the trust assets between August 1995 and May 1996. Lane knew that there was a life insurance policy payable to Jane Bennett, that Dick Bennett knew about the policy, that Dick Bennett had not disclosed the existence of the policy, that the proceeds had been deposited into a joint account to which Dick Bennett had access and that, in fact, Dick Bennett had denied that there was any insurance policy. In light of the above facts, we conclude that Lane proved by a preponderance of the evidence the applicability of Rule 1.6(b) as an exception to Rule 1.9. Accordingly, the evidence supports the referee's finding that Lane reasonably believed that his disclosure was necessary to prevent future criminal activity by Dick Bennett, see RSA 638:11, I. ...

Petition denied.

INQUIRY

Self-Protective Measures.   For their own protection, lawyers sometimes need to disclose client information without client authority. Model Rule 1.6(b)(4) authorizes a lawyer to disclose client information to get advice about the conduct rules. For example, a lawyer might call the state bar's ethics hotline to discuss whether the lawyer could do as a corporate client's president had asked in undertaking the dual representation of the corporation and president in defense of a shareholder-oppression claim. Model Rule 1.6(b)(5) contains a similar self-protection exception. A client may dispute a bill, requiring the lawyer to disclose client information reasonably necessary to respond to the dispute. *See* In re Rules of Prof. Conduct, 2 P.3d 806 (Mont. 2000) (limit disclosures to that reasonably necessary unless client consents). A client may sue for malpractice or file a grievance against a lawyer, once again requiring the lawyer to disclose client information. *See* Pappas v. Holloway, 787 P.2d 30 (Wash. 1990) (disclosure permitted to defend malpractice claim). Model Rule 1.6 provides the client with a shield, not a sword. If the client chooses to maintain a defense or claim, or pursue a charge or grievance against the client's lawyer, then the lawyer may disclose client information in self-protection. If law or court order require a lawyer to disclose client information, then Model Rule 1.6(b)(6) authorizes that disclosure. On the other hand, a lawyer must not use the threat of disclosure to induce the client to forgo a claim or waive a defense in a fee dispute.

See In re Bolter, 985 P.2d 328 (Wash. 1999) (threat to reveal client's alleged lies to IRS).

   Organization Clients.   As the above section on organization clients alludes, communications by an organization constituent within that constituent's organization role are communications within Model Rule 1.6's duty of confidentiality. The lawyer who represents a corporate client must maintain as confidential information that a corporate representative brings to the lawyer. Comment [2] to ABA Model Rule 1.13 gives as an example the corporate lawyer who interviews corporate employees to investigate wrongdoing. The employees' information is corporate-client information that the lawyer must maintain as confidential under Model Rule 1.6. Comment [2] to Model Rule 1.13 also states the other aspect of the same circumstance, cautioning further that the lawyer must not share with the employee corporate-client information that the corporate client's duly authorized constituent has not authorized the lawyer to share. The lawyer should not tell the employee all about the corporation's matter simply because the employee works for the corporation. Lawyers share confidential corporate information with corporate decisionmakers, not just any corporate employee.

   Attorney-Client Privilege.   As the beginning of this section indicates, Model Rule 1.6's duty of confidentiality is different from and broader than the attorney-client privilege. Unlike the conduct rule, which applies outside of court, the attorney-client privilege is an evidentiary privilege against compelled disclosure relating to court proceedings. The attorney-client privilege is thus a subject of your civil procedure and evidence courses, as is the work-product privilege protecting materials prepared in anticipation of litigation. *See* FED. R. CIV. P. 26(b)(3). Unlike the conduct rule, the attorney-client privilege protects only confidential communications made between lawyer and client, meaning that communications made in the presence of others who do not have a common interest are not privileged. *See, e.g.,* Cooney v. Booth, 198 F.R.D. 62 (E.D. Pa. 2000) (lawyer-client teleconference with adversary physician not privileged); Calvin Klein Trademark Trust v. Wachner, 198 F.R.D. 53 (S.D. N.Y. 2000) (communications shared with public-relations firm not privileged). Like the conduct rule, the privilege has a crime-fraud exception. *See* United States v. Zolin, 491 U.S. 554 (1989). A client's confidential threat to kill someone is not privileged, *see* United States v. Alexander, 287 F.3d 811 (9th Cir. 2002), just as the conduct rule would not require a lawyer to keep it confidential.

Career and Professional Development

Communication is also a skill relating to your career choice and professional development. Indeed, clarity and purpose in your communication may be your single most important skill in developing the professional network through which you will find and prosper in a law or law-related job. Whether your communication involves electronic messages or printed letters and resumes, you should follow the conventions for sound and attractive professional communication. Follow rules like writing in complete sentences using proper grammar and correct spelling. Use appropriately formal forms of address when the communications are to strangers. Maintain appropriately professional forms of address in all professional settings. Respond to communications promptly. Review your communications for tone, content, and format before sending, and proofread. Organize your communications so that they serve the needs and interests of the recipient. Career-related communications indicate how effective you will be as a professional when communicating. Be consistent and thorough in keeping your communications professional, and your reward will follow.

CHAPTER V

PRODUCTIVITY

Fees, Client Property, Lawyer Supervision, Supervision of Nonlawyer Assistants, Sale of a Law Practice

Money often costs too much.
> — *Ralph Waldo Emerson*

Man has in fact been granted the power not only of knowing the different things which he meets in this universe, of comparing them and of forming new notions in regard to them, but also the ability to foresee what he is going to do, to bestir himself to accomplish it, to shape it to a certain norm and a certain end, and to infer what the result will be; and further, to judge whether things already done conform to rule.
> — *Samuel Von Pufendorf*

OBJECTIVE: Given private practice in a law-firm setting, articulate how to set fees, safekeep client property, and supervise subordinate lawyers and nonlawyer assistants, in a productive and accountable manner consistent with the conduct rules.

Applicable Rules

1.5 Fees

1.15 Safekeeping Property

1.17 Sale of Law Practice

5.1 Responsibilities of Partners, Managers, and Supervisory Lawyers

5.2 Responsibilities of a Subordinate Lawyer

5.3 Responsibilities Regarding Nonlawyer Assistants

A lawyer must not merely be an obedient citizen of a nation and member of a profession whose authenticity supports client relationship. A lawyer must also be productive. Lawyers are economic drivers. They are wealth producers. The corporations that they form and advise, and to which they help attract capital, are critical to the national and world economy. The families that they help protect in their relationships, members, and property, are the fundamental economic and social unit of regenerative society. Lawyers invest significant capital in their education and training precisely to become and remain productive participants in local, regional, national, and world economies. The way that lawyers ensure that they are productive in the manner that their investment warrants is through fair fee agreements and billing, safekeeping of client property, and sound supervisory relationships within law firms. This chapter addresses these essential subjects.

A. Fees

Types of Fees. How do lawyers bill, that either keeps them productive or gets them into trouble? Ever since the Supreme Court held lawyer minimum fee schedules to be an antitrust violation, *see* Goldfarb v. Virginia State Bar, 421 U.S. 773 (1975), the hourly fee has been the prevalent form of lawyer billing. Lawyers calculate hourly fees by multiplying the number of hours that they work on a matter times an hourly rate. Lawyers tend to bill monthly for hourly fees, requiring clients to pay monthly. When not billing hourly, lawyers may work on fixed or flat fees, charging clients a single predetermined fee for specific work or work product, perhaps a will or to incorporate a business. Lawyers may also work on contingency fees, meaning fees calculated as a percentage (often one-third) of the client's total recovery. Contingency fees tend to work best in litigation involving a probable damage award. A proportional fee is another form, in which client agrees to pay lawyer a percentage of the value of the transaction for which lawyer provides services. Lawyers also sometimes modify or blend different fee forms, perhaps agreeing to convert from hourly to contingency fee after a certain point in a matter, or setting minimum fees or maximum fees, or using sliding scales for fees, intending these efforts to reflect value billing. The trend has also been away from hourly billing. Some clients resist hourly fees because of perceived abuses, particularly overbilling by working more hours than the task justifies. Some lawyers resist hourly fees either because hourly work may not reward innovation and investment in the work product or because it implies drudgery. Now, consider a case involving yet another type of fee, this one controversial, known as a premium or bonus fee.

Sheresky Aronson & Mayefsky, LLP v. Whitmore,
New York Supreme Court
851 N.Y.S.2d 61 (2007), *affd.*, 861 N.Y.S.2d 44 (2008)

... In 2002, defendant retained the Law Firm to represent her against her former husband in a divorce action. ... [D]efendant and the Law Firm executed a retainer agreement. The retainer agreement ... contained a "Premium Fee" clause, which allowed for an additional fee and is the gravamen of the dispute in the instant action.

The Divorce Action was subsequently settled in accordance with a settlement agreement executed by defendant and her former husband ... which provided, inter alia, for payment of 100% of the plaintiff's legal fees, which totaled approximately $350,000. [C] At some juncture during the Law Firm's representation of defendant, defendant agreed to pay the Law Firm a "Premium Fee," i.e., a bonus, of $150,000.00 payable in three payments. The first installment of $50,000 was paid in July 2005. Subsequently, however, defendant notified the Law Firm, inter alia, that "after looking over the total billing figures and [her] after-settlement bonus to the firm of $50,000, [she has] decided [that] this bonus is sufficient and that [she would] not be making any more bonus payments."

The Law Firm thereafter commenced this action against defendant for breach of the "Premium Fee" clause of the retainer agreement.... .

The pivotal issue raised by the parties is whether the Law Firm complied with the matrimonial rules of procedure for attorneys in domestic relations matters, i.e., the Rule[, 22 NYCRR 1400.3], in connection with its claimed entitlement to the payment of the premium fee agreed to by defendant.

... The requirement that attorneys execute written retainer agreements with matrimonial clients is found not only in the Rule, but also in Code of Professional Responsibility, in Disciplinary Rule (DR) 2-106(c)(2)(b), which forbids attorneys from collecting "[a]ny fee in a domestic relations matter ... unless a written agreement is signed by the lawyer and client setting forth in plain language the nature of the relationship and the details of the fee arrangement." It is well settled that an attorney's noncompliance with the Rule generally precludes the attorney's recovery of fees in domestic relations matters ([cc]). The relevant portions of the Rule relied on by the defendant provide as follows:

> An attorney who undertakes to represent a party and enters into
> an arrangement for, charges or collects any fee from a client shall

execute a written agreement with the client setting forth in plain language the terms of the compensation and the nature of services to be rendered. The agreement, and any amendment thereto, shall be signed by both client and attorney, and in actions in Supreme Court, a copy of the signed agreement shall be filed with the court with the statement of net worth... . A copy of a signed amendment shall be filed within 15 days of signing... .

8. Any clause providing for a fee in addition to the agreed-upon rate, such as a reasonable minimum fee clause, must be defined in plain language and set forth the circumstances under which such fee may be incurred and how it will be calculated. (22 NYCRR 1400.3 & 1400.3[8])

... It is undisputed that the retainer agreement signed by the parties in 2002 was properly filed, and that the Law Firm received payment in full from defendant's ex-husband for its representation of the defendant during the Divorce Action. However, the fee being sought in this action by the Law Firm consists of an additional fee characterized in the retainer agreement as a premium fee, pursuant to the "Premium Fee" clause therein. This clause provides as follows: "We reserve the right to discuss with you at the conclusion of the matter your payment of a reasonable additional fee to us, in excess of the actual time and disbursements, for exceptional results achieved, time expended, responsiveness accorded, or complexity involved in your case. However, no such fee will be charged to you without your consent."

Since this clause provides for an additional fee, in addition to the agreed-upon compensation, it must comply with the requisites of the Rule, which, based on its plain language, clearly requires that any clause for an additional fee must define in "plain language," inter alia, how the additional fee "will be calculated" (22 NYCRR 1400.3[8]).

Here, the "Premium Fee" clause merely reserves the Law Firm's right to have a future discussion with defendant regarding the payment of the premium fee. This clause is devoid of any language explicitly setting forth how this fee was to be calculated (22 NYCRR 1400.3[8]). Additionally, the "Premium Clause" fails to clearly provide the circumstances under which the premium fee "may be incurred" (*id.*). Although this clause indicates that the payment of an additional fee would be for "exceptional results achieved, time expended, responsiveness accorded, or complexity involved in your case," it does not define in "plain language" how these factors would trigger the additional fee, particularly when the Law Firm was being compensated pursuant to the hourly billing rates set forth in the retainer agreement. Further, an additional fee based on exceptional results could be viewed as a contingent fee, which is clearly prohibited by DR 2-106(C)(2). Thus, the "Premium Fee" Clause fails to set forth in "plain language" the factors mandated by the Rule (22 NYCRR 1400.3[8]). ...

Thus, based upon the omission of the requisite language in the "Premium Fee" Clause as required by the Rule, and the failure of the filing of a writing amending the "Premium Fee" Clause to include the necessary language, the Law Firm failed to comply with the Rule. Accordingly, the Law Firm's noncompliance results in its inability to collect the additional fee they seek in this action ([c]). ...

Accordingly, it is

ORDERED that the motion by defendant Holly Whitmore for an order dismissing the complaint is granted . . .

INQUIRY

Attitude Toward Fees. Do not mistake the subject of fees as either necessary evil or opportunity for personal enrichment. Either of those attitudes—that the whole subject of fees and billing is one better avoided or fees are the central reason for law practice—will mislead you. Fees and billing are evidence of sound practice and judgment. They are proof that you are conducting yourself in a responsible manner that means something for the community and field within which you practice. Timekeeping in particular is not a chore but a privilege. When you track your time for billing and practice-management purposes, you hold yourself accountable to your client, firm, family, profession, and own goals and education. Fee arrangements can also be peculiar to certain practice areas and local customs. Learning and following those conventions, while ensuring that they meet all conduct rules, can be a good way to ensure good client relationships.

Practice

The out-of-state lawyer took one look at the local counsel's invoice for legal services and laughed. The invoice said simply, "Legal services: $20,000." The out-of-state lawyer had consented to the client retaining the local counsel who, as it turned out, they had not needed for the case. For each service for which the out-of-state lawyer had billed the client, the out-of-state lawyer had the date, time expended to the tenth of an hour, and detailed description of the work performed. By contrast, the local counsel had sent the single opaque invoice with the nice big round number, after the matter resolved just before trial. When the client protested the bill, the local counsel had said that was how they always did it in that region and field. The client now wanted the out-of-state lawyer's opinion about the bill. The out-of-state lawyer simply showed the client the conduct rule, glad at having followed what the out-of-state lawyer knew to be the responsible billing convention.

Regulation of Fees.   Nowhere is a lawyer's interest more naturally in conflict with the client's interest than over fee agreements.   To address this inherent conflict, the ABA Model Rules take several default stances protecting clients. The Model Rules, similar state rules, and state statutes like the one in the *Whitmore* case above, prohibit lawyers from using certain revenue-generating techniques that may be common in other professions or businesses. The Model Rules make you a lawyer first and business owner second. As you study fee and property rules, identify these divergences of interest and how the Rules favor clients in fee agreements. For instance, Model Rule 1.5 on fees mandates that you treat your client fairly when forming an agreement for fees, charging fees, and collecting them. How significant is this restriction? How does it likely influence how lawyers price their legal services?   Model Rule 1.5 also urges (and in the case of contingency fees requires) that at the outset you write your fee agreement with the client.   It also addresses how lawyers from different firms may divide fees that they earn on the same matter. Consider a similar state version of Model Rule 1.5.

INDIANA R. PROF. CONDUCT 1.5: Fees.
(a) A lawyer shall not make an agreement for, charge, or collect an unreasonable fee or an unreasonable amount for expenses. The factors to be considered in determining the reasonableness of a fee include the following:
(1) the time and labor required, the novelty and difficulty of the questions involved, and the skill requisite to perform the legal service properly;
(2) the likelihood, if apparent to the client, that the acceptance of the particular employment will preclude other employment by the lawyer;
(3) the fee customarily charged in the locality for similar legal services;
(4) the amount involved and the results obtained;
(5) the time limitations imposed by the client or by the circumstances;
(6) the nature and length of the professional relationship with the client;
(7) the experience, reputation, and ability of the lawyer or lawyers performing the services; and
(8) whether the fee is fixed or contingent.
(b) The scope of the representation and the basis or rate of the fee and expenses for which the client will be responsible shall be communicated to the client, preferably in writing, before or within a reasonable time after commencing the representation, except when the lawyer will charge a regularly represented client on the same basis or rate. Any changes in the basis or rate of the fee or expenses shall also be communicated to the client.
(c) A fee may be contingent on the outcome of the matter for which the service is rendered, except in a matter in which a contingent fee is prohibited by paragraph (d) or other law. A contingent fee agreement shall be in a writing signed by the client and shall state the method by which the

fee is to be determined, including the percentage or percentages that shall accrue to the lawyer in the event of settlement, trial or appeal; litigation and other expenses to be deducted from the recovery; and whether such expenses are to be deducted before or after the contingent fee is calculated. The agreement must clearly notify the client of any expenses for which the client will be liable whether or not the client is the prevailing party. Upon conclusion of a contingent fee matter, the lawyer shall provide the client with a written statement stating the outcome of the matter and, if there is a recovery, showing the remittance to the client and the method of its determination.

(d) A lawyer shall not enter into an arrangement for, charge, or collect:

(1) any fee in a domestic relations matter, the payment or amount of which is contingent upon the securing of a dissolution or upon the amount of maintenance, support, or property settlement, or obtaining custody of a child; or

(2) a contingent fee for representing a defendant in a criminal case.

This provision does not preclude a contract for a contingent fee for legal representation in a domestic relations post-judgment collection action, provided the attorney clearly advises his or her client in writing of the alternative measures available for the collection of such debt and, in all other particulars, complies with Prof. Cond. R. 1.5(c).

(e) A division of a fee between lawyers who are not in the same firm may be made only if:

(1) the division is in proportion to the services performed by each lawyer or each lawyer assumes joint responsibility for the representation;

(2) the client agrees to the arrangement, including the share each lawyer will receive, and the agreement is confirmed in writing; and

(3) the total fee is reasonable.

INQUIRY

Reasonableness of Fees. ABA Model Rule 1.5 requires that all fees be reasonable. There is no precise formula for determining what constitutes a reasonable fee. Model Rule 1.5(a) lists eight factors, the first of which dominates in many instances: the time involved in the matter, together with the level of skill and difficulty. In any pursuit, not just the law profession, the time and skill that work takes should ordinarily correlate with the compensation. Even if a lawyer is not billing hourly, the fee should bear some reasonable relationship in most cases to the time that the work took the lawyer. What time increment should you use in hourly billing? Most lawyers probably use one-tenth hour (.10) increments. Those who instead use one-quarter hour (.25) increments should know that not all courts will approve. *See* Swisher v. United States, 262 F. Supp.2d 1203 (D. Kan 2003) (quarter-hour increments unreasonable). Subrule 1.5(a)(3) indicates the fee should also ordinarily bear some relationship to the fees other lawyers charge, that is, to the market for fees. The next factor in Subrule 1.5(a)(4), the amount involved and results obtained, encourages a lawyer to be economically efficient. Small matters should not ordinarily warrant large fees. Under Subrule 1.5(a)(7), an experienced lawyer of high standing may charge more than an inexperienced lawyer of no particular standing, reflecting the efficiency that often comes with experience and value that often comes with standing. Subrule 1.5(a)(8) permits a higher rate for a contingent fee than an hourly fee, given the risk that the lawyer shares with the client. Consider the following discipline case addressing some of these factors.

In the Matter of Green,
Colorado Supreme Court
11 P.3d 1078 (2000)

PER CURIAM.

Lawrence Jamalian Green, the respondent in this lawyer regulation case, was admitted to practice law in Colorado in 1979.... The hearing board found that Green charged an excessive fee in a civil case.... [W]e agree that Green violated Colo. RPC 1.5 charging an unreasonable fee[... but] determine that public censure is an adequate sanction this case.

I.   FACTS AND PROCEDURAL HISTORY

... A tile contractor hired Green in 1991 to sue a homeowner and her husband for failure to pay for the contractor's installation of ceramic tile in their house. Green filed an action ... on behalf of the contractor against the homeowners for breach of contract and to foreclose a mechanics' lien in the amount of $7,422.33. The defendants counterclaimed, asserting that the contractor breached implied warranties of fitness for a particular purpose and merchantability. The contract between the tile contractor and the homeowners entitled the party who prevailed at trial to attorney's fees and costs. Green and his client agreed that if the client prevailed, then Green would accept as his fee whatever amount the court awarded. Otherwise, the client would owe Green nothing.

After a bench trial, the trial judge issued findings of fact, conclusions of law, and an order. The court sustained the contractor's breach of contract claim and dismissed the homeowners' counterclaim. The judge awarded Green's client damages in the amount of $7,422.33, plus costs, interest, and attorney's fees. The court directed Green to file an affidavit for fees and costs within fifteen days.

In an affidavit filed following trial, Green requested attorney's fees in the amount of $29,554.80, which he calculated by multiplying his hourly rate of $165 by the 179.12 hours he claimed to have worked on the case. After a hearing, the trial judge determined that Green's billing rate was reasonable, but that the itemized list of services Green personally performed included secretarial or other non-attorney services that are not usually billed to clients. Thus, the judge ruled that the amount Green claimed was excessive and that a reasonable fee under the circumstances was $12,000... .

The homeowners appealed the trial court's judgment in the contractor's favor on the breach of contract claim. The contractor and Green cross-appealed the amount of the fee award. The court of appeals affirmed the trial court's judgment regarding the contractor's breach of contract claim and dismissal of the homeowners' counterclaim... . However, the court of appeals reversed the trial court's judgment on the issue of Green's fees, holding that it was not supported by the trial court's findings:

> [T]he record does not reflect that the trial court actually derived the amount of fees awarded by considering both a reasonable hourly rate and a reasonable number of hours, then making any necessary adjustments. In particular, the trial court's order does not indicate its finding as to the reasonable number of hours expended on the claims involving the homeowners.

[C] Remanding the case, the court of appeals directed the trial court to reconsider the issue of Green's fees and make additional findings on the reasonableness of the hours Green worked on the case. ...

Before the trial court finished reconsidering Green's fees, Green filed a supplementary affidavit for attorney's fees in addition to those he had already claimed. Green stated that, through trial and the appeal, he had expended 618.13 hours of time and that his hourly fee rate was $165, amounting to $101,991.45 in attorney's fees. Subtracting the amount of fees he had previously claimed for the trial ($29,554.80), Green asked for $72,436.65 in attorney's fees for his work on the appeal. ...

The trial court issued its order reconsidering the award of attorney's fees... . The judge first subtracted the hours the judge found were related to the performance of secretarial functions from the total number of hours that Green claimed to have expended on the case, arriving at a total of 124.275 hours. The court then adjusted that amount by considering factors such as the amount of the plaintiff's recovery, Green's defense against the homeowners' counterclaim, the actual trial time devoted to the case, and the discovery that Green performed. The trial court adjusted the total of hours to 100 hours. Based on Green's hourly rate of $165, which the court found reasonable, the court awarded Green a total of $16,500 in attorney's fees for Green's work on the trial. The trial court also ruled that it did "not believe that it has jurisdiction to determine attorney fees on appeal and suggests that those issues are more appropriately addressed to the Colorado Court of Appeals." ...

Disciplinary counsel brought a complaint against Green, charging him with violating Colo. RPC 1.5(a) (charging an excessive fee). . . .

II. DISCUSSION
B. Unreasonable Fee

... The hearing board found, by clear and convincing evidence, that Green violated Colo. RPC 1.5(a), stating that particularly in light of the fee's amount in relation to the recovery, the fee was "outrageous on its face" and "grossly unreasonable":[fn]

> The sheer amount of the Respondent's fee demand is outrageous on its face, and reflects a disturbing lack of judgment and perspective on his part. The Board notes that the Colorado Rules of Professional Conduct set forth eight factors to be considered in determining the reasonableness of a fee. Applying each of these factors to this case, and in particular, § 1.5(a)(4) (the amount involved and the results obtained), the Board concludes that the Respondent charged a grossly unreasonable fee in violation of Colo. 1.5(a).

... [W]e consider only the attorney's fees Green charged for the appeal. ...

Arguably, the $69,000 Green charged for the appeal is unreasonable per se because of the relatively small judgment of $7,400 involved. However, the issue is more complex. For instance, the attorney for the homeowners, who represented the losing party on all of the critical issues on appeal, testified that *his* attorney's fees for the appeal "were in the $30,000 to $40,000 range."

Green's affidavit setting forth his time entries for work performed on the appeal contains unreasonable charges. There are charges reflecting time Green spent on tasks that could have been done by a non-lawyer at a significantly lower rate than $165 per hour. For example, there are multiple entries reflecting the faxing of documents to the client and opposing counsel, entries for calls made to the court of appeals clerk's office, and the delivery of documents to opposing counsel. Colo. RPC 1.5(a)(1) indicates that one factor in determining the reasonableness of a fee is "the novelty and difficulty of the questions involved, and the skill requisite to perform the legal service properly." Under this principle, charging an attorney's hourly rate for clerical services that are generally performed by a non-lawyer, and thus for which an attorney's professional skill and knowledge add no value to the service, is unreasonable as a matter of law. ...

In addition, some entries for time spent on legal work are

excessive. For example, there is an entry for receiving and reviewing the court of appeals decision and faxing it to the client. The court of appeals' opinion is twelve pages long. Green represents that he spent 6.0 hours performing these services. At $165 per hour, Green therefore charged $990 for reviewing and faxing a twelve page decision. This is an unreasonable charge as a matter of law for one of two alternative reasons. If the time was spent merely in "reviewing," in other words reading the appellate opinion with minimal additional legal analysis or research involved, it was an excessive and inefficient use of the attorney's time and it is unreasonable to charge for the lawyer's own inefficiencies.... .

If, on the other hand, his time involved more extensive work, then the billing statement is so vague that it fails reasonably to identify the nature of the services performed. ... Either of these two bases is a sufficient rationale to conclude that this charge was unreasonable.

Thus, our review of the entire record, and specifically Green's affidavit for fees charged for the appeal, supports the hearing board's conclusion to the extent that it determined that Green charged an unreasonable fee on the appeal in violation ...

DISCIPLINE

... [W]e now address the appropriate level of discipline. Under the American Bar Association *Standards for Imposing Lawyer Sanctions,* public censure "is generally appropriate when a lawyer negligently engages in conduct that is a violation of a duty owed to the profession, and causes injury or potential injury to a client, the public, or the legal system." ABA *Standards for Imposing Lawyer Sanctions* at 7.3 (1991 & Supp.1992) (hereinafter ABA *Standards*). ...

The commentary to standard 7.3 states, "Courts typically impose reprimands when lawyers engage in a single instance of charging an excessive or improper fee." We have recently found a public censure appropriate when a lawyer charges an excessive fee. ...

The hearing board found the existence of a mitigating factor and several aggravating factors. The only mitigating factor found by the hearing board was that Green had cooperated in these proceedings. [C] Aggravating factors included the presence of a prior disciplinary offense, [c]; that Green had a dishonest or selfish motive, [c]; ... that Green refused to acknowledge the wrongful nature of his conduct, [c]; and that Green has substantial experience in the practice of law, [c]. ...

Considering the seriousness of the misconduct, together with the aggravating and mitigating factors, we conclude that a public censure is an adequate and appropriate sanction. Accordingly, we reject the hearing board's and panel's recommendation of suspension....

INQUIRY

Determining Reasonableness. As the above case illustrates, the reasonableness standard applies to the fee from the outset of the representation all the way to its conclusion. ABA Model Rule 1.5(a) also prohibits not only collecting an unreasonable fee but also forming an agreement for an unreasonable fee and billing for an unreasonable fee. A client does not have to pay an unreasonable bill in order for officials to discipline a lawyer for charging an unreasonable fee. If changed circumstances make the original fee unreasonable, then the lawyer must adjust the fee to ensure it is reasonable. Who judges whether a fee is reasonable? The lawyer's opinion alone does not control. A client charged an unreasonable fee may file a complaint with discipline officials who may discipline the lawyer. Many state and local bar associations have fee arbitration programs. Some programs require lawyers to take fee disputes to mandatory arbitration before suing to recover fees. What advantage is there to a lawyer to arbitrate fee disputes? Fee disputes are a common source for other complaints against lawyers. Rightly or wrongly, the lawyer who sues for fees runs the risk of counterclaim for malpractice and grievance to discipline officials.

Biography

Practitioners so widely admired Kimberly Cahill, a small-firm practitioner in suburban Detroit, that she rose to become the 72nd president of the State Bar of Michigan before she passed away at the age of 47. Anyone who met Ms. Cahill instantly felt her humanity and warmth, but it was her monthly presidential columns in the Michigan Bar Journal that most illustrated her great leadership gifts. She urged that lawyers mold the profession to meet its coming changes rather than simply react from crisis to crisis. Ms. Cahill challenged lawyers to represent the downtrodden, minority, and outcast even in the face of public hostility, but to do so with warm civility. Most of all, she encouraged us to celebrate the quiet lawyer heroes among us, those who stand solidly beside their clients without fanfare, at the time of their clients' greatest challenges.

Billing Practices. The above *In re Green* case illustrates two billing practices—grossly inefficient work and billing at lawyer rates for non-lawyer work—that courts routinely condemn as unreasonable. Can you imagine any other unreasonable billing practices? Lawyers working for hourly fees get into trouble when they forget that they are billing for their time actually spent on the client's matter, not for their willingness to lend their talents. For example, some lawyers may routinely round fractional time up to the next larger fraction of an hour (three minutes to six minutes, 22 minutes to 30 minutes, etc.), dishonestly padding a bill in small increments. For another example, lawyers often charge for travel time en route to depositions and meetings. A lawyer might legitimately bill for time spent on an airplane if the fee agreement provides for travel time, especially if the lawyer uses that time efficiently by working on the client's matter. Yet whom should the lawyer charge if the lawyer works on one client's matter while traveling to another client's matter? Double billing both clients for the same time would be per se unreasonable. Similarly, a lawyer may take three hours to prepare a document for one client and then take just 10 minutes to modify it for the same use by another client. Double billing both clients for three hours would be per se unreasonable. Can you articulate a fair solution for a reasonable fee for the latter work? Fixed fees and value billing are permissible alternatives to hourly fees when disclosed, agreed to, and reasonable.

Documenting Fees. Does it surprise you that Model Rule 1.5, written by and for lawyers about contracts between lawyer and client, does not (excepting contingent fees) require fee agreements to be in writing? Most wise practitioners ignore the rule's permissive standard, put all fee agreements in writing, and have the client sign the fee agreement. Practitioners may include the fee agreement in a broader contract called a retainer agreement or have the client countersign a letter of retention documenting the fee and other terms. You may hear that a fee agreement protects the lawyer as much as the client. Can you imagine how? A retainer agreement or retention letter usually spells specific rights and duties such as the scope of representation, duties of cooperation and communication, how the parties will handle expenses, and who will be working on the client's matter. ABA Model Rule 1.4's duty to communicate fully with the client includes communicating the basis and rate of the fee. Sending regular monthly billing statements to the client is a common and reliable way to keep clients informed, freeing you from avoidable inquiries. If your monthly bills are consistent and thorough in describing the work you do, then they will provide a detailed account for the client as to precisely what you are accomplishing on their behalf. Good billing practice is one of the best relationship management and marketing techniques. Some lawyers even send a monthly billing statement to clients whose matter is on a contingency fee, simply to inform the client of case tasks and progress.

Reasonable Expenses. Model Rule 1.5(a) also prohibits forming an agreement for, charging, or collecting unreasonable expenses, also requiring in Subrule 1.5(b) that a lawyer communicate expenses preferably in writing. Expenses can vary widely depending on the type of work. For example, certain kinds of litigation may require substantial expert-witness fees, deposition-transcript costs, and travel (airfare and hotel) expenses, occasionally running into tens of thousands of dollars. Those cases require clear communication of the size, scope, and necessity of expenses before and as incurred, even in contingency-fee cases when the lawyer is advancing the expenses. In the more usual work, though, expenses may involve court filing and motion fees, copying and mailing costs, and possibly mileage expenses to and from court or other locations. To be reasonable, copying and mileage expenses should approximate actual costs, rather than turning an expense into a profit center. Lawyers should treat other costs, like electronic-research fees, secretarial expense, and ordinary telephone expense, as overhead rather than expenses.

Some lawyers charge interest on unpaid fees and expenses. Statutes known as usury laws may regulate interest. *See, e.g.,* MICH. COMP. L. §438.31 (7% maximum for written obligations, 5% maximum for oral obligations). To be reasonable, interest on fees and expenses must comply with statutes. Indeed, keep in mind that fee agreements are contracts subject to all laws governing contracts. In disputes, the courts will construe ambiguities against their drafter (the lawyer), examine for unconscionability, bar parol evidence, and otherwise treat them as they would other contracts.

Retainer Fees. Lawyers working on hourly fees may also request a retainer fee. As our discussion turns to retainer fees, non-refundable fees, and engagement fees, recognize that usage of these terms differ among lawyers, fields of practice, and geographic regions. Learn the local lexicon. Here, though, by a *retainer fee*, we mean a certain amount as an advance on the hourly fees that the lawyer will charge as the client's matter progresses. A retainer fee ensures that a lawyer receives at least some fee even if the client later refuses to pay the hourly billing and remains uncollectible. Retainer fees are common in divorce actions, criminal defense, and other fields where the client's continuing ability to pay is uncertain. Although intended as an advance against billed hourly fees, the retainer becomes a flat fee in many cases. Some lawyers request subsequent additional retainer fees when the billing exhausts the first retainer, in this way transferring to the client the risk of non-representation rather than allowing the client to transfer to the lawyer the risk of non-payment.

Non-Refundable Fees. You will sometimes see the term *non-refundable fee*. These fees attorneys characterize as earned on receipt, with no portion refundable to the client. If a fee must always be reasonable, how can a non-refundable fee be reasonable, for instance, if the representation is interrupted before the end of the case? Some states brand non-refundable fees as per se unreasonable. *See* In re Kendall, 804 N.E.2d 1152 (Ind. 2004). A good general rule is that even if labeled non-refundable, the fee is still nonetheless an advance on future fees, any unused portion of which the lawyer must return to the client. *See* ABA Model Rule 1.5, Comment 4; *but see* Grievance Administrator v. Cooper, 757 N.W.2d 867 (Mich. 2008) (approving that lawyer retain $4,000 non-refundable minimum fee for retention where written agreement so provided).

Charging Liens. In his unpublished notes for a lecture he wrote for law students but probably never gave, Abraham Lincoln urged that lawyers not take fees up front on retainer because doing so would remove the payment incentive for working. He instead recommended taking an advance note for the fees, presumably to eliminate enforcement disputes on non-payment later. Lincoln's awkward accommodation illustrates that thankfully, his acumen was presidential, not managerial. Lawyers do, though, occasionally seek security for their fees. There are two types of lawyer liens, the *charging lien* and the *retaining lien*. A charging lien grants a lawyer security against the proceeds of a settlement or judgment that the lawyer helped the client obtain. Because negotiating a charging lien with a client is a direct conflict of interest between lawyer and client, lawyers must follow ABA Model Rule 1.8(a) governing business transactions with a client. The charging lien must also comply with all other applicable statutes and regulations governing liens, and not unduly interfere with the client's property. *See* In re Adkins, 596 S.E.2d 1 (2004) (disbarment for charging liens exceeding amounts due).

Retaining Liens. A retaining lien allows an attorney to retain the file until the client pays fees. However, recall the lawyer's duty under ABA Model Rule 1.16 to protect the client's interest on termination of representation, including surrending papers and property to which the law entitles the client. Generally, an attorney cannot withhold the client's file if doing so would prejudice the client, as when the client terminated the lawyer in the midde of the representation and needs the file to secure successor counsel to conclude the representation. *See* MICH. ETHICS OPIN. RI-203. A lawyer may not ethically exercise a retaining lien on client property if the client needs the property to pursue the client's legal rights or when a refusal to turn over the file would prejudice the client's case, making retaining liens at best problematic.

Engagement Fees. A client may agree to pay an *engagement fee* simply to assure that the lawyer will be available on a matter if needed. A client pays an engagement fee, perhaps better described as an availability fee, even though the lawyer has not yet provided any service. Discipline officials scrutinize engagement fees, making them particularly perilous for practitioners.

Few circumstances warrant engagement fees. The lawyer must offer unique or scarce services or level of representation, and the client must be sophisticated enough to understand the fee and its benefit. *See, e.g.,* Raymark Indus., Inc. v. Butera, Beausang, Cohen & Brennan, 193 F.3d 210 (3d Cir. 1999) (approving $1 million engagement fee paid by corporate client). So, for example, one of a handful of lawyers with the experience and resources to handle very high-end, financially complex divorce cases might charge a sophisticated client an engagement fee for a divorce action if marital counseling proved unsuccessful. By contrast, a general practitioner would have little justification to charge a client an engagement fee for any work if the client could obtain equally sufficient representation from another local general practitioner. *See, e.g.,* In re Cooperman, 633 N.E.2d 1069 (N.Y. Ct. App. 1994) (two-year suspension for non-refundable engagement fees between $5,000 and $10,000 in criminal cases). The less sophisticated the client, the less reasonable an engagement fee becomes.

Contingency Fees. Federal and state statutes and rules limit the percentage contingency fee allowed in certain types of cases. *See, e.g.,* CAL. BUS. & PROF. CODE §6146 (sliding scale beginning at 40% and going down as recovery increases); MICH. CT. RULE 8.121(B) (one third of recovery in personal-injury and wrongful-death cases). Subrule (d) of ABA Model Rule 1.5 prohibits contingency fees to obtain a divorce (though not to collect divorce-judgment obligations post-judgment) and in criminal cases. Subrule (c) permits other contingency fees but requires that agreements for them be in a writing stating the percentage, expenses, and whether the lawyer will take reimbursement of expenses before or after taking the percentage fee. Which method—taking expenses before or after the fee—favors the client? Advancing expenses raises another issue beyond calculating repayment. ABA Model Rule 1.8 prohibits an attorney from providing financial assistance to a client such as a loan for living expenses. Client loans would give lawyers too much influence over the resolution of client matters. Yet, an attorney may advance costs and expenses of litigation. How, if at all, is an advance of litigation expenses different from a loan for living expenses? Litigation might not be possible without it, particularly for indigent clients. Another issue arises in that not every contingency-fee case results in a recovery. Model Rule 1.5(c) requires the contingency-fee agreement to state whether repayment of expenses is contingent on a successful outcome. In the event of no recovery (a litigation loss), you and your firm may decide not to pursue reimbursement particularly from an indigent client. If you do intend to seek reimbursement from the client in the event of no recovery, then the contingency-fee agreement must state. Consider how the following sample agreement addresses these issues. Then consider a case illustrating a risk inherent in contingency fees.

<u>FEE AGREEMENT</u>

Client retains Attorneys to represent Client as legal counsel to maintain a civil action for damages in connection with a motor vehicle accident on or about July 28, 2007. Unless otherwise agreed in writing, the representation does include pursuing the personal injury claim arising out of that incident through trial but does not include appeals from orders or judgments in the matter or claims for property-damage collision-coverage insurance benefits. THE TERMS OF THE REPRESENTATION ARE AS FOLLOWS:

This document is the entire agreement. Oral promises or statements do not modify it. Attorneys have made no promises or guarantees regarding the outcome of Client's matter. Attorneys will devote their professional skills to Client's matter. Client will cooperate with Attorneys. Client will maintain with Attorneys a current address, failing which Attorneys may terminate this agreement. Client binds Client's personal representatives, conservators, and assigns to this agreement. ***Attorneys will communicate settlement offers to Client for Client's decision.***

Attorneys will advance costs (e.g., transcripts, court fees, expert-witness fees, process-server fees, copying, mail and courier, and travel). Client will reimburse Attorneys for costs. Client will pay Attorneys one third of the recovery after reimbursing costs. ***If Client makes no recovery, then Client will pay no fee.*** Attorneys have offered Client hourly and per-day fee arrangements that Client has declined. Client approves that Attorneys will share their fee with referring attorney John Doe. Attorneys may withdraw without cause, in which event Client will owe no fee to Attorneys. If Attorneys withdraw due to Client misconduct or Client discharges Attorneys, then Client will reimburse costs and pay Attorneys at the higher of $200 per hour or one third of the amounts last offered by opposing parties. If Client recovers costs and attorney's fees, then Attorneys have the option of receiving the costs and attorney's fees or adding the costs and attorneys' fees to the other money recovered and receiving one third of the total. If the recovery includes future payments, Attorneys will use the present value of the future payments to calculate the one-third fee. Attorneys have a fee and costs lien on Client's file and recovery.

Client authorizes Attorneys to pay insurance or other liens or assignments out of the recovery. Attorneys own Client's file except for specifically identified Client property such as stock certificates, personal photographs, original wills, contracts, and unrecorded deeds. Attorneys will destroy Client files without notice to the client five years from the last date of service, except that Attorneys will retain indefinitely Client property such as stock certificates, personal photographs, and original wills, contracts, and unrecorded deeds, or return those items to Client if Client has kept Attorneys advised of a current address. Client agrees to pay a reasonable search and copying charge for file requests.

ATTORNEYS   CLIENT

_____/_____   _____/_____

Culpepper & Carroll, PLLC v. Cole,
Louisiana Supreme Court
929 So.2d 1224 (2006)

PER CURIAM.

Connie Daniel Cole seeks review of a judgment of the court of appeal affirming an award of attorney's fees to his former counsel. For the reasons that follow, we reverse the judgment of the court of appeal.

FACTS AND PROCEDURAL HISTORY

Connie Daniel Cole retained attorney Bobby Culpepper of the law firm of Culpepper & Carroll, PLLC, to represent him in a contest of his mother's will. Mr. Cole requested that the firm handle the matter on one-third contingent fee basis, and Mr. Culpepper agreed to do so. On September 20, 2000, Mr. Culpepper sent Mr. Cole a letter in which he confirmed that he would accept the representation on a contingent fee basis of one-third "of whatever additional property or money we can get for you."

After negotiation between Mr. Culpepper and counsel for the estate of Mr. Cole's mother, Mr. Cole was offered property worth $21,600.03 over and above what he would have received under the terms of the decedent's will. Mr. Culpepper thought the compromise was reasonable and recommended to Mr. Cole that he accept the offer. However, Mr. Cole refused to settle his claim for that amount, believing he was entitled to a larger share of his mother's succession as a forced heir. When Mr. Culpepper refused to file suit in the matter, Mr. Cole terminated his representation. Mr. Cole then proceeded in proper person to challenge his mother's will, but he was unsuccessful and recovered nothing.

On April 12, 2004, Mr. Culpepper filed a "Petition on Open Account" on behalf of the Culpepper law firm. The suit was filed in Ruston City Court against Mr. Cole, seeking the sum of $6,950.01 plus legal interest, together with 25% on the principal and interest as additional attorney's fees. Attached to the petition were Mr. Culpepper's invoice for attorney's fees and a demand letter to Mr. Cole seeking the payment of "the entire balance of $6,950.01 that you owe Culpepper & Carroll, PLLC."

Mr. Cole, appearing in proper person, answered the law firm's petition and denied that he owed any money. Mr. Cole explained in his answer that "Mr. Culpepper did this on a contingency fee basis," that Mr. Culpepper "quit the case," and that Mr. Cole paid court costs but Mr. Culpepper "would not go to court."

Following a trial on the merits, at which both parties testified, the city court rendered judgment in favor of the law firm, awarding the sum of $6,950.01, plus legal interest from the date of judicial demand until paid, together with 25% on the principal and interest as additional attorney's fees, and costs. ... The court noted that "work was accomplished" by Mr. Culpepper and further noted that, according to the testimony, the settlement would have produced a better result than if the case had gone to trial on the issue of forced heirship. Thus, the court was satisfied that the law firm met its burden of proof.

Mr. Cole appealed the city court's judgment, and in a 2-1 ruling, the court of appeal amended the judgment and affirmed. [C] The majority agreed that a valid contingent fee contract existed between Mr. Cole and Mr. Culpepper, and found that by refusing to sign the "favorable settlement" negotiated by Mr. Culpepper before he was discharged, Mr. Cole was in effect depriving Mr. Culpepper of the contingent fee he had already earned. Accordingly, the court of appeal affirmed the award to Mr. Culpepper of $6,950.01 in attorney's fees, plus legal interest. However, the court of appeal found that the money owing in this case does not derive from an open account, but rather from a contractual obligation in the form of a contingent fee agreement. Based on this reasoning, the court of appeal amended the trial court's judgment to delete the award to the law firm of 25% additional attorney's fees plus costs under the open account statute. ...

Upon Mr. Cole's application, we granted certiorari to review the correctness of the court of appeal's ruling. [C]

DISCUSSION

As a threshold matter, we note the trial court made a finding of fact that a contingent fee contract existed between Mr. Cole and Mr. Culpepper. Based on our review of the record, we find no manifest error in this determination.

Having found a contingent fee contract exists, we now turn to the question of whether Mr. Culpepper is entitled to recover any attorney's fees under this contract. Pursuant to the parties' agreement, Mr. Culpepper is entitled to one-third "of whatever additional property or money" he obtained on behalf of Mr. Cole. It is undisputed that Mr. Cole recovered no additional property or money as a result of the litigation against his mother's estate. Because Mr. Cole obtained no recovery, it follows that Mr. Culpepper is not entitled to any contingent fee.

Nonetheless, Mr. Culpepper urges us to find that his contingency should attach to the settlement offer he obtained on behalf of his client, even though his client refused to accept that offer. According to Mr. Culpepper, he did the work for which Mr. Cole retained him, and he is therefore entitled to one-third of the amount offered in settlement, notwithstanding Mr. Cole's rejection of the settlement offer.

With the benefit of hindsight, it would have been in Mr. Cole's best interest to accept the settlement offer obtained by Mr. Culpepper.

However, it is clear that the decision to accept a settlement belongs to the client alone. *See* Rule 1.2(a) of the Rules of Professional Conduct ("A lawyer shall abide by a client's decision whether to settle a matter."). Therefore, regardless of the wisdom of Mr. Cole's decision, his refusal to accept the settlement was binding on Mr. Culpepper.

To allow Mr. Culpepper to recover a contingent fee under these circumstances would penalize Mr. Cole for exercising his right to reject the settlement. We find no statutory or jurisprudential support for such a proposition. Indeed, this court has rejected any interpretation of the Rules of Professional Conduct which would place restrictions on the client's fundamental right to control the case. ...

In summary, we find that Mr. Culpepper did not obtain any recovery on behalf of Mr. Cole. In the absence of a recovery, it follows that Mr. Culpepper cannot collect a contingent fee for his services. Accordingly, we must reverse the judgment of the court of appeal awarding a contingent fee to Mr. Culpepper.

INQUIRY

Reasonableness of Contingency Fees. The United States is unusual in allowing contingency fees, due in part to its American Rule that each party bears its own fees in the absence of statute. *See, e.g.,* 42 U.S.C. §1988 (civil rights actions); *see also* Blum v. Stenson, 465 U.S. 886 (1984) (fees paid as percentage of common fund). Many other nations following the English Rule under which the losing party pays the prevailing party's attorney's fees. Without the prospect for fee shifting, either under the English Rule, a contract clause, or a fee-shifting statute, lawyers would be reluctant or unwilling to represent indigent parties unless they could recover their fees from the parties' recovery. Contingency fees allow for representation when a party has no financial means by which to retain counsel other than the anticipated benefit from the representation. Yet ABA Model Rule 1.5(a) still requires that the contingency fee be reasonable. Contingency fees present special opportunities for abuse because they do not always depend on the time that a lawyer spends on the client's matter. If a major contingency-fee claim settles with a few demand letters and telephone calls, then the resulting fee may be so high when calculated on an hourly basis that the fee is unreasonable. The contingency-fee lawyer bears a risk that the hourly fee lawyer does not, and risk is a factor in judging a fee's reasonableness, but risk alone does not justify an exorbitant fee. Contingency-fee lawyers can address some of this concern by using sliding-fee scales where the percentage fee is smaller if the case settles at an earlier stage, but in any case, the fee must still be reasonable. Consider the following case.

In re Calahan,
Louisiana Supreme Court
930 So.2d 916 (2006)

PER CURIAM.

This disciplinary matter arises from formal charges filed by the Office of Disciplinary Counsel ("ODC") against respondent, Pressley Charles Calahan, an attorney licensed to practice law in Louisiana.

UNDERLYING FACTS AND PROCEDURAL HISTORY

... Count I—The Hebert Matter

David Hebert retained an attorney to represent him in a maritime personal injury case. When the case settled in the fall of 1998, Mr. Hebert paid attorney's fees of more than $36,000. Believing this sum to be excessive, Mr. Hebert retained respondent in late September 2000 to assist him in recovering a portion of the fee. Respondent informed Mr. Hebert that his fee in such matters customarily ranged from 40%-50% of the amount recovered, and he presented Mr. Hebert with a contingent fee agreement to that effect. However, Mr. Hebert refused to sign the agreement, as he understood from prior discussions with respondent that the fee would be based upon an hourly rate. On October 2, 2000, respondent faxed Mr. Hebert's former attorney a one-page letter demanding the return of the excessive legal fee.... .

On October 4, 2000, two days after receiving respondent's letter, the attorney refunded $30,000 to respondent on Mr. Hebert's behalf. Respondent paid $17,500 to Mr. Hebert by check drawn on his client trust account dated October 5, 2000, and retained $12,500 as his attorney's fee. Though Mr. Hebert had specifically refused to sign a contingent fee agreement in connection with respondent's representation, the legal fee that respondent collected was approximately 40% of the amount he recovered. Mr. Hebert subsequently retained new counsel and filed both a disciplinary complaint and a civil suit against respondent with respect to the $12,500 fee. ...

Hearing Committee Recommendation

In Count I, the Hebert matter, the hearing committee found that respondent attempted to enforce a contingent fee against his former client, but when it became apparent that effort was failing, he shifted his argument to an hourly arrangement in an attempt to justify the fee. Respondent's reconstructed time records reflect 81 hours, which would have supported the $12,500 fee if truly spent on the case.

However, the committee found respondent was not credible in his assertion that he spent 81 hours working on Mr. Hebert's case. The committee determined that respondent worked no more than five to ten hours in the matter, and that the $12,500 fee was excessive. Based on these factual findings, the committee found that respondent charged an unreasonable fee, in violation of Rules 1.5(a) and 8.4(a). Respondent also violated Rule 1.5(b) by failing to communicate whether the fee was to be a contingent fee or an hourly fee, and violated Rule 1.5(c) by failing to have a contingent fee agreement in writing. Respondent produced a written contingent fee agreement that Mr. Hebert refused to sign, but respondent nevertheless proceeded to collect his fee and defend the suit against him on the basis that a contingent fee contract was in place. ...

DISCUSSION

... Respondent has clearly engaged in professional misconduct. In ... the Hebert matter, respondent charged his client a $12,500 legal fee to write a one-page demand letter to another lawyer who, ironically, had charged the client an excessive legal fee. Mr. Hebert had specifically refused to pay respondent's proposed 40%-50% contingent fee in connection with the endeavor, but nevertheless, the legal fee respondent charged was approximately 40% of the amount recovered from the first lawyer. When Mr. Hebert questioned the amount of the fee, respondent refused to acknowledge his client's justifiable concerns, telling him in a rather cavalier fashion to "do what you got to do."

Mr. Hebert took respondent's advice and filed a disciplinary complaint and a civil suit against respondent. In the disciplinary matter, respondent began with the argument that the fee was negotiated and was not a contingent fee. Meanwhile, in the civil suit, respondent argued that he did have a contingent fee agreement. When it became apparent that argument was going to be unsuccessful because the contingent fee agreement was not in writing, respondent said the fee was calculated on an hourly basis. In support of that argument, respondent conjured up a timesheet showing that he worked on Mr. Hebert's case for **81 hours,** which coincidentally was enough time to justify the entirety of the $12,500 fee. The trial court correctly rejected this fabrication, but respondent persisted in that argument during his disciplinary hearing. He continues to maintain that he is entitled to the exorbitant fee because it was fully earned (reasoning that the successful oil well has to pay for the "dry holes"), and indeed questions why his client objected in the first place, since the $17,500 Mr. Hebert received was more than what he started out with. We find respondent's conduct in this case is serious, and his defense of the matter has bordered on perjury. Standing alone, the misconduct in Count I warrants a lengthy suspension from the practice of law. [C] ...

[The court also held that the respondent had defrauded a legally blind woman into signing a contingency-fee agreement, forging an endorsement on a settlement check, and forging a signature on an affidavit, among other misconduct.]

DECREE

... [I]t is ordered that Pressley Charles Calahan ... be and he hereby is disbarred. His name shall be stricken from the roll of attorneys and his license to practice law in the State of Louisiana shall be revoked. ...

INQUIRY

Quantum Meruit. What should happen if, as in the above case, there is no clear fee agreement or if the agreement in place does not cover what happens in the representation? Lawyers who comply with conduct rules and fee statutes may recover in quantum meruit when a client accepts and benefits from legal services not covered by formal fee agreement. One such instance may occur when a client discharges a lawyer in a contingency-fee case after the lawyer has provided substantial services but before the lawyer and client have ascertained the recovery. A wise lawyer would provide in the contingency-fee agreement for that and other eventualities. A contingency-fee agreement might define an hourly or percentage fee recovery if the client terminates the representation early. A lawyer may also negotiate with successor counsel regarding the quantum meruit fee, as soon as successor counsel assumes the representation and can evaluate the value of the prior lawyer's services. A lawyer is likely to have a fee claim against the client who terminates the lawyer without cause, *see* Malonis v. Harrington, 816 N.E.2d 115 (Mass. 2004), especially if the client attempts duplicitously to fire the lawyer after having agreed to a settlement out of which the client had contracted to pay the lawyer a contingency fee, *see* Dweck Law Firm, L.L.P. v. Mann, 340 F. Supp.2d 353 (S.D. N.Y. 2004) (breach of covenant of good faith and fair dealing). Should it make a difference if the client terminates the prior lawyer with cause, or if the prior lawyer withdrew without cause? *See* Rus, Miliband & Smith v. Conkle & Olesten, 6 Cal.Rptr.3d 612 (Cal. Ct. App. 2003) (no fee due on lawyer's withdrawal without cause from contingency-fee case resulting in $1.875 million settlement). Consider one quantum-meruit case illustrating the challenges of negotiating or calculating a reasonable fee.

Keys v. Mercy Hospital,
Louisiana Court of Appeals
537 So.2d 1223 (1989)

In this case attorneys John T. Cooper and Richard I. Farmer intervened in an action for damages to protect their rights under a contingency fee contract. Prior to judgment being rendered John Cooper settled his claim. Richard Farmer appeals a judgment reducing his fee of one-sixth of the total recovery as required by the contigency fee contract to $4,600 plus legal interest from date of judicial demand. ... We affirm.

Elphage Keys' wife died in Mercy Hospital... . Keys employed attorneys Richard Farmer and John Cooper to represent h[im] and his minor son in a claim for damages. On October 23, 1978, Keys executed a contingency fee contract assigning one-third interest in the case to Farmer and Cooper.

Keys testified that on June 24, 1981, March 4, 1982, and August 18, 1982, he sent letters to Farmer discharging him. On October 27, 1982, Donna Condie enrolled as counsel of record and trial attorney in this matter. Farmer and Cooper then intervened in an attempt to preserve their contingency fee. Upon completion of trial on the damages issue, judgment was rendered awarding Keys damages totalling $350,000 ($200,000 to Keys and $150,000 to his minor child). That judgment is now final.

Following trial of the intervention, the district court entered judgment limiting Farmer's recovery to quantum meruit and awarding him $4,600 for legal services rendered.

On appeal Farmer ... alleges the trial court erred in finding he was discharged for cause and in not awarding him his full contingency fee.
...

The Louisiana jurisprudence has clearly stated that where a party to a contingency fee agreement discharges his attorney before the fee is earned the attorney's mandate is revoked, the contract is dissolved and quantum meruit provides the proper basis for recovery. [Cc] The phrase, quantum meruit, means as much as is deserved. [C] The determination of an attorney's compensation under a quantum meruit analysis is predicated upon an evaluation of the facts in the record and an application of the criteria listed in Disciplinary Rule 2-106(B) of the Code of Professional Responsibility. [C] A quantum meruit analysis properly evaluates not merely the laws expended, but the results and benefits obtained. [C] Therefore, recovery is limited to the actual value of the service rendered. [C]

In awarding Farmer $4,600 the trial judge indicated, in his reasons for judgment, that he relied heavily on a finding that the work product of Farmer and Cooper was of little or no assistance to subsequent counsel at trial on the merits or on appellate review. These conclusions are well supported by the record.

The record reflects that Farmer's role in handling this matter was limited to obtaining medical authorization forms and the autopsy report, discussing the composition of and representation before the Medical Review Panel, obtaining nurse's notes, assisting co-counsel with responsive pleadings, but not in the pleadings themselves, and generally discussing with his associate and Keys the legal aspects of the case under litigation. His efforts before the Medical Review Panel were unsuccessful. Suit was filed on behalf of his client on August 11, 1982. His testimony and the evidence reflect that the theory of recovery employed by Farmer is not the theory on which the case was successfully litigated. We therefore, find the trial court correctly compensated Farmer for the limited benefit which his efforts rendered his client.

For the foregoing reasons, the judgment of the district court is affirmed. ...

INQUIRY

Fee Divisions. Lawyers who are in the same firm may divide fees earned by a single lawyer's services to a single client in whatever fashion the lawyers' partnership agreement so provides. Some firms are more entrepreneurial, permitting lawyers to keep more of the fees that they earn, whether by salary increases, draws, or bonuses. Other firms are more collegial, requiring lawyers to share more of the fees that they earn. The conduct rules do not address fee divisions within firms. ABA Model Rule 1.5(e) addresses divisions of fees between lawyers who are not the same firm, permitting a fee division only in proportion to services performed or if both lawyers share joint responsibility for the client's matter. The client must also agree to the share that each lawyer will receive, with that agreement confirmed in writing, and the total fee remaining reasonable. *See* Chambers v. Kay, 56 P.3d 645 (Cal. 2002) (fee-sharing agreement unenforceable without client disclosure and consent). What concern does Model Rule 1.5(e) address? When lawyers refer matters to other lawyers, they may wish to do so in exchange for a referral fee. The advertising and prominence of some lawyers give them the opportunity to earn substantial referral fees in arrangements that make them more like brokers than practicing lawyers. If the client is unaware that the lawyer with whom they initially deal is little more than a broker of claims, then the referral arrangement will have misled them into a relationship with the lawyer receiving the referral. Model Rule 1.5(e) makes referral arrangements transparent and reduces brokered claims, although some states permit referral fees with fewer restrictions. *See* MICH. R. PROF. CONDUCT 1.5(e).

Money Laundering. The United States Supreme Court has held that criminal defendants have no right to pay their lawyers with funds derived from criminal activity. *See* United States v. Monsanto, 109 S. Ct. 2657 (1989); Caplin & Drysdale v. United States, 109 S.Ct. 2667 (1989). The Supreme Court's stance leaves criminal-defense lawyers who receive large sums of money from their clients with the concern that they may be targeted for prosecution for money laundering, even though the federal Money Laundering Act of 1986, 18 U.S.C. §1957, does not directly prohibit criminal defendants from paying their attorneys fees with criminally derived funds. How can criminal-defense lawyers taking large retainers protect themselves from money-laundering charges? Another provision about which all lawyers must be aware is the IRS requirement that any person who who receives more than $10,000 in cash from one person or entity while conducting their trade or business must file a Form 8300 with the IRS. The $10,000 transfer may occur in a single transaction or two or more related transactions that result in an excess of $10,000 being received by the business owner within a 12-month period. Is it ethical to ask the client to have someone else pay the fee or pay the fee in small amounts over time?

B. Client Property

Fiduciary Practice. Lawyers handle the funds and property of clients and others as a matter of course in many different practice circumstances. Lawyers gather, manage, and distribute assets of estates in probate, guardianship, and conservatorship proceedings. *See* Idaho State Bar v. Frazier, 28 P.3d 363 (Idaho 2001) (discipline relating to theft of estate jewelry from lawyer's briefcase). They retain original wills and deeds. *See* In re Blackmon, 629 S.E.2d 369 (S.C. 2006). They receive and disburse litigation settlement funds. They act as escrow agents in real-estate and business transactions, and when persons or entities dispute title to property or rights to funds. They hold property in trust for clients under treatment or prosecution. *See* Florida Bar v. Grosso, 760 So.2d 940 (Fla. 2000) (lawyer disciplined for failure to return client's firearms after successful completion of prosecution). They also hold client advances on fees. A large part of the value of lawyer services lies in their willingness and ability to act responsibly when holding others' property. The lack of that trust would seriously handicap lawyers, their clients, and others in legal and financial transactions. To build and maintain that trust, lawyers accept the responsibility of fiduciaries when holding others' property. They act with the greatest care as to others' property and with the greatest degree of loyalty to the interest of those others in that property. ABA Model Rule 1.15 articulates several specific obligations carrying out these fiduciary obligations, including to hold others' property separately rather than to commingle it with the lawyer's property and not to take property as to which the lawyer has a claim while the claim remains in dispute. Consider a similar state version of Model Rule 1.15 followed by a case illustrating the core duty.

> UTAH R. PROF. CONDUCT 1.15: **Safekeeping Property.**
> (a) A lawyer shall hold property of clients or third persons that is in a lawyer's possession in connection with a representation separate from the lawyer's own property. Funds shall be kept in a separate account maintained in the state where the lawyer's office is situated or elsewhere with the consent of the client or third person. The account may only be maintained in a financial institution that agrees to report to the Office of Professional Conduct in the event any instrument in properly payable form is presented against an attorney trust account containing insufficient funds, irrespective of whether or not the instrument is honored. Other property shall be identified as such and appropriately safeguarded. Complete records of such account funds and other property shall be kept by the lawyer and shall be preserved for a period of five years after termination of the representation.
> (b) A lawyer may deposit the lawyer's own funds in a client trust account for the sole purpose of paying bank service charges on that account, but only in an amount necessary for that purpose.
> (c) A lawyer shall deposit into a client trust account legal fees and expenses that have been paid in advance, to be withdrawn by the lawyer only as fees are earned or expenses incurred.
> (d) Upon receiving funds or other property in which a client or third person has an interest, a lawyer shall promptly notify the client or third person. Except as stated in this Rule or otherwise permitted by law or by agreement with the client, a lawyer shall promptly deliver to the client or third person any funds or other property that the client or third person is entitled to receive and, upon request by the client or third person, shall promptly render a full accounting regarding such property.
> (e) When in the course of representation a lawyer is in possession of property in which two or more persons (one of whom may be the lawyer) claim interests, the property shall be kept separate by the lawyer until the dispute is resolved. The lawyer shall promptly distribute all portions of the property as to which the interests are not in dispute.

_____

In the Matter of Disciplinary Proceedings Against Strnad,
Wisconsin Supreme Court
505 N.W.2d 134 (1993)

... In our order granting reconsideration, we directed the parties to address in their briefs the issue of whether an attorney's taking trust account funds awarded by a court to a client and applying those funds to the attorney's fees while there is a dispute between the attorney and the client as to the fee to which the attorney is entitled violates SCR 20:1.15 concerning a lawyer's safekeeping of client property. The court stayed pending reconsideration the 60-day suspension of Attorney Strnad's license it imposed.

... In his report to the court in this proceeding, the referee made findings that on two occasions Attorney Strnad withdrew from his trust account and applied to his fee funds previously ordered by the circuit court to be held in a trust account pending further order and that he did so without a court order allowing or approving such withdrawal. ...

We reject Attorney Strnad's argument that the court impermissibly relied on the settlement of his fee he and his client ultimately reached as evidence that he did not reasonably believe he was entitled to apply to his fee the full amount of the client's funds he took from his trust account. ... Neither the referee nor the court made a determination concerning the amount to which Attorney Strnad was entitled as his fee for representing the client.

We next address the issue we directed the parties to address in this reconsideration: whether Attorney Strnad's withdrawal of his client's funds from his trust account as partial payment of his fee while there was a dispute between himself and his client as to that fee violated the court's rules concerning a lawyer's safekeeping of client property. Attorney Strnad contended that the moment the circuit court awarded the funds he was holding to his client, those funds "belonged" to him, not to the client, as he had a lien on them by virtue of the services he had rendered to the client. He further argued that the judgment awarding the funds to his client terminated the account in which he held those funds and, as a result, SCR 20.50(1)(b) no longer was applicable. Those arguments have no merit, neither does Attorney Strnad's attempt to find ambiguity in the word "belonging" as used in that rule.

The Board correctly asserted that the issue is controlled by Disciplinary Proceedings Against Marine, 82 Wis.2d 602, 264 N.W.2d 285 (1978). There, the court determined that in order for an attorney to unilaterally withdraw from a trust account funds belonging to a client, there must be an agreement between the client and the attorney on three points: the right of the attorney to look to the client for the payment of the attorney's fee, the amount to which the attorney is entitled and the time at which payment will be expected. The court said, "Absent an agreement as to these matters it is difficult to see how any reasonably prudent attorney could assume that part of his client's trust funds could legally be withdrawn, because the requirement that they be withdrawn only in the absence of a dispute clearly assumes that the client has at least been advised as to these matters."

The modification of our opinion we make herein does not affect our determination of discipline to be imposed for Attorney Strnad's professional misconduct. ...   [A]n order of the trial court was anticipated in order to establish Attorney Strand's entitlement to any portion of the client funds he held, as well as any amount in excess thereof. Because there was no order from the court determining his fee and because his client had not approved or even knew of his withdrawals of her funds and because he knew the client was disputing his fee, Attorney Strnad violated former SCR 20.50(1)(b).

IT IS FURTHER ORDERED that the license suspension ordered by the court on November 12, 1992 shall commence November 1, 1993. ...

————————————

I N Q U I R Y

Rule Against Commingling. ABA Model Rule 1.15(a) begins with a rule against commingling, requiring that lawyers hold client property separate from the lawyer's property. The anti-commingling rule accomplishes several goals. It discourages lawyers from purposefully or mistakenly using client property. *See, e.g.,* In re Baxter, 940 P.2d 37 (Kan. 1997) (mistaken use of client's settlement check deposited into firm's account). It simplifies and makes more transparent the lawyer's accounting for client funds. It prevents client property from being drawn into disputes over lawyer funds. It also keeps third parties from garnishing or otherwise executing on client property when enforcing rights against the lawyer. *See* In re Glorioso, 819 So.2d 320 (La. 2002) (commingling client funds risked tax seizure for lawyer's unpaid obligations); In re Anonymous, 698 N.E.2d 808 (Ind. 1998) (commingling subjects client funds to attachment for lawyer obligations). And it prevents lawyers from using client funds to hide their own funds from execution and reporting. *See* In re Lund, 19 P.3d 110 (Kan. 2001) (lawyer hiding funds from ex-wife in client trust account); In re Betancourt, 661 N.Y.S.2d 208 (App. Div. 1997) (lawyer uses trust account to prevent garnishment by creditor). Any misuse, intentional or not, of client funds is likely to result in discipline. *See, e.g.,* In re Asher, 772 A.2d 1161 (D.C. 2001) (per se offense).

Intentional misuse of client funds is likely to result in severe discipline. *See* State ex rel. NSBA v. Frederiksen, 635 N.W.2d 427 (Neb. 2001) (three-year suspension for theft of $15,000 by lawyer dissatisfied with compensation). Yet the worst scheme, sure to result in disbarment for the multiple clients it would harm, would be for a lawyer to misuse client funds for the lawyer's own purpose while replenishing those funds with other client funds, in a pyramid or kiting scheme. *See, e.g.,* In re Freimark, 702 A.2d 1286 (N.J. 1997).

   Lawyer Trust Accounts.   Although some lawyers may hold and control real or personal property belonging to others, nearly all lawyers find it necessary and expedient from time to time to hold funds belonging to others. Lawyers do so in trust accounts. What do you think is the purpose of ABA Model Rule 1.15(a)'s provision for a trust-account bank reporting insufficient-funds notices to discipline officials? Irregularities in trust accounts are among the most common of sources for client loss and lawyer discipline. Bars have found that early warning of trust-account irregularities can prevent larger problems later. What must lawyers do when they need to draw on trust-account funds to pay the practice's expenses and are entitled to do so by, for instance, having earned the advanced fee? Lawyers do not use a trust account to pay the practice's expenses. They will have an office account out of which to do so. If the circumstances entitle a lawyer to some or all of the funds in a trust account, for instance as an earned and undisputed fee, then the lawyer will transfer those funds from the trust account into the office account for further disbursement for wages and expenses. If only funds belonging to clients and others are to go into a trust account, then how can a lawyer keep a trust account open when the host bank needs to withdraw an account fee? ABA Model Rule 1.15(b) permits a lawyer to place the lawyer's own money into a trust account solely to pay bank charges.

   Interest on Lawyer Trust Accounts.   Who gets the interest that a properly managed trust account may earn? States have enacted interest-on-lawyer-trust-account (IOLTA) laws that require banks holding lawyer trust accounts to convey the interest into state funds for representation of the indigent. *See, e.g.,* TENN. SUP. CT. R. 43; *see also* Brown v. Legal Fdn., 538 U.S. 216 (2003) (state law requiring state receive interest on lawyer trust accounts is not a regulatory taking). Lawyers occasionally hold large sums of money, particularly in settlement of major personal-injury or wrongful-death cases, where even the daily interest can be substantial. In those instances, state IOLTA laws may permit lawyers to open a separate special trust account for the client's large sum and pay the interest to the client. The important point is that lawyers do not make money holding others' funds. *See* Florida bar v. Dancu, 490 So.2d 40 (Fla. 1986) (rule violation for lawyer to keep interest on client funds without client knowledge and consent).

Client-Protection Funds. State bars maintain client-protection funds out of which to provide compensation to clients who suffer loss due to intentional lawyer misconduct. State bar dues fund client-protection funds. Most lawyers insure against malpractice liability, and many clients who suffer harm can obtain a malpractice-insurance recovery. Yet insurance does not cover loss caused by intentional wrongs. For instance, when a lawyer absconds with a client's settlement funds, insurance recovery may be unlikely. In those cases, a client-protection fund can provide at least some recovery. Because state bars can divert only a limited portion of their modest dues to client protection, client-protection funds are limited. Most state bars cap recovery at amounts ranging from $10,000 to $50,000. Given that lawyers can handle far larger sums in certain practice areas, client-protection funds offer only a limited remedy for serious misconduct. They do not protect loss from carelessness. In a few states, restitution in a disciplinary proceeding is also possible.

C. Lawyer Supervision

Managerial Authority. The work that lawyers do with other lawyers increases their productivity. Law firms tend to structure lawyers into a hierarchy of partners and associates, in some larger firms with classes of senior and junior partners, and senior and junior associates. Even in firms with a less formal structure, more experienced lawyers with larger client bases may assign work to less experienced lawyers who have fewer clients. Every firm has some form of management structure, formal or informal, through which the firm ensures efficient service to clients. With management comes responsibility. ABA Model Rule 5.1 requires that partners and lawyers with comparable managerial authority ensure that all lawyers in the firm follow the conduct rules. Law firm managers must not allow practice to devolve to sink-or-swim conditions that foster rule violations. *See* In re Yacavino, 494 A.2d 801 (N.J. 1985). Model Rule 5.1 requires specifically that supervising lawyers take reasonable care to ensure that subordinate lawyers follow the conduct rules. Less experienced lawyers require more supervision. *See* Fla. Bar v. Nowacki, 697 So.2d 828 (Fla. 1997) (discipline for leaving entire caseload to new associate while undergoing cancer treatment). Model Rule 5.1 also provides for a limited kind of managerial responsibility for partners, managers, and supervising lawyers when they learn of a violation but fail to take reasonable remedial action. *See* In re Myers, 584 S.E.2d 357 (S.C. 2003) (supervisory lawyer violates Rule 5.1 by not notifying opposing counsel when subordinate should have);   In re Bailey, 821 A.2d 851 (Del. 2003) (enhanced duty of managing partner to ensure every lawyer's compliance).   Consider an identical state version of ABA Model Rule 5.1, followed by a case discussing that managerial responsibility.

DELAWARE R. PROF. CONDUCT 5.1:   **Responsibilities of Partners, Managers, and Supervisory Lawyers.**
(a) A partner in a law firm, and a lawyer who individually or together with other lawyers possesses comparable managerial authority in a law firm, shall make reasonable efforts to ensure that the firm has in effect measures giving reasonable assurance that all lawyers in the firm conform to the Rules of Professional Conduct.
(b) A lawyer having direct supervisory authority over another lawyer shall make reasonable efforts to ensure that the other lawyer conforms to the Rules of Professional Conduct.
(c) A lawyer shall be responsible for another lawyer's violation of the Rules of Professional Conduct if:
(1) the lawyer orders or, with knowledge of the specific conduct, ratifies the conduct involved; or
(2) the lawyer is a partner or has comparable managerial authority in the law firm in which the other lawyer practices, or has direct supervisory authority over the other lawyer, and knows of the conduct at a time when its consequences can be avoided or mitigated but fails to take reasonable remedial action.

In re Cohen,
District of Columbia Court of Appeals
847 A.2d 1162 (2004)

PER CURIAM.[fn]
This disciplinary proceeding arises from one count of formal charges filed by the Office of Disciplinary Counsel ("ODC") against respondent, Neal W. Wilkinson, an attorney licensed to practice law in the State of Louisiana.

UNDERLYING FACTS
In   August,   1996,   Kimberly   Saucier   Emanuel   approached respondent about handling the succession of her father, who had passed away, leaving Mrs. Emanuel as executrix of his estate. Respondent advised Mrs. Emanuel that he could not take the case because he was involved in an election campaign.   However, he introduced Mrs. Emanuel to Paul Doug Stewart, a Mississippi law school graduate who was working as a law clerk in respondent's office and had taken the Louisiana bar examination in July, 1996. Respondent advised Mrs. Emanuel that Mr. Stewart could handle the necessary   preliminary   matters   in   the   case   under   respondent's

supervision, and then fully assume the representation once he was admitted to the bar. Based on respondent's assertions, Mrs. Emanuel agreed to the arrangement, and gave respondent $650, which he agreed to hold in trust for Mr. Stewart's anticipated expenses. According to respondent, he cautioned Mr. Stewart not to give any legal advice to Mrs. Emanuel.

Days following the meeting, Mr. Stewart drafted a letter to Mrs. Emanuel, under both his name and respondent's name, confirming that respondent's law firm would be handling the succession matter. The letter promised to keep Mrs. Emanuel informed on a variety of issues on which she might need "further legal advice." Respondent was generally made aware of the contents of the letter by telephone, and directed his secretary to send it out under his signature. Mr. Stewart also signed the letter.

The following day, respondent sent a letter to the will's notary and witnesses asking them to execute affidavits to permit the probate of the will. After sending these letters, respondent had no further involvement in the succession. He never spoke with Mrs. Emanuel again, nor did he ever review her file. Although he discussed the fee arrangement with Mr. Stewart, respondent never specifically inquired about the details of Mr. Stewart's handling of the succession proceeding.

In early September, 1996, still prior to Mr. Stewart's bar admission, the heirs began receiving notices from one of the mortgage creditors. While Mr. Stewart attempted to resolve the matter with the mortgage company, he was unable to successfully handle the problem. Mr. Stewart never advised respondent of the problems with the mortgage company.

In October, 1996, Mr. Stewart was admitted to the practice of law in Louisiana. Approximately four months later, Mr. Stewart left respondent's firm for other employment. Mr. Stewart specifically advised respondent's secretary that he was leaving the succession file. The file sat unattended for several months in respondent's office.

DISCIPLINARY PROCEEDINGS

Subsequently, Mrs. Emanuel learned that incorrect advice given by Mr. Stewart resulted in creditors foreclosing on certain succession property. As a result, Mrs. Emanuel filed a disciplinary complaint against Mr. Stewart for mishandling the succession. The ODC ultimately closed its investigation into the complaint because Mr. Stewart was not admitted to the bar at the time of the misconduct.

However, the ODC initiated its own investigation into respondent's conduct, based on his failure to supervise Mr. Stewart during the time in question. As a result of this investigation, the ODC filed one count of formal charges against respondent alleging violations of Rules 1.1

(incompetence), 1.2 (lack of due diligence), 5.1 (failure of attorney to supervise a subordinate attorney) and 5.3 (failure to properly supervise a non lawyer assistant) of the Rules of Professional Conduct. Subsequently, it amended the formal charges to include a violation of Rule 5.5 (assisting a nonmember of the bar to engage in the unauthorized practice of law). Respondent filed answers denying any misconduct on his part.

Formal Hearing

At the formal hearing, Mr. Stewart … conceded he gave Mrs. Emanuel erroneous legal advice regarding the property, but stated respondent was unaware he had given this advice. Mr. Stewart testified respondent had instructed him not to give any legal advice, but noted that respondent did not make any attempts to determine whether he had given advice to her during their meeting, which occurred in respondent's absence. …

Respondent testified Mrs. Emanuel knew he had no interest in handling her case. As to his referring the matter to Mr. Stewart, respondent asserted he never thought he placed his client at risk because he believed the case was a simple succession matter that would not require any initial legal advice. Respondent stated he had no knowledge Mr. Stewart had given erroneous legal advice, and that he was unaware there were any problems with the succession until the complaint was filed against Mr. Stewart. As to the letter of representation forwarded to Mrs. Emanuel, respondent alleged he was only generally made aware of the contents of the letter by telephone, whereupon he instructed his secretary to sign and mail the letter out. He maintained that had he known the full contents of the letter, he probably would not have sent the letter out. While he asserted he did not violate the Rules of Professional Conduct, respondent admitted if he had known about the problem earlier, he would have stepped in to do something about it.

In mitigation, respondent noted, at the time in question, his wife was suffering from a terminal illness. He traveled to New Orleans after work each day, where she was hospitalized, and returned each evening to care for his children. His wife passed away soon after. …

DISCUSSION

… While respondent may have not been directly responsible for the incorrect legal advice given by Mr. Stewart to Mrs. Emanuel, we find he breached his professional obligation to Mrs. Emanuel by failing to properly supervise Mr. Stewart. Respondent essentially turned the case over to Mr. Stewart, knowing at the time that Mr. Stewart was not licensed to practice law in Louisiana and was unfamiliar with Louisiana succession law. Respondent did not speak with Mrs. Emanuel after his initial meeting, nor did he review her file.

Under these circumstances, we conclude respondent breached his fundamental obligations to Mrs. Emanuel under Rules 5.1(b) and 5.3(b) to ensure the actions of his non-lawyer assistant (and later subordinate attorney) conformed to the rules of professional conduct. Although the evidence indicated respondent did not know Mr. Stewart gave the incorrect advice to Mrs. Emanuel, respondent, as the client's attorney, retains compete responsibility for the representation. As we explained in *Louisiana State Bar Ass'n v. Edwins,* 540 So.2d 294, 299 (La.1989): "A lawyer often delegates tasks to clerks, secretaries, and other lay persons. Such delegation is proper if the lawyer maintains a direct relationship with his client, supervises the delegated work, and has complete professional responsibility for the work product ... A lawyer cannot delegate his professional responsibility to a law student employed in his office ... The student in all his work must act as agent for the lawyer employing him, who must supervise his work and be responsible for his good conduct." ...

Having found respondent violated Rules 5.1(b) and 5.3(b) in failing to supervise Mr. Stewart's handling of the matter, the sole question remaining is the appropriate sanction for this misconduct. ...

Respondent's misconduct caused actual harm to his client, causing the succession to pay nearly $10,000 to redeem the foreclosed property. Aggravating factors are present, including respondent's refusal to acknowledge the wrongful nature of his misconduct and his substantial experience in the practice of law. We also recognize the presence of mitigating factors, including respondent's personal problems and the lack of a dishonest or selfish motive.

Having considered these factors, we conclude the appropriate sanction for respondent's misconduct is a sixty-day suspension from the practice of law. ...

INQUIRY

Subordinate Lawyers.   Supervision raises its own issues for subordinate lawyers. ABA Model Rule 5.2(a) requires subordinate lawyers to comply with the conduct rules even when directed by a supervisory partner to violate them. Is that requirement fair? Model Rule 5.2(a) addresses the so-called Nuremberg defense raised in the Nazi war-crimes trials. In effect, Model Rule 5.2(a) means that it does not matter if the boss is Hitler—you still follow the rules. Yet Model Rule 5.2(b) provides a narrow safe harbor for the subordinate lawyer when the supervisory lawyer resolves reasonably an arguable conduct-rule question. If, in other words, after research the subordinate lawyer is still unsure of how a conduct rule applies, the subordinate lawyer may accept a supervisory lawyer's reasonable resolution. Is that safe harbor necessary or helpful? If so, is it large enough, too large, or just about right? Lawyers practice in part by applying accepted professional conventions with the conventions defining otherwise uncertain boundaries on arguable questions of duty. What may look somewhat like a questionable shortcut may in fact be a reliable safe harbor that lawyers have developed and agreed to over time. Yet the question must first be arguable for a supervisory lawyer to resolve it contrary to the subordinate lawyer's better inclination. *See, e.g.,* Holland v. The Gordy Company, 2003 WL 19858000 (Mich. Ct. App. April 29, 2003) (associate not entitled to rely on partners whom he called for directions after discovering that opposing counsel had inadvertently produced counsel's litigation file for inspection). A subordinate lawyer must refuse a supervisory lawyer's instruction when the subordinate lawyer knows that it will result in a conduct rule violation. Consider an identical state version of ABA Model Rule 5.2, followed by a case in which a subordinate lawyer unwisely relied on the unreasonable advice of superiors.

> **DELAWARE R. PROF. CONDUCT 5.2:   Responsibilities of a Subordinate Lawyer.**
> (a) A lawyer is bound by the Rules of Professional Conduct notwithstanding that the lawyer acted at the direction of another person.
> (b) A subordinate lawyer does not violate the Rules of Professional Conduct if that lawyer acts in accordance with a supervisory lawyer's reasonable resolution of an arguable question of professional duty.

In re Lightfoot,
United States Court of Appeals for the Seventh Circuit
217 F.3d 914 (2000)

POSNER, Chief Judge.

... [W]e directed Assistant U.S. Attorney Lori Lightfoot to show cause why she should not be disciplined for conduct unbecoming a member of the bar of this court. [C] She responded by submitting a brief and a number of supporting documents, including testimonials to her character from lawyers whom she has appeared opposite to in court, and the Department of Justice submitted an amicus curiae brief in her support. At her request we held an oral hearing at which she, her lawyer, and the U.S. Attorney for the Northern District of Illinois presented argument to us and answered our questions.

... [O]n August 19 of last year, at about 1:00 p.m., the U.S. Marshals Service, equipped with a certification of extraditability and a surrender warrant, brought Lars Lindstrom to the garage of the federal courthouse in Chicago, where they met two Norwegian policemen. A marshal drove Lindstrom and the two Norwegians (Lindstrom is Swedish) to O'Hare Airport. They had tickets to fly to Norway on a plane scheduled to depart at 5:00. At 2:20, about twenty minutes after the marshal and his passengers arrived at O'Hare, Lindstrom's lawyer applied to this court for an emergency stay of extradition, which Judge Rovner granted forthwith in order to have time to consider the merits of a stay pending appeal of an order that the district court had issued denying Lindstrom's petition for habeas corpus. Assistant U.S. Attorney Lightfoot, who was handling the government's defense against Lindstrom's challenge to his extradition, was notified by this court of Judge Rovner's grant of the stay at 2:55. After consulting with Deputy U.S. Attorney Joan Safford, who is in charge of international affairs for the U.S. Attorney's office for the Northern District of Illinois and who in turn consulted Randy Toledo, a lawyer in the Office of International Affairs in the criminal division of the Justice Department in Washington, Lightfoot at 4:40 p.m. filed with the court a motion to lift the stay that Judge Rovner had granted. The motion was referred to Judge Rovner and by her immediately denied, but by the time word of the denial was relayed to the marshal who had driven Lindstrom and the Norwegian policemen to the airport, the plane had left with the trio on it. As we held in our previous decision, Lindstrom's departure from the territory of the United States mooted his challenge to his extradition to Norway.

Safford and Toledo advised Lightfoot during the afternoon of August 19 that the extradition had occurred at the meeting with the Norwegian policemen in the garage of the federal courthouse, and so the stay of extradition granted by Judge Rovner was moot. We rejected this position in our previous opinion.... What seemed clear to us, and what we take this opportunity to repeat in view of doubts intimated in the briefs, is that the courts of the extraditing jurisdiction, in this case the federal courts, do not lose jurisdiction over the person of the individual to be extradited as long as he is still within United States territory. Our garage did not become Norway when Lindstrom entered the car with the Norwegian police; nor did O'Hare become Norway when he and his captors arrived there.

Our ruling established the power of Judge Rovner to issue a stay even though Lindstrom was already at O'Hare when she issued it. ... The purpose of the stay, after all, was to allow the court to consider Lindstrom's appeal from the denial of his petition for habeas corpus, and that purpose would be thwarted if the stay were interpreted as an empty gesture.

All this seems to us so clear that the contrary advice tendered by Safford and Toledo was not only unsound, but unreasonable. ...

The motion filed by attorney Lightfoot ... was misleading. It is one thing for a lawyer to advocate an unreasonable position to a court; usually the court can prevent any serious harm to anyone just by rejecting the position. It is another thing for a lawyer to defeat an opposing party's claims by misleading the court, whether by a misrepresentation or by a pregnant omission. That is misconduct, [cc], and is what happened here. To the extent, unilluminated by the record, that Safford was (as Lightfoot argues) complicit in Lightfoot's violation of the duty of candor, the fact that Safford is Lightfoot's superior would not get Lightfoot off the hook. Reliance on a superior's orders is a defense to a charge of misconduct only when reasonable, *In re Howes,* 123 N.M. 311, 940 P.2d 159, 164-65 (N.M.1997) (per curiam); ABA Model Rule of Professional Conduct 5.2, comment [2] (1995), and it is not reasonable to believe that one is authorized to mislead a court. *People v. Casey,* 948 P.2d 1014, 1016-17 (Colo.1997) (per curiam).

The motion that Lightfoot filed asked this court to lift the stay that had been "imposed regarding the surrender of Lars Lindstrom to Norwegian authorities." The natural meaning to be ascribed to this statement is that the government interpreted the stay to be a prohibition against allowing the Norwegians to remove Lindstrom from the United States and thus from the court's jurisdiction. ...

Anyone reading this motion would suppose that the government understood the stay to be a prohibition against Lindstrom's being removed from the United States. ... The motion thus created a thoroughly false impression of the government's position, an impression that could not but cause Judge Rovner to believe that unless she vacated the stay Lindstrom would remain in the United States until the merits of his appeal could be considered. The impression was false because we know that the Justice Department was proceeding on the premise that the stay which Judge Rovner had issued did not stay the removal of Lindstrom from the United States— the stay had no effect, was moot, would not prevent the 5:00 p.m. departure. Had Judge Rovner received timely notice that her stay was being so interpreted by the officials to whom it was directed, she would no doubt have issued a further order making clear that the stay was a stay of removal and not merely of some metaphysical act of "extradition" that had occurred hours before in the basement of the federal courthouse. Had Lightfoot's motion informed the court that unless it took further action Lindstrom would be on his way to Norway within minutes, Judge Rovner might have issued an order directly to the airline, and the order might have been timely; for the motion was filed at 4:40, and the plane didn't take off until 5:45. Of course it would have been much better had Lightfoot informed the court of the Justice

Department's interpretation of the stay much earlier; for remember that she learned before 3:00 p.m. that the stay had been issued.

For a government lawyer to file with a court a misleading statement the effect of which is to moot a petition for habeas corpus is professional misconduct. Lightfoot's motion was bound to lull Judge Rovner into thinking that the stay had had the intended effect of preventing Lindstrom's appeal from becoming moot.

Because the motion was (and had to be) filed hurriedly, and Lightfoot had received misleading advice from her superiors concerning a novel situation that she had never before confronted, and because her record as a lawyer is otherwise unblemished, as attested by the glowing testimonials that we have received concerning her character and her professional competence and performance, we do not think a severe sanction, such as suspension or disbarment from the bar of this court, or a recommendation to Illinois's Attorney Registration and Disciplinary Committee for disciplinary action, is warranted. We are disposed instead to regard the episode as an isolated lapse deserving only of a reprimand. We are more troubled by the attitudes and behavior of the Justice Department. The U.S. Attorney for the Northern District of Illinois in his brief and in his oral statement at the disciplinary hearing emphasized the importance of hierarchy in the Justice Department. The inference we draw is not the intended one, but that the more serious misconduct in this matter was institutional rather than personal. Considering that extradition to foreign countries is not a novel or infrequent occurrence, we are surprised to read in the U.S. Attorney's amicus brief that "it did not occur to AUSA Lightfoot *or her supervisor* at that time [i.e., after custody of Lindstrom had been transferred to the Norwegians but before the plane took off] that this Court could issue any further orders to stop the already completed extradition" (emphasis added). Remember that the supervisor in question was the Deputy U.S. Attorney who is in charge of international matters in the U.S. Attorney's office and that she was consulting a specialist in the Justice Department's home office. ...

We are troubled, finally, by the U.S. Attorney's request that we "depublish" our previous decision. ... The request to vacate our decision, which we of course deny, suggests to us that the U.S. Attorney still does not appreciate the gravity of the situation demonstrated by the uncontested facts, which reveal that the Justice Department's failure to equip its attorneys with the necessary expertise to opine on difficult issues relating to extradition precipitated the filing of a misleading motion by the Department that caused this court to lose jurisdiction over an appeal by a person who claims that he had been ordered extradited in violation of law.

Mitigating Factors. The *In re Lightfoot* case above illustrates one situation that can challenge subordinate lawyers, when supervisory lawyers in effect charge them to accomplish illicit ends. Should the supervisor's illicit charge mitigate an inexperienced subordinate's rule violation? Some courts have held that it does. *See* People v. Casey, 948 P.2d 1014 (Colo. 1997); In re Rivers, 331 S.E.2d 332 (S.C. 1984). Should the subordinate lawyer's cooperation in the investigation resulting in discipline of the supervisory lawyer mitigate the subordinate lawyer's discipline? *See* In re Segall, 638 N.Y.S.2d 444 (App. Div. 1996) (subordinate's cooperation in prosecution of $1.2 million overbilling scheme reduces subordinate's discipline to censure). Can you think of other situations that can challenge subordinate lawyers? Supervisory lawyers may fail to appreciate diligence issues that a subordinate lawyer can face when unable to keep up with an unreasonable workload. *See, e.g.,* Attorney Grievance Commn. v. Mooney, 753 A.2d 17 (Md. 2000) (case-assignment system must ensure associates have time for trial preparation). The subordinate lawyer must in those instances notify the supervisory lawyer that the subordinate lawyer cannot complete the work while fulfilling duties of diligence. Yet the supervisory lawyer also bears responsibility for workload issues. *See* Davis v. Alabama State Bar, 676 So.2d 306 (Ala. 1996) (suspension of partners for assigning associates huge caseloads).

D. Supervision of Nonlawyer Assistants

Delegating Responsibly. Lawyers can be substantially more productive with the help of qualified non-lawyer assistants like office managers, bookkeepers, paralegals or legal assistants, secretaries, and investigators. *See* Missouri v. Jenkins, 491 U.S. 274n.10 (1989) (recognizing efficiency of employing paraprofessionals). Yet the opportunity to rely on the help of non-lawyer assistants carries with it the responsibility to supervise those non-lawyer assistants. Strictly speaking, non-lawyers are not subject to lawyer conduct rules because they hold no license subject to discipline. Disciplinary authorities have no direct sway over non-lawyers. Non-lawyers cannot be disbarred or suspended from practice because they hold no license to practice. ABA Model Rule 5.3 instead makes the lawyer who employs non-lawyer assistants responsible for ensuring the integrity of the non-lawyer's assistance. *See* Mays v. Neal, 928 S.W.2d 830 (Ark. 1997) (lawyer retains ultimate responsibility for assistant's work). ABA Model Rule 5.3(a) and (b) require managing and supervisory lawyers to ensure that non-lawyer assistants conform their conduct to the professional obligations of the firm's lawyers. ABA Model Rule 5.3(c) makes those lawyers responsible for non-lawyer assistant actions that would violate conduct rules if those assistants were lawyers, if the managing and supervisory lawyers fail to take reasonable remedial action. Consider an identical state version of ABA Model Rule 5.3.

DELAWARE R. PROF. CONDUCT 5.3: Responsibilities Regarding Non-Lawyer Assistants.

With respect to a nonlawyer employed or retained by or associated with a lawyer:

(a) a partner in a law firm, and a lawyer who individually or together with other lawyers possesses comparable managerial authority in a law firm, shall make reasonable efforts to ensure that the firm has in effect measures giving reasonable assurance that the person's conduct is compatible with the professional obligations of the lawyer;

(b) a lawyer having direct supervisory authority over the nonlawyer shall make reasonable efforts to ensure that the person's conduct is compatible with the professional obligations of the lawyer; and

(c) a lawyer shall be responsible for conduct of such a person that would be a violation of the Rules of Professional Conduct if engaged in by a lawyer if:

(1) the lawyer orders or, with the knowledge of the specific conduct, ratifies the conduct involved; or

(2) the lawyer is a partner or has comparable managerial authority in the law firm in which the person is employed, or has direct supervisory authority over the person, and knows of the conduct at a time when its consequences can be avoided or mitigated but fails to take reasonable remedial action.

In re Meltzer,

New York Supreme Court, Appellate Division
741 N.Y.S.2d 240 (2002)

PER CURIAM.

Respondent Curt Meltzer was admitted to the practice of law in the State of New York by the Second Judicial Department on February 20, 1980, as Curt Owen Meltzer. At all times relevant hereto, respondent has maintained an office for the practice of law within the First Department.

On May 25, 2001, petitioner Departmental Disciplinary Committee ("DDC") served respondent with a Notice and Statement of Charges charging respondent with ten counts of professional misconduct. Respondent was charged with engaging in conduct reflecting adversely on his fitness to practice law in violation of Disciplinary Rule ("DR") 1-

102(A)(7); being responsible for the neglect of three legal matters by a non-lawyer under his supervision in violation of DR 1-104(D)(2); aiding a non-lawyer in the unauthorized practice of law in violation of DR 3-101; sharing legal fees with a non-lawyer in violation of DR 3-102; forming a corporation with a non-lawyer, which entity was engaged in the practice of law, in violation of DR 3-103; and neglecting a legal matter entrusted to him in violation of DR 6-101(A)(3). Respondent filed an Answer admitting all but one of the charges. ...

The relevant facts are undisputed. In August 1996, respondent and his long-time paralegal/office manager, Annie Chan-Eng, formed a corporation, Golden Mountain International, Inc. ("GM"), in which respondent had a 50% ownership interest and a 50% interest in any profits generated. GM, through Ms. Chan-Eng, a non-lawyer, provided legal services in immigration matters to individual clients, and respondent associated with GM in his capacity as a lawyer. In addition, respondent neglected, and was responsible for Ms. Chan-Eng's neglect of, immigration law matters for three different clients. For example, important papers were not timely filed with the Immigration and Naturalization Service, as clients had been promised, or such papers were filed without required supporting information. In one matter, Ms. Chan-Eng dishonestly concealed the neglect from the client. Further, when two of the clients made inquiry of respondent and demanded that their fees be refunded, respondent sent the clients angry correspondence baselessly claiming that all work promised had been done in a timely fashion, and, in one case, threatening to call the police if the client appeared at his office again without an appointment. ...

Although respondent's guilt of misconduct as alleged by the DDC staff is undisputed, the Referee and the Hearing Panel recommended that the sanction of public censure be imposed based on the existence of substantial mitigating factors, as established by respondent's testimony and that of his treating psychiatrist. Respondent has no prior disciplinary record, and performed pro bono work for about 10 years. During the period of the relevant events, respondent's 21-year marriage came to an end, resulting in his loss of regular contact with his two sons. In addition, respondent experienced financial difficulties as the result of the break-up of his law firm and ensuing litigation. Respondent was evicted from his former office on one month's notice, his family home was auctioned, and he was forced to deplete his IRA to make mortgage payments and to support his family. During the relevant period, respondent was diagnosed as suffering from major depression, for which he received psychiatric treatment. At present, respondent continues to receive psychiatric counseling, which appears to have stabilized his personal and professional life sufficiently to allow him to properly represent his present clients and to rebuild his practice.

Respondent has expressed remorse for his misconduct, which expression the Referee and the Hearing Panel found to be genuine. In addition, respondent had already made refunds of fees to two of the complainants prior to the hearing. Respondent assured the Hearing Panel that he has reduced his workload to avoid further neglect of client matters, and that he now personally reviews all documents before they leave his office.

… In prior cases, we have imposed the sanction of public censure, rather than suspension, based on evidence that the attorney's misconduct arose from serious financial or psychological problems or traumatic life events, and that the attorney had taken steps to resolve the problems which contributed to the misconduct ([cc]). We are also influenced by respondent's sincere remorse and acknowledgment of wrongdoing, his cooperation with the DDC staff, and his otherwise unblemished record.

Accordingly, the petition of the DDC for an order … confirming the findings of fact and conclusions of law of the Referee and the Hearing Panel should be granted, and respondent publicly censured.

Petition granted and respondent publicly censured.

All concur.

INQUIRY

Conduct Compatible with Lawyer Obligations. ABA Model Rule 5.3 applies not only to law firm employees but also to persons whom the lawyer retains or with whom the lawyer associates. Who might those non-employee persons be? Cases and ethics opinions indicate that lawyers may be responsible for the actions of a document-preparation company with which a lawyer contracts, investigators, interpreters, marketing firms, software providers and computer consultants, collection agencies, and in one case, even a client. *See* In re Cline, 756 So.2d 284 (La. 2000) (lawyer entrusting settlement checks to client without appropriate supervision to ensure compliance). Because these persons are not subject to lawyer conduct rules, the lawyer's responsibility for their actions depends on their relationship to the lawyer. Model Rule 5.3(a)'s key phrase is that the person's conduct must be compatible with the lawyer's professional obligations. Confidentiality is an example. *See* Stewart v. Bee-Dee Neon & Signs, Inc., 751 So.2d 196 (Fla. Dist. Ct. App. 2000) (instruct nonlawyer employees not to discuss confidential information).

Unauthorized practice of law is another example. *See* In re Farmer, 950 P.2d 713 (Kan. 1997) (lawyer must tell nonlawyer assistants not to give legal advice). Honesty is another example. *See* State ex rel. Okla. Bar Assn. v. Patmon, 939 P.2d 1155 (Okla. 1997) (secretary signing lawyer's name to misleading motion). Should discipline officials hold a lawyer responsible for a nonlawyer assistant's single violation? *See* People v. Milner, 35 P.3d 670 (Colo. O.P.D.J. 2001) (no lawyer responsibility for paralegal's extraordinary outburst); Attorney Grievance Commn. v. Ficker, 706 A.2d 1045 (Md. 1998) (lawyer not responsible for client's arrest due to assistant's one missed message).

Supervising Trust Accounts. One area where lawyers should be particularly wary and discipline officials are particularly vigilant involves nonlawyer management of lawyer trust accounts. Lawyers must not leave trust-account management entirely to nonlawyers. At a minimum, lawyers must maintain some system of supervision such as independent review of bank statements, failing which they will be subject to discipline for a nonlawyer assistant's defalcation. *See* In re Cater, 887 A.2d 1 (D.C. 2005) (lawyer discipline for secretary's embezzlement of $47,000); In re Kaszynski, 620 N.W.2d 708 (Minn. 2001) (lawyer discipline for legal assistant's theft of client money from trust account using forged checks); Curtis v. Kentucky Bar Assn., 959 S.W.2d 94 (Ky. 1998) (lawyer discipline for spouse bookkeeper's purchase of dog using trust account loan). For a lawyer to sign multiple blank checks out of a trust account for nonlawyers to complete for trust-account disbursements is not appropriate supervision and will result in discipline on the account's mismanagement. *See* In re Struthers, 877 P2d 789 (Ariz. 1994). For a lawyer to give blanket authorization to an office-manager spouse who then commingled lawyer and client funds will also result in discipline. *See* In re Moore, 704 A.2d 1187 (D.C. 1997).

E. Sale of a Law Practice

Client Autonomy. One mark of a productive lawyer is a thriving and valuable law practice. May a lawyer sell a law practice, realizing its value? Some practices lend themselves to conveyance, particularly in estate planning where a long-serving lawyer may have built up a wills bank on which to draw for estate work. Other transactional practices where client relationships are stable and long term may also lend themselves to sale. Yet as you might imagine, special considerations attend the sale of a law practice. One has to consider what value the selling lawyer is transferring. Certainly, lawyers may without restriction convey a building, office equipment, and other physical assets that support a law practice. Yet ABA Model Rule 1.17 and similar state rules require that the lawyer satisfy several conditions if conveying the practice itself. Those requirements indicate that client relationships, files, and goodwill are the central assets constituting the practice, toward which the lawyer must give special attention. After all, clients get to decide who their lawyer is. As Comment [1] to Model Rule 1.17 states, "Clients are not commodities that can be purchased and sold at will." As you read the following identical state version of Model Rule 1.17, notice how the rule ensures reasonable client autonomy. What other goals does the rule promote?

> **DELAWARE R. PROF. CONDUCT 1.17: Sale of a Law Practice.**
> A lawyer or a law firm may sell or purchase a law practice, or an area of law practice, including good will, if the following conditions are satisfied:
> (a) The seller ceases to engage in the private practice of law, or in the area of practice that has been sold in the jurisdiction in which the practice has been conducted;
> (b) The entire practice, or the entire area of practice, is sold to one or more lawyers or law firms;
> (c) The seller gives written notice to each of the seller's clients regarding:
> (1) the proposed sale;
> (2) the client's right to retain other counsel or to take possession of the file; and
> (3) the client's consent to the transfer of the client's files will be presumed if the client does not take any action or does not otherwise object within ninety (90) days of receipt of the notice.
> In a matter of pending litigation, if a client cannot be given notice, the representation of that client may be transferred to the purchaser only upon entry of an order so authorizing by a court having jurisdiction. The seller may disclose to the court in camera information relating to the representation only to the extent necessary to obtain an order authorizing the transfer of a file. If approval of the substitution of the purchasing lawyer for the selling lawyer is required by the rules of any tribunal in which a matter is pending, such approval must be obtained before the matter can be included in the sale.
> (d) The fees charged clients shall not be increased by reason of the sale.

INQUIRY

Conditions of Sale. Model Rule 1.17 imposes three basic conditions of sale: (1) that the selling lawyer stop practicing in that area; (2) that the lawyer sell the whole practice substance area; and (3) that the lawyer notify clients of the sale. The practice prohibition and whole-sale conditions make a practice sale a once-in-a-career retirement proposition. Lawyers do not generally work to build value in a law practice, sell the practice, and start over, as persons in business might. The first two conditions also prevent confusing and unseemly competition between seller and buyer over clients. The third condition for client notice ensures client autonomy and confidentiality of files. These conditions and the concerns that they address highlight the challenges that prohibited practice sales in general until Model Rule 1.17's relatively recent adoption in 1990. Practice sales help retiring sole practitioners more than large-firm lawyers, who may be able to transfer their partnership share to other lawyers in the firm without practice-sale conditions. Should conduct rules permit a suspended or disbarred lawyer to sell a law practice? Ethics opinions disagree. *Contrast* SOUTH CAROLINA ETHICS OPIN. 2003-06 (2003) (no), *with* MAINE ETHICS OPIN. 178 (2002) (yes).

Career and Professional Development

Employers of lawyers value productivity perhaps as much as they value reputation, ethics, collegiality, and other attributes. Productivity links with those other attributes. The lawyer who maintains good supervisory and subordinate relationships is productive. The lawyer who relies appropriately on nonlawyer assistants increases the quantity and efficiency of the lawyer's work, pleasing law firm and clients. As Cicero liked to say, there is no real difference between the moral and the expedient. Expedient actions are not shortcuts. They are right routes to right ends for right reasons. Prove your productivity to yourself and future employers. Develop a portfolio in law school showing the quantity and quality of your work. Improve your technology skills to leverage your time and talents. Understand what makes you productive, and be ready to explain and demonstrate it to prospective employers and clients.

CHAPTER VI

RESPECT

Toward Others, For Opposing Parties and Counsel, As Prosecutor, For Judges and Jurors

Men are respectable only as they respect.
— Ralph Waldo Emerson

Being brilliant is no great feat if you respect nothing.
— Goethe

... [T]he life and the liberty of the individual and the fruits of his labor are not more sacred after they have been declared by a written law to be inviolable than they were before; and the legitimate province of constitutions is to furnish them with due and adequate protection instead of providing the means whereby the individual may be robbed by the organized society he enters, of either or all.
— Justice Thomas M. Cooley

OBJECTIVE: Given a lawyer's need to constantly interact with clients, witnesses, opposing parties and counsel, judges, and court staff, articulate the conduct rules that require the lawyer to show respect for the individual and justice system in all of those interactions.

Applicable Rules

3.4 Fairness to Opposing Party and Counsel

3.8 Special Responsibilities of a Prosecutor

4.4 Respect for Rights of Third Persons

8.2 Judicial and Legal Officials

You saw in the previous chapter that citizenship and membership carry responsibilities. In this chapter, you learn that one of those responsibilities is to *respect* all individuals in the justice system and the system itself. You may have heard the maxim that one should have to earn respect. That maxim is wrong, turning the concept of respect on its head. Respect is respect because it is given rather than earned. One accords respect to another based on the role that the other occupies, whether a familiar role like mother, father, sister, or brother, or a professional role like witness, client, opposing party or counsel, judge, or juror. It is a lawyer's responsibility to treat these persons according to the privileges of their role, even when they do not fulfill the attributes of their roles. Voluntary respect is the duty that a lawyer owes all persons involved in the justice system at all times—and owes the justice system itself. Consider in this chapter specific conduct rules that call our attention to specific individual roles toward which lawyers owe respect. "Actions speak louder than words." We judge others based on their actions, not on what they say. Do not underestimate the subject of respect. The interests these rules protect are primary. The profession and public would lose much if conduct rules did not require lawyers to respect. As you study these rules, see if you can identify the interests that they serve. See, too, if you can imagine from the cases and discussion what would happen if the profession did not have these rules, and lawyers' words did not match their actions.

A. Toward Others

The Public. When we think of the people with whom lawyers interact commonly, we think of clients, other lawyers, and judges. Subsequent sections of this chapter address the respect that lawyers owe those persons. Yet lawyers also interact relatively frequently with other individuals who are only incidentally involved in the justice system. Those persons sometimes include witnesses but also often include clients' employers, medical-care providers, family members, acquaintances, and business associates. Lawyers deal constantly with the public, not just with clients and other lawyers. How lawyers treat members of the public is important to public confidence in the law and law profession. It is also important to public access to the justice system. The person whom a lawyer has offended and embarrassed is less likely to trust lawyers and the legal system. The person whom a lawyer has shown respect will more likely trust lawyers and the legal system when that person needs them. We should respect our fellow citizens, even when and especially when they are only indirectly involved in the legal system. ABA MODEL RULE OF PROFESSIONAL CONDUCT 4.4, an identical state version of which is below, ensures that lawyers conform their conduct toward members of the public in a way that engenders public trust and confidence.

> SOUTH CAROLINA R. PROF. CONDUCT 4.4:   Respect for Rights of Third Persons.
> **(a)** In representing a client, a lawyer shall not use means that have no substantial purpose other than to embarrass, delay, or burden a third person, or use methods of obtaining evidence that violate the legal rights of such a person.
> **(b)** A lawyer who receives a document relating to the representation of the lawyer's client and knows or reasonably should know that the document was inadvertently sent shall promptly notify the sender.

INQUIRY

Limitations.   At first glance, Model Rule 4.4(a) seems straightforward, offering little with which to disagree. Yet look closer. Notice that Model Rule 4.4 defines respect in negative terms, as a prohibition against certain conduct. Is respect merely the absence of conduct that a lawyer intends to burden, delay, and embarrass? Can you articulate affirmative actions associated with respect? *See* Dondi Props. Corp. v. Commerce Sav. & Loan Assn., 121 F.R.D. 284, 288 (N.D. Tex. 1988) (specific standards of courtesy the breach of which may lead to sanctions). Civility codes are relatively common, particularly in the federal courts. *See, e.g.,* STANDARDS FOR PROFESSIONAL CONDUCT WITHIN THE SEVENTH FEDERAL JUDICIAL CIRCUIT. Notice, too, an important limitation on the lawyer's duty in that it arises only in the course of the lawyer representing a client. One supposes, then, that lawyers are free to act obnoxiously, intending to burden, delay, and embarrass others, so long as they do not do so while representing a client. Should conduct rules regulate a lawyer's non-professional conduct? Does Model Rule 4.4 go far enough? To whom does Model Rule 4.4(a) refer when it states a "third person"? Some state versions of Model Rule 4.4 replace "third persons" with "others," perhaps making clearer that the rule applies to protect all members of the public. *See* ARIZ. R. PROF. CONDUCT 4.4. The situations in which Rule 4.4(a) may apply are diverse. *See* In re Disciplinary Action Against Bunch, 784 N.W.2d 64 (Minn. 2010) (public reprimand for false affidavit filed to delay former tenants from enforcing rights). Consider the following case.

In re Campbell,
Kansas Supreme Court
199 P.3d 776 (2009)

PER CURIAM.

This is an uncontested, original proceeding in discipline filed by the office of the Disciplinary Administrator against Respondent Frederick B. Campbell, a Garnett attorney licensed to practice in this state since 1998.

The Disciplinary Administrator filed a formal complaint against Respondent for his conduct in connection with his performance as county attorney for Anderson County, Kansas, alleging violations of Kansas Rules of Professional Conduct (KRPC) 4.4(a) [] (embarrassment, delay, burden to third person); KRPC 8.4(d) [] (conduct prejudicial to administration of justice); and KRPC 8.4(g) (conduct adversely reflecting on fitness to practice law).

Hearing Panel's Findings of Fact and Conclusions of Law

The facts as found by Respondent's disciplinary hearing panel included the following:

In early May 2007, certain minors attended a Greeley-area party at which beer was consumed. One minor girl, C.H., who had drunk approximately six beers, was photographed by other partygoers while she had sexual intercourse with a foreign exchange student, M.V. The amateur photographers also recorded certain minors drinking beer at the party.

Within a few days, C.H. informed her school counselor that M.V. had sexually assaulted her at the party. Law enforcement was notified. During this same time period, the Anderson County Sheriff's office was also investigating a similar report about M.V. from a second female high school student.

Law enforcement officers obtained some of the photographs taken at the May party and forwarded them to Respondent. Respondent altered the photographs to obscure faces and certain body parts but not others. He concluded that he would not pursue prosecution of M.V. because Respondent believed the sexual conduct depicted in the photographs to have been consensual.

The Anderson County Review newspaper ran an article in early July 2007 in which it discussed Respondent's view of the incident. The newspaper further reported that Respondent planned to show the photographs from the May party to the parents of minors who had attended.

Upon reading the article, C.H.'s mother contacted Respondent to tell him that he did not have her permission to show the photographs of her minor daughter to others. The Respondent challenged the mother, saying he did not need her permission. Thereafter, Respondent proceeded with his plan to show the photographs to several parents of minors who attended the party.

The newspaper ran a follow-up article regarding the photographs as well as an editorial written by Sandy Barnett, Executive Director of the Kansas Coalition Against Sexual and Domestic Violence. After counsel for C.H. and her mother contacted Respondent about sealing the photographs from public view, Respondent wrote a return letter, stating,

> As the photographs you refer to are evidence of criminal activity by several minors and as I cannot lawfully withhold evidence, I have allowed and will continue to allow the parents of potential respondents to view altered versions of them, in my office... .
>
> ... I further want to thank you for any future litigation that you pursue in this matter as it will inevitably generate a large amount of publicity for the issue of underage drinking, hosting of minors and the harmful effects of minors engaging in public sexual acts. I was beginning to fear that nothing would be done and that this issue would fade from the public eye.

C.H. was subjected to public ridicule as a result of these events, and she now suffers from depression.

Based on the foregoing facts, the hearing panel concluded that Respondent violated KRPC 4.4 and KRPC 8.4(d) and (g), writing:

> The Respondent allowed adults to view photographs of minors consuming alcoholic beverages, photographs of C.H. partially clothed, and photographs of sexual intercourse between C.H. and M.V. The Respondent explained that his purpose in doing so was to shock the parents as to what occurs at teenage parties. The Respondent further explained that his overall goal is to decrease underage drinking. At the hearing on this matter, the Respondent acknowledged that he could have achieved his goal without allowing others to view the photographs. Further, allowing parents of minors attending the party to view photographs of C.H. partially clothed and photographs of sexual intercourse between C.H. and M.V. bears no relation to decreasing underage drinking. Thus, when the Respondent showed the pictures to the parents of the minors attending the party, he had no valid substantial legal purpose, other than to embarrass, delay, or burden third persons. Accordingly, the Hearing Panel concludes that the Respondent violated KRPC 4.4.

... K.S.A. [] 38-2310(c) provides [that information identifying victims and alleged victims of sex offenses shall not be disclosed or open to public inspection under any circumstances]... .

... In this case, the Respondent engaged in "conduct that is prejudicial to the administration of justice" when he violated K.S.A. 38-2310(c) by allowing parents of minors who attended the May 11, 2007, party to view the photographs. ...

Disposition

Before this court, the Disciplinary Administrator changed his recommendation to a 90-day suspension, taking the position that Respondent had abused the power of his office and done actual harm to C.H. The Disciplinary Administrator also noted Respondent's testimony that he had reviewed the KRPCs before showing the parents the photographs; although he thought his planned conduct would raise a close question under the rules, he proceeded.

Counsel for Respondent argued to us that, although his client's conduct was egregious, it arose out of a "right reason," i.e., a zeal to end underage drinking. Counsel also asserted that the record on appeal contained evidence that his client suffered from Asperger's Syndrome, a malady that impairs his ability to empathize with others and that his client had apologized to C.H.'s mother after the disciplinary hearing concluded. ...

There are no disputed facts in this case. And the facts, as established, amply support the conclusions about violations of KRPC 4.4 and KRPC 8.4(d) and (g) at which the disciplinary hearing panel arrived. We therefore adopt the findings of fact and conclusions of law of the panel.

This court is empowered to impose any form of discipline or conditions separate from or connected to any type of discipline it deems appropriate, regardless of whether that form or type of discipline has been recommended by a hearing panel. Supreme Court Rule 203(a)(5) []. In view of what we discern as Respondent's continued inability or unwillingness to come to grips with the devastation his conduct has wrought in at least one life and the potential for it to chill reports from victims of future sex crimes and their cooperation with prosecutions of dangerous offenders, we believe a 90-day suspension to be an inadequate sanction. We instead order a 6-month suspension from the practice of law and shall require Respondent to follow the procedure outlined in Supreme Court Rule 219 [] to be reinstated. A minority of the court would impose a longer period of suspension. In addition, because Respondent and his counsel raised substantial concerns at oral argument about the possibility that a medical or psychological condition may have contributed to the sanctioned conduct, the existence and/or effect of such a condition on Respondent's future behavior should be among the issues addressed by the Rule 219 procedure.

IT IS THEREFORE ORDERED that Frederick B. Campbell be suspended for 6 months from the practice of law and that he shall follow the procedure outlined in Rule 219 to be reinstated.

IT IS FURTHER ORDERED that the costs of the proceeding be assessed to Respondent.

INQUIRY

Obtaining Evidence. There are other ways that Model Rule 4.4(a) requires lawyers to show respect to others. Model Rule 4.4(a) also includes a prohibition against a lawyer obtaining evidence in the course of a representation, in a way that violates a legal right of others. Every prohibition of the ABA MODEL RULES OF PROFESSIONAL CONDUCT addresses some misconduct in which lawyers have engaged. What do you think lawyers do to obtain evidence from others that violates the rights of those others? *See, e.g.,* In re Hagedorn, 904 N.E.2d 659 (Ind. 2009) (public reprimand imposed for subpoenaing third parties for medical and other records without requisite notice to opposing party). Lawyers may interview witnesses under circumstances where the witnesses might not speak if the lawyer disclosed whom the lawyer represented. Is that respectful, to get information or documents from someone that they would not give to you if they knew your role? Surreptitious investigation, while occasionally productive in the individual cause, can yet undermine public confidence, create suspicion, and lead to the withholding or destruction of evidence. Do you see how important it is to not mislead others regarding the lawyer's role and reason for seeking information from others?

Inadvertent Document Disclosure. Respect can also require action when someone makes a mistake. Back in the good old days of facsimile machines, lawyers associated Model Rule 4.4(b)'s inadvertent-document-disclosure rule with mistaken facsimile transmissions. Most lawyers of the fax era have sent or received an inadvertent fax. What is the risk today? How common is inadvertent document disclosure today, given the prevalence of emails and other electronic communications and storage? *See* Stengart v. Loving Care Agency, Inc., 990 A.2d 650 (N.J. 2010) (lawyer's continuing to review privileged emails recovered from opposing party's computer violates Rule 4.4(b)). Notice that Model Rule 4.4(b) limits the lawyer's notify-the-sender duty to instances where the inadvertent document relates to the lawyer's representation of a client. Some state versions of Model Rule 4.4(b) broaden the duty to include any documents, not just those that relate to a representation. *See* ARIZ. R. PROF. CONDUCT 4.4(b) ("A lawyer who receives a document and knows or reasonably should know that the document was inadvertently sent shall promptly notify the sender... .").

Metadata. A related concern to inadvertent emails and facsimile transmissions is confidential information contained in the metadata of an electronic document. For example, whether or not a lawyer deliberately embeds comments and uses track-changes features when finalizing a word-processing document, the document in its electronic form will often contain information regarding the author, storage location, document-creation date, revision dates, and contents of earlier versions, that the lawyer would not want revealed. Does inadvertently discovering that metadata or deliberately mining that metadata, without notifying opposing counsel, constitute a violation of Model Rule 4.4(b)? The ABA Ethics Committee and several jurisdictions say no, thus permitting review of metadata, while other jurisdictions say yes, thus prohibiting that review. The difference may also depend on whether it becomes apparent to reviewing counsel that the inclusion of metadata was inadvertent. *See* Rico v. Mitsubishi Motors Corp., 42 Cal.4th 807 (Cal. 2007) (stop reviewing metadata when inadvertent disclosure becomes reasonably apparent).

Waiver. Notice that the conduct rule on inadvertent disclosure simply requires that the lawyer receiving the document notify the sender. Model Rule 4.4(b) does not say what the recipient lawyer must then do with the document. The notice requirement of Model Rule 4.4(b) gives the holder of the privilege an opportunity to assert the privilege and demand the document's return or destruction. Intentional disclosure of a privileged document waives the privilege. A person may also waive a privilege by not raising the privilege when circumstances warrant that the person do so. *See* Kaye Scholer LLP v. Zalis, 878 So.2d 447 (Fla. App. 2004). Yet knowing waiver is different from inadvertent waiver. Whether the privilege disappears when its holder inadvertently discloses a document depends on state privilege law. *See* Carbis Walker, LLP v. Hill, Barth and King, LLC, 930 A.2d 573 (Pa. Super. Ct. 2007) (five-factor test including precautions, number and extent of disclosures, delay in rectifying, and interests of justice). If you have given the notice required by Model Rule 4.4(b) and privilege law does not require that you return an inadvertently disclosed document, can you still see reasons why it might be better that you do return the document, or would your duty to your client prevent you from doing so? How would you wish the recipient to treat you if you inadvertently disclosed a privileged document? Think of the role that building trust, confidence, and respect has in law practice.

B. For Opposing Parties and Counsel

Respect for Adversaries.   The lawyer's duty to respect others extends not just to the public but also to opposing parties and counsel. There is a natural tendency to mistreat one's adversaries. It is a counter-productive tendency that lawyers must resist if they are to comply with the conduct rules. Lawyers who do any significant amount of litigation or even negotiation over the terms of agreements outside of litigation spend a lot of time communicating with opposing counsel. The interests of a lawyer's client often seem and sometimes are diametrically opposed to the interests of opposing counsel's client. Yet there is little good and much harm to being unkind to one's adversaries. Instead, lawyers use their skills to help clients discern broader interests, identify interim objectives pursuing those interests, and generate options and implement plans toward achieving those objectives. Those activities often depend on improving relationships with others who have different interests, meaning those whom a client perceives to be adversaries. To help their clients, lawyers must often make an adversarial relationship less so, in order to generate, maintain, and improve communications that lead to compromise. Read the following similar state version of ABA MODEL RULE OF PROFESSIONAL CONDUCT 3.4 addressing respect toward one's adversaries, followed by an illustrative order.

> MICHIGAN R. PROF. CONDUCT 3.4:   **Fairness to Opposing Party and Counsel.** A lawyer shall not:
> (a) unlawfully obstruct another party's access to evidence; unlawfully alter, destroy, or conceal a document or other material having potential evidentiary value; or counsel or assist another person to do any such act;
> (b) falsify evidence, counsel or assist a witness to testify falsely, or offer an inducement to a witness that is prohibited by law;
> (c) knowingly disobey an obligation under the rules of a tribunal except for an open refusal based on an assertion that no valid obligation exists;
> (d) in pretrial procedure, make a frivolous discovery request or fail to make reasonably diligent efforts to comply with a legally proper discovery request by an opposing party;
> (e) during trial, allude to any matter that the lawyer does not reasonably believe is relevant or that will not be supported by admissible evidence, assert personal knowledge of facts in issue except when testifying as a witness, or state a personal opinion as to the justness of a cause, the credibility of a witness, the culpability of a civil litigant, or the guilt or innocence of an accused; or
> (f) request a person other than a client to refrain from voluntarily giving relevant information to another party, unless:

(1) the person is a relative or an employee or other agent of a client; and
(2) the lawyer reasonably believes that the person's interests will not be adversely affected by refraining from giving such information.

Jayhawk Capital Mgt., LLC v LSB Industries, Inc.,
United States Disrict Court for the District of Kansas
Case No. 2:08-cv-02561-EFM (April 12, 2011)

ORDER ON MOTION TO CONTINUE

"He who is his own lawyer has a fool for a client" is one of every lawyer's favorite proverbs.

Among the several reasons why this is undoubtedly true, is that lawyers are trained to handle disputes skillfully but without the emotional rancor that will mask the actual parties' reason and good sense.[fn] Regrettably, many attorneys lose sight of their role as professionals, and personalize the dispute; converting the parties' disagreement into a lawyers' spat. This is unfortunate, and unprofessional, but sadly not uncommon. Before the Court, however, is an uncommon example of this unhappy trend.

This matter is currently set for trial commencing June 14, 2011. Defendants seek a brief continuance, noting that one of their counsel, Bryan Erman, along with his wife, is expecting their first child due on July 3. Given the proposed length of trial and the famous disregard that newborns (especially first-borns) have for such schedules, and given that the trial is scheduled in Kansas City while the new Erman's arrival is scheduled in Dallas, Defendants move this Court for a continuance.

This in itself would not be remarkable, but in reviewing the motion the Court was more than somewhat surprised to read that "Plaintiffs have refused to agree to continue the trial setting and have indicated that they intend to oppose this Motion."

Well, every party is entitled to file an opposition to a motion, and hoping that perhaps Defendants' had mis-characterized the vigor of Plaintiffs' opposition, we have eagerly awaited Plaintiffs defense of its opposition. The Memorandum in Opposition arrived yesterday, and it was, sadly, as advertised.

First, Plaintiffs make a lengthy and spirited argument about when Defendants should have known this would happen, even citing a pretrial conference occurring in early November as a time when Mr. Erman "most certainly" would have known of the due date of his child, and even more astonishingly arguing that "utilizing simple math, the due date for Mr. Erman's child's birth would have been known on approximately Oct. 3, or shortly thereafter." For reasons of good taste which should be (though, apparently, are not) too obvious to explain, the Court declines to accept Plaintiffs' invitation to speculate on the time of conception of the Ermans' child.

Further, Plaintiffs assert that there are currently five attorneys from two different firms on Defendants' signature block. While the Court might be inclined to agree with Plaintiffs that this seems like a plethora of attorneys, it can't help but note that, entered and active on behalf of Plaintiffs in this case, are also five attorneys, from three different firms; so perhaps Plaintiffs are illequipped to argue that Defendants have too many attorneys.

Finally, Plaintiffs argue that surely Mr. Erman will have sufficient time to make it from the Kansas City trial to the Dallas birth, even helpfully pointing out the number of daily, non-stop flights between the two cities; and in any event complain of the inconvenience of this late requested continuance. Certainly this judge is convinced of the importance of federal court, but he has always tried not to confuse what he does with who he is, nor to distort the priorities of his day job with his life's role. Counsel are encouraged to order their priorities similarly.

Defendants' Motion is **GRANTED**. The Ermans are **CONGRATULATED**.

IT IS SO ORDERED.

Dated this 12th day of April, 2011.

INQUIRY

Zealous Advocacy. Despite the plain terms of Model Rule 3.4 requiring fairness to opposing party and counsel, there remains a prevailing sense, captured by the phrase "zealous advocacy," that lawyers should make things especially hard for their adversaries. A zealot is a fanatical partisan or member of a fanatical sect. The ABA MODEL RULES OF PROFESSIONAL CONDUCT do not call for zealous advocacy, at least not in that sense of a fanatical partisan. As we will study in the next chapter, ABA Model Rule 1.3 requires a lawyer to act "with reasonable diligence and promptness" when representing a client. It is only in the Comment to ABA Model Rule 1.3 that the phrase "zeal in advocacy on the client's behalf" appears. In that context of a rule requiring *reasonable* diligence, the zeal to which the Comment refers means eagerness and strong interest, rather than partisan fanaticism. Some in the profession nonetheless seize on the concept of zealotry to attempt to excuse misconduct. As you read the following cases as examples, develop in mind the distinction between constant fairness, reasonable diligence, and strong interest on one hand and rule-breaking zealotry on the other hand.

Traxler v. Ford Motor Co.,
Michigan Court of Appeals
576 N.W.2d 398 (1998)

WAHLS, Judge.

Defendants Ford Motor Company and Ford Motor Company of Canada (hereinafter Ford) appeal by leave granted from an order of default. We affirm in part, reverse in part, and remand.

This case stems from an automobile accident in 1990. At the time of the accident, two-month-old Sarah Traxler was strapped into a child safety seat in the back of her parents' 1986 Ford Tempo. Her mother was driving, and her father was seated next to her in the back seat. As the Traxlers were waiting to make a left turn, they were rear-ended by another vehicle traveling at approximately fifty miles an hour. The force of the collision caused the driver's seat of the Traxler's car to move rearward into the back seat, striking Sarah in the head. Sarah was left with severe and permanent injuries. Apparently, no one else was injured in the crash.

Plaintiffs filed suit against the driver of the other vehicle, the maker of the child safety seat, and Ford. This appeal involves only Ford.[fn] Plaintiffs' theory regarding Ford's liability revolved around the design of the driver's seat in the Ford Tempo. Their discovery requests thus focused on Ford's design process, on Ford's knowledge regarding the tendency of its seats to give way in rear-end collisions, and on other lawsuits filed against Ford alleging front-seat design defects. Discovery took place over more than two years and was marked by Ford's numerous objections and by plaintiffs' repeated motions to compel. Most of plaintiffs' motions to compel were withdrawn before the trial court could hear them, apparently because the parties agreed to work out their differences between themselves. Eventually, however, the trial court heard and granted one of plaintiffs' motions to compel. In granting the motion, the trial court warned Ford that its failure to comply with the discovery order would result in a default. In response to the trial court's order, Ford provided plaintiffs with sixty-two boxes of documents. After reviewing this new information, plaintiffs asked the trial court to order a default against Ford. They argued that the documents produced as a result of the trial court's order should have been produced far earlier and that the delay had prejudiced them to the point that default was the only appropriate remedy. The trial court agreed and entered an order of default against

Ford. In its written opinion, the trial court lambasted Ford for its conduct during discovery:

> What plaintiffs' counsel discovered when they read those documents was disgusting; no other word would be accurate. For over two years, Ford had concealed very significant documents and information, and, worse, had blatantly lied about those documents and about the information in them; any word other than "lied" would understate what Ford did... . After carefully reviewing plaintiffs' discovery requests and some of Ford's responses (hundreds of pages), studying several rounds of briefs, and listening to counsels' very helpful oral argument, this Court had to agree that an outrageous fraud has been perpetrated by Ford... and that the sanction of a default... is the appropriate response. ...

Ford ... argues that the evidence in the record does not support the trial court's conclusion that Ford lied or committed fraud. We disagree. ...

The parties and the trial court address numerous examples of Ford's conduct during discovery. Here, we simply address two interrogatories that are illustrative. We begin with an interrogatory and a response that highlight Ford's position during the early stages of discovery:

> 35. How many 4-door Ford Tempos were sold in 1986 by Ford dealers in the United States and Canada?
>
> [*ANSWER:*]
>
> 35. Ford objects to this Interrogatory on the ground that it is overly broad, vague, irrelevant, oppressive and not calculated to lead to the discovery of admissible evidence. Without waiving its objections and in the spirit of discovery, Ford states 176,976 Four-Door Tempo vehicles were sold in the United States and Canada.

This exchange is significant for two reasons. First, it illustrates the fact that Ford objected to interrogatories even where its objections were groundless on their face; how can an interrogatory that asks for a simple numerical answer be overly broad or vague? What is the purpose of objecting on the ground that a request is oppressive when the objection is followed by the answer to the request? How could Ford argue that information regarding the number of products sold is irrelevant or not calculated to lead to the discovery of admissible evidence in a products liability suit? Clearly, Ford's objections were boilerplate... . The significance of these observations becomes clear when we review one of the more important interrogatories. The parties and the trial court offer contrasting interpretations of the following interrogatory and answer:

10. State whether the same left front driver's seat and right front passenger seat tracks and seat backs, as identified previously in this set of interrogatories as having been installed on the subject vehicle, were ever installed on any other Ford Motor Company vehicle, including but not limited to Mustang, [Capri], Escort, Lynx station wagon, Thunderbird, Cougar, Taurus, Sable, Topaz, and Tempo, of any model year. If the answer is yes, state which vehicles, which model years and which seat (driver or passenger).

ANSWER:

10. Ford objects to this Interrogatory on the ground that it is overly broad, vague, irrelevant, oppressive and not calculated to lead to the discovery of admissible evidence. Without waiving its objections and in the spirit of discovery, Ford states that the seat track assemblies used in the Tempo are unique to the Tempo/Topaz car lines only.

... According to the trial court: "That answer was not true. Plaintiffs have learned that the Tempo/Topaz seat was derived from the Escort/Lynx seat and that that seat had been used in numerous other models. Ford admits that now, but only after having been caught in a lie."

... Ford insists that it is true that "the seat track assemblies used in the Tempo are unique to the Tempo/Topaz car lines only." That may be, but the question asked of Ford was not so limited. Ford was asked whether the front "seat tracks and seat backs" installed in 1986 Tempos "were ever installed on any other Ford Motor Company vehicle." ... Ford ... responded that "the seat track assemblies used in the Tempo are unique to the Tempo/Topaz car lines only." What it did was craftily reformulate the question to ask only what it wanted to say, namely: that the seat track assemblies, not the seats themselves, were unique, thereby creating the misleading impression that the seats had not been used in any other vehicles. ... That was as dishonest as saying in so many words that the seats, not just the seat track assemblies, were unique to the vehicle.... Ford's answer was not simply a precise answer to a poor question; it was a dishonest answer, carefully crafted to mislead the reader. ...

... If Ford meant to say that only the seat tracks were unique, and that the other components were so common that answering the interrogatory would be unduly burdensome, it needed only say so. Instead, Ford gave what it now claims was a "partial" answer, which clearly omitted relevant information. By doing so, Ford created the appearance that it was lying or intentionally concealing relevant information. We cannot conclude that the trial court's findings in this regard were clearly erroneous. ...

... It is clear that the trial court considered the nature of Ford's errors and concluded that they were not simple mistakes or oversights. Instead, the trial court concluded that Ford had lied and perpetrated "an outrageous fraud." We find no evidence in the record to contradict the trial court's findings, and they are not clearly erroneous. Ford's related argument, that the trial court failed to consider whether a default should be ordered against Ford for the conduct of its attorneys, is without merit. The trial court had the authority to order a default against Ford even if its attorneys were responsible for the misconduct. [Cc]

... Ford argues, and we agree, that it is entitled to an evidentiary hearing where it may introduce evidence (1) that its failure to comply with plaintiffs' discovery requests was accidental or involuntary and (2) that plaintiffs were not prejudiced by Ford's mistakes. We believe that due process requires such a hearing... .

For the foregoing reasons, we affirm the trial court's conclusion that it had the power to order a default where Ford lied or committed fraud. However, we reverse the trial court's order of default against Ford and remand for an evidentiary hearing in accordance with this opinion. ...

RICHARD ALLEN GRIFFIN, P.J., concur.

GRIBBS, Judge (concurring in part and dissenting in part).

... I would affirm the trial court's order of default against Ford and remand for a determination of plaintiffs' damages. ...

... [I]n a comprehensive, single-spaced 11-page opinion[FN1] *[Eds. note: see the full appellate opinion for the trial court's detailed opinion]* the trial court already found and ably explained its conclusion that Ford committed "wanton and flagrant violation of its discovery obligation." ... It could not be clearer from the trial court's opinion that it has *already* found that Ford's conduct was deliberate, conscious, and by careful design. ...

Contrary to the trial court's July 16 order, Ford continued to conceal and withhold documents relating to its Seat Back Task Force and it appears that plaintiffs became aware of the existence of such task force activity through an independent investigation. ... The [trial court's] opinion specified in detail various deceptions, including the failure to reveal the Seat Back Task Force study, pursuant to the court order of July, 1996, but only in response to plaintiffs' Motion for Default:

> The impact of Ford's deception was made abundantly clear by its latest discovery disclosures. Plaintiffs had asked Ford to identify and produce all tests done to establish the integrity of the seats used in 1986 Ford Tempos, as well as the same or similar seats used in other vehicles. Ford responded that it had performed 48 rear impact tests on the Tempo/Topaz seat between 1984 and 1994. The discovery disgorged in response to this Court's July order revealed that there have been

hundreds of such tests performed on the same seats in numerous other models. Those tests are all highly relevant to this case and were requested by plaintiffs. By the way it responded to plaintiffs' interrogatories that the Tempo/Topaz seat was unique, Ford hid all those other tests.

Concealing those tests concealed something highly significant to this case. In those tests, the front seats routinely collapsed into the back seat on the slightest impact. Throughout this case, Ford has insisted that its seats, including those in 1986 Tempos, are designed to "yield." Ford has persistently taken great exception to any characterizations of seats having "failed," "broke", or "collapsed," but the test reports just disclosed repeatedly use those very terms to describe what happened to Ford seats in collisions just like that which occurred in this case. What Ford disclosed also revealed that, years ago, it had developed, but never used, a seat capable of withstanding much greater rear-end impacts than that which injured Sarah. Until last August, Ford has disclosed none of that.

Ford also failed to disclose that it had convened a Task Force to study seat back performance, that that Task Force had had numerous tests performed on Ford seat backs, and that a report was drafted, but apparently never issued. ...

One more example of Ford's mendacity will suffice. Another of plaintiffs' 1994 interrogatories asked Ford to identify all lawsuits against it which complained about defects in the seat backs and/or seat tracks of the 1986 Ford Tempos and other Ford vehicles utilizing the same or similar seats. At first, Ford identified only 2 such lawsuits. Later Ford reported that there had been 48 lawsuits, but no particulars were ever disclosed. The recently-produced documents reveal that Ford has defended the Tempo/Topaz seat in 91 lawsuits. Some 19 of those lawsuits were brought on behalf of minor children who were injured due to seat failures, several of them having been back seat passengers injured just like Sarah Traxler, by a collapsing front seat. Even more startling is the revelation in the documents disclosed in response to this Court's July order that Ford has defended hundreds of lawsuits involving the same seat in other models. Nothing was disclosed about those numerous lawsuits until August, 1996... .

Ford's conduct has badly prejudiced plaintiffs and this Court. Plaintiffs' counsel has had to spend considerable effort and incur great expense acquiring from other sources information which Ford should have disclosed. More significantly, Ford's misconduct has frustrated plaintiffs in the development of information vital to a persuasive presentation of their claims. What Ford has belatedly revealed about its testing of the car seat at issue in this case, what it appears to have learned from those tests, the availability of a safer seat, and the fact that a safer seat was never used, all go directly to what a plaintiff must prove in a case like this one... . To enable plaintiffs to respond, discovery needs to start anew. Plaintiffs' experts need to start all over, and a tremendous amount of follow-up inquiries must be made of Ford and its pertinent personnel. That would put off trial until next year, which would be very unfair to plaintiffs. ...

As the majority agrees, the trial court's findings and conclusions are supported by the record. Because of Ford's egregious and intentional conduct, because plaintiffs have been severely harmed by the prolonged and needless delay and concealment that will necessitate beginning discovery all over again, and because Ford has been provided *years* of due process in this matter, I would affirm.

"What Were They Thinking?"
If you cannot universalize your contemplated action into a reasonable rule that you would have others follow when dealing with you, then think twice about taking that action. *Traxler v. Ford Motor Co.* represents an extreme example of unfairness to an opposing party and counsel. Why would defense counsel have acted as they did in concealing through artful language mountains of material evidence? They must have expected to get away with it, that is, that no one would discover their concealment. Do you think that they had successfully concealed evidence in prior cases? Fraud and newly discovered evidence are grounds to reopen cases. They are also grounds to discipline and even disbar a lawyer. Can you see the hazard of instrumental reasoning that just because it might have worked before does not make it the right action again—or ever? Would defense counsel have concealed the evidence if they had reasoned morally?

INQUIRY

Discovery Abuses. Can you see why some of the more common abuses of the relationship with opposing counsel occur around discovery in civil litigation, and why Model Rule 3.4 thus prohibits those specific abuses? Discovery is one area in which lawyers often exercise delegated authority without the direct involvement or supervision of the court. Many procedures require court involvement, such as the issuing of a summons for service with a complaint, the issuing of a garnishment writ to enforce a money judgment, and obtaining an order to show cause why the court should not hold a party in contempt. Yet when it comes to discovery, lawyers have much greater freedom to make others take action. It is precisely where lawyers have the greatest freedom that we should take the greatest care to keep our actions within the grant of authority. See, for example, State Bar of Georgia Formal Advisory Opinion 05-10 (Ga. Sup. Ct. April 25, 2006), providing that the state bar can discipline local counsel who permits, through willful blindness, his co-counsel to destroy documentary evidence or commit other discovery abuses. *See also* Feld's Case, 815 A.2d 383 (N.H. 2002) (suspension for preparing interrogatory answers the lawyer knew to be false); Jones's Case, 628 A.2d 254 (N.H. 1993) (disbarment for concealing evidence).

Threatening Opposing Counsel. What are the ethics of threatening opposing counsel with a disciplinary complaint? While lawyers have the duty to report misconduct that calls into question another lawyer's substantial fitness, *see* ABA Model Rule 8.3(a), lawyers must not use baseless threats of a disciplinary complaint to manipulate opposing counsel. While Model Rule 3.4 requiring fairness to opposing counsel does not expressly prohibit baseless threats, ABA Comm. on Ethics & Prof. Resp. Formal Opin. No. 94-383 held that ABA Model Rules 3.1, 4.1, 4.4, and 8.4(b) do at least by implication prohibit that action. *See also* In re Discipline of Eicher, 661 N.W.2d 354 (S.D. 2003) (misconduct to decline client's appeal in exchange for opposing counsel's withdrawal of discipline complaint). The better course may be not to make any such threats, valid or otherwise. If there is cause to make a complaint, then make the complaint. If there is no cause, then make no threat. *See* The Florida Bar v. Frederick, 756 So.2d 79 (Fla. 2000) (bargaining away disciplinary complaint is misconduct prejudicial to the administration of justice). What do you think?

Economics of Unfairness. The above *Traxler v. Ford Motor Co.* decision illustrates that the court in which the misconduct occurs can impose sanctions up to default. If the default was the lawyers' responsibility, then there could also be civil (malpractice) liability on the lawyers' part, if the client (in that case, Ford) can establish causation. A lesser but more common court sanction is to make the lawyer pay the costs that an opposing party incurs because of the lawyer's concealing evidence or engaging in other unfair conduct. Judges have other lawful ways of punishing lawyers for unfairness to opposing parties and counsel. Unfairness can be expensive even when a lawyer wins. Consider the following case resulting in a judge's million-dollar-plus reduction in lawyer fees to the prevailing party.

Lee v. American Eagle Airlines, Inc.,
United States District Court for the Southern District of Florida
93 F. Supp.2d 1322 (2000)

ORDER ON ATTORNEY'S FEES AND COSTS
MIDDLEBROOKS, District Judge. ...

I. Introduction

"Let's kick some ass," Marvin Kurzban said loudly to his client, Anthony Lee, and his co-counsel, Ira Kurzban. I had taken the bench, and Court was in session. Opposing counsel and their client representatives were seated across the aisle. The jury was waiting to be called into the courtroom. Mr. Kurzban's comment was suited more to a locker room than a courtroom of the United States, and the conduct of Plaintiff's counsel that followed disrupted the adversary system and interfered with the resolution of a civil dispute.

The trial of this case lasted approximately fourteen days. The jury found that American Eagle Airlines had subjected Mr. Lee to a racially hostile work environment in violation of Title VII of the Civil Rights Act of 1964, 42 U.S.C. §2000e, *et seq.*, and 42 U.S.C. §1981. As compensation, the jury awarded Mr. Lee $300,000. In addition, the jury awarded Mr. Lee $650,000 in punitive damages. ... This motion seeking attorney's fees and costs pursuant to 42 U.S.C. § 1988 followed.[fn]

As the prevailing party in a Title VII action, the Plaintiff now seeks $1,611,910.50 in attorney's fees. This request presents the question of whether unprofessional and disruptive conduct of counsel which prolongs the proceedings and creates animosity which interferes with the resolution of a cause can be considered in determining an award of attorney's fees.

In their post-trial motions, counsel for the parties filed opposing affidavits concerning additional misconduct that was not directly observed by the Court. ...

These issues have been distasteful and time consuming. There is a great temptation to simply move on and ignore the issue. It is unpleasant to hear lawyers accusing each other of lies and misrepresentations. Unprofessionalism on the part of lawyers is a distraction and takes time away from other pending cases; it also embroils the Court in charges and counter charges. However, the functioning of our adversary system depends upon being able to rely upon what a lawyer says. So, confronted by affidavits of counsel that were directly contradictory, I decided to hear testimony and make credibility findings. These findings are based upon direct observations by the Court, the transcript of the trial, and the evidentiary hearing.

In addition, we contacted the Florida Bar to determine whether counsel had been the subject of complaints regarding unprofessional conduct. The Florida Bar forwarded a record of a previous complaint by a state court judge concerning the conduct of Marvin Kurzban. In response to that complaint, and immediately before the trial in this cause, the Florida Bar had directed Mr. Kurzban to attend an ethics class and pay a fine.

II. Findings of Fact Pertaining to Misconduct by Counsel

Discovery in this case was rancorous from the beginning. As is often the case, counsel for both sides contributed to the lack of civility. The tone of depositions was harsh, witnesses were treated with discourtesy, and discovery disputes were abundant. The transcripts of the depositions in this case are weighted down with bitter exchanges between the lawyers. [Cc]

Testimony at the evidentiary hearing reflected that this uncivil conduct also continued during conversations between counsel. The testimony of a young lawyer formerly with the Defendant's counsel's law firm was particularly poignant. This lawyer testified that during telephone conversations with Ira Kurzban, she was hung up on, told that she had only been assigned to work on the case because she was African-American, and wrongly accused of misrepresentations. She testified that her experience with opposing counsel in this case was a factor in her decision to leave her litigation practice.

This testimony was not only powerful and credible, but it also reflects the corrosive impact this type of unprofessional behavior can have upon the bar itself. A litigation practice is stressful and often exhausting. Unprofessional litigation tactics affect everyone exposed to such behavior and the ripple effect of incivility is spread throughout the bar.

The trial began. Testimony at the evidentiary hearing reveals that Mr. Kurzban's "Let's kick some ass" comment was not an aberration. A client representative of the Defendant, a lawyer for American Airlines, testified that she and others were subjected to a barrage of comments out of the hearing of the Court and jury which she likened to trash talk at a sporting event. Local counsel for the Defendant was called a "Second Rate Loser" by Marvin Kurzban. She testified that each day as court began, Marvin Kurzban would say, "Let the pounding begin." In front of defense counsel's client, Mr. Kurzban would ask, "How are you going to feel when I take all of your client's money?" When walking out of the courtroom, Marvin Kurzban would exclaim, "Yuppies out of the way."

Other than Mr. Kurzban's opening comment, I was unaware of this conduct towards opposing counsel and their client's representatives, although counsel for the Defendants alluded to it during the trial. [C] However, I observed continuing misconduct during the trial itself.

Early in the trial, an episode occurred when defense counsel brought to the Court's attention that after an instruction to a witness not to discuss his testimony during a break in his testimony for lunch, Ira and Marvin Kurzban had approached the witness and had a discussion—with an open deposition transcript in hand. Marvin Kurzban responded, "That's a lie." The Kurzbans then explained that they had the transcript open because they were looking at it, but that they were not talking with the witness about it. Their explanation was that they were talking about where they were going for lunch. I accepted the explanation, but with the observation that it was an exercise of poor judgment. [C]

Shortly afterward, Marvin Kurzban objected to a question, and I overruled his objection. He continued to argue his point, then he visibly expressed his dismay with the ruling. I asked counsel to approach for a sidebar conference, wherein I advised him that for the third time he had made visible displays of disagreement with rulings by nodding his head or looking upward at the ceiling. I told him to stop that conduct and to cease making speaking objections. [C]

Subsequently, I warned both counsel again; once before the jury [c], and again at the close of the mornings testimony. [C] Ira Kurzban responded that he was way beyond acrimony with opposing counsel.

After this warning, defense counsel followed the Court's admonition and refused to respond to provocations from opposing counsel. Later that day, Marvin Kurzban interrupted an appropriate cross-examination and requested a sidebar to accuse counsel of intentionally delaying the examination so that he could not reach a witness. [C]

Despite repeated warnings, Plaintiff's counsel continued to address comments to opposing counsel rather than to the Court [c] and interject inappropriate comments before the jury. [C]

The belligerence of Plaintiff's counsel, particularly Marvin Kurzban, spread like a contagion through the courtroom. ...

... [T]he Court Reporter indicated that at a break, which was a brief break for him inasmuch as we had a calendar call scheduled during that luncheon break, Marvin Kurzban asked him for a portion of transcript. The reporter responded that he could not produce those pages over the break (because he had to report the calendar call). Marvin Kurzban responded, "What are you here for, just to look pretty?" ...

I learned that accusations of bias followed any disagreement with positions espoused by Plaintiff's counsel: "There's no question that he's entitled to it, so it's no—if I understand what Your Honor's saying, you don't want it to go in front of the jury for whatever reason." [C]

"Your Honor, I know you're angry at me, but I hope you're not taking it out on my client." [C] "In fact, I think that the Court has exhibited extreme bias in this case and your rulings on objections." [C] "Well, Your Honor, I respectfully disagree with you, that's for a court of appeals ultimately to decide, but to put a motive on it I think it exhibits a substantial amount of bias on behalf of Your Honor." [C] "And I concur with what my brother has said. There's been clear animous by this Court to this side." [C] "I've practiced 26 years and I've tried over 50 cases, and I've won multimillion dollar verdicts on more than a dozen cases. I don't need for this Court to allow a witness to have his wife introduced. I can't think of any reason or purpose, other than prejudice, that this Court would allow such an act to occur." [C]

Disturbing behavior by both Marvin Kurzban and Ira Kurzban occurred repeatedly during the trial. When confronted about their conduct, they would deny that which I had just observed and then lash out in a personal attack. For instance, after I overruled an objection made by Ira Kurzban, Marvin Kurzban laughed. [C] Other examples of their conduct following rulings include Marvin Kurzban tossing a pen; Ira Kurzban exclaiming, "This is outrageous"; the rolling of eyes; exasperated looks at the ceiling; and flailing of arms. I warned counsel about this behavior. [C]

After the episode of Marvin Kurzban laughing at my ruling, I asked counsel to approach the bench. Marvin Kurzban responded: "I didn't laugh. What I started doing was writing a note, saying to my brother ... I didn't realize I was saying it out loud—we're not trying his case. That's what the objection was, because he's telling about his problems." Ira Kurzban then interjected: "I'd like to add, Your Honor, there's a continuing pattern of conduct we believe shows enormous bias and has turned this trial into a circus-like atmosphere." [C] ...

Shortly thereafter, during a discussion between the Court, Marvin Kurzban, and defense counsel about the admissibility of an exhibit a witness had allegedly drawn during a videotaped deposition but which was not on the Plaintiff's exhibit list, Ira Kurzban walked to the video machine and begin playing the videotape of the deposition in front of the jury. I directed that the machine be turned off and we took a fifteen minute break. [C] ...

During a cross-examination concerning how much time the witness spent on various shifts, Marvin Kurzban held a file towards the witness and asked: ... "I have your personnel file (indicating). How many times did you have to work between 1992 and 1994, sir? Do you think it was more than a handful of times?" [C]

After an objection, and out of the presence of the jury, I asked Mr. Kurzban for the witness's personnel file[, which Mr. Kurzban did not have in the courtroom. The Court concluded, "]I believe, frankly, that it is inappropriate to make a deliberate misrepresentation to a witness or to ask, implying in your questioning something that is not true.["] ...

Mr. Kurzban insisted that he had the personnel file back at his office. He was asked to produce it and he responded that he would the following day. The file was never produced.

At the end of the trial, defense counsel Connor approached Ira Kurzban and offered his hand in congratulations. Mr. Kurzban refused to shake his hand. The trial ended much like it had begun.

At the evidentiary hearing, Plaintiff's counsel were unrepentant, attacking opposing counsel and accepting no responsibility for their own actions. They argued that the perceived misconduct was only a matter of style and the exercise of first amendment rights. In keeping with that "style," Marvin Kurzban ended the hearing with the proclamation that he had called his opponent a loser, but not a second-rate loser because, "I don't rate losers." Mr. Kurzban's testimony reflects that he has no clue about what it means to be a lawyer.

III. Analysis

Courts presiding over civil rights actions may, in their discretion, award the prevailing party[fn] a "reasonable attorney's fee (including expert fees)" as part of its costs. [Cc] Although the presiding court has discretion, a prevailing plaintiff is to be awarded attorney's fees "in all but special circumstances." *Christiansburg Garment Co. v. EEOC*, 434 U.S. 412, 417[] (1978); [cc]. ...

... As explained more fully in the findings of misconduct, contained in Section II, *supra,* the conduct of Ira Kurzban and Marvin Kurzban both during and prior to trial was very troubling. In my estimation, the manner in which a lawyer interacts with opposing counsel and conducts himself before the Court is as indicative of the lawyer's ability and skill as is mastery of the rules of evidence. Upon review of the trial transcripts and the evidence presented during the evidentiary hearing on attorney conduct and based on observations at trial, I find that the conduct of Ira Kurzban and Marvin Kurzban in the litigation of this case fell far below acceptable standards, especially in light of the $300 hourly rate the attorneys claim. Accordingly, I find "special circumstances" justifying a departure from counsels' requested rates: Ira Kurzban shall be awarded $150 per hour for his pretrial work and $0 for his trial work; Marvin Kurzban's rate for this action is $0. [Cc].[fn]

... The Court is more concerned about the excessive number of hours billed in this case in light of its nature. This case involved racial harassment endured by a single plaintiff at a single site of employment. Although this matter was hotly contested, due in large part to overzealousness on both sides, the $1,611,910.50 in fees sought by Plaintiff's counsel based on 3,269.54 hours is clearly excessive. ...

To account for the excessive number of hours claimed in this case, we reduce Plaintiff's counsels' hours by 40% across-the-board. ...

V. Conclusion

... [A] letter recently received from a trial lawyer... stated: "... I do not think that problem is that lawyers do not know how to act in a civil manner. Rather, I think some lawyers will simply do that with which they can get away."

Special masters, grievance committees and educational seminars are not as effective as a sanction for uncivil behavior.

I know our federal court is quite busy and that the time it takes to consider uncivil behavior may have to be taken from some other pending case. However, I would submit that eliminating uncivil behavior not only helps that case, but every other case in which that lawyer is involved. Moreover, as the word spreads as to the price to be paid for unprofessionalism, other lawyers and other cases will be implicated.[fn]

I believe that this reduction in attorney fees is an appropriate response to the conduct by Plaintiff's counsel in this case, but I am not convinced it will deter future misconduct. I frankly considered denying fees altogether... .

For the foregoing reasons, it is hereby ORDERED AND ADJUDGED that ... we award Plaintiff **$312,324.63** in fees and costs.

Furthermore, because of the misconduct of counsel which occurred in this case, a copy of this order shall be sent to the Florida Bar and the Peer Review Committee for the Southern District of Florida for any action deemed appropriate.

"What Were They Thinking?"

What belief system were the plaintiffs' lawyers in the above case following that would cost them over a million dollars in fees because of their misconduct? The opinion documents the desultory effects of a "kick-ass" ethic, illustrating a different form of unfairness from the prior case, in this instance overzealous advocacy. In *The Moral Labyrinth of Zealous Advocacy*, 1992 CAP. UNIV. L.REV. 735, Professor James Elkins points to a "moral malaise" that law students first encounter in law school and that gradually destroys healthy professional identity. He traces lawyers' moral malaise to a pathological adversarialism. Professor Elkins argues that when lawyers substitute an ethic of zealousness for common morality, they separate themselves from the public at their own peril and the peril of the profession. We get to make choices of how to construct our identity. Choose wisely.

INQUIRY

Discipline for Unfairness. The default of a client, court sanctions, and loss of fees are only some of the consequences for treating opposing parties and counsel unfairly. Notice that the *Lee v. American Eagles Airline, Inc.* opinion ended with the referral of the overzealous lawyers to the Florida Bar and the federal district court's peer-review committee. Those referrals placed at risk the lawyers' law licenses and, separately, their ability to practice in that federal district court. Federal district courts grant separate admission to lawyers. Just because a lawyer is admitted to practice in the state courts does not mean that they have the privilege to practice in the federal district courts within that state. Lawyers must apply separately to the federal district court, which then has its own review procedures for terminating admission for misconduct. How do you think the lawyers in the above case fared in each forum, before the state bar grievance officials and before the peer-review committee of the federal court? Consider the following discipline case for violating Rule 3.4 on fairness to opposing parties and counsel.

Matter of Geisler,
Indiana Supreme Court
614 N.E.2d 939 (1993)

PER CURIAM.
   The respondent, David M. Geisler, was charged in a complaint for disciplinary action with engaging in conduct prejudicial to the administration of justice by obstructing the prosecuting attorney's access to evidence, in violation of Rules 3.4(a), 8.4(c) and (d) of the *Rules of Professional Conduct* and Rule 7-102(A)(7) of the preceding *Code of Professional Responsibility*. The disciplinary charges arose out of his representing Larry Baughman on child molesting charges. ...
   ... [T]he respondent... was retained by Larry Baughman to represent him on six counts of child molesting and attempted child molesting. ... The complaining witness was Carolyn Baughman, Larry Baughman's wife, and the victim was their daughter. The defendant had threatened Carolyn Baughman, and she feared physical violence from her husband. Nonetheless, no CHINS petition was filed nor was there any legal restriction preventing the defendant from contacting or residing with the family during the pendency of his prosecution. After the arrest, the defendant was released on bail and for some two or three months preceding his trial lived with the victim and the complaining witness.

... Carolyn Baughman did not want her daughter to testify at trial and made respondent aware of her feelings. The hearing officer concluded that she feared her husband and also did not want to expose her daughter to the trauma of the criminal process. There was some testimony that perhaps she was fearful of breaking up her marriage and being unable to manage on her own. Whatever her reasons, it was clear that she did not want her daughter to testify at trial. ...

... Mrs. Baughman continued in her conviction not to testify or allow her daughter to testify. Although Mrs. Baughman made this clear to the prosecuting attorney, he firmly believed that both would ultimately do so, if necessary, and, therefore, he issued no subpoenas until he grew leery some few days prior to trial.

The hearing officer found that during the early phases of preparing a defense strategy, Mrs. Baughman sought to learn the outcome and effect on the trial if the daughter was unavailable to testify. ... In response to this sort of inquiry, the Respondent discussed relevant case law with the Baughmans and provided them with copies of two cases, [cc]. ... The two cases follow the *Patterson*[fn] exception to the hearsay rule which provides that a prior statement of a witness is admissible, not only for the purposes of impeachment, but also as substantive evidence provided the statement is admitted and the witness is present at trial for cross-examination.

On January 30, 1987, at the last scheduled pretrial conference, the respondent urged his client to accept a plea agreement, but Baughman rejected the proposal. ...

The testimony as to what transpired after the rejection of the plea is conflicting and hotly contested. Mrs. Baughman testified that the respondent advised her to leave the state, go as far as she could, and that he did not want to know where. It was his assessment, that without her and her daughter's testimony, the case would have to be dismissed. Larry Baughman corroborated this testimony. Respondent's secretary, Janis Sims, also testified that she overheard respondent's telephone conversation with Mrs. Baughman, within two weeks of the trial, during which he advised Mrs. Baughman to take her daughter out of school and leave so that she could not be served with a subpoena and would not be under a court order to appear. Respondent denied these accusations and insisted that he advised Mrs. Baughman not to leave, but if she did, she was to call the judge and let him know she would not appear at the trial. ...

Mrs. Baughman and her daughter in fact went to Marshall County where they stayed with friends. They returned to their home on Friday, February 13, to acquire more clothes. While they were there, a deputy sheriff approached the home in an attempt to serve them with subpoenas, but was advised by Larry Baughman that they were not present and that Baughman was unaware of their whereabouts. In fact, Baughman helped them escape through a rear window.

Baughman testified that he advised respondent of his own actions. He testified that the respondent had advised him to deny knowing his wife and daughter's whereabouts, but both Baughman and the respondent agree that respondent advised him to testify truthfully at the scheduled trial. Baughman's criminal trial was continued, and he and Mrs. Baughman were charged with obstruction of justice.

The hearing officer also found that the evidence is undisputed that respondent made little or no effort to prepare for the trial.

Shortly after the trial was continued, the county Department of Public Welfare filed a CHINS petition, and the daughter was removed from the custody of the Baughmans. Respondent withdrew his appearance from the Baughman case, and sometime thereafter Larry Baughman accepted a plea agreement. The charge of obstruction of justice against Mrs. Baughman was dismissed pursuant to the terms of Larry Baughman's plea agreement, and ultimately the daughter was returned to the mother's custody.

Respondent challenged the credibility of the three adverse witnesses. He argued that the Baughmans decided between themselves that Mrs. Baughman and the daughter should be unavailable for service and trial. He claimed that they misinterpreted the cases to which he had referred them causing him to regret his action. ... Respondent also attributed their adverse testimony to a need to blame someone for their criminal obstruction of justice. Respondent attacked Janis Sims's credibility contending that her ability to overhear was impaired and that her memory of some of the surrounding events was not clear.

The hearing officer ... determined that the respondent did in fact assist Carolyn Baughman and her daughter in obstructing the prosecuting attorney's access to evidence. ... Our examination of the record indicates that the evidence for his conclusions is clear and convincing. ...

... [C]ircumstances corroborate the testimony of the three witnesses leading us to the inescapable conclusion that respondent was fully aware that Mrs. Baughman and her daughter would not avail themselves to service partly due to respondent's advice. We agree with the hearing officer's conclusion that the respondent exploited his knowledge gained from inappropriate contact with the State's material witnesses and stood by silently while the State's case was impeded. He fully expected that the prosecution's witnesses would not testify and, rather than prepare for trial, prepared to challenge the requested continuance.

The extent of Respondent's contact with Mrs. Baughman, his knowledge of her firm intent not to attend the trial, his knowledge that she relied on the case law provided by him, his preparation not for trial but to contest a motion for continuance, all indicate, at best, respondent's collusion in the obstruction of justice. Such conduct frustrates the orderly administration of justice and reflects negatively on the legal profession. We conclude that by his conduct the respondent assisted the Baughmans in their effort to withhold evidence and to frustrate the orderly administration of justice.

Having determined that Respondent engaged in misconduct, we must assess an appropriate sanction. This involves an analysis of the offense, actual or potential injury, the state of mind of the respondent, the duty of this court to preserve the integrity of the profession, the risk to the public, and matters in mitigation or aggravation. [C] The procedure of the adversary system contemplates that the evidence in a case is to be marshalled competitively by the contending parties. Fair competition in the adversary system is secured by prohibitions against destruction or concealment of evidence, improperly influencing witnesses, obstructive tactics in discovery procedure and the like. Comment to Rule 3.4 of the *Rules of Professional Conduct.* This offense strikes at the heart of an orderly system of justice. Respondent breached his ethical duty as a lawyer to the legal system, the public and the legal profession. ...

Under these circumstances, we find that a period of suspension with automatic reinstatement appropriately addresses the severity of the offense and reflects the particular circumstances of Respondent's conduct. It is, therefore, ordered, that the respondent David M. Geisler, is suspended from the practice of law for a period of ninety (90) days, at the expiration of which he will be automatically reinstated. ...

Costs are assessed against the respondent.

INQUIRY

Interfering with Witnesses. When Model Rule 3.4(f) prohibits a lawyer from encouraging witnesses to refrain from sharing their information with an opposing party, it memorializes the principle that everyone should have the same access to evidence. *See* State ex rel. Bar Assn v. Cox, 48 P.3d 780 (Okla. 2002) (60-day suspension for lawyer trying to induce friend not to testify as expert for other side). Every litigator knows the rule not to discourage witness non-attendance or non-disclosure. You can see from the above *Matter of Geisler* case how easily an opponent and judge can construe a lawyer's actions as interfering. Rule 3.4(f) contains some exceptions, though.

The first exception is for a client. Lawyers do advise clients not to voluntarily give information to the other side. A common instruction is to speak to another about the litigated matter only with the lawyer's approval. Opposing lawyers will not surreptitiously contact a lawyer's client but insurance representatives may do so. What other conditions do lawyers place on that advice? Lawyers certainly advise clients to comply fully with discovery requests, obey subpoenas, and testify completely and truthfully. Rule 3.4(f) applies only to the *voluntary* sharing of information, meaning when a person is under no compulsion (no subpoena or authorized request) to share information. Lawyers do advise clients to speak only when and where so advised.

Advising Agents. Model Rule 3.4(f)'s other exception is for a client's relatives, employees, and other agents, so long as the person's interests will not be adversely affected by refraining from sharing information. Can you see why the rule permits lawyers to advise a client's family members and agents to refrain from voluntarily sharing information? A lawyer could gain much information by surreptitiously interviewing the spouse, corporate manager, or other family member or agent of an opposing party. Yet damaging private disclosures to an opponent can undermine those important relationships. The attorney-client privilege, interspousal and confidential-communications privileges, and other privileges already recognize the value of trust and confidence within marriages, families, workplaces, and agency relationships. Model Rule 3.4(f) in effect permits a lawyer to patrol and preserve those privileges.

Violating Court Rules. Be sure that you appreciate each other specific prohibition of Model Rule 3.4. The above cases illustrate the prohibitions of subrules (a) and (b) against obstructing access to evidence, altering, destroying, or concealing potential evidence, urging or helping others to do so, falsifying evidence, and urging and assisting false testimony or offering illegal inducements to witnesses. As the *Matter of Geisler* opinion states, these actions strike against the core of the justice system. Model Rule 3.4(c) then turns knowing violations of court rules into misconduct, expanding the lawyer's ethical duty to encompass obeying those rules. Do not miss the significance of Model Rule 3.4(c): if you knowingly disobey court rules, you are engaging in misconduct for which a judge, opposing counsel, party, or non-party witness could report you and grievance officials could discipline. Model Rule 3.4(c) does grant lawyers the right to challenge openly the applicability of a court rule. Model Rule 3.4(d) then addresses litigation discovery, that lawyers must not make frivolous discovery requests and must make reasonably diligent efforts to comply with credible requests. The messages are clear: litigate by the court rules because not to do so may be an ethics violation.

Trial Procedures. Model Rule 3.4(e) addresses misconduct at trial. It first prohibits lawyers from alluding to inadmissible matters, a prohibition that turns the evidence rules (like the court rules) into conduct rules. Lawyers who misbehave in the courtroom run the risk of not only affecting the proceeding adversely and facing court sanction but also facing ethics grievance. Rule 3.4(e) also prohibits lawyers from stating personal knowledge and opinions at trial. You might wonder how lawyers manage to give opening statements and closing arguments without stating knowledge or opinions. Trial lawyers learn quickly that it is perfectly permissible to urge, "The evidence shows" certain facts while it is impermissible to urge, "I believe" in those facts. *See, e.g.,* State v. Goltz, 111 S.W.3d 1 (Tenn. Crim. App. 2003) (mistrial for prosecutor vouching in closing argument, "I know for a fact that [witness] Carl Hutchinson is honest"); *see also* Reetz v. Kinsman Marine Transit Co., 330 N.W.2d 638 (Mich. 1982) (mistrial for closing argument asserting, "We know about millions of dollars being awarded for certain kinds of injuries; we know of that kind of thing; we know of millions of dollars being awarded for injuries.").

C. As Prosecutor

Special Duties. To this point, the chapter has addressed the general duty of any lawyer to act fairly toward others. Prosecutors have special duties of fairness because of their special role. *See* Berger v. United States, 295 U.S. 78 (1935) (prosecutor represents "a sovereignty whose obligation is to govern impartially"). Some of the cases cited above involved prosecutors, to whom Model Rule 3.4 certainly applies. A separate rule, ABA MODEL RULE OF PROFESSIONAL CONDUCT 3.8, a similar state version of which is below, states the special duties of a prosecutor. Rule 3.8 articulates the prosecutor's special role around the principle that the public must have the greatest trust in and respect for the criminal justice system if it is to fulfill its proper function. Prosecution is not adversarial in quite the way that civil litigation is adversarial. Prosecutors owe duties not just to the government, the public, and victims of crime but also to those whom prosecutors charge with crime. That duty begins with not to over-charge crime. *See* Iowa Supreme Ct. Atty. Discipline Bd. v. Howe, 706 N.W.2d 360 (Iowa 2005) (suspending prosecutor for charging under a 1920s statute requiring vehicles to bear cowl lamps). It is when prosecutors forget their duty to the charged defendant that prosecutors most risk public trust and confidence. As you read the following state version of Model Rule 3.8, note in particular the prosecutor's duty not to charge without probable cause and the duty to make timely disclosure of exonerating evidence.

WASH. R. PROF. CONDUCT 3.8: Special Responsibilities of a Prosecutor.
The prosecutor in a criminal case shall:
(a) refrain from prosecuting a charge that the prosecutor knows is not supported by probable cause;
(b) make reasonable efforts to assure that the accused has been advised of the right to, and the procedure for obtaining, counsel and has been given reasonable opportunity to obtain counsel;
(c) not seek to obtain from an unrepresented accused a waiver of important pretrial rights, such as the right to a preliminary hearing;
(d) make timely disclosure to the defense of all evidence or information known to the prosecutor that tends to negate the guilt of the accused or mitigates the offense, and, in connection with sentencing, disclose to the defense and to the tribunal all mitigating information known to the prosecutor, except when the prosecutor is relieved of this responsibility by a protective order of the tribunal;
(e) not subpoena a lawyer in a grand jury or other criminal proceeding to present evidence about a past or present client unless the prosecutor reasonably believes:
(1) the information sought is not protected from disclosure by any applicable privilege;
(2) the evidence sought is essential to the successful completion of an ongoing investigation or prosecution; and
(3) there is no other feasible alternative to obtain the information;
(f) except for statements that are necessary to inform the public of the nature and extent of the prosecutor's action and that serve a legitimate law enforcement purpose, refrain from making extrajudicial comments that have a substantial likelihood of heightening public condemnation of the accused and exercise reasonable care to prevent investigators, law enforcement personnel, employees or other persons assisting or associated with the prosecutor in a criminal case from making an extrajudicial statement that the prosecutor would be prohibited from making under Rule 3.6 or this Rule.

INQUIRY

Suppressing Evidence. Consistent with the prosecutor's public role, ABA Model Rule 3.8(d) requires a prosecutor to disclose timely all evidence and information tending to negate guilt or mitigate an offense. Model Rule 3.8(d) has a constitutional basis, although the conduct rule is somewhat broader than the Constitution's requirement. In Brady v. United States, 373 U.S. 83 (1963), the Supreme Court held that a prosecutor violates due process when suppressing material negating or mitigating evidence for which the defense made a request. Unlike the Constitution, Model Rule 3.8(d) requires disclosure whether or not the defense makes a request. ABA

Formal Ethics Opin. 09-454 further holds that the Rule 3.8(d) requires disclosure whenever the evidence has a "minimal tendency" to negate or mitigate. The materiality standard of *Brady* is higher, meaning again that the rule is broader than the Constitution. Prosecutors must also not turn a blind eye toward negating or mitigating evidence held not by the prosecutor but by police. *See* Kyles v. Whitley, 514 U.S. 419, 437 (1995) (prosecutor's duty extends to disclosing evidence held by other government actors including police). Consider one very well known instance of prosecutor suppression, in which Durham, North Carolina prosecutor Michael Nifong charged three Duke lacrosse team members with rape while suppressing DNA test results reportedly showing that the complainant's clothing and body had genetic material from several other men but none from the lacrosse players, and publicly denying the existence of that exculpatory evidence. The court dismissed the charges, and a discipline committee disbarred Nifong.

The North Carolina State Bar v. Nifong,
Disciplinary Hearing Commission
06-DHC-35 (June 16, 2007)

[The following remarks by Hearing Panel Chair F. Lane Williamson constituted Phase Two of the hearing, following Phase One in which the panel found specific violations. The panel included a second attorney member and a public member.]

Thank you for your patience. The hearing committee has deliberated and we are in unanimous agreement that there's no discipline short of disbarment that would be appropriate in this case given the magnitude of the offenses we have found and the effect upon the profession and the public.

I do want to make some remarks as to why we reached our conclusion. This matter has been a fiasco. There is no doubt about it. It has been a fiasco for a number of people, starting with the defendants and moving out from there to the justice system in general. We've heard evidence over the last several days of how that came about. Though we are lawyers and a school administrator—we're not psychologists—you have to ask yourself, "Why? Why did we get to the place that we got?"

It seems that at the root of it is self-deception arising out of self-interest. Mark Twain said that "when a person cannot deceive himself the chances are against his being able to deceive other people."

Well, what we have here, it seems, is that we had a prosecutor who was faced with a very unusual situation in which the confluence of his self-interest collided with a very volatile mix of race, sex and class, a situation that if it were a plot of a John Grisham novel it would be considered to be perhaps too contrived. At that time he was facing a primary and yes he was politically naive. But we can draw no other conclusion that that those initial statements that he made were to forward his political ambitions. But having once done that and having seen the facts as he hoped they would be, in his mind the facts remained that way in the face of developing evidence that that was not in fact the case.

And even today one must say that in the face of a declaration of innocence by the attorney general of North Carolina, it appears the defendant still believes the facts to be one way and the world now knows that is not the case.

We are required under our rules to consider certain aggravating and mitigating factors... . And those are set forth in the rule and I'm going to say what aggravating and mitigating factors we have found.

We have found as aggravating factors dishonest or selfish motive, a pattern of misconduct, multiple offenses, refusal to acknowledge wrongful nature of conduct—in the respect of the handling of the DNA evidence; we do find that he has made some acknowledgement of his wrongful conduct in regard to the pretrial statements—the vulnerability of the victim—or the victims in this case and primarily the victims are the three young men who were wrongfully charged. And we find also as an aggravating factor substantial experience in the practice of law.

As mitigating factors we find absence of a prior disciplinary record, a reputation for character. We expressly find that the aggravating factors outweigh the mitigating factors.

This matter appears to be an aberration in a couple of respects. It appears to be an aberration in the life and career of Michael Nifong. It appears also to be an aberration in the way justice is handled in North Carolina. It's an illustration of the fact that character—good character—is not a constant. Character is dependent upon the situation. Probably any one of us could be faced with a situation at some point that would test our good character and we would prove wanting. And that has happened to Mike Nifong. But the fact that it has happened and the fact that we have found dishonesty and deceitful conduct requires us in the interest of protection of the public to enter the most severe sanction that we can enter, which is disbarment.

I want to say something about who the victims are here. The victims are the three young men to start with, their families, the entire lacrosse team and their coach, Duke University, the justice system in North Carolina and elsewhere. And indeed prosecutors—honest, ethical, hard-working prosecutors throughout the nation—as we've heard through anecdotal evidence are victims of this conduct. And in particular the justice system is a victim of the way this was taken out of ... the courtroom and put in the hands of the public and not only the public in general but into a media frenzy unprecedented in anyone's experience. ...

As I think anyone who has sat through this entire proceeding— we've been here now on the fifth day—that you can't do justice in the media, you can't do justice on sound bites. The way to arrive at a determination of the facts is to hear in a fair and open proceeding all of the evidence and then for the trier of fact to determine what the facts are. And we've done that this week.

That did not happen and was not going to happen apparently in the Duke lacrosse case. The justice system righted itself somehow so that at the end of the day there was indeed a declaration of innocence of these three young men. But it was done with backup systems in a way that was never designed to work as the justice system should work. Perhaps that was set in motion by the state bar's initial complaint, filed on December 28, 2006, that shortly thereafter led to the recusal of Mr. Nifong from the Duke lacrosse cases. That was a controversial decision, I believe. Certainly unprecedented that the state bar would take disciplinary action against a prosecutor during the pendency of the case when indeed the presiding judge had concurrent and coextensive disciplinary jurisdiction. That was the step—although we were not privy to the decision to do that—I am sure that was a matter of serious debate as to whether to do that because that in itself took the justice system off track.

The other mechanism by which the system more or less righted itself was the involvement of the attorney general and the special prosecutors, who looked at it from a standpoint of prosecutors who were cognizant of their duty... . And that led to something really very extraordinary, a declaration of actual innocence of the three defendants—something that could never have been accomplished even if the criminal case had proceeded before Judge Smith. And while we don't know, it seems reasonably clear that one would predict that at the suppression hearing in February the case would have been dismissed. But it would have been dismissed with no declaration of innocence and indeed this entire controversy regarding the wrongful prosecution still hanging over the heads of the defendants and the justice system of North Carolina.

So perhaps that was the good thing that happened if one can find much of anything good out of this situation.

But the fact that if these extraordinary [events] had not come to pass, leading to that declaration of innocence, raises another point that we should all be aware of, which is that the person who is the most powerful in the criminal justice system is not the judge and except at the end of the process it's not the jury, it's the prosecutor who makes the charging decision to start with.

The prosecutor, as any defense lawyer will tell you, is imbued with an aura that if he says its so it must be so. And even with all the constitutional rights that are afforded criminal defendants, the prosecutor merely by asserting a charge against defendants already has a leg up. And when that power is abused, as it was here, it puts constitutional rights in jeopardy. We have a justice system but the justice system only works if the people who participate in it are people of good faith and respect those rights.

And Mr. Nifong it must be said for whatever reason it does appear to us to be out of self-interest and self-deception, not necessarily out of an evil motive, but that his judgment was so clouded by his own self-interest that he lost sight of it and wandered off the path of justice and had to be put back on course again by again very extraordinary means.

This is also a case where due to the initial strong statements, unequivocal statements, made by Mr. Nifong, there was a deception perpetrated upon the public. And many people were made to look foolish because they simply accepted that if this prosecutor said it was true, it must be true.

When I think back to those early days in the spring of last year and we think of how public opinion was so overwhelmingly against these defendants and you think of the public aggravation that they suffered and then you look at how the truth came out slowly in small increments and look at the situation now as to what public opinion is there is a 180-degree turn. And those who made a rush to judgment based upon an unquestioning faith in what a prosecutor had told them were made to look foolish and many still do look foolish.

It is very difficult to find any good in this situation that brings us here. I can only think of a couple things. One is that there are very few deterrents upon prosecutorial misconduct. For very good policy reasons, prosecutors are virtually immune from civil liability. About the worst that can happen to them for the conduct of a case is that the case can be overturned. The only significant deterrent upon a prosecutor is the possibility of disciplinary sanction. And here the most severe sanction is warranted. ...

Every case is different but the case we have here is a clear case of intentional prosecutorial misconduct. So in addition to this being a deterrent to any prosecutorial misconduct, I would say that this should be a reminder to everyone that it's the facts that matter. It's not the allegations. And if you sit as a juror or if you sit at home watching your television about court proceedings, you have to carefully consider the facts and the evidence before you make a conclusion about something and not just trust someone who tells who it is so because that is someone who's in a position who is supposed to know.

The other thing that may be good about this is to say that this ... has given an opportunity to air some but not all of the evidence that may relate to this matter. ... [W]e've had an opportunity over the last several days to hear additional evidence—and while it is really not within the purview of the panel to make such a pronouncement—I want to say again that we acknowledge the actual innocence of the defendants. And there is nothing here that has done anything but support that assertion. ...

... It's been truly—a fiasco is not too strong a word. But it could have resulted from a lapse of character of practically anyone, not just in particular Mike Nifong. We've heard anecdotal evidence of the harm that it has caused. The actual harm is very difficult to get one's arms around. But I certainly hope that this process will help assuage the harm and stop the ripples that seemed to start when the stone was thrown in the pond. They just got bigger and bigger. But hopefully they will ebb from this point forward. ...

So unless there is anything further for us to address, this proceeding is concluded. Thank you.

INQUIRY

Public Statements.   Notice that ABA Model Rule 3.8(f) limits the public statements that a prosecutor can make. One concern Rule 3.8(f) addresses is that public comments may taint the jury pool. The court and defense counsel would strike jurors who heard news reports of the matter, but not all jurors admit to their knowledge. Rule 3.8(f) also requires a prosecutor to take reasonable steps to ensure that other law-enforcement personnel do not make unnecessary public comments that would have the same effect.   Despite Rule 3.8(f), prosecutors and other law-enforcement officials do frequently make public comments. You may recall news conferences and other alerts. Rule 3.8(f) permits these public statements for "legitimate law enforcement purposes... ." Can you think of examples? Rule 3.8(f) presumably permits a prosecutor to alert or allow others to alert the public of a safety threat relating to an ongoing or recent crime, the need to discover witnesses or recover evidence, and make similar statements. Can you think of statements that a prosecutor must not make or allow other law-enforcement officials to make? See the *Nifong* findings omitted from the above excerpt.

Exoneration.   The above state version of ABA Model Rule 3.8 says nothing directly about a prosecutor discovering post-conviction evidence of innocence. In 2009, the American Bar Association adopted amendments (reproduced below) to Model Rule 3.8 to address the prosecutor's special duty to assist with exonerations. Were the amendments necessary? Recall the *In re Riehlman* case from Chapter II, in which a prosecutor just diagnosed with a terminal illness revealed a wrongful conviction to the respondent criminal-defense lawyer. Should it take a death-bed conversion to make a prosecutor come clean? Prosecutors have acted diligently, even heroically, to exonerate the wrongfully convicted. In one instance, prosecutors assigned an assistant to defend two murder convictions when evidence surfaced that the proceedings had wrongfully convicted the murderers. When investigation convinced the assistant that the defendants were innocent, he helped them with locating witnesses and developing defense strategy. Wayne D. Garris, Jr., *Model Rule of Professional Conduct 3.8: The ABA Takes a Stand Against Wrongful Convictions*, 22 GEO. J. LEGAL ETHICS 829 (2009). The new Subrule (g) of Model Rule 3.8 may not be necessary to alert the prosecutor's conscience, but then again, it may be helpful to assistant prosecutors who act at their supervisor's commands. Should all lawyers, not just public prosecutors, have a similar duty to disclose to the other side evidence that they discover post proceeding? Why does Model Rule 3.8(g) stop at prosecutors?

ABA MODEL RULE OF PROF. CONDUCT 3.8: Special Responsibilities of a Prosecutor.

...

(g) When a prosecutor knows of new, credible and material evidence creating a reasonable likelihood that a convicted defendant did not commit an offense of which the defendant was convicted, the prosecutor shall:

(1) promptly disclose that evidence to an appropriate court or authority, and

(2) if the conviction was obtained in the prosecutor's jurisdiction,

(i) promptly disclose that evidence to the defendant unless a court authorizes delay, and

(ii) undertake further investigation, or make reasonable efforts to cause an investigation, to determine whether the defendant was convicted of an offense that the defendant did not commit.

(h) When a prosecutor knows of clear and convincing evidence establishing that a defendant in the prosecutor's jurisdiction was convicted of an offense that the defendant did not commit, the prosecutor shall seek to remedy the conviction.

INQUIRY

Cross-Examination. Cross-examination of witnesses at trial is another area where prosecutors may have different obligations than defense lawyers. The American Bar Association's Criminal Justice Section has published standards relating to both the defense function and the prosecution function of lawyers practicing in the criminal-justice system. ABA Defense Function Standard 4-7.6(b) permits a defense lawyer to cross-examine a witness even if the lawyer believes that the witness is telling the truth. Can you articulate why? By contrast, ABA Prosecution Function Standard 3-5.7(b) states, "A prosecutor should not use the power of cross-examination to discredit or undermine a witness if the prosecutor knows the witness is testifying truthfully." Can you articulate why?

Plea Negotiation. ABA Model Rule 3.8 makes no mention of plea bargains, even though plea negotiation is central to a prosecutor's role. Indeed, plea bargaining is so central to prosecution that ABA Prosecution Function Standard 3-4.1(a) urges prosecutors to "have and make known a general policy or willingness to consult with defense counsel" over pleas. In other words, it may be wrong (even if not a discipline offense) for a prosecutor to refuse as a matter of policy to discuss pleas. What limits are there on what a prosecutor may threaten or promise in order to induce a plea bargain? Prosecutors must not make false statements of law or fact in plea discussions. ABA Prosecution Function Standard 3-4.1(c). While prosecutors may agree that they will seek a certain sentence, they must not promise that the court will impose a certain sentence. ABA Prosecution Function Standard 3-4.2(a). While a prosecutor must not threaten false charges (that much Rule 3.8(a)'s prohibition at least implies), prosecutors may constitutionally threaten to increase charges to that which probable cause supports, in order to induce a defendant to plea to the charged crime. *See* Bordenkircher v. Hayes, 434 U.S. 357, 364 (1978). Prosecutors may also promise leniency in exchange for truthful testimony in another prosecution. *See* United States v. Singleton, 165 F.3d 1297 (10th Cir. 1999).

Federal Prosecutors. From the late 1980s through the 1990s, the United States Department of Justice held that its federal prosecutors (United States attorneys) were not subject to state conduct rules when those state rules conflicted with federal law and practice. Congress then provided otherwise in the Citizens Protection Act, 28 U.S.C. §530(b), making federal prosecutors "subject to State laws and rules" where the prosecutors practiced "to the same extent and in the same manner as other attorneys in that State." When it comes to state and federal prosecution practice, one size now fits all, except to the extent that the different state and federal courts have different local procedural rules, customs, and practices, or the laws under which the prosecution takes place require different conduct of those prosecutors.

D. For Judges

Knowing False Statements. The duty of lawyers to respect others extends to respecting judges and other public legal officials. Model Rule 8.2 titled "Judicial and Legal Officials," addresses the respect that lawyers owe a judge, magistrate, referee, or other adjudicatory officer or public legal official. Rule 8.2 prohibits a lawyer from making intentional or reckless false statements about a judge's or other public legal official's qualifications or integrity. Lawyers must not gossip or trash-talk about judges. To use false statements to attack a judge's qualifications or integrity destroys public confidence in the justice system. Rule 8.2's protection of judicial candidates in addition to judges indicates that lawyers must respect both the role of the public legal official and the person who occupies or wishes to occupy the role. Read the following similar state version of Model Rule 8.2 for these requirements, followed by a case involving a lawyer making one of the most damning of false statements that a lawyer could possibly make in disrespect for judges.

ARIZONA R. PROF. CONDUCT 8.2: Judicial and Legal Officials.

(a) A lawyer shall not make a statement that the lawyer knows to be false or with reckless disregard as to its truth or falsity concerning the qualifications or integrity of a judge, adjudicatory officer or public legal officer, or of a candidate for election or appointment to judicial or legal office.

(b) A lawyer who is a candidate for judicial office shall comply with the applicable provisions of the Code of Judicial Conduct.

Dayton Bar Assn. v. O'Brien,
Ohio Supreme Court
812 N.E.2d 1263 (2004)

O'DONNELL, J.

{¶1} We are called upon to determine the appropriate sanction for an attorney who has told his client that the trial judge who presided over his criminal case and who was preparing to sentence him might be persuaded to grant a motion to withdraw the client's guilty plea if the client had the money "to afford that kind of treatment."

{¶2} A three-member panel of the Board of Commissioners on Grievances and Discipline recommended a six-month stayed suspension and upon review, the entire board recommended a public reprimand. We reject both recommendations. For the following reasons, the conduct in question warrants an indefinite suspension from the practice of law.

{¶3} Relator, the Dayton Bar Association, filed a complaint against respondent, attorney Daniel L. O'Brien... after receiving a complaint from Kurtis Wallace, one of O'Brien's clients. O'Brien has been licensed to practice law in Ohio since 1999 and has previously represented Wallace in several legal matters. In the instant case, Wallace hired O'Brien to represent him in connection with criminal charges of identity theft and forgery before Montgomery County Court of Common Pleas Judge Michael T. Hall. O'Brien entered into plea negotiations with the prosecutor, and as a result, Wallace pled guilty to identity theft in exchange for the dismissal of the forgery charge. The court continued the matter for sentencing.

{¶4} On the day of sentencing, O'Brien met with the prosecutor in Judge Hall's chambers, where the judge informed them that he declined to impose a sentence of community control and that he intended to incarcerate Wallace. O'Brien left the chambers and informed Wallace of the judge's intentions. Upset with the pending sentence, Wallace fled the courthouse and failed to appear in the courtroom for sentencing.

{¶5} Several days later, Wallace contacted O'Brien by telephone and advised him that his brother could lend him $12,000 to pay for the withdrawal of his guilty plea. Wallace called O'Brien a second time and made a secret tape recording of their conversation, in which O'Brien stated that with $12,000, he (O'Brien) might be able to find someone to whom Judge Hall owed a favor who could persuade the judge to permit the withdrawal of Wallace's plea. A transcript of the recorded conversation reveals that O'Brien stated:

{¶6} "If you want a first class legal defense you gotta pay for a first class defense and if that means that I look around, then I say who does the judge owe a favor to, I'm walking around talking with the best of the best and I say I need you to come in on one favor, I need to withdraw the guilty plea and we need to show up there together and I need you to bring it. If I don't think I can bring it, I get somebody who does. You know what I mean? That's the kind of thing that you pay for and that way once he's got what we need done, we send him out, we come back in and we deal with the rest of it. I mean if you want high priced stuff that's how you get it and we've done big magic, big magic for people who had the money to be able to afford that kind of treatment."

{¶7} Wallace never paid any money to O'Brien; instead, he hired another attorney to represent him and he filed a grievance against O'Brien with the Dayton Bar Association. Wallace's new counsel provided the tape to Judge Hall, who had the case transferred.

Following investigation, a panel of the Board of Commissioners on Grievances and Discipline ... found that O'Brien violated DR1-102(A)(5) ... provid[ing] that a lawyer shall not "[e]ngage in conduct that is prejudicial to the administration of justice" [and] DR 9-101(C) stat[ing] that "a lawyer shall not state or imply that he is able to influence improperly or upon irrelevant grounds any tribunal, legislative body, or public official." EC 9-4 states the rationale for DR 9-101(C): "Because the very essence of the legal system is to provide procedures by which matters can be presented in an impartial manner so that they may be decided solely upon the merits, any statement or suggestion by a lawyer that he can or would attempt to circumvent those procedures is detrimental to the legal system and tends to undermine public confidence in it." ...

{¶12} ... [W]e have repeatedly stressed our disdain for any statements by an attorney that imply the corruptibility of the judicial system or that the attorney can improperly influence a judicial officer. We have consistently imposed severe sanctions on attorneys who choose to engage in such misconduct. This case warrants a similar sanction. The board's recommendation of a public reprimand fails to consider the seriousness of O'Brien's conduct. His statements expressly suggested corruption in the court system, impugned the integrity of the judiciary, and maligned the reputation of Judge Hall. It is irrelevant that O'Brien failed to collect any money from Wallace or never acted on his statements. The suggestion of improper influence to affect the outcome of a matter pending before Judge Hall constituted an egregious violation of the Code of Professional Responsibility and warrants a severe sanction.

{¶13} Lawyers are officers of the court and, as such, they must strive to uphold the integrity of judicial officers before whom they appear. By their oath, lawyers are charged with high ethical standards which, as professionals, they are expected to uphold at all times. Lawyers who engage in errant behavior do so at their own peril. O'Brien eroded and impugned the integrity of a judicial officer and intimated to a client that, for $12,000, he could improperly influence the outcome of a criminal case; in so doing, he falsely represented the judicial process to be corrupt and thereby risked diminishing the public's perception of, and confidence in, the judiciary. Accordingly, he is hereby indefinitely suspended from the practice of law.

{¶14} Costs are taxed to respondent.

Judgment accordingly.

INQUIRY

Criticizing Judges. Why do the rules protect judges against certain kinds of lawyer criticism? Do you think that the rules need to do so? Model Rule 8.2 prohibiting knowingly or recklessly false statements about a judge has both public and private functions. The private function is to keep lawyers from undermining the reputation of specific judges. Judges, like lawyers, have an interest in their reputation. When a party loses a case, the party has a natural inclination to blame the judge. Model Rule 8.2 prohibits a lawyer from fueling a client's natural inclination with false statements denigrating the judge's integrity. Model Rule 8.2's public function has to do with maintaining respect not just for a specific judge but for the judiciary and justice system generally. Court orders and judgments are not self-executing. The justice system's functioning depends on sufficient public respect that individual members of the public comply voluntarily with those orders and judgments. Resist the temptation to blame the judge. Do not attack a judge's integrity without factual basis, even in the privacy of one's own office. Remember the proverb that a king inevitably hears the confidential criticism of a courtier. Consider the following case involving one of the most damning of implications a lawyer could make against a judge.

Practice

It had been an exhausting day of trial. The unrepresented plaintiff, whose out-of-control actions had made the trial seem like a circus, had already left the courtroom. The two lawyers representing the two defendants were packing their trial cases as one of the defendants complained about the day. The defendant's complaints gradually turned from the out-of-control plaintiff to the judge's unwillingness or inability to control the plaintiff and trial. One of the lawyers quietly backed away, his bags packed, heading for the courtroom door, not liking the way the conversation had turned. The other lawyer whose client was complaining joined in the complaint. Suddenly, the door to chambers flew open, and the red-faced trial judge emerged in a rage, berating the complainers whose words the courtroom microphones had been playing into the judicial office. Although the defendants won the jury trial of the out-of-control plaintiff's bizarre claims, the atmosphere for the rest of the trial was decidedly cool between the trial judge, parties, and counsel.

Judicial Campaigns. Model Rule 8.2 also prohibits knowingly or recklessly tellling falsehoods about a candidate for judicial or legal office. Some may misconstrue Model Rule 8.2 to be a violation of a lawyer's First Amendment rights to speak freely about an important public issue. How do adopted state versions of Model Rule 8.2 pass constitutional muster? While the First Amendment protects false statements about public figures and officials that the speaker does not know to be false, it does not protect false statements that the speaker makes with actual malice, meaning with a knowing or reckless disregard for the statements' falsity. *See* New York Times v. Sullivan, 376 U.S. 254 (1964); *see also* St. Amant v. Thompson, 390 U.S. 727 (1968) (recklessness includes subjective serious doubt as to the statement's truth); Garrison v. State of Louisiana, 379 U.S. 64 (1964) (recklessness includes high degree of awareness of falsity). Model Rule 8.2 permits a lawyer to make a false statement, just not a knowing or reckless false statement. Both members of the public and lawyers should take care to speak only what they believe to be the truth about a candidate for judicial or other legal office. Model Rule 8.2 puts a lawyer's license on the line when a lawyer speaks a knowing or reckless falsehood about a candidate for judicial or legal office.

Career and Professional Development

One way in which lawyers show respect to one another, judges, clients, and others, while at the same time working on their career and professional development, is to join and participate in the activities of professional, industry, and trade organizations. In law school, students start and join student organizations. When joining the profession, new lawyers join local bar associations where they meet, socialize with, and address local professional issues with the local lawyers and judges. As a lawyer develops a niche practice, the lawyer may join specialty bars and bar sections. When lawyers begin to develop their own clientele within a specific industry, trade, or profession, they may join industry, trade, and professional associations,l where they learn more about their client's needs and interests. Lawyers also join affinity bars around ethnicity, culture, and heritage, for the social and professional support that affinity offers. Consider what professional associations you will join, and plan to do so. Many bar associations and sections accept student members at low or no cost, where students can find mentors and job leads, and work on networks and professional development.

CHAPTER VII

HONESTY

Toward Others, When Dealing with Unrepresented and Represented Persons, Toward Tribunals

The principle with which we are now dealing is that one which is called Expediency. The usage of this word has been corrupted and perverted and has gradually come to the point where, separating moral rectitude from expediency, it is accepted that a thing may be morally right without being expedient, and expedient without being morally right. No more pernicious doctrine than this could be introduced into human life.

— Cicero

OBJECTIVE: Given client representations in which you must communicate information to others in various situations including in courts or other tribunals, articulate your responsibility to be honest in your communications and dealings.

Applicable Rules

3.3   Candor to the Tribunal

4.1   Truthfulness in Statements to Others

4.2   Communication with Person Represented by Counsel

4.3   Dealing with Unrepresented Persons

Committed, earnest, productive, and authentic lawyers who have excellent professional relationships communicate with others in a variety of practice settings. Some of those settings involve persons over whom the lawyer has a distinct advantage. Each of those situations requires the lawyer's honesty. In many instances, honesty also includes candor, meaning an openness, forthrightness, outspokenness, and bluntness, as to the lawyer's advice, role, and objectives. Although honesty seems like a simple construct, practice settings make honesty's pursuit more complex. A lawyer must follow appropriate professional norms and applicable conduct rules to ensure the lawyer's honesty and candor. An example is a lawyer dealing with an unrepresented person. Training makes a lawyer good at convincing others in order to get what the lawyer wants. Lawyers must show candor not to exercise undue advantage when dealing with unrepresented persons. Likewise, a lawyer will have occasional contact with a person whom another lawyer represents but when that other lawyer is not present. Again, the lawyer having direct contact with a represented person whose representative is not present must show candor not to take undue advantage of that opportunity. Finally, lawyers make arguments and present evidence in tribunals, encountering judges, jurors, and others who do not know the facts or even the controlling law. Lawyers must exercise special care not to take undue advantage in these forums and instead to communicate truthfully and with candor. Consider each of these situations in turn, after exploring the basic duty of honesty in all representations.

A. Statements to Others

Course of the Representation. Lawyers must be honest, but when must they be so? ABA Model Rule 4.1(a) prohibits knowing false statements of material fact to third persons in the course of representing a client. Statements, of course, include both oral statements and writings. *See* Columbus Bar Assn. v. Battisti, 739 N.E.2d 344 (Ohio 2000) (false affidavits). It is understandable that Model Rule 4.1 should qualify the duty to apply "[i]n the course of [the lawyer] representing a client... ." Professional conduct rules apply generally to professional behavior. Perhaps discipline officials should have no particular interest in ensuring that a lawyer is honest in playing a card game with friends even if the lawyer would be a better friend if the lawyer were honest even then. Model Rule 4.1 prohibits false statements only in the course of a representation, such as in litigation, *see* In re Gross, 759 N.E.2d 288 (Mass. 2001) (impersonation scheme at trial), and negotiation, *see* In re Eadie, 36 P.3d 468 (Or. 2001). Yet ABA Model Rule 8.4(c) includes a broader prohibition on lawyer dishonesty, not restricted to the course of representation. *See* In re Albin, 982 P.2d 385 (Kan. 1999) (lawyer's scam legal mail to non-client prisoner violates Rule 8.4, not 4.1). Read the identical state version of Model Rule 4.1 below, followed by a case illustrating the rule's application. While reading Model Rule 4.1 for its other limitations, keep in mind that there are times when a lawyer should not be parsing a rule for its exception. Honesty may always be the best policy.

> **ARKANSAS R. PROF. CONDUCT 4.1: Truthfulness in Statements to Others.**
> In the course of representing a client a lawyer shall not knowingly:
> (a) make a false statement of material fact or law to a third person; or
> (b) fail to disclose a material fact when disclosure is necessary to avoid assisting a criminal or fraudulent act by a client, unless disclosure is prohibited by Rule 1.6.

Matter of Apt,
Kansas Supreme Court
946 P.2d 1002 (1997)

PER CURIAM:

This is an original proceeding in discipline filed by the office of the Disciplinary Administrator against Frederick G. Apt, Jr. ... an attorney licensed to practice law in the state of Kansas. Complaints against respondent alleged that respondent violated ... MRPC 4.1 [] (truthfulness in statements to others)... .

... Frederick G. Apt, Jr., was retained by Robert and Hazel Irwin of Iola, Kansas, to prepare their wills in May 1981. In July 1993, he prepared joint and mutual durable powers of attorney for them. In October 1993, he prepared new wills for the Irwins.

In January 1995, both Irwins were in poor health. Mr. Irwin was living in a nursing home and receiving Medicaid benefits through the Kansas Department of Social and Rehabilitation Services (SRS). Mrs. Irwin was living at home but preparing to move to a nursing home. Their son, Robert Irwin, Jr., (Robert Jr.) who had their powers of attorney, contacted respondent and requested preparation of documents for the future sale of his parents' home. ... On January 16, 1995, respondent prepared a deed that showed both of the Irwins as sellers and with no buyer named. ...

Prior to the property being listed for sale with a realtor, Mrs. Irwin died testate on January 18, 1995, leaving all of her personalty to her children. At her death, the home passed to her husband pursuant to joint tenancy survivorship. Subsequent to his mother's death, Robert Jr. contacted Allen County Realty regarding listing and selling his father's house. ...

On February 20, 1995, a potential buyer, James Akers, ... deposited $500 earnest money for purchase of the house. Akers later canceled his option to purchase and forfeited the $500 deposit. Prior to Akers' cancellation, respondent had entered Akers' name as grantee on the deed... . In June 1995, Terry and Cheryl Sparks purchased the house.

In preparation for the June sale to the Sparks, respondent directed his secretary to prepare a new first page of the deed because the original deed listed Akers as the buyer. ... The deed was signed again by Robert Jr. shortly prior to the June 1995 sale. The deed delivered to the Sparks in June 1995 was dated January 16, 1995, and named both Robert Irwin, Sr., and the deceased, Hazel Irwin, as grantors.

On June 15, 1995, respondent wrote to the Iola SRS office claiming that Mr. and Mrs. Irwin had sold their home to Terry and Cheryl Sparks by warranty deed dated January 16, 1995, and that Mrs. Irwin had passed away shortly after the sale. Respondent claimed that because Hazel Irwin had died after the sale of the house, one-half of the sale proceeds were included in her estate (to be divided between her son and daughter). Respondent also claimed the remaining half belonged to the surviving husband and could be credited as an asset against his future Medicaid benefits. The panel determined that the respondent's statements of fact and law were false.

On August 14, 1995, following SRS's request for information regarding the sale, respondent wrote a letter again stating that the house had been sold prior to Mrs. Irwin's January 18, 1995, death and that they "were waiting for title requirements and financing by the purchaser." The panel pointed out that a prospective buyer had not been located until February 1995, and the title report was not available until March 1995. Respondent's letter further stated that "[t]he deed was signed and ready for delivery prior to [Mrs. Irwin's] death," even though the purchasers were not located until 5 months after the death, and the deed which was ultimately delivered to the buyers had been signed in June 1995. Respondent's letter also stated: "Since [Mrs. Irwin's] death [occurred] after the sale, those proceeds go to her two children." The panel found that this letter contained false statements of fact and law.

On September 28, 1995, legal counsel for SRS, Reid Stacey, complainant, wrote respondent requesting an explanation for the factual discrepancies contained in respondent's letters. Even though the house had not been listed prior to Mrs. Irwin's death and there was no buyer, respondent wrote Reid Stacey on October 2, 1995, asserting that "[p]rior to Mrs. Irwin's death a valid oral purchase contract was entered into with both parties concerned." Respondent then stated that title and plumbing work was being completed at the time of Mrs. Irwin's death "to meet buyer requirements." He further stated a $500 down payment, which had actually been paid by James Akers, was paid by the Sparks prior to Mrs. Irwin's death. The panel found that these were also false statements of fact.

A complaint was filed. In preparing his response to the complaint, respondent prepared affidavits for others to sign which were false. ...

In his testimony before the hearing panel, respondent ... defended his handling of the Irwin deeds as "just using what we already had prepared," but admitted such procedure was "laziness or shortcutting." ...

The panel concluded that ... respondent was, for all practical purposes, committing welfare fraud. ...

The hearing panel found that the facts established the following violations of the Model Rules of Professional Conduct by clear and convincing evidence: ... "Rule 4.1—Truthfulness in Statements to Others—The hearing panel found that respondent made false statements of material facts and law to the Iola SRS office, to the SRS attorney in Topeka, and to the office of the Disciplinary Administrator." ...

On July 1, 1997, respondent sent a letter to the Clerk of the Kansas Appellate Courts notifying the Clerk that he had retired from the practice of law effective that date.

When respondent appeared before this court on September 12, 1997, his attorney stated that respondent... had by a plea agreement entered a plea of no contest to attempted welfare fraud, a misdemeanor... .

... A majority of the court is of the opinion that respondent's conduct warrants published censure. A minority views respondent's conduct as being more egregious than conduct where published censure is imposed and would impose a more severe sanction.

IT IS ORDERED THAT Frederick G. Apt, Jr., be and he is hereby disciplined by published censure... .

IT IS FURTHER ORDERED THAT the costs of these proceedings be assessed to respondent and that this order be published in the official Kansas Reports.

INQUIRY

Knowledge of Falsity. Model Rule 4.1(a) prohibits only knowing falsehoods. Model Rule 4.1(a) does not impose a duty of care on a lawyer to ascertain the truth. *See* In re Tocco, 984 P.2d 539 (Ariz. 1999) (actual knowledge, not should have known). On the other hand, discipline officials may determine knowledge based on circumstantial evidence. A lawyer is unlikely to defend successfully a charge of dishonesty where the circumstances make it appear that the lawyer knew of the truth but recklessly disregarded it in re-asserting a falsehood. *See* In re Eliasen, 913 P.2d 1163 (Idaho 1996). Model Rule 4.1(a) also refers only to facts, meaning that lawyers are generally free to give opinions on price, value, settlement prospects, and the like, without implicating Model Rule 4.1(a)'s admonition to truthtelling, as its Comment [2] indicates. Does Model Rule 4.1(a) require an affirmative statement, or is an omission enough? Comment [1] suggests that Model Rule 4.1(a) also prohibits partially true statements that a lawyer combines with a misleading omission producing the effect of an affirmative false statement. The lawyer must know and intend the omission, though. *See* In re Summer 105 P.3d 848 (Or. 2005).

Participating or Authorizing Ruses. Some lawyers believe, erroneously, that they are entitled to participate in "sting operations," to send their agents "undercover," or to use other false pretenses in order to gain access to persons or places to investigate. Unless there is a statute, regulation, or court rule allowing an attorney to participate in a ruse such as a sting operation (exceptions usually limited to prosecutors), misrepresenting yourself or your intentions constitutes a violation of Model Rule 4.1. For a current example, a lawyer or lawyer's agent may not "friend" someone on Facebook or other social media in order to obtain information to use in representing a client. Doing so would violate Model Rule 4.1 because the lawyer's ruse induces the target to grant access to the network site that the target would not have granted if the target knew the lawyer's intentions. *See* PHILADELPHIA BAR ASSN. PROF. GUIDANCE COMM. OPIN. 2009-02 (March 2009). Consider the following illustrative case of a lawyer using a false statement of material fact to gain admission to a reservation to serve a subpoena, by telling tribal representatives that she wanted to give away coupons for free beer.

In the Matter of Leyh,
Disciplinary Commission of the Arizona Supreme Court
Disciplinary Commn. Rpt. 06-0600 (2006)

... The State Bar asserts that Respondent violated ER 4.1(a) by making false statements of material fact to third persons and by misleading them through withholding relevant material facts. Respondent falsely state[d] that Zephyr Lager does exist and that she was a marketing representative for the company that was testing this new beer. Respondent falsely told Ms. Kill that Ms. Kill had to provide Respondent her contact information before Ms. Kill could obtain the (non existent) beer. Responsdent's false statements were material and were substantial and important as to influence the tribe members and affected the outcome. ... [T]he success of her ruse depended on the materiality of her false representations.

... Respondent admits that she did not sufficiently undertake an analysis of what false statement of material fact or law was made, nor did she analyze the materiality of such misstatements. ...

... The eight members of the Disciplinary Commission by a majority of seven recommend accepting and adopting the Hearing Officer's findings of fact, conclusions of law and recommendation for censure, one year of probation... , and costs of these disciplinary proceedings. ...

"What were they thinking?"

Recognize that the lawyer in the above case probably had a good reason, and perhaps even a compelling reason, to serve the subpoena. Sometimes, a lawyer will get into trouble because the lawyer focuses only on the fact that the lawyer is pursuing a good end, forgetting that the lawyer must also consider the quality of the means. In law, ends do not justify means. A lawyer must always go about the practice of the profession in a lawful, honest, and decorous fashion.

INQUIRY

Immaterial Falsehoods. Model Rule 4.1(a) prohibits only material falsehoods. Model Rule 4.1(a) does not impose a duty to tell the truth regarding irrelevant facts. Rule 4.1(a)'s materiality requirement clarifies the rule's purpose, which is to keep a lawyer's falsehoods from influencing others in their actions. Discipline cases equate a false statement's calculation to influence with materiality. *See* In re Merkel, 138 P.3d 847 (Or. 2006). Interestingly, though, cases have not required that the lawyer's false statement actually influence, only that the falsehood is a statement that could influence. *See* In re Winthrop, 848 N.E.2d 961 (Ill. 2006). Notice, though, that Model Rule 4.1(a) prohibits false statements only "to a third person," the implication being that a lawyer's false statement to a client does not violate Rule 4.1. *See* State ex rel. Oklahoma Bar Assn. v. Bolusky, 23 P.2d 268 (Okla. 2001). How does Model Rule 4.1 treat misstatements that lawyers may make in negotiation about a client's "last offer," "highest offer," or "lowest demand"? Comment [2] to Model Rule 4.1 recognizes that generally accepted negotiation conventions may permit strategic misstatements as to a party's intention, taken either as immaterial or as predictions rather than false statements of fact. *But cf.* Fire Ins. Exchange v. Bell, 643 N.E.2d 310 (Ind. 1994) (fraud for lawyer to misrepresent insurance policy limits to induce settlement).

Disclosure to Prevent Assisted Crime or Fraud. Model Rule 4.1(a) prohibits only affirmative false statements, not the omission to speak. Model Rule 4.1(a) imposes no duty on the part of a lawyer to speak when the lawyer determines it better not to speak. On the other hand, if the client uses the lawyer's services to commit a crime or fraud, then Model Rule 4.1(b) does impose a duty to speak, so long as speaking would comply with the duty of confidentiality imposed by Model Rule 1.6. Recall from Chapter 4 that Model Rule 1.6(b)(2) permits a lawyer to reveal confidential information when the lawyer reasonably believes that doing so is necessary to prevent reasonably certain and substantial injury from the client's use of the lawyer's services. What, then, does Model Rule 4.1(b) add? Recall that Model Rule 1.6(b)(2) only *permits* a lawyer to reveal information to prevent substantial injury using the lawyer's services. Model Rule 4.1(b) *requires* a lawyer to reveal information to prevent assisting a client with crime or fraud. Putting the two rules together requires a lawyer to reveal information to prevent a client crime or fraud using the lawyer's services reasonably certain to result in substantial injury.

B. Unrepresented Persons

Disclosing Interests. Students may assume that lawyers deal primarily with other lawyers. In fact, though, lawyers deal with unrepresented persons in a variety of settings. Depending on the practice area, lawyers may deal primarily with unrepresented opposing litigants, for example in collections work, or beneficiaries, creditors, and claimants, for example in estate work. Lawyers often deal with clients' unrepresented family members, employers, business associates, medical treaters, and other witnesses. In each of those instances, the lawyer deals with the unrepresented person to gain that person's information, documents, agreement, authorization, waiver, consent, or other advantage to the lawyer and client. *See* MONTANA ETHICS OPIN. 011115 (2001) (lawyer for defendant client may interview alleged victims only when disclosing role). In many of those instances, what the lawyer seeks to gain from the unrepresented person is to the unrepresented person's real or potential disadvantage. Thus, when a lawyer deals with an unrepresented person, ABA Model Rule 4.3 first requires that the lawyer not mislead the person into thinking that the lawyer is disinterested. *See* In re Air Crash Disaster, 909 F. Supp. 1116 (N.D. Ill. 1995) (trial lawyer misrepresents case investigation as independent survey to defendant pilots); *see also* Disciplinary Counsel v. Rich, 633 N.E.2d 1114 (Ohio 1994) (discipline for arranging for mother to approve dismissal of paternity action against client without disclosing representation). The lawyer must make reasonable efforts to prevent and correct misunderstandings, which will often require the lawyer to tell the unrepresented person why the lawyer is dealing with the person, if not also whom the lawyer is representing. Read the following identical state version of Model Rule 4.3 for that and its other significant prohibition. Then consider an illustrative case.

> **ARKANSAS R. PROF. CONDUCT 4.3: Dealing with Unrepresented Person.**
> In dealing on behalf of a client with a person who is not represented by counsel, a lawyer shall not state or imply that the lawyer is disinterested. When the lawyer knows or reasonably should know that the unrepresented person misunderstands the lawyer's role in the matter, the lawyer shall make reasonable efforts to correct the misunderstanding. The lawyer shall not give legal advice to an unrepresented person, other than the advice to secure counsel, if the lawyer knows or reasonably should know that the interests of such a person are or have a reasonable possibility of being in conflict with the interests of the client.

In re Pautler,
Colorado Supreme Court
47 P.3d 1175 (2002)

Justice KOURLIS delivered the Opinion of the Court.

"I will employ such means as are consistent with Truth and Honor; I will treat all persons whom I encounter through my practice of law with fairness, courtesy, respect, and honesty." Oath of Admission-Colorado State Bar, 2002.[fn]

In this proceeding we reaffirm that members of our profession must adhere to the highest moral and ethical standards. Those standards apply regardless of motive. Purposeful deception by an attorney licensed in our state is intolerable, even when it is undertaken as a part of attempting to secure the surrender of a murder suspect. A prosecutor may not deceive an unrepresented person by impersonating a public defender. ...

I.

... On June 8th, 1998, Chief Deputy District Attorney Mark Pautler arrived at a gruesome crime scene where three women lay murdered. All died from blows to the head with a wood splitting maul. While at the scene ("Chenango apartment"), Pautler learned that three other individuals had contacted the sheriff's department with information about the murders. Pautler drove to the location where those witnesses waited ("Belleview apartment"). Upon arrival, he learned that the killer was William Neal. Neal had apparently abducted the three murder victims one at a time, killing the first two at the Chenango apartment over a three-day period. One of the witnesses at the Belleview apartment, J.D.Y., was the third woman abducted. ...

When Pautler reached the Belleview apartment, Deputy Sheriff Cheryl Moore had already paged Neal according to the instructions Neal had left. Neal answered the page by phoning the apartment.... .

At one point, Neal made it clear he would not surrender without legal representation; Moore passed a message to that effect to Pautler. ...

... Instead of contacting the PD's office, or otherwise contacting defense counsel, Pautler offered to impersonate a PD, and those law enforcement agents at the scene agreed.

When Neal again requested to speak to an attorney, Sheriff Moore told him that "the PD has just walked in," and that the PD's name was "Mark Palmer," a pseudonym Pautler had chosen for himself. Moore proceeded to brief "Palmer" on the events thus far, with Neal listening over the telephone. Moore then introduced Pautler to Neal as a PD. Pautler took the telephone and engaged Neal in conversation. Neal communicated to Pautler that he sought three guarantees from the sheriff's office before he would surrender: 1) that he would be isolated from other detainees, 2) that he could smoke cigarettes, and 3) that "his lawyer" would be present. To the latter request, Pautler answered, "Right, I'll be present."

Neal also asked, "Now, um, at this point, I want to know, um, what my rights are—you feel my rights are right now." Pautler did not answer the question directly, but asked for clarification. Neal then indicated he sought assurance that the sheriff's office would honor the promises made. Pautler communicated to Neal that he believed the sheriff's department would keep him isolated as requested. Pautler did not explain to Neal any additional rights, nor did Neal request more information on the topic. In later conversations, it was clear that Neal believed "Mark Palmer" from the PD's office represented him.

Neal eventually surrendered to law enforcement without incident. ... Pautler was at the scene but did not speak with Neal, although he asked the officer to tell Neal that the attorney was indeed present. Evidence at the hearing indicated that Neal was put into a holding cell by himself and received his requested cigarettes as well as a telephone call.

Pautler made no effort to correct his misrepresentations to Neal that evening, nor in the days following. James Aber, head of the Jefferson County Public Defender's office, eventually undertook Neal's defense. Aber only learned of the deception two weeks later when listening to the tapes of the conversation whereupon he recognized Pautler's voice. Aber testified at Pautler's trial that he was confused when Neal initially said that a Mark Palmer already represented him. Aber told the board that he had difficulty establishing a trusting relationship with the defendant after he told Neal that no Mark Palmer existed within the PD's office. Several months later Neal dismissed the PD's office and continued his case pro se, with advisory counsel appointed by the court. Ultimately, Neal was convicted of the murders and received the death penalty. ...

II.

... The jokes, cynicism, and falling public confidence related to lawyers and the legal system may signal that we are not living up to our obligation; but, they certainly do not signal that the obligation itself has eroded. ... Lawyers themselves are recognizing that the public perception that lawyers twist words to meet their own goals and pay little attention to the truth, strikes at the very heart of the profession—as well as at the heart of the system of justice. Lawyers serve our system of justice, and if lawyers are dishonest, then there is a perception that the system, too, must be dishonest. ...

IV.

The complaint ... charges Pautler with violating Rule 4.3.... . This rule targets precisely the conduct in which Pautler engaged. At all times relevant, Pautler represented the People of the State of Colorado.[fn] The parties stipulated that Neal was an unrepresented person. Pautler deceived Neal and then took no steps to correct the misunderstanding either at the time of arrest or in the days following. Pautler's failure in this respect was an opportunity lost. Where he could have tempered the negative consequences resulting from the deception, he instead allowed them to linger.

While it is unclear whether Pautler actually gave advice to Neal, he certainly did not inform Neal to retain counsel. In addition, Pautler went further than implying he was disinterested; he purported to represent Neal. Without doubt, Pautler's conduct violated the letter of Colo. RPC 4.3. ...

V.

The hearing board suspended Pautler for three months and then stayed that suspension during twelve months of probation. During the probationary period, Pautler was to fulfill various conditions including retaking the MPRE. ...

The board found that Pautler violated duties to the legal system, the profession, and the public. It also ruled that his mental state was "not only knowing, it was intentional." Further, the board found actual injury to the administration of justice in that Pautler's conduct "contributed to a perceived lack of trust between Neal and his lawyers, adversely impacted subsequent judicial proceedings and resulted in additional hearings to explore factual and legal issues created by the deceptive conduct." The board ruled the harm was perhaps unquantifiable, but certainly present. The board also found substantial "potential injury" because, had Neal discovered Pautler's deception, the "negotiating gains made by Sheriff Moore might be lost, Neal could terminate communication and resume or escalate his murderous crime spree." The board also considered the implications of whether Pautler actually became Neal's lawyer. ...

We conclude that the hearing board's discipline was reasonable. ...

In sum, we agree with the hearing board that deceitful conduct done knowingly or intentionally typically warrants suspension, or even disbarment. ... This sanction reaffirms for all attorneys, as well as the public, that purposeful deception by lawyers is unethical and will not go unpunished. At the same time, it acknowledges Pautler's character and motive.

VI.

Therefore, we affirm the hearing board's ruling that Pautler violated Rules 8.4(c) and 4.3 of the Colorado Rules of Professional Conduct. We also affirm the hearing board's probationary period, with a three-month suspension to be imposed only if Pautler violates the terms of that probation. Finally, Pautler is to pay the costs of this proceeding as ordered by the hearing board.

"What Were They Thinking?"

In your view, is Prosecutor Pautler a hero or a goat? Satisfying the demands of a murderer on the loose and apprehending that murderer for the public's safety clearly motivated Mr. Pautler. Do ends, especially compelling ends, justify the means? In this case, the ruse worked. Yet just because it worked this time does not mean that doing it here or elsewhere would be a practice to endorse. One has to ask other questions before reaching that conclusion. Was the ruse truly necessary, or would the murderer have turned himself in anyway? Did this ruse lead other dangerous criminals not to trust law enforcement in subsequent similar cases? It may have led this murderer to discharge his counsel, resulting in the death penalty. When we seek ends by illicit means, we are probably ignoring a host of other considerations in the broader picture. In the end, the court gave Prosecutor Pautler no suspension so long as he complied with other terms, allowing the court to condemn the practice without condemning the well-intentioned practitioner.

INQUIRY

Advising the Unrepresented. In addition to not misleading the unrepresented into thinking that a lawyer is disinterested, ABA Model Rule 4.3's other prohibition is against advising the unrepresented person whose interests may be adverse to the client's interests, other than to secure counsel. A lawyer may give advice to persons who have not formally retained the lawyer. So long as a lawyer has adequate information about the person, the person's adversaries, and the person's matter, there is nothing generally wrong about a lawyer giving a person advice. Those persons may be prospective clients. A lawyer may be able to help an unrepresented person with a few minutes of informal advice, whether or not that person later becomes the lawyer's client. A lawyer may also deal as opposing counsel with an unrepresented person, so long as the person knows that the lawyer is acting as an adversary. *See, e.g.,* Barrett v. Virginia State Bar, 611 S.E.2d 375 (Va. 2005) (no violation for lawyer to give bad advice to his own wife during disputed separation). What Model Rule 4.3 prohibits is the lawyer *giving advice* when the person's interests may conflict with the interests of the lawyer's client, meaning that the person does not appreciate the lawyer's adversarial role and that any such advice would entail the lawyer's conflict of interest. *See, e.g.,* Hopkins v. Troutner, 4 P.3d 557 (Idaho 2000) (defense lawyer should not advise opposing party on case settlement value without disclosing representation). For example, a lawyer would violate Model Rule 4.3 by telling an unrepresented person that the person has no claims or defenses against the lawyer's client, when the person does not know the lawyer represents that client and takes the lawyer's statement as independent advice rather than an opposing counsel's advocacy. *See, e.g.,* Attorney Q v. Miss. State Bar, 587 So.2d 228 (Miss. 1991) (private reprimand for lawyer telling unrepresented opponent not to contact insurance representative when served, without disclosing role as opposing counsel).

C. Represented Persons

Preventing Overreaching. The above section addressed how a lawyer must communicate with a person who has *no* counsel. What candor must a lawyer show when communicating with a person who *does* have counsel? Three interests are at stake when a person has counsel but the counsel is not present when another lawyer communicates with that person. The person has an interest in not giving up rights that counsel would have protected if counsel had been present. The missing counsel has an interest in serving the client, ensuring that the client has the best outcome in the matter the client entrusted to counsel. In addition, the lawyer who communicates with the represented person has an interest in preserving the professional relationship with missing counsel. ABA Model Rule 4.2 preserves all three interests—that of the represented person, the missing counsel, and the lawyer who communicates with the represented person—by requiring the lawyer to obtain the consent of counsel when communicating with the person about the subject of the representation. Put plainly, there is no going around the back of opposing counsel, no overreaching with a represented person when the person's counsel is not there to protect the person. *See* State v. Gilliam, 748 So.2d 622 (La. Ct. App. 1999) (protects clients from unintended harmful admissions). Consider the following identical state version of Model Rule 4.2.

> TENN. R. PROF. CONDUCT 4.2: **Communication with a Person Represented by Counsel.**
> In representing a client, a lawyer shall not communicate about the subject of the representation with a person the lawyer knows to be represented by another lawyer in the matter, unless the lawyer has the consent of the other lawyer or is authorized to do so by law or a court order.

INQUIRY

Communication Authorized by Law. Model Rule 4.2 ends with an exception that a lawyer may communicate with a represented person when authorized by law or court order to do so. Service of process is an example. If a court rule or statute requires that a lawyer send certain pleadings or court papers to a represented person, then the lawyer does not violate Model Rule 4.2 by doing so. *See, e.g.,* Wilkerson v. Brown, 995 P.2d 393 (Kan. Ct. App. 1999) (approving service of offer of judgment on represented party). Similarly, if the represented person holds a government office to which a lawyer has a right of petition, then the person's representation does not prohibit that communication. See American Canoe Assn., Inc. v. City of St. Albans, 18 F. Supp.2d 620 (S.D. W.Va. 1998). Indeed, state lawyer-officials such as prosecutors may have their own lawful responsibility to communicate with represented persons, satisfying Model Rule 4.2's exception. *See* United States v. Joseph Binder Schweizer Empl. Co., 167 F. Supp.2d 862 (E.D. N.C. 2001) (approving ex-parte preindictment interviews). Following disagreement over whether federal prosecutors had the same liberty, Congress resolved that they are now explicitly subject to state ethics rules including state versions of Model Rule 4.2. *See* U.S.C. §530B (1998); United States v. Brown, 356 F. Supp.2d 470 (M.D. Pa. 2005). Yet counsel should take care not to extend the authorization beyond its strict terms. Court rule or statute may authorize a lawyer to serve a subpoena on a represented person to attend a deposition, but it would not authorize the lawyer to take the deposition outside of the represented person's counsel. *See* Parker v. Pepsi-Cola Gen. Bottlers, Inc., 249 F. Supp.2d 1006 (N.D. Ill. 2003).

Communication Between Clients. A principal salutary effect of Model Rule 4.2 is to facilitate that lawyers communicate with one another mediating and negotiating their respective clients' matters.

Model Rule 4.2 effectively routes two-way communications between the parties' lawyers rather than three-way or four-way communications that could muddy and confuse communications. Clients benefit from that orderly and mediated communication. On the other hand, Model Rule 4.2 does not prohibit one lawyer's client from communicating with another lawyer's client. In certain cases, for example in non-contentious business transactions, represented parties should on occasion communicate directly with one another. May a lawyer use a client to skirt Model Rule 4.2, arming the client with advice to share with an opposing party outside of the presence of that party's counsel? Decisions discourage that kind of manipulation. *See, e.g.,* Holdren v. General Motors Corp., 13 F. Supp.2d 1192 (D. Kan. 1998) (protective order preventing client from obtaining affidavits from opposing party's employees on lawyer's instructions); Trumbull County Bar Assn. v. Makridis, 671 N.E.2d 31 (Ohio 1996) (reprimanding lawyer who instructed client to call opposing party and then hand telephone to lawyer). For a related example, Model Rule 4.2 would prohibit a lawyer from preparing a document for execution by a represented party on the urging of the lawyer's client. *See* In re Pyle, 91 P.3d 1222 (Kan. 2004) (public reprimand and ethics school for plaintiff's lawyer who used client to get defendant boyfriend's signature on adverse affidavit prepared by plaintiff's lawyer).

Biography

President Clinton commissioned Victoria A. Roberts to serve as a United States District Judge for the Eastern District of Michigan, with the unanimous advice and consent of the United States Senate. Judge Roberts was in private practice before her appointment, also serving as a court appointed special master and arbitrator in pending litigation matters. While on the federal bench, Judge Roberts became the 62nd president of the State Bar of Michigan and the first African-American female to hold that position. Her term expired in September 1997, the same year that Michigan Lawyers Weekly named her Lawyer of the Year. An elegant and dignified woman, Judge Roberts is a role model for many women lawyers as to how to balance femininity and grace with determined and successful advocacy. Judge Roberts holds lawyers to the same high standards of professionalism and competence for which she is renowned.

Inducing Others. Just as it is improper for a lawyer to use a client to skirt Model Rule 4.2's prohibition on communicating with represented persons outside of the presence of counsel, so, too, is it improper for a lawyer to use others for the same purpose. Model Rule 8.4 states that it is professional misconduct for a lawyer to violate or attempt to violate the Rules of Professional Conduct through the acts of another person. A lawyer does not violate Model Rule 4.2 by accepting fortuitous assistance from others in obtaining information from a represented person. *See* Hayes v. Commonwealth, 25 S.W. 3d 463 (Ky. 2000) (prosecutor does not violate rule when detective obtains represented person's statement independent of any request by prosecutor); State v. P.Z., 703 A.2d 901 (N.J. 1997) (same as to social worker obtaining defendant's statement). Yet a lawyer does violate Model Rule 4.2 if the lawyer requests a third person to communicate with a represented person for the lawyer's benefit in the subject matter of the representation. *See* Allen v. International Truck & Engine, 2006 WL 2578896 (S.D. Ind. Sept. 6, 2006) (lawyers use investigators to contact adverse parties).

Subject Matter of Representation. Model Rule 4.2 does not prohibit greeting a person who arrives at court or in the office before the person's counsel arrives. A lawyer may speak politely with a represented person about the weather, the holidays, or other non-consequential small talk, when the person's counsel is not present and without counsel's consent. Indeed, if the represented person occupies a role that requires the lawyer to communicate with the person on other subjects, such in a court or other government agency, then the lawyer may communicate with the person on other consequential subjects outside of the representation. *See* Model Rule 4.2, Comment [4]. Yet a lawyer must not broach the subject of the representation without counsel's presence or consent. May the person consent? Significantly, the person does not hold the privilege. Only the person's counsel may consent. The person is not the only one who has an interest. The person's counsel also has an interest in the communication when it touches on the subject of the representation. Comment [3] to Model Rule 4.2 makes clear, "The Rule applies even though the represented person initiates or consents to the communication." Would you consent to your client speaking with opposing counsel outside of your presence? Lawyers do rarely consent, although when they do, they may limit the consent to specific issues, particularly those that do not implicate the client's substantial rights. Consider a case illustrating that Model Rule 4.2 requires consent only to communicate about the subject of the representation.

State ex rel. Okla. Bar Assn. v. Harper,
Oklahoma Supreme Court
995 P.2d 1143 (2000)

HODGES, J.

... II. FACTS

¶2 At the time of the alleged misconduct, Respondent represented Government Employees Insurance Company (GEICO). The representation arose out of an automobile accident involving Bobbie Tenequer (Tenequer), GEICO's insured. The allegations are that Respondent violated rule 4.2 of the ORPC by communicating with Tenequer concerning the accident without first getting the consent of Tenequer's attorney even though he knew that she was represented in the matter.

¶3 ... On December 23, 1997, Tenequer, John McIntosh (Tenequer's boyfriend), and their baby were traveling on a rural road near Ponca City. The vehicle in which they were traveling was owned by Tenequer's father and insured through him by GEICO. The pickup struck some cattle which were in the roadway. It is unclear whether, at the time of the accident, Tenequer or her boyfriend was driving the pickup, but the police report shows that Tenequer was driving.

... ¶5 On January 13, 1998, attorney Kenny Jean (Jean) wrote two letters to GEICO. In the first letter, he identifies John McIntosh and Tenequer as his clients. Jean advised GEICO that he has been retained to represent McIntosh and Tenequer in their claims for benefits under the medical payment provision of the policy and possibly claims under the uninsured motorist provision of the policy. In the second letter, Jean identifies only McIntosh as his client on a personal injury claim for negligence against Tenequer. ...

¶6 On March 4, 1998, Jean sent GEICO a demand letter on behalf of the baby, Marxus. Jean claimed $411.30 on behalf of Marxus for medical bills and $3,000.00 for pain and suffering and offered to settle for $2,500.00. In the letter, Jean made it clear that he was representing interests adverse to Tenequer's... . In a letter written on behalf of McIntosh to GEICO on March 18, 1998, Jean made this same statement regarding Tenequer's negligence.

¶7 In March of 1998, GEICO paid Tenequer's claim under the medical payments provision of the policy. Jean averred that the settlement of Tenequer's claim for medical payments left Tenequer with a possible uninsured motorist claim against GEICO and a liability claim against the owner of the cattle. Complainant asserts that Jean still represented Tenequer on these claims. ...

¶9 GEICO's claim log notes show that on August 12, 1998, Tenequer called GEICO to obtain the status of her son's claim. At the time, she informed GEICO that she was dismissing Jean as of that day. She was told to have Jean notify GEICO immediately.

¶10 Then on August 19, 1998, believing that Tenequer was no longer represented by an attorney, Wimberly conducted a telephone interview with Tenequer. Tenequer's comments during the interview prompted Wimberly to ask Tenequer if Jean still represented her. Tenequer replied that Jean told her that she did not have a case against the cattle owner, that it was up to her to discover how the cattle got out of the fence, and that Jean had basically done nothing.

¶11 At the end of the interview, Tenequer informed Wimberly that, contrary to her previous statements, McIntosh was actually driving the vehicle at the time of the accident. An entry in GEICO's files on August 21, 1998, indicates Wimberly thought Tenequer was not represented by an attorney. Because of Tenequer's change in testimony in which she stated that McIntosh was driving, GEICO contacted Respondent and asked him to take Tenequer's statement under oath. ...

¶13 At the beginning of the statement, Respondent asked Tenequer if she would like to have a lawyer present. Tenequer replied that she saw no need to have a lawyer present. She did not mention that she was represented by Jean. ...

III. PROCEDURAL HISTORY

¶14 Jean filed a grievance... alleging that Respondent had violated rule 4.2 of the ORPC by communicating with Tenequer even though he knew that she was represented by an attorney. ... Jean testified that, when Respondent took Tenequer's statement, Jean still represented Tenequer on an uninsured motorist claim. Jean posited that he was investigating the possibility that the cattle were on the road because of a connection with a vehicle, giving Tenequer a possible claim under the uninsured motorist provisions of the policy. ...

¶15 ... [T]he subject of Respondent's communication with Tenequer was GEICO's responsibility for liability claims made against Tenequer by McIntosh. ... Respondent's uncontradicted testimony was that, at the time he took her statement, he did not know that Jean represented Tenequer. ... The testimony was that it would be highly unusual for the same attorney to represent both the insured driver of a vehicle and the passenger making a claim against the driver. Complainant presented no evidence that Respondent had actual knowledge that Jean represented Tenequer at the time of the hearing.

IV. ANALYSIS

... ¶17 ... The comments [to Rule 4.2] state: "The prohibition of communication with a represented person only applies, however, in circumstances where the lawyer knows that the person is in fact represented in the matter to be discussed. *This means that a lawyer had actual knowledge of the fact of the representation*; but such actual knowledge may be inferred from the circumstances. ... Thus, a lawyer cannot evade the requirement of obtaining the consent of counsel by closing eyes to the obvious." (Emphasis added.) Rule 4.2 has three requirements: (1) a communication, (2) with a person known to be represented by an attorney, (3) on the matter of the representation. ...

¶19 We reject Complainant's request to rewrite rule 4.2 to abrogate the requirement that a lawyer's knowledge of representation must be actual. The explicit language of the rule requires actual knowledge of the representation on the matter of the subject of the communication. [C] Further, the comments leave no question that, without actual knowledge of the representation, there is no violation of rule 4.2. [C] ...

¶20 There is no question that Respondent communicated with Tenequer. The inquiry then is (1) whether Respondent's communication with Tenequer was about the subject of the matter on which Jean represented Tenequer, and (2) whether Respondent had actual knowledge that Jean represented Tenequer on the matter. ... Jean alleged that he represented Tenequer on a claim against the cattle owner and on an uninsured motorist claim. Tenequer's uninsured motorist claim was not the subject of the communication. Thus, Respondent did not communicate about a subject in a matter for which Jean represented her. [C]

¶21 Complainant argues that the subject of the matter on which Jean represented Tenequer was the accident. It would be foreign to most lawyers representing an insurance company that Jean could have represented Tenequer generally regarding the accident as well as the passenger filing a claim against her. ... Thus, the communication at the time of Tenequer's statement could not have been the subject on the matter of Jean's representation of Tenequer.

¶22 Even if the communications in the statement were about a subject in a matter in which Jean represented Tenequer, Respondent had no knowledge of the representation. ...

¶24 Complainant relies on an ethics opinion issued by the American Bar Association which states: "When the represented party declares that counsel has been discharged, (the) sensible course would be confirm whether (the) lawyer had been effectively discharged." ABA Formal Opinion 95-396. We agree that this is the sensible course. In fact, GEICO probably should have confirmed that Tenequer had discharged Jean. This information is not imputed to Respondent for purposes of a rule 4.2 violation. ...

V. CONCLUSION

¶25 Complainant has failed to show by clear and convincing evidence that Respondent violated rule 4.2 of the Rules of Professional Conduct. ...

RESPONDENT EXONERATED.....

INQUIRY

Second Opinions. The above *Oklahoma Bar Assn. v. Harper* case intimates that when a person states that they have discharged their counsel, a lawyer wishing to communicate with that person about the subject of the representation should first confirm the putative discharge with counsel. *See* In re Capper, 757 N.E.2d 138 (Ind. 2001) (contact opposing counsel if person alleges discharge); *see also* Iowa Supreme Ct. Atty. Disc. Bd. v. Box, 715 N.W.2d 758 (Iowa 2006) (renouncing representation not sufficient); ABA FORMAL ETHICS OP. 95-396 (1995) (same—contact opposing counsel). What should you do in the event that a represented person meets with you for a second opinion, perhaps considering whether to retain you as co-counsel or replacement counsel? A strict reading of Model Rule 4.2 would seem to prohibit you from communicating with a person seeking a second opinion, without counsel's consent. Is that Model Rule 4.2's purpose? Counsel might be unwilling to grant consent particularly if counsel fears losing the client or having a lawyer contradict counsel's advice. Yet clients should get to choose their counsel and have second opinions if they wish, without their counsel choosing who gets to give the second opinions. Comment [4] to Model Rule 4.2, added in 2002, indicates that Model Rule 4.2 does *not* prohibit a lawyer from communicating with a represented person when giving a second opinion: "Nor does this Rule preclude communication with a represented person who is seeking advice from a lawyer who is not otherwise representing a client in the matter." *See, e.g.,* State ex rel. Okla. Bar Assn. v. Butner, 976 P.2d 542 (Okla. 1998). Even if Model Rule 4.2 does not require consent, should you contact the other counsel anyway? If you did, then you might preserve professional relationships while also learning important information about the client and matter. Telling a prospective client who seeks your second opinion that you would prefer first to speak with the client's current counsel shows the client an admirable level of professionalism.

Managerial Employees of Represented Corporations. Recall the discussion from Chapter 4's section on ABA Model Rule 1.13 "Organization as Client" that a lawyer with a corporate client represents the corporation, not its employees. What, then, does Model Rule 4.2 require of a lawyer who encounters employees of a corporation represented by an opposing lawyer? Under Model Rule 4.2, a lawyer must not speak to those employees of a represented corporation if the employees manage for the corporation, act in ways that bind the corporation, or carry out the lawyer's advice for the corporation. *See* Palmer v. Pioneer Inn Assocs., Ltd., 257 F.3d 999 (9th Cir. 2001) (no ex-parte interviews of those who manage or speak for represented corporation); Featherstone v. Schaerrer, 34 P.3d 194 (Utah 2001) (no ex-parte interview of corporate secretary of represented corporation). Those managerial employees are, in effect, the represented corporation. For a lawyer to communicate with those managerial employees without corporate counsel's consent would violate Model Rule 4.2's prohibition. Comment [7] to Model Rule 4.2 authorizes contact with former employees, *see, e.g.,* Smith v. Kalamazoo Ophthalmology, 322 F. Supp.2d 883 (W.D. Mich. 2004), but Comment [7] is a relatively recent 2002 addition as to which there is some contrary prior authority, *see* United States v. W.R. Grace, 401 F. Supp.2d 1065 (D. Mont. 2005).

Other Employees of Represented Corporations. What, though, about non-managerial employees of a represented corporation—may counsel communicate with those lower-level employees? Model Rule 4.2 does not prohibit a lawyer from speaking to non-managerial employees of a represented corporation, meaning those who manage or speak for the organization, or carry out the lawyer's advice for the corporation. *See* NAACP v. Fla. Dept. of Corr., 122 F. Supp. 2d 1335 (M.D. Fla. 2000) (ex-parte interviews of line employees permissible). Query what a lawyer gains by speaking to low-level corporate employees who do not have managerial authority, cannot bind the corporation, and are not acting on corporate counsel's advice. *See* Cole v. Appalachian Power Co., 903 F. Supp. 975 (S.D. W.Va. 1995) (approving interviews of employees to obtain basic data). There may be little reason for a lawyer to pursue those communications. Here, too, is where Model Rule 4.3's admonition to not mislead the unrepresented into thinking that an interviewing lawyer is disinterested takes on special meaning. While a lawyer may communicate with those non-managerial employees, the lawyer must not mislead them into thinking that the lawyer is disinterested. *See, e.g.,* McCallum v. CSX Transp., Inc., 149 F.R.D. 104 (M.D. N.C. 1993) (full disclosure required before interviewing non-management employee). In pending litigation, courts have even prescribed specific scripts for lawyers to follow when communicating with those employees. *See* In re Envtl. Ins. Dec. Judgment Actions, 600 A.2d 165 (N.J. Super. Ct. Law Div. 1991); Monsanto Co. v. Aetna Cas. & Sur. Co., 593 A.2d 1013 (Del. Super. Ct. 1990). Those employees will properly be on their guard, even in the unlikely case that they have helpful information. These limitations are likely as they should be, given the need for fairness to organizations, their managers, and their non-management employees, as to all others.

D. Statements in Tribunals

Candor Toward Tribunals. The above sections treat three specific interactions—with unrepresented persons, represented persons, and clients of diminished capacity—that require candor, recognizing a lawyer's undue advantage in dealing with others. A broader area requiring candor and sensitivity involves legal service within a tribunal. ABA Model Rule 3.3 requires candor toward the tribunal, invoking candor's broad meaning of truthtelling, disclosing facts and authority, presenting no false evidence, and preventing and remediating frauds on the tribunal. To be just, and to meet the other needs and expectations of a civil society, adjudication requires a special forum. While the adjudicative officer bears a large responsibility for the quality of the adjudicative forum, lawyers make an equal or greater contribution. Lawyers do far more communicating in court than judges do. The quality of adjudication depends largely on the lawyers' candor and sensitivity to the forum's requirements. As you read an identical state version of Model Rule 3.3, see if you can anticipate the special situations and issues that it addresses.

ARKANSAS R. PROF. CONDUCT 3.3: **Candor Toward the Tribunal.**
(a) A lawyer shall not knowingly:
(1) make a false statement of fact or law to a tribunal; or fail to correct a false statement of material fact or law previously made to the tribunal by the lawyer;
(2) fail to disclose to the tribunal legal authority in the controlling jurisdiction known to the lawyer to be directly adverse to the position of the client and not disclosed by opposing counsel; or
(3) offer evidence that the lawyer knows to be false. If a lawyer, the lawyer's client, or a witness called by the lawyer, has offered material evidence and the lawyer comes to know of its falsity, the lawyer shall take reasonable remedial measures including, if necessary, disclosure to the tribunal. A lawyer may refuse to offer evidence, other than the testimony of a defendant in a criminal matter, that the lawyer reasonably believes is false.
(b) A lawyer who represents a client in an adjudicative proceeding and who knows that a person intends to engage, is engaging or had engaged in criminal or fraudulent conduct related to the proceeding shall take reasonable remedial measures, including if necessary, disclosure to the tribunal.
(c) The duties stated in paragraphs (a) and (b) continue to the conclusion of the proceeding, and apply even if compliance requires disclosure of information otherwise protected by Rule 1.6.

(d) In an ex parte proceeding, a lawyer shall inform the tribunal of all material facts known to the lawyer which will enable the tribunal to make an informed decision, whether or not the facts are adverse.

INQUIRY

False Statements.   Model Rule 3.3 begins simply with the admonition not to make a false statement of fact to the tribunal. Lawyers make fact statements to tribunals in two ways. Lawyers first file pleadings and other papers and make other communications to tribunals, that contain factual assertions. *See, e.g,* In re Cleaver-Bascombe, 892 A.2d 396 (D.C. 2006) (Rule 3.3 violation to submit false fee voucher to court). They then make appearances before tribunals. Model Rule 3.3(a)(1)'s opening prohibition applies to both written and oral fact statements. Lawyers may properly rely on others—clients and witnesses—for facts. When those others are wrong about the facts, their error does not implicate the lawyer who reasonably relies on their information. Yet when the lawyer is asserting personal knowledge of facts, then the lawyer must ensure that those assertions are truthful. Lawyers do on occasion prepare and sign their own affidavits and otherwise represent personal knowledge of certain matters, often facts relating to procedures like service. A sound lawyer will pause before doing so, ensuring that every fact statement is accurate. Consider the following example of another common instance when lawyers make fact assertions to courts regarding the results of tests and contents of reports.

In re Discipline of Wilka,
South Dakota Supreme Court
638 N.W.2d 245 (2001)

GILBERTSON, Chief Justice.

[¶1.] Attorney Timothy J. Wilka (Wilka) was reported to the Disciplinary Board of the State Bar of South Dakota by Second Circuit Judge Glen Severson for violations of the Model Rules of Professional Conduct, stemming from Wilka's use of an incomplete drug report during a visitation hearing and his misleading responses to Judge Severson's questions regarding the report. The Board recommended discipline in the form of a public censure. We agree.

FACTS AND PROCEDURE

[¶2.] Wilka ... was admitted to practice in South Dakota in 1983. He is currently engaged in private practice with one associate in Sioux Falls, South Dakota.

[¶3.] In July 2000, Wilka was representing Travis Van Overbeke (Client) in a divorce action against Carla Van Overbeke (Mother). Mother was seeking to restrict Client's visitation rights with his three-year-old daughter to supervised visitation on the basis that Client was using methamphetamines. ... A hearing was scheduled before Judge Severson for July 31, 2000.

[¶4.] In preparation for the hearing, Wilka counseled Client to undergo a urinalysis test for methamphetamines at Avera McKennan Hospital in Sioux Falls. Client was tested on July 18, 2000. However, the test conducted by McKennan screened for a battery of drugs. While Client tested negative for methamphetamines, he did test positive for cannabinoids, which signaled recent use of marijuana.

[¶5.] The lab technician who performed the analysis telephoned the results to Wilka, who later received a printed report of the substance abuse screen. The screen showed the positive result for cannabinoids and a "not detected" result for seven other substances, including methamphetamines. Wilka then contacted the technician and informed her that, because there were no allegations of marijuana use in his case, he needed a report only indicating the methamphetamine results. He requested a new test be completed, one that screens only for methamphetamine use. The technician informed Wilka that they were unable to separate the screen but that she could provide him with a second report, one without the cannabinoids result. The technician accomplished this by simply tearing or cutting off the bottom portion of the drug screen results, omitting the positive result for cannabinoids.

[¶6.] Following the receipt of the partial report, Wilka made a copy of the report and sent it to opposing counsel, Doug Thesenvitz (Thesenvitz), to refute the charge of methamphetamine use by Client. Thesenvitz had indicated that he would withdraw his motion for supervised visitation if Client tested negative for methamphetamine use. As a former prosecutor, however, Thesenvitz was apparently familiar with the drug screen report and noticed that the cannabinoids result was conspicuously missing. Therefore, he decided to proceed with the hearing.

[¶7.] During the July 31 hearing, Wilka had the partial report marked as Exhibit A and presented it to Client's wife initially for impeachment purposes on cross-examination. Wilka then asked that the partial report be admitted into evidence and it was received by the court. Immediately upon admission, the court asked "Is this cut off or is this the entire—" Wilka responded, "That's what I was provided by the hospital, Your Honor." Again, the court inquired "Is this the entire thing?" Wilka replied "That's what I have Judge. That's what I asked them to screen for."

[¶8.] Before closing statements, the court again addressed the partial report by stating "Mr. Wilka, this wasn't offered for the truth of what the results are. It was—" Wilka responded with "—to show that on July 18th there was no methamphetamine or any of the other drugs detected in his system." The court informed Wilka that the irregularities of the partial report, its torn uneven appearance, made the report "suspect" and it was not competent evidence. Wilka responded "I understand. This is exactly what was provided to me by the people at McKennan Hospital, and if you don't want to receive it, Your Honor, then I understand." Finally, the court ordered Client to undergo an additional drug screen, which came back negative for all drugs, and directed Wilka to provide a certified result of Exhibit A. Wilka did disclose the entire report to the court and opposing counsel while the case was still pending, with no apparent harm being done to either party.

[¶9.] Judge Severson reported Wilka's conduct to the Minnehaha County State's Attorney, the Disciplinary Board and to this Court. Criminal charges pursuant to SDCL 22-11-21, 22-11-22 and 22-29-6 were initiated by the State's attorney but were ultimately pled down to a civil contempt charge.[FN1The State's attorney also elected to notify the press of the contempt proceedings.] On November 7, 2000, Wilka appeared before Judge Severson and entered the following statement: "Your Honor, I sincerely apologize to the Court for failing to fully disclose to the Court that the report I offered as evidence on July 31, 2000, is incomplete. My answers to the Court's questions were misleading and I am sorry." Wilka was found in contempt and fined $100.

[¶10.] After the disciplinary hearing was conducted on June 15, 2001, the Board concluded that Wilka had violated the following Rules of Professional conduct: 3.3(a)(1), (2) and (4)[fn] and 3.3(b) concerning candor toward the tribunal; 3.4(a) concerning fairness; 4.1(a) concerning truthfulness; and 8.4(a), (c) and (d) concerning professional misconduct. The Board also found that Wilka "showed little genuine remorse for his conduct" and recommended public censure. ...

ANALYSIS AND DECISION

[¶13.] ... Wilka's conduct in this case, as well as his prior record,[FN5] lead us to conclude that public censure is appropriate. [FN5. Wilka ... has received discipline in the form of two cautions, two admonitions and two private reprimands.] ...

[¶15.] Clearly, the requirement of candor towards the tribunal goes beyond simply telling a portion of the truth. It requires every attorney to be fully honest and forthright. ... There is no allowance for interpretation.

[¶ 16.] Wilka's intent to mislead the court is not mitigated by his concerns over Client's right to confidentiality. The dilemma in which Wilka found himself was one of his own making. Options other than evading the questions of the court remained open to him. ... We respect Wilka's desire to represent Client without betraying confidentiality. Nevertheless, there is a line that even the zealous advocate cannot cross. Herein, the referee found Wilka's conduct to be "deceitful and he misled Judge Severson and this was intentional in nature." Such conduct clearly crosses the line into improper and unprofessional conduct.

[¶17.] Wilka argues that what he has had to endure because of this incident already amounts, in reality, to a public censure. He points to having been the subject of criminal investigations, the recipient of a $100 fine for civil contempt and to the corresponding press coverage that apparently was substantial. We have consistently refused to recognize such claims for leniency to avoid professional discipline. [Cc] The purpose of a criminal prosecution is to punish a crime against the State. The purpose of civil contempt is to punish the wrongdoer. The purpose of attorney disciplinary proceedings is not to punish the attorney anew, but rather to take sufficient measures for the protection of the public and its legal system from a repetition of these types of incidents. [C]

[¶18.] The Referee also found that Wilka was "remorseful and contrite." When he appeared before this Court, he personally expressed this remorse. At this point in these proceedings, we have no reason to doubt the sincerity of his statement.

[¶19.] Therefore, based on a totality of the circumstances, Timothy J. Wilka is hereby publicly censured. [C] In accordance with this censure, we require Wilka to submit an affidavit addressed to this Court within 30 days from the date of this opinion in which he states under oath that: a) he has reviewed the Rules of Professional Conduct; b) he recognizes fully that his conduct (in evading the questions of and misleading the court with respect to the admission as evidence of the partial drug report) violated the Rules of Professional Conduct by which he is bound; and c) he pledges he will devote every effort in his future practice to fully abide by the South Dakota Rules of Professional Conduct. In addition, we require that Wilka pay the Clerk of this Court for the expenses of these proceedings within 30 days of the date that he is notified of the amount thereof.

"What Were They Thinking?"

A detection ethic is a poor conduct guide. The lawyer in the above case at least three times made judgments that others would not detect his actions: first when he had the lab technician tear off the bottom of the report; second when he submitted the torn-off report as Exhibit A in the hearing; and third when he answered the judge's questions with indirection rather than a truthful disclosure of what the lawyer must have known the judge was asking. The question is not the lawyer's poor judgment for failing to recognize that both the opposing counsel (a former prosecutor) and trial judge would recognize that the report was incomplete. The issue is instead the lawyer's acting on a mindset that his conduct would be acceptable so long as others did not discover his corruption. Do you think his six prior disciplines might illustrate the unreliability of a detection ethic? What would the lawyer have done in each instance if instead of a detection ethic, the lawyer had followed an ethic of transparency, candor, and integrity? Keep in mind that the lawyer owed the client a duty of confidentiality as to the positive results for the other drug, which was not initially in dispute in the proceeding. The above opinion states that the lawyer had other options. Can you articulate them?

INQUIRY

Misleading Silence. As the above *In re Wilka* case illustrates, Model Rule 3.3's prohibition against false statements also reaches misleading statements and omissions. Lawyers have been reprimanded or disciplined for sitting silent at counsel table while a law partner misrepresents facts, *see* Daniels v. Alander, 844 A.2d 182 (Conn. 2004); standing silently by while a client conceals a criminal record, *see* In re Cardwell, 50 P.3d 897 (Colo. 2002); failing to disclose other pending charges when disclosure was necessary for judge to make a sound decision, *see* In re Seelig, 850 A.2d 477 (N.J. 2004); conducting sham proceedings after a secret settlement, *see* In re Alcorn, 41 P.3d 600 (Ariz. 2002); offering a stipulated order with which the parties had secretly agreed not to comply, *see* In re Ortner, 699 N.W.2d 865 (S.D. 2005); and requesting sanctions for failure to produce when the lawyer had already obtained the requested discovery by other means, *see* In re Eicher, 661 N.W.2d 354 (S.D. 2003). Take no comfort that your mouth remains pure while misconduct darkens your heart and soul. The conduct rules address the whole lawyer.

Temptation Abounds. Lawyers violate Model Rule 3.3's prohibition against false statements to tribunals in many ways, but the violations do fall into general patterns. Some of the more common ways in which lawyers violate Model Rule 3.3's false-statement prohibition include: misrepresentations to frustrate discovery, *see, e.g.,* In re Hermina, 907 A.2d 790 (D.C. 2006) (false claim that an order in another case prevented discovery response); misrepresenting licensure, *see* In re Cohen, 612 S.E.2d 294 (Ga. 2005) (lawyer files pleadings while on inactive status); misrepresenting the lawyer's role, *see, e.g.,* In re Roose, 69 P.3d 43 (Colo. 2003) (lawyer misidentifies herself as client's current appointed counsel); and notarizing signatures on documents, *see, e.g.,* In re Porter, 930 So.2d 875 (La. 2006) (lawyer notarizes client husband signing client wife's signature). Watch out for these areas. Temptation abounds. Do you see anything in common about these areas? Is it the detection ethic mentioned in the box above, that lawyers think that these are the areas where they can most likely get away with a little dishonesty? At other times, lawyers appear to make false statements for strategic purposes to gain an advantage in a proceeding. *See, e.g.,* Office of Disc. Counsel v. Wrona, 908 A.2d 1281 (Pa. 2006) (false accusations that judge altered audiotapes regarding support hearing); Attorney Grievance Commn. v. DeMaio, 842 A.2d 802 (Md. 2004) (false accusations of judicial conspiracy to frustrate appeal).

Defining Tribunals. Appreciate the breadth of proceedings to which Model Rule 3.3 applies. Model Rule 3.3 applies to more than just court proceedings. ABA Model Rule 1.0(m) defines a tribunal as a body that acts in an adjudicative capacity. The definition includes not only courts but also arbitration and administrative hearings including compliance and license proceedings. *See* Andrews v. Kentucky Bar Assn., 169 S.W.3d 862 (Ky. 2005) (Rule 3.3 applies to letters to discipline official); In re Diggs, 544 S.E.2d 628 (S.C. 2001) (Rule 3.3 applies to submission to commission on legal education certifying continuing-legal-education compliance); *but see* Florida Bar v. Rotstein, 835 So.2d 241 (Fla. 2002) (Rule 3.3 does not apply to statement to grievance committee); *see also* ABA Model Rule 8.1 (requiring honesty in lawyer admission and discipline proceedings). Model Rule 3.3 also applies to court-annexed proceedings like depositions conducted in a law office ancillary to a court-filed case, *see* Model Rule 3.3 Comment [1], and to rule-making and policy-making bodies, *see* Model Rule 3.9 Comment [1]. Perhaps we should not be too concerned about Model Rule 3.3's boundaries, though, given a lawyer's other even broader duties of candor and honesty. A good practice may be to follow the spirit of Model Rule 3.3 in every forum (excepting the disclosure of confidential information), whether or not an adjudicative tribunal.

Beyond Representation. Some conduct rules apply only to situations in which a lawyer is representing a client. Notice Model Rule 3.3's ambiguity in that respect. *Contrast* In re Whitney, 120 P.3d

550 (Wash. 2005) (Rule 3.3 applies to lawyer testimony), *with* State ex rel. Okla. Bar Assn. v. Dobbs, 94 P.3d 31 (Okla. 2004) (Rule 3.3 does not apply to lawyer testimony). While Model Rule 3.3(a)(1) has no explicit condition that the lawyer be representing a client in order for the rule to apply, Subrules (a)(2) and (a)(3) at least imply if not directly require that the lawyer must be acting as an advocate on behalf of a client for the rule to apply. In other words, a lawyer who is not representing a client may not have the same duties of candor toward tribunals. Interestingly, though, discipline proceedings routinely apply Rule 3.3 to lawyers who are parties, perhaps confirming the adage that the lawyer who represents him- or herself has a fool for a client. *See* In re O'Meara, 834 A.2d 235 (N.H. 2003) (discipline for false statements in lawyer's own divorce case); In re Scott, 657 N.W.2d 567 (Minn. 2003) (same); In re Harris, 847 So.2d 1185 (La. 2003) (discipline for false statements in lawyer's own discipline proceeding); People v. Albright, 91 P.3d 1063 (Colo. O.P.D.J. 2003) (discipline for false statements in lawyer's own bankruptcy filing). Consider one such case.

In re Barker,
South Carolina Supreme Court
572 S.E.2d 460 (2002)

PER CURIAM:

In this attorney disciplinary matter, the Subpanel and the full Panel recommended respondent Douglas A. Barker be definitely suspended for nine months. We impose a six-month definite suspension.

FACTS

On October 12, 1998, respondent, acting *pro se,* initiated a divorce action against his wife, Diana Spreeuw Barker (Wife). Respondent alleged that "since September 26, 1997, the parties hereto have lived separate and apart due to irreconcilable differences and seek a decree of divorce on the ground of separation for a period of one year." The complaint also sought joint custody for the couple's two daughters. Respondent prepared Wife's *pro se* Answer admitting to the allegations in the Complaint and asking the family court to adopt their settlement agreement.

On October 26, 1998, both respondent and Wife appeared *pro se* before the family court. At the hearing, respondent testified that he and his wife had "been living separate and apart since September 26, 1997." In addition, respondent called a corroborating witness who testified that respondent and Wife had been living separate and apart since September 1997. The family court granted respondent a divorce based on one year's continuous separation and approved the settlement agreement which included a joint custody arrangement for the couple's two children.

Respondent and Wife, however, had not been continuously separated for that year. In April 1999, respondent filed a Rule 60, SCRCP, motion with the family court informing the court of this fact.[FN1Respondent also filed a self-report with Disciplinary Counsel.] As a result of the false statements made by respondent, the family court vacated the divorce as well as the approval of their agreement.

In addition to the false statements regarding the couple's continuous separation, respondent was charged with making a false statement to the family court on the financial declaration he filed at the October 1998 hearing. Respondent listed no creditors on the declaration, and no entry was made regarding a retirement fund. During the divorce litigation that ensued after the October 1998 divorce order was vacated, respondent listed several debts and a retirement fund.

Respondent testified at the hearing before the Subpanel. He admitted that the statements regarding continuous separation in the divorce complaint and at the hearing were false and that he made the misrepresentations to the family court with the intention of getting both the divorce granted and the settlement agreement approved. Moreover, he stated the corroborating witness knew her testimony was false. He explained his primary concern was joint custody of the children because he was their primary caregiver. Regarding the financial declaration, respondent stated that any omissions were not made with the intent to deceive Wife. Respondent acknowledged, however, that he did not make full financial disclosure **to the court** at the October 1998 divorce hearing.

DISCUSSION

The Subpanel recommended a definite suspension for nine months and that respondent pay the costs of the disciplinary proceedings. Respondent filed exceptions, but the Full Panel adopted the Subpanel's report. ...

Respondent has admitted the above facts and clearly has committed numerous acts of misconduct. Specifically, we find respondent violated the following Rules of Professional Conduct, Rule 407, SCACR: (1) Rule 1.1 (failing to provide competent representation); (2) Rule 1.7 (conflict of interest in representing both himself and Wife in the 1998 divorce proceeding); (3) Rule 3.1 (presenting a claim that was not meritorious in the 1998 divorce proceeding); (4) Rule 3.3 (candor towards the tribunal, by making false statements of fact and law to the family court); (5) Rule 3.4 (fairness to opposing party); (6) Rule 4.1 (truthfulness in statements to others); and (7) Rule 8.4... .

In mitigation, respondent asks the Court to recognize he was under the emotional stress of a divorce and acted solely out of concern for his children.

We conclude a six-month definite suspension is the appropriate sanction. *See In re Diggs,* 344 S.C. 397, 544 S.E.2d 628 (2001) (90-day suspension imposed on attorney who gave false statements under oath on his CLE compliance report); *In re Blake,* 343 S.C. 441, 539 S.E.2d 710 (2000) (four-month definite suspension imposed on attorney who made false representations to the family court as to why he needed a continuance for a client's hearing); *In re Murphy,* 336 S.C. 196, 519 S.E.2d 791 (1999) (nine-month definite suspension imposed where attorney, *inter alia,* made misrepresentations to the probate court while acting as co-personal representative of his aunt's estate).

Accordingly, we definitely suspend respondent for six months and order him to pay the costs of these disciplinary proceedings. ...

DEFINITE SUSPENSION.

INQUIRY

Correcting False Statements. The second clause of Model Rule 3.3(a)(1) requiring that lawyers correct previous false statements made to the tribunal addresses a special situation. On occasion, a lawyer will make a statement to a tribunal believing it to be true but learns later that the statement was false. Model Rule 3.3(a)(1) refers to that situation, requiring the lawyer to correct the previously made false statement. Lawyers make those corrections in the most expedient manner by amending a pleading, supplementing a brief, corresponding with the judge or other adjudicative officer, or placing the correction on the record at the next opportunity. Appreciate the limited duration of the duty of candor toward the tribunal. Model Rule 3.3(c) states that the duty continues until the conclusion of the proceeding, which Comment [13] then defines to be "when final judgment in the proceeding has been affirmed on appeal or the time for review has passed." So, in the usual court case, a lawyer need not correct a falsehood that comes to light after the appeal has concluded or the appeal period has expired. *See* Daniels v. Alander, 844 A.2d 182 (Conn. 2004) (exhaustion of appeals includes time for petition for writ of certiorari); ARIZ. ETHICS OP. 05-05 (2005) (duty continues in unemployment proceeding as long as client continues to receive benefits). Yet if while an appeal is pending a client admits to having testified falsely at trial, then the lawyer must remonstrate with the client and, if unsuccessful, notify the court to satisfy the duty to correct false testimony offered through the lawyer. *See* MD. ETHICS OP. 2005-15 (2005).

Disclosing Legal Authority. The next special situation that Model Rule 3.3 addresses surprises some students. Model Rule 3.3(a)(2) requires lawyers to disclose to the tribunal *adverse* authority from a controlling jurisdiction, that the other side fails to disclose. One might assume from a lawyer's advocacy role that lawyers only disclose authority favorable to their own client's position. Model Rule 3.3(a)(2) requires the opposite, although only when the authority is from a controlling jurisdiction, *see* Former Employees of Chevron Prods. Co. v. U.S. Secy. of Labor, 245 F. Supp.2d 1312 (Ct. Intl. Trade 2002), and only when the other side has not disclosed that authority. Lawyers may disagree over what is controlling authority. Which way would you lean in a close call, to disclose or not to disclose? One of the surest ways to build a solid professional reputation is to err on the side of disclosure. Judges and other adjudicative officers need to make sound decisions. The judge who makes a decision not knowing controlling authority is more likely to err. As the following case demonstrates, error may seem to one party adventitious at the time but in the long term helps no one. Model Rule 3.3(a)(2) does not require a lawyer to argue the other side's case, but it does establish a figurative floor so that the lawyer does not by arguing the client's side mislead the tribunal into believing that there is no contrary controlling authority. As we shall see again in more detail in the last chapter, a lawyer's relationship to authority determines the character of the lawyer.

Massey v. Prince George's County,
United States District Court for the District of Maryland
907 F. Supp. 138 (1995)

MESSITTE, District Judge.

I.

The Court takes this occasion to address the matter of counsel's responsibility for bringing legal authority to its attention in appropriate fashion.

What the Court *sua sponte* decides is to reverse its earlier decision dismissing certain causes of action in this case and to keep the matter in federal court; the manner in which this reversal has come about, however, merits discussion in its own right.

II.

Plaintiff Willie Massey alleges that in the early morning hours of November 4, 1992 he was sleeping in a vacant or abandoned building in Cheverly, Maryland. He contends that all of a sudden he was awakened by Prince George's County police officers who, without warning, set their police dog upon him. Massey says that although he offered no resistance, the animal proceeded to bite him and inflict painful and permanent injury all over his body. In his Third Amended Complaint before the Court, Massey has sued the individual officers for assault and battery under Maryland law and for deprivation of his Fourth Amendment rights, i.e. for use of excessive force, under 42 U.S.C. §1983.[fn] The officers have denied liability, claiming that Massey was warned about the dog in a loud voice and that he resisted their efforts to arrest him.

Earlier in these proceedings, Defendants filed a fifteen page Motion for Summary Judgment to which excerpts from depositions of Plaintiff and various officers were appended. With regard to the Section 1983 claims, Defendants argued that their seizure of Plaintiff and the force used by them were reasonable as a matter of law. After citing general Supreme Court law regarding such claims,[fn] defense counsel invited the Court's attention to the case of *Robinette v. Barnes,* 854 F.2d 909 (6th Cir.1988), in which the U.S. Court of Appeals for the Sixth Circuit concluded that the use of a trained police dog in circumstances comparable to those in the case at bar was reasonable as a matter of law. ...

In the present case, Plaintiff's Response to Defendants' Motion for Summary Judgment consisted of a single page, his Statement of Material Facts in Dispute barely more than two. In these, Plaintiff's counsel cited one case and one alone, namely the *Robinette* case already cited by defense counsel, which Plaintiff's counsel did no more than attempt to distinguish on its facts.

When the matter came on for oral argument, defense counsel again argued the applicability of *Robinette* to the present case, while Plaintiff's counsel again tried to distinguish *Robinette* on its facts, offering no further citation to authority.

At the conclusion of oral argument, largely on the strength of *Robinette,* the Court announced its decision to dismiss the two counts of excessive force, finding the officers' actions reasonable as a matter of law. What remained open, however, was the issue of whether Plaintiff's state law cause of action for assault and battery could survive in the face of the Court's ruling with regard to the two federal constitutional torts. The parties were invited to submit supplemental statements with regard to that limited issue.

III.

Defense counsel has now submitted a one-page letter brief in conformity with the Court's request. Plaintiff's counsel has submitted a six-page letter [that] ... invites the Court to reconsider its dismissal of the two federal constitutional counts. ... [F]or the first time Plaintiff's counsel cites legal authority directly on point to the case at bar. The case, *Kopf v. Wing*, 942 F.2d 265 (4th Cir.1991), is not only an excessive force case involving a police dog, but is the controlling law in this Circuit. ... [T]hat case clearly mandates denial of Defendants' Motion for Summary Judgment, which is to say reinstatement of the excessive force claims the Court recently dismissed. But the fact that *Kopf* has been cited for the first time by Plaintiff's counsel in a supplemental letter—well after the filing of his threadbare initial response to Defendants' Motion for Summary Judgment and his equally scant oral argument on the motion—is a cause for considerable concern. At the same time, the fact that this case has never been cited by defense counsel in his initial pleadings, in oral argument or indeed to this day, gives cause for even greater concern.

IV.

... The parallels between *Kopf* and the case at bar are striking and need little elaboration. The Court accepts without question that, on the authority of *Kopf*, Plaintiff ought to have prevailed as against Defendants' Motion for Summary Judgment. Notwithstanding this, neither Plaintiff's nor Defendants' counsel brought the case to the Court's attention even through oral argument. Thereafter, only Plaintiff's counsel, never defense counsel, cited the case, and then only because the Court had directed briefing on another point of law.

V.

One must assume that had Plaintiff's counsel, in preparing his initial Opposition to the Motion for Summary Judgment, exhibited the same degree of diligence that ultimately permitted him to locate the case in untimely fashion, he could have located the case in timely fashion. Instead, counsel offered only the sketchiest statement of grounds, reflecting a bare minimum of legal research, showing every sign of having been dictated on the run. The net effect of this truncated effort was to consume valuable court time in oral argument and the preparation of supplemental briefs (not to mention preparation of the present Opinion), all of which could have been avoided by earlier diligence on counsel's part. ...

The action of defense counsel in this case raises a far more serious concern. It is possible that defense counsel also overlooked the *Kopf* precedent, but if he did, the oversight was glaring and extremely troublesome. *Kopf* not only deals with a claim of excessive force against police where a police dog was involved; individual Prince George's County police officers and the County itself were defendants in that case. Indeed, at least one attorney for Prince George's County in *Kopf*, as shown in the reported case, was an individual, whom the Court judicially notices, was still in the County Attorney's office at the time of the filing of the present Motion for Summary Judgment.[fn]

The regrettable inference is that defense counsel in the instant case may in fact have deliberately failed to disclose to the Court directly controlling authority from this Circuit. If so, the action would constitute a clear violation of the Rules of Professional Conduct.

Thus, Rule 3.3(a)(3) provides that "a lawyer shall not knowingly ... fail to disclose to the tribunal legal authority in the controlling jurisdiction known to the lawyer to be directly adverse to the position of the client and not disclosed by opposing counsel." In federal court, the "controlling jurisdiction" is the circuit in which the district court sits. [C] Particularly disturbing is the type of case encountered here— a litigant who was an unsuccessful party to a directly relevant adverse precedent who has failed to cite that precedent to the court. [C] The Court cannot help but ponder the County's actions.

Under the circumstances, the Court will direct defense counsel to show cause to the Court in writing within thirty (30) days why citation to the *Kopf* case was omitted from his Motion for Summary Judgment, oral argument, and indeed from any pleading or communication to date.

The Court also recollects that in the last several months counsel for Prince George's County was before the Court in at least one other police dog excessive force case in which a Motion for Summary Judgment in favor of the County was granted. It may be that *Kopf* was omitted from the pleading in that proceeding as well. Accordingly, the Court directs defense counsel and the Office of the Prince George's County attorney, within sixty (60) days to disclose to the Court the status of that case and any and all police dog excessive force cases involving Prince George's County that were pending as of August 9, 1991, the date *Kopf* was decided by the Fourth Circuit, or that have been filed from that date to the present. The Court's Show-Cause Order, entered simultaneously with this Opinion, spells out the information that is to be provided. Any further sanctions that may be imposed by the Court will depend on the County's showing of cause pursuant to this directive.

Enough has been said for now. No formal Motion for Reconsideration need be filed by Plaintiff's counsel since, as indicated, *Kopf* clearly dictates reinstatement of the excessive force claims. In consequence, the state court claim for assault and battery also remains in the case. ...

———————————

INQUIRY

Offering False Evidence. The next special situation that Model Rule 3.3 addresses has to do with offering false evidence. In the same way that Model Rule 3.3(a)(1) prohibits a lawyer from making false statements of fact and requires their correction, Model Rule 3.3(a)(3) prohibits a lawyer from offering false evidence while also requiring that a lawyer remediate the offering if learning about it later. The first duty not to offer false evidence is straightforward. *See* In re Steele, 868 A.2d 146 (D.C. 2005) (discipline for submitting fabricated subpoena to excuse non-appearance). The second duty to remediate prior offers of false evidence requires a more complex response. For example, if a client surprises a lawyer by testifying falsely at deposition or trial, the lawyer would urge the client confidentially to correct the false testimony, explaining its consequences including that the lawyer would correct the statement and withdraw from the representation, that the court may sanction the client, and that the perjury charges are possible, if the client does not make the correction. *See* Model Rule 3.3 Comment [10]; *see also* Idaho State Bar v. Warrick, 44 P.3d 1141 (Idaho 2002) (take action immediately rather than waiting for others to find out). Consider the following case illustrating the violations of making false statements of fact and submitting false evidence, followed by a case illustrating the violation of failing to correct false testimony.

In re Bailey,
Louisiana Supreme Court
848 So.2d 530 (2003)

PER CURIAM.

This disciplinary matter arises from two counts of formal charges filed by the Office of Disciplinary Counsel ("ODC") against respondent, Gary W. Bailey, an attorney licensed to practice law in Louisiana.

FORMAL CHARGES
Count I-The Matthews Matter

Respondent represented the plaintiff in the [*Matthews* case]... . In the course of the litigation, the defendants filed an exception of prescription which was set for hearing on Monday, July 26, 1999. On July 20, 1999, respondent filed a motion to continue the hearing, representing that he could not be present because he was "scheduled for trial" in a Texas personal injury case[, the *Bailey* case,] beginning on July 22, 1999... , anticipated to last three to five days.

The judge presiding in the *Matthews* case, Judge Timothy E. Kelley, subsequently learned that the *Bailey* trial had been completed in May 1999, two months prior to the prescription hearing in *Matthews,* and that the only matter remaining on that docket was a motion for new trial which was to be heard on Thursday, July 22, 1999, four days prior to the prescription hearing. Based upon this information, Judge Kelley denied respondent's motion for a continuance.

On July 26, 1999, respondent did not appear at the hearing in the *Matthews* case, nor did he file any pleading on his client's behalf.[fn] Following a hearing on August 2, 1999, Judge Kelley sanctioned respondent for misrepresenting facts to the court. On August 20, 1999, Judge Kelley filed a complaint against respondent with the ODC. ...

Count II-The Wagner Matter

Respondent represented the plaintiff in the [*Wagner* case]. Plaintiff's petitiom alleged that she had been the victim of a battery committed at her home by her neighbors. At the trial of the matter on August 8, 2000, respondent attempted to introduce into the record a medical narrative report authored by Dr. Nicholas J. Campo. However, the report was altered on its face. Specifically, although the original narrative report referred to the plaintiff's history of being "accosted at work," the words "at work" had been deleted from the copy of respondent's exhibit that he attempted to introduce at trial.

On August 11, 2000, defense counsel filed a complaint against respondent with the ODC. ...

Hearing Committee Recommendation

After considering the evidence presented at the hearing, the hearing committee found that respondent intentionally misrepresented to Judge Kelley a professional conflict in a Texas proceeding in connection with his seeking a continuance of the hearing on the exception of prescription pending before Judge Kelley... .

In connection with Count II, the committee found respondent either altered or was aware of the altering of Dr. Campo's report at the time he attempted to file it into evidence in the *Wagner* case. The committee noted that the original report was never found or produced by respondent; rather, the only version of the report produced by respondent "was a copy with the alteration that deleted the work reference. This Committee does not accept respondent's explanation that the report in that condition was simply consistent with sloppy work done by doctors, and feels that at the very least the report in that condition should have prompted an inquiry by respondent to Dr. Campo's office as to the obvious irregularity of that sentence. ..." ...

Based upon these factual findings, the committee determined that respondent violated the Rules of Professional Conduct as charged in the formal charges. ...

... [N]oting that it was "particularly influenced" by "the multiplicity of sanctionable conduct committed by respondent and by his total refusal to acknowledge the wrongful nature of his conduct," the committee recommended that respondent be suspended from the practice of law for two years.

Respondent filed an objection to the hearing committee's report and recommendation.

Disciplinary Board Recommendation

After reviewing this matter, the disciplinary board generally adopted the hearing committee's findings of fact and conclusions of law, and agreed that respondent should be suspended from the practice of law for two years. ...

DISCUSSION

... We agree that the factual findings of the hearing committee are well supported by the evidence. We also agree that these factual findings support the conclusion that respondent has violated the Louisiana Rules of Professional Conduct. ...

Each instance of respondent's misconduct is serious in nature. In 1999, respondent filed a motion for continuance in which he knowingly misrepresented to the trial court that he had a scheduling conflict (i.e., a trial that would last three to five days), when he had no reason to believe his statements were in any way truthful or accurate. In 2000, respondent filed a medical report into evidence at trial when he clearly knew that the report had been altered. It is particularly disturbing to us that the alteration pertained to an issue that was central to respondent's case (i.e., whether his client's alleged injury occurred at home, as she claimed, or at work). After reviewing the record, we agree with the hearing committee and the disciplinary board that such serious misconduct justifies a lengthy suspension from the practice of law. Accordingly, we will accept the disciplinary board's recommendation and suspend respondent from the practice of law for two years.

DECREE

Upon review of the findings and recommendation of the hearing committee and disciplinary board, and considering the record, it is ordered that Gary W. Bailey, Louisiana Bar Roll number 21996, be suspended from the practice of law in Louisiana for a period of two years. All costs and expenses in the matter are assessed against respondent... .

In re Page,
Indiana Supreme Court
774 N.E.2d 49 (2002)

PER CURIAM.

The respondent here, Paul J. Page, failed to take action while, in open court with his client, the client testified that he had not driven a car in nine years when in fact the client had, a statement the respondent had reason to believe was untruthful. We find the respondent violated Ind.Professional Conduct Rule 3.3(a)(2).

The respondent and the Disciplinary Commission have submitted for our approval a *Statement of Circumstances and Conditional Agreement for Discipline* in which the respondent admits to his misconduct and agrees to be publicly reprimanded for it. The opinion that follows includes a summary of the facts underlying the parties' proffered resolution.

The respondent was admitted to practice law in this state of Indiana on October 15, 1990, and practices in Indianapolis. On March 6, 1991, the Indiana Bureau of Motor Vehicles determined that an individual (hereinafter "the client") was an habitual traffic violator, and his license was suspended for ten years. On March 10, 1999, the client was driving a motor vehicle in Shelbyville, Indiana when he was stopped for making an illegal u-turn. On March 11, 1999, authorities charged the client with driving a motor vehicle while his license was suspended, pursuant to IC 9-30-10-16, in a criminal case docketed in the Shelby Superior Court 2. On October 4, 1999, the respondent entered his appearance as the client's attorney. The respondent never asked the client whether he had been driving a motor vehicle on March 10, 1999, and, in discussing his available defenses with the respondent, the client did not claim that he had not been driving that day. ...

On October 28, 1999, the respondent prepared and filed a verified petition for probationary license for the client in Marion Circuit Court in a separate case... . The petition also stated that the client "has not violated the terms of his suspension by operating a vehicle[.]"

At a November 15, 1999 hearing on the petition, the presiding commissioner asked the client, "Have you driven an automobile in the last nine years, sir?" The client, under oath, answered "No." The respondent attended the hearing as the client's counsel and was present in the courtroom during the exchange. Although the client's answer to the commissioner's question was untrue and the respondent had reason to believe the client's answer was untrue, the respondent did not take any steps to convince the client to disclose the untruthfulness of the answer, and continued to represent the client. In the criminal case, on January 21, 2000, the client, through the respondent, stipulated that he was driving a motor vehicle on March 10, 1999. ...

Professional Conduct Rule 3.3(a)(2) provides that a lawyer shall not fail to disclose a material fact to a tribunal where disclosure is necessary to avoid assisting a criminal or fraudulent act against a tribunal by a client. We find that the respondent violated that rule by remaining silent and taking no action before the Marion Circuit Court when he knew of credible evidence that his client had driven an automobile within nine years of the hearing. We recognize the tension between the duty to keep a client confidence under Prof.Cond.R. 1.6

and the obligation to disclose under Prof.Cond.R. 3.3(a)(2). [C] In some circumstances (such as where the lawyer's services will be used by the client in materially furthering a course of criminal or fraudulent conduct),[fn] resignation is the appropriate step. [C] However, doing nothing, as the respondent did here, is not an acceptable option.[fn]

Having found misconduct, we now turn to the issue of appropriate sanction for it. In this regard, the parties have stipulated to several factors in mitigation of the respondent's misconduct: he has not been sanctioned by this Court for a violation of the *Rules of Professional Conduct* prior to the present misconduct; he made full and complete disclosure of the facts underlying this disciplinary matter and maintained a cooperative attitude toward the disciplinary process; he enjoys a reputation for integrity and truthfulness in the community and among his peers in the bar; and with the exception of this act of misconduct, the respondent has otherwise conducted himself in a professional manner as a member of the Bar. ...

... Pursuant to their agreed resolution, the Commission and the respondent ask us to approve a public reprimand in this case. In light of the agreement, the mitigating factors, and precedent, we find that the sanction should be approved.

Accordingly, the respondent, Paul J. Page, is hereby reprimanded and admonished for the misconduct set forth herein. ...

Costs of this proceeding are assessed against the respondent.

INQUIRY

Knowledge of Falsity. Notice that the prohibition that a lawyer "shall not" offer such evidence applies only to evidence that the lawyer "knows to be false." The lawyer must *know* of the evidence's falsity, not merely suspect it, for the prohibition to be mandatory, especially in criminal cases with their higher beyond-a-reasonable-doubt burden of proof. *See* United States v. Midgett, 342 F.3d 321 (4th Cir. 2003) (strong belief not sufficient knowledge to refuse to offer client's testimony in criminal case); State v. McDowell, 669 N.W.2d 204 (Wis. Ct. App. 2003) (criminal-defense lawyer "knows" only in extraordinary circumstances). The *In re Page* case above provides a good illustration of the lower standard in a civil case. The opinion states that the lawyer "had reason to believe" that the client's testimony was untruthful, but the lawyer's admission and stipulation in the driving action established that the lawyer actually knew. What do you think of the rule's limitation to actual knowledge? Keep in mind that ABA Model Rule 1.0(f) provides that a lawyer's "knowledge may be inferred from circumstances." There is a fine line between inferred knowledge and unreasonable belief. The latter can easily look more like the former. Should the rule also be mandatory if the lawyer *suspects* that evidence is false? Just as for Model Rule 3.3(a)(1) on correcting false statements, Model Rule 3.3(c) provides that the lawyer's duty under Model Rule 3.3(a)(3) to remediate an offering of false evidence continues until the proceeding concludes. If after the proceeding concludes the lawyer discovers that some of the offered evidence was false, then the lawyer need not correct it.

Refusing to Offer False Evidence. Model Rule 3.3(a)(3) permits a lawyer to refuse to offer evidence that the lawyer *reasonably believes* to be false, in all instances except one. Who would urge a lawyer to offer false evidence? Model Rule 3.3(a)(3)'s silent reference is primarily to the client, although non-party witnesses may also offer false evidence. Clients have strong interests in litigation, particularly in criminal cases involving long-term incarceration. If, as you might suspect, persons charged with simple traffic violations will on occasion testify untruthfully, then you can be sure that clients having significantly greater property and liberty interests will also on occasion offer testimony that the lawyer reasonably believes to be false. Lawyers may refuse those offers in all but one situation, addressed below. Does it surprise you that as to evidence that the lawyer reasonably believes to be false (as opposed to evidence that the lawyer *knows* to be false), Model Rule 3.3(a)(3) is permissive ("may refuse") rather than mandatory ("must refuse")? Model Rule 3.3(a)(3) gives a lawyer important discretion when the lawyer remains uncertain of the evidence's falsity and believes that there remains some likelihood that the evidence is true, even though there is strong indication that the evidence is in fact false. That discretion enables a lawyer to make important judgments about the lawyer's own morality, while alternatively allowing the lawyer to rely on the tribunal's factfinding in appropriate cases. Sometimes, rules must point us toward principles rather than answers.

Constitutional Rights to Testify. Model Rule 3.3(a)(3) does not permit a lawyer to refuse to offer the testimony of a client criminal defendant, when the lawyer reasonably believes that the client will testify falsely. The lawyer must allow the client criminal defendant to testify falsely. This exception accommodates a criminal defendant's constitutional right to testify. The accommodation is not as simple as it looks, though. The lawyer retains the lawyer's own duty not to present false evidence to the tribunal. In effect, the lawyer must allow the client criminal defendant to testify falsely while distancing the lawyer from the false testimony. Lawyers do so by moving to withdraw from the representation. *See Lucas v. State*, 572 S.E.2d 274 (S.C. 2002) (motion to withdraw is appropriate response, although court retains discretion to deny motion). Some authority supports an alternative narrative approach in which the lawyer presents the client's truthful testimony in the usual manner of questions and answers under direct examination but then alerts the tribunal that the client will testify in the narrative rather than by question and answer as to the false testimony. *See* People v. Jennings, 83 Cal. Rptr.2d 33 (Cal. Ct. App. 1999). This unusual accommodation, disapproved by the Supreme Court, *see* Nix v. Whiteside, 475 U.S. 157 (1986), and ABA Formal Ethics Op. 87-353 (1987), but recognized in Model Rule 3.3 Comment [7], enables the lawyer not to induce the false testimony or otherwise appear to be a part of it. The lawyer thus ensures that the trial judge knows of the perjury, *see* People v. DePallo, 754 N.E.2d 751 (N.Y. 2001), although presumably jurors do not know.

Criminal or Fraudulent Conduct. Model Rule 3.3(b) requires a lawyer to take reasonable remedial measures including if necessary notifying the tribunal, whenever a person engages in criminal or fraudulent conduct relating to the proceeding. An example would be if the lawyer learned that the client had submitted a false petition or schedule in, say, a bankruptcy proceeding, to attempt to gain an advantage in discharge. Model Rule 3.3(b) would then require the lawyer to notify the court if doing so was still necessary after the lawyer remonstrated unsuccessfully with the client. The American Bar Association amended Model Rule 3.3(b) in 2002 to expand its reach. The prior rule required a lawyer to remediate a client's crime or fraud relating to the proceeding only if the client used the unwitting lawyer's services to perpetrate the crime or fraud. *See, e.g.,* In re Winthrop, 848 N.E.2d 961 (Ill. 2006) (no discipline under former Rule 3.3 where lawyer's service was not involved in fraud on the court). Today's Model Rule 3.3(b) requires the lawyer to remediate the crime or fraud even if the client did not use the lawyer's services in perpetrating it on the tribunal.

Ex-Parte Proceedings. Lawyers on occasion initiate and conduct ex-parte proceedings in a tribunal, meaning a proceeding in which the opposing side is not present or represented and has no notice of the proceeding. An example is a request for a temporary restraining order in which notice of the request would cause the other side to take the action that the requesting party wishes to prevent. In those ex-parte proceedings, Model Rule 3.3(d) requires a lawyer to disclose to the tribunal facts adverse to the requesting party, sufficient for the tribunal to make an informed decision. *See, e.g.,* In re Mullins, 649 N.E.2d 1024 (Ind. 1995) (lawyer should have told judge in emergency guardianship proceeding that another action was already underway). Judges and other adjudicative officers are sensitive to the lawyer's duty in ex-parte proceedings. Judges will inquire specifically of counsel whether there are such adverse facts. Lawyers pay close attention to Model Rule 3.3(d) in ex-parte proceedings. Lawyers requesting ex-parte relief know that as soon as the tribunal issues the requested relief, the opposing party will learn of it and bring adverse facts to the tribunal's attention. Consider the following illustrative case.

Ndreko v. Ridge,
United States District Court for the District of Minnesota
351 F. Supp.2d 904 (2004)

DAVIS, District Judge.
... II. FACTUAL BACKGROUND
Petitioner Elton Ndreko is a native of Albania. He left Albania in 1992 and entered the United States on approximately April 13, 1998, as a non-immigrant crewman. He was authorized to remain in the United States until May 11, 1998. He remained in the United States past May 11, and was provided with a Notice to Appear, charging him as removable for remaining in the United States without authorization after the expiration of the non-immigrant crewman authorization. Ndreko admitted that he was deportable, but filed an application for asylum and withholding of removal and for relief under the Convention against Torture.

After a hearing, at which Ndreko was represented by attorney Michael York, the Immigration Law Judge denied Ndreko's application. The Immigration Law Judge found that Ndreko was not credible, based, in part, on the conclusion that he had submitted fraudulent medical documents in support of his claim for asylum. ...

The Immigration Law Judge denied Ndreko's request for asylum and ordered that Ndreko be removed from the United States to Albania. Ndreko appealed the Immigration Judge's decision to the Board of Immigration Appeals ("BIA"), which dismissed his appeal on September 10, 2003. On that date, Ndreko was subject to an administratively final order of removal.

Ndreko, *pro se,* then appealed the BIA decision to the Eighth Circuit Court of Appeals. Ndreko was taken into custody on August 15, 2004. On August 20, 2004, he filed a motion to stay deportation with the Eighth Circuit. On September 10, 2004, the Eighth Circuit denied his motion to stay.

On September 16, Ndreko, through his counsel, Patricia Mattos, filed a request for reconsideration of the September 10 Order. ... October 8, the Eighth Circuit denied Ndreko's motion for reconsideration. ...

On December 8, Ndreko learned that he was being put on a plane for removal to Albania. ...

At approximated 4:57 p.m. on the evening of December 8, Ndreko filed a Petition for Writ of Habeas Corpus [Docket No. 1] and a Motion for Temporary Restraining Order [Docket No. 2]. Based on Mattos's representation of the situation, the Court held an immediate telephonic hearing. Mattos did not mention the existence of the pending petition for review before the Eighth Circuit in this matter in the Petition for Writ of Habeas Corpus, in the Motion for Temporary Restraining Order, or during the telephonic hearing. She did request that the Court order Ndreko's Amsterdam-bound plane to change course and land in the United States.

The Court granted the motion for a temporary restraining order the same day. [Docket No. 3] As ordered by the Court, the Government met Ndreko when his flight landed in Amsterdam and gave him a plane ticket for an immediate nonstop return flight to Minneapolis, Minnesota. He returned to Minnesota on December 9. On December 15, the Government filed a motion to dismiss. ...

III. DISCUSSION

... B. Jurisdiction

The Court agrees that under 8 U.S.C. § 1252, it is without jurisdiction to consider Ndreko's habeas corpus petition and stay his removal. ...

... [T]he Government's Motion to Dismiss is granted.

IV. SANCTIONS: FINDINGS OF FACT AND CONCLUSIONS OF LAW

When applying for the temporary restraining order, Ndreko's counsel, Patricia Mattos, failed to inform the Court that Ndreko's case is currently pending before the Eighth Circuit and that, in recent months, that court has twice rejected his motions to stay removal. ...

Mattos omitted these facts, both in her moving papers and during the telephone hearing on the motion for a temporary restraining order, despite the fact that Mattos is Ndreko's counsel of record in the matter before the Eighth Circuit. In fact, Mattos filed the motion for reconsideration of the motion to stay that was denied by the Eighth Circuit in October.

At the same time that Mattos hid these facts from the Court, she asked the Court to land a plane that had already taken flight. At oral argument on December 17, Mattos first characterized this complete lack of candor as an "oversight"... . Mattos's statements demonstrate that her lack of candor was not an "oversight;" rather, she made a calculated decision to hide the existence of the Eighth Circuit proceeding from this Court.

Counsel's statements at oral argument, combined with the fact that Mattos is Ndreko's appellate counsel and the obviously vital importance of the Eighth Circuit proceedings, lead the Court to conclude that Mattos's lack of candor was wilful and in bad faith. Having lost petitioner's motions to stay before the Eighth Circuit, Mattos intentionally misled this Court, during an emergency hearing after normal Court hours, in order to circumvent the Eighth Circuit's clear intention that Ndreko's removal not be stayed. Because she did not achieve the desired result before the proper court, Mattos employed an intentional lack of candor to mislead this Court into issuing an order that it was without jurisdiction to issue and that was in direct conflict with not one, but two clear orders from a superior court.

Mattos's conduct violated the general duty of candor to the tribunal imposed on all officers of the court. [C] ...

At Mattos's request, a telephonic hearing on the motion for the temporary restraining order was immediately held on Wednesday evening, after normal working hours, less than one hour after the petition for habeas corpus and the motion were filed. By filing the motion with the Court after Ndreko's airplane had departed the airport, Mattos created an emergency situation, which disadvantaged both the Court and the Government, and induced the Court to rely on Mattos's representations regarding the "emergency" before it. ... Minnesota Rule of Professional Conduct 3.3(d) notes that "[i]n an ex parte proceeding, a lawyer shall inform the tribunal of all material facts known to the lawyer which will enable the tribunal to make an informed decision, whether or not the facts are adverse." Clearly, Mattos failed to inform the Court of material facts in this case. ...

Because of the serious consequences of Mattos's conduct and the lack of judgment demonstrated by her actions, the Court imposes the following sanctions under its inherent power: Mattos is suspended from practicing law before the undersigned judge, and she is ordered to attend a continuing legal education course on attorney ethics within the next year. These sanctions are intended to punish Mattos for her actions and to deter her from repeating those actions. The Court hopes that both this opinion and the continuing legal education class will teach Mattos how to better carry out her duties as both an attorney and an officer of the court. She did no favor to her client by having him flown across the globe under false pretenses and without hope of relief from a Court that had no power to decide his case. Finally, because Mattos's conduct violated the Minnesota Rules of Professional Conduct, a copy of this opinion is being forwarded to the Office of Lawyers Professional Responsibility. ...

Career and Professional Development

This chapter on candor forces us to think about our own character, including especially our willingness to recognize the humanity of others. reading it may have made you think of your personality. Some of us are extroverts who draw energy from interaction, while others are introverts whom interaction distracts. Some of us sense in the moment, while others of us strategize intuitively for the future. Some of us feel our way through situations, while others of us tend more to think and reason. Some of us close and finish matters judgmentally, while others of us remain perceptive keeping things open, flexible, and incomplete. The point is not that one trait or set of traits is better than another trait or set of traits. The point is that while personality influences behavior, it can also be an important bridge to your career and professional development. Take the Myers-Briggs Type Indicator test or a similar personality test to see what you can learn about your traits and how they connect with careers and your personal and professional responsibility.

CHAPTER VIII

INTEGRITY

Merit, Expeditiousness, Impartiality, Decorum, Consistency

> *Integrity is telling myself the truth. And honesty is telling the truth to other people.*
>
> — *Spencer Johnson*

> *I should never act except in such a way that I can also will that my maxim should become a universal law.*
>
> — *Immanuel Kant*

OBJECTIVE: Given the opportunity to advocate in adjudicative and nonadjudicative proceedings, articulate your responsibility to show integrity in your contentions, public actions, private influences, and advocate's role.

Applicable Rules

3.1 Meritorious Claims and Contentions

3.2 Expediting Litigation

3.5 Impartiality and Decorum of the Tribunal

3.6 Trial Publicity

3.7 Lawyer as Witness

3.9 Advocate in Nonadjudicative Proceeding

Everyone agrees that lawyers should be honest, even though the prior chapter showed that honesty in a professional setting could require more than is immediately obvious. Spencer Johnson's above quote, though, suggests that while honesty in communications to others is critical, beyond basic honesty a lawyer must also have integrity, meaning a consistency between that which a lawyer reflects outwardly and that which the lawyer believes internally. Perhaps thankfully, conduct rules cannot delve a lawyer's professional soul to determine a lawyer's merit. Yet if a lawyer is merely honest in communications without having the deeper kind of integrity that law practice demands, then the lawyer is likely to violate other conduct rules that demand that integrity. The lawyer may communicate truthfully but still make frivolous contentions, impede litigation, disrupt the tribunal's decorum, and exhibit an inconsistency in roles that detract from the quality of adjudication. This chapter explores those conduct rules that require lawyers to go beyond facial honesty to professional integrity.

A. Meritorious Contentions

Bringing and Defending Proceedings. Lawyers start lawsuits in court and start other legal proceedings before administrative or other adjudicatory bodies. ABA Model Rule 3.1 requires that lawyers initiate and defend those proceedings, and contest issues in them, only when the legal and factual basis for doing so is not frivolous. Model Rule 3.1's requirement has more to it than the mere honesty required by ABA Model Rule 3.3 "Candor Toward the Tribunal" and 4.1 "Truthfulness in Statements to Others." While a proceeding may be frivolous under Model Rule 3.1 because the allegations on which it relies are false, implicating a party's honesty if not also the lawyer's honesty, yet a proceeding may also be frivolous in a deeper sense that although the allegations on which it relies are true, they do not make a meritorious contention. There is a difference between dishonest contentions and frivolous contentions. To be frivolous with one's contentions is not necessarily to be dishonest. Merit goes deeper than truthfulness, implying worth or value to the proceeding. Lawyers can even be wrong in their allegations, so long as they first make reasonable investigation. *See, e.g.,* Storey v. Cello Holdings, L.L.C., 347 F.3d 370 (2d Cir. 2003) (sanction only contentions "utterly lacking in support). Yet to make allegations that even if true do not merit contention is to violate Model Rule 3.1. Under Model Rule 3.1, a lawyer must look beyond the facial truth of the contentions to whether they advance a just claim or defense. Consider how an identical state version of Model Rule 3.1 demands integrity.

> ARKANSAS R. PROF. CONDUCT 3.1: **Meritorious Claims and Contentions.**
> A lawyer shall not bring or defend a proceeding, or assert or controvert an issue therein, unless there is a basis in law and fact for doing so that is not frivolous, which includes a good faith argument for an extension, modification or reversal of existing law. A lawyer for the defendant in a criminal proceeding, or the respondent in a proceeding that could result in incarceration, may nevertheless so defend the proceeding as to require that every element of the case be established.

INQUIRY

Parallel Sanctions. You should already know from your torts, civil-procedure, and other law studies that lawyers must not make frivolous contentions. Lawyers suffer discipline when violating Model Rule 3.1 by making frivolous contentions. *See, e.g.,* In re Levine, 847 P.2d 1093 (Ariz. 1993) (three-month suspension); Dodrill v. Executive Director, 842 S.W.2d 383 (Ark. 1992) (one-year suspension). Yet Model Rule 3.1 reflects only the discipline hazard—the possibility that someone will notify discipline officials, resulting in misconduct charges—when a lawyer makes frivolous arguments. The risks of other immediate hazards may be as great as or greater than the risk of license discipline. Courts operate under rules and statutes that permit them to sanction the lawyer and the lawyer's client within the proceeding. *See, e.g,* 18 U.S.C. §3006A (vexatious initiation of federal criminal proceedings); 28 U.S.C. §1912 (frivolous federal appeals); 28 U.S.C. §1927 (vexatious multiplication of proceedings); FED. R. APP. P. 38 (frivolous appeals); FED. R. CIV. P. 11; MICH. CT. R. 2.114; *see also* Obert v. Republic Western Ins. Co., 264 F. Supp.2d 106 (D. R.I. 2003) (both court-rule and conduct-rule sanctions); In re Boone, 66 P.3d 896 (Kan. 2003) (state discipline following federal sanction). Litigation sanctions are often monetary but may also include default, dismissal, or even findings of contempt. *See* 18 U.S.C. §401-402; In re Hampton, 919 So.2d 949 (Miss. 2006) (contempt finding for failure to appear). Malpractice claims and unpaid bills are other possibilities, although with malpractice, the lawyer's frivolous contention would have had to cause the client some loss, which may not be the case unless the lawyer overlooked a meritorious contention when making the frivolous one. Lawyers have more to fear than license discipline when making frivolous contentions. Consider one case illustrating parallel sanctions while holding that the findings of frivolous contentions in the underlying case bind the lawyer in the discipline case.

In re Caranchini,
Missouri Supreme Court
956 S.W.2d 910 (1997)

LIMBAUGH, Judge.
ORIGINAL DISCIPLINARY PROCEEDING
... The Chief Disciplinary Counsel ("Informant") charges Gwen G. Caranchini ("Respondent") with numerous violations of the Missouri Rules of Professional Conduct ("Missouri Rules") based upon

Respondent's misconduct in four separate federal court cases. The federal courts have sanctioned Respondent for her misconduct. After consideration of the propriety of sanctions under the Missouri Rules based on the findings of misconduct in those federal cases, this Court orders that Respondent be disbarred. ...

I. OFFENSIVE NON–MUTUAL COLLATERAL ESTOPPEL

Respondent claimed in the proceeding before the master, and continues to claim before this Court, that she is entitled to a hearing on the underlying facts of the federal sanction decisions. The master determined that the doctrine of offensive non-mutual collateral estoppel precludes Respondent from relitigating the federal courts' factual determinations. This Court agrees. ...

... [T]he application of offensive non-mutual collateral estoppel in this case is consistent with the underlying principles of protecting litigants from the burden of relitigating issues and the promotion of judicial economy. *Parklane Hosiery[Co. v. Shore]*, 439 U.S. [322,] 326[(1979)]. Under this doctrine, the federal court findings have properly been used as the basis for this disciplinary action.

II. DOUBLE JEOPARDY

Respondent's next point is that the double jeopardy clause of the federal and state constitutions prohibits further disciplinary action by this Court because the federal courts have already sanctioned her for her misconduct. ... Even assuming, *arguendo,* that the federal court sanctions do constitute punishment for double jeopardy purposes, this Court holds that state disciplinary actions do not. Without state punishment, therefore, no double jeopardy violation exists.[fn] ...

III. SANCTIONABLE MISCONDUCT

... [T]his Court must now consider the specific charges against Respondent. ...

A. Count One: White v. General Motors Corporation

In *White v. General Motors Corp.*, 699 F.Supp. 1485 (Kan.1988), Respondent represented two clients... who brought claims against General Motors Corporation ("GM") for wrongful discharge and breach of contract. ... The district court found insufficient legal and factual bases to support these claims and ordered summary judgment for GM. Subsequently, the district court imposed sanctions against Respondent after finding that she had engaged in numerous acts of misconduct. *White v. General Motors Corp.*, 126 F.R.D. 563 (Kan.1989). The district court's findings in the *White* case may be summarized as follows: 1. Respondent failed to make a reasonable factual inquiry before filing the wrongful discharge complaint. [C] Both of her clients had previously executed documents releasing GM from employment-related claims, and she knew of the existence of the releases before she filed the wrongful discharge complaint. [C] ... 2. Respondent pursued

White's slander claim without making a reasonable inquiry to determine whether that claim was well-founded in fact. [C] ... 3. Respondent disregarded well-established Kansas law by arguing that the determination of whether the facts surrounding the signing of the release constituted duress was initially a jury question, rather than a question of law. [C] ... 4. Respondent's argument that the releases signed by plaintiffs were ambiguous, which was her excuse for continuing to use the releases, was not well-founded in fact or law. [C] 5. Respondent advanced the action for an improper purpose, not only by filing suit, but also by threatening to contact the media and government agencies before suit was ever filed. [C] ... 6. Respondent needlessly increased the cost of litigation by making voluminous discovery requests that would not have been necessary had she made a reasonable inquiry to determine that the claims were well-founded in the first place. [C]

Based on these findings, the district court ordered Respondent to pay GM's costs and attorney's fees totaling $172,382.19. *White v. General Motors Corp.*, 908 F.2d 675, 678 (10th Cir.1990). The Tenth Circuit affirmed the district court's findings but remanded for reconsideration of the appropriate amount of sanctions. *Id.* at 683. On remand, the district court reduced the amount of sanction to $50,000, *White v. General Motors Corp.*, 139 F.R.D. 178, 183 (Kan.1991), and the Tenth Circuit affirmed the sanction on appeal. *White v. General Motors Corp.*, 977 F.2d 499, 503 (10th Cir.1992).

Informant charges in Count I that the conduct for which Respondent was sanctioned in the *White* case also constitutes a violation of Rules 4–3.1, 4–3.2, 4–8.4(a), and 4–8.4(d) of the Missouri Rules.

Rule 4–3.1 forbids an attorney from bringing a proceeding or asserting an issue unless there is a non-frivolous basis for doing so. A claim "is not frivolous merely because the facts have not first been fully substantiated." Rule 4–3.1 (Comment). However, continuing to pursue a claim once it becomes apparent that there is no factual basis to support that claim is clearly contrary to the requirements of the rule. By pursuing White's slander claim even after it became apparent that there was no factual basis for that claim, Respondent violated Rule 4–3.1. ...

B. Count Two: Pope v. Federal Express Corporation

In *Pope v. Federal Express Corp.*, 138 F.R.D. 675 (W.D.Mo.1990), the court found that Respondent attempted to use a forged document to support the plaintiff's sexual harassment claim. [C] This document was a computer generated report on which a forged handwritten note had been added. The note read: "Carol, *you* "feel" good! Danny." [C] The court also found that Respondent continued to rely on this document as support for her client's claim long after she learned that the document was a forgery. [C] ... After rejecting Respondent's theory that the forged document was manufactured by some unknown person in an attempt to discredit her client, *Pope v. Federal Express Corp.*, 138 F.R.D. 684, 688–89 (W.D.Mo.1991), the court imposed monetary sanctions of $30,000. [C] ... Subsequently, the Eighth Circuit affirmed the district court's reduced sanction of $25,000 noting that Respondent "knowingly offered a falsified document into evidence." *Pope v. Federal Express Corp.*, 49 F.3d 1327, 1328 (8th Cir.1995).

Informant charges in Count II that Respondent has violated Rules 4–3.1, 4–3.2, 4–3.3(a)(4), 4–3.4(b), 4–8.4(a), 4–8.4(c), and 4–8.4(d) of the Missouri Rules.

This Court holds that Respondent violated Rule 4–3.1 by pursuing a claim that lacked a non-frivolous basis because she pursued her client's claim after it had become apparent that the claim was not well-founded in fact. ...

C. Count Three: Perkins v. General Motors Corporation

In *Perkins v. General Motors Corp.*, 129 F.R.D. 655 (W.D.Mo.1990), Respondent represented her client in bringing a Title VII claim against GM. [C] After the court had reached a final judgment on the underlying claim, the court considered defendant's motion for sanctions and found that Respondent had engaged in numerous acts of misconduct. [C] The following is a brief summary of the district court's findings in the *Perkins* case: 1. Respondent made unsupported allegations that a GM manager had been the subject of prior sexual harassment charges. [C] ... 2. Respondent made an affirmative misrepresentation regarding the date when she learned that a potential party's place of residence had changed. [C] ... 3. Respondent intentionally withheld the name of a senior GM manager who could potentially serve as a significant witness in her client's case. [C] ... 4. Respondent deliberately misrepresented her ability to connect the testimony of several witnesses to her client. [C] ... 5. Respondent filed a recusal motion that had no reasonable basis in fact or law. [C] The Eighth Circuit subsequently affirmed the district court's findings regarding all aspects of Respondent's misconduct. *Perkins v. General Motors Corp.*, 965 F.2d 597, 600–02 (8th Cir.1992).

As a result of this misconduct, Informant charges in Count III that Respondent has violated Rules 4–3.1, 4–3.2, 4–3.3(a)(1), 4–3.4(a), 4–3.4(d), 4–8.4(a), and 4–8.4(d) of the Missouri Rules.

This Court holds that Respondent violated Rule 4–3.1 by 1) alleging the misconduct of a GM manager when that allegation had no factual support and 2) filing a frivolous recusal motion that lacked any basis in fact or law. ...

D. Count Four: Platt v. Jack Cooper Transport

In *Platt v. Jack Cooper Transport, Co.*, 959 F.2d 91 (8th Cir.1992), the Eighth Circuit found that Respondent had previously filed a frivolous sanctions motion against opposing counsel in the trial court and was pursuing a frivolous appeal from the denial of that motion. [C] ... For this misconduct, the court imposed sanctions of $2500. [C]

Informant charges in this final Count that Respondent has violated Rules 4–3.1, 4–3.2, 4–8.4(a), and 4–8.4(d) of the Missouri Rules. We hold that Respondent violated Rule 4–3.1 by pursuing the sanction motion and appeal, which were proceedings for which she lacked a non-frivolous basis. ...

IV. THE SANCTION

... [T]he record in this case clearly establishes that Respondent intentionally submitted a false document, intentionally made false statements, and intentionally withheld material information. This misconduct is an affront to the fundamental and indispensable principle that a lawyer must proceed with absolute candor towards the tribunal. In the absence of that candor, the legal system cannot properly function. Unfortunately, Respondent has shown a consistent willingness to forego this duty of candor to the tribunal. ... Under these circumstances, the protection of the public and the maintenance of the integrity of the legal profession require the most severe sanction available.

This Court orders Gwen G. Caranchini disbarred. ...

INQUIRY

Determining Frivolousness. Was the court in the above case applying a subjective or objective standard as to whether the lawyer's contentions were frivolous? ABA Model Rule 3.1 does not refer to the lawyer's state of mind. Instead, it requires a basis in law and fact for each contention. Model Rule 3.1 thus imposes an objective standard for a lawyer's contentions, not a subjective standard. *See* Lawyer Disc. Bd. v. Neely, 528 S.E.2d 468 (W. Va. 1998). If a lawyer makes a frivolous argument because the lawyer is a fool rather than malicious, then the lawyer has still violated Model Rule 3.1. *See, e.g.,* Idaho State Bar v. Hawkley, 92 P.3d 1069 (Idaho 2002) (discipline whether the lawyer is naïve or malicious). Yet as the above case intimates, a lawyer's motive can affect how discipline officials will view a contention. A lawyer whose motives are pure, in the sense that the lawyer seeks solely to advance a client's just cause or defense, probably has greater leeway in making arguments that approach the line of frivolousness. At least, discipline cases under state versions of

Model Rule 3.1 often take note of lawyer motives. *See, e.g.,* State ex rel. Oklahoma Bar Assn. v. Bedford, 956 P.2d 148 (Okla. 1997) (frivolous claim to hinder just collection effort); In re Yao, 661 N.Y.S.2d 199 (N.Y. App. Div. 1997) (extortionate claims based on embarrassing a wealthy person). A suitably illustrative worst case is Attorney Grievance Commn. v. Culver, 849 A.2d 423 (Md. 2004), in which a lawyer who had a sexual affair with a current client whose divorce matter the lawyer bungled counterclaimed frivolously to oppress and dissuade her when she justly sued him for malpractice and unreasonable fees.

Reasonable Investigation. Model Rule 3.1 effectively imposes a duty to investigate law before contending. *See, e.g.,* Attorney Grievance Commn. v. Zdravkovich, 762 A.2d 950 (Md. 2000) (lawyer should read statute before purporting to rely on it); In re Richard, 986 P.2d 1117 (N.M. 1999) (lawyer should read case before purporting to rely on it). Model Rule 3.1 also imposes a duty to investigate facts before contending. *See, e.g,* In re Zohdy, 892 So.2d 1277 (La. 2005) (lawyer should confirm fact before alleging). On the other hand, when an allegation for which the lawyer had a reasonable basis later proves false, the lawyer is not subject to discipline. *See, e.g.,* Lawyer Disc. Bd. v. Neely, 528 S.E.2d 468 (W. Va. 1998). A lawyer may also need discovery to confirm or contradict an allegation for which there are reasonable initial inferences. *Id.* Discipline officials will also consider the time constraints within which a lawyer must work when not investigating allegations and instead relying on the client or another lawyer, so long as those constraints are genuine and the lawyer makes reasonable requests for time extensions. *See* OR. ETHICS OPIN. 2005-59 (2005). A lawyer may also reasonably rely on another lawyer whose competence is not in question. *See, e.g.,* In re Ruffin, 610 S.E.2d. 803 (S.C. 2005) (reasonable reliance on retained counsel). Consider an illustrative case of a lawyer's reasonable investigation.

Lawyer Disc. Bd. v. Neely,
West Virginia Supreme Court
528 S.E.2d 468 (1998)

PER CURIAM:[fn]

This disciplinary proceeding was instituted by the complainant, Office of Disciplinary Counsel [hereinafter "ODC"] of the West Virginia State Bar against Roger D. Hunter and Richard F. Neely, members of the Bar. Mr. Hunter and Mr. Neely were charged with violating Rule 3.1 of the West Virginia Rules of Professional Conduct. ...

I

The proceeding against Mr. Hunter and Mr. Neely involved their representation of Linda and Quewanncoii Stephens. Mr. and Mrs.

Stephens have a son, Quinton, who is autistic. In September 1990, when Quinton was approximately nine months old, he was enrolled in the Fort Hill Child Development Center [hereinafter Center].

On December 2, 1994, Mrs. Stephens received a phone call from a staff member at the Center asking her to pick up Quinton because the day care employee who was responsible for his supervision was not at work, and Quinton was disrupting the other children during nap time. When Mrs. Stephens arrived at the Center, she found Quinton alone in the director's office strapped to a posture correcting chair, which she had provided, with his hands and face covered with partly-dried fecal material. According to Mrs. Stephens, the room was dark and the blinds were drawn. The employee who had been watching Quinton claimed that she left him alone for about ninety seconds to get a change of diaper for him. Mrs. Stephens immediately removed Quinton from the Center, and shortly thereafter, she and her husband consulted with Mr. Hunter... .

Subsequently, Mr. Hunter ... became a partner of Neely & Hunter. Mr. Hunter took the Stephens' case with him, and Mr. Neely took the lead in preparing the pleadings and handling of the case. On June 12, 1995, Mr. Neely filed a civil action in the name of Linda, Quewanncoii, and Quinton Stephens against the Center and Ms. Hawks.

The complaint alleged that Mr. and Mrs. Stephens and Quinton had suffered intentional infliction of emotional distress based upon the outrageous conduct of the defendants and that Quinton had suffered damages from an intentional battery on December 2, 1994. The complaint further alleged that as a result of interviews with persons associated with the Center, the plaintiffs believed that the December 2, 1994 incident was "but one of many instances in which an autistic child ... was strapped to a chair in a dark room for many hours and left alone as a result of his mental and physical handicap." ...

Thereafter, Mr. Hunter submitted answers to interrogatories on behalf of the plaintiffs listing the names of several individuals who served as the basis for the allegation that Quinton had in many instances been left alone in a dark room for many hours. However, none of the individuals testified to such incidents during discovery.

On December 11, 1995, the defendants moved for summary judgment. The court dismissed Mr. and Mrs. Stephens causes of action for intentional infliction of emotional distress. The court also dismissed Quinton's claim for intentional infliction of emotional distress for the "many instances" in which he was allegedly strapped in a chair in a dark room for many hours. This claim was dismissed because the only evidence plaintiffs produced during discovery was the testimony of Mary Ellen Davis, Quinton's special education teacher, that one day she found Quinton in the chair in his classroom when all the other children were up and about in the same room. ... Only Quinton's claim for intentional infliction of emotional distress was permitted to go forward.

Subsequently, the plaintiffs requested a voluntary dismissal of the remaining claim in order to appeal the summary judgment order. The defendants then filed a motion for sanctions under Rule 11 of the West Virginia Rules of Civil Procedure.[fn] Thereafter, the parties reached an agreement whereby the plaintiffs agreed to dismiss the appeal and all claims with prejudice in return for the defendants dismissing the Rule 11 motion and agreeing not to seek attorney sanctions against either Mr. Hunter or Mr. Neely.

On March 17, 1997, the Investigative Panel of the Board filed a Statement of Charges in this matter. ... Mr. Neely and Mr. Hunter were both charged with violating Rule 3.1[fn] in that the complaint filed by Mr. Neely asserted emotional distress counts on behalf of Linda and Quewanncoii Stephens, a count of intentional battery on behalf of Quinton Stephens, and a count of emotional distress based on many alleged instances where Quinton had been left alone in a dark room for many hours.

On October 10, 1997, the Hearing Panel Subcommittee issued a report, which ... by majority vote, found a violation of Rule 3.1 by both Mr. Hunter and Mr. Neely. The Board recommended admonishment. ...

II

... In this proceeding, the Board found a violation of Rule 3.1 based solely on the allegations set forth in paragraph VII of the complaint.[fn] The Board concluded that a reasonable attorney should have known that the allegations set forth in paragraph VII were unwarranted and that Mr. Hunter and Mr. Neely knew they were without basis. In reaching this decision, the Board recognized that the entire lawsuit was not baseless or frivolous because Quinton Stephens' intentional tort claim survived the motion for summary judgment. In effect, the Board seeks to admonish Mr. Hunter and Mr. Neely for factual assertions set forth in a single paragraph of a complaint that later proved to be false.

This case illustrates the difficulties in determining what is a frivolous lawsuit. ...

With the adoption of the Rules of Professional Conduct, and more specifically Rule 3.1, an objective standard was established to determine the propriety of pleadings and other court papers.[fn] Nonetheless, the term "frivolous," now a part of the rule, remains undefined. However, the Comment to the rule is instructive regarding what conduct is permissible and what constitutes frivolousness. The Comment provides, in pertinent part:

The filing of an action ... is not frivolous merely because the facts have not first been fully substantiated or because the lawyer expects to develop vital evidence only by discovery.   Such action is not frivolous even though the lawyer believes that the client's position ultimately will not prevail.   The action is frivolous, however, if the client desires to have the action taken primarily for the purpose of harassing or maliciously injuring a person or if the lawyer is unable either to make a good faith argument on the merits of the action taken or to support the action taken by a good faith argument for an extension, modification or reversal of existing law.

It is obvious that the drafters of the rules acknowledged that when lawyers prepare and file pleadings in civil actions, they routinely make factual allegations in support of their theories of liability and assert defenses in response thereto, some of which ultimately prove to be unsubstantiated.   The Comment suggests that these practices do not warrant discipline under Rule 3.1. ...

While we remain concerned about the increasing number of cases that clog our court dockets, we recognize that there are instances where an attorney has exhausted all avenues of pre-suit investigation and needs the tools of discovery to complete factual development of the case.   An action or claim is not frivolous if after a reasonable investigation, all the facts have not been first substantiated.   A complaint may be filed if evidence is expected to be developed by discovery.   A lawyer may not normally be sanctioned for alleging facts in a complaint that are later determined to be untrue.

As previously discussed, the specific allegations in paragraph VII of the Stephens' complaint were not ultimately supported by the facts developed during discovery.   Nonetheless, the record indicates that Mr. Hunter and Mr. Neely conducted a reasonable investigation of the case. Because of his autism, Quinton was unable to provide any information about his care at the Center.   However, Mrs. Stephens provided the details of what happened on December 2, 1994.   In addition, she related at least three other incidents which suggested that the Center may not have been rendering adequate supervision of Quinton.[fn] Mrs. Stephens also told Mr. Neely about conversations she had with some of the employees at the Center which caused her to believe that Quinton's posture correcting chair had been used for discipline or management purposes against her specific directions.[fn]   The record indicates that Mr. Hunter and Mr. Neely received no cooperation from the defendants during their investigation.   In the end, they were left with the choice of advising the Stephenses to give up or file the complaint and proceed with discovery.   Given these circumstances, we find that Mr. Hunter and Mr. Neely did not violate Rule 3.1

Accordingly, based on all of the above, the complaint filed against Mr. Hunter and Mr. Neely is dismissed.

Charges dismissed.

INQUIRY

Extending, Modifying, or Reversing Law. Although Model Rule 3.1 applies an objective standard to determine a contention's frivolousness, a lawyer's good faith is clearly relevant when the lawyer argues for a change in law. Why does Model Rule 3.1 add that a meritorious contention includes a good faith argument to extend, modify, or reverse law? Is that additional statement an exception to Model Rule 3.1's requirement that contentions must have merit? Practitioners do not treat arguments to extend, modify, or reverse law as an opportunity to make frivolous arguments. To the contrary, Model Rule 3.1 makes clear that a meritorious contention *includes* one made in good faith to extend, modify, or reverse law. Law changes by the good faith arguments of lawyers. Model Rule 3.1 permits lawyers to argue for law change when there are reasonable grounds for it. What does this liberty mean practically? If every time that a lawyer needed to argue in good faith for a change in law the lawyer had to worry about misconduct allegations, then law practice would be significantly more constrained and hazardous. Practitioners instead seldom give serious thought to misconduct allegations when arguing in good faith that the law should change to meet the demands of justice. Frivolous contentions do not include arguments that the law should change to satisfy justice in changing circumstances. Consider now a contention that the court found to have crossed the line.

Smith v. Commonwealth,
Pennsylvania Supreme Court
574 A.2d 558 (1990)

NIX, Chief Justice.

This appeal, one of six such appeals consolidated for our review, asks that we consider the propriety of an order of the Commonwealth Court assessing attorney's fees and costs against appointed counsel for prosecuting what the court determined to be a frivolous appeal. ...

On January 25, 1985, appellant Pernell Smith was convicted of robbery and sentenced to a term of imprisonment... . He was paroled on October 3, 1986, subject to the special condition that he maintain employment once obtained. Subsequently, the Board of Probation and Parole *503 ("Board") discovered that he had failed to report to work, and appellant was arrested for a technical violation of the special condition of his probation. Appellant waived his right to counsel and to a full Board hearing and admitted to the technical violation. His arguments that he wanted a better paying job were rejected, and appellant was recommitted... . After receiving notice of his recommitment, appellant requested and was appointed counsel from the Lancaster County Public Defender's Office. He filed a Petition for Administrative Relief, which was denied. He then filed a Petition for Review with the Commonwealth Court. The court determined appellant's appeal to be frivolous because the court had repeatedly held that it would not review the discretionary recommitment when the recommitment period is within the presumptive range. On that basis, the Commonwealth Court granted the Board's petition for attorney's fees... .

Here the Board's action was the recommitment of appellant to prison after a determination that he was a technical parole violator. This determination was based upon a finding that he had violated Special Condition No. 6 of his parole, maintaining employment once secured. Appellant does not challenge the Board's action as being a violation of his constitutional rights or the law, nor does he dispute that he failed to maintain employment. Rather, his allegations are premised upon the belief that the Board did not give adequate consideration to the evidence he presented as a mitigating circumstance. We affirm that this aspect of the recommitment order is not appealable. ...

Generally, an appeal which is determined to lack any basis in law or fact is considered to be frivolous. *McCoy v. Court of Appeals,* 486 U.S. 429[] (1988). An appeal is not frivolous merely because it lacks merit. *Commonwealth v. Greer,* 455 Pa. 106, 314 A.2d 513 (1974). ...

The concept of frivolity should not be construed as disfavoring legitimate attempts to change existing law. Even where long-standing case law on a particular point is contrary to an appellant's point of view, there may be a reasonable basis for arguing for the re-evaluation of that law. [C] In this context a distinction must be made as to situations where the repetitive appeal is being sought to perpetuate a concededly discredited position.

Here, appellant insists that his appeal to the Commonwealth Court was not frivolous because this Court has never considered the merits of the issue raised herein. Certainly, where an issue has not been addressed in this Court, its introduction in a lower court for the purpose of bringing it before this Court is not necessarily frivolous, even though the lower tribunal may have established a firm policy to the contrary. [C] However, where such an approach is followed, it must be supported by a reasonble belief that this Court will be persuaded to change that existing policy. In view of the statutory and policy reasons for the Commonwealth Court's standard of review in this area, appellant's counsel could not legitimately argue that he held such a belief. ...

We now hold that despite the constitutional right to counsel in an appeal from a criminal conviction, costs and attorney's fees may be assessed against court-appointed appellate counsel for the filing of a frivolous appeal.

Both the federal and state constitutions guarantee an indigent the right to have counsel appointed for the purpose of appealing a criminal conviction. *McCoy v. Court of Appeals, supra; Bronson v. Pennsylvania Board of Probation and Parole,* 491 Pa. 549, 421 A.2d 1021 (1980), *cert. denied,* 450 U.S. 1050[] (1981). This right guarantees the opportunity to assert a legitimate basis for challenging the ruling of a lower court. *See McCoy, supra.* The right does not justify the assertion of patently frivolous claims, or give counsel license to engage in dilatory, obdurate, or vexatious conduct. As stated in *McCoy, supra:* "*A lawyer,* after all, *has* no duty, *indeed no right, to pester a court with frivolous arguments,* which is to say arguments that cannot conceivably persuade the court, so if he believes in good faith that there are no other arguments that he can make on his client's behalf he is honorbound [sic] to so advise the court and seek leave to withdraw as counsel. *United States v. Edwards,* 777 F.2d 364, 365 (7th Cir.1985)." 486 U.S. at 436[]. ... This Court has concluded that the proper procedure, once counsel has determined that no basis exists for the assertion of a legitimate claim has been set forth in *Anders v. California,* [386 U.S. 738, 744 (1967)]:

> ... [I]f counsel finds his case to be wholly frivolous, after a conscientious examination of it, he should so advise the court and request permission to withdraw. That request must, however, be accompanied by a brief referring to anything in the record that might arguably support the appeal. A copy of counsel's brief should be furnished the indigent and time allowed him to raise any points that he chooses; the court—not counsel—then proceeds, after a full examination of all the proceedings, to decide whether the case is wholly frivolous. If it so finds it may grant counsel's request to withdraw and dismiss the appeal insofar as federal requirements are concerned, or proceed to a decision on the merits, if state law so requires. On the other hand, if it finds any of the legal points arguable on their merits (and therefore not frivolous) it must, prior to decision, afford the indigent the assistance of counsel to argue the appeal. (Footnote omitted.)

The Board correctly highlights the distinction between offering an argument presented with an acknowledgement of its frivolousness and the same argument endorsed by counsel as being worthy of review. By filing an *Anders* brief, a lawyer does not advocate arguments he believes are "wholly frivolous"; rather, he presents them for the court's confirmation of his belief. Counsel serves the interests of both the client and the court by diligently investigating the possible grounds for appeal and advising the court of his decision that no legitimate grounds exist. *McCoy, supra,* at 436[]; *Ellis v. United States,* 356 U.S. 674, 675[] (1958). Pursuing a concededly frivolous argument engages the attorney in conduct which is deliberately designed to mislead the tribunal. *Polk County v. Dodson,* 454 U.S. 312, 323[] (1981).

Accordingly, the order of the Commonwealth Court is affirmed.

INQUIRY

Client Directives. What must a lawyer do if a client instructs the lawyer to make a frivolous contention, insisting that the lawyer do so? ABA Model Rule 1.2(a) requires a lawyer to abide by a client's decision on objectives and to consult as to the means the lawyer will use to achieve the objective. To contend frivolously is a means, not an objective, and a poor means at that. Model Rule 3.1 works together with Model Rule 1.2(a) to ensure that lawyers not use frivolous contentions to attempt to advance client objectives, even if the client insists. ABA Model Rule 1.16(a)(1) requires a lawyer to terminate and withdraw from the representation if continuing the representation will result in violation of the Model Rules. Lawyers have every right, rule, and reason to resist client directives to make frivolous contentions, and the duty to do so. *See* VA. ETHICS OPIN. 1530 (1993).

Biography

Sandra Day O'Connor was the first female to serve on the United States Supreme Court, appointed by President Ronald Reagan in 1981. Justice O'Connor faced many challenges getting there. The Arizona ranch on which her parents raised her had no running water or electricity until she was seven years old, she had no siblings until age eight, and the nearest neighbors lived 25 miles away. So she learned to drive at age seven and mastered shooting firearms and riding horses by age eight. Having learned hard work and self-reliance from an early age, Justice O'Connor would later take only two years to earn her law degree, graduating 3rd out of a class of 102—just behind Chief Justice William H. Rehnquist. Despite proven intellectual ability, Justice O'Connor found that no law firm in California wanted to hire her and only one offered her a position as a legal secretary. So Justice O'Connor persevered, taking positions in public service and opening her own law firm, eventually building a career that took her to the United States Supreme Court. Respect Justice O'Connor for her hard work, perseverance, and faith charting her own path. She is a shining example of the principles that the Founding Fathers celebrated in the Declaration of Independent and enshrined in the Constitution. They would not be surprised at the freedoms and opportunities Justice O'Connor and others have found to reach their greatest potential.

Defending Criminal Cases. Notice Model Rule 3.1's explanation regarding when a lawyer defends a criminal proceeding or other proceeding that could result in the client's incarceration. Why does it permit a lawyer to defend those proceedings by requiring the prosecutor to establish every element? Would it be a frivolous defense to make a prosecutor prove what the defendant knows to be true? The 14th Amendment's due-process clause requires states to prove each element of a criminal charge. *See* Patterson v. New York, 432 U.S. 197 (1977). The Constitution also guarantees a privilege against self-incrimination and effective assistance of counsel in criminal proceedings. Those guarantees would not be worth much if it were misconduct for the lawyer defending a criminal charge to make the prosecutor prove each element. If it were not for Model Rule 3.1's explanation, a criminal-defense lawyer might in effect have to admit the charge or elements of the charge, effectively undermining the defendant client's Fifth Amendment privilege against self-incrimination. Instead, a lawyer may file court papers and make arguments that require the court to ensure that the prosecution has established each element of the charged crime, so long as the lawyer does not affirmatively make frivolous arguments. *See* Smith v. Robbins, 528 U.S. 259 (2000). Notice again that Model Rule 3.1's explanation extends not only to the defense of criminal charges but also to the defense of proceedings that may result in the client's incarceration such as contempt or special administrative proceedings.

B. Expediting Litigation

Dilatory Actions to Impede. Just as integrity requires that a lawyer make only meritorious contentions considering the deeper value or worth of a proceeding in advancing a just claim or defense, integrity also requires that the lawyer expedite proceedings. It is not simply that a lawyer must initiate and defend proceedings only on meritorious contentions, as ABA Model Rule 3.1 requires. ABA Model Rule 3.2 then requires that the lawyer pursue the litigation on a timetable that advances it toward its just end. Lawyers could use frivolous claims and defenses to impede justice, although in doing so they would violate Model Rule 3.1. Yet lawyers could also employ deliberate procedures to frustrate *just* (rather than frivolous) claims or defenses, to impede and delay others from the justice that the claims and defenses represent. Doing so would violate Model Rule 3.2 requiring expeditious resolution. When lawyers use permissible litigation procedures not for the ends those procedures warrant but to impede and delay others in concluding the proceeding, they violate the duty Model Rule 3.2 imposes to expedite litigation. Consider an identical state version of Model Rule 3.2 followed by an illustrative case.

> **MISSISSIPPI R. PROF. CONDUCT 3.2: Expediting Litigation.**
> A lawyer shall make reasonable efforts to expedite litigation consistent with the interests of the courts.

Columbus Bar Assn. v. Finneran,
Ohio Supreme Court
687 N.E. 2d 405(1997)

Per Curiam. Attorneys must use the tools of our legal system as they were intended. Our Ethical Considerations expressed in EC 7-1 state that "[t]he duty of a lawyer, both to his client and to the legal system, is to represent his client zealously *within the bounds of the law.*" (Emphasis added.) Therefore, while the advocate has a duty to use legal procedure to benefit the client's cause, the advocate also has a duty not to abuse legal procedure. The law, both procedural and substantive, establishes the limits within which an advocate may proceed. We conclude from the facts in this case that respondent has abused the tools of the system to the detriment of both his clients and our system of justice. ...

The transcripts of hearings in the various cases before the common pleas court attached to the motion for default make clear that respondent repeatedly failed to respond to the discovery requests of his opponents. When a case for which respondent was responsible was about to be dismissed for failure to respond to discovery requests, respondent's practice was to voluntarily dismiss the case under Civ.R. 41 and then refile the same action within a year. Respondent would repeat this process several times for each matter. When asked at a hearing in common pleas court why he did not respond to discovery, respondent provided rambling answers about the magnitude of his caseload, the difficulty he had in contacting clients, the fact that his paralegal had been "hired away" or injured, and, significantly, the small amount offered by the defendant to settle the case. Thus it appears that after respondent filed a case, he would undertake no further action until confronted by the possibility of dismissal with prejudice for failure to respond to the defendant's discovery requests. Then respondent would keep the cause of action alive by the stratagem of voluntary dismissal and serial refiling, all in the hopes of obtaining an acceptable settlement offer. In short, respondent consistently employed tactics of evasion and delay, a strategy out of keeping with the purpose and intent of our system of orderly procedures.

We conclude that the tactics employed by respondent to circumvent discovery, in several instances for more than five years, were prejudicial to the administration of justice and a violation of DR 1-102(A)(5).

One of the goals of our legal system is the prompt resolution of disputes. Our Civil Rules are designed to achieve this result. Civ.R. 1(B) states that "[t]hese rules shall be construed and applied to effect just results by eliminating delay, unnecessary expense and all other impediments to the expeditious administration of justice." Civ.R. 11 states, "The signature of an attorney * * * constitutes a certificate * * * that * * * [the document] is not interposed for delay."

DR 7-102(A)(1) provides that a lawyer shall not "conduct a defense, delay a trial, or take other action on behalf of his client * * * when it is obvious that such action would serve merely to harass or maliciously injure another." Dilatory practices bring the administration of justice into disrepute. As the American Bar Association stated in its Comment to Rule 3.2 of its Model Rules of Professional Conduct, "Delay should not be indulged merely for the convenience of the advocates, or for the purpose of frustrating an opposing party's attempt to obtain rightful redress or repose." [C] Engaging, as respondent did, in a procedure or tactic that had no substantial purpose other than delay constituted representation outside the bounds of the spirit and intent of our law. We conclude that the tactic of delay employed by respondent violated DR 7-102(A)(1). ...

We hereby indefinitely suspend respondent from the practice of law in Ohio. Costs taxed to respondent.

Judgment accordingly.

INQUIRY

Causes and Motives for Delay. The above *Finneran* case suggests a few of the case-management causes for delay and improper motives that lawyers may have for delay. Lawyers can avoid or remedy some of the causes with practice management including monitoring caseloads, practicing within fields of competence, and ensuring adequate staffing. The motives tend to be more nefarious. Authorities have cited gamesmanship, Collins v. CSX Transp., 441 S.E.2d 150 (N.C. 1994), helping a client postpone paying a just claim, N.C. ETHICS OPIN. 2003-1 (2003), and even hoping for a change in the law during the delay, In re Boone, 7 P.3d 270 (Kan. 2000).

Types of Delay. Lawyers can violate Model Rule 3.2 either intentionally or unintentionally in a variety of ways. Dilatory tactics may involve taking a client's retainer fee but doing nothing, *see, e.g.,* Carter v. Mississippi Bar, 654 So.2d 505 (Miss. 1995), leading clients to believe that the lawyer had filed cases that the lawyer had not filed, *see, e.g.,* In re Mozingo, 497 S.E.2d 729 (S.C. 1998), drafting but not filing a complaint when the lawyer should file it, *see, e.g.,* Attorney Grievance Commn. v. Rose, 892 A.2d 469 (Md. 2006) (delay in filing divorce action), not serving a case once filed, *id.*, not correcting an inaccurate pleading, *see, e.g.,* Attorney Grievance Commn. v. Wallace, 793 A.2d 535 (Md. 2002), failing to advance a case once filed and served, *see, e.g.,* In re Tweedly, 20 P.3d 1245 (Kan. 2001), failing to comply with discovery requests, *see, e.g.,* In re Graham, 503 N.W.2d 476 (Minn. 1993), failing to respond to a court's docket call, *see, e.g.,* In re Kight, 685 N.E.2d 472 (Ind. 1997), failing to meet the court's scheduling order, *see, e.g.,* In re White, 699 So.2d 375 (La. 1997), failing to appear in court on the noticed date, *see, e.g.,* In re Mitchell, 946 P.2d 999 (Kan. 1997), sending unprepared associates in the lawyer's place, *see, e.g.,* In re Zeitler, 866 A.2d 171 (N.J. 2005), failing to prepare and file court orders once obtained, *see, e.g.,* In re Romero, 690 N.E.2d 707 (Ind. 1998), refusing to obey court orders, *see, e.g.,* In re Ring, 692 N.E.2d 35 (Mass. 1998), and failing to seek anticipated post-petition relief, *see, e.g.,* In re Cherry, 715 N.E.2d 382 (Ind. 1999). These examples show you more clearly how expediting litigation relates to integrity.

C. The Tribunal's Decorum

Improper Influence and Communications. The previous chapter addressed a lawyer's duty under ABA Model Rule 3.3 to be truthful toward a tribunal. The distinction shown above between simply being honest in one's statements or going further to make only meritorious contentions, applies equally to being merely honest in court or going further to support the court's appropriate impartiality and decorum, as ABA Model Rule 3.5 requires. Do not think of Model Rule 3.5's mandate to support the court's decorum as quaint or anachronistic. The impartiality and decoum that Model Rule 3.5 requires take several specific and robust forms. Model Rule 3.5 prohibits lawyers from seeking to influence unduly judges, jurors, prospective jurors, or other officials by means prohibited by law. Rule 3.5 specifically prohibits lawyers from seeking to communicate secretly with judges and jurors without authorization during a proceeding, or communicate with jurors after discharge when the court or law prohibits communication or the juror desires not to communicate, or in a way that misleads the juror. Federal and state statutes also make interfering with judges and jurors a crime. *See, e.g.,* 18 U.S.C. §1503 (crime to intimidate by threat of force); 18 U.S.C. §1504 (crime to influence juror in writing). Rule 3.5 also has a catch-all provision prohibiting conduct that disrupts a tribunal. Consider an identical state version of Model Rule 3.5 followed by two convincing cases illustrating different ways in which lawyers can improperly inhibit tribunal decorum.

> **WASHINGTON R. PROF. CONDUCT 3.5: Impartiality and Decorum of the Tribunal.**
> A lawyer shall not:
> (a) seek to influence a judge, juror, prospective juror or other official by means prohibited by law;
> (b) communicate ex parte with such a person during the proceeding unless authorized to do so by law or court order;
> (c) communicate with a juror or prospective juror after discharge of the jury if:
> (1) the communication is prohibited by law or court order;
> (2) the juror has made known to the lawyer a desire not to communicate; or
> (3) the communication involves misrepresentation, coercion, duress or harassment; or
> (d) engage in conduct intended to disrupt a tribunal.

United States v. Thoreen,
United States Court of Appeals for the Ninth Circuit
653 F.2d 1332 (1981)

EUGENE A. WRIGHT, Circuit Judge:
I. INTRODUCTION

The issue before us is whether an attorney may be found in criminal contempt for pursuing a course of aggressive advocacy while representing his client in a criminal proceeding such that, without the court's permission or knowledge, he substitutes someone for his client at counsel table with the intent to cause a misidentification, resulting in the misleading of the court, counsel, and witnesses; a delay while the government reopened its case to identify the defendant; and violation of a court order and custom.

We affirm the district court's finding of criminal contempt. ...

II. FACTS

By February 1980, Thoreen, an attorney, had practiced law for almost five years.

In February 1980, he represented Sibbett, a commercial fisher, during Sibbett's non-jury trial before Judge Tanner for criminal contempt for three violations of a preliminary injunction against salmon fishing.[fn]   In preparing for trial, Thoreen hoped that the government agent who had cited Sibbett could not identify him. He decided to test the witness's identification.

He placed next to him at counsel table Clark Mason, who resembled Sibbett and had Mason dressed in outdoor clothing denims, heavy shoes, a plaid shirt, and a jacket-vest.

Sibbett wore a business suit, large round glasses, and sat behind the rail in a row normally reserved for the press.

Thoreen neither asked the court's permission for, nor notified it or government counsel of, the substitution.

On Thoreen's motion at the start of the trial, the court ordered all witnesses excluded from the courtroom. Mason remained at counsel table.

Throughout the trial, Thoreen made and allowed to go uncorrected numerous misrepresentations. He gestured to Mason as though he was his client and gave Mason a yellow legal pad on which to take notes. The two conferred. Thoreen did not correct the court when it expressly referred to Mason as the defendant and caused the record to show identification of Mason as Sibbett.

Because of the conduct, two government witnesses misidentified Mason as Sibbett. Following the government's case, Thoreen called Mason as a witness and disclosed the substitution. The court then called a recess.

When the trial resumed, the government reopened and recalled the government agent who had cited Sibbett for two of the violations. He identified Sibbett, who was convicted of all three violations.

On February 20, 1980, Thoreen was ordered to appear on February 27 and show cause why he should not be held in criminal contempt. At the hearing, Judge Tanner found him in criminal contempt. ...

III. DISCUSSION ...

B. CONTEMPT

Judge Tanner found Thoreen in criminal contempt for the substitution because it was imposed on the court and counsel without permission or prior knowledge; the claimed identification issue did not exist; it disrupted the trial; it deceived the court and frustrated its responsibility to administer justice; and it violated a court custom. He found Mason's presence in the courtroom after giving the order excluding witnesses another ground for contempt because Thoreen planned that Mason would testify when the misidentification occurred. Judge Tanner held also that Thoreen's conduct conflicted with DR 1-102(A)(4)[(against engaging in deceit)], DR 7-102(A)(6)[(against presenting false evidence)], and DR 7-106(C)(5)[(failing to comply with local customs)] of the Washington Code of Professional Responsibility.

Thoreen's principal defense is that his conduct was a good faith tactic in aid of cross-examination and falls within the protected realm of zealous advocacy. He argues that as defense counsel he has no obligation to ascertain or present the truth and may seek to confuse witnesses with misleading questions, gestures, or appearances. [C] ...

1. Zealous Advocacy

While we agree that defense counsel should represent his client vigorously, regardless of counsel's view of guilt or innocence, [cc], we conclude that Thoreen's conduct falls outside this protected behavior.

Vigorous advocacy by defense counsel may properly entail impeaching or confusing a witness, even if counsel thinks the witness is truthful, and refraining from presenting evidence even if he knows the truth. [C] When we review this conduct and find that the line between vigorous advocacy and actual obstruction is close, our doubts should be resolved in favor of the former. [C]

The latitude allowed an attorney is not unlimited. He must represent his client within the bounds of the law. [Cc] As an officer of the court, he must "preserve and promote the efficient operation of our system of justice." Chapman v. Pacific Tel. & Tel., 613 F.2d 193, 197 (9th Cir.1979).

Thoreen's view of appropriate cross-examination, which encompasses his substitution, crossed over the line from zealous advocacy to actual obstruction because, as we discuss later, it impeded the court's search for truth, resulted in delays, and violated a court custom and rule. Moreover, this conduct harms rather than enhances an attorney's effectiveness as an advocate.

It is fundamental that in relations with the court, defense counsel must be scrupulously candid and truthful in representations of any matter before the court. This is not only a basic ethical requirement, but it is essential if the lawyer is to be effective in the role of advocate, for if the lawyer's reputation for veracity is suspect, he or she will lack the confidence of the court when it is needed most to serve the client.
...

Substituting a person for the defendant in a criminal case without a court's knowledge has been noted as an example of unethical behavior by the ABA Committee on Professional Ethics. See Informal Opinion No. 914, 2/24/66 (decided under the former ABA Code of Professional Responsibility).

Ethical standards establish the outermost limits of appropriate and sanctioned attorney conduct. While we acknowledge that a court's power to discipline or disbar an attorney "'proceeds upon very different grounds' from those which support a court's power to punish for contempt," Cammer v. United States, 350 U.S. 399, 408 n.7[] (1956) (quoting Ex Parte Robinson, 86 U.S. 505[]), we consider and apply ethical benchmarks when determining whether an attorney's conduct is inappropriate to his role and thus constitutes contumacious misbehavior. ...

The record supports Judge Tanner's conclusion that Thoreen's substitution was misbehavior that obstructed justice. It was inappropriate because it was done without consent, and violated a court custom to allow only counsel, parties, and others having the court's permission to sit forward of the rail. This conduct is deemed unprofessional and may subject an attorney to disciplinary measures in Washington. [C]

Thoreen's argument that he may not be held in contempt for violating the custom and practice because he lacked notice of it is unpersuasive. ... [A] contemnor need not have specific warning or be aware that his acts may subject him to criminal sanctions as opposed to other penalties. [C] Certain conduct is inherently inappropriate and self-noticing. [C]

In federal and state courts of general jurisdiction, only attorneys and parties customarily sit at counsel table. Others do so only with the court's permission.

Thoreen's years in practice included trial and pretrial experience in Judge Tanner's court and presumably in other courts. Viewing the evidence in the light most favorable to the government, we cannot accept Thoreen's contention that he was unaware of this widespread custom.

His violation of the order to exclude witnesses by keeping Mason at counsel table is both a second example of misbehavior and independent grounds for contempt... .

Thoreen admits he planned and intended the substitution, but defends by asserting that (1) it was a good faith effort to prove misidentification and attack the credibility of the government witnesses; (2) he never intended to misrepresent any facts to the court or to obstruct justice; and (3) he believed the court knew Sibbett's identity from the pretrial hearing.

The record shows that Sibbett's identification was not an issue, contradicting the need to attack credibility. The testimony about Sibbett's violations was thorough, credible, and not in conflict.

Thoreen's alleged belief that the court would remember Sibbett from a pretrial proceeding is unrealistic because that hearing took place several months earlier and Sibbett was but one of many persons cited for violating the salmon fishing injunction.

His alleged lack of intent to deceive the court or to obstruct justice is irrelevant. [The contempt statute] does not require specific intent. It suffices that he should have been aware that his conduct exceeded reasonable limits and hindered the search for truth.

CONCLUSION

Thoreen's error in judgment was unfortunate. The court's ire and this criminal contempt conviction could have been avoided easily and the admirable goal of representing his client zealously preserved if only he had given the court and opposing counsel prior notice and sought the court's consent.[FN7. While finding Thoreen's tactic misleading and obstructive of justice, we acknowledge that certain variations are acceptable. If identification is at issue, an attorney could test a witness's credibility by notifying the court and counsel that it is and by seeking the court's permission to (1) seat two or more persons at counsel table without identifying the defendant; [C]; (2) have no one at counsel table; (3) hold an in-court lineup.]

Nonetheless, viewing the evidence in the light most favorable to the government, we find that there is sufficient evidence to find beyond a reasonable doubt that Thoreen violated 18 U.S.C. §401(1) and (3). [C] The district court's findings were not clearly erroneous. [C] We AFFIRM the contempt conviction. ...

In the Matter of Abbott,
Delaware Supreme Court
925 A.2d 482 (2007)

PER CURIAM:

This is an attorney discipline matter involving charges of professional misconduct against Richard L. Abbott... . This matter originates from the arguments set forth in the opening and reply briefs filed by Mr. Abbott in an appeal to the Superior Court from a decision of the New Castle County Board of License, Inspection & Review ("LIRB"). The petition ... alleges that in those briefs, the Respondent's "written advocacy [was] undignified, discourteous, and degrading to the tribunal, as well as prejudicial to the administration of justice." ...

We have determined that the Respondent's behavior violates both Rules 3.5(d) and 8.4(d) of the Rules of Professional Conduct and goes beyond being *merely* unprofessional. ...

Respondent's Conduct

... [T]he ODC identifies the following statements contained in the Respondent's opening and reply briefs:

- A *fictionalized* account of the hearing written by lawyers.
- Miraculously, with the aid of legal counsel's imaginative and creative writing skills, the supposed reasoning for the LIRB's decision became dramatically more extensive and well-reasoned.
- *Fictional* account of the LIRB hearing prepared weeks later.
- The written decision creates an *imaginary, make-believe* set of reasons for the LIRB's findings.
- The County cites no legal authority to support its assertion that the LIRB's attorney may *fabricate conclusions* of the LIRB in the written decision.
- Certainly the County does not believe that the LIRB's attorney truly has the authority to *write decisions from whole cloth.*
- *Laughably,* the County found that the violation was not resolved based on an *illogical and irrational dissertation.*
- Why would the County want to start making decisions on the merits when it could continue to run 395 into the ground for *sport* based on whatever *whimsical speculation* the County could conjure up?
- The County's argument ... constitutes *pure sophistry.*
- "The County's own answering brief provides the legal authority to quickly dispense with this *ridiculous argument.*"
- Never one to miss an opportunity to deny a party the right to a fair and impartial hearing on the merits.
- Otherwise the County would be permitted to *appoint a group of monkeys* to the LIRB, and simply *allow the attorney to interpret the grunts and groans of the ape members and reach whatever conclusion the attorney wished* from the documents of record.
- [T]he ... Code cannot be *magically transmuted.*

Third, ODC alleges that the Respondent improperly implied that the Superior Court might rule on a basis other than the merits of the case. In support of this allegation, the ODC relies upon the following passage in the Respondent's reply brief: "This is a typical tactic used by the County, in an effort to prejudice the Court against [respondent's client] based on the hope that the Court will decide the matter based upon any potential bias or prejudice that it may have against [the client's representative], rather than on merits."

Accusations Against Counsel/Inflammatory Characterizations

... In this case, we conclude that the Respondent's written statements in his briefs filed with the Superior Court ... violate Rule 3.5(d). First, the Respondent directly accused a fellow member of the Bar of fabricating the basis of the LIRB's decision. Second, the Respondent engaged in "discourteous conduct that is degrading to a tribunal."

Judicial Bias Allegation

The Respondent's briefs also suggested that the Superior Court might rule on a basis other than the merits of the case. We hold that those "unfounded accusations impugning the integrity" of the tribunal violated Rule 3.5(d). ...

Delaware Attorney's Oath

The Respondent, like so many before him and so many since, took the following oath upon his admission to the Delaware Bar in 1989: "I, ..., do solemnly swear that I will support the Constitution of the United States and the Constitution of the State of Delaware; that I will behave myself in the office of an Attorney within the Courts according to the best of my learning and ability and with all good fidelity as well to the Court as to the client; that I will use no falsehood nor delay any person's cause through lucre or malice."

This oath is, in its essential language, the same one taken by Delaware lawyers since colonial days. ...

Thus, the ideal that a Delaware lawyer will "behave ... in the office of an Attorney" is a first principle of the Delaware Bar that dates back a hundred years before the Revolutionary War. Today, that principle remains a fundamental tenet of the American legal profession. As former Chief Justice of the United States, Warren E. Burger, stated: "lawyers who know how to think but have not learned how to behave are a menace and a liability not an asset to the administration of justice. ... I suggest the necessity for civility is relevant to lawyers because they are the living exemplars—and thus teachers—everyday in every case and in every court; and their worst conduct will be emulated ... more readily than their best."

Zealousness Within Boundaries

All members of the Delaware Bar are officers of the Court. Although a lawyer has a duty to his or her client, each Delaware lawyer has sworn an oath to practice "with all good fidelity as well to the Court as to the client." This responsibility to the "Court" takes precedence over the interests of the client because officers of the Court are obligated to represent these clients zealously *within* the bounds of both the positive law and the rules of ethics. ...

Civil behavior towards the tribunal and opposing counsel does not compromise an attorney's efforts to diligently and zealously represent his or her clients. ... This Court has frequently quoted the following remarks of Justice Sandra Day O'Connor:

> I believe that the justice system cannot function effectively when the professionals charged with administering it cannot even be polite to one another. Stress and frustration drive down productivity and make the process more time-consuming and expensive. Many of the best people get driven away from the field. The profession and the system itself lose esteem in the public's eyes.
>
> * * *
>
> In my view, incivility disserves the client because it wastes time

and energy—time that is billed to the client at hundreds of dollars an hour, and energy that is better spent working on the case than working over the opponent.

... Zealous advocacy never requires disruptive, disrespectful, degrading or disparaging rhetoric. The use of such rhetoric crosses the line from acceptable forceful advocacy into unethical conduct that violates the Delaware Lawyers' Rules of Professional Conduct. ...

During his confirmation hearing, the Chief Justice of the United States, John G. Roberts, Jr., ... used a baseball analogy: "Judges are like umpires. Umpires don't make the rules; they apply them. The role of an umpire is critical. They make sure everybody plays by the rules." Like umpires, judges must decide which hits by an advocate are fair and which hard hits by an advocate are foul. In this case, the hits in the briefs filed by the Respondent were not only foul but were so far beyond the boundaries of propriety that they were unethical.

Conclusion

We hold that the appropriate sanction for the Respondent in this matter is a public reprimand. . . .

INQUIRY

Interviewing Jurors. A lawyer's actions outside the tribunal could also improperly disrupt the tribunal. For example, lawyers can learn a lot about their case and professional performance by interviewing jurors after the court has discharged them. How does a lawyer do so without violating Model Rule 3.5? A good first step is to speak with the trial judge during trial about the judge's intentions. If the trial judge orders no juror contact following jurors' discharge, then obviously, the trial lawyers must have none. On the other hand, a few judges make special provision for the lawyers to have a few minutes with the jurors after their discharge, with the judge or a court staff member present. Many more judges leave the question of post-discharge juror contact entirely to counsel. In those instances, some counsel wait in the courtroom or a hallway for jurors to gather their personal effects from the jury room, and then greet and chat with them. Other lawyers find immediate post-verdict encounters with jurors to be potentially unsettling to both counsel and jurors, and prefer instead to contact jurors later by telephone or, perhaps better yet, have a secretary or other law-firm staff member do so. Sometimes, a juror will show more candor to a secretary than to the trial lawyer whose performance the juror criticizes. In any case, though, the lawyer must be sure that law or local rule does not prohibit post-discharge contact with jurors and be sure that any contact avoids anything that might look like disrespect. Consider now a case illustrating another kind of disruption occurring outside of the tribunal.

Cook v. American Steamship,
United States Court of Appeals for the Sixth Circuit
134 F.3d 771 (1998)

CLAY, Circuit Judge.

Leonard C. Jaques appeals from the district court's ... orders imposing sanctions upon him pursuant to 28 U.S.C. §1927. For the reasons set forth below, we **AFFIRM** the district court's orders regarding imposition of sanctions.

I.

This appeal arises out of an incident that occurred ... at the end of the first day of retrial in the underlying suit, in the courtroom of the lower court. In his June 13, 1996, opinion and order... , Judge Bernard Friedman, the United States District Court Judge assigned to the case, noted that, on that day, at approximately 5:00 p.m., the court had adjourned, and the judge had just left the bench. In the courtroom remained plaintiff's expert witness, Dr. Kresta, the court reporter, Fred Pratt, the parties and their counsel. Mr. Jaques was counsel to the plaintiff in the underlying suit, and Mr. Emery was counsel to the defendant. Thereafter, Fred Pratt entered Judge Friedman's chambers, exclaiming "Judge, Mr. Jaques just hit Mr. Emery!" Judge Friedman returned to the courtroom and inquired into what had just happened. Mr. Emery responded that he was just assaulted by Mr. Jaques. Federal Protective Service ("FPS") officers were called, and they took [the following] statements from witnesses.

> ...
>
> **Fred Pratt**—Witness was examining rope exhibit. Mr. Emery accused witness of being too rough with exhibit, and was in process of removing it. Argument ensued between witness, Mr. Jacques [sic] and Mr. Emery. Mr. Jacques [sic] said something to the effect, "You S.O.B., I ought to hit you." With that said, Mr. Jacques [sic] reached up and appeared to have grabbed Mr. Emery by the hair, pulling him head first into floor. I then went and got Judge Friedman, who came in courtroom and informed the parties he would call Fed. Police so reports could be made.
>
> **Thomas Lenney**—Mr. Emery asked the gentleman not to mishandle the rope or touch it without Mr. Emery watching. In disregard of this request, the gentleman continued to manipulate the rope. Mr. Emery proceeded to attempt to take the rope away stating: "You don't handle my property that way." At this time, Mr. Emery bent over to

pick up the rope. It was at this point that Mr. Jacques [sic] reached over grabbing Mr. Emery by the head & hair and ultimately throwing him to the ground yelling: "You bring that back here."

Richard Keaton—Mr. Emery took the rope out of the box for examination by Mr. Jaques and his witness. He asked them to be careful. Mr. Jaques [sic] witness started recklessly handling the evidence. Tom Emery objected to this and said the exam was over. Leonard Jaques then started yelling at Tom Emery that he couldn't do that. Tom Emery continued packing the rope away. Leonard Jaques started calling him names and then all of the sudden grabbed Tom Emery by the hair on top of his head. He pulled Tom Emery over at the waist, then threw him to the ground. I was about 2 feet away from Tom the whole time.

In their statements to FPS, Mr. Emery and Mr. Jaques claimed the following:

Mr. Emery—I was holding a large (2' x 1') box in both hands that contained evidence (a large rope). I had told Mr. Jaques and his expert—Kresta—that they could not examine the rope, had put it away and had turned to put it against the wall when Mr. Jaques grabbed the hair on the top of my head and threw me to the floor, ripping hair from the top of my head.

Mr. Jaques—Dr. Kresta, my expert, began to assess the severed end of the rope when Mr. Emery in a bellecose [sic] voice shouted to my expert, "don't handle my rope, god damn you, you are not going to [illegible] my rope at all!" Emery was ballistic and he was shouting to Dr. Kresta and I was afraid Emery was going to hit Dr. Kresta who is recovering from heart surgery, so I reached atop Emery's head and pulled his head back with the flat of my left hand, to separate him from my expert, whereupon Emery hit the floor, feining [sic] an attack and deliberately acted as if he had been assaulted and knocked down.

When court convened the next morning, defendant moved for a 24-hour adjournment and for disqualification of plaintiff's counsel from the trial. The lower court denied defendant's motion to disqualify Mr. Jaques. Defense counsel then moved for a mistrial, claiming that he was emotionally distraught from what occurred the preceding day, and thus, was unable to continue with the trial. The lower court granted the motion and declared a mistrial, noting that whoever was found responsible for the mistrial would be assessed costs. The lower court also indicated that factual findings would not be made at that point, but the FPS and the U.S. Marshals' report would play a role in that determination. ...

... [T]he court made an initial determination ... that Mr. Jaques was responsible for the assault that caused the mistrial. Moreover, the court ordered Mr. Jaques to show cause... as to why he should not be assessed costs, expenses and attorney fees pursuant to 28 U.S.C. §1927[FN3] and the court's inherent power. [FN3. 28 U.S.C. §1927 provides that: "Any attorney or other person admitted to conduct cases in any court of the United States or any Territory thereof who so multiplies the proceedings in any case unreasonably and vexatiously may be required by the court to satisfy personally the excess costs, expenses, and attorneys' fees reasonably incurred because of such conduct. ..."] ... [A]dditional sanctions were imposed upon Mr. Jaques, pursuant again to 28 U.S.C. § 1927, for the defendant's costs, expenses, and attorney fees. Mr. Jaques filed a timely notice of appeal.... .

II.

... The lower court had all it needed to make a determination of fault; it had all of the witnesses' statements as well as Mr. Jaques' rendition of the incident. Moreover, Judge Friedman was very familiar with the conduct of the attorneys, having presided over the underlying proceeding since 1993; who could better assess the conduct of the attorneys than someone who was not only familiar with the attorneys but with the witnesses as well. We find nothing in the record to indicate that a hearing was needed to assist the court in its decision that Mr. Jaques acted without justification in laying his hands on Mr. Emery. Therefore, it was proper for the lower court to assess sanctions upon Mr. Jaques pursuant to §1927 without holding an evidentiary hearing. ...

... Mr. Jaques' final argument is that he should be excused for his actions because he was going to the aid of another, his expert witness, Dr. Kresta. Specifically, Mr. Jaques asserts that he feared that Mr. Emery was going to assault Dr. Kresta. ...

Upon careful review of the witnesses' statements we do not believe that Mr. Jaques honestly believed that Dr. Kresta was about to be assaulted; thus, no force was needed. In his statement to the FPS, Dr. Kresta stated that "Mr. Emery *arrogantly* took the rope from [his] hands and prevented [him] from inspection of the rope." [C] Donald Krispin, co-counsel to Mr. Jaques, stated to the FPS, that Mr. Emery *"shouted and threatened* Mr. Jaques and Dr. Kresta pulling the exhibit from plaintiffs expert and pulling the box away from Mr. Jaques." [C] ...

There is no indication that Mr. Emery attempted to assault Dr. Kresta. Dr. Kresta himself never said he was in fear of assault, and therefore, in need of assistance. All that is clear is that Mr. Emery took the rope from Dr. Kresta. Moreover, the fact that Mr. Emery "shouted" at Dr. Kresta and Mr. Jaques does not justify the use of physical force. Force can seldom be justified when used as a response to mere words, no matter how vile the words may be. ...

III.

Mr. Jaques' conduct was deplorable and fell short of the behavior and demeanor expected of a member of the bar. His actions were unreasonable and caused additional expense to the opposing party. Therefore, the lower court did not abuse its discretion in determining that Mr. Jaques acted without justification in laying his hands on Mr. Emery; thus, sanctions pursuant to §1927 were warranted.

For the foregoing reasons we **AFFIRM** the district court's ... orders regarding imposition of sanctions.

> ### *"What Were They Thinking?"*
> What do you think of the conduct of both attorneys? Why do you think they behaved this way? As lawyers, we are supposed to *help* our clients solve their problems, not compound them. Clients contend with unchecked emotion, but when they do, the lawyers should maintain a mediating presence. The sanctioned lawyer in the above case did not advance, and very likely instead delayed, the client's cause. Do you think that when these lawyers were in law school they ever imagined one day behaving as they did? What happened to them to make them change?

INQUIRY

Means Prohibited by Law. Model Rule 3.5(a) prohibits attempts at influencing "by means prohibited by law.... ." Why include the qualifier "means prohibited by law"? A lawyer's role as an advocate requires that the lawyer seek constantly and purposely to influence judges, jurors, and other officials through permissible direct advocacy. Influence through advocacy is what we do. Lawyers must not influence through bribery, extortion, fraud, other crimes and torts, or in ways that violate other rules and statutes. Are there other means, in addition to direct advocacy, of influencing a judge that law allows, such as socializing at the country club or gym? Some degree of socializing can be appropriate, although not to influence officials. The lawyer who socializes with a judge simply to curry favor is a sycophant and fool, and judges know it. In addition, appearances of propriety at all times remain important. Chapter 13 addresses this subject in greater depth from the standpoint of the judicial-conduct rules. May a judge and lawyer be Facebook friends? There is authority that a judge may not "friend" on a social-network page lawyers who appear before the judge. FLORIDA SUP. CT. ADV. OPIN. 2009-20. Other authority suggests that a judge may Facebook-friend law-enforcement and court-employee professional acquaintances so long as not discussing matters related to the judge's position. S.C. ADV. COMM. ON STDS. OF JUD. CONDUCT OPIN. 17-2009.

Ex Parte Communications. Model Rule 3.5(b) prohibits unauthorized ex-parte communications with judges, jurors, and other officials during a proceeding, meaning communications made by one lawyer outside of the presence of the proceeding's other lawyers. Rule 3.5(b) prohibits what some would consider casual, friendly chats, when they turn to litigated matters. There is no stopping by the judge's chambers to chat about a pending case with the other side's lawyer not present. Approaching a juror in the hallway on a trial break is another prohibited communication. New lawyers must take special care to respect this important limitation. Judges in some courts, especially state courts where there may be less formality than in federal courts, may permit some incidental ex-parte contact—a greeting in the early morning before trial, a polite inquiry about a mutual professional acquaintance during a mid-day break in the proceeding, and so forth. Those incidental contacts are generally permissible so long as the lawyer does not communicate about the proceeding. Lawyers need not be impolite when a judge is willing to engage in small talk about the weather or sports, for instance, although *any* such ex-parte contact with a juror would create an appearance of impropriety. Yet lawyers must ensure that the small talk does not turn to the pending proceeding. Polite is one thing. Secretive is another.

Trial Publicity. A lawyer's integrity and the impartiality and decorum of the tribunal also depend on how a lawyer treats trial publicity. Lawyers will on occasion represent parties in litigation that draws public interest. Lawyers conducting prominent litigation may receive a telephone call or electronic communication from a reporter. How must lawyers treat trial publicity? On those occasions, a lawyer would be wise to study once again the applicable conduct rule. Lawyers, like prosecutors and prominent public defenders, who deal frequently with cases of public interest will know and follow scrupulously the applicable conduct rule because of both the discipline risk and risk of court sanctions. ABA Model Rule 3.6 begins by prohibiting lawyers from making extrajudicial statements that the lawyer should know might prejudice a proceeding. In other words, Model Rule 3.6 prohibits trying a case through the press. Yet Model Rule 3.6 provides for several exceptions. As you read an identical state version of Model Rule 3.6, see if you can articulate the policy reasons for the rule and the First Amendment basis and other reasons for its several exceptions.

WASHINGTON R. PROF. CONDUCT 3.6: Trial Publicity.

(a) A lawyer who is participating or has participated in the investigation or litigation of a matter shall not make an extrajudicial statement that the lawyer knows or reasonably should know will be disseminated by means of public communication and will have a substantial likelihood of materially prejudicing an adjudicative proceeding in the matter.

(b) Notwithstanding paragraph (a), a lawyer may state:

(1) the claim, offense or defense involved and, except when prohibited by law, the identity of the persons involved;

(2) information contained in a public record;

(3) that an investigation of a matter is in progress;

(4) the scheduling or result of any step in litigation;

(5) a request for assistance in obtaining evidence and information necessary thereto;

(6) a warning of danger concerning the behavior of a person involved, when there is reason to believe that there exists the likelihood of substantial harm to an individual or to the public interest; and

(7) in a criminal case, in addition to subparagraphs (1) through (6);

(i) the identity, residence, occupation and family status of the accused;

(ii) if the accused has not been apprehended, information necessary to aid in apprehension of that person;

(iii) the fact time and place of arrest; and

(iv) the identity of investigating and arresting officers or agencies and the length of the investigation.

(c) Notwithstanding paragraph (a), a lawyer may make a statement that a reasonable lawyer would believe is required to protect a client from the substantial undue prejudicial effect of recent publicity not initiated by the lawyer or the lawyer's client. A statement made pursuant to this paragraph shall be limited to such information as is necessary to mitigate the recent adverse publicity.

(d) No lawyer associated in a firm or government agency with a lawyer subject to paragraph (a) shall make a statement prohibited by paragraph (a).

INQUIRY

Prejudicing a Proceeding. Why would a lawyer want to prejudice a proceeding? Cases have shown several improper reasons for lawyers to manipulate trial publicity. Trial publicity may harm a party's reputation biasing a jury against the party, *see, e.g.,* Kramer v. Tribe, 156 F.R.D. 96 (D. N.J. 1994), affd., 52 F.3d 315 (3rd Cir. 1995), create an atmosphere of distrust for law-enforcement authorities in a criminal trial, *see, e.g.,* In re Duncan, 533 S.E.2d 894 (S.C. 2000) (reproduced below), or form the ground for a desired motion for change of venue, *see, e.g.,* In re Litz, 721 N.E.2d 258 (Ind. 1999). What standard does Model Rule 3.6 apply to restrict trial publicity? Parties have substantial interests in their litigation matters, just as the public has a substantial interest in knowing about those matters. In Gentile v. State

Bar, 501 U.S. 1030 (1991), the Supreme Court balanced these trial-publicity interests advanced by free speech against the interest of the parties and public in having a fair proceeding before an impartial tribunal—advanced by restricting free speech. In *Gentile*, the Supreme Court approved the substantial-likelihood-of-prejudice standard adopted later in Model Rule 3.6(a). The Supreme Court could have adopted a higher clear-and-present-danger standard, giving greater freedom to lawyers to speak publicly about important trials. Which do you favor, and why? Notice that Model Rule 3.6(a) only restricts lawyers who investigated or participated in the proceeding from trial publicity. Model Rule 3.6(d) also restricts other members of the firm or government agency of which the restricted lawyer is a part. Non-involved lawyers may still speak. *See* Model Rule 3.6 Comment [3] ("the public value of informed commentary is great"). Now consider an illustrative case.

In re Duncan,

South Carolina Supreme Court
533 S.E.2d 894 (2000)

PER CURIAM:

In this attorney grievance proceeding, respondent admits that he has committed ethical violations and consents to the imposition of a sanction to be determined by this Court. We accept respondent's admission and find an indefinite suspension is the appropriate sanction. ...

... Respondent represented a client who was under investigation in Lexington County for several crimes, including murder. On or about May 29, 1995, the client was questioned by law enforcement personnel in the polygraph room of the Lexington County Law Enforcement Center. When the questioning was interrupted, respondent, who had been present in the Law Enforcement Center, but not in the polygraph room, entered the polygraph room and engaged in a conversation with his client. Because respondent and his client were alone in the polygraph room, there was an expectation of privacy for purposes of engaging in privileged and confidential attorney-client communications. However, unbeknownst to respondent, his conversation with the client was being recorded on videotape by personnel of the Lexington County Sheriff's Department who were stationed in an adjacent room. Immediately after leaving the polygraph room, respondent's client was arrested on the charge of murder. He was later charged with first degree burglary, armed robbery, assault and battery with intent to kill and possession of a firearm during the commission of a violent crime, all in connection with the matters under investigation at the time of the unauthorized taping.

Respondent did not learn of the unauthorized taping until August 1997. Respondent obtained a copy of the tape from the public defender who, along with another court appointed attorney, had taken over representation of the client. Respondent contacted a reporter for a local television station about the tape. Respondent gave the tape to the reporter, or caused the tape to be given to the reporter, in reliance on an agreement between the two that the television station would copy the tape, but that only the video portion of the tape would be broadcast. The reporter also agreed not to reveal the source from which the copy of the tape was obtained.

Respondent gave the tape to the reporter with knowledge that the tape and the news reports related thereto would most likely be broadcast extensively in the midlands of South Carolina, including Lexington County, where the client would eventually be tried, as well as throughout the State. It was respondent's intent, in giving the tape to the reporter, to influence the upcoming trial to the client's advantage and to make known the actions of the Lexington County Sheriff's Department in taping his client. Following broadcast of the tape, respondent provided an affidavit for use in the client's trial wherein he stated he did not believe that either the State or the client could receive a fair trial in Lexington County as a result of the release of the tape to the news media. Respondent acknowledges that the release of the tape created considerable additional work for the parties and the courts of this State.

On or about March 18, 1998, respondent was called to testify before a federal grand jury which was conducting an investigation into whether the unauthorized taping by personnel of the Lexington County Sheriff's Department violated federal wiretapping laws. While under oath, respondent knowingly made a false material declaration to the grand jury. Specifically, respondent testified that he did not provide the tape to the media and that he did not know who provided the tape to the media. On or about July 29, 1999, respondent pled guilty to one count of making a false declaration to a grand jury in violation of 18 U.S.C. § 1623. He was sentenced to four months in prison, four months under home confinement, and two years of supervised release, and fined $33,386.92. ...

Respondent ... admits that he has violated ... Rule 3.6(a) (making an extrajudicial statement about a case that the lawyer would expect to be disseminated by the media knowing that it will have a substantial likelihood of materially prejudicing an adjudicative proceeding in the matter) ... [and several other conduct rules].

It is therefore ordered that respondent shall be indefinitely suspended from the practice of law in this State. ...
INDEFINITE SUSPENSION.

INQUIRY

Timing Is Everything. As the above case illustrates, implicit in Model Rule 3.6 is that the timing of trial publicity matters greatly. Cases consider that timing when deciding whether to impose discipline for a lawyer's trial publicity. Defense counsel's appearance in a criminal case can be one dramatic moment heightening the effects of public statements. *See, e.g.,* State v. Grossberg, 705 A.2d 608 (Del. Super. Ct. 1997). Extra-judicial statements made during grand-jury proceedings can affect whether a grand jury brings an indictment. *See, e.g.,* Lawyer Disc. Bd. v. Sims, 574 S.E.2d 795 (W. Va. 2002). The eve of trial as jury draw approaches tends to be another moment when trial publicity could color the jury's attitude about the case before it hears instructions and evidence. *See, e.g.,* United States v. Bingham, 769 F. Supp. 1039 (N.D. Ill. 1991). By contrast, extra-judicial statements made months or years before trial may have insufficiently prejudicial impact to impose discipline, *see, e.g.,* Iowa Sup. Ct. Bd. of Prof. Ethics & Conduct v. Visser, 629 N.W.2d 376 (Iowa 2001), even when the statement would have been prejudicial but for the cooling-off time, *see, e.g.,* Commonwealth v. McCullum, 602 A.2d 313 (Pa. 1992).

Gag Orders. May a trial court impose a stricter gag order than the substantial-likelihood-of-prejudice standard that the Supreme Court approved in *Gentile*? Although the law is not crystal clear, when the Supreme Court struck the First Amendment balance in *Gentile*, it probably prevented trial courts from imposing substantially greater restrictions on lawyer trial publicity than Model Rule 3.6 imposes. A trial court may prudently remind the lawyers of their obligation to the profession, public, and court to ensure a fair proceeding, but it may be that the trial court can constitutionally do little more than incorporate Model Rule 3.6 into its pretrial orders. *See, e.g.,* Constand v. Cosby, 229 F.R.D. 472 (E.D. Pa. 2005) (adopting Model Rule 3.6); Atlanta-Journal Constitution v. State, 596 S.E.2d 694 (Ga. Ct. App. 2004) ("no comment" gag order reversed in favor of Model Rule 3.6); Twohig v. Blackmer, 918 P.2d 332 (N.M. 1996) (complete gag order invalid); *but see* United States v. McVeigh, 964 F. Supp. 313 (D. Colo. 1997) (imposing complete gag order on trial counsel). After all, lawyers should already appreciate their obligation to show integrity with respect to their trial proceedings and public statements. One should not hinder the other.

Integrity suggests consistency between how a lawyer thinks and acts, from one place to another.

Practice

The lawyer chuckled as he listened to the reporter saying, "So, up to your old tricks, huh? Could you send me a copy of what your client filed with the Department of Civil Rights?" "No," the lawyer would politely reply again this time, as he had each time before, "We have no comment on any pending matter." The lawyer would take these calls each time because he knew that the reporter would fill him in on what others were doing and saying. There was no sense in ignoring even an only marginally reliable source for information. The lawyer would not, though, be drawn into confirming, denying, or sharing information. The calls usually lasted little more than a minute. Yet he always enjoyed hearing how the reporter was piecing together a story about which the lawyer knew much more—but was not about to be sharing.

Permitted Extrajudicial Statements. Model Rule 3.6(b) lists information that a lawyer restricted from trial publicity may nonetheless share publicly. Can you articulate the purpose behind these exceptions? Some examples are obvious, such as when Model Rule 3.6(b)(7)(ii) permits a lawyer (presumably a prosecutor) to make extrajudicial statements aiding the apprehension of an accused. Model Rule 3.6(b)(5), permitting public requests for help in obtaining evidence, and Model Rule 3.6(b)(6), permitting public warnings of danger, are other examples of appropriate trial publicity, although you can probably imagine how an artful lawyer might manipulate those exceptions to achieve improper purposes such as to taint a jury pool. In that regard, notice how specific is the information that Model Rule 3.6(b) allows. Can you see now why prosecutors tend to read carefully written extrajudicial statements without holding freewheeling press conferences? Does Model Rule 3.6(b) address adequately the First Amendment interests? In other words, does it allow trial lawyers to say what you think trial lawyers should say? Model Rule 3.6(b) is a roadmap for lawyer integrity on the subject of trial publicity. If a restricted lawyer makes extrajudicial statements outside of Model Rule 3.6(b), then there is a good chance that the motive and display show a lack of integrity.

D. Role Consistency

Advocate as Witness. Integrity has another aspect having to do with the consistency of a lawyer's roles. One cannot easily wear two hats. Anytime that a lawyer takes on more than one simultaneous role, there are opportunities for misunderstanding and mischief. The problems are twofold. A person may misunderstand the lawyer's role, unwisely relying on that misunderstanding. Dual or multiple roles may also cause the lawyer to distort one of those roles, through a conflict of interests created by the different expectations within each role. The prime example is when a lawyer serves as both an advocate and a witness at a trial. Advocates argue, while witnesses testify truthfully. A lawyer who plays both roles could confuse jurors into thinking that advocacy is testimony or testimony advocacy. *See, e.g.,* People v. Donaldson, 113 Cal. Rptr. 538 (Ct. App. 2001) (prosecutor taking witness stand to contradict other testimony and then arguing prosecutor's own testimony in closing). Moreover, a lawyer who plays both roles may shape the advocacy to fit the testimony or shape the testimony to fit the advocacy. In either case, much harm may result. *See, e.g.,* People v. Finley, 141 P.3d 911 (Colo. Ct. App. 2006) (lawyer testifies against client while representing at subsequent sentencing). A lawyer of integrity thus gives thought to the lawyer's role in any situation while ensuring consistency whenever the lawyer has multiple roles. ABA Model Rule 3.7 prohibits a lawyer from acting as both an advocate and witness at trial, with certain exceptions. As you read an identical state version of Model Rule 3.7, see if you can articulate the reasons for its exceptions. In addition, consider an illustrative case.

> **NEW JERSEY R. PROF. CONDUCT 3.7: Lawyer as Witness.**
> (a) A lawyer shall not act as advocate at a trial in which the lawyer is likely to be a necessary witness unless:
> (1) the testimony relates to an uncontested issue;
> (2) the testimony relates to the nature and value of legal services rendered in the case; or
> (3) disqualification of the lawyer would work substantial hardship on the client.
> (b) A lawyer may act as advocate in a trial in which another lawyer in the lawyer's firm is likely to be called as a witness unless precluded from doing so by RPC 1.7 or RPC 1.9.

In re Atwater,
South Carolina Supreme Court
586 S.E.2d 589 (2003)

PER CURIAM:

... Prior to respondent's admission to the South Carolina Bar, he was employed as a paralegal in a law firm. While employed as a paralegal, respondent assisted an attorney in the formation of a corporation for a college friend (Husband) and the friend's wife (Wife).

After being admitted to the South Carolina Bar, respondent represented Wife and her son with regard to several traffic violations.

In 1999, respondent was retained by Husband to pursue a divorce action against Wife. Wife's counsel filed a motion seeking respondent's disqualification. The trial court, in its order granting the motion, recognized that the corporation was to be equitably divided and would more than likely be a contested issue at trial. The trial court was concerned about the possible conflict of interest that could result from respondent's representation of Husband as well as the possibility that respondent could be called as a witness.

Following the issuance of the order, Wife contacted the Office of Disciplinary Counsel to initiate a disciplinary complaint against respondent. Respondent failed to respond to requests by the Office of Disciplinary Counsel for information regarding respondent's representation of Husband.

Respondent admits that undertaking representation of Husband was an error in judgment. He also admits he failed to respond to inquiries made by the Office of Disciplinary Counsel and that he did not initially cooperate in the investigation being conducted by the Office of Disciplinary Counsel.

However, in mitigation, respondent states that Wife's complaint was raised long after he had been involved in representation of Husband and in retaliation for the aggressive manner in which he represented Husband. Respondent maintains Wife's attorneys litigated the case without objection to respondent representing Husband and even negotiated with respondent over a period of time in an attempt to settle the matters in dispute. Respondent contends there would have never been a complaint about his representation of Husband if the matters had been settled as Wife and her counsel desired. Respondent also contends the family court order specifically stated there was no evidence of a conflict of interest in his representation of Husband. He states that although Wife's complaint alleged he was a possible witness, he was never called as a witness because Wife's assertions that respondent could be a witness were not true. ...

Respondent admits that by his conduct he has violated ... Rule 3.7 (a lawyer shall not act as an advocate at a trial in which the lawyer is likely to be a necessary witness except under limited circumstances)... [among many other rules]. ...

We find, after consideration of the mitigating circumstances, that respondent's misconduct warrants a public reprimand. Accordingly, we accept the Agreement for Discipline by Consent and publicly reprimand respondent for his actions.

PUBLIC REPRIMAND.

Inquiry

Permissible Dual Roles. The first exception to Model Rule 3.7(a)'s prohibition against advocates acting simultaneously as witnesses is testimony as to an uncontested issue. Can you think of any examples where a court should permit a lawyer to testify on an uncontested issue? Occasionally, a court may require lawyer testimony on routine matters such as authentication of an undisputed original document, verification of undisputed fees, or introduction of an undisputed calculation or summary. Model Rule 3.7(a)(1) permits a lawyer to offer that testimony even while acting as an advocate. Occasionally, a lawyer must establish the nature and value of the lawyer's services, perhaps for a prevailing-party fee award or to sue a client who has not paid fees. Model Rule 3.7(a)(2) permits a lawyer to do so. *See, e.g.,* Bernier v. DuPont, 715 N.E.2d 442 (Mass. Ct. App. 1999) (error to disqualify estate lawyer testifying to support fee request). Notice, too, that Model Rule 3.7 refers to not acting as a witness and advocate "at a trial" rather than before a tribunal. Cases interpret the reference to trial to mean court proceedings, not agency proceedings. A lawyer may act as an advocate and witness in an administrative hearing. *See, e.g.,* Heard v. Foxshire Assocs., LLC, 806 A.2d 348 (Md. Ct. Spec. App. 2002). May a lawyer act as advocate if the client agrees that the lawyer need not testify? *See* Freeman v. Vicchiarelli, 827 F. Supp. 300 (D. N.J. 1993) (lawyer still disqualified if testimony is likely necessary).

Disqualification as Substantial Hardship. Given Model Rule 3.7's prohibition against witness advocates, lawyers take care not to make themselves witnesses. The contingency-fee lawyer who suddenly finds that the lawyer must serve as a witness could lose a substantial contingency fee to another lawyer. Disqualification as advocate in order to testify as witness means loss of an opportunity to earn fees. Lawyers adopt prudent practices to prevent becoming a witness in a client matter. *Cf.* State ex rel. Oklahoma Bar Assn. v. Downes, 121 P.3d 1058 (Okla. 2005) (discipline for sex with divorce client where lawyer should have anticipated having to testify as to sex). For example, lawyers employ investigators to take statements and inspect scenes so that the investigator is the witness in the event of a dispute over a statement or scene. Model Rule 3.7(b) offers an alternative solution: allow another lawyer from the same firm to act as an advocate in the trial in which the other lawyer testifies. *See, e.g.,* Cunningham v. Sams, 588 S.E.2d 484 (N.C. Ct. App. 2003) (disqualifying lawyer but not law firm). This accommodation removes juror confusion over a lawyer's dual roles even if not fully resolving the lawyer's conflict of interest—

which is why Model Rule 3.7(b) requires that the lawyer acting as advocate comply with the conflict-of-interest rules, ABA Model Rules 1.7 and 1.9. *See, e.g.,* Weigel v. Farmers Ins. Co., 158 S.W.3d 147 (Ark. 2004) (disqualifying lawyer and law firm where lawyer would testify for opposing party). Model Rule 3.7(a)(3) provides another exception allowing an advocating lawyer to testify if disqualification would work substantial hardship on the client. How do you think the courts measure hardship? The cost, quality, and availability of alternative lawyer services, and the occasioned delay, are all factors. Consider an illustrative case.

_____

D.J. Inv. Group, L.L.C. v. DAE/Westbrook, L.L.C.,
Utah Supreme Court
147 P.3d 414 (2006)

DURRANT, Justice:
INTRODUCTION

¶1 Rule 3.7(a) of the Utah Rules of Professional Conduct generally prohibits a lawyer from "act[ing] as [an] advocate at a trial in which the lawyer is likely to be a necessary witness," but provides an exception where disqualification of the lawyer would "work substantial hardship on the client."[fn] In this interlocutory appeal, we granted certiorari on a single question ... whether the substantial hardship exception was properly applied in this case. ...

BACKGROUND

¶3 ... SunCrest seeks to disqualify Snuffer and his firm, Nelson, Snuffer, Dahle & Poulsen, P.C., from representing D.J. as an advocate at trial based on Snuffer's involvement in a November 16, 2000 settlement agreement ("the Agreement") between SunCrest and D.J. that is now a subject of dispute in the present case.

¶4 The Agreement was intended to resolve an October 2000 lawsuit brought by D.J. against SunCrest for an alleged trespass. In provision 14 of the Agreement, SunCrest promised to allow D.J. to use a "Southerly Roadway" that would be built across property belonging to third party Micron Technology, Inc. ("Micron"). In return, D.J. agreed to dismiss its prior lawsuit and to allow SunCrest to use an access road that SunCrest had built over D.J.'s property. Snuffer acted as D.J.'s lawyer at all times during these events and has continued to represent D.J. through the present proceedings. The extent of his involvement in negotiating the November 2000 Agreement is disputed.

¶5 A short time after the parties signed the Agreement, the dispute between the parties was rekindled. ... D.J. filed the present lawsuit. It seeks to rescind the Agreement... .

¶6 ... [O]ver two and one-half years after D.J. filed its complaint, SunCrest moved pursuant to rule 3.7 of the Utah Rules of Professional Conduct to disqualify Snuffer from representing D.J. at trial, arguing that Snuffer is a necessary witness in the case. SunCrest alleges that Snuffer played an important role in drafting provision 14 of the Agreement ... and that his testimony regarding the intent of the parties will be crucial. ...

¶7 Upon hearing oral arguments on SunCrest's motion to disqualify Snuffer, the district court issued a written ruling declining to disqualify Snuffer and his firm from representing D.J. at trial. It reasoned that it need not determine whether Snuffer was likely to be a necessary witness because his disqualification would cause substantial hardship to D.J. and thus fell within the exception provided by rule 3.7(a)(3). After noting that it had weighed the interests of the two parties in accordance with the comments to rule 3.7, the district court stated,

> [T]he parties have conducted a significant amount of discovery in connection with this litigation. Most, if not all, of the key witnesses have been deposed and written discovery has been sent out and answered by both parties. All things considered, the parties have engaged in a substantial amount of work. Indeed, the Court file now fills seven exceptionally thick folders and addresses some very complex legal issues. The Clerk of the Court has just opened the eighth file. Under these circumstances, the Court doubts that another attorney could be brought up to speed in this matter and recognizes that such an effort would require D.J. to expend an exorbitant amount of time and money. ...

ANALYSIS

... ¶12 We initially hold that ... the substantial hardship exception of rule 3.7(a)(3) requires a balancing of the hardship that a lawyer's disqualification would cause to the lawyer's client against the prejudice that the opposing party would suffer if the lawyer were to act as an advocate-witness at trial. ... [T]he balancing contemplated by the substantial hardship exception also calls for consideration of the interests of the tribunal.... .

¶13 Rule 3.7(a)(3) ... does not indicate how much hardship may be imposed on a client before the hardship becomes "substantial."[fn] ... The comment further explains,

> Whether the tribunal is likely to be misled or the opposing party is likely to suffer prejudice depends on the nature of the case, the importance and probable tenor of the lawyer's testimony, and the probability that the lawyer's testimony will conflict with that of other witnesses. Even if there is a risk of such prejudice, in determining whether the lawyer should be disqualified, due regard must be given to the effect of disqualification on the lawyer's client.

It is relevant that one or both parties could reasonably foresee that the lawyer would probably be a witness.[fn]

... ¶29 The advisory committee's comment to rule 3.7 mentions five factors that are relevant in assessing the interests of the parties.[fn] The first three are relevant to the prejudice that an advocate-witness would impose on the opposing party and the tribunal.[fn] The fourth factor considers the effect that the lawyer's disqualification will have on the client and specifies that "due regard must be given" to this effect even if there is risk of prejudice to the opposing party.[fn] Finally, the fifth factor states, "It is relevant that one or both parties could reasonably foresee that the lawyer would probably be a witness."[fn]

... ¶32 ... [T]he district court's interpretation of the factors in the context of this case appears to be quite reasonable.

¶33 A delay in filing a motion to disqualify counsel or in notifying opposing counsel that a motion to disqualify is likely raises concerns that the party who delays may be using the motion as a manipulative litigation tactic.[fn] This concern naturally enters into the balancing of interests and is addressed, in part, by the "foreseeability" factor from the advisory committee's comment to rule 3.7.[fn] ...

¶34 Ultimately, it appears that the district court concluded that SunCrest's culpability in filing an untimely motion was the factor most relevant to the weight of its interests and that, given SunCrest's weak claim to prejudice, the hardship to D.J. was significant enough for the substantial hardship exception to apply in this case. In so finding, the district court was acting within its broad discretion to control the conduct of the attorneys in a matter before the court. ...

CONCLUSION

¶39 ... [W]e conclude that the district court's substantial hardship determination is a mixed question of fact and law that implicates the district court's broad discretion to control the conduct of the lawyers before it. We therefore give significant deference to the district court's substantial hardship determination. Finally, we hold that the court of appeals correctly concluded that the district court did not abuse its discretion when it weighed the interests of the parties and decided that, in light of SunCrest's delay in filing the motion to disqualify and the financial and tactical hardship that would be suffered by D.J. if Snuffer were disqualified, the substantial hardship exception applied in this case. We therefore affirm.

INQUIRY

Tactical Abuse. The above case hints that parties and their lawyers have attempted to use Rule 3.7 motions to disqualify for tactical advantage in pending litigation. A grievance to discipline officials is not the only remedy. Parties may move to disqualify opposing counsel, which is often how the role-conflict issue arises. Because disqualifying the opposing side's lawyer can give a party a distinct advantage in litigation, courts are sensitive to potential abuses of motions to disqualify. *See, e.g.,* In re Bahn, 13 S.W.3d 865 (Tex. Ct. App. 2000) (require showing of actual prejudice); Klupt v. Krongard, 728 A.2d 727 (Md. Ct. Spec. App. 1999) (scrutinize motions to disqualify closely). Even if an opposing party is successful, the disqualified lawyer may still be able to assist the lawyer's client even if not acting as an advocate at trial. *See, e.g.,* Lowe v. Experian, 328 F. Supp.2d 1122 (D. Kan. 2004) (disqualified counsel permitted to assist client, just not act as advocate at trial); Merrill Lynch Bus. Fin. Services, Inc. v. Nudell, 239 F. Supp.2d 1170 (D. Colo. 2003) (disqualified counsel may participate in pretrial hearings and conferences).

Advocacy in Nonadjudicative Proceedings. Consider one final area where lawyers must show integrity beyond mere honesty in communications. Lawyers find occasion to appear for clients in federal and state legislative hearings, city council and county commission meetings, school board meetings, administrative hearings, and other nonadjudicative proceedings. The legislative and administrative bodies who hear lawyers should know for whom a lawyer speaks. When a lawyer advocates before a legislative or administrative body, the lawyer's representation shapes the lawyer's advocacy. To conceal one's role as a representative is to misrepresent one's statements as if independent and disinterested. The members of those bodies hearing the lawyer's advocacy should know for whom the lawyer speaks in order that they may better evaluate the lawyer's statements or testimony. A lawyer's disclosure in a legislative or administrative forum is especially important because, unlike in courts, non-lawyers have equal access to those forums. Members could easily mistake a lawyer's advocacy for an independent statement of a non-lawyer. For these reasons, ABA Model Rule 3.9 requires that a lawyer representing a client before a nonadjudicative body disclose the lawyer's representative capacity. Consider an identical state version of Model Rule 3.9.

CHAPTER VIII   INTEGRITY   369

PENNSYLVANIA R. PROF. CONDUCT 3.9:   Advocate in Nonadjudicative Proceedings.
A lawyer representing a client before a legislative body or administrative agency in a nonadjudicative proceeding shall disclose that the appearance is in a representative capacity and shall conform to the provisions of Rules 3.3(a) through (c), 3.4(a) through (c), and 3.5.

Career and Professional Development

Beyond the above conduct rules, integrity can play a large part in a lawyer's career and professional development.   The behaviors toward tribunals that the above rules require are behaviors that law firms and other employers of lawyers also expect of lawyers when not in court. One survey indicates that 74% of hiring partners expect new hires to be sensitive to ethics issues, ranking ethics sensitivity as more important than knowledge of substantive law.   James E. Moliterno, *Professional Preparedness: A Comparative Study of Law Graduates Perceived Readiness for Professional Ethics Issues,* 58 LAW & CONTEMP. PROBS. 259, 273 (1995), citing Bryant G. Garth & Joanne Martin, *Law Schools and the Construction of Competence,* 43 J. LEGAL EDUC. 469, 490 (1993). Lawyers should be contending only with merit in transactional and law-office-management matters, too, not just in tribunals.   Lawyers should be expediting transactional and law-office management, too, just as they should expedite litigation. Lawyers should generally not be having frequent secretive communications with decisionmakers who do not happen to be public officials, when others who have an interest in the decision are not present. Apply the above conduct rules more broadly to your behavior toward lawyers in all professional and non-professional settings, not just in tribunals, and your career and professional development should benefit.

CHAPTER IX

LOYALTY

Avoiding Conflicts of Interest

Fidelity is the sister of justice.
— *Horace*

Away, then, with sharp practice and trickery, which desires, of course, to pass for wisdom, but is far from it and totally unlike it. For the function of wisdom is to discriminate between good and evil; whereas, inasmuch as all things morally wrong are evil, trickery prefers the evil to the good.
— *Cicero*

OBJECTIVE: Given common and conflicting interests of different clients, former clients, and prospective clients, articulate the rules and conventions to follow to comply with the conduct rules and demonstrate your loyalty.

Applicable Rules

1.7   Conflict of Interest: Current Clients

1.8   Conflict of Interest: Current Clients: Specific Rules

1.9   Duties to Former Clients

1.18 Duties to Prospective Clients

A. Conflicts Framework

Loyalty's Value. Think about the basic dynamic underlying every lawyer-client relationship. The client, whether person or entity, pays to have the lawyer represent them in a vital matter. The client cannot manage the matter without help, and its outcome will have great impact, such as whether their child will continue to live with them, they will receive money for medical care after serious injury, they will get to continue to enjoy a worklife, or their business will survive. Most clients do not see a lawyer because things are going well. They seek a lawyer because they have a problem they need badly to address. When a client seeks a lawyer, the lawyer's obedience, relationship, competence, diligence, honesty, and integrity are all important. Yet the quality that clients expect most from their lawyer is that the lawyer will keep their best interest at heart. Above all, clients want their lawyer's loyalty. Clients place critical trust in lawyers. There is no greater offense to a client than to have a lawyer violate that trust.

Specificity of Conflicts Rules. The lawyer's duty of loyalty underlies all aspects of the lawyer-client relationship, yet nowhere is that duty codified more clearly than in the conflict of interest rules. The conflict of interest rules differ significantly from the other ABA MODEL RULES OF PROFESSIONAL CONDUCT. Unlike many of the Model Rules written in broad and general language, the conflict of interest rules are technical and precise. Each subsection of the conflicts rules addresses a specific situation with tests and exceptions that vary from subsection to subsection. Even though several conduct rules may apply to a situation, there is usually one conflict-rule subsection that applies specifically to any one conflict situation. Unlike in horseshoe games, close does not count in conflicts analyses. To succeed on the Multistate Professional Responsibility Exam and bar exam, and in practice, you must usually find and follow the one conflicts-rule subsection that governs the situation.

Difficulty of Conflicts Rules. Conflicts of interest are notoriously difficult to discern. New lawyers, especially, may not see arising conflicts of interest shrouded in a thicket of communications and relationships. Yet the primary reason why lawyers sometimes overlook conflicts of interest may surprise you. It is not that they are so hard to discern but that we tend not to want to see them. Self interest clouds our vision, silences our conscience, and masks our judgment. Thus, the more lucrative the case and more prestigious the client, the more likely the lawyer will ignore an evident interest conflict. Spotting conflicts of interest on law school exams, although still difficult, is in that respect your easier time because you have no incentive to ignore them. Expect to find conflicts more difficult to spot in practice because of the basic human nature that we seek what is in our own interest more than what is in others' interest. In conflicts situations, we fight the basest of human instincts.

Conflict-Recognition Techniques. As you begin this shrouded journey into the technical and precise world of conflicts of interest, several techniques will help you. First, remember that people and events usually bring or create the interest conflicts. Often, a new client or new lawyer brings the conflict with them into a situation. Think of these situations as involving *interest* conflicts. Less often, the facts or procedural posture of a matter create the conflict. Think of these situations as involving *positional* conflicts. Another technique is to evaluate the situation from the perspective of each other party, turning the lawyer's self interest from a shroud into a tool. What would each party in the matter think about the lawyer and the lawyer's role? What would the lawyer's client and former client think? This technique helps you spot conflicts not seen easily from the lawyer's vantage point. In addition, it is easy to know your own thoughts on a matter. Keep in mind that the test of conflicts is whether other reasonable people think that you can be loyal in a certain situation. Judge conflicts not by your own view but by what you suspect others will view. In sum, as you analyze these situations, ask who is bringing the conflict, what is causing the conflict, and what is each person's interest in the situation. If you answer those questions consistently, then you will do much better at preventing and resolving conflicts of interest.

Client Consent to Conflicts. Each conflict rule contains a consent provision that may allow a lawyer to proceed with a representation despite the conflict of interest that the rule addresses. These consent provisions are contingent. They may be available in some situations but not others. They may require the lawyer to obtain consent in a certain form, by a certain process, or from a certain person. Do not think of consent as a panacea. Consent is usually a narrow exception to the broader rule defining and prohibiting the conflict. Clients may also revoke consent at any time, requiring the lawyer to withdraw from representation. Resisting client revocation and enforcing client consent within litigation is a distasteful and expensive process that few lawyers win. If you were a judge, to whom would you give the benefit of the doubt, a client who claims they did not understand the implications of the waiver they signed or the lawyer trying to enforce the waiver to continue with the representation against the wishes of a previous or current client? In most instances, courts uphold waivers of conflicts of interest only against sophisticated corporate clients or individuals who had the benefit of independent counsel at the time they signed the waiver and because of their sophistication cannot realistically claim that they did not know the implications of what they were signing.

Client Relations and Expense. Another practical reality underlies conflicts of interest. If someone thinks you have a conflict of interest, then you have a public-relations problem, even if there is no actual conflict of interest. A client, former client, prospective client, or other person perceives disloyalty. Is the new representation that you are considering undertaking—that which created the impression of disloyalty—worth the price to your reputation? Even if the conflict allegation against you is simply a litigation tactic, then you would still have duties under ABA Model Rules 1.2 and 1.4 to advise your prospective clients that they will have to expend additional attorney fees to litigate a disqualification motion if they want to retain you as a lawyer—not a productive or fun conversation to have with a prospective client.

Remedies against lawyers who violate conflict of interest rules include disqualification from the representation, civil liability for breach of contract or malpractice, professional discipline, or a combination of these remedies. Just because a conduct rule indicates you may do something, does not mean you should do so. It may very well be in your long-term best interest to decline borderline representations than risk disqualification or worse. Keep this framework in mind as in the next three sections you study conflict-of-interest rules relating to current, former, and prospective clients. In the next chapter, you will study other conflict-of-interest rules regulating lawyer conduct, not directly involving current, former, or prospective clients.

B. Current-Client Conflicts

Concurrent Conflicts of Interest. The first kind of lawyer conflict of interest involves representing a current client while other interests affect the lawyer's service to that client. ABA Model Rule 1.7 calls that kind of primary, direct conflict of interest—the first kind that you should recognize and avoid—a *concurrent* conflict of interest. Model Rule 1.7 defines a concurrent conflict, first, as one in which the lawyer's representation of one client is directly adverse to another client, or second, one with a significant risk that the lawyer's own interest or an interest of another will limit the lawyer's service to the client. The principle is simply that you should not at one moment (concurrently) serve two masters, whether those two masters are two different clients or one client and the attorney's own interest. A current client has the right to your full devotion, undiluted by the interest of another client or your own interest or the interest of another. Read the following similar state version of Model Rule 1.7 for this understanding and for the rule's exception. Then read two straightforward cases illustrating concurrent conflicts. The first case involves a lawyer who apparently did not realize that he was helping a client who was opposing another of his clients but was still disciplined. The second case illustrates the hazard of representing a client while having a strong contrary personal interest—and what to do about it.

SOUTH DAKOTA R. PROF. CONDUCT 1.7: **Conflict of Interest: Current Clients.**

(a) Except as provided by paragraph (b), a lawyer shall not represent a client if the representation involves a concurrent conflict of interest. A concurrent conflict of interest exists if:

(1) the representation of one client will be directly adverse to another client; or

(2) there is a significant risk that the representation of one or more clients will be materially limited by the lawyer's responsibilities to another client, a former client or a third person or by a personal interest of the lawyer.

(b) Notwithstanding the existence of a concurrent conflict of interest under paragraph (a), a lawyer may represent a client if:

(1) the lawyer reasonably believes that the lawyer will be able to provide competent and diligent representation to each affected client;

(2) the representation is not prohibited by law;

(3) the representation does not involve the assertion of a claim by one client against another client represented by the lawyer in the same litigation or same matter before a tribunal; and

(4) each affected client gives informed consent, confirmed in writing.

State ex rel. Nebraska State Bar Assn. v. Frank,
Nebraska Supreme Court
631 N.W.2d 485 (2001)

...FACTS

... Frank was admitted to practice law in the State of Nebraska on January 25, 1973. Since 1981, he has been employed as an attorney employee of the ... Sodoro firm in Omaha... . The Sodoro firm concentrates its practice primarily in the area of insurance defense litigation. One of its primary clients is St. Paul Insurance Company (St. Paul), which the Sodoro firm represents in both Iowa and Nebraska. During the period from 1992 through 1997, Frank, on behalf of the Sodoro firm, represented St. Paul in insurance defense matters.

In 1992, Frank served as cocounsel in a claim involving Iowa law with Sheldon Gallner, a licensed Iowa attorney. The claim concerned Donald Peterson, a workers' compensation and personal injury client, who had contacted Frank to represent him in an Iowa workers' compensation claim. Believing Gallner to be an experienced Iowa workers' compensation attorney, Frank referred Peterson to Gallner. Frank had no agreement with Gallner or Peterson regarding the extent of Frank's involvement in the claim or his fees. Frank worked on the Peterson claim, providing Gallner with copies of Peterson's medical records, as well as conducting telephone conferences with Peterson and Gallner. Frank did not participate in any discovery meetings with expert witnesses or document evaluation. Frank did not prepare pleadings or correspondence. In October 1992, Frank received $20,670 in fees from Gallner for his work on the Peterson claim.

Prior to his participation in the Peterson matter, Frank did not determine whether or not he had a conflict of interest in representing Peterson in Peterson's Iowa workers' compensation claim. In particular, Frank did not attempt to discover the identity of the employer's insurance carrier defending against Peterson's claim in Iowa until 1998. The insurance carrier was St. Paul.

The referee concluded that Frank was representing Peterson in a claim against St. Paul at the same time he was representing St. Paul in other matters. The referee found that although Frank did not know he was representing clients with differing interests, he was not excused by his ignorance, concluding that such representation may have diluted Frank's loyalty or undermined his efforts to represent either or both of his clients effectively.

In addition to the facts recited above, the referee noted in his report that the conflict of interest arose from Frank's "negligence" rather than an intentional act to benefit himself or another client. The referee found no evidence that any client was harmed. The referee also noted that Frank had cooperated fully in the disciplinary proceedings and had shown an attitude of regret and remorse. The referee found that Frank was not a threat to the public.

The referee found that Frank had demonstrated his commitment to the legal profession and the community by serving as the chair of the Nebraska State Bar Association's workers' compensation section, serving on the Omaha Bar Association's domestic relations committee, presenting continuing legal education seminars, contributing to the workers' compensation manual, and serving on Omaha's human relations board.

The referee stated that the record contained 27 affidavits from lawyers and judges whom Frank knew professionally as a result of his years in practice. The affidavits attested to Frank's competence, professionalism, honesty, integrity, commitment to his clients, and fitness to practice law. Some of the affidavits referred to Frank's civic and community involvement, his volunteer coaching of youth sports, his commitment to his profession, and his dedication to his family.

... [T]he referee recommended that Frank be publicly reprimanded.

ANALYSIS

... The evidence in the present case establishes ... that at the time he was representing Peterson in a claim against St. Paul, Frank was also representing St. Paul in unrelated litigation. Pursuant to DR 5-105, Frank had an ethical obligation to decline representation involving differing interests, and to discontinue representing multiple clients if such representation involved differing interests. See DR 5-105(A) and

(B). As a result of his conduct, Frank has violated DR 5-105(A) and (B).... Frank has also violated his oath as an attorney. ...

... Upon due consideration, this court agrees with the referee's recommendation and finds that Frank should be publicly reprimanded. Thus, Frank is hereby publicly reprimanded for conduct in violation of the Code of Professional Responsibility and his oath of office as a member of the Nebraska State Bar Association. ...

Haley v. Boles,
Texas Court of Appeals
824 S.W.2d 796 (1992)

... This is an original proceeding in which the Relator, Victor Haley ("Haley"), seeks a writ of mandamus requiring the Respondent,[fn] Judge Bennie C. Boles, to revoke his order denying Haley's motion to withdraw as appointed defense counsel in a criminal case. We have granted Haley's petition.

On May 8, 1990, Judge Boles notified Haley by letter that he had appointed him to represent Larry Christopher, the defendant in a criminal case in Shelby County, Texas. On October 10, 1990, Haley filed his motion to withdraw as counsel for Christopher. Haley alleged that a conflict of interest arises from his representation of the defendant, because the Shelby County district attorney, Karren Price, is the spouse of Haley's law partner, John Price. On July 17, 1991, Judge Boles denied Haley's motion to withdraw. Haley then filed this mandamus proceeding. There was no response to Haley's petition.

... The propriety of attorneys/spouses representing opposing parties in a criminal trial is one of first impression. It is clear, however, that if there be impropriety in spouses representing adversaries, the disqualification extends to the partners and associates of the spouse....

As an attorney "conflict of interest" issue, without legal precedent, we look to the TEXAS RULES OF PROFESSIONAL CONDUCT. Its Preamble provides: "7. In the nature of law practice, conflicting responsibilities are encountered. Virtually all difficult ethical problems arise from apparent conflict between a lawyer's responsibilities to clients, to the legal system and to the lawyer's own interests." There is at least the appearance of tension with respect to each of these three areas of responsibility in the case before us.

First, the *client's* interest is a serious concern. Haley is appointed counsel for an indigent criminal defendant. Christopher's right to the services of appointed counsel is one of constitutional dimensions. The indigent defendant, however, does not participate in the selection of the lawyer assigned by the trial court to defend his rights and freedom.

The sixth amendment has been interpreted as assuring the right to conflict-free representation. *Glasser v. United States,* 315 U.S. 60, 69-70[] (1941). We conclude that the Prices' marital relationship creates the appearance of having compromised and limited the defendant's constitutional right to effective assistance of counsel. For this reason alone, Haley's petition must be granted; our ruling here is, therefore, limited to the representation of indigent defendants in criminal cases by court-appointed counsel.

... As mentioned, there are other considerations that impact the representation of this indigent defendant by counsel whose partner is married to the prosecuting attorney. These relationships affect our *legal system* itself. The cornerstone of the system is effective, independent representation of the respective litigants by professional counsel. Our concern is further erosion of public confidence in our system. Here, the appearance of independence of the trial counsel is diminished. Furthermore, should the case not be tried, but dismissed or a plea bargain reached, the close personal relationship between the adversaries' lawyers creates at least an appearance that the disposition resulted from less than arm's length negotiations.

Finally, as to the spousal relationship's impact upon the *lawyer's own interests,* we note the effect of the Texas community property laws: one-half of the district attorney's salary becomes a part of the adversary/husband's community estate. Karren Price's prosecutorial success and continued service in that office is beneficial to John Price. ...

... Even had Christopher affirmatively consented to Haley's continued representation, the above-enumerated concerns would not have been laid to rest. ... The indigent defendant's consent to continued representation ... does not embody the same degree of free choice as that of the paying client. ...

We hold that the Respondent clearly abused his discretion in denying Haley's motion to withdraw as the indigent defendant's counsel. If Haley is required to raise this matter by appeal, his client will have to submit to a trial of this case without the benefit of conflict-free representation. Haley, therefore, does not have an adequate remedy at law. ...

INQUIRY

Positional Conflicts. The above two cases illustrate how either the client (as in the *Frank* case) or lawyer (as in the *Haley v. Boles* case) can bring interests to a representation that create a conflict of interest. A slightly different kind of conflict that also falls under Model Rule 1.7

involves when the lawyer must take conflicting positions within litigation that affect materially the lawyer's ability to represent a client. These positional conflicts arise out of the facts, law, or procedural posture of one or more unrelated matters, not out of what the lawyer or client bring to the representation. For example, a lawyer may properly represent one client in one case and a different client in a different case, taking contrary positions on the law in each case, so long as doing so does not undermine the lawyer's credibility, although the two cases would likely need to be in different courts. *See* Model Rule 1.7 Comment [24]; *see also* Simpson Perf. Prods. v. Horn, 92 P.3d 283 (Wyo. 2004) (permissible to represent client suing NASCAR and client supplying NASCAR). If instead both matters were before the same judge or appealed to the same appellate court, then the lawyer's conflicting positions in each case would likely impair the lawyer's ability to represent both clients, barring the representation under Model Rule 1.7. *See, e.g.,* Williams v. State, 805 A.2d 880 (Del. 2002) (arguing different weight to jury's recommendations in two capital cases, one recommendation sparing life and the other taking it). Consider an even more obvious case of a positional conflict involving a lawyer representing a client against the lawyer's own self.

Attorney General v. Michigan Public Service Commn.,
Michigan Court of Appeals
625 N.W.2d 16 (2001)

RICHARD ALLEN GRIFFIN, J.

... At the time of oral arguments in this appeal, the Attorney General was both appellant and counsel for appellee [Public Service Commission]. Upon calling the case, the Court raised the issue of the apparent conflict of interest of the Attorney General regarding her dual roles. ... Thereafter, appellee PSC requested that the Attorney General appoint a special assistant attorney general to represent its interests. By mutual agreement, the Attorney General eventually appointed attorney Allan Falk as special assistant attorney general for the PSC. ...

Dual Roles and "Conflict Wall"

The Attorney General is one of only three constitutionally mandated single executives heading principal departments of state government. Const. 1963, art. 5, §3, ¶1. An elective official, Const. 1963, art. 5, §21, the Attorney General and her designated assistants provide legal services to the state of Michigan and its hundreds of agencies, boards, commissions, officials, and employees... .

The Attorney General represents that until the present case, her dual roles in these cases had never been questioned, even though the practice has existed "for approximately three decades." Indeed, until the advent of this case, the judiciary has not focused on the ethical strictures that govern the conduct of the Attorney General and her assistants. ...

The Attorney General argues there is no conflict of interest in her dual roles. In the alternative, she asserts that were there a conflict of interest, it has been remedied by the erection of a "conflict wall".... .

... [S]he acknowledges and represents: "*While all Assistants and Special Assistants derive their authority from the Attorney General,* neither the Attorney General personally, nor any supervisor, nor anyone else has access to the files and records of both parties." (Emphasis added.)

The special assistant attorney general claims that the Attorney General's "conflict wall" may have been breached in the present case. Appellee PSC alleges that the briefs on the conflict of interest issue originally prepared by the assistant attorneys general for the public service division and the special litigation division were nearly identical.

We find it unnecessary to resolve the factual dispute regarding whether there has been a breach of the "conflict wall." Whether the purported wall has been penetrated is simply not dispositive to our resolution of the issue. ...

Rules of Professional Conduct

"An attorney owes undivided allegiance to a client and usually may not represent parties on both sides of a dispute." ... This maxim governing the practice of law stems from the Michigan Rules of Professional Conduct (MRPC), Rule 1.7, Conflict of Interest: General Rule... .

The Attorney General contends that by virtue of her unique office, she is "authorized by law to appear on both sides of a case or take conflicting positions when a private lawyer would be prohibited from doing so," and that she "does not stand in the same shoes worn by any other counsel" with regard to issues of conflict of interest. The special assistant attorney general asserts otherwise... .

In our analysis of this important question, we begin by acknowledging the unique status of the Attorney General as a constitutional officer of the state of Michigan and her concomitant statutory authority to represent the state as its chief legal counsel. However, in this capacity, the Attorney General is not immune from application of the rules of professional conduct... .

The Legislature has ... created a traditional attorney-client relationship between the Attorney General and the state officers he is required to represent. It is well settled that in the control of litigation, the Attorney General has the duty to conform his conduct to that prescribed by the rules of professional ethics. ... As a lawyer and an officer of the courts of this State, the Attorney General is subject to the rules of this Court governing the practice of law and the conduct of lawyers, which have the force and effect of law. ...

... [T]he Attorney General's unique status *requires accommodation, not exemption, under the rules of professional conduct.* ...

Under our scheme of laws, the attorney general has the duty as a constitutional officer possessed with common law as well as statutory powers and duties to represent or furnish legal counsel to many interests-the State, its agencies, the public interest and others designated by statute.

Paramount to all of his duties, of course, is his duty to protect the interest of the general public. ...

In fact, nearly all the decisions from other jurisdictions cited by appellant in support of her position that the Attorney General may represent opposing state agencies also provide that the Attorney General may do so only "where he or she is not an actual party" in the dispute. ...

Thus, in the present case, because the Attorney General is a named party, the authorities on which she relies do not support her position. On the contrary, this line of authority holds that when the Attorney General is an actual party to the litigation, independent counsel should be appointed for the state agency in order to remedy the ethical impediment to the legal action brought by the Attorney General. ...

The common, consistent rationale that can be gleaned from these cases is that the rules of professional conduct do apply to the office of attorney general; while mechanical application of these rules is not possible because of the unique nature of that office, thus allowing dual representation in certain circumstances not otherwise permitted in the arena of private practice, the rules do recognize a clear conflict of interest when the Attorney General acts as a party litigant in opposition to an agency or department that she also represents in the same cause of action. We agree with the view of the majority of other jurisdictions on this issue. We hold that a conflict of interest arises when the Attorney General intervenes as a party in opposition to a state agency that she represents as counsel.

We find no idiosyncrasies in Michigan law that would warrant rejection of this reasoning; on the contrary, MRPC 1.7 fully supports this conclusion. ...

... We hold only that pursuant to the rules of professional conduct, if the Attorney General chooses to stand in opposition to a state agency or department *as an actual party litigant* and yet simultaneously attempts to represent that state agency in the litigation, such dual representation creates a conflict of interest that must be addressed and rectified.

The effect of our ruling is also tempered by its remedy, since we conclude that the consequence of such a conflict is not necessarily automatic disqualification of the Attorney General as counsel for the state agency or, conversely, a bar to the ability of the Attorney General to pursue an action as a active party. Rather, consistent with MRPC 1.7, dual representation is permissible if "the lawyer reasonably believes the representation will not adversely affect the relationship with the other client" and "each client consents [to dual representation] after consultation." MRPC 1.7(a).

In order to remedy the conflict of interest, the Court directs ... that appellant Attorney General file within twenty-one days either a stipulation for substitution of counsel for appellee PSC or a consent of client for continuation of counsel after consultation regarding the conflict. MRPC 1.7(a)(2). ...

INQUIRY

Nonconsentable Concurrent Conflicts. As the above case intimates, Model Rule 1.7(b) permits a lawyer to maintain a concurrent conflict of interest if the lawyer satisfies four conditions, ending in the client's written informed consent. The first three conditions, though, involve conflicts that are (as the rule's Comments articulate) *nonconsentable*. The first condition may be the most hazardous, which is that the lawyer must make a reasonable judgment about whether the lawyer will be able to provide sound representation to each client whom the conflict affects. If not, then the conflict is nonconsentable. Keep in mind that although Model Rule 1.7(b)(1) authorizes the lawyer to make that judgment, the judgment must still be reasonable, and the affected client may also be making that judgment at a later time when the representation fails to achieve its objective. *See* FMC Techs., Inc. v. Edwards, 420 F. Supp.2d 1153 (W.D. Wash. 2006) (clients and former clients may move to disqualify counsel). Model Rule 1.7(b)(2)'s second condition requires the lawyer to ensure that another conduct rule or other law does not prohibit the conflicted representation. If another rule prohibits the representation, then the representation is nonconsentable.

Multiple Adverse Representations. Model Rule 1.7(b)(3)'s third condition—the easiest to recognize and with which to comply—prohibits consent if the lawyer would simultaneously be representing two clients who are litigating against one another. Appearing for both the plaintiff and defendant in the same case is nonconsentable. For example, when a divorcing couple approaches a lawyer to represent them both in obtaining the divorce, the lawyer must explain that as amicable as the proceeding may remain, the lawyer may represent only one of them. *See* Vinson v. Vinson, 588 S.E.2d 392 (Va. Ct. App. 2003) ("gross conflict"). Model Rule 1.7(b)(3)'s prohibition applies even if the lawyer represents the two adverse clients in two different cases involving unrelated matters. *See* Morse v. Clark, 890 So.2d 496 (Fla. Dist. Ct. App. 2004). If both are current clients, then the lawyer must not represent one in one proceeding and the other in another proceeding even if the two proceedings are unrelated. *See, e.g.,* In re Toups, 773 So.2d 709 (La. 2000) (district attorney prohibited from continuing representation of husband in divorce action when wife filed criminal complaint for attorney to prosecute against husband). A lawyer may represent multiple parties whose litigation interests align. *See, e.g.,* Patterson v. Balsamico, 440 F.3d 104 (2d Cir. 2006) (lawyer permitted to represent multiple defendants in civil rights case, where all were employed by defendant city).

Informed Consent. The fourth and final condition to a permitted concurrent conflict of interest is that the lawyer obtains the client's informed consent in writing. *See* Model Rule 1.7(b)(4). ABA Model Rule 1.0(e) defines informed consent to be a person's agreement to "after the lawyer has communicated adequate information and explanation about the material risks of and reasonably available alternatives to the proposed course of conduct." There is no holding back. The lawyer must communicate the material risks, meaning all of those things that might make the representation go poorly. The lawyer must also communicate the alternatives, meaning the means by which the client could obtain equivalent representation without the conflict. Model Rule 1.7(b)(4) requires that the client's consent be in writing. If you were to draft that writing for the client to sign, what would you include? Prudence suggests including the verbatim conduct rule under which the lawyer obtains the client's consent, a complete disclosure of the conflict and its material risks, and the alternatives. Some situations—call them non-consentable or non-waiveable—are so fraught with conflict that a lawyer could not reasonably seek the client's consent. *See* Model Rule 1.7(b)(1) (lawyer's belief that lawyer can represent client competently must be reasonable). Consider one such case that also illustrates that conflicts of interest can have constitutional dimensions in criminal cases involving appointment of counsel.

Holloway v. Arkansas,

United States Supreme Court
435 U.S. 475 (1978)

Mr. Chief Justice BURGER delivered the opinion of the Court.

Petitioners, codefendants at trial, made timely motions for appointment of separate counsel, based on the representations of their appointed counsel that, because of confidential information received from the codefendants, he was confronted with the risk of representing conflicting interests and could not, therefore, provide effective assistance for each client. We granted certiorari to decide whether petitioners were deprived of the effective assistance of counsel by the denial of those motions. ...

Early in the morning of June 1, 1975, three men entered a Little Rock, Ark., restaurant and robbed and terrorized the five employees of the restaurant. During the course of the robbery, one of the two female employees was raped once; the other, twice. ...

On July 29, 1975, the three defendants were each charged with one count of robbery and two counts of rape. On August 5, the trial court appointed Harold Hall, a public defender, to represent all three defendants. ... Two days later, their cases were set for a consolidated trial to commence September 4.

On August 13 Hall moved the court to appoint separate counsel for each petitioner because "the defendants ha[d] stated to him that there is a possibility of a conflict of interest in each of their cases... ." ... [T]he court declined to appoint separate counsel. ...

On September 4, before the jury was empaneled, Hall renewed the motion for appointment of separate counsel "on the grounds that one or two of the defendants may testify and if they do, then I will not be able to cross-examine them because I have received confidential information from them." The court responded, "I don't know why you wouldn't," and again denied the motion. ...

On the second day of trial, after the prosecution had rested its case, Hall advised the court that, against his recommendation, all three defendants had decided to testify. He then stated:

"Now, since I have been appointed, I had previously filed a motion asking the Court to appoint a separate attorney for each defendant because of a possible conflict of interest. This conflict will probably be now coming up since each one of them wants to testify."

"THE COURT: That's all right; let them testify. There is no conflict of interest. Every time I try more than one person in this court each one blames it on the other one."

"MR. HALL: I have talked to each one of these defendants, and I have talked to them individually, not collectively."

"THE COURT: Now talk to them collectively."

The court then indicated satisfaction that each petitioner understood the nature and consequences of his right to testify on his own behalf, whereupon Hall observed:

"I am in a position now where I am more or less muzzled as to any cross-examination."

"THE COURT: You have no right to cross-examine your own witness."

"MR. HALL: Or to examine them."

"THE COURT: You have a right to examine them, but have no right to cross-examine them. The prosecuting attorney does that."

"MR. HALL: If one [defendant] takes the stand, somebody needs to protect the other two's interest while that one is testifying, and I can't do that since I have talked to each one individually."

"THE COURT: Well, you have talked to them, I assume, individually and collectively, too. They all say they want to testify. I think it's perfectly alright [sic] for them to testify if they want to, or not. It's their business."

"Each defendant said he wants to testify, and there will be no cross-examination of these witnesses, just a direct examination by you."

"MR. HALL: Your Honor, I can't even put them on direct examination because if I ask them—"

"THE COURT: (Interposing) You can just put them on the stand and tell the Court that you have advised them of their rights and they want to testify; then you tell the man to go ahead and relate what he wants to. That's all you need to do."

Holloway then took the stand on his own behalf, testifying that during the time described as the time of the robbery he was at his brother's home. His brother had previously given similar testimony. When Welch took the witness stand, the record shows Hall advised him, as he had Holloway, that "I cannot ask you any questions that might tend to incriminate any one of the three of you.... Now, the only thing I can say is tell these ladies and gentlemen of the jury what you know about this case... ." Welch responded that he did not "have any kind of speech ready for the jury or anything. I thought I was going to be questioned." When Welch denied, from the witness stand, that he was at the restaurant the night of the robbery, Holloway interrupted, asking:

"Your Honor, are we allowed to make an objection?"

"THE COURT: No, sir. Your counsel will take care of any objections."

"MR. HALL: Your Honor, that is what I am trying to say. I can't cross-examine them."

"THE COURT: You proceed like I tell you to, Mr. Hall. You have no right to cross-examine your own witnesses anyhow."

Welch proceeded with his unguided direct testimony, denying any involvement in the crime and stating that he was at his home at the time it occurred. Campbell gave similar testimony when he took the stand. He also denied making any confession to the arresting officers.

The jury rejected the versions of events presented by the three defendants and the alibi witness, and returned guilty verdicts on all counts. On appeal to the Arkansas Supreme Court, petitioners raised the claim that their representation by a single appointed attorney, over their objection, violated federal constitutional guarantees of effective assistance of counsel. In resolving this issue, the court relied on what it characterized as the majority rule: "[T]he record must show some material basis for an alleged conflict of interest, before reversible error occurs in single representation of co-defendants." ...

... Here trial counsel, by the pretrial motions of August 13 and September 4 and by his accompanying representations, made as an officer of the court, focused explicitly on the probable risk of a conflict of interests. The judge then failed either to appoint separate counsel or to take adequate steps to ascertain whether the risk was too remote to warrant separate counsel. We hold that the failure, in the face of the representations made by counsel weeks before trial and again before the jury was empaneled, deprived petitioners of the guarantee of "assistance of counsel." ...

... [F]rom the cases cited it is clear that the prejudice [to the defendants] is presumed regardless of whether it was independently shown. ...

Moreover, this Court has concluded that the assistance of counsel is among those "constitutional rights so basic to a fair trial that their infraction can never be treated as harmless error." *Chapman v. California,* [386 U.S. 18,] 23[(1967)]. Accordingly, when a defendant is deprived of the presence and assistance of his attorney, either throughout the prosecution or during a critical stage in, at least, the prosecution of a capital offense, reversal is automatic. [Cc]

That an attorney representing multiple defendants with conflicting interests is physically present at pretrial proceedings, during trial, and at sentencing does not warrant departure from this general rule. Joint representation of conflicting interests is suspect because of what it tends to prevent the attorney from doing. For example, in this case it may well have precluded defense counsel for Campbell from exploring possible plea negotiations and the possibility of an agreement to testify for the prosecution, provided a lesser charge or a favorable sentencing recommendation would be acceptable. Generally speaking, a conflict may also prevent an attorney from challenging the admission of evidence prejudicial to one client but perhaps favorable to another, or from arguing at the sentencing hearing the relative involvement and culpability of his clients in order to minimize the culpability of one by emphasizing that of another. Examples can be readily multiplied. The mere physical presence of an attorney does not fulfill the Sixth

Amendment guarantee when the advocate's conflicting obligations have effectively sealed his lips on crucial matters.

Finally, a rule requiring a defendant to show that a conflict of interests—which he and his counsel tried to avoid by timely objections to the joint representation—prejudiced him in some specific fashion would not be susceptible of intelligent, evenhanded application. ... But in a case of joint representation of conflicting interests the evil—it bears repeating—is in what the advocate finds himself compelled to *refrain* from doing, not only at trial but also as to possible pretrial plea negotiations and in the sentencing process. It may be possible in some cases to identify from the record the prejudice resulting from an attorney's failure to undertake certain trial tasks, but even with a record of the sentencing hearing available it would be difficult to judge intelligently the impact of a conflict on the attorney's representation of a client. And to assess the impact of a conflict of interests on the attorney's options, tactics, and decisions in plea negotiations would be virtually impossible. Thus, an inquiry into a claim of harmless error here would require, unlike most cases, unguided speculation.

Accordingly, we reverse and remand for further proceedings not inconsistent with this opinion....

"What Were They Thinking?"

Does the trial court judge's reaction in *Holloway* surprise you? What blinded the trial judge to the appointed lawyer's conflict? One of the keys to being a successful litigator is learning to deal with biased judges (whether the bias involves ideology, race, gender, or just a bad mood that day) and those who are disorganized or just "don't get it." Do you agree that the lawyer in *Holloway* did a good job of making a record without arguing with, annoying, and disrespecting the judge? How should a lawyer disagree with a judge? Lawyers defending multiple defendants in a single criminal case sometimes enter joint-defense agreements to cooperate. Could three lawyers have done so in the above *Holloway* case, or would there still have been an unavoidable conflict?

INQUIRY

Transactional Conflicts. Many of the illustrations in this chapter involve litigation conflicts. Conflicts can exist almost as readily in transactional matters. Model Rule 1.7 Comment [27] gives as examples the drafting of wills for husband and wife or for several other family members. Each family member may have differing and even adverse interests in providing or not providing for one another. Comment [27] also gives estate administration as an example where transactional conflicts may arise. Jurisdictions differ over whether the client is the estate administrator or the estate itself including its creditors and beneficiaries. Yet in either case, the estate lawyer must make clear who is and is not the lawyer's client, and must refrain from advocating as a representative of anyone whose interests are adverse to the lawyer's estate client. Comment [28] gives as yet another example the negotiation of a joint venture. A lawyer might represent the venture assisting all of those who form it without contention, but the lawyer would ordinarily not be able to represent one constituent against another when interests diverge. Each would then obtain their own counsel. On occasion, a lawyer will represent two clients in two different matters in which it develops that the interests of one current client becomes adverse to the interests of the other current client, requiring the lawyer to withdraw. *See, e.g.,* Andrew Corp. v. Beverly Mfg. Co., 415 F. Supp.2d 919 (N.D. Ill. 2006).

Specific Conflicts. You might have surmised from the above three conflicts cases that conflicts tend to arise around common patterns. ABA Model Rule 1.7 provides only a general framework for addressing conflicts of interest. Why not address some of the common conflicts situations specifically? ABA Model Rule 1.8 does so, setting the conditions for when a lawyer may permissibly enter into a business transaction with a client, use client information against the client, accept a gift from a client, acquire literary or media rights relating to a representation, provide financial assistance to a client, accept compensation from someone other than the client to represent the client, and do several other things that implicate conflicts of interest. A conflict of interest under Model Rule 1.8 is a conflict under Model Rule 1.7. Read the following state version of Model Rule 1.8 for the conditions attached to each special conflict situation. Then read a case that cost a lawyer $33 million for not satisfying those conditions.

SOUTH DAKOTA R. PROF. CONDUCT 1.8: **Conflict of Interest: Current Clients, Specific Rules.**
(a) A lawyer shall not enter into a business transaction with a client or knowingly acquire an ownership, possessory, security or other pecuniary interest adverse to a client unless:
(1) the transaction and terms on which the lawyer acquires the interest are fair and reasonable to the client and are fully disclosed and transmitted in writing in a manner that can be reasonably understood by the client;
(2) the client is advised in writing of the desirability of seeking and is given a reasonable opportunity to seek the advice of independent legal counsel on the transaction; and
(3) the client gives informed consent, in a writing signed by the client, to the essential terms of the transaction and the lawyer's role in the transaction, including whether the lawyer is representing the client in the transaction.

(b) A lawyer shall not use information relating to representation of a client to the disadvantage of the client unless the client gives informed consent, except as permitted or required by these Rules.

(c) A lawyer shall not solicit any substantial gift from a client, including a testamentary gift, or prepare on behalf of a client an instrument giving the lawyer or a person related to the lawyer any substantial gift unless the lawyer or other recipient of the gift is related to the client and the gift is not significantly disproportionate to those given to other donees similarly related to donor. For purposes of this paragraph, related persons include a spouse, child, grandchild, parent, grandparent or other relative or individual with whom the lawyer or the client maintains a close, familial relationship.

(d) Prior to the conclusion of representation of a client, a lawyer shall not make or negotiate an agreement giving the lawyer literary or media rights to a portrayal or account based in substantial part on information relating to the representation.

(e) A lawyer shall not provide financial assistance to a client in connection with pending or contemplated litigation, except that:

(1) a lawyer may advance court costs and expenses of litigation, the repayment of which may be contingent on the outcome of the matter; and

(2) a lawyer representing an indigent client may pay court costs and expenses of litigation on behalf of the client.

(f) A lawyer shall not accept compensation for representing a client from one other than the client unless:

(1) the client gives informed consent;

(2) there is no interference with the lawyer's independence of professional judgment or with the client-lawyer relationship; and

(3) information relating to representation of a client is protected as required by Rule 1.6.

(g) A lawyer who represents two or more clients shall not participate in making an aggregate settlement of the claims of or against the clients, or in a criminal case an aggregated agreement as to guilty or nolo contendere pleas, unless each client gives informed consent, in a writing signed by the client. The lawyer's disclosure shall include the existence and nature of all the claims or pleas involved and of the participation of each person in the settlement.

(h) A lawyer shall not:

(1) make an agreement prospectively limiting the lawyer's liability to a client for malpractice unless the client is independently represented in making the agreement, or

(2) settle a claim or potential claim for such liability with an unrepresented client or former client unless that person is advised in writing of the desirability of seeking and is given a reasonable opportunity to seek the advice of independent legal counsel in connection therewith.

(i) A lawyer shall not acquire a proprietary interest in the cause of action or subject matter of litigation the lawyer is conducting for a client, except that the lawyer may:

(1) acquire a lien authorized by law to secure the lawyer's fee or expenses; and

(2) contract with a client for a reasonable contingent fee in a civil case.

(j) A lawyer shall not have sexual relations with a client unless a consensual sexual relationship existed between them before the client-lawyer relationship commenced.

(k) While lawyers are associated in a firm, a prohibition in the foregoing paragraphs (a) through (i) that applies to any one of them shall apply to all of them.

Passante v. McWilliam,
California Court of Appeal
62 Cal. Rptr.2d 298 (1997)

SILLS, Presiding Justice.

As someone once said, if you build it they will come. And by the same token, if you make a baseball card that can't be counterfeited, they will buy it. Which brings us to the case at hand.

In 1988 the Upper Deck Company was a rookie baseball card company with an idea for a better baseball card: one that had a hologram on it. Holograms protect credit cards from counterfeiting, and the promoters of the company thought they could protect baseball cards as well. By the 1990's the Upper Deck would become a major corporation whose value was at least a quarter of a billion dollars. Collecting baseball cards, like baseball itself, is big business.

But the outlook wasn't brilliant for the Upper Deck back in the summer of 1988. It lacked the funds for a $100,000 deposit it needed to buy some special paper by August 1, and without that deposit its contract with the major league baseball players association would have been jeopardized.

The Upper Deck's corporate attorney, Anthony Passante, then came through in the clutch. Passante found the money from the brother of his law partner, and, on the morning of July 29, had it wired to a company controlled by one of the directors. That evening, the directors of the company accepted the loan and, in gratitude, agreed among themselves that the corporate attorney should have three percent of the firm's stock. The rest is history. Instead of striking out, the Upper Deck struck it rich.

At this point, if we may be forgiven the mixed metaphor, we must change gears. No good deed goes unpunished. Anthony Passante never sought to collect the inchoate gift of stock, and later, the company just outright reneged on its promise. Passante sued for breach of oral contract, and the jury awarded him close to $33 million—the value of three percent of the Upper Deck at the time of trial in 1993.

The trial judge, however, granted a judgment notwithstanding the verdict, largely because he concluded that Passante had violated his ethical duty as a lawyer to his client. There was no dispute that Passante did not tell the board that it might want to consult with another lawyer before it made its promise. Nor did Passante advise the board of the complications which might arise from his being given three percent of the stock.

The board had a clear moral obligation to honor its promise to Passante. He had, as the baseball cliché goes, stepped up to the plate and homered on the Upper Deck's behalf. And if this court could enforce such moral obligations, we would advise the company even yet to pay something in honor of its promise.

But the trial judge was right. If the promise was *bargained for,* it was obtained in violation of Passante's ethical obligations as an attorney. If, on the other hand, it was not bargained for—as the record here clearly shows—it was gratuitous. It was therefore legally unenforceable, even though it might have moral force. We must therefore, with perhaps a degree of reluctance, affirm the judgment of the trial court. ...

DISCUSSION

In his opening brief Passante asserts that "[a]n enforceable contract requires only a promise capable of being enforced and consideration to support the promise." As framed, the assertion is incomplete. Consideration must also be given in exchange for the promise. Past consideration cannot support a contract. [C]

Cases relied on by Passante merely demonstrate the rule that the extinguishment of a preexisting obligation, or the rendering of past services *with the expectation of future payment,* constitute sufficient consideration for a contract. ...

As a matter of law, any claim by Passante for breach of contract necessarily founders on the rule that consideration must result from a bargain. ...

Thus if the stock promise was truly bargained for, then he had an obligation to the Upper Deck, as its counsel, to give the firm the opportunity to have separate counsel represent it in the course of that bargaining. The legal profession has certain rules regarding business transactions with clients. Rule 3–300 of the California Rules of Professional Conduct (formerly rule 5–101) forbids members from entering "a business transaction with a client" without first advising the client "in writing that the client may seek the advice of an independent lawyer of the client's choice."

Here it is undisputed that Passante did not advise the Upper Deck of the need for independent counsel in connection with its promise, either in writing or even orally. Had he done so *before* the Upper Deck made its promise, the board of directors might or might not have been so enthusiastic about his finding the money as to give away three percent of the stock. ... *Bargaining* between the parties might have resulted in Passante settling for just a reasonable finder's fee. Independent counsel would likely have at least reminded the board members of the obvious—that a grant of stock to Passante might complicate future capital acquisition.

For better or worse, there is an inherent conflict of interest created by any situation in which the corporate attorney for a fledgling company in need of capital accepts stock as a reward for past service. As events in this case proved out, had the gift of 3 percent of the company's stock been completed, it would have made the subsequent capital acquisition much more difficult.

Passante's rejoinder to the ethics issue is, as we have noted, to point to the evidence that the stock was virtually thrust at him in return for what he had done. The terms were totally dictated by the Upper Deck board. And that is it, precisely. There was no bargaining.

But a close reading of the facts shows that the stock had not been bargained for in exchange for arranging the loan; Passante had already arranged the loan (even though the loan had not been formally accepted by the board) before the idea of giving him stock was ever brought up. There is no evidence that Passante had any expectation that he be given stock in return for arranging the $100,000 loan. Clearly, all of Passante's services had already been rendered by the time the idea of giving Passante some stock was proposed. ...

CONCLUSION

The promise of three percent of the stock was not a reward contract.... It was simply, to use a phrase usually associated with life insurance contracts, an inchoate gift—that is, an unenforceable promise from a grateful corporate board. ... [I]t represented a moral obligation. ... [I]t was legally unenforceable. ... The judgments in favor of McWilliam, the Upper Deck, and Korbel are affirmed.

INQUIRY

Business Transactions with a Client. The *Passante* case is an extreme example of a common situation in which a lawyer has an opportunity to benefit from sharing in the client's success. *See, e.g.,* In re Nelson, 681 N.W.2d 352 (Minn. 2004) (lawyer induces clients to invest millions with lawyer); In re Davis, 740 N.E.2d 855 (Ind. 2001) (client invests settlement in lawyer's business). Model Rule 1.8(a) requires that the transaction be fair and fully disclosed in an understandable writing, that the lawyer write the client advising review by independent counsel, and that the client sign consent detailing the transaction. *See* In re Trewin, 684 N.W2d 121 (Wis.

2004) (client's signature on note not consent in writing); Cotton v. Kronenberg, 44 P.3d 878 (Wash. Ct. App. 2002) ($42,000 mobile home for $30,000 fee not fair). Whether lawyer and client can meet this standard depends on the nature and terms of the business transaction. Notice, too, that a lawyer must meet Model Rule 1.8(a)'s several conditions when the lawyer takes a security or other pecuniary interest adverse to a client. Lawyers may wish to secure their fees with a mortgage or lien in client property but must meet the rule's several conditions when doing so. *See, e.g.,* Valley/50th Ave., L.L.C. v. Stewart, 153 P.3d 186 (Wash. 2007); Ankerman v. Mancuso, 860 A.2d 244 (Conn. 2004) (note to secure fees permissible). Model Rule 1.8(i) prohibits a lawyer from taking a security interest in the subject of the litigation other than a charging or retaining lien allowed by law and, of course, a lien on proceeds in connection with a contingency-fee agreement. *See* People v. Mason, 938 P.2d 133 (Colo. 1997) (violation to take interest in cabin that would be subject of litigation representation). Can you see how a lawyer's security interest in the litigation's subject matter (a parcel of real property, for example) would give the lawyer too much control over the course and resolution of the litigation?

Biography

Isaac Hecht practiced law in downtown Baltimore for 65 years in a tax, corporate, and estate practice. About the quality of Mr. Hecht's advocacy, his law partner Bruce Chapper said, "In the 27 years that I've been his partner, I've never seen anyone fight harder or be more devoted to his clients' interests." Mr. Hecht's public service, though, made an equal or greater mark. Mr. Hecht was treasurer of the Maryland Client Security Trust Fund from its creation in 1967 until his death in 2003. He served on ABA committees encouraging such funds to the point that there is now one in every U.S. state and Canada province. The American Bar Association gives the Isaac Hecht Client Protection Fund Award once a year in recognition of those who excel in client protection. John Gleason, president of the National Client Protection Organization, said that Mr. Hecht "believed that the trust of law clients is the essential linchpin in every lawyer-client relationship, and that client protection funds represent the legal profession at its best." Mr. Hecht and his wife, to whom Mr. Hecht was married for 61 years, established several scholarships at Maryland educational institutions. Mr. Hecht was at his office working until a few weeks before he died at the age of eighty nine.

Substantial Gifts from Clients. The above *Passante* case involved a client's unsolicited gift to a lawyer. Model Rule 1.8(c) prohibits a lawyer from asking a client for a substantial gift. Model Rule 1.8 Comment [6] makes clear that a lawyer may accept a token of appreciation such as a present given at a holiday. Model Rule 1.8(c) prohibits only substantial gifts and, by its strict terms, prohibits only a lawyer soliciting (not receiving) a substantial gift. Whether solicited or not, the risk of overreaching is particularly acute when a lawyer prepares a will for a vulnerable client who has substantial property. *See, e.g.,* In re Boulger, 637 N.W.2d 710 (N.D. 2001); In re Goebel, 735 N.E.2d 1178 (Ind. 2000). The will should ordinarily not convey anything of substantial value to the lawyer or lawyer's relative. Although the practice is probably unwise, lawyers do on occasion prepare a will for a family member who desires to leave the lawyer a share of the estate proportionate to shares left to similar family members. Model Rule 1.8(c) permits those transactions. Can you see why it might still be better for the lawyer to suggest the help of another lawyer who is not a family member? Consider a case in which a lawyer conducted business transactions with clients and accepted a substantial gift from a relative without meeting Model Rule 1.8's requirements.

In re Lupo,
Massa chusetts Supreme Court
851 N.E.2d 404 (2006)

... The respondent, a solo practitioner concentrating in the practice of real estate law, has been a member of the Massachusetts bar since December, 1974. He became a licensed real estate broker in January, 1975, and owns a number of rental properties. ...

a. *Count one.* The first count concerns the respondent's representation as both lawyer and real estate broker of five elderly sisters, the termination of that relationship, and the respondent's subsequent lawsuit against the sisters and their new attorney. Central for our purposes is the conflict of interest arising from the respondent's dual role. Briefly stated, the sisters sought to sell an undeveloped parcel of land they had jointly inherited. ... The eldest sister first retained the respondent to provide legal representation to the sisters in the matter while the sisters engaged a real estate broker, Martin Coleman, to broker the sale of their property.... .

After receiving and rejecting several offers, the sisters, through Coleman, contacted Mark Rogers, a prospective buyer-developer who had previously expressed interest in the property, requesting a higher figure than he had offered. Rogers responded to Coleman with an offer of the requested amount. ... [O]n March 25, 1998, at the request of the husband of one sister, Coleman communicated the Rogers offer to the respondent (but not the sisters).... .

In the meantime, the respondent sought to become the broker for the sisters. ... The respondent asked the sisters to sign a standard form listing agreement providing for an exclusive right to sell the property. ... [T]he sisters had difficulty filling in the forms, and the respondent asked them to sign the forms with some of the information, including his fee, not yet specified. The hearing committee found that there was "no meeting of the minds as to the amount of the commission."

... On March 25, 1998, Coleman communicated the Rogers offer to the respondent. On May 5, 1998, after the property had been listed on MLS, the respondent received a second offer from a different prospective purchaser. The respondent did not inform his clients of either offer until a meeting with two of the sisters on May 21, 1998, at which he described the offers generally, informing the sisters falsely that both offers had come through the MLS listing. He also told the two sisters that he could not "move forward" with the offers until the listing agreement was signed by all five sisters, one of whom had not yet signed it.

On June 3, 1998, the respondent met with the sisters, Randall Jacobs, and attorney Kathleen Pendergast, the daughter of one of the sisters. The parties discussed the legal services agreement and the listing agreement. They amended the former to reflect the respondent's prior oral agreement to defer charging for his services until the property was sold. ... At Pendergast's request, the respondent provided the sisters with the listing agreement signed on March 11, 1998. The sisters then noted that a commission fee in the amount of ten per cent had been written into the space that had previously been blank, and a dispute ensued. ... The parties then agreed to a broker's fee of eight per cent of the sale price of the land up to $1.5 million and six per cent for any amount over $1.5 million. After they signed the agreement, the respondent then discussed the two offers he had received. The sisters agreed to pursue the Rogers offer, which ultimately was not successful. As of October, 2002, the property had not been sold.

The sisters subsequently learned that the Rogers offer presented to them by the respondent in June was the same offer that Coleman had received earlier. They then retained Pendergast as their lawyer and in July, 1998, Pendergast terminated the respondent's services as the sisters' lawyer and broker. She also filed a grievance concerning the respondent with the Office of Bar Counsel. ...

b. *Count two.* This count concerns claims of self-dealing by the respondent in connection with his providing legal services, including estate planning services, for his elderly aunt, Eleanor L. Lupo. In late 1999 and early 2000, the respondent's aunt sought his advice concerning payment of her living expenses from assets she held, including her house in Newton. The respondent discussed with his aunt her eligibility for Medicaid assistance in the event that she should enter a nursing home, and advised her, as the hearing committee found, that she would have to "spend-down" her funds if she sold her house in order to qualify for such assistance.

The respondent's aunt entered a nursing home in January, 2000. In March, 2000, the respondent purchased his aunt's house from her for $170,000. ... [A]t the time of the purchase, the respondent knew that the fair market value of his aunt's property was "substantially" more than his purchase price, and was at least $240,000. He failed to inform his aunt of this fact. The hearing committee concluded that the respondent "knowingly misrepresented" the value of the property to his aunt in order to purchase it from her for substantially less than its fair market value.

The hearing committee also found that the respondent did not advise his aunt to obtain the advice of independent counsel regarding Medicaid eligibility and the advisability of selling her house to the respondent. Despite the respondent's claim to the contrary, the hearing committee found that the respondent was not "simply acting as a nephew" in advising his aunt, but was "providing his aunt with legal services." The hearing committee noted that the respondent had a fiduciary obligation to his aunt under the power of attorney and a "personal business interest," as one who owned and rented residential properties, in acquiring his aunt's house for himself.

In 2000, another nephew of the respondent's aunt, Thomas Gallinelli, learned of the house transaction between the respondent and his aunt. He retained an attorney to ascertain the facts. ...

The hearing committee ... concluded that the respondent violated Mass. R. Prof. C. 1.8(a), [c], because he had not fully disclosed to his clients the ramifications of his actions and because his clients were not given any opportunity to seek the advice of independent counsel. ... By continuing to represent the sisters as their attorney after the parties entered into the listing agreement, the hearing committee concluded, the respondent had violated Mass. R. Prof. C. 1.7(b), [c]. ...

... The hearing committee also concluded that the respondent's conduct in having his aunt sign the deed conveying her house to him, where the terms of the transaction were not fair and reasonable to his aunt and were not fully disclosed in a manner she could reasonably understand, and where she was not given an opportunity to seek the advice of independent counsel, violated rule 1.8(a).....

... As to count one, we have reviewed the entire record and are satisfied that there was more than adequate evidence to support each of the violations found by the board. ...

As to count two, the respondent ... claims that "it simply would have taken longer" for his aunt to "spend-down her assets and obtain Medicaid coverage" had she received a higher purchase price. The respondent's posture is an extraordinary one: he paid his aunt less than the fair market value in order to hasten her qualification for Medicaid coverage, all for his own benefit. This court declines to give its imprimatur to any such fraudulent scheme. The record is clear that at the time of this nefarious transaction his aunt was elderly, and dependent on him as her only caregiver. ...

... We now turn to the issue of an appropriate sanction.

... In two separate matters, the respondent engaged in "clear, personal conflicts of interest with elderly, unsophisticated and vulnerable clients," in the words of the hearing committee. The respondent's conduct reflects an insensitivity to his obligation of absolute fiduciary fidelity to those whom he counselled, combined with a pattern of self-dealing and self-enrichment at their expense. His conduct is particularly egregious as concerns his aunt who, the record is clear, relied on him for advice and counsel. The obligation of an attorney to those he advises does not terminate because of the existence of a familial or close relationship, or because he is not compensated for his services. Such a relationship requires that the attorney exercise the greatest care because the level of trust placed in his advice will likely be all the greater. For these reasons, we agree with bar counsel that a two-year suspension "does not give full weight to the extended and predatory nature of the respondent's misconduct."
...

... We ... conclude that an indefinite suspension is appropriate ... [and] that restitution to the aunt's estate is appropriate. ... An order shall enter forthwith suspending the respondent indefinitely from the practice of law. ...

INQUIRY

Financial Assistance. Model Rule 1.8(e) prohibits a lawyer from providing financial assistance to a client in connection with pending or contemplated litigation, except to advance costs in a contingency-fee matter or to pay expenses for an indigent client's representation. Historically, financing litigation was controversial and outlawed as champerty. The concern was that shifting the financial incentive and risk from lawyer to client would lead to an increase of litigation and loss of client control over it. Contingency-fee arrangements and litigation assistance for the indigent are established policy exceptions promoting access to justice. A contingency-fee lawyer may advance expenses for filing fees, deposition transcripts, and other litigation expenses but may not give or loan money to a client for food, rent, medical care, or other necessities. *See* State v. Smolen, 17 P.3d 456

(Okla. 2000) (prohibiting humanitarian exception for disabled client's living expenses); *cf.* Florida Bar v. Taylor, 648 So.2d 1190 (Fla. 1994) (permitting humanitarian aid for child's clothing). Model Rule 1.8(e)'s restriction is in some respects welcome for contingency-fee lawyers who already bear the burden of advancing expenses and should not have to entertain client demands for personal assistance. The restriction also prevents contingency-fee lawyers from competing for and, in essence, buying the claims of desireable contingency-fee clients.

Collateral Compensation. Model Rule 1.8(f) prohibits a lawyer from letting someone else pay for a client's representation unless the client gives informed consent, the payor does not interfere with the representation, and the lawyer does not share with the payor confidential information about the representation. When would someone pay a lawyer to represent another? Lawyers face common instances when one person pays for the representation of another including parents for representing a child, employers an employee, and insurers the insured. *See, e.g.,* Nevada Yellow Cab Corp. v. Eighth Jud. Dist. Ct., 152 P.3d 737 (Nev. 2007) (insurer and insured are effectively both clients, even though primary duty is to insured). Can you discern why the restrictions of Model Rule 1.8(f) are necessary? Just because someone pays for another's representation should not give the payor control over the outcome. The payor may desire to control the outcome—what parent or employer on occasion would not?—but the lawyer must keep the client's interest at heart. *See, e.g.,* United States v. Schwarz, 283 F.3d 76 (2d Cir. 2002) (ineffective assistance for lawyer to accept retainer from police union to defend officers). Payment is one thing, devotion another.

Aggregate Settlements. Model Rule 1.8(g) prohibits a lawyer from settling multiple clients' claims in the aggregate without obtaining written informed consent. In personal-injury cases, lawyers may occasionally represent two or more plaintiffs or defendants, provided that they can do so without conflict under Model Rule 1.7. Negotiations may then proceed around establishing a fair lump-sum amount to settle all claims, leaving for later the division of the lump sum among the plaintiffs or division of payment among the defendants. Model Rule 1.8(g) ensures that the lawyer representing multiple clients does not settle a case in the aggregate without first giving each client all information necessary to evaluate the settlement and then obtaining each client's written consent. *See* In re Hoffman, 883 So.2d 425 (La. 2004) (communicate each client's share to each client rather than dealing through one client). The conflict problem becomes particularly acute when the available insurance limits are less than the aggregated settlement value. *See, e.g,* Straubinger v. Schmitt,

CHAPTER IX LOYALTY 399

792 A.2d 481 (N.J. Sup. Ct. App. Div. 2002). Model Rule 1.8(g) applies as well to settling a criminal case by aggregated agreement.

Limiting and Settling Malpractice Claims. Model Rule 1.8(h) prohibits a lawyer from limiting and settling malpractice claims without advising the client in writing to seek independent counsel and giving the client a chance to do so. Lawyers are prudent drafters. They know how to manage and allocate risk. A lawyer might draft a fee agreement that required a client to waive future potential malpractice claims. Model Rule 1.8(h)(1) prohibits prophylactic malpractice-waiver agreements in most cases. The only place that one is likely to see a prospective waiver of malpractice claims is with a sophisticated corporate client who asks a lawyer to take on extraordinary risk in the representation. Model Rule 1.8(h)(2) addresses the settlement of an actual rather than prospective malpractice claim. A lawyer may settle a malpractice claim with an unrepresented current or former client only if the lawyer advises the client in writing that it is in their best interest to seek the advice of an independent attorney and if the attorney gives the client a reasonable opportunity to seek the counsel of another attorney. *See* In re Braun, 734 N.E.2d 535 (Ind. 2000) (failure to advise client to seek independent counsel). What if the client cannot afford to hire independent counsel? May the attorney seeking to settle the malpractice claim hire an independent lawyer to represent the client in settling the malpractice claim? Reconsider Model Rule 1.8(f).

Sexual Relations. Model Rule 1.8(j), a 2002 amendment, prohibits a lawyer from having sexual relations with a client unless the sexual relationship existed before the client became a client of the lawyer. Comment [19] to Model Rule 1.8 cautions that when the client is an organization, Model Rule 1.8(j)'s prohibition applies to "a constituent of the organization who supervises, directs or regularly consults with that lawyer concerning the organization's legal matters." Can you discern the hazards that sexual intimacy between lawyer and client create? Clients, particularly those who are involved in divorce and criminal matters, are often vulnerable emotionally, socially, psychologically, and spiritually. *See, e.g.,* In re Berg, 955 P.2d 1240 (Kan. 1998) (undue advantage over divorce clients to induce sexual relationships); In re Rinella, 677 N.E.2d 909 (Ill. 1997) (same). They may attempt to transfer their personal desires and relationships from their proper objects within their families and social circles to the professional relationship with the lawyer—a phenomenon with which psychologists and therapists are quite familiar. Lawyers must keep relationships professional for the benefit of the clients and for their own good. Their loyalties must be to the client, not for the satisfaction of their own interests and desires. Many jurisdictions have yet to adopt Model Rule 1.8(j), but some without the specific prohibition have nonetheless held sexual relations with a client to violate Model Rule 1.7's general prohibition on conflicts of interest. *See, e.g,,* State v. Downes, 121 P.3d 1058 (Okla. 2005); In re Tsoutsouris, 748 N.E.2d 856 (Ind. 2001).

C. Former-Client Conflicts

Persistent Loyalty. A lawyer's loyalty to a client does not end when the representation ends. Loyalty extends beyond the period of legal service. Lawyers learn things about clients and their matters in the course of a representation that others could use against the client, if a lawyer gave those others the opportunity. If when the representation ended a lawyer could use against the client and for the benefit of a new client what the lawyer learned in the representation, then clients would be less willing or unwilling to consult with lawyers. To ensure a lawyer's continuing loyalty to former clients, ABA Model Rule 1.9(a) prohibits a lawyer from representing a person whose interests are adverse in the same or substantially related matter in which the lawyer represented a former client, unless the former client gives written informed consent. Model Rule 1.9(c) extends the prohibition beyond representing an adverse client in the same or substantially related matter, to even using information to the disadvantage of the former client outside of a representation, except as the rules otherwise permit (for example, to prove a fee claim against a client). Read a similar state version of Model Rule 1.9 for these fundamentals and for its rule of imputed disqualification.

> **SOUTH DAKOTA R. PROF. CONDUCT 1.9: Duties to Former Clients.**
> (a) A lawyer who has formerly represented a client in a matter shall not thereafter represent another person in the same or a substantially related matter in which that person's interests are materially adverse to the interests of the former client unless the former client gives informed consent, confirmed in writing.
> (b) A lawyer shall not knowingly represent a person in the same or a substantially related matter in which a firm with which the lawyer formerly was associated had previously represented a client
> (1) whose interests are materially adverse to that person; and
> (2) about whom the lawyer had acquired information protected by Rules 1.6 and 1.9(c) that is material to the matter; unless the former client gives informed consent, confirmed in writing.
> (c) A lawyer who has formerly represented a client in a matter or whose present or former firm has formerly represented a client in a matter shall not thereafter:
> (1) Use information relating to the representation to the disadvantage of the former client except as these Rules would permit or require with

respect to a client, or when the information has become generally known; or

(2) Reveal information relating to the representation except as these Rules would permit or require with respect to a client.

INQUIRY

Distinguishing Current from Former Clients. A challenging but critical distinction to make is whether a client is a current client or a former client. To what events or circumstances would you look to determine whether a client is a current client or former client? *See, e.g.,* Oxford Sys., Inc. v. Cellpro, Inc., 45 F. Supp.2d 1055 (W.D. Wash. 1999) (current, not former, client based on long-term ongoing relationship); Hatfield v. Seville Centrifugal Bronze, 732 N.E.2d 1077 (Ohio C.P. 2000) (current, not former, client based on annual advice without termination notice). The distinction is critical because the standards in Model Rule 1.7 and Model Rule 1.9 are different. Clients cannot consent to some concurrent conflicts under Model Rule 1.7, particularly representing adverse parties in the same litigation. If a lawyer saw an opportunity to represent a desireable prospective client but would have to drop a current client in order to eliminate a concurrent conflict, may the lawyer do so? *See* Santacroce v. Neff, 134 F. Supp.2d 366 (D. N.J. 2001) (disqualifying law firm over "hot potato" gambit); *see also* RESTATEMENT OF THE LAW GOVERNING LAWYERS §132, Comment c ("The present client conflict may not be transformed into a former-client conflict by the lawyer's withdrawal from the representation of the existing client."). By contrast, former clients may under Model Rule 1.9 consent to any conflict, if the lawyer meets each of the rule's requirements. The question of when a current client becomes a former client is also likely to determine when the statute of limitations will begin to run on the client's potential malpractice claims against the lawyer.

Substantially Related Matters. Perhaps the biggest distinction between the treatment of current and former clients, though, is that Model Rule 1.9 former-client conflicts prohibit a lawyer from representing an adverse client only in the "same or substantially related matter," not, as in Model Rule 1.7, any other matter. Conflicts between current clients turn on whether the interests of the clients are adverse even if the clients are involved in entirely unrelated matters. Conflicts between a former and current client depend on showing the substantial relationship of the two matters. A relationship between matters is substantial if they arose out of the same transaction. *See, e.g.,* Franklin v. Callum, 782 A.2d 884 (N.H. 2001). On the other hand, if the relationship between matters is only incidental and not substantial, then there is no disqualifying conflict of interest. *See* S.D. Warren Co. v. Duff-Norton, 302 F. Supp.2d 762 (W.D. Mich. 2004); Duvall v. Bledsoe, 617 S.E.2d 601 (Ga. 2005). Courts have frequently addressed these definitions and tests. *See* In re Carey, 89 S.W.3d 477 (Mo. 2002) ("gallons of ink" trying to define them). The critical concern that they approximate is whether the lawyer will have adverse information from the prior representation. *See* County of L.A. v. United States Dist. Ct., 223 F.3d 990 (9th Cir. 2000). General knowledge of a former client's business may not be enough to disqualify a lawyer from representing a subsequent client with an adverse interest. *See, e.g.,* State ex rel. Ogden Newspapers, Inc. v. Wilkes, 566 S.E.2d 560 (W. Va. 2002). Consider the following case showing the significance and difficulty of determining whether matters are substantially related and introducing Model Rule 1.9's rule of imputed disqualification.

Haagen-Dazs Co. v. Perche No! Gelato, Inc.,
United States District Court for the Northern District of California
639 F. Supp. 282 (1986)

This is a motion by the Pillsbury Company, Inc., ("Pillsbury"), the parent company of Haagen-Dazs Company, Inc. ("Haagen-Dazs"), for the disqualification of counsel for Double Rainbow Gourmet Ice Cream, Inc. ("Double Rainbow") in this antitrust litigation.

Double Rainbow is ... engaged in the manufacture and sale of super premium ice cream. Pillsbury... entered the super premium ice cream market when it purchased Haagen-Dazs in 1983. Haagen-Dazs ... manufactures and sells super premium ice cream. Haagen-Dazs and Double Rainbow are competitors. The main issue presently raised by this litigation is whether Haagen-Dazs' distribution policies violate the antitrust laws. ...

Pillsbury and Haagen-Dazs filed this motion to disqualify both San Francisco and Minneapolis counsel from representing Double Rainbow in this series of actions.... .

The basis for this motion is the past and present employment of Mr. Franklin C. Jesse, Esq., an attorney formerly employed as in-house counsel in the Pillsbury Company legal department, and currently associated with Double Rainbow's Minneapolis counsel, Gray, Plant, Mooty, Mooty & Bennett ("the Gray firm"). Haagen-Dazs and Pillsbury contend that Mr. Jesse's former employment with Pillsbury and current employment with the Gray firm require disqualification of Mr. Jesse. They assert that, as a Pillsbury attorney for ten years, Mr. Jesse was aware of Haagen-Dazs' distribution policies, and had access to confidential information relating to the issues underlying this litigation. They also seek an order disqualifying the Gray firm. In addition, they claim that, due to the long-standing affiliation of the Gray firm with Double Rainbow's San Francisco counsel, Alioto & Alioto ("Alioto"), that firm must also be disqualified from participation in this litigation.

The record discloses that Mr. Jesse went to work in the Pillsbury legal department in 1974 and remained until October 1984. During that period, Mr. Jesse held various positions, including general attorney, senior attorney, international group counsel, and senior corporate counsel. From 1980 until October 1984, Mr. Jesse was also a member of the legal department's administration committee.

It appears that Mr. Jesse worked primarily on international business and legal matters while employed by Pillsbury. ... Haagen-Dazs alleges that Mr. Jesse has knowledge of Pillsbury's acquisition and marketing strategy, since he was a member of the legal department at the time the policy for entering the super premium ice cream market was adopted. Finally, Mr. Jesse was in the legal department in 1984 at the time that office defended a claim brought by Ben & Jerry's Homemade, Inc., another manufacturer of super premium ice cream, which involved issues identical or similar to those raised in this series of cases.

At the present time, Mr. Jesse is an associate "international counsel" with the Gray firm. Since joining that firm on November 1, 1984, his practice has involved primarily international business matters. Mr. Jesse has stated in a declaration and in a deposition that he has no present knowledge of the distribution policies which are challenged here, and that he was not privy to confidences concerning the issues raised by this litigation. Furthermore, Mr. Jesse states that he has not worked on these cases, or on any of the related cases, and that his only connection with this litigation has been in response to this motion made by Pillsbury and Haagen-Dazs. ...

Rule 1.9(a) of the American Bar Association Model Rules of Professional Conduct (1983) provides that: "A lawyer who has formerly represented a client in a matter shall not thereafter: (a) represent another person in the same or a substantially related matter in which that person's interests are materially adverse to the interests of the former client unless the former client consents after consultation. ..."

The Ninth Circuit has specifically adopted this "substantial relationship" test, and in *Trone v. Smith,* 621 F.2d 994 (9th Cir.1980), the court elaborated on the standard by stating that the test is met if the factual contexts of the two representations are similar or related, regardless of "whether confidences were in fact imparted to the lawyer by the client" in the prior representation. *Id.* at 998-99. ... "If there is a *reasonable probability* that confidences were disclosed which could be used against the client in a later, adverse representation, a substantial relation between the two cases is presumed." *Id.* at 998 (emphasis added). ...

Thus, to make the showing necessary for disqualification of Double Rainbow's counsel, Haagen-Dazs and Pillsbury must establish that Mr. Jesse, while at Pillsbury, worked on matters substantially related to this litigation, or that there is a reasonable probability that Mr. Jesse received confidential information. If there is a showing that Mr. Jesse was privy to client confidences substantially related to this litigation, Double Rainbow may then attempt to show that Mr. Jesse had no personal involvement in the substantially related matters.

Regardless of the particular language used by the courts and the rules of professional conduct to define the standards, a common principle underlies all of them: the interests of the clients are primary, and the interests of the lawyers are secondary. ...

The court has reviewed the exhibits and memoranda submitted by both parties and in light of the above standards concludes that, while at Pillsbury, Mr. Jesse worked on matters substantially related to this litigation, and that there is a reasonable basis for concluding that he received confidential information relevant to this litigation. ...

... The record here discloses substantial similarities in the legal employments of Mr. Jesse and the legal and business matters involved in those employments. While Mr. Jesse and the Gray firm have attempted to show that his distribution-related work was limited to international matters, it appears that Mr. Jesse had information concerning Haagen-Dazs' domestic distribution strategies as well. Mr. Jesse worked for a lengthy period of time in the Pillsbury legal department, and it is reasonable to conclude that, as a senior attorney in that office, he also had significant contact with Pillsbury management during the formulation of its super premium ice cream acquisition and marketing strategy. While Mr. Jesse states that he was not aware of Haagen-Dazs' distribution policies, his presence in the legal department at the time Pillsbury entered the super premium ice cream market suggests that he was at least exposed to management's and the legal department's consideration of distribution policies. In addition, his employment during the Ben & Jerry's litigation raises an inference that he was privy to information about that litigation which is, in itself, substantially related to this litigation. ...

The court further finds that the presumptions in favor of Pillsbury's and Haagen-Dazs' position have not been rebutted. The record demonstrates that Mr. Jesse did have personal involvement in legal matters which the court finds are substantially related to the issues in this case, and that he did receive certain relevant confidential information.

The court concludes that disqualification of Mr. Jesse is necessary to protect Haagen-Dazs' and Pillsbury's confidences and to avoid the appearance of impropriety. ...

Since the court has concluded that Mr. Jesse must be disqualified, it follows under the rule set forth in the *Trone* case and the Model rule that the law firm of Gray, Plant, Mooty, Mooty & Bennett must also be disqualified from further representation in this litigation.

The Gray firm has argued that its disqualification is not mandated because it instituted a screening procedure whereby all files and information relating to this litigation were sealed off from Mr. Jesse. The Ninth Circuit has considered this so-called "Chinese Wall" defense twice, but has left open the question whether such a screening procedure is sufficient to defeat a disqualification motion when a member of the firm has previously worked on matters substantially related to the pending litigation. ... At the least, the burden is shifted to the law firm to establish the effectiveness of its "Chinese Wall" procedures.

In this case, it appears that the Gray firm did not institute the "Chinese Wall" measures until *after* the first of these suits had been filed. ... In light of the fact that the screening procedures were not instituted until after the litigation commenced, and one year after Mr. Jesse's employment, the court concludes that Double Rainbow's "Chinese Wall" defense will not insulate the firm from disqualification.
...

Haagen-Dazs and Pillsbury argue that the Gray firm and the Alioto firm have a long-standing relationship "characterized by continuous exchange of information, strategy and advice," and that the Alioto firm must therefore be disqualified on the basis of its affiliation with the Gray firm. ...

In evaluating the association of these two firms, the court notes that there is nothing on the record to suggest that Mr. Jesse had any direct contact with the Alioto firm. ...

... [T]he court finds that while the two firms have worked together on this and other litigation, the association between Alioto & Alioto and the Gray firm does not warrant disqualification of the Alioto firm. In the court's view, the risk of disclosure of client confidences will be virtually eliminated by the disqualification of the Gray firm. That disqualification should also greatly reduce any appearance of impropriety. The record does not warrant the extension of vicarious disqualification to another level. ...

THEREFORE, IT IS ORDERED that:

(1) Mr. Franklin Jesse is disqualified from further representation of

any party to this litigation;

(2) Gray, Plant, Mooty, Mooty & Bennett, are disqualified from further representation of any party to this litigation;

(3) The requested disqualification of Alioto & Alioto is denied; ... .

INQUIRY

Imputed Disqualification. Imputed disqualification involves the vicarious disqualification of a law firm and the rest of its lawyers because of the direct disqualification of one or more of its lawyers. The next chapter addresses more completely and directly the imputed disqualification of lawyers and law firms. Imputed disqualification is the whole subject of ABA Model Rule 1.10 addressed in the next chapter. For now, though, appreciate that Model Rule 1.9(b) embeds its own imputed-disqualification rule within the rules on conflicts of interest involving former clients. The reason for Model Rule 1.9(b) to treat imputed disqualification rather than leaving it for Model Rule 1.10 is that Model Rule 1.9(b)'s rule of imputed disqualification involving former clients is limited, not general like Model Rule 1.10. For Model Rule 1.9(b) to disqualify the other lawyers and law firm, the lawyer who formerly represented the client must have acquired confidential information material to the matter from which the other lawyers and law firm are to be disqualified. When the conflicts analysis bases imputed disqualification on a lawyer's representation of a former rather than current client, the lawyer must have had confidential information from that former client. The concern must be actual, not theoretical. Presumably, the lawyer can no longer acquire information from a former client, so there is no reason to disqualify other lawyers and firms simply because the lawyer once represented the former client.

Lawyers Changing Firms. Another reason that Model Rule 1.9(b) limits imputed disqualification to associates of lawyers who have actual knowledge of the former client's adverse matter is to facilitate movement of lawyers from firm to firm. *See* Model Rule 1.9 Comments [4]-[7]. In essence, when a lawyer changes firms, the lawyer brings along a set of conflicts of interest that impute disqualification to members of the new law firm. In narrow fields in which there are few clients each having large needs for legal services, imputed disqualification can ruin a firm. By limiting Model Rule 1.9(b) to imputed disqualification based only on actual knowledge, lawyers have a better chance to move from firm to firm, even though movement is still restricted. *See* Healthnet, Inc. v. Health Net, Inc., 289

CHAPTER IX LOYALTY 407

F. Supp.2d 755 (S.D. W. Va. 2003) (inadequate screening of lawyer who moved to firm). We will return to these subjects in the next chapter.

D. Prospective-Client Conflicts

Loyalty to Prospective Clients. A lawyer's loyalty also extends to prospective clients. ABA Model Rule 1.18(a) defines a prospective client as someone who discusses with a lawyer the possibility of forming a lawyer-client relationship. By definition, prospective clients do not become "retained" clients of the lawyer. Lawyers can and do provide substantial legal services to prospective clients, merely by discussing the possibility of representation.   In brief initial consultations with a lawyer, prospective clients learn about the nature of their legal rights, whether they have legal claims or defenses, and how to protect their legal rights, pursue claims, and raise defenses. Prospective clients learn how lawyers deliver and price legal services, while lawyers learn facts and circumstances from their prospective clients. Lawyers must maintain confidentiality and ensure loyalty in these initial consultations with prospective clients, to ensure the free exchange of information. If lawyers owed no duties to prospective clients, then those prospective clients would guard their words, and lawyers would have little opportunity to learn what they needed to determine whether to undertake the representation. It does not matter whether a prospective client ever retains counsel. Model Rule1.18 binds to loyalty and confidentiality the lawyer with whom the prospective client consults, in essence making it a conflict of interest for the lawyer to disclose or use the prospective client's information, or represent a client adverse to the prospective client after receiving the prospective client's information. Read the following similar state version of Model Rule 1.18, followed by an illustrative case.

> **SOUTH DAKOTA R. PROF. CONDUCT 1.18: Duties to Prospective Client.**
> (a) A person who discusses with a lawyer the possibility of forming a client-lawyer relationship with respect to a matter is a prospective client.
> (b) Even when no client-lawyer relationship ensues, a lawyer who has had discussions with a prospective client shall not use or reveal information learned in the consultation, except as in Rule 1.9 would permit with respect to information of a former client.
> (c) A lawyer subject to paragraph (b) shall not represent a client with interests materially adverse to those of a prospective client in the same or a substantially related matter if the lawyer received information from the prospective client that could be significantly harmful to that person in the matter, except as provided in paragraph (d). If a lawyer is disqualified from representation under this paragraph, no lawyer in a firm with which that lawyer is associated may knowingly undertake or continue representation in such a matter, except as provided in paragraph (d).

(d) When the lawyer has received disqualifying information as defined in paragraph (c), representation is permissible if:

(1) both the affected client and the prospective client have given informed consent, confirmed in writing, or

(2) the lawyer who received the information took reasonable measures to avoid exposure to more disqualifying information than was reasonably necessary to determine whether to represent the prospective client; and

(i) the disqualified lawyer is timely screened from any participation in the matter and is apportioned no part of the fee therefrom; and

(ii) written notice is promptly given to the prospective client.

Sturdivant v. Sturdivant,
Arkansas Supreme Court
241 S.W.3d 740 (2006)

ANNABELLE CLINTON IMBER, Justice.

This is a case of first impression involving the interpretation of the Arkansas Rules of Professional Conduct, more specifically Rule 1.18 (2006). The question raised on appeal is whether the circuit court erred in disqualifying attorney James L. Tripcony and his law firm from representing Appellant Sharon J. Sturdivant in a post-divorce custody proceeding against Appellee Timothy L. Sturdivant. We affirm the order of the circuit court.

... On February 15, 2005, the Pulaski County Circuit Court entered an amended decree and order that gave Timothy physical custody of his minor children from Sunday evening of every week until Thursday evening, as well as alternating weekend visitation. At that time, Sharon's attorney of record was Dee Scritchfield and Timothy's attorney of record was Linda Shepherd.

Two months later, on April 25, 2005, James L. Tripcony filed his entry of appearance as Sharon's attorney of record in the divorce proceeding. Timothy's counsel sent a letter to Tripcony, notifying him that the Tripcony Law Firm had a conflict of interest that would require his immediate withdrawal as Sharon's attorney. Specifically, the letter stated that Timothy had consulted with Heather May of the Tripcony Law Firm about a change of custody before he retained the Shepherd Law Firm to represent him in the same matter. After receiving the notice of a potential conflict, Sharon's attorney filed a motion for relief from order.

According to testimony elicited at a hearing on the motion, Timothy retained Linda Shepherd to represent him in the divorce proceeding after a "lengthy consultation" with Heather May of the Tripcony Law Firm about his desire to seek a change of custody. May took notes during the consultation and Timothy gave her a copy of a journal in which he had recorded matters involving him, Sharon, and the children. He also disclosed facts that were not in the journal and told May everything he knew regarding the children and his concerns about his former wife. The journal was eventually disclosed to opposing counsel in the earlier custody proceeding that culminated in the entry of the February 15, 2005 amended decree and order. Finally, Timothy confirmed that he did not retain the Tripcony Law Firm to represent him in the custody proceeding.

Tripcony advised the court that when he was notified of the potential conflict, he and May checked their office files to find out whether Timothy had been in the office. Upon discovering that Timothy had indeed consulted with May, Tripcony consulted the newly revised rules of professional conduct concerning prospective clients. *See* Ark. R. Prof'l Conduct 1.18 (2006). He further stated that he and May reviewed her notes and determined that they had no information that would be harmful to Timothy. Following his review of May's consultation notes and the Arkansas Rules of Professional Conduct, Tripcony concluded that disqualification would not be warranted under Rule 1.18.

The circuit court ruled otherwise in an order entered on September 1, 2005, that disqualified Tripcony and his law firm from representing Sharon. Specifically, the court found that prior to Shepherd being retained by Timothy in the change-of-custody proceeding, Timothy had consulted with, received legal advice from, and provided confidential information to May concerning the custody proceeding. From that order, Sharon filed a timely notice of appeal. ...

For her sole point on appeal, Sharon asserts that the circuit court erred when it applied Rule 1.9 of the Arkansas Rules of Professional Conduct to disqualify Tripcony and his law firm. She claims that disqualification of her attorney is not warranted under Ark. R. Prof'l Conduct 1.18. As support for that claim, she asserts that the Tripcony Law Firm received no information that could be "significantly harmful" to her former husband. ...

Here, Sharon asserts that Rule 1.18 was adopted in 2005 to give guidance to attorneys in their duties owed to prospective clients, as opposed to Rule 1.9, which deals with former clients. Specifically, she relies upon Rule 1.18(c), which bars an attorney from representing a client with adverse interests to those of a prospective client in a substantially related matter if the attorney "received information from the prospective client that could be significantly harmful to that person in the matter." ... As further support for her position, Sharon cites Comment 1 to Ark. R. Prof'l Conduct 1.18, which states, "A lawyer's discussions with a prospective client usually are limited in time and depth and leave both the prospective client and the lawyer free (and sometimes required) to proceed no further. Hence, prospective clients should receive some but not all of the protection afforded clients."

In applying the provisions of Rule 1.18 to the facts of this case, it is undisputed that Timothy was a prospective client under the terms of Rule 1.18(a) when he consulted with Heather May of the Tripcony Law Firm. Moreover, as a result of that communication, May was prohibited from using or revealing information learned in her meeting with Timothy, "except Rule 1.9 would permit with respect to information of a former client." Ark. R. Prof'l Conduct 1.18(b)(2006). Thus, the duty May owed to Timothy as a prospective client under Rule 1.18(b) would be coextensive with the duty an attorney owes to a former client under Rule 1.9(c). Furthermore, the duty to a prospective client exists regardless of how brief the initial conference may have been and regardless of the fact that no client-attorney relationship ensued. Comment 3 to Ark. R. Prof'l Conduct 1.18 (2006).

As a lawyer subject to the provisions of Rule 1.18(b), May would also be prohibited from representing a client with interests materially adverse to those of her prospective client, Timothy, in the same or a substantially related matter if she received information from Timothy "that could be significantly harmful to [him] in the matter." Ark. R. Prof'l Conduct 1.18(c)(2006). The circuit court correctly concluded that Timothy was a prospective client of the Tripcony Law Firm and that the current action is the same custody proceeding for which Timothy consulted May of the Tripcony Law Firm. Likewise, Sharon does not contest the fact that her interests are materially adverse to those of her former husband, Timothy. ...

... [W]e cannot say that the circuit court clearly erred in finding that harmful information would have been forthcoming during Timothy's conference with Heather May of the Tripcony Law Firm about this change-of-custody proceeding. As stated earlier, Timothy testified that in addition to giving May a copy of his journal, he also told her about facts that were not in the journal, and he disclosed everything he knew and his concerns about the children and his former wife. According to Timothy, he acted upon advice received from May during the consultation with her. As to whether May received information that "could be significantly harmful" to Timothy, we agree with the circuit court that a lawyer who consults with a prospective client about a change-of-custody proceeding will necessarily become privy to information that could be used to the disadvantage of that person in the same proceeding. ...

Affirmed.

INQUIRY

Intake Procedures. Model Rule 1.18 imposes certain opportunity costs on a lawyer who interviews a prospective client. Can you articulate how it does so? Lawyers must be cautious about whom they interview as a prospective client. As the above case illustrates, meeting with a prospective client can effectively disqualify the lawyer from representing any other adverse party in the ensuing matter. If the prospective client's matter involves an adverse party whom the lawyer ordinarily represents or wishes to represent, then meeting with the prospective client will have cost the lawyer that opportunity. Indeed, a conniving prospective client might just meet deliberately with a lawyer whom the prospective client did not want to retain but also did not want an adverse party to retain, thereby disqualifying the lawyer. Lawyers craft and employ intake procedures to lower these opportunity costs. Can you discern what those procedures might be? Office assistants can record minimal information regarding the adverse parties in the prospective client's matter before the lawyer meets with the prospective client, giving the lawyer the opportunity to ensure that the prospective client's communications will not disqualify the lawyer from desireable representations. *See, e.g.,* Pro-Hand Services Trust v. Monthei, 49 P.3d 56 (Mont. 2002) (no disqualification based on secretary's preliminary communications).

Imputed Disqualification. As was the case in Model Rule 1.9 addressing conflicts of interest over former clients, Model Rule 1.18 addressing conflicts of interest over prospective clients also includes a rule for imputed disqualification. Model Rule 1.18(c) provides that if a lawyer is disqualified from representing a new client because of having received information from a prospective client that could harm the prospective client in a matter adverse to the new client, then other lawyers with whom the disqualified lawyer is associated are also disqualified. Model Rule 1.18(d) offers those other lawyers a reprieve, if they can show either that the prospective client and new client give written informed consent. Model Rule 1.18(d) offers those lawyers a second reprieve, if they can show that the lawyer who received the prospective client's information took care to receive as little information as necessary to decide on the representation and the other lawyers in the firm screened that lawyer from participating in or receiving fees from the matter, with notice to the prospective client. Notice to the prospective client enables the prospective client to challenge the exception's application and the adequacy of screening procedures. Can you articulate from the above cases what would constitute reasonable screening procedures?

Career and Professional Development

Prospective employers value loyalty, just as clients do. Law firms and other employers of lawyers invest heavily in recruiting and training new lawyers. When one of those new lawyers leaves the employment early, the employer loses a substantial investment. When you interview with a law firm or other employer, you may focus on communicating your interest in a job offer. The employer may be focusing on whether and how long you will stay after accepting an offer. If you are interested in working as a lawyer for an organization, whether as corporate counsel or in a law firm, then think carefully about how clearly you express institutional loyalty. Lawyers do not like working in law firms with other lawyers whose loyalty depends on little more than the size and security of the next paycheck. Connect your interests and commitments with prospective employers. Be prepared in interviews to demonstrate those connections, making your loyalty more and more apparent.

CHAPTER X

TRANSPARENCY

Imputed and Special Conflicts of Interest

What is written clearly is not worth much, it's the transparency that counts.

— *Louis Ferdinand Celine*

OBJECTIVE: Given varying law practice, law firm, government, and adjudicative roles implicating different alignments and interests, articulate the rules and conventions to follow to demonstrate to others your transparency.

Applicable Rules

1.10 Imputation of Conflicts of Interest: General Rule

1.11 Special Conflicts of Interest for Government Employees

1.12 Former Judge, Arbitrator, Mediator

2.3   Evaluation for Use by Third Persons

2.4   Lawyer Serving as Third-Party Neutral

You saw in the last chapter that lawyers play different roles representing different interests, and that those different interests implicate a lawyer's loyalty to prospective, current, and former clients. The last chapter dealt primarily with the lone lawyer in private practice. Yet lawyers occupy other special roles that implicate additional interests, requiring additional conflicts rules. Each of the conflicts rules that this chapter explores involves lawyers performing unique roles that implicate important principles. These additional conflicts rules emphasize the lawyer's need for transparency in every role and in these special roles in particular. As you read this chapter, try to identify the larger purposes each conflicts rule serves and discern why transparency is such an important attribute in the situations contemplated by each rule.

A. Imputed Conflicts

Imputed Disqualification in Firms. To impute is to presume a condition or quality based on circumstance rather than proof, such as on one's relationship with another. The concept of an imputed conflict is that even though a lawyer has no direct conflict—there is no evidence that the lawyer has an interest adverse to a client—the lawyer nonetheless associates with other lawyers in a way that the law will attribute the other lawyers' conflicts to the conflict-free lawyer. The prior chapter already introduced you to subrules of imputed disqualification embedded in the conflicts rules regarding former (Model Rule 1.8(k)) and prospective clients (Model Rule 1.9(b) and (c)). The primary rule of imputed disqualification, though, is ABA Model Rule 1.10 addressing *current* clients. Model Rule 1.10 provides that when one lawyer in a law firm has a conflict of interest prohibiting that lawyer from representing a certain client, then all other lawyers in the same law firm share that conflict. Model Rule 1.10(a) offers only one exception to imputed disqualification, when the conflict is due to a personal interest of the lawyer that will not limit the work of the firm's other lawyers. Consider a similar state version of Model Rule 1.10.

LOUISIANA R. PROF. CONDUCT 1.10: **Imputation of Conflicts of Interest: General Rule.**
(a) While lawyers are associated in a firm, none of them shall knowingly represent a client when any one of them practicing alone would be prohibited from doing so by Rules 1.7 or 1.9, unless the prohibition is based on a personal interest of the prohibited lawyer and does not present a significant risk of materially limiting the representation of the client by the remaining lawyers in the firm.
(b) When a lawyer has terminated an association with a firm, the firm is not prohibited from thereafter representing a person with interests materially adverse to those of a client represented by the formerly associated lawyer and not currently represented by the firm, unless:
(1) the matter is the same or substantially related to that in which the formerly associated lawyer represented the client; and
(2) any lawyer remaining in the firm has information protected by Rules 1.6 and 1.9(c) that is material to the matter.
(c) A disqualification prescribed by this rule may be waived by the affected client under the conditions stated in Rule 1.7.
(d) The disqualification of lawyers associated in a firm with former or current government lawyers is governed by Rule 1.11.

INQUIRY

Associated in a Firm. Model Rule 1.10 imputes conflicts when lawyers are "associated in a firm... ." *See* Model Rule 1.10 Comment [4] (non-lawyer assistant's conflicts not imputed to lawyers in firm provided assistant is screened). In most cases, association in a firm will be evident. Lawyers either are or are not partners or associates of a firm. Imputed conflicts end at the boundary of the firm. If two lawyers from different firms represent a single client as co-counsel, then their individual conflicts remain imputed only to their own firms. *See, e.g.,* Jones v. Beverly Health & Rehab. Services, 68 F. Supp.2d 1304 (N.D. Fla. 1999). Yet lawyers associate through other relationships such as when a lawyer, though not a partner or associate, is *of counsel* to a law firm. Of-counsel relationships tend to involve use of letterhead, conference space, and minimal secretarial services without sharing fees or other compensation arrangements. Whether Model Rule 1.10 would impute the conflicts of a lawyer who is of counsel to a firm, to the firm, probably depends on how close the of counsel relationship is. *Contrast* Smith & Nephew, Inc. v. Ethicon, Inc., 98 F. Supp.2d 106 (D. Mass. 2000) (imputed conflicts extend to of counsel relationship between firms), *with* Gray v. Memorial Med. Ctr., Inc., 855 F. Supp. 377 (S.D. Ga. 1994) (imputed conflicts do not extend to lawyers who are of counsel to firm). Sharing office space with another lawyer may be enough to treat the lawyers as if they were "associated in a firm" for purposes of Model Rule 1.10, at least where the lawyers share access to confidential files. *See* Monroe v. City of Topeka, 988 P.2d 228 (Kan. 1999).

Considering Screening. If one lawyer in a firm has a conflict of interest, then the possibility exists that the firm might simply screen that lawyer from from having any contact with another matter handled by other lawyers in the firm, where the conflict could be harmful. The *Haagen Dazs* case in the prior chapter introduced you to the concept of screening a lawyer, sometimes referred to as maintaining a proverbial Chinese Wall—an image of a long, winding, impenetrable barrier topped by lookouts. Does Model Rule 1.10 permit screening? The similar state version of Model Rule 1.10 above, identical to Model Rule 1.10 until its 2009 amendment, has no screening exception. Neither do most jurisdictions. Under those rules, one lawyer of a firm may not represent a client while any other lawyer of the firm would have a conflict of interest in doing so either because of a current or former client. Screening makes no difference. Can you articulate why most state rules and the predecessor to the current Model Rule 1.10 do not authorize screening? How much would lawyers sacrifice in public trust to adopt conduct rules that permit more screening? Model Rule

1.10(c) does make imputed disqualification consentable. The client affected by the imputed conflict may waive it with written informed consent.

Amendment to Permit Screening. The current Model Rule 1.10, amended in 2009 but not yet widely adopted, does permit screening, following a trend to permit screening in some instances. *See, e.g.,* Hempstead Video, Inc. v. Incorporated Village of Valley Stream, 409 F.3d 127 (2d Cir. 2005). The current Model Rule 1.10(a) replaces the Rule 1.10(a) shown in the state version above with the following:

> While lawyers are associated in a firm, none of them shall knowingly represent a client when any one of them practicing alone would be prohibited from doing so by Rules 1.7 or 1.9, unless
> (1) the prohibition is based on a personal interest of the lawyer and does not present a significant risk of materially limiting the representation of the client by the remaining lawyer's association with a prior firm, and
> (2) the prohibition is based upon Rule 1.9(a) or (b), and arises out of the disqualified lawyer's association with a prior firm, and
> (i) the disqualified lawyer is timely screened from any participation in the matter and is apportioned no part of the fee therefrom;
> (ii) written notice is promptly given to any affected former client to enable the former client to ascertain compliance with the provisions of this Rule, which shall include a description of the firms and of the screened lawyer's compliance with these Rules; a statement that review may be available before a tribunal; and an agreement by the firm to respond promptly to any written inquiries or objections by the former client about the screening procedures; and
> (iii) certifications of compliance with these Rules and with the screening procedures are provided to the former client by the screened lawyer and by a partner of the firm, at reasonable intervals upon the former client's written request and upon termination of the screening procedures.

Adequacy of Screening. If states were to adopt the current Model Rule 1.10(a)(2) permitting screening, then what would screening entail? The court in Kala v. Aluminum Smelting & Refining, Co., 688 N.E.2d 258 (1998), stated the following factors to determine adequate screening procedures:

> Factors to be considered in deciding whether an effective screen has been created are whether the law firm is sufficiently large and whether the structural divisions of the firm are sufficiently separate so as to minimize contact between the quarantined attorney and the specific attorney responsible for the the current representation, the existence of safeguards or procedures which prevent the quarantined attorney from access to relevant files or other information relevant to the present litigation, prohibited access to file and other information on the case, locked case filed with keys distributed to a select few, secret codes necessary to access pertinent

information on electronic hardware, instructions given to all members of a new firm regarding the ban on exchange of information and the prohibition of sharing of fees from such litigation.

The critical thing to remember about screening is that even if a state were to permit it by adopting the current version of Model Rule 1.10(a)(2), screening would remain an exception to imputed disqualification. Screening does not cure the underlying conflict. If a screen is inadequately constructed, then imputed disqualification applies and the law firm is disqualified from the representation. Consider an illustrative case recognizing that screening is not permitted under the applicable state law.

Hitachi, Ltd. v. Tatung Co.,
United States District Court for the Northern District of California
419 F. Supp.2d 1158 (2006)

BREYER, District Judge.

Plaintiff, Hitachi, Ltd. ("Hitachi"), filed a complaint alleging that defendants, Tatung Co. and Tatung Co. of America, Inc. (collectively "Tatung"), infringed three Hitachi patents. Plaintiff now moves to disqualify defense counsel, Greenberg Traurig, LLP, on the ground that Greenberg's representation of defendants constitutes a conflict of interest under Rule 3-310(E) of the Rules of Professional Conduct of the State Bar of California.

BACKGROUND

... Hitachi is represented by McDermott, Will & Emery LLP ("McDermott").

Between December 2003 and November 2004, McDermott represented Hitachi in ... [the] TVP case[]. In the TVP case, Hitachi asserted the *same three patents* asserted in this lawsuit against Tatung. Hitachi claims that the accused products in the TVP case operate virtually identically to the accused Tatung products. Further, the defenses alleged in the TVP case were substantively identical to those raised by Tatung in this case.

Until mid-October 2005, Mr. Jong P. Hong was an associate at McDermott. He represented Hitachi in the TVP case and billed 340 hours to the case over six months, until the time the case settled. The parties dispute the extent of Mr. Hong's involvement in the TVP case. Tatung claims Mr. Hong had limited knowledge of the TVP case which primarily was derived from document review. Hitachi claims, however, that Mr. Hong was involved with most areas of the case and even attended meetings concerning case strategy and preparations for mediation.

McDermott filed the present action on behalf of Hitachi in June 2005. Although Mr. Hong was still employed at McDermott until October 2005, he did not work on the present matter and billed no time to it.

Tatung originally retained a different firm, Baum and Weems, as counsel in this case. Tatung substituted Greenberg Traurig, LLP ("Greenberg") as counsel in this case in January 2006. ...

Mr. Hong is currently an associate at Greenberg. Mr. Hong began working at Greenberg in October 2005, before Tatung retained Greenberg in this matter. Greenberg has 28 offices and four affiliate offices. Most of the work relating to the present matter, however, is being conducted out of the Silicon Valley office, where Mr. Hong is located. Only 14 attorneys are listed on the Greenberg website as being in the Greenberg Silicon Valley intellectual property department. Only six attorneys are listed as being a member of only the intellectual property or intellectual property litigation groups, of which Mr. Hong is one. Another attorney listing only intellectual property and intellectual property litigation as areas of practice is Mr. Korea, one of three attorneys of record for Tatung.

Prior to entering an appearance in this case, Greenberg implemented an ethical wall. The firm notified Mr. Hong that his employment would be terminated if he shared any confidential information related to Hitachi with anyone at Greenberg. The firm's information technology ("IT") department set up a separate "library" to house documents in the case, which Mr. Hong cannot access. Further, the firm sent a memorandum highlighting the conflict and screening procedures to the entire Silicon Valley office, the intellectual property and records department in the Los Angeles office, and the entire intellectual property department firmwide. The firm instituted a "closed door" policy when their attorneys are discussing the Tatung matter. Finally, Mr. Hong has declared that he has not disclosed any confidential information related to, derived from, or in any way connected to his representation of Hitachi.

DISCUSSION

Plaintiff argues that Mr. Hong is an associate at Greenberg, that Mr. Hong formerly represented Hitachi in a substantially related matter, that ethical walls, as a matter of law in California, are insufficient to prevent the vicarious disqualification of Greenberg, and that the ethical wall here provides ineffective protections of confidential information. Defendants do not dispute that Mr. Hong, an associate at Greenberg, formerly represented Hitachi in a substantially related matter. Rather, they argue that vicarious disqualification of Greenberg is unwarranted because the firm properly instituted an ethical wall to prevent the sharing of confidential information. However, if necessary to satisfy the Court, Tatung offers to transfer the Tatung litigation matter to another Greenberg office.

I. LEGAL STANDARDS

Motions to disqualify counsel are decided under state law. [C] ...

Under California law the starting point for deciding a motion to disqualify counsel is the recognition of interests implicated by such a motion. ...

II. DISQUALIFICATION OF MR. HONG: SUBSTANTIALLY RELATED REPRESENTATION

Mr. Hong must be disqualified from representing Tatung in this matter. Rule 3-310(E) of the Rules of Professional Conduct of the State Bar of California states: "A member shall not, without the informed written consent of the client or former client, accept employment adverse to the client or former client where, by reason of the representation of the client or former client, the member has obtained confidential information material to the employment." ...   Because Tatung does not dispute that this case constitutes a substantially related matter to the TVP case, Mr. Hong must be disqualified from representing Tatung in this matter. Tatung does not dispute Mr. Hong's disqualification.

III. DISQUALIFICATION OF GREENBERG: ETHICAL WALLS

A. Legal Background

The established rule in California is that where an attorney is disqualified from representing a client because that attorney had previously represented a party with adverse interests in a substantially related matter that attorney's entire firm must be disqualified as well, regardless of efforts to erect an ethical wall.[fn] [Cc] Nonetheless, recent California and Federal decisions may indicate an increased willingness in California to allow timely and effective ethical walls to prevent vicarious disqualification. [C] No California case, however, has yet expressly altered the established rule.

The established law in California rejects ethical walls... . Thus, although the law in California may be at a critical shift, this Court is bound to follow California law as it presently exists. Accordingly, as a matter of California law, the Court finds that Greenberg's ethical screening procedures cannot prevent vicarious disqualification and Greenberg is disqualified from representing Tatung in this matter.

B. Even if Ethical Walls Were Permissible the Court Would Still Disqualify Greenberg

Even if California law permitted ethical walls to prevent disqualification where an attorney moves from one private firm to another, in the particular circumstances of this case, the Court, in its discretion, would disqualify Greenberg.

As set forth above, Greenberg promptly recognized and attempted to resolve the ethical conflict. Greenberg immediately initiated an ethical wall, instituting its screening procedures prior entering an appearance in this case without being compelled by Hitachi. Greenberg isolated Mr. Hong from the present case by warning him and other members of the firm, denied him access to case files, and instituted a closed door policy for discussions relating to the present case. Short of transferring the matter to another office, which they have offered if the Court finds necessary, Greenberg could not substantially improve the efficacy of their ethical screening procedures.

Nonetheless, the Court finds that disqualification is warranted, in part because this action and the action in which Mr. Hong represented Hitachi are so substantially related-indeed, they are nearly identical. ... Tatung has not cited a single case in which a court held that an ethical wall prevented the vicarious disqualification of a firm where the two matters were as closely related as the two at issue here, and where the disqualified attorney had billed such a significant amount of time on the earlier matter.

The Court also finds it troubling that the present case is handled primarily out of the same office that Mr. Hong is located. ... [T]he close proximity of Mr. Hong and the attorneys handling the Tatung matter undoubtedly increases the unease of Hitachi that their confidential information will be improperly disclosed. Moreover, the close proximity increases the actual risk of intentional or unintentional disclosure of Hitachi confidential information.

The small size of Greenberg's Silicon Valley intellectual property department exacerbates the problem of proximity and leads the Court to conclude that the ethical wall is insufficient. Because of the small number attorneys practicing intellectual property in Greenberg's Silicon Valley office, and the even smaller number of attorneys practicing only intellectual property and intellectual property litigation, Mr. Hong likely has substantial contact with the Greenberg intellectual property attorneys handling this case. Further, although Greenberg has instituted a "closed door" policy when their attorneys are discussing the Tatung matter, Greenberg has not otherwise isolated Mr. Hong from the Tatung legal team. ...

IV. CONCLUSION

Mr. Hong must be disqualified from the present matter as he previously represented Hitachi in a substantially related matter. Greenberg must also be disqualified. The vicarious disqualification of Mr. Hong's entire firm is compelled as a matter of California law.

Further, even if the Court were to accept a more flexible approach to the use of ethical walls, in the particular circumstances of this case the screening procedures utilized in this case are insufficient to adequately protect Hitachi confidential information and prevent the appearance of impropriety.

IT IS SO ORDERED.

> ***Biography***
>
> In 1973, a court appointed Frank Armani and another lawyer Francis Belge to defend Robert Garrow for the murder of Philip Domblewski. Garrow admitted to Armani and Belge that he had killed Domblewski, raped and murdered the man's female companion, and raped and murdered a 16-year-old girl. Garrow told his lawyers where he had left his two female victims, information they confirmed by photographing the remains. Armani and Belge kept their client Garrow's secret until Garrow confessed to the murders at trial a year later. Lawyers supported Armani and Belge, who had complied with their professional duties to Garrow, but the public reviled them. Their thriving law practices withered, while they received hate mail and death threats. Longtime friends stopped speaking to them. They had to move out of their homes. A grand jury investigated both lawyers, indicting Belge, causing Armani to suffer a heart attack, even though the trial judge later dismissed the charge and lauded Belge. Belge eventually gave up his law practice, while Armani slowly rebuilt his. Belge died in 1989. The legal profession now regards Amani, age 79 and semiretired, as a hero. He received a distinguished-lawyer award from the Onondaga County (N.Y.) Bar Association and nomination for the national Michael Franck Award presented by the ABA Center for Professional Responsibility. In 2010, Armani received a standing ovation when he appeared at a program about the Garrow case at the Center's National Conference on Professional Responsibility. Armani co-authored the book *Privileged Information* on the case, which was also the basis for the 1987 feature film "Sworn to Silence."

INQUIRY

Lawyers Leaving a Firm. Do imputed conflicts persist after the lawyer whose representation generated the conflicts leaves a law firm? Model Rule 1.10(b) addresses the situation in which a lawyer leaves a law firm, and the clients whose matters generated the conflicts are no longer clients of the firm. (The lawyer may have taken the clients with the lawyer, or their matters may have concluded.) May the law firm then represent new clients whose matters are adverse to the departed clients of the lawyer who left the firm? Model Rule 1.10(b) in essence holds that the departed lawyer takes the conflicts with the lawyer, leaving the firm free to represent clients adverse to the departed clients. Even though the departed lawyer could not represent adverse clients in the same or substantially related matter (*see* Model Rule 1.9), the law firm now may represent adverse clients, so long as no lawyer remaining in the firm has a departed client's confidential information material to the same or a substantially related matter in which the firm represents the new client.

Lawyers Joining a Firm. On the other hand, a lawyer who joins a new firm brings the lawyer's conflicts with the lawyer, even if the lawyer does not bring the clients whose representation created the conflict. *See, e.g.,* State ex rel. Cosenza v. Hill, 607 S.E.2d 811 (W. Va. 2004). The lawyer joining a new firm, though, does not bring the former firm's imputed conflicts, only those conflicts that the lawyer actually holds. That is, the lawyer may be able to show that the lawyer did not obtain any confidential information involving clients of other lawyers of the former firm, to bring to the new firm creating imputed disqualification of members of the new firm. *See, e.g.,* United States v. Ketner, 370 F. Supp.2d 1045 (C.D. Cal. 2005). Interestingly, the lawyer who joins a new firm with conflict information imputed to disqualify other members of the new firm and who leaves the new firm before disclosing that information to other lawyers in the new firm, leaves the members of the new firm without the imputed disqualification. *See, e.g.,* Reilly v. Computer Assocs. Long-Term Disability Plan, 423 F. Supp.2d 5 (E.D. N.Y. 2006). In short, Model Rule 1.10(a) imputes disqualification among current members of the firm without asking what information a lawyer has learned, but Model Rule 1.10(b) disqualifies only those lawyers who receive confidential client information when a lawyer leaves or joins a firm. *See* Monroe v. City of Topeka, 988 P.2d 228 (Kan. 1999).

B. Conflicts of Government Lawyers

Government Service of Lawyers. Lawyers move into and out of government service. A lawyer's government service might be as a judge, prosecutor, attorney general, agency lawyer, or in any of dozens of similar roles. Lawyers in government service often come into contact with a wide variety of matters. For example, judges and prosecutors entertain hundreds of matters involving thousands of parties. If when these lawyers left government service to join a law firm their imputed conflicts came with them, then law firms could not hire many former government lawyers, whom conflicts would bar from much private practice. Both the law firms and former government lawyers would suffer, as would the public. Former government lawyers bring substantial value to the clients and communities they serve in private practice, and to their law firms. Conduct rules should enable lawyers to move in and out of government service with relative ease, for the benefit of the government, public, and profession. Read ABA Model Rule 1.11(a) addressing how to treat conflicts of interest involving a former government lawyer.

PENNSYLVANIA R. PROF. CONDUCT 1.11: Special Conflicts of Interest for Former and Current Government Officers and Employees.
(a) Except as law may otherwise expressly permit, a lawyer who has formerly served as a public officer or employee of the government:
(1) is subject to Rule 1.9(c); and
(2) shall not otherwise represent a private client in connection with a matter in which the lawyer participated personally and substantially as a public officer or employee, unless the appropriate government agency gives its informed consent to the representation.
(b) When a lawyer is disqualified from representation under paragraph (a), no lawyer in a firm with which that lawyer is associated may knowingly undertake or continue representation in such a matter unless:
(1) the disqualified lawyer is screened from any participation in the matter and is apportioned no part of the fee therefrom; and
(2) written notice is promptly given to the appropriate government agency to enable it to ascertain compliance with the provisions of this rule.
(c) Except as law may otherwise expressly permit, a lawyer having information that the lawyer knows is confidential government information about a person acquired when the lawyer was a public officer or employee may not represent a private client whose interests are adverse to that person in a matter in which the information could be used to the material disadvantage of that person. As used in this Rule, the term "confidential government information" means information that has been obtained under governmental authority and which, at the time this Rule is applied, the government is prohibited by law from disclosing to the public or has a legal privilege not to disclose and which is not otherwise available to the public. A firm with which that lawyer is associated may undertake or continue representation in the matter only if the disqualified lawyer is screened from any participation in the matter and is apportioned no part of the fee therefrom.
(d) Except as law may otherwise expressly permit, a lawyer currently serving as a public officer or employee:
(1) is subject to Rules 1.7 and 1.9; and
(2) shall not:
(i) participate in a matter in which the lawyer participated personally and substantially while in private practice or nongovernmental employment, unless the appropriate government agency gives its informed consent; or
(ii) negotiate for private employment with any person who is involved as a party or as a lawyer for a party in a matter in which the lawyer is participating personally and substantially, except that a lawyer serving as a law clerk to a judge, other adjudicative officer or arbitrator may negotiate for private employment as permitted by Rule 1.12(b) and subject to the conditions stated in Rule 1.12(b).
(e) As used in this Rule, the term "matter" includes:

(1) any judicial or other proceeding, application, request for a ruling or other determination, contract, claim, controversy, investigation, charge, accusation, arrest or other particular matter involving a specific party or parties; and

(2) any other matter covered by the conflict of interest rules of the appropriate government agency.

INQUIRY

Former Government Lawyers. Model Rule 1.11(a)(1) makes a former government lawyer subject to Model Rule 1.9(c), which prohibits a lawyer from using the information of a former client against the former client or revealing that information. Model Rule 1.11(a)(2) further prohibits the former government lawyer from representing a client in a matter in which the lawyer participated substantially as a government lawyer, unless the government agency consent. For example, a judge could not leave the bench for private practice and then represent a party in the same case in which the judge conducted pretrial matters. As to what circumstances trigger a conflict, Model Rule 1.11(a)(2) employs a personal-and-substantial-participation standard that is different from the directly adverse or materially limited standards Model Rule 1.7(a) employs and the materially adverse standard that Model Rule 1.9(a) employs. Model Rule 1.11 adopts its personal-and-substantial-participation standard from the federal Ethics in Government Act, 18 U.S.C. §207, with regulations defining that standard as "more than official responsibility, knowledge, perfunctory involvement, or involvement on an administrative or peripheral issue," 5 C.F.R. §2637.201(d). Can you see how government service might require that different standard? It may be difficult for a government lawyer to identify who is the client. Model Rule 1.11(a)(2) links the conflict to personal and substantial participation in a government matter rather than to a specific client. Consider a case illustrating the standard.

Park-N-Shop, Ltd. v. City of Highwood,
United States District Court for the Northern District of Illinois
864 F. Supp. 82 (1994)

ASPEN, District Judge:

Presently before the court is defendants' motion to disqualify Joe Obenberger as plaintiffs' attorney. Defendants ... argue that Obenberger's participation in this case violates Rule 1.11(a) of the Illinois Rules of Professional Conduct. In relevant part, that rule provides: "[A] lawyer shall not represent a private client in connection with a matter in which the lawyer participated personally and substantially as a public officer or employee. ..."

It is undisputed that Obenberger was not a member of the Highwood City Council in the mid-1980s, when the City Council amended the liquor ordinance to provide for an initial fee of $10,000, followed by an annual renewal fee of approximately $2,000.[fn] It is also undisputed that Obenberger was not a member of the Highwood City Council in 1994, when the City published the liquor ordinance that is the subject of the present lawsuit. Indeed, the only connection between Obenberger's service as a Highwood alderman and this lawsuit is that Obenberger sat on the City Council when Mayor Fidel Ghini, as Liquor Commissioner, issued plaintiff Park-N-Shop its license. Defendants suggest that this connection is sufficient to establish Obenberger's "participation".... . As noted above, however, Rule 1.11(a) only applies where the participation is *personal* and *substantial.* Even if defendants' non-specific argument about Obenberger were enough to support a claim that he participated in the granting of Park-N-Shop's license, with the accompanying assurance of annual renewal, such participation is, at best, tangential. Obenberger played no role in establishing the renewal policy, in drafting or passing the legislation setting the fees, or in ultimately eliminating that legislation. Furthermore, defendants do not, and presumably can not, assert that the issuing of a license to Park-N-Shop specifically was ever the subject of formal, or even informal, debate or discussion among members of the City Council. As a result, we simply can not conclude that Obenberger's "participation" in the granting of Park-N-Shop's license was either personal or substantial. Accordingly, defendants' argument based on Rule 1.11(a) must fail. ...

Finally, defendants suggest that Obenberger should be disqualified because he could take advantage of confidential information he learned while an alderman. ... Although Obenberger offered the council his legal advice while sitting as an alderman, and on one occasion oversaw settlement negotiations with the city's attorneys, it is undisputed that Obenberger was never appointed as an attorney for the city, never appeared on behalf of the city, and never received any compensation for his law-related comments or assistance. Accordingly, we can not conclude that Obenberger acted as an attorney for the city. ...

... [E]ven if Obenberger's activities amount to legal representation of the city, defendants have failed to demonstrate that such representation was on a matter "substantially related" to the ordinances at issue. ...

... Because defendants have failed to identify any basis for Obenberger's disqualification, their motion must be denied. It is so ordered.

INQUIRY

Imputed Disqualification. Model Rule 1.11(b) provides for the imputed disqualification of the lawyers in a firm whose former government lawyer has a conflict of interest. Model Rule 1.11(b) does permit screening on the by-now-familiar condition that no part of the fee reach the former government lawyer and on notice to the lawyer's former government agency to allow it to ensure screening compliance.

Negotiating for Private Employment. Government lawyers who wish to return to private practice would have a natural interest in negotiating that return before relinquishing their government employment. Law firms may even have a strong interest in bidding for the services of prominent government lawyers whose return to private practice they anticipate. Think, for instance, of the turnover of prominent government lawyers during a change in political administrations. The problem is that the common interest of government lawyer and law firm in negotiating a future relationship may influence the work of both while the government lawyer remains in government service. An unscrupulous government lawyer and law firm could conceivably trade favorable government treatment for future employment. What the profession needs is what lawyers know as a *revolving-door rule.* Model Rule 1.11(d)(2)(ii) addresses the concern by prohibiting any such negotiation between the government lawyer and a party or lawyer appearing in a matter in which the government lawyer participates personally and substantially. *See, e.g.,* Commonwealth v. Maricle, 10 S.W.3d 117 (Ky. 1999). Model Rule 1.11(d)(2)(ii) makes an exception for law clerks who notify their adjudicative officer of their negotiations. Courts properly anticipate the departure of their law clerks. Consider a case illustrative of the revolving-door rule.

In re Sofaer,
District of Columbia Court of Appeals
728 A.2d 625 (1999)

This case [involves] ... an informal admonition to respondent for having violated Rule 1.11(a) of the District of Columbia Rules of Professional Conduct. The rule states in relevant part: "A lawyer shall not accept other employment in connection with a matter which is the same as, or substantially related to, a matter in which the lawyer participated personally and substantially as a public officer or employee."

A hearing committee and the Board both concluded that respondent had violated this rule by undertaking to represent the government of Libya in connection with criminal and civil disputes and litigation arising from the 1988 bombing of Pan American Flight 103 over Lockerbie, Scotland, after respondent, while serving as Legal Advisor in the United States Department of State, took part personally and substantially in the government's investigation of the bombing and in related diplomatic and legal activities. ...

Respondent argues that in defining the "matter" in which he took part... , the [Discipline] Board bundled together activities so diverse in nature as to give him no fair warning of a potential overlap when he accepted the private representation of Libya. We are not persuaded. The activities in question, including diplomatic intervention with an unnamed country, attendance at confidential briefings on the criminal investigation, and overseeing the State Department's response to civil third-party subpoenas, all centered about ... "... why and how Pan Am 103 blew up over Lockerbie." The contours of the bombing and the government's investigation and related responses to it were defined sharply enough to constitute a "matter" under the Rule.

... Respondent contends that his work as Legal Advisor concerned the Pan Am 103 bombing in ways that were too marginal, infrequent, or passive to amount to "personal and substantial" participation in the matter. ... [Respondent] asserts[that his role] consisted largely of a routine response to a third-party subpoena issued by Pan Am in furtherance of its theory that the U.S. government had advance warning of the bombing but failed to act.

... [B]ut his participation went further. After Pan Am voiced its theory of government foreknowledge at a meeting with the Secretary of State which respondent either attended or knew of, respondent's judgment was sought on whether, or how fully, to inform the Department's designated witness in the subpoena matter of the meeting, in preparation for his testimony. ...

Moreover, respondent's actions take on added significance when viewed in the context of his participation, as one of a small number of senior State Department officials, in confidential oral and written briefings which periodically included information about the progress of the criminal investigation and related diplomatic actions. The fact that respondent played no role in the investigation itself and was not shown to have recommended or taken action based on the briefings is not critical. As the Board explained, "Respondent was much more than the passive recipient of general agency information. As chief legal officer of the State Department, [he] was kept abreast of the progress of the investigation and the diplomatic efforts in response to the bombing precisely so that he could provide legal advice and perform legal duties concerning the bombing when called upon to do so."

All told, respondent's active participation in the Pan Am 103 matter bears no resemblance to the merely peripheral or formal involvement in a matter which the Rule does not encompass. [C] ...

... Rule 1.11(a) prohibits a lawyer from accepting employment in connection with a matter "the same as, or substantially related to," a matter in which he or she took part as a public officer or employee. The inquiry is a practical one asking whether the two matters substantially overlap. Respondent insists that he stayed clear of that overlap by restricting the terms of his agreement to represent Libya so as to "assum[e] Libya's culpability for the [Pan Am 103] bombing." A lawyer may, of course, limit the objectives of a representation with client consent. Rule 1.2(c). But respondent's retainer agreement exemplifies why, in our view, limiting the private representation rarely will succeed in avoiding the convergence addressed by Rule 1.11(a). While stating that "[the firm's] efforts will not include substantial activities as litigators but rather would be limited to activities associated with agreed upon measures, including consensual dispositions," the agreement emphasized that "[m]easures will be taken only with your [*i.e.,* Libya's] prior consent, and *without admission of liability.*" (emphasis added). The proposed activities included "investigating the facts and legal proceedings, preparing legal analyses, providing legal advice and proposing legal steps to deal with" the "ongoing civil and criminal disputes and litigation" stemming from the destruction of Pan Am 103—all clearly features of a comprehensive attorney-client relationship. We do not question the sincerity of respondent's belief that the representation could be insulated, factually and ethically, from the investigation and diplomatic efforts of which he had been part. The "substantially related" test by its terms, however, is meant to induce a former government lawyer considering a representation to err well on the side of caution. Respondent did not do so. ...

... Joined by *amici curiae* who are former government officials, respondent urges that finding an ethical violation in this case will deter District of Columbia lawyers from entering the government or serving for long once there, lest Rule 1.11(a) trip them up after they enter private practice. We are sensitive to the concern ... that over-zealous application of the revolving-door rule would be "at the cost of creating an insular, permanent legal bureaucracy." ... But that concern is misplaced here. Our finding that respondent violated Rule 1.11(a) is well within the heartland of Rule 1.11(a)'s application. Further, Bar

Counsel aptly states why no lawyer need find himself inadvertently in the position of risk that respondent and amicus hypothesize:

> A former government lawyer in the Respondent's position is free to solicit the views of his or her former agency concerning the proposed private legal undertaking (which the Respondent deliberately elected not to do in this case), or to consult with ethics advisers in his or her law firm (which, again, the Respondent seems not to have done concerning Rule 1.11) or with the Legal Ethics Committee of the Bar (which the Respondent never suggested he did). If, while in government service or while contemplating entry into such service, the attorney deliberates the prospect that Rule 1.11 will narrow somewhat the career choices and client selections available to the attorney following departure from the government, then the Rule will have served one of its salutary objectives.

We affirm the Board's conclusion that respondent violated Rule 1.11(a) and the Board's order directing Bar Counsel to issue an informal admonition.

So ordered.

INQUIRY

Confidential Government Information.   The authority of government to investigate enables government lawyers to learn secrets about individuals whether or not the lawyers participate personally and substantially in the matters involving those individuals. Legal work in prosecutor offices, administrative agencies, and other government offices may expose a lawyer to confidential information that the lawyer could potentially use once in private practice. Model Rule 1.11(c) disqualifies a former government lawyer from representing a client in whose matter the lawyer could use confidential government information against a person. The former government lawyer must actually have that information, not merely have had access to it in the former government employment. *See* Walker v. State Dept. of Transp. & Dev., 817 So.2d 57 (La. 2002). Model Rule 1.11(c) imputes disqualification but permits screening on the usual condition that the conflicted lawyer not share in earned fees. Consider another case illustrative of the revolving-door concern.

In re White,
District of Columbia Court of Appeals
11 A.3d 1226 (2011)

The Board on Professional Responsibility has filed two separate reports and recommendations with this court concerning respondent, Lucille Saundra White, arising from separate matters that occurred during the same period. In its first report, issued on August 20, 2009, the Board recommended that respondent be suspended for six months and be required to demonstrate fitness as a condition for reinstatement for violating Rule 1.11 of the District of Columbia Rules of Professional Conduct (conflict in successive government and private employment). Respondent filed exception.... In a second report, ... the Board recommended that respondent be disbarred....

August 20, 2009 Report

On August 20, 2009, the Board on Professional Responsibility concluded that respondent violated D.C. Bar Rule 1.11 (conflict in successive government and private employment), stemming from respondent's representation of Ms. Gladys Thomas. During respondent's tenure as head of the investigating unit at the District of Columbia Office of Human Rights ("OHR"), she had supervised the investigation of an age discrimination complaint filed by Ms. Thomas arising out of her discharge from a position with the Department of Consumer and Regulatory Affairs. The investigating agent had provided respondent with a draft Letter of Determination ("LOD") concerning Ms. Thomas's complaint in July 2002; OHR's final LOD advised Ms. Thomas that there was no probable cause to support her complaint.

Ms. Thomas pursued her age discrimination allegation by filing suit in the United States District Court for the District of Columbia on January 9, 2003, the same month that respondent was terminated from OHR. In an e-mail between Ms. Thomas's counsel, Ms. Janet Cooper, and respondent dated January 6, 2004, the two discussed entering a "co-counsel" relationship for Ms. Thomas's suit. In mid-December 2003, respondent had telephoned an unidentified representative at the D.C. Bar Ethics Counsel to inquire about engaging in this representation; however respondent provided only "a partial description of the relevant facts" during that call and specifically omitted her involvement with the Thomas case while she was at OHR. Thereafter, respondent participated in reviewing and editing court filings, including a draft motion on behalf of Ms. Thomas, and attended a deposition of a witness in the case, Bernard Ferguson. Following respondent's attendance at the Ferguson deposition on January 13, 2004, Michael Bruckheim, the attorney representing the District, contacted Ms. Cooper to complain about respondent's involvement as a violation of Rule 1.11; he filed a motion to disqualify respondent and Ms. Cooper after Ms. Cooper refused to withdraw. Ms. Cooper and respondent each filed an affidavit asserting that respondent had not played a substantive role concerning Ms. Thomas's case while at OHR.

On June 29, 2004, U.S. District Court Judge Royce C. Lamberth granted the motion to disqualify both respondent and Ms. Cooper, on the basis that respondent was the supervisor overseeing the investigation of Ms. Thomas's claim while she was at OHR. Bar Counsel filed charges against respondent on July 6, 2005, alleging that she had violated Rule 1.11 and Rule 8.4(d) (serious interference with the administration of justice), and evidentiary hearings followed from December 2005 through April 2006.

On April 9, 2007, Hearing Committee Number Five found that respondent's representation of Ms. Thomas was adverse to the District of Columbia government, and was on a matter in which respondent had been personally and substantially involved when she worked in OHR. ...

On August 20, 2009, the Board issued a report agreeing with the Hearing Committee that respondent had violated Rule 1.11. . . and recommended that respondent be suspended for six months and be required to demonstrate fitness as a condition of reinstatement. On November 9, 2009, this court suspended respondent pending final action on the Board's report. . . .

We adopt the Board's conclusion as to the Rule 1.11 violation. ...

Sanctions

... [T]he Board's report as amended on July 28, 2010, focuses on the seriousness of the conduct, the prior offense (referring to the August 20, 2009, report dealing with the representation of Ms. Thomas), the prejudice it caused to the reputation of OIG employees, and especially the respondent's attitude throughout the proceedings. Regarding respondent's attitude during its investigations, the Board emphasized that "[a]t no point did [r]espondent express any hint of regret or remorse for anything that has happened since 2001 or any acknowledgment of wrongdoing." It also noted her "erratic" behavior, citing her accusation that the Hearing Committee chairman was biased against her. The Board also considered the impact of the prior disciplinary proceedings—referring to the recommended sanctions for respondent's misconduct in connection with her representation of Ms. Thomas—as further evidence of inconsistencies in her testimony before the Board. Based on these considerations, the Board concluded that there are no mitigating factors and that disbarment is warranted based on the severity of the misconduct. ...

ORDERED that Lucille Saundra White is disbarred from the practice of law in the District of Columbia, effective thirty days from the date of this opinion. ... Respondent shall not be eligible for reinstatement for five years from the effective date of disbarment, pursuant to D.C. Bar R. XI, § 16(a).

So ordered.

INQUIRY

Current Government Lawyers. Model Rule 1.11(d) provides that lawyers who were once in private practice and currently serve in government must follow the same conflict rules Model Rule 1.7 as to current clients and Model Rule 1.9 as to former clients as lawyers who are in private practice. Just as a former government lawyer must not participate in a private matter in which the lawyer participated personally and substantially while in government service, so, too, must a current government lawyer not participate in a matter in which the lawyer participated personally and substantially while in private practice. Importantly, Model Rule 1.11(d) conflicts out only the current government lawyer, not other members of the government agency. In other words, there is no imputed disqualification of other government lawyers when a lawyer from private practice joins the government service with disqualifying information, so long as the government agency screens the new lawyer from sharing confidential information with the other government lawyers who are working on the matter from which the rule bans the new lawyer. *See, e.g.,* United States v. Goot, 894 F.2d 231 (7th Cir. 1990); State ex rel. Tyler v. MacQueen, 447 S.E.2d 289 (W. Va. 1994). Under Model Rule 1.11(d)(2)(i), the agency for which the government lawyer works may consent to the government lawyer's participation in those matters.

C. Conflicts of Third-Party Neutrals

Former Third-Party Neutrals. Loyalty takes on a different meaning when the subject involves a former judge, arbitrator, mediator, or other professional who participated as a neutral independent resolution specialist in a case—what lawyers call a *third-party neutral*—but is now in private practice. In those cases, the third-party neutral had no prior allegiance to any specific party. Instead, the neutral's loyalty was to the role of an independent case-resolution specialist. Once a third-party neutral leaves that role, the loyalty to the role does not end. Just as with the revolving-door concern with government lawyers, a third-party neutral who left the role to join forces with one side or the other in a case in which the neutral had served would create an appearance of impropriety. Either side might feel as if they were in a bidding war for the allegiance of the neutral. ABA Model Rule 1.12 resolves that concern by prohibiting a judge, arbitrator, mediator, or other third-party neutral from representing anyone in a matter in which the neutral participated personally and substantially, unless all parties consent. *See, e.g.*, Pappas v. Waggoner's Heating & Air, Inc., 108 P.3d 9 (Okla. Ct. Civ. App. 2004) (disqualification of mediator). So long as the matters are the same, *cf.* Schultz v. Schultz, 783 So.2d 329 (Fla. Dist. Ct. App. 2001) (arbitrator in husband's shareholder suit may later represent wife in divorce because matters were different), and the neutral had personal and substantial participation in the matter, *see, e.g.*, In re Hoffman, 670 N.W.2d 500 (N.D. 2003) (granting default judgment in divorce case was personal and substantial participation), the neutral may not later represent any party in that matter. Consider a similar state version of Model Rule 1.12 followed by an illustrative case.

> **PENNSYLVANIA R. PROF. CONDUCT 1.12: Former Judge, Arbitrator, Mediator or Other Third-Party Neutral.**
> (a) Except as stated in paragraph (d), a lawyer shall not represent anyone in connection with a matter in which the lawyer participated personally and substantially as a judge or other adjudicative officer, third-party neutral (including arbitrator or mediator) or law clerk to such a person, unless all parties to the proceeding give informed consent.
> (b) A lawyer shall not negotiate for employment with any person who is involved as a party or as lawyer for a party in which the lawyer is participating personally and substantially as a judge or other adjudicative officer, or third-party neutral. A lawyer serving as a law clerk to a judge, other adjudicative officer or third-party neutral may negotiate for employment with a party or lawyer involved in a matter in which the clerk is participating personally and substantially, but only after the lawyer has notified the judge, other adjudicative officer or third-party neutral.
> (c) If a lawyer is disqualified by paragraph (a), no lawyer in a firm with which the lawyer is associated may knowingly undertake or continue representation in the matter unless:
> (1) the disqualified lawyer is screened from any participation in the matter and is apportioned no part of the fee therefrom; and
> (2) written notice is promptly given to the parties and any appropriate tribunal to enable them to ascertain compliance with the provisions of this Rule.
> (d) An arbitrator selected as a partisan of a party in a multi-member arbitration panel is not prohibited from subsequently representing that party.

James v. Mississippi,
Mississippi Supreme Court
962 So.2d 528 (2007)

In this attorney discipline case we are asked whether a former judge may represent a party in a case related to one over which she formerly presided. Because the Rules of Professional Conduct squarely prohibit such a situation, we hold that she may not.

FACTS AND PROCEDURAL HISTORY

... Attorney Ceola James served as a Chancellor in the Ninth Chancery District, which is composed of Humphreys, Issaquena, Sunflower, Warren, and Washington Counties. The case of *J.N.W.E. v. W.D.W.*, which triggered the complaint at hand, arose in the Chancery Court of Washington County, where Ms. James was chancellor.

Styled a "Petition for Protection from Domestic Abuse," *J.N.W.E.* was brought by a mother seeking court-ordered protection for her child, who had allegedly been physically abused by her husband, W.D.W. The couple was in the process of a divorce action situated in Yazoo County.

J.N.W.E. moved the court for a protective order that would prevent her husband, W.D.W., from visiting with their child, alleging that the child was subject to physical harm by the father. At an emergency hearing on November 21, 2001, ... Ms. James entered an order staying any unsupervised visitation by the child's father on that same day.

On December 14, 2001, Ms. James held a final hearing on the issue in which the defendant appeared and acknowledged he had indeed signed the statement previously admitted as evidence, while contesting that he had actually done the acts portrayed in the statement. After this hearing, Ms. James entered another order on January 23, 2002 extending the previous order and barring W.D.W. from any unsupervised visitation with the child. ...

On June 20, 2002, a final judgment of divorce was entered in Yazoo County. Over a year later, on November 24, 2004, an ex parte order was entered substituting Ms. James as counsel of record for J.N.W.E. in the Yazoo County divorce action. Opposing counsel quickly filed a motion to disqualify Ms. James as attorney of record, citing her previous involvement in the related child abuse case and the prohibition set forth in Mississippi Rule of Professional Conduct 1.12. After the failure of Ms. James to respond to the motion or appear at the hearing, the trial court disqualified her as J.N.W.E.'s attorney.

Ms. James responded with a motion to reconsider that ruling, arguing that she did not receive proper notice regarding the motion to disqualify, and also filed a motion to disqualify the attorney of W.D.W. and a motion for recusal against the trial judge. The trial judge set aside the original order to disqualify Ms. James and allowed a hearing on the merits.

After this hearing, the trial judge found again that Ms. James had violated Rule 1.12 and, accordingly, could not represent J.N.W.E. The court also denied the motions for disqualification of attorney and recusal filed by Ms. James, finding that they had no merit.

Ms. James then appealed to this Court to review the decision of the trial court. We assigned the case to our Court of Appeals for decision, but notified the Mississippi Bar of the possible violation of Rule 1.12. As noted *supra,* the Court of Appeals found that the trial court was correct in disqualifying Ms. James as attorney of record for J.N.W.E. because of the Rule 1.12 conflict, and we denied certiorari to review that decision.

Concerned that a breach of ethics had occurred, the Bar notified the Committee on Professional Responsibility, which investigated the alleged attorney misconduct. ... The Committee found a violation of Rule 1.12 had occurred, and a public reprimand for violation of Rule 1.12 was issued to Ms. James on January 24, 2005.

Pursuant to M.R.D. 7(c), Ms. James requested a formal proceeding to review the decision of the committee, and a three-member Complaint Tribunal convened for a trial of the matter on June 29, 2005. The Complaint Tribunal found—as had the Court of Appeals and the Committee on Professional Responsibility—that Ms. James had violated Rule 1.12. It recommended a public reprimand as penalty for the violation.

Ms. James appealed this decision, at which time the Bar filed a motion asking for damages, as the Bar considered the appeal frivolous. The Bar argued that because multiple bodies had found a violation of Rule 1.12—including the trial court; the Court of Appeals; this Court by implication, as we denied certiorari; the Committee on Professional Responsibility; and the Complaint Tribunal—Ms. James' appeal was wholly frivolous.

We denied the motion, citing Rule 9 of the Rules of Discipline, which allow that "the accused attorney may, *as a matter of right,* appeal any disposition of the Tribunal to the [Supreme] Court." (emphasis added). For even an attorney who admits that her conduct was a violation of our rules may still appeal "the extent or absence of discipline" assessed by the Complaint Tribunal. M.R.D. 9(b).

Ms. James asks us to review twelve issues, and the Bar tells us there is but one. There are actually two: was there a violation of Rule 1.12? And, if so, is a public reprimand warranted? After a full review, we conclude there was a violation and that a public reprimand is warranted. ...

DISCUSSION

The Rule.

Rule 1.12(a) of the Mississippi Rules of Professional Conduct states, in pertinent part, that "a lawyer shall not represent anyone in connection with a matter in which the lawyer participated personally and substantially as a judge." ...

The Rule's purpose is to safeguard the integrity of the legal profession in Mississippi. ...

Substantial Participation.

... In the case at hand, Ms. James urges that ... she did not participate substantially in the case. "Substantial participation" is not as simple as a mathematical formula, although the extent of the judge's repeated participation should be assessed. The extent of the judge's interaction with the case and the litigants should be the primary focus of the inquiry.

The facts are undisputed that while acting as chancellor Ms. James entered three orders in the child abuse case in Washington County and presided over two hearings. The first hearing was apparently ex parte and not transcribed. The second hearing was transcribed and runs to thirty-two pages, which does not include the arguments of counsel, which were not transcribed. Ms. James questioned both attorneys about the case and specifically directed inquiries to W.D.W. about whether he had indeed abused his child or signed a statement admitting he had.

One of the orders crafted a temporary injunction against W.D.W. preventing him from having any unsupervised visitation with his child. Another converted this temporary injunction to a permanent one pending the outcome of the Yazoo County divorce case.

Accordingly, Ms. James substantially participated in the case. She read motions, conducted hearings, heard testimony, and entered orders. In fact, she handled the entirety of the child abuse case.

"Matter" Defined.

Ms. James further argues that even if she had participated substantially as a judge in the Washington County child abuse case, the Yazoo County divorce case is not the same "matter" as contemplated by Rule 1.12. The cases were certainly situated in different counties and had different cause numbers, and the Bar does not contend Ms. James was originally involved in the Yazoo County case. The question thus turns on what "a matter" means as contemplated by Rule 1.12.

The Comment to Rule 1.12 begins by noting that "[t]his Rule generally parallels Rule 1.11," which defines "matter." Rule 1.11(d)(1) sets forth that "the term 'matter' includes ... any judicial or other proceeding, application, request for a ruling or other determination, contract, claim, controversy, investigation, charge, accusation, arrest or other particular matter involving a specific party or parties."

Application to the Case at Hand.

Ms. James oversaw the Washington County child abuse petition, not the Yazoo County divorce action. However, the two cases were greatly intertwined. The parties, J.N.W.E. and W.D.W., are the same. The initial pleading filed before Ms. James by J.N.W.E., styled a "Petition for Protection from Domestic Abuse," discusses the evolution of the divorce case in Yazoo County. It further reveals that the Yazoo County

Chancery Court had ruled previously on the custody issue between J.N.W.E. and W.D.W., which was the sole subject of the Washington County case. At the second hearing in the Washington County child abuse case, Ms. James acknowledged that information regarding the alleged child abuse "w[as] presented to the Yazoo Chancery Court."

It is also indisputable that any divorce action will include a discussion and ruling by the chancery court on custody of any children to the marriage. Ms. James ruled explicitly on the rights of W.D.W. to have visitation with his child. Custody and visitation are inextricably bound to the divorce action in Yazoo County where Ms. James later attempted to represent J.N.W.E.

While the two cases do not share the same docket number, they do involve the same parties, the same issues, and the same concerns. As a judge, Ms. James personally and substantially participated in the Washington County child abuse action, which was focused exclusively on the visitation of the minor child.

Critically, Ms. James admits she was hired by J.N.W.E. to obtain a modification of the Yazoo County divorce order, specifically a "modification so [J.N.W.E.] could get custody." Custody of the minor child is exactly the matter Ms. James oversaw in the Washington County child abuse case.

Because she substantially participated in the custody matter as a judge, Ms. James cannot now represent J.N.W.E.—nor, for that matter, could she represent the father, W.D.W. The only circumstance in which Ms. James could have represented "anyone in connection [in the] matter" is if "all parties to the proceeding give informed consent confirmed in writing." M.R.P.C. 1.12(a). As signaled by his motion to disqualify, W.D.W. expressly did not consent to Ms. James representing his ex-wife, J.N.W.E.

The Discipline Imposed.

... Ms. James has violated Rule 1.12, which is designed to preserve the integrity of the legal system from real or potential conflicts of interest. There is a compelling need to deter members of the Bench and Bar from this type of conduct and protect the public from this type of behavior. The Comment to Rule 1.11 is illustrative in this respect, as enforcement of that Rule, as well as Rule 1.12, "prevents a lawyer from exploiting public office for the advantage of a private client." At all times we must protect the public from these types of conflicts of interest. ...

CONCLUSION

In order to protect the integrity of our profession, our Rules of Professional Conduct specifically prohibit attorneys who are former judges from later representing anyone in a matter in which they personally and substantially participated as a judge. Because Ms.

James violated this prohibition, she must be publicly reprimanded.

CEOLA JAMES SHALL BE PUBLICLY REPRIMANDED IN OPEN COURT BY THE PRESIDING JUDGE ON THE FIRST DAY OF THE NEXT TERM OF THE WARREN COUNTY CIRCUIT COURT.

"What Were They Thinking?"

You probably sensed the complainant's consternation that the former judge in the above case continued to maintain that she had *not* violated Rule 1.12 notwithstanding that five bodies had each held that she *had* violated the rule. How might she have justified her thinking? When the application of a conduct rule appears to be a judgment call, is it a good time to rely on the thinking of independent others? Do you think that the judge might have lacked a mentor to encourage her to accept the wisdom of the first, second, third, or fourth bodies before pursuing her appeal to a published opinion before the fifth body?

INQUIRY

Negotiating for Employment. Model Rule 1.12(b) includes the same restriction against negotiating for employment while a third-party neutral, that Model Rule 1.11(d)(2)(ii) includes for government lawyers. Judges and other third-party neutrals must not negotiate for employment with parties or lawyers who appear before them, except that law clerks may do so with notice to their third-party neutral employer. Once again, as in other government service, judicial law clerks tend to serve for a short term with the expectation that they are preparing for a career of representing litigants in the same or similar tribunals. Parties should also have less concern that a law clerk may influence an outcome.

Imputed Disqualification and Screening. As you read the similar state version of Model Rule 1.12 above, you should have noticed its now-familiar rule for imputed disqualification in Model Rule 1.12(c) including its exception permitting screening on condition of notice to the involved parties and tribunal, and that no fee from the representation flow to the disqualified third-party neutral. States have accepted screening in the case of government lawyers and third-party neutrals, even though not yet done so widely in the case of lawyers moving from firm to firm. *See, e.g.,* In re County of L.A., 223 F.3d 990 (9th Cir. 2000) (timely screening of former judge defeats imputation of conflict to other members of firm). What is the difference? It may in part be a matter of quantity, that more lawyers move from firm to firm than government lawyers and third-party neutrals move into law firms. Screening may simply be easier when the screened lawyer is a former government employee or third-party neutral because there are fewer of them and their distinction makes them easier to mark for screening. The trust we hold for them may also be a factor, as may the need for distinguished public servants to move in and out of that service. Consider an illustrative case involving a firm's effort to screen a former judge who joined the firm after participating in a proceeding in which the firm would represent a client. Remember, screening is an imperfect solution.

Cho v. Superior Court,
California Court of Appeals
45 Cal. Rptr.2d 863 (1995)

... The issue in this case is whether a law firm must be disqualified as counsel in a lawsuit after employing the retired judge who had presided over the action and had received ex parte confidences from the opposing party in the course of settlement conferences. We conclude that screening procedures are not sufficient to preserve public trust in the justice system in these circumstances and therefore the firm must be disqualified.

Factual and Procedural Summary
Petitioner is the plaintiff in an action entitled Cho v. Cho Hung Bank [c] (the action) pending in respondent court. This writ proceeding stems from the denial of petitioner's motion to disqualify the law firm of Graham & James, counsel for real party in interest Cho Hung Bank, after Eric E. Younger, the judge who had presided over the action, retired and joined Graham & James in an "of counsel" capacity.

Judge Younger was assigned to the action and held three settlement conferences at various stages of the proceedings. The petition for writ of mandate states: "Petitioner's posture in the settlement conferences accordingly changed at such stages, not the least of which was disclosure of Petitioner's bottom line settlement." A declaration by David Zweig, counsel for petitioner, submitted in support of her motion to disqualify, stated that Judge Younger had been privy to confidences relating to the merits of petitioner's case. Mr. Zweig declared: "Before Judge Younger left the bench at the end of 1994, His Honor made effort to settle the case and held at least 3 settlement conferences. In separate conference, Judge Younger asked plaintiff's counsel to speak candidly about the strengths and weaknesses of plaintiff's case, to which counsel responded openly and divulged information to His Honor in confidence. No such information would have been divulged but for the fact that it was in a confidential setting." Irwin Friedman, another attorney for petitioner, declared that confidential information, including petitioner's "'bottom line' settlement" had been divulged to Judge Younger in settlement conferences.

Judge Younger retired in late December 1994, with the action still pending. Graham & James substituted into the lawsuit as counsel for real party in interest Cho Hung Bank on February 17, 1995. Within the next few days, a partner at Graham & James, Stephen Owens, reviewed the court docket sheet and discovered for the first time that Judge Younger had presided over the case until his retirement. Mr. Owens had heard that Judge Younger was joining the firm, and he told the managing partner, Henry David, of Judge Younger's role in the action. After researching the issues, Graham & James decided to impose a "'cone of silence'" around Judge Younger before he began his formal relationship with the firm. A memorandum was circulated throughout Graham & James directing all personnel that Judge Younger was not to be involved in the action in any way; that it was not to be discussed in his presence; that Judge Younger was not to discuss his role or any information he had obtained; and that he was not to have access to any files or written materials about the action.

Judge Younger began his work with Graham & James on March 1, 1995. Petitioner's attorney first learned of this from Jang W. Lee at a deposition on March 22, 1995. Mr. Lee is a former attorney for Cho Hung Bank, and is a real party in interest in these proceedings. On the same day that petitioner's counsel learned of Judge Younger's affiliation with Graham & James, a letter from that firm was delivered to the court and counsel in the action formally informing them of Judge Younger's relationship with that firm, and of the steps taken to screen him from any involvement in the action.

Petitioner moved to recuse or disqualify Graham & James in March 1995. In opposition to the motion, real party in interest Cho Hung Bank submitted the declaration of Judge Younger, which stated that "While I did conduct settlement discussions in chambers with each side (in the other's absence), I do not believe I ever learned any confidential information from plaintiff; if I did, I certainly did not remember it for any period of time."[fn] ...

Discussion

This case presents an issue of first impression in California-whether a law firm must be disqualified when it employs a former judge who in his official capacity received ex parte confidences, bearing on the merits of a lawsuit over which he was presiding, from an adverse party in the identical litigation in which the motion to disqualify is brought. We conclude that the firm must be disqualified.

...

The parties acknowledge that Judge Younger is disqualified from participating in the action by virtue of his role as judge. There is no

California rule of professional conduct which governs the issue of disqualification of Graham & James. ...

The protection of the confidences of litigants has been a primary focus of rules of professional conduct in California and as drafted by the American Bar Association. ... [U]nder the Model Rules, a former judge may not represent anyone in connection with a matter in which he or she "participated personally and substantially as a judge ...." (Model Rules, rule 1.12(a).) The rule on vicarious disqualification of the law firm employing a former judicial officer parallels the rule for former public attorneys: the disqualified attorney must be screened from participation, receive no share of the fee, and notice must be given to the appropriate tribunal. (Model Rules, rule 1.12(c).)

The integrity of the judicial process demands that litigants have confidence that a judicial officer who has been privy to revelations regarding the case in the course of settlement conferences will not later become aligned with the opposition. Unlike the disqualification of a former private sector attorney who has governmental information, here the former judge became privy to the confidences of private parties to the litigation.

We are presented with a situation in which the judge's role *did* include receiving confidences from petitioner's counsel ex parte during repeated settlement conferences. The case is analogous to that of a mediator who was disqualified from representing a litigant in a subsequent matter related to an earlier case in which the mediator had received confidences from the parties. ...

We agree ... that disqualification of both the individual attorney and his or her firm is required where the attorney has been privy to confidences of a litigant while acting as a neutral mediator. We also agree with the distinction drawn between adjudicators and mediators, so long as the adjudicator does not become a mediator and, in doing so, receive confidences from the parties going to the essential merits of the dispute. Where a judicial officer has presided over settlement conferences which included ex parte communication, we presume the revelation of confidences relating to the merits of a litigant's case. The same principles ... demand disqualification of both the former judge and his or her new firm in such circumstances. The case for disqualification of the judge is even more compelling than the case of the mediator, who has a far more limited role in a matter than a judge. ...

All manner of issues are discussed in confidence at a settlement conference, including the strengths and weaknesses of each party's case, and the amount the party is willing to pay or receive in settlement. "[A] settlement conference judge does not decide anything—he merely uses his judicial status to help the parties reach a settlement if reasonably possible. To this end it has been said that the judge should actively participate in the negotiating process to 'break the ice' between litigants who may be reluctant to settle. The judge should also use any expertise he may have in the subject area of the litigation to express his opinions of the settlement value of the various causes of action against the different defendants or of the range in which negotiations may realistically proceed. He should listen to and carefully evaluate the parties' personal contentions so they will feel they have had their 'day in court' if the case is settled. ...

No amount of assurances or screening procedures, no "cone of silence," could ever convince the opposing party that the confidences would not be used to its disadvantage. When a litigant has bared its soul in confidential settlement conferences with a judicial officer, that litigant could not help but be horrified to find that the judicial officer has resigned to join the opposing law firm—which is now pressing or defending the lawsuit against that litigant.[fn] No one could have confidence in the integrity of a legal process in which this is permitted to occur without the parties' consent. ...

Disposition

Let a peremptory writ of mandate issue directing the superior court to vacate its order denying petitioner's motion to disqualify Graham & James and to enter a new order granting the motion. ...

INQUIRY

Current Third-Party Neutrals. Model Rule 1.12 addresses only former judges, arbitrators, mediators, and other third-party neutrals who have moved to private law practice. What duties of loyalty do current third-party neutrals have regarding their roles? The primary concern, addressed by ABA Model Rule 2.4, is that parties who employ third-party neutrals understand that the third-party neutral does not represent any party in the matter but is indeed neutral. Arbitrators, mediators, case evaluators, and other dispute-resolution professionals can at times appear to be giving counsel to one party or another, especially when the dispute-resolution procedure permits private caucuses with only one side present. After Model Rule 2.4(a) defines a third-party neutral, Model Rule 2.4(b) requires the neutral to ensure that parties understand the difference between the neutral's role and the role of a lawyer representative. Read a similar state version of Model Rule 2.4, followed by a case illustrating the sensitivity that a third-party neutral needs to show in disclosing potential conflicts of interest.

WASHINGTON R. PROF. CONDUCT 2.4:   Lawyer Serving as Third-Party Neutral.

(a) A lawyer serves as a third-party neutral when the lawyer assists two or more persons who are not clients of the lawyer to reach a resolution of a dispute or other matter that has arisen between them. Service as a third-party neutral may include service as an arbitrator, a mediator or in such other capacity as will enable the lawyer to assist the parties to resolve the matter.

(b) A lawyer serving as a third-party neutral shall inform unrepresented parties that the lawyer is not representing them. When the lawyer knows or reasonably should know that a party does not understand the lawyer's role in the matter, the lawyer shall explain the difference between the lawyer's role as a third-party neutral and a lawyer's role as one who represents a client.

La Serena Properties, L.L.C. v. Weisbach,
California Court of Appeals
112 Cal. Rptr.3d 597 (2010)

INTRODUCTION

Plaintiffs La Serena Properties, LLC, Casa Margaritaville, Inc., and Steven Yates (appellants) appeal from a judgment entered after the trial court sustained the demurrers of defendants Gerald Weisbach (Weisbach) and the American Arbitration Association (AAA) (respondents) without leave to amend. Appellants sued respondents for damages, as well as other relief, alleging five separate causes of action, all of which arise out of the alleged failure of arbitrator Weisbach to disclose a certain conflict of interest during the appointment process.

We agree with the trial court that the alleged claims of misconduct, no matter how pleaded, all arise out of the conflict of interest disclosure procedure that is integrally part of the arbitration process. Thus, respondents are protected from liability by the common law arbitral immunity for quasi-judicial acts. Accordingly, we affirm the judgment.

II.
FACTUAL AND PROCEDURAL BACKGROUNDS

... The complaint alleges that appellants entered into a construction contract and a subsequent promissory note with Merchant Builders, Inc. (MBI) in 2002, both of which included mandatory AAA arbitration provisions. Subsequently, a dispute arose between appellants and MBI, and appellants demanded arbitration under the AAA arbitration clauses contained in the contract and note. ...

After being compelled to go to arbitration, it is alleged that MBI's lawyers conspired among themselves to persuade appellants to accept Weisbach as the arbitrator, without disclosing that Weisbach had a longstanding "family relationship" with one of MBI's counsel, David Baskin (Baskin), in that Weisbach was the "boyfriend" of Baskin's sister. Appellants then "tentatively agreed" to Weisbach serving as the arbitrator.

A "Notice of Appointment" was sent to Weisbach by AAA, indicating that he had been selected as arbitrator. The notice included a conflicts of interest disclosure form.... .

Weisbach completed the form disclosing only a former association with Gerald K. Carroll, an attorney who worked with Long & Levit while Weisbach served as "of counsel" to the firm. Weisbach dated the disclosure form September 7, 2005, and signed it.

The complaint also alleges that Weisbach joined the conspiracy with MBI's counsel at "some time prior to September 12." "Hours later," on September 12, 2005, Weisbach sent an email to AAA stating that he had just received a call from Baskin informing Weisbach that Baskin was representing MBI in the dispute. Weisbach then stated: "David is a personal friend. While I do not believe that our relationship would prejudice my hearing of this matter, this relationship does present a potential conflict. Please so inform the parties and advise." A copy of the email was faxed to counsel in the case, along with a cover letter from AAA, asking that AAA be advised within 15 days if there was any objection to the appointment of Weisbach. Apparently, neither side then objected to Weisbach's service as arbitrator.

With the agreement of MBI's counsel, Weisbach did not disclose his "familial" relationship with Baskin, or the "depth and character of his relationship with the Baskin family," including the fact that he "was in a romantic relationship with Baskin's sister." Appellants claim that the partial disclosures of Weisbach's relationship with Carroll and Baskin were intended to appear as if complete disclosures had been made when the full nature of the conflict was concealed from appellants.

The arbitration commenced on March 26, 2006, and extended over 10 days. MBI was represented by Baskin and his son, Caleb Baskin. An arbitration award was issued by Weisbach on July 20, 2006, and was clarified in an amended award on September 26, 2006. The final award denied more than 20 claims made by appellants against MBI, including eight fraud claims, but awarded appellants a total of $12,336.44 for two claims. Appellants were also awarded $4,112.15 in attorney fees, and reimbursement of $5,250.01, which they previously had paid in excess of their allocated 50 percent share of the costs of the arbitration.

Almost two years later, on May 28, 2008, the president of MBI wrote to the AAA, complaining about the failure of Weisbach to disclose his "intimate" involvement with Baskin's sister.   MBI complained that this conflict caused Weisbach to struggle to render an impartial "verdict," and ultimately resulted in a "'non-decision'" or "'split verdict.'"   Appellants alleged that prior to their receipt of their copy of this letter they had no knowledge of this relationship and Weisbach's failure to disclose it.

Subsequently, court proceedings were commenced in the Santa Cruz County Superior Court seeking to set aside the arbitration award. That relief was ultimately granted on October 16, 2008.

Appellants filed the complaint in this action [alleging]... fraud, fraudulent concealment, breach of contract, unfair business practices, and negligence.   Appellants sought an award of damages, disgorgement of profits, punitive damages, prejudgment interest, and costs, including attorney fees. ...

III.
ANALYSIS

... Central to impartial decision-making by arbitrators and judges alike is the need for them to make disclosures that may give rise to a challenge to the judge's impartiality by one of the parties, even if the judge or arbitrator concludes that he or she is not disqualified. ...

... [A] person serving as an arbitrator pursuant to an arbitration agreement has statutory and ethical duties to comply with certain disclosure requirements. Code of Civil Procedure section 1281.9, subdivision (a) mandates that a person "proposed" to serve as a neutral arbitrator "shall disclose all matters that could cause a person aware of the facts to reasonably entertain a doubt that the proposed neutral arbitrator would be able to be impartial... ." The section goes on to describe those types of relationships that must be disclosed, including "[a]ny professional or significant personal relationship the proposed neutral arbitrator ... has or has had with any party to the arbitration proceeding or lawyer for a party." [C] ...

While the parties have not cited a California case directly on point, and we have not found one, we have no doubt that the alleged failure to make adequate disclosures of potential conflicts of interest falls within the scope of the absolute immunity for quasi-judicial acts. ...

... While disclosures take place before the arbitrator's appointment becomes final, and certainly before the commencement of the arbitration itself, it is an integral part of the arbitration process. Indeed, the rules and statutes governing the disclosures by arbitrators make it clear that such disclosures are to occur when the arbitrator is "proposed."   Similarly, judges are expected to make the disclosures required of them before the adjudicative function of the courts begin.

... Therefore, any claimed misconduct by the arbitrator in association with the failure to make a required disclosure at the inception of his or her selection was sufficiently associated with the arbitration process itself to justify the application of arbitral immunity. ...

Courts have observed that the public interest appellants seek to protect is sufficiently advanced by the remedy of vacation of the arbitration award, which constitutes the sole remedy for arbitrator misconduct. [C] ...

Accordingly, we agree with the trial court that the common law absolute immunity for quasi-judicial acts applies to the misconduct alleged in the complaint, thereby precluding appellants' civil lawsuit for damages against Weisbach and the AAA.

IV.
DISPOSITION

The judgment in favor of respondents is affirmed. Costs on appeal are awarded to respondents.

D. Evaluations for Third Persons

Opinion Letters. One final area in which lawyers face questions of loyalty has to do with lawyers providing evaluations at the request of a client but for the benefit of third persons. Lawyers on occasion evaluate the legal status of a matter or the client's "compliance" with regulatory law, or analyze for the benefit of a third person risk that a client faces, just as accountants do for banks and buyers relating to a client's financial condition. Lawyers often call those evaluations *opinion letters* referring to a third person needing the lawyer's opinion regarding the client's legal circumstances. An opinion letter may be necessary for the sale of a client's business, the insuring or bonding of a client's risk, or the extension of credit to the client. Opinion letters may go to buyers, insurance and bond companies, banks, and others. When they do, the lawyers who write them must ensure that they can do so in all candor without adversely affecting the client. For example, the lawyer who is defending a client in litigation may find it unwise to issue to a third person an opinion concerning the risks of the litigation, lest that opinion fall into the hands of the litigation opposition. A lawyer who owes a duty of advocacy to a client may find it difficult to set aside that role as advocate long enough to assess bluntly the real risks of the litigation. At a minimum, the lawyer would need the client's consent to reveal confidential information, but even with that consent, the role of both representing the client and giving an evaluation to a third person is so fraught with conflict that, while permissible, a more prudent approach may be to require that the client hire an independent evaluator for that opinion. Consider ABA Model

Rule 2.3 on the subject, followed by a case illustrating the hazards of a dual role of client representative and evaluator for a third person.

WASHINGTON R. PROF. CONDUCT 2.3: Evaluation for Use by Third Persons.
(a) A lawyer may provide an evaluation of a matter affecting a client for the use of someone other than the client if the lawyer reasonably believes that making the evaluation is compatible with other aspects of the lawyer's relationship with the client.
(b) When the lawyer knows or reasonably should know that the evaluation is likely to affect the client's interests materially and adversely, the lawyer shall not provide the evaluation unless the client gives informed consent.
(c) Except as disclosure is authorized in connection with a report of an evaluation, information relating to the evaluation is otherwise protected by Rule 1.6.

Mehaffy, Rider, Windholz & Wilson v. Central Bank Denver, N.A.,

Colorado Supreme Court
892 P.2d 230 (1995)

... Petitioners represented the town of Winter Park (Town) and the Winter Park Development Authority (Authority) in connection with notes and bonds issued by the Authority in 1984 and 1985. Central Bank Denver, (respondent), purchased the notes and bonds. Respondent's claims against petitioners are predicated on opinion letters that petitioners prepared at the request of their clients in connection with the offering and sale of the notes and bonds of the Authority. The court of appeals held that an attorney who issues an opinion letter for the purpose of inducing a non-client to purchase municipal notes or bonds can be liable for negligent misrepresentation when the opinion letter contains material misstatements of fact. We agree with the court of appeals and the remand of respondent's negligent misrepresentation claim against petitioners to the district court for trial.

In January 1983, the Winter Park Town Council (Town Council) created the Authority to improve certain blighted areas within the Town's limits. The Authority adopted an urban renewal plan (Plan) to construct projects paid for by property tax increment financing. The Town Council set a public hearing on the proposed Plan as required by section 31-25-107(3), 12B C.R.S. (1986). Instead of holding a public hearing or making the factual findings required under section 31-25-107(4), 12B C.R.S. (1986), the Town Council submitted the Plan to the electorate for approval at a special election. After the voters approved the Plan and the Town Council adopted the Plan, the Authority issued $4 million in Notes (1984 Notes) to finance the construction of a parking garage. Hanifen Imhoff, Inc. (Hanifen) was the underwriter for the 1984 Notes. Respondent expressed interest in purchasing the 1984 Notes and began negotiating the terms and conditions of the purchase.

Before respondent purchased the 1984 Notes, East Grand County School District and other governmental entities (school district) filed a lawsuit against the Town, the Town Council, and the Authority in the district court, claiming that the Town Council had failed to make certain findings of fact required by section 31-25-107(4). Respondent informed Hanifen that it would not purchase the 1984 Notes if there was any risk that the lawsuit would succeed and cause a default on the 1984 Notes.

Hanifen assured respondent that the lawsuit had no merit, and that bond counsel, O'Connor & Hannan, would certify that all necessary steps to secure the tax revenue required to finance the 1984 Notes had been taken. Respondent contacted Arnold Kaplan of O'Connor & Hannan. Kaplan assured respondent that an opinion letter, stating that the lawsuit had no merit, would be issued by Mehaffy, Rider, Windholz & Wilson, counsel for the Town and the Authority. Mehaffy, Rider, Windholz & Wilson, issued an opinion letter on September 24, 1984, stating that the lawsuit did not have merit. On September 24, 1984, O'Connor & Hannan issued an opinion letter stating that the 1984 Notes were validly issued and agreed that the lawsuit had no merit. These opinion letters were provided to respondent, and respondent purchased the 1984 Notes from Hanifen for $4 million in reliance on counsels' representations.

In February 1985, the Authority issued $4.5 million in Notes (1985 Notes), in order to retire the 1984 Notes. Mehaffy and Kaplan advised the respondent that the 1985 Notes were valid, and that the lawsuit had no merit. These opinion letters were provided to respondent. Windholz, who had been retained to defend the Authority against the lawsuit, prepared a letter to Kaplan and respondent that expressed his opinion that the allegations in the lawsuit were without merit.

On February 28, 1985, respondent submitted a private placement letter (referred to by the parties as a "comfort letter") to the Town and the Authority, in which respondent stated that it was relying on its own investigation of all material facts relating to the transaction. Respondent purchased the 1985 Notes on February 28, 1985. ...

... [T]he Authority [then] issued Winter Park Development Authority Tax Increment Refunding and Improvement Bonds, Series 1985A (1985A Bonds) to retire the 1985 Notes. In connection with the issuance of the 1985A Bonds, respondent issued a second comfort letter, dated October 16, 1985, that was identical in all material respects to the February 28, 1985, comfort letter. Respondent refused to purchase the 1985A Bonds without assurances from petitioners that the lawsuit was without merit. Mehaffy, Kaplan, and Windholz each issued opinion letters stating that the 1985A Bonds were valid, and advised the respondent that the lawsuit had no merit. On October 24, 1985, respondent purchased the 1985A Bonds for $5,015,000.

On March 11, 1986, the district court granted the school district's motion for partial summary judgment invalidating the Town Council's approval of the Plan, and invalidating the financing for the 1985A Bonds. ... [T]he court of appeals affirmed the district court. Because the financing for the 1985A Bonds was invalidated, Grand County refused to remit incremental property tax revenues to the Authority. The Authority was unable to provide sufficient funds to the trustee to make the interest payments for the 1985A Bonds, and the 1985A Bonds went into default.

Respondent filed a complaint against the petitioners... .

Generally, an attorney is not liable to a non-client absent a finding of fraud or malicious conduct by the attorney. ... An attorney's liability to non-clients has been limited for various reasons, including the potential liability of an attorney to an unforeseeable and unlimited number of third parties, as well as the adversarial nature of litigation.
...

... The tort of negligent misrepresentation provides a remedy when money is lost due to misrepresentation in a business transaction. ... To establish a claim for negligent misrepresentation, it must be shown that the defendant supplied false information to others in a business transaction, and failed to exercise reasonable care or competence in obtaining or communicating information on which other parties justifiably relied. ...

In the present case, respondent requested that the Town and the Authority issue opinion letters because of the potential damage of the lawsuit on the Authority's ability to pay off the 1984 and 1985 Notes and the 1985A Bonds. Petitioners' opinion letters were prepared for the benefit of respondent and most of the letters were addressed to the respondent. The letters assured respondent that the lawsuit did not have merit. The opinion letters were not issued in the context of an adversarial relationship, but were issued in order to secure respondent's participation in a business relationship that would mutually benefit the Town, the Authority, and respondent. Accordingly, by issuing legal opinion letters for the purpose of inducing respondent to purchase the 1984 and 1985 Notes and 1985A Bonds, petitioners may be liable to respondent for negligent misrepresentation. ...

The opinion letters state that the Town and the Authority complied with section 31-25-107(4) before adopting the Plan. Compliance with section 31-25-107(4) requires that particular factual findings be made before the Plan is adopted. ... [T]he court of appeals held that the statutorily required factual findings under section 31-25-107(4), regarding the need for an urban renewal program, were not made by the Town Council before the matter was referred to the electorate. ...

Respondent's investigation of the transactions was limited to the extent it believed necessary. By inquiring whether the lawsuit had merit, respondent sought assurances from petitioners about the likelihood of success of the lawsuit. Because petitioners issued opinion letters that stated that the lawsuit did not have merit, respondent may have been influenced not to conduct further investigations into the merits of the lawsuit. Whether respondent's comfort letters disclaimed its reliance on petitioners' opinion letters is a material issue of fact that precludes summary judgment. ...

Accordingly, we affirm the judgment of the court of appeals and the remand of respondent's negligent misrepresentation claim against petitioners to the district court for trial.

INQUIRY

Loss of Confidentiality and Privilege. There is little or no dispute that a lawyer's sharing an evaluation with a third person destroys the confidential and privileged nature of the lawyer's communications on the subject of the evaluation. The evaluation is generally not privileged in the hands of the third person and is intead discoverable by others including the client's adversaries in litigation. *See, e.g.,* Burden-Meeks v. Welch, 319 F.3d 897 (7th Cir. 2003). On the other hand, there is some authority that the lawyer and client may preserve the confidentiality of the lawyer's evaluation if they take substantial steps to bind the third person to that confidentiality, as is often done when prospective purchasers demand to inspect confidential business information. *See, e.g.,* Hewlett-Packard Co. v. Bausch & Lomb, Inc., 115 F.R.D. 308 (N.D. Cal. 1987).

Sarbanes-Oxley Act. As a prior chapter intimated, lawyers who give opinions for third persons to use relating to the sale of registered securities owe duties under the Sarbanes-Oxley Act of 2002, 15 U.S.C. §78d. The Act gave the Securities Exchange Commission authority to enact regulations under which the Commission can discipline lawyers for failing to comply with its regulations. *See* 17 C.F.R. §§205.1-205.7. As previously indicated, the regulations authorize lawyers to disclose information to the Commission regarding a client's compliance with federal securities laws. Transparency is critically important to more than just clients. It plays a role in the largest movements on the largest stages.

Career and Professional Development

Transparency is an important aspect of a new lawyer's career and professional development. Law firms and other employers of lawyers want to know whom they are hiring. While certain information is and should always remain private, professional secrets—those matters that are likely to become public and also likely to affect future professional relationships—are generally not good for anyone when forming new employment relationships. Many times, chances are good that interviewers who ask specific questions requiring transparency already know information that the interviewee might prefer to withhold. Frank disclosure of that information, whether of prior careers and employment, prior associations and activities, or the like, may be all that a prospective employer needs to feel confident that the candidate has no other secrets that might disqualify the candidate from employment. The key is to be transparent at the right time and with the right persons. Get counsel from trained and experienced placement professionals when you have questions regarding transparency. Get started on the right foot.

CHAPTER XI

R E P U T A T I O N

Advertising, Marketing, Soliciting, Specializing

> *It takes twenty years to build a reputation and five minutes to ruin it. If you think about that, you'll do things differently.*
> — *Warren Buffett*

> *Nobody raises his reputation by lowering others.*
> — *Unknown*

> *[Americans] have found out that in their country and their age man is brought home to himself by an irresistible force; and losing all hope of stopping that force, they turn all their thoughts to the direction of it. They therefore do not deny that every man may follow his own interest; but they endeavor to prove that it is the interest of every man to be virtuous.*
> — *Alexis de Tocqueville*

OBJECTIVE: Given the need to develop and expand a law practice through marketing activities, articulate the rules and conventions to follow to uphold and improve your reputation.

Applicable Rules

7.1   Communications Regarding a Lawyer's Services

7.2   Advertising

7.3   Direct Contact with Prospective Clients

7.4   Communications of Fields of Practice and Specialization

7.5   Firm Names and Letterheads

7.6   Political Contributions to Obtain Government Legal Engagements

---

Respect is granted, reputation earned. Giving the profession's oath, accepting professional membership, and entering into client and other professional relationships afford one a substantial degree of respect.

Yet it is productivity, honesty, integrity, loyalty, and transparency that earn lawyers strong positive reputation. The profession is of course concerned with the reputation and image of lawyers. You, too, should be concerned with your reputation, if you plan to have a meaningful career, represent your family and associates well—and keep your law license. In some respect, all of the conduct rules address reputation. Several conduct rules address reputation directly. Conduct rules regulate how a lawyer communicates about the lawyer's services, advertises the lawyer's licensure, services, and specialization, contacts prospective clients, and obtains engagements through political contributions. In this chapter, consider some ground rules regarding communication about a lawyer's services before studying specifics of those other rules. Good reputation is one of the more satisfying aspects of law practice.

A. Communication

False or Misleading Communications. Before considering advertising specifically, a lawyer must recognize the need of prospective clients and others to have accurate information regarding a lawyer's services. Advertising, addressed in a later section, raises special issues. Yet in any circumstances, whether part of a lawyer's marketing program or not, lawyers should not be misleading the public about the nature or quality of their legal services. *See, e.g.,* North Carolina State Bar v. Culbertson, 627 S.E.2d 644 (N.C. 2006) (misleading for lawyer arguing federal cases to claim that he was published in Federal Law Reports); In re Zang, 741 P.2d 267 (Ariz. 1987) (advertisement of personal-injury lawyers arguing to jury misleading when none had actually tried a personal-injury case to conclusion). Ignore for a moment the lawyer's duty to speak truthfully about matters that the lawyer is handling. If lawyers are to have good reputation among members of the public, then the public should be able to rely on statements that lawyers make about their services. The reputation of the profession and its individual members depends in the first instance on what lawyers say about their own services. ABA Model Rule 7.1 prohibits a lawyer from making false or misleading communications about the lawyer's services. Model Rule 7.1 applies not only to advertising but to any other communication a lawyer makes about the lawyer's services. Consider an identical state version of Model Rule 7.1.

> MINNESOTA R. PROF. CONDUCT 7.1: **Communications Concerning a Lawyer's Services.**

A lawyer shall not make a false or misleading communication about the lawyer or the lawyer's services. A communication is false or misleading if it contains a material misrepresentation of fact or law, or omits a fact necessary to make the statement considered as a whole not materially misleading.

INQUIRY

Unjustified Expectations.   Model Rule 7.1 defines false or misleading communications as those that include a material misrepresentation of fact or law or omit facts necessary to make the communication not materially misleading. Model Rule 7.1 prohibits not only false communications but also misleading ones. Some statements may be perfectly accurate but nevertheless mislead a person into believing something about a lawyer's services that is not true.   Model Rule 7.1 Comment [3] gives creating unjustified expectations as the first of two examples of a misleading communication. For example, a lawyer might state that the lawyer settled the lawyer's last three cases each for over $500,000. While a statement of that kind may be true, it may cause a prospective client to believe that the lawyer means that the client's case will also settle for $500,000, when that value may be an unjustified expectation. *See, e.g.,* In re Coale, 775 N.E.2d 1079 (Ind. 2002) (advertising $225,000,000 in total compensation for plaintiffs creates unjustified expectations).

A Historic Example. Vinson & Elkin is the formerly prestigious Texas law firm that represented the defunct energy-trading company Enron. Just before its historic collapse, Enron retained Vinson & Elkin to investigate the now-infamous accounting irregularities an Enron insider alleged regarding Enron partnerships. According to a *Forbes* report, the investigation had the character of whitewash. Failing to interview key witnesses and asking few tough questions enabled Vinson & Elkin to issue a report blessing the controversial partnerships just one day before Enron restated its financial statements due to the partnerships' failure. According to a *Houston Chronicle* report, Vinson & Elkins paid dearly, settling with Enron's bankruptcy estate for $30,000,000 to avert civil litigation against the firm for allegedly aiding and abetting fraud in the company's collapse. Many retirees lost their retirement savings in that collapse. Would they agree with Vinson & Elkins' website touting that "[o]ur reputation and our people are our principle assets," "our success depends on maintaining an impeccable professional reputation," and "[w]e are committed to the highest ethical standards, both in our service to clients and in our personal lives." Is the firm's website misleading?

Unsubstantiated Comparisons. The second example that Model Rule 7.1 Comment [3] gives of a misleading communication is when a lawyer makes a comparison that a prospective client cannot substantiate. For example, a lawyer might state that the lawyer charges the lowest fees for the highest quality service in town, when although those comparisons could in theory be true, a prospective client would not be able to substantiate them given the variety of fee structures other lawyers in the community use and variety of quality criteria. *See, e.g.,* In re Wamsley, 725 N.E.2d 25 (Ind. 2000) (misleading to advertise that lawyer could get the best settlement in the least time); In re Anonymous, 637 N.E.2d 171 (Ind. 1994) (unsubstantiated comparison to advertise as premier personal-injury firm). Similarly, a lawyer who claims 20 years of Marine Corps experience without disclosing that none of it had to do with law practice, or who claims to be an assistant professor at a prominent university when the professorship had nothing to do with law, misleads the public into thinking that the lawyer has qualifications and experience that other lawyers do not have. *See* In re Huelskamp, 740 N.E.2d 846 (Ind. 2000). Avoid creating unjustified expectations or making unsubstantiated comparisons.

Another Historic Example. Honesty regarding a lawyer's services means something. Let another story illustrate just how much it means. Federal prosecutors indicted the formerly prestigious silk-stocking New York law firm Milberg Weiss (now known as Milberg LLP) and several of its prominent partners for allegedly paying to plaintiffs $11,400,000 in illegal kickbacks in 180 federal securities cases—and then lying to the courts about it. Three partners pled guilty to the criminal scheme, which involved paying another lawyer (who also pled guilty to federal charges) to act as a plaintiff or get family members to act as plaintiffs in dozens of securities cases. Nevertheless, the firm's home page boasts proudly that the firm's lawyers are "[e]xperts in protecting victims of corporate fraud and other public misconduct." The firm was apparently not so expert in protecting its own prominent partners from fraudulent schemes. Perhaps in order to make Milberg's home page non-deceptive and not misleading, it should add a disclaimer stating "Except Our Own."

Biography

The legend of lawyers is so powerful that the most famous lawyers are often fictional. Atticus Finch was the main character in Harper Lee's novel *To Kill A Mockingbird*, representing an African-American man charged with rape in the Jim Crow south. In the 1962 film version, Gregory Peck portrayed Finch's unwavering devotion to human dignity, equality, integrity, and compassion so effectively that the American Film Institute declared Atticus

Finch as the Greatest Film Hero of All Time. The character has certainly garnered a strong foothold in lawyers' collective psyche. The Southern Poverty Law Center's Morris Dees shares that Finch was why he became a lawyer. Federal Judge Richard Matsch, who presided over the McVeigh trial, cites Finch as a major influence on his judging. A Notre Dame law professor cites *To Kill a Mockingbird* as the most influential teaching text. A Michigan Law Review article asserts that no real lawyer has done more than Atticus Finch has done for the positive public perception of lawyers. Some have accused Harper Lee of making Finch an accomplice and accommodator to Jim Crow laws. No lawyer has done all that can be done. There is always more. Yet Finch serves as a great example for many lawyers.

Law-Firm Names. The need of prospective clients and others to have certain basic accurate information regarding a lawyer's services extends to how a lawyer chooses and uses a law-firm name. Law-firm names are significant—so much so that a special conduct rule ABA Model Rule 7.5 governs them. Law-firm names imply associations, sometimes with a partnership history, culture, and tradition, or with a prominent lawyer, or simply among several lawyers. For example, the lawyer Monroe who designates the firm "Monroe & Associates" presumably has associates, right? *See* Disciplinary Counsel v. Furth, 754 N.E.2d 219 (Ohio 2001) (impermissible for sole practitioner to use "and Associates" in firm name); Medina County Bar Assn. v. Grieselhuber, 678 N.E.2d 535 (Ohio 1997) (misleading for unaffiliated sole practitioner to include "and Affiliates" in firm name). Model Rule 7.5 first ensures that law-firm names comply with Model Rule 7.1 requiring truth in lawyer communications about services including in particular whether they practice in a firm of lawyers. *See* Friedman v. Rogers, 440 U.S. 1 (1979) (upholding constitutionality of rule prohibiting misleading professional trade names). Model Rule 7.5 next prohibits a lawyer in private practice from using a firm name that implies a connection with government, a government official, or a charity, on the same principle that to do so would be misleading. *See, e.g.,* Mezrano v. Alabama State Bar, 434 SO.2d 732 (Ala. 1983) (suspension due in part to use of "University Legal Center" trade name when firm, although on University Boulevard, had no association with nearby university). Ending the firm name with an appellation like "Agency Services," "Legal Clinic," and "Legal Aid" may run afoul of Model Rule 7.5's prohibition. *See, e.g.,* In re Vincenti, 704 A.2d 927 (N.J. 1998) (prohibiting use of "legal clinic" on letterhead without disclaimer).

Disclosing Licensure. Finally, Model Rule 7.5 requires a law firm with offices in more than one state to indicate when lawyers in the firm are not licensed in an office's state. *See, e.g.,* In re Franco, 66 P.3d

805 (Kan. 2003) (business card misleads when indicating practice in two states when lawyer was licensed in only one state); Attorney Grievance Commn. v. Alsafty, 838 A.2d 1213 (Md. 2003) (discipline for using business card from office in state when lawyer not licensed in state and cards gave no indication). It is traditional and rule-compliant for letterheard to indicate the licensure of lawyers who are licensed in other states and not licensed in the state in which the office is located. Read Rule 7.5 for these provisions, followed by an illustrative case.

> **MINNESOTA R. PROF. CONDUCT 7.5: Firm Names and Letterheads.**
>
> (a) A lawyer shall not use a firm name, letterhead, or other professional designation that violates Rule 7.1. A trade name may be used by a lawyer in private practice if it does not imply a connection with a government agency or with a public or charitable legal services organization and is not otherwise in violation of Rule 7.1.
>
> (b) A law firm with offices in more than one jurisdiction may use the same name or other professional designation in each jurisdiction, but identification of the lawyers in an office of the firm shall indicate the jurisdictional limitations on those not licensed to practice in the jurisdiction where the office is located.
>
> (c) The name of a lawyer holding a public office shall not be used in the name of a law firm, or in communications on its behalf, during any substantial period in which the lawyer is not actively and regularly practicing with the firm.
>
> (d) Lawyers may state or imply that they practice in a partnership or other organization only when that is the fact.

Karlena Zachery,
Massachusetts Board of Bar Overseers
Pub. Reprimand No. 2007-3 (Jan. 26, 2007)

SUMMARY

During 2004, the respondent was practicing law in Massachusetts as a solo practitioner. While practicing in this capacity, the respondent utilized stationery that identified her practice as "Williams & Zachery." The respondent was not in a partnership with an attorney named Williams during 2004, or at any other time. By intentionally holding herself out as a member of a law firm called "Williams & Zachery" the respondent misled clients, courts and opposing counsel into believing that she was practicing in a partnership, thus making a false and misleading statement about her services.

During a portion of 2004, the respondent utilized letterhead listing two other attorneys as "of counsel" to "Williams & Zachery." Neither attorney listed as "of counsel" on respondent's letterhead had any affiliation with the respondent or authorized the respondent to list him on her letterhead as "of counsel." By intentionally misrepresenting that the two attorneys were "of counsel" to a law firm in which the respondent was a member, the respondent misled clients, courts and opposing counsel into believing that she was affiliated with the two listed counsel. In so doing, the respondent made a false and misleading statement about her services.

By using a firm name and letterhead that made false and misleading statements about her affiliations with other lawyers, the respondent violated Mass. R. Prof. C. 7.1 and 7.5(a).

This matter came before the Board of Bar Overseers on a stipulation of facts and a joint recommendation that a sanction of public reprimand be imposed. On January 8, 2007, the Board voted to accept the stipulation of the parties and to administer a public reprimand to the respondent.

B. Soliciting

Prohibition Against Solicitation.   You now have a sense of some basic restrictions regarding the truth of a lawyer's communications about the lawyer's services.   The next significant restriction after communicating truthfully has to do with the traditional prohibition against in-person, telephonic, and other real-time contacts to solicit paying practice.   ABA Model Rule 7.3's anti-solicitation provision changes the nature of law practice, making it less like a business and more like a profession. Lawyers market their services, but they do not do so in person to persons whom they know to be in need of those services.   Most lawyers consider Model Rule 7.3's anti-solicitation provision to be a limitation on advertising, which it is, although it is also a more-fundamental rule about how lawyers relate to others who might need their services.   Read an identical state version of Model Rule 7.3 for its general role and specific contours before considering a case that upheld an anti-solicitation provision against constitutional attack. The case articulates the concern Model Rule 7.3 addresses.

> DELAWARE R. PROF. CONDUCT 7.3:   **Direct Contact with Prospective Clients.**
> (a) A lawyer shall not by in-person, live telephone or real-time electronic contact solicit professional employment from a prospective client when a significant motive for the lawyer's doing so is the lawyer's pecuniary gain, unless the person contacted:
> (1) is a lawyer; or
> (2) has a family, close personal, or prior professional relationship with the lawyer.
> (b) A lawyer shall not solicit professional employment from a prospective client by written, recorded or electronic communication or by in-person,

telephone or real-time electronic contact even when not otherwise prohibited by paragraph (a), if:

(1) the prospective client has made known to the lawyer a desire not to be solicited by the lawyer; or

(2) the solicitation involves coercion, duress or harassment.

(c) Every written, recorded or electronic communication from a lawyer soliciting professional employment from a prospective client known to be in need of legal services in a particular matter shall include the words "Advertising Material" on the outside envelope, if any, and at the beginning and ending of any recorded or electronic communication, unless the recipient of the communication is a person specified in paragraphs (a)(1) or (a)(2).

(d) Notwithstanding the prohibitions in paragraph (a), a lawyer may participate with a prepaid or group legal service plan operated by an organization not owned or directed by the lawyer that uses in-person or telephone contact to solicit memberships or subscriptions for the plan from persons who are not known to need legal services in a particular matter covered by the plan.

Ohralik v. Ohio State Bar Association,

United States Supreme Court
436 U.S. 447 (1978)

... Today we ... hold that the State—or the Bar acting with state authorization—constitutionally may discipline a lawyer for soliciting clients in person, for pecuniary gain, under circumstances likely to pose dangers that the State has a right to prevent.

I

Appellant, a member of the Ohio Bar, ... learned from the postmaster's brother about an automobile accident that had taken place on February 2 in which Carol McClintock, a young woman with whom appellant was casually acquainted, [and Wanda Lou Holbert, a passenger in Carol McClintock's vehicle,] had been injured. Appellant made a telephone call to Ms. McClintock's parents, who informed him that their daughter was in the hospital. Appellant suggested that he might visit Carol in the hospital. ...

Appellant proceeded to the hospital, where he found Carol lying in traction in her room. After a brief conversation about her condition,[fn] appellant told Carol he would represent her and asked her to sign an agreement. Carol said she would have to discuss the matter with her parents. She did not sign the agreement, but asked appellant to have her parents come to see her.[fn] Appellant also attempted to see Wanda Lou Holbert, but learned that she had just been released from the hospital. [C] He then departed for another visit with the McClintocks.

On his way appellant detoured to the scene of the accident, where he took a set of photographs. He also picked up a tape recorder, which he concealed under his raincoat before arriving at the McClintocks' residence. Once there, he re-examined their automobile insurance policy, discussed with them the law applicable to passengers, and explained the consequences of the fact that the driver who struck Carol's car was an uninsured motorist. Appellant discovered that the McClintocks' insurance policy would provide benefits of up to $12,500 each for Carol and Wanda Lou under an uninsured-motorist clause. ... The McClintocks ... told appellant that Carol had phoned to say that appellant could "go ahead" with her representation. Two days later appellant returned to Carol's hospital room to have her sign a contract, which provided that he would receive one-third of her recovery.

In the meantime, appellant obtained Wanda Lou's name and address from the McClintocks after telling them he wanted to ask her some questions about the accident. He then visited Wanda Lou at her home, without having been invited. He again concealed his tape recorder and recorded most of the conversation with Wanda Lou.[fn] After a brief, unproductive inquiry about the facts of the accident, appellant told Wanda Lou that he was representing Carol and that he had a "little tip" for Wanda Lou: the McClintocks' insurance policy contained an uninsured-motorist clause which might provide her with a recovery of up to $12,500. The young woman, who was 18 years of age and not a high school graduate at the time, replied to appellant's query about whether she was going to file a claim by stating that she really did not understand what was going on. Appellant offered to represent her, also, for a contingent fee of one-third of any recovery, and Wanda Lou stated "O. K."[fn]

Wanda's mother attempted to repudiate her daughter's oral assent the following day, when appellant called on the telephone to speak to Wanda. Mrs. Holbert informed appellant that she and her daughter did not want to sue anyone or to have appellant represent them, and that if they decided to sue they would consult their own lawyer. Appellant insisted that Wanda had entered into a binding agreement. A month later Wanda confirmed in writing that she wanted neither to sue nor to be represented by appellant. She requested that appellant notify the insurance company that he was not her lawyer, as the company would not release a check to her until he did so.[fn] Carol also eventually discharged appellant. Although another lawyer represented her in concluding a settlement with the insurance company, she paid appellant one-third of her recovery[fn] in settlement of his lawsuit against her for breach of contract.[fn]

Both Carol McClintock and Wanda Lou Holbert filed complaints against appellant with the Grievance Committee of the Geauga County Bar Association. The County Bar Association referred the grievance to appellee, which filed a formal complaint with the Board of Commissioners on Grievances and Discipline of the Supreme Court of Ohio.[fn] After a hearing, the Board found that appellant had violated [two anti-solicitation provisions] of the Ohio Code of Professional Responsibility.[fn] The Board rejected appellant's defense that his conduct was protected under the First and Fourteenth Amendments. The Supreme Court of Ohio adopted the findings of the Board,[fn] reiterated that appellant's conduct was not constitutionally protected, and increased the sanction of a public reprimand recommended by the Board to indefinite suspension.

... We now affirm the judgment of the Supreme Court of Ohio.

II

The solicitation of business by a lawyer through direct, in-person communication with the prospective client has long been viewed as inconsistent with the profession's ideal of the attorney-client relationship and as posing a significant potential for harm to the prospective client. It has been proscribed by the organized Bar for many years.[fn] Last Term the Court ruled that the justifications for prohibiting truthful, "restrained" advertising concerning "the availability and terms of routine legal services" are insufficient to override society's interest, safeguarded by the First and Fourteenth Amendments, in assuring the free flow of commercial information. *Bates[v. State Bar of Arizona]*, 433 U.S.[350], 384[(1977)]; see *Virginia Pharmacy Board v. Virginia Citizens Consumer Council,* 425 U.S. 748[] (1976). ...

A

Appellant contends that his solicitation of the two young women as clients is indistinguishable, for purposes of constitutional analysis, from the advertisement in *Bates.* ... But in-person solicitation of professional employment by a lawyer does not stand on a par with truthful advertising about the availability and terms of routine legal services, let alone with forms of speech more traditionally within the concern of the First Amendment. ...

Moreover, "it has never been deemed an abridgment of freedom of speech or press to make a course of conduct illegal merely because the conduct was in part initiated, evidenced, or carried out by means of language, either spoken, written, or printed." *Giboney v. Empire Storage & Ice Co.,* 336 U.S. 490, 502[] (1949). ...

In-person solicitation by a lawyer of remunerative employment is a business transaction in which speech is an essential but subordinate component. While this does not remove the speech from the protection of the First Amendment, as was held in *Bates* and *Virginia Pharmacy,* it lowers the level of appropriate judicial scrutiny. ...

... Unlike a public advertisement, which simply provides

information and leaves the recipient free to act upon it or not, in-person solicitation may exert pressure and often demands an immediate response, without providing an opportunity for comparison or reflection.[fn] The aim and effect of in-person solicitation may be to provide a one-sided presentation and to encourage speedy and perhaps uninformed decisionmaking; there is no opportunity for intervention or counter-education by agencies of the Bar, supervisory authorities, or persons close to the solicited individual. ... In-person solicitation is as likely as not to discourage persons needing counsel from engaging in a critical comparison of the "availability, nature, and prices" of legal services, cf. *Bates*, 433 U.S. at 364[], it actually may disserve the individual and societal interest, identified in *Bates,* in facilitating "informed and reliable decisionmaking." *Ibid.*[fn] ...

B

The state interests implicated in this case are particularly strong. In addition to its general interest in protecting consumers and regulating commercial transactions, the State bears a special responsibility for maintaining standards among members of the licensed professions. See *Williamson v. Lee Optical Co.,* 348 U.S. 483[] (1955); *Semler v. Oregon State Bd. of Dental Examiners,* 294 U.S. 608[] (1935). "The interest of the States in regulating lawyers is especially great since lawyers are essential to the primary governmental function of administering justice, and have historically been 'officers of the courts.'" *Goldfarb v. Virginia State Bar,* 421 U.S. 773, 792[] (1975). While lawyers act in part as "self-employed businessmen," they also act "as trusted agents of their clients, and as assistants to the court in search of a just solution to disputes." *Cohen v. Hurley,* 366 U.S. 117, 124[] (1961). ...

The substantive evils of solicitation have been stated over the years in sweeping terms: stirring up litigation, assertion of fraudulent claims, debasing the legal profession, and potential harm to the solicited client in the form of overreaching, overcharging, underrepresentation, and misrepresentation.[fn] The American Bar Association, as *amicus curiae,* defends the rule against solicitation primarily on three broad grounds: It is said ... to reduce the likelihood of overreaching and the exertion of undue influence on lay persons, to protect the privacy of individuals, and to avoid situations where the lawyer's exercise of judgment on behalf of the client will be clouded by his own pecuniary self-interest.[fn]

III

... The Rules were applied in this case to discipline a lawyer for soliciting employment for pecuniary gain under circumstances likely to result in the adverse consequences the State seeks to avert. In such a situation, which is inherently conducive to overreaching and other forms of misconduct, the State has a strong interest in adopting and enforcing rules of conduct designed to protect the public from harmful solicitation by lawyers whom it has licensed.

The State's perception of the potential for harm in circumstances such as those presented in this case is well founded.[fn] ... [T]he potential for overreaching is significantly greater when a lawyer, a professional trained in the art of persuasion, personally solicits an unsophisticated, injured, or distressed lay person.[fn] Such an individual may place his trust in a lawyer, regardless of the latter's qualifications or the individual's actual need for legal representation, simply in response to persuasion under circumstances conducive to uninformed acquiescence. Although it is argued that personal solicitation is valuable because it may apprise a victim of misfortune of his legal rights, the very plight of that person not only makes him more vulnerable to influence but also may make advice all the more intrusive. Thus, under these adverse conditions the overtures of an uninvited lawyer may distress the solicited individual simply because of their obtrusiveness and the invasion of the individual's privacy,[fn] even when no other harm materalizes.[fn] ...

On the basis of the undisputed facts of record, we conclude that the Disciplinary Rules constitutionally could be applied to appellant. He approached two young accident victims at a time when they were especially incapable of making informed judgments or of assessing and protecting their own interests. He solicited Carol McClintock in a hospital room where she lay in traction and sought out Wanda Lou Holbert on the day she came home from the hospital, knowing from his prior inquiries that she had just been released. Appellant urged his services upon the young women and used the information he had obtained from the McClintocks, and the fact of his agreement with Carol, to induce Wanda to say "O. K." in response to his solicitation. He employed a concealed tape recorder, seemingly to insure that he would have evidence of Wanda's oral assent to the representation. He emphasized that his fee would come out of the recovery, thereby tempting the young women with what sounded like a cost-free and therefore irresistible offer. He refused to withdraw when Mrs. Holbert requested him to do so only a day after the initial meeting between appellant and Wanda Lou and continued to represent himself to the insurance company as Wanda Holbert's lawyer. ...

Accordingly, the judgment of the Supreme Court of Ohio is
Affirmed.

Mr. Justice BRENNAN took no part in the consideration or decision of this case.

Mr. Justice REHNQUIST, concurring in the judgment.

For the reasons stated in my dissenting opinion in *In re Primus,* 436

U.S. 412[], I concur in the affirmance of the judgment of the Supreme Court of Ohio.

INQUIRY

Real-Time Communications. Notice that Model Rule 7.3 prohibits more than just in-person solicitation. It also prohibits solicitation by telephone and other electronic means, such as a real-time chat-room discussion, that involve real-time communications. Having read the *Ohralik* case, can you now articulate the concern sufficiently to make the distinction between real-time communications and other communications a meaningful one? Notice, too, that Model Rule 7.3(a) has exceptions for lawyer-to-lawyer solicitations, solicitation of family members and close personal friends, and solicitation of prior clients. *See, e.g.,* In re Appert, 315 N.W.2d 204 (Minn. 1981) (no solicitation based on close relationship). Once again, can you articulate why Model Rule 7.3(a) would permit solicitation of members of each of those groups? Even as to those groups, though, Model Rule 7.3(b) prohibits solicitation when the prospective client has indicated not to solicit or when the solicitation would be coercive or harassing. Can you think of examples when solicitation would be coercive or harassing?

Ambulance Chasing. The one behavior in which lawyers have engaged that most irritates the public and reduces the reputation of lawyers is probably the solicitation of victims and their families immediately after an accident, a practice going by the pejorative phrase of *ambulance chasing.* Aggressive pitches for legal representation as to liability claims can be a sign of disrespect, burdening those who are seeking medical care for serious injury or grieving immediate-family survivors. That burden is surely in part why Model Rule 7.3(c) requires lawyers to mark written solicitations as *Advertising Material* in a conspicuous manner including on the outside of any envelope. Individuals take seriously letters from lawyers. If they want not to be solicited, then they should be able to disregard advertising materials before opening. It can look like unprofessional money-grubbing at a time when victims need care and healing. Importantly, a lawyer who responds to a plea for legal assistance is not soliciting. *See* In re Blaylock, 978 P.2d 381 (Or. 1999) (permissible to respond to telephone call from family or immediate aid of injured prospective client). Solicitation involves *initiating* the contact, not responding to inquiries from others, a line that can be hard to discern in some instances. *See, e.g.,* In re D'Amico, 668 So.2d 730 (La. 1996) (no solicitation where prospective client did not perceive lawyer's call to be an offer for services). Other cases of solicitation are clearer. Consider a more-extreme and nefarious case than the above *Ohralik* case.

The Florida Bar v. Barrett,
Florida Supreme Court
897 So.2d 1269 (2005)

PER CURIAM.

We have for review a referee's report regarding alleged ethical breaches by attorney David A. Barrett. ... We approve the referee's findings of fact and recommendations as to guilt. For the reasons explained below, we decline to approve the recommended sanction of a one-year suspension and instead disbar Barrett.

I. FACTS

... Barrett was the senior partner and managing partner in the Tallahassee law firm of Barrett, Hoffman, and Hall, P.A. In approximately January 1993, Barrett hired Chad Everett Cooper, an ordained minister, as a "paralegal." Although Cooper had previously worked for a law firm in Quincy, Florida, Cooper's primary duty at Barrett's law firm was to bring in new clients. As Cooper testified, Barrett told him to "do whatever you need to do to bring in some business" and "go out and ... get some clients." Cooper was paid a salary averaging $20,000 and, in addition to his salary, yearly "bonuses" which generally exceeded his yearly salary. In fact, Cooper testified that Barrett offered him $100,000 if he brought in a large case.

To help Cooper bring in more personal injury clients to the law firm, Barrett devised a plan so that Cooper could access the emergency areas of a hospital and thus be able to solicit patients and their families. In order to gain such access, Barrett paid for Cooper to attend a hospital chaplain's course offered by Tallahassee Memorial Hospital.

In approximately March of 1994, Molly Glass's son was critically injured when he was struck by an automobile while on his bicycle. While her son was being treated in the intensive care unit at Tallahassee Memorial Hospital, Cooper met the Glass family. Cooper, who dressed in "clothing that resembled a pastor," identified himself to the family as a chaplain and offered to pray with them. Thereafter, Cooper gave a family member of Molly Glass the business card of attorney Eric Hoffman, one of the partners in Barrett's law firm, and suggested that the family call the firm. Neither Barrett nor Cooper knew Molly Glass prior to Cooper's solicitation at the hospital. After her son died, Molly Glass retained Barrett's law firm in a wrongful death action. A settlement was negotiated, and she was pleased with the result until May of 1999, when she read a newspaper article about improper solicitation of clients and realized that Cooper's actions in the hospital constituted inappropriate solicitation. The referee specifically found that Cooper was Barrett's agent at the time that Cooper solicited Molly Glass and that Barrett ordered the conduct and ratified it by paying Cooper a salary and bonuses.

In April 1994, Cooper referred his friend, Terry Charleston, to Barrett's law firm. Charleston was an automobile accident victim whose injuries left him a quadriplegic. After the case was settled for over $3 million, Cooper was paid a bonus that year of $47,500.[fn] Barrett attempted to justify the extremely large bonus, contending that the bonus was based on personal services, pastoral services, and companionship that Cooper provided to Charleston. The referee rejected this explanation, finding that Barrett lied about the reason for the bonus. Instead, the referee found that Barrett gave Cooper the bonus for bringing in the case, and thus Barrett engaged in an illegal fee-splitting plan.

On September 19, 1997, Barrett, who had the ultimate authority for hiring and firing in his law firm, fired Cooper. In the words of Barrett's now-deceased partner, Eric Hoffman, Barrett fired Cooper because "it was getting pretty hot and he was afraid that everyone would get caught."[fn] However, even after Cooper was fired, his relationship with Barrett did not end.

While Cooper obtained accident reports and solicited patients for a chiropractor, he also continued to solicit clients for Barrett. After the patients were seen by the chiropractor, the accident reports were forwarded to Barrett's law partner, Hoffman. Cooper was paid $200 for each client who was brought into the law firm. The referee specifically found that Barrett knew about this scheme and that he ratified the conduct of Hoffman and Cooper. Barrett micromanaged the office, especially the finances, and personally signed the checks to Cooper in the amount of $200 per client for soliciting eight clients. Moreover, Barrett inquired as to whether there was insurance coverage before authorizing the firm's checks written to Cooper for soliciting clients. In addition to Molly Glass, the referee found that Barrett improperly solicited twenty-one other clients in violation of the Rules of Professional Conduct.

Finally, in May 1996, Barrett sent Cooper to Miami and Chicago in order to solicit clients as a result of the Value Jet airplane crash in the Everglades. Although Barrett denied any knowledge about this, his own business records show that $974.24 was paid for Cooper's travel expenses. The referee found that Barrett's testimony regarding this matter was not credible. While neither solicitation resulted in clients for Barrett's firm, the referee concluded these were inappropriate solicitation attempts directed by Barrett.

Based on the above factual findings, the referee found that Barrett was guilty of violating ... [Florida Bar Rule] 4-7.4(a) (solicitation)....

II. ANALYSIS

... While there may be conflicting evidence, the overwhelming record evidence supports the referee's findings of fact. Therefore, we reject Barrett's contention that the findings of fact in the referee's report are not properly supported by the evidence. Because competent, substantial evidence in the record supports the referee's findings, we adopt the findings of fact and further approve without further discussion the referee's recommendation that Barrett be found guilty of violating the above rules. ...

Both parties appeal the recommended discipline of a one-year suspension. Barrett argues that a twenty-day suspension is appropriate based on previous solicitation cases. The Bar argues that the appropriate discipline for such egregious ethical misconduct is disbarment. We agree with the Bar. ...

... Barrett used deception to gain access to hospital patients by paying for Cooper to complete a hospital chaplain's course and sending him under the guise of providing spiritual comfort to people in their most needy time, when at the time Cooper was an attorney's employee being paid to obtain clients. Barrett then changed his scheme when "it was getting pretty hot," instead relying on Cooper to obtain clients while he worked for a chiropractor. His schemes resulted in twenty-two improperly solicited clients. Additionally, Barrett also engaged in an illegal fee-splitting plan with Cooper. ... Moreover, this is not a situation where Barrett failed to realize his actions were wrong; he engaged in the conduct intentionally and then fired Cooper when he became concerned about the possibility of being caught. ... Any discipline less than disbarment is far too lenient based on the amount and type of misconduct which occurred here and would not fulfill the three purposes of lawyer discipline.

In sum, members of The Florida Bar are ethically prohibited from the solicitation of clients in the manner engaged in by Barrett. The Court expects that its rules will be respected and followed. This type of violation brings dishonor and disgrace not only upon the attorney who has broken the rules but upon the entire legal profession, a burden that all attorneys must bear since it affects all of our reputations. Moreover, such violations harm people who are already in a vulnerable condition, which is one of the very reasons these types of solicitations are barred. Therefore, this Court will strictly enforce the rules that prohibit these improper solicitations and impose severe sanctions on those who commit violations of them.

III. CONCLUSION

We approve the referee's findings of fact and recommendations as to guilt, but we decline to approve the recommended discipline of a one-year suspension and instead disbar respondent. ...

It is so ordered.

PARIENTE, C.J., and WELLS, ANSTEAD, LEWIS, QUINCE, CANTERO, and BELL, JJ., concur.

INQUIRY

Group Legal Services. Model Rule 7.3(d) permits a lawyer to participate in a legal-service plan that solicits memberships. What is a pre-paid legal plan or a group legal services plan? Pre-paid legal plans are a type of legal insurance plan. Subscribers pay a monthly premium similar to other insurances like auto, life or health, which then provides them access to legal services that they may not otherwise be able to afford, usually by the pre-paid legal plan referring the insured to a "participating attorney" who receives modest fixed fees for the work. Who does Model Rule 7.3(d) presume is doing the in-person soliciting? Model Rule 7.3(d) does not authorize the participating lawyer to solicit memberships for services, only other representatives of the plan. Model Rule 7.3(d) further prohibits a participating lawyer from owning an interest in the plan. Can you see why these restrictions might be necessary? Recall the concerns articulated in *Ohralik.* On the other hand, nonlawyers may have strong associational rights and interest in encouraging prospective clients to see specific lawyers, with which a state bar must not interfere. *See* United Transp. Union v. Michigan State Bar, 401 U.S. 576 (1971).

Access to Legal Services. Is all other in-person solicitation banned? You should have noticed that Model Rule 7.3 only prohibits solicitation for compensation. A lawyer may offer pro-bono legal services without running afoul of Model Rule 7.3. The associated right to counsel has constitutional dimensions. Consider In re Primus, 436 U.S. 412 (1978). Edna Smith Primus was an ACLU attorney when she met with pregnant mothers on public assistance who were being sterilized or threatened with sterilization as a condition of the continued receipt of medical assistance under the Medicaid program. Her purpose was to offer the ACLU's free legal assistance. The Bar and Supreme Court of South Carolina reprimanded Primus publicly for solicitation, but the United States Supreme Court held that South Carolina could not prohibit in-person solicitation where a legal-aid organization "offers its services free of charge to individuals who may be in need of legal assistance and may lack the financial means and sophistication necessary to tap alternative sources of such aid." Courts have also recognized a judicial privilege for class counsel to mail notices to prospective class members. *See, e.g.,* Kittler v. Eckberg, Lammers, Briggs, Wolff & Vierling, 535 N.W.2d 653 (Minn. Ct. App. 1995).

Educational Information. Another question of access has to do with public education about the law. The public should be able to learn from qualified lawyers about their legal rights and interests. A popular marketing tool for some lawyers is to present an informative seminar to members of the public or to set up a booth at an event in hopes of attracting prospective clients. Does Model Rule 7.3 allow this form of marketing? If so, then where do you think the lines would be to prevent overt solicitation? See Maryland State Bar Assn. Comm. on Ethics Op. 2004-29 (2004). Some lawyers attempt to mitigate conduct that approaches or crosses the line on permissible advertising and marketing by including a disclaimer. What should be the effect of a disclaimer? *See* In re Keller, 792 N.E.2d 865 (Ind. 2003) ("no specific result implied" disclaimer on television advertising does not correct misleading suggestion that "insurance companies know" firm's name and reputation for enhanced settlements); In re Foos, 770 N.E.2d 335 (Ind. 2002) (small-type disclaimer does not negate standard-type misleading advertisement).

C. Marketing

Lawyer Advertising. The above discussion should have indicated to you that lawyers do market their law practices within certain norms, conventions, and restrictions. Consider lawyer advertising, now that you appreciate the basic obligation to be truthful when describing the legal services that you plan to offer and the prohibition against solicitation. Thinking about lawyer advertising will lead you to broader questions like what exactly reputation is. How does the consumer of legal services define reputation? What is reputation's source? What control do lawyers really have over their reputations? Advertising gives lawyers some control over their reputation among members of the public. At least, advertising may be the first communication a prospective client receives from the client's eventual lawyer. Advertising is also a powerful statement about a lawyer's values and demeanor, and, usually, a good hint as to the lawyer's worldview, meaning the paradigm through which the lawyer views the world. *See* ABA Model Rule 7.2 Comment [3] ("Questions of effectiveness and taste in advertising are matters of speculation and judgment."). ABA Model Rule 7.2 authorizes lawyer advertising within certain bounds. Read a similar state version of Model Rule 7.2 before considering a few of the issues that it raises.

WASHINGTON R. PROF. CONDUCT 7.2: Advertising.
(a) Subject to the requirements of Rules 7.1 and 7.3, a lawyer may advertise services through written, recorded or electronic communication, including public media.
(b) A lawyer shall not give anything of value to a person for recommending the lawyer's services, except that a lawyer may
(1) pay the reasonable costs of advertisements or communications permitted by this Rule;
(2) pay the usual charges of a legal service plan or a not-for-profit lawyer referral service;
(3) pay for a law practice in accordance with Rule 1.17; and
(4) refer clients to another lawyer pursuant to an agreement not otherwise prohibited under these Rules that provides for the other person to refer clients or customers to the lawyer, if
(i) the reciprocal referral agreement is not exclusive, and
(ii) the client is informed of the existence and nature of the agreement.
(c) Any communication made pursuant to this Rule shall include the name and office address of at least one lawyer or law firm responsible for its content.

I N Q U I R Y

Lawyer Referral Services. Model Rule 7.2(b)(2) authorizes a lawyer to remit to a non-profit lawyer referral service the nominal charges that those services often charge. Local bar associations often establish lawyer referral services as a service to the public and to their member lawyers. Members of the public may contact the local bar's referral service for referral to a local lawyer who has assured the service that the lawyer will consult with the client for a nominal fee remitted to the service to pay for its non-profit cost of operation. If the lawyer can help the client, then the lawyer and client may negotiate the fee. Lawyers use lawyer referral services to build practice experience and expand the practice's client base. Model Rule 7.2 adds a sentence to the state version of Rule 7.2(b)(2) above that, "A qualified lawyer referral service is a lawyer referral service that has been approved by an appropriate regulatory authority." Bar officials have disciplined lawyers for paying non-approved for-profit referral services. *See, e.g,* People v. Zimmerman, 938 P.2d 131 (Colo. 1997).

Paying Others for Referrals. Model Rule 7.2(b) outlines an important aspect of many lawyers' marketing practice. Lawyers, especially those in small firms and solo practice, maintain informal professional networks through which they refer clients back and forth when the service that the client requires is not within their practice specialty. A tax lawyer, business lawyer, estate lawyer, civil litigator, and family lawyer may each maintain a solo practice but share client referrals much as would partners and associates within a large law firm. Model Rule 7.2(b) prohibits a lawyer from paying referral fees to nonlawyers. For example, a lawyer may not provide a stack of professional cards to a tow-truck operator and offer to pay the operator to distribute the cards to injured accident victims at the scene. Doing so would violate both the anti-solicitation provision of Model Rule 7.3 and the referral-fee provision of Model Rule 7.2. *See, e.g.,* In re Goff, 837 So.2d 1201 (La. 2003) (suspension for using nonlawyer runners to solicit personal-injury cases); Cincinnati Bar Assn. v. Haas, 699 N.E.2d 919 (Ohio 1998) (same for paying insurance agent for referrals).

Lawyer-to-Lawyer Referrals. Model Rule 7.2 does permit a lawyer to refer clients to other lawyers and accept referrals in return, so long as the client approves, the referral arrangement is not exclusive, and the involved lawyers pay no referral fees. *See, e.g.,* Colorado v. Carpenter, 893 P.2d 777 (Colo. 1997) (censure of lawyer who charged modest monthly referral fee to other lawyers). ABA Model Rule 1.5 would permit a referral fee if the referring lawyer retains responsibility for the matter and the fee is commensurate with the value of the referring lawyer's services—effectively making it compensation for services rather than a pure referral fee. A few states go farther, permitting pure referral fees among lawyers, *see, e.g.,* KAN. R. PROF. CONDUCT 1.5(g), or nearly pure fees where the referring lawyer does little or no further work but retains responsibility for the file, *see, e.g.,* ILLINOIS R. PROF. CONDUCT 1.5(g); Corcoran v. Northeast Illinois Regional Commuter R.R. Co., 803 N.E.2d 807 (Ill. Ct. App. 2003). For example, in one of those states a business lawyer might refer a personal-injury client to a personal-injury lawyer and accept a portion of the contingency fee (often one third of the one-third fee), with or without continuing responsibility depending on the special rules of the jurisdiction.

First Amendment Protection. The *Ohralik* case in the above section on solicitation introduced you to the concept of First Amendment and Fourteenth Amendment protection of lawyer advertising. The Supreme Court's decision in Bates v. State Bar of Arizona, 433 U.S. 350 (1977), threw open the previously highly restrictive gates to lawyer advertising. *Bates* held constitutionally protected a lawyer's newspaper advertisement of specific services at specific fees, against a regulation that banned virtually all lawyer advertising. Until *Bates*, state laws and conduct rules kept lawyer advertising to a minimum. *Bates* revolutionized lawyer advertising. Model Rule 7.2's broad authorization of lawyer advertising with only a few specific restrictions designed to address specific concerns is a product of the *Bates* decision and the series of Supreme Court decisions and rule changes that followed it.   Zauderer v. Office of Disciplinary Counsel, 471 U.S. 626 (1985), is an example in which the Supreme Court held that bar officials could not constitutionally discipline a contingency-fee lawyer who advertised in the newspaper for clients with claims against the manufacturer of the Dalkon Shield contraceptive intrauterine device.   Consider two subsequent Supreme Court cases applying the First Amendment principles and framework under which the states continue to regulate lawyer advertising.

Shapero v. Kentucky Bar Association,
United States Supreme Court
486 U.S. 466 (1988)

In 1985, petitioner, a member of Kentucky's integrated Bar Association, [c], applied to the Kentucky Attorneys Advertising Commission[fn] for approval of a letter that he proposed to send "to potential clients who have had a foreclosure suit filed against them." The proposed letter read as follows:

> "It has come to my attention that your home is being foreclosed on. If this is true, you may be about to lose your home. Federal law may allow you to keep your home by *ORDERING* your creditor [*sic*] to *STOP* and give you more time to pay them.
>
> "You may call my office anytime from 8:30 a.m. to 5:00 p.m. for *FREE* information on how you can keep your home.
>
> "Call *NOW,* don't wait. It may surprise you what I may be able to do for you. Just call and tell me that you got this letter. Remember it is *FREE,* there is *NO* charge for calling."

The Commission did not find the letter false or misleading. Nevertheless, it declined to approve petitioner's proposal on the ground that a then-existing Kentucky Supreme Court Rule prohibited the mailing or delivery of written advertisements "precipitated by a specific event or occurrence involving or relating to the addressee or addressees as distinct from the general public." [C][fn] ...

... [T]he Kentucky Supreme Court felt "compelled by the decision in *Zauderer [v. Office of Disc. Counsel,* 471 U.S. 626 (1985),] to order [the rule] deleted," [c], and replaced it with the ABA's [prior] Rule 7.3, which provides in [part]:   "A lawyer may not solicit professional employment from a prospective client with whom the lawyer has no family or prior professional relationship, by mail, in-person or otherwise, when a significant motive for the lawyer's doing so is the lawyer's pecuniary gain. ..." ...

... Rule 7.3 like its predecessor, prohibits targeted, direct-mail solicitation by lawyers for pecuniary gain, without a particularized finding that the solicitation is false or misleading.   We granted certiorari to resolve whether such a blanket prohibition is consistent with the First Amendment, made applicable to the States through the Fourteenth Amendment, [c], and now reverse.[fn]

II

Lawyer advertising is in the category of constitutionally protected commercial speech. See *Bates v. State Bar of Arizona,* 433 U.S. 350[] (1977). The First Amendment principles governing state regulation of lawyer solicitations for pecuniary gain are by now familiar: "Commercial speech that is not false or deceptive and does not concern unlawful activities ... may be restricted only in the service of a substantial governmental interest, and only through means that directly advance that interest." *Zauderer, supra,* 471 U.S. at 638[] (citing *Central Hudson Gas & Electric Corp. v. Public Service Comm'n of New York,* 447 U.S. 557, 566[] (1980)). Since state regulation of commercial speech "may extend only as far as the interest it serves," *Central Hudson, supra,* at 565[], state rules that are designed to prevent the "potential for deception and confusion ... may be no broader than reasonably necessary to prevent the" perceived evil. *In re R.M.J.,* 455 U.S. 191, 203[] (1982).

In *Zauderer,* application of these principles required that we strike an Ohio rule that categorically prohibited solicitation of legal employment for pecuniary gain through advertisements containing information or advice, even if truthful and nondeceptive, regarding a specific legal problem. We distinguished written advertisements containing such information or advice from in-person solicitation by lawyers for profit, which we held in *Ohralik v. Ohio State Bar Assn.,* 436 U.S. 447[] (1978), a State may categorically ban. The "unique features of in-person solicitation by lawyers [that] justified a prophylactic rule prohibiting lawyers from engaging in such solicitation for pecuniary gain," we observed, are "not present" in the context of written advertisements. *Zauderer, supra,* 471 U.S. at 641-642[].

Our lawyer advertising cases have never distinguished among various modes of written advertising to the general public. See, *e.g., Bates, supra* (newspaper advertising); *id.,* 433 U.S. at 372n.26[] (equating advertising in telephone directory with newspaper advertising); *In re R.M.J., supra* (mailed announcement cards treated same as newspaper and telephone directory advertisements). Thus, Ohio could no more prevent Zauderer from mass-mailing to a general population his offer to represent women injured by the Dalkon Shield than it could prohibit his publication of the advertisement in local newspapers. Similarly, if petitioner's letter is neither false nor deceptive, Kentucky could not constitutionally prohibit him from sending at large an identical letter opening with the query, "Is your home being foreclosed on?," rather than his observation to the targeted individuals that "It has come to my attention that your home is being foreclosed on." ...

The court below disapproved petitioner's proposed letter solely because it targeted only persons who were "known to need [the] legal services" offered in his letter, [c], rather than the broader group of persons "so situated that they might in general find such services useful." Generally, unless the advertiser is inept, the latter group would include members of the former. The only reason to disseminate an advertisement of particular legal services among those persons who are "so situated that they might in general find such services useful" is to reach individuals who *actually* "need legal services of the kind provided [and advertised] by the lawyer." But the First Amendment does not permit a ban on certain speech merely because it is more efficient; the State may not constitutionally ban a particular letter on the theory that to mail it only to those whom it would most interest is somehow inherently objectionable. ...

... [A] particular potential client will feel equally "overwhelmed" by his legal troubles and will have the same "impaired capacity for good judgment" regardless of whether a lawyer mails him an untargeted letter or exposes him to a newspaper advertisement—concededly constitutionally protected activities—or instead mails a targeted letter. The relevant inquiry is not whether there exist potential clients whose "condition" makes them susceptible to undue influence, but whether the mode of communication poses a serious danger that lawyers will exploit any such susceptibility. [C] ...

... In assessing the potential for overreaching and undue influence, the mode of communication makes all the difference. Our decision in *Ohralik* that a State could categorically ban all in-person solicitation turned on two factors. First was our characterization of face-to-face solicitation as "a practice rife with possibilities for overreaching, invasion of privacy, the exercise of undue influence, and outright fraud." *Zauderer,* 471 U.S. at 641[]. See *Ohralik, supra,* 436 U.S. at 457-458, 464-465[]. Second, "unique ... difficulties," *Zauderer, supra,* 471 U.S. at 641[], would frustrate any attempt at state regulation of in-person solicitation short of an absolute ban because such solicitation is "not visible or otherwise open to public scrutiny." *Ohralik,* 436 U.S. at 466[]. See also *ibid.* ("[I]n-person solicitation would be virtually immune to effective oversight and regulation by the State or by the legal profession") (footnote omitted). Targeted, direct-mail solicitation is distinguishable from the in-person solicitation in each respect. ...

... [M]erely because targeted, direct-mail solicitation presents lawyers with opportunities for isolated abuses or mistakes does not justify a total ban on that mode of protected commercial speech. See *In re R.M.J.,* 455 U.S. at 203[]. The State can regulate such abuses and minimize mistakes through far less restrictive and more precise means, the most obvious of which is to require the lawyer to file any solicitation letter with a state agency, *id.,* at 206[], giving the State ample opportunity to supervise mailings and penalize actual abuses. ...

The record before us furnishes no evidence that scrutiny of targeted solicitation letters will be appreciably more burdensome or less reliable than scrutiny of advertisements. [C] As a general matter, evaluating a targeted advertisement does not require specific information about the recipient's identity and legal problems any more than evaluating a newspaper advertisement requires like information about all readers. If the targeted letter specifies facts that relate to particular recipients (*e.g.,* "It has come to my attention that your home is being foreclosed on"), the reviewing agency has innumerable options to minimize mistakes. It might, for example, require the lawyer to prove the truth of the fact stated (by supplying copies of the court documents or material that led the lawyer to the fact); it could require the lawyer to explain briefly how he or she discovered the fact and verified its accuracy; or it could require the letter to bear a label identifying it as an advertisement, [cc], or directing the recipient how to report inaccurate or misleading letters. To be sure, a state agency or bar association that reviews solicitation letters might have more work than one that does not. But "[o]ur recent decisions involving commercial speech have been grounded in the faith that the free flow of commercial information is valuable enough to justify imposing on would-be regulators the costs of distinguishing the truthful from the false, the helpful from the misleading, and the harmless from the harmful." *Zauderer, supra,* 471 U.S. at 646[].

III

... [R]espondent identifies two features of the letter before us that, in its view, coalesce to convert the proposed letter into "high pressure solicitation, overbearing solicitation," Brief for Respondent 20, which is not protected. First, respondent asserts that the letter's liberal use of underscored, uppercase letters (*e.g.,* "Call *NOW,* don't wait"; "it is *FREE,* there is *NO* charge for calling") "fairly shouts at the recipient ... that he should employ Shapero." [Cc] Second, respondent objects that the letter contains assertions (*e.g.,* "It may surprise you what I may be able to do for you") that "stat[e] no affirmative or objective fact," but constitute "pure salesman puffery, enticement for the unsophisticated, which commits Shapero to nothing." [C]

The pitch or style of a letter's type and its inclusion of subjective predictions of client satisfaction might catch the recipient's attention more than would a bland statement of purely objective facts in small type. But a truthful and nondeceptive letter, no matter how big its type and how much it speculates can never "shou[t] at the recipient" or "gras[p] him by the lapels," [c], as can a lawyer engaging in face-to-face solicitation. The letter simply presents no comparable risk of overreaching. ...

To be sure, a letter may be misleading if it unduly emphasizes trivial or "relatively uninformative fact[s]," *In re R.M.J., supra,* at 205[] (lawyer's statement, "in large capital letters, that he was a member of the Bar of the Supreme Court of the United States"), or offers overblown assurances of client satisfaction, cf. *In re Von Wiegen,* [] 481 N.Y.S.2d 40, 49, 470 N.E.2d 838, 847 (1984) (solicitation letter to victims of massive disaster informs them that "it is [the lawyer's] opinion that the liability of the defendants is clear"), cert. denied, 472 U.S. 1007[] (1985); *Bates, supra,* 433 U.S. at 383-384[] ("[A]dvertising claims as to the quality of legal services ... may be so likely to be misleading as to warrant restriction"). Respondent does not argue before us that petitioner's letter was misleading in those respects. Nor does respondent contend that the letter is false or misleading in any other respect. Of course, respondent is free to raise, and the Kentucky courts are free to consider, any such argument on remand.

The judgment of the Supreme Court of Kentucky is reversed, and the case is remanded for further proceedings not inconsistent with this opinion.

It is so ordered.

Justice WHITE, with whom Justice STEVENS joins, concurring in part and dissenting in part[, omitted].

Justice O'CONNOR, with whom THE CHIEF JUSTICE and Justice SCALIA join, dissenting[, omitted].

Florida Bar v. Went for It, Inc.,
United States Supreme Court
515 U.S. 618 (1995)

Justice O'CONNOR delivered the opinion of the Court.

Rules of the Florida Bar prohibit personal injury lawyers from sending targeted direct-mail solicitations to victims and their relatives for 30 days following an accident or disaster. This case asks us to consider whether such Rules violate the First and Fourteenth Amendments of the Constitution. We hold that in the circumstances presented here, they do not.

I

In 1989, the Florida Bar (Bar) completed a 2-year study of the effects of lawyer advertising on public opinion. After conducting hearings, commissioning surveys, and reviewing extensive public commentary, the Bar determined that several changes to its advertising rules were in order. In late 1990, the Florida Supreme Court adopted the Bar's proposed amendments with some modifications. [C] Two of these amendments are at issue in this case. ... Together, these Rules create a brief 30-day blackout period after an accident during which lawyers may not, directly or indirectly, single out accident victims or their relatives in order to solicit their business.

In March 1992, G. Stewart McHenry and his wholly owned lawyer referral service, Went For It, Inc., filed this action for declaratory and injunctive relief in the United States District Court for the Middle District of Florida challenging Rules 4-7.4(b)(1) and 4-7.8(a) as violative of the First and Fourteenth Amendments to the Constitution. McHenry alleged that he routinely sent targeted solicitations to accident victims or their survivors within 30 days after accidents and that he wished to continue doing so in the future. Went For It, Inc., represented that it wished to contact accident victims or their survivors within 30 days of accidents and to refer potential clients to participating Florida lawyers. In October 1992, McHenry was disbarred for reasons unrelated to this suit, [c]. Another Florida lawyer, John T. Blakely, was substituted in his stead. ...

The District Court referred the parties' competing summary judgment motions to a Magistrate Judge, who ... recommended that the District Court grant the Bar's motion for summary judgment on the ground that the Rules pass constitutional muster.

The District Court rejected the Magistrate Judge's report and recommendations and entered summary judgment for the plaintiffs, [c], relying on *Bates v. State Bar of Ariz.,* 433 U.S. 350[] (1977), and subsequent cases. The Eleventh Circuit affirmed on similar grounds, [c]. ... We granted certiorari, [c], and now reverse.

II

A

... In *Virginia Bd. of Pharmacy v. Virginia Citizens Consumer Council, Inc.,* 425 U.S. 748[(1976)], we invalidated a state statute barring pharmacists from advertising prescription drug prices. ...

In *Virginia Bd.,* the Court limited its holding to advertising by pharmacists, noting that "[p]hysicians and lawyers ... do not dispense standardized products; they render professional *services* of almost infinite variety and nature, with the consequent enhanced possibility for confusion and deception if they were to undertake certain kinds of advertising." *Id.,* at 773n.25[] (emphasis in original). One year later, however, the Court applied the *Virginia Bd.* principles to invalidate a state rule prohibiting lawyers from advertising in newspapers and other media. In *Bates v. State Bar of Arizona, supra,* the Court struck a ban on price advertising for what it deemed "routine" legal services: "the uncontested divorce, the simple adoption, the uncontested personal bankruptcy, the change of name, and the like." 433 U.S. at 372[]. Expressing confidence that legal advertising would only be practicable for such simple, standardized services, the Court rejected the State's proffered justifications for regulation.

Nearly two decades of cases have built upon the foundation laid by *Bates.* It is now well established that lawyer advertising is commercial speech and, as such, is accorded a measure of First Amendment protection. See, *e.g., Shapero v. Kentucky Bar Assn.,* 486 U.S. 466, 472[] (1988); *Zauderer v. Office of Disciplinary Counsel of Supreme Court of Ohio,* 471 U.S. 626, 637[] (1985); *In re R.M.J.,* 455 U.S. 191, 199[] (1982). Such First Amendment protection, of course, is not absolute. We have always been careful to distinguish commercial speech from speech at the First Amendment's core. ...

Mindful of these concerns, we engage in "intermediate" scrutiny of restrictions on commercial speech, analyzing them under the framework set forth in *Central Hudson Gas & Elec. Corp. v. Public Serv. Comm'n of N.Y.,* 447 U.S. 557[] (1980). Under *Central Hudson,* the government may freely regulate commercial speech that concerns unlawful activity or is misleading. [C] Commercial speech that falls into neither of those categories, like the advertising at issue here, may be regulated if the government satisfies a test consisting of three related prongs: First, the government must assert a substantial interest in support of its regulation; second, the government must demonstrate that the restriction on commercial speech directly and materially advances that interest; and third, the regulation must be "'narrowly drawn.'" *Id.,* at 564-565[]. ...

B

... The Bar asserts that it has a substantial interest in protecting the privacy and tranquility of personal injury victims and their loved ones against intrusive, unsolicited contact by lawyers. [C][fn] ... Because direct-mail solicitations in the wake of accidents are perceived by the public as intrusive, the Bar argues, the reputation of the legal profession in the eyes of Floridians has suffered commensurately. [C] The regulation, then, is an effort to protect the flagging reputations of Florida lawyers by preventing them from engaging in conduct that, the Bar maintains, "'is universally regarded as deplorable and beneath common decency because of its intrusion upon the special vulnerability and private grief of victims or their families.'" [Cc]

We have little trouble crediting the Bar's interest as substantial. On various occasions we have accepted the proposition that "States have a compelling interest in the practice of professions within their boundaries, and ... as part of their power to protect the public health, safety, and other valid interests they have broad power to establish standards for licensing practitioners and regulating the practice of professions." *Goldfarb v. Virginia State Bar,* 421 U.S. 773, 792 [] (1975); see also *Ohralik, supra,* 436 U.S. at 460[]; *Cohen v. Hurley,* 366 U.S. 117, 124[] (1961). ... In other contexts, we have consistently recognized that "[t]he State's interest in protecting the well-being, tranquility, and privacy of the home is certainly of the highest order in a free and civilized society." *Carey v. Brown,* 447 U.S. 455, 471[] (1980). Indeed, we have noted that "a special benefit of the privacy all citizens enjoy within their own walls, which the State may legislate to protect, is an ability to avoid intrusions." *Frisby v. Schultz,* 487 U.S. 474, 484-485[] (1988).

... The Bar submitted a 106-page summary of its 2-year study of lawyer advertising and solicitation to the District Court. That summary contains data—both statistical and anecdotal—supporting the Bar's contentions that the Florida public views direct-mail solicitations in the immediate wake of accidents as an intrusion on privacy that reflects poorly upon the profession. As of June 1989, lawyers mailed 700,000 direct solicitations in Florida annually, 40% of which were aimed at accident victims or their survivors. [C] A survey of Florida adults commissioned by the Bar indicated that Floridians "have negative feelings about those attorneys who use direct mail advertising." [C] Fifty-four percent of the general population surveyed said that contacting persons concerning accidents or similar events is a violation of privacy. [C] A random sampling of persons who received direct-mail advertising from lawyers in 1987 revealed that 45% believed that direct-mail solicitation is "designed to take advantage of gullible or unstable people"; 34% found such tactics "annoying or irritating"; 26% found it "an invasion of your privacy"; and 24% reported that it "made you angry." [C] Significantly, 27% of direct-mail recipients reported that their regard for the legal profession and for the judicial process as a whole was "lower" as a result of receiving the direct mail. [C] ...

In light of this showing[,] ... we conclude that the Bar has satisfied the second prong of the *Central Hudson* test. ...

In reaching a contrary conclusion, the Court of Appeals determined that this case was governed squarely by *Shapero v. Kentucky Bar Assn.,* 486 U.S. 466[] (1988). ...

While some of *Shapero* 's language might be read to support the Court of Appeals' interpretation, *Shapero* differs in several fundamental respects from the case before us. First and foremost, *Shapero* 's treatment of privacy was casual. ... Second, in contrast to this case, *Shapero* dealt with a broad ban on *all* direct-mail solicitations, whatever the time frame and whoever the recipient.

Finally, the State in *Shapero* assembled no evidence attempting to demonstrate any actual harm caused by targeted direct mail. ...

We find the Court's perfunctory treatment of privacy in *Shapero* to be of little utility in assessing this ban on targeted solicitation of victims in the immediate aftermath of accidents. ... The intrusion targeted by the Bar's regulation stems not from ... the lawyer's confrontation of victims or relatives with such information, while wounds are still open, in order to solicit their business. In this respect, an untargeted letter mailed to society at large is different in kind from a targeted solicitation; the untargeted letter involves no willful or knowing affront to or invasion of the tranquility of bereaved or injured individuals and simply does not cause the same kind of reputational harm to the profession unearthed by the Bar's study. ...

Here, ... the harm targeted by the Bar cannot be eliminated by a brief journey to the trash can. The purpose of the 30-day targeted direct-mail ban is to forestall the outrage and irritation with the state-licensed legal profession that the practice of direct solicitation only days after accidents has engendered. ...

Passing to *Central Hudson*'s third prong, we examine the relationship between the Bar's interests and the means chosen to serve them. [C] ...

... The Bar's rule is reasonably well tailored to its stated objective of eliminating targeted mailings whose type and timing are a source of distress to Floridians, distress that has caused many of them to lose respect for the legal profession. ...

... Our lawyer advertising cases have afforded lawyers a great deal of leeway to devise innovative ways to attract new business. Florida permits lawyers to advertise on prime-time television and radio as well as in newspapers and other media. They may rent space on billboards. They may send untargeted letters to the general population, or to discrete segments thereof. There are, of course, pages upon pages devoted to lawyers in the Yellow Pages of Florida telephone directories. ... Finding no basis to question the commonsense conclusion that the many alternative channels for communicating necessary information about attorneys are sufficient, we see no defect in Florida's regulation.

III

... This case... concerns pure commercial advertising, for which we have always reserved a lesser degree of protection under the First Amendment. ...

We believe that the Bar's 30-day restriction on targeted direct-mail solicitation of accident victims and their relatives withstands scrutiny under the three-pronged *Central Hudson* test that we have devised for this context. The Bar has substantial interest both in protecting injured Floridians from invasive conduct by lawyers and in preventing the erosion of confidence in the profession that such repeated invasions have engendered. The Bar's proffered study, unrebutted by respondents below, provides evidence indicating that the harms it targets are far from illusory. The palliative devised by the Bar to address these harms is narrow both in scope and in duration. The Constitution, in our view, requires nothing more.

The judgment of the Court of Appeals, accordingly, is *Reversed.*

Justice KENNEDY, with whom Justice STEVENS, Justice SOUTER, and Justice GINSBURG join, dissenting[, omitted].

INQUIRY

Specific Advertisements.   So, in the wake of these First Amendment cases, what lawyer advertising must discipline officials allow, and what advertising may they regulate? Cases continue to be clear that state bars may regulate untruthful and misleading advertising. *See, e.g.,* Farrin v. Thigpen, 173 F. Supp.2d 427 (M.D. N.C. 2001) (upholding ban on misleading television advertisement showing fictional lawyers intimidated by advertiser lawyers into agreeing to settlement demands); In re Cole, 738 N.E.2d 1035 (Ind. 2000) (upholding discipline of lawyer for calling himself the county prosecutor when he was only an appointed deputy). For the courts to uphold the regulation, though, the public harm must be real, not theoretical. *See* Mason v. Florida Bar, 208 F.3d 952 (11th Cir. 2000) (holding unconstitutional a rule requiring a disclaimer on advertising lawyer ratings). The following case is one of the more interesting cases to be decided under the established First Amendment regime. May lawyers compare their services to the work of pitbulls or piranhas? Would doing so violate Model Rule 7.1 requiring that lawyers make no unsubstantiated comparisons? What is behind the prosecution of lawyers engaging in that sort of advertising? There is a myth that only small-firm lawyers violate conduct rules due to the lack of mentor opportunities provided in the larger firms. While mentor opportunities are important, do not fall for the myth, even when it comes to advertising. Keep in mind the above Milberg Weiss and Vinson & Elkin examples. Every firm and lawyer must think carefully about its advertising.

Florida Bar v. Pape,
Florida Supreme Court
918 So.2d 240 (2005)

PARIENTE, C.J.

In this case we impose discipline on two attorneys for their use of television advertising devices that violate the Rules of Professional Conduct. These devices, which invoke the breed of dog known as the pit bull, demean all lawyers and thereby harm both the legal profession and the public's trust and confidence in our system of justice.[fn]

We conclude that attorneys Pape and Chandler ("the attorneys") violated Rules Regulating the Florida Bar 4-7.2(b)(3) and 4-7.2(b)(4) by using the image of a pit bull and displaying the term "pit bull" as part of their firm's phone number in their commercial. Further, because the use of an image of a pit bull and the phrase "pit bull" in the firm's advertisement and logo does not assist the public in ensuring that an informed decision is made prior to the selection of the attorney, we conclude that the First Amendment does not prevent this Court from sanctioning the attorneys based on the rule violations. We determine that the appropriate sanctions for the attorneys' misconduct are public reprimands and required attendance at the Florida Bar Advertising Workshop.

BACKGROUND AND PROCEDURAL HISTORY

On January 12, 2004, The Florida Bar filed complaints against the attorneys, alleging that their law firm's television advertisement was an improper communication concerning the services provided, in violation of the Rules of Professional Conduct. The advertisement included a logo that featured an image of a pit bull wearing a spiked collar and prominently displayed the firm's phone number, 1-800-PIT-BULL. ...

The referee found that the attorneys did not violate rule 4-7.2(b)(3), relying on the distinction that the logo and telephone number "describe qualities of the respondent attorneys" but do not describe or characterize "the quality of the lawyer services." ...

The referee also concluded that the ad was protected speech and therefore that an interpretation of rules 4-7.2(b)(3) and 4-7.2(b)(4) to prohibit the ad would render the rules unconstitutional as applied.

ANALYSIS
... A. Violation of Attorney Advertising Rules

As a preliminary matter, the pit bull logo and 1-800-PIT-BULL telephone number in the ad by the attorneys do not comport with the general criteria for permissible attorney advertisements set forth in the comments to section 4-7 of the Rules of Professional Conduct. The rules contained in section 4-7 are designed to permit lawyer advertisements that provide objective information about the cost of legal services, the experience and qualifications of the lawyer and law firm, and the types of cases the lawyer handles. [C] The comment to rule 4-7.1 provides that "a lawyer's advertisement should provide only useful, factual information presented in a nonsensational manner. Advertisements using slogans ... fail to meet these standards and diminish public confidence in the legal system." The television commercial at issue here uses both a sensationalistic image and a slogan,[fn] contrary to the purpose of section 4-7.

More specifically, the attorneys' ad violated rule 4-7.2(b)(3), which prohibits the use of statements describing or characterizing the quality of the lawyer's services. In *Florida Bar v. Lange,* 711 So.2d 518, 521-22 (Fla.1998), we approved the referee's finding that an advertisement that stated "When the Best is Simply Essential" violated the predecessor provision to rule 4-7.2(b)(3) because it was self-laudatory and purported to describe the quality of the lawyer's services. In this case, the simultaneous display of the pit bull logo and the 1-800-PIT-BULL phone number conveys both the characteristics of the attorneys and the quality of the services they purport to provide. At the very least, the printed words and the image of a pit bull in the television commercial could certainly be perceived by prospective clients as characterizing the quality of the lawyers' services. ...

... From the perspective of a prospective client unfamiliar with the legal system and in need of counsel, a lawyer's character and personality traits are indistinguishable from the quality of the services that the lawyer provides. A courteous lawyer can be expected to be well mannered in court, a hard-working lawyer well prepared, and a "pit bull" lawyer vicious to the opposition. ... [The advertisements] lead a reasonable consumer to conclude that the attorneys are advertising themselves as providers of "pit bull"-style representation. We consider this a characterization of the quality of the lawyers' services in violation of rule 4-7.2(b)(3).

We also conclude that the ad violates rule 4-7.2(b)(4), which requires that visual or verbal depictions be "objectively relevant" to the selection of an attorney, and prohibits depictions that are "deceptive, misleading, or manipulative." The comment to this rule explains that it "prohibits visual or verbal descriptions, depictions, or portrayals in any advertisement which create suspense, or contain exaggerations or *appeals to the emotions,* call for legal services, or create consumer problems through characterization and dialogue ending with the lawyer solving the problem. ... As an example, *a drawing of a fist, to suggest the lawyer's ability to achieve results, would be barred.* Examples of permissible illustrations would include a graphic rendering of the scales of justice to indicate that the advertising attorney practices law, a picture of the lawyer, or a map of the office location." (Emphasis supplied.) The logo of the pit bull wearing a spiked collar and the prominent display of the phone number 1-800-PIT-BULL are more manipulative and misleading than a drawing of a fist. These advertising devices would suggest to many persons not only that the lawyers can achieve results but also that they engage in a combative style of advocacy. The suggestion is inherently deceptive because there is no way to measure whether the attorneys in fact conduct themselves like pit bulls so as to ascertain whether this logo and phone number convey accurate information.

In addition, the image of a pit bull and the on-screen display of the words "PIT-BULL" as part of the firm's phone number are not objectively relevant to the selection of an attorney. The referee found that the qualities of a pit bull as depicted by the logo are loyalty, persistence, tenacity, and aggressiveness.   We consider this a charitable set of associations that ignores the darker side of the qualities often also associated with pit bulls: malevolence, viciousness, and unpredictability. Further, although some may associate pit bulls with loyalty to their owners,[fn] the manner in which the pit bull is depicted in the attorneys' ad in this case certainly does not emphasize this association. The dog, which is wearing a spiked collar, directly faces the viewer and is shown alone, with no indication that it is fulfilling its traditional role as "man's best friend." ...

This Court would not condone an advertisement that stated that a lawyer will get results through combative and vicious tactics that will maim, scar, or harm the opposing party, conduct that would violate our Rules of Professional Conduct. [C] Yet this is precisely the type of unethical and unprofessional conduct that is conveyed by the image of a pit bull and the display of the 1-800-PIT-BULL phone number. ...

Indeed, permitting this type of advertisement would make a mockery of our dedication to promoting public trust and confidence in our system of justice.[fn] Prohibiting advertisements such as the one in this case is one step we can take to maintain the dignity of lawyers, as well as the integrity of, and public confidence in, the legal system. Were we to approve the referee's finding, images of sharks, wolves, crocodiles, and piranhas could follow. For the good of the legal profession and the justice system, and consistent with our Rules of Professional Conduct, this type of non-factual advertising cannot be permitted. We therefore conclude that the 1-800-PIT-BULL ad aired by the attorneys violates rules 4-7.2(b)(3) and 4-7.2(b)(4).

B. First Amendment Protection of Lawyer Advertising

We also disagree with the referee's conclusion that the application of rules 4-7.2(b)(3) and 4-7.2(b)(4) to prohibit this advertisement violates the First Amendment. Lawyer advertising enjoys First Amendment protection only to the extent that it provides accurate factual information that can be objectively verified. This thread runs throughout the pertinent United State Supreme Court precedent. ...

C. Discipline

... [W]e have in the past approved public reprimands for attorneys who have been found guilty of violating the advertising rules. [Cc] We have also required that attorneys attend the Florida Bar Advertising Workshop. [C] We conclude that similar discipline is warranted in this case.

CONCLUSION

... We find John Robert **Pape** and Marc Andrew **Chandler** guilty of violating rules 4-7.2(b)(3) and 4-7.2(b)(4) of the Rules Regulating the **Florida Bar**. We order that each attorney receive a public reprimand... . We also direct **Pape** and **Chandler** to attend and complete the **Florida Bar** Advertising Workshop within six months of the date of this opinion.

It is so ordered.

WELLS, ANSTEAD, LEWIS, QUINCE, CANTERO, and BELL, JJ., concur.

INQUIRY

Law-Firm Websites. The conduct rules governing advertising also govern marketing through websites. Websites should tell viewers where the lawyers hold a license. They should ensure that viewers understand that the lawyers do not yet represent them, even if they click through various screens. Soliciting specific inquiries can be especially hazardous. If a website includes legal information, then the website should state that the information does not substitute for consultation with a lawyer. While websites should provide contact routes, state bars may require that they show a physical address within the state in addition to email addresses. The American Bar Association's eLawyering Task Force, Standing Committee on the Delivery of Legal Services, and Law Practice Management Section offer *Best Practice Guidelines for Legal Information Web Site Providers* (2003) available through the American Bar Association's website. We reproduce below a key ABA Formal Opinion on websites.

Interactive Websites. The interactive nature of websites, particularly those that provide substantial legal information and encourage viewers to post inquiries, poses special problems for lawyers. For instance, imagine the potential loss of clients to the firm if any prospective client could disqualify all members of a law firm simply by disclosing confidential information to members of the firm using a "contact us" feature of the firm's website.   Several ethics opinions hold that prospective clients have no confidentiality when they send unsolicited emails to lawyers, although they caution lawyers to add that disclaimer to their websites if they expect to be able to use any such information. *See* Ca. Formal Ethics Opin. 2005-168 (2005); San Diego County Bar Assn. Ethics Opin. 2006-1 (2006); N.Y. City Bar Assn. Ethics Opin. 2001-1 (March 1, 2001); *see also* Fla. Bar Opin. 07-3 (Jan. 16, 2009). Websites should also caution viewers not to interpret general legal information to apply to their specific legal issues. They should also warn viewers, preferably through click-through disclaimers, *see* Va. Legal Ethics Opinion 1842 (Sept. 30, 2008), that any action they take in viewing screens and links, using a "contact us" feature, or posting inquiries will not create a client-lawyer relationship or implicate duties of confidentiality or loyalty.   Read the following excerpts of Formal Opinion 10-457 to see if you can discern its other cautions.

Lawyer Websites
ABA Formal Opinion 10-457
(August 5, 2010)

Websites have become a common means by which lawyers communicate with the public. Lawyers must not include misleading information on websites, must be mindful of the expectations created by the website, and must carefully manage inquiries invited through the website. Websites that invite inquiries may create a prospective client-lawyer relationship under Rule 1.18. Lawyers who respond to website-initiated inquiries about legal services should consider the possibility that Rule 1.18 may apply.[Footnotes throughout omitted.]
I. Introduction
Many lawyers and law firms have established websites as a means of communicating with the public. A lawyer website can provide to anyone with Internet access a wide array of information about the law, legal institutions, and the value of legal services. Websites also offer lawyers a twenty-four hour marketing tool by calling attention to the particular qualifications of a lawyer or a law firm, explaining the scope of the legal services they provide and describing their clientele, and adding an electronic link to contact an individual lawyer. The obvious benefit of this information can diminish or disappear if the website visitor misunderstands or is misled by website information and features. A website visitor might rely on general legal information to answer a personal legal question.   Another might assume that a website's provision of direct electronic contact to a

lawyer implies that the lawyer agrees to preserve the confidentiality of information disclosed by website visitors.

For lawyers, website marketing can give rise to the problem of unanticipated reliance or unexpected inquiries or information from website visitors seeking legal advice. This opinion addresses some of the ethical obligations that lawyers should address in considering the content and features of their websites.

II. Website Content

A. Information about Lawyers, their Law Firm, or their Clients

Lawyer websites may provide biographical information about lawyers, including educational background, experience, area of practice, and contact information (telephone, facsimile and e-mail address). A website also may add information about the law firm, such as its history, experience, and areas of practice, including general descriptions about prior engagements. More specific information about a lawyer or law firm's former or current clients, including clients' identities, matters handled, or results obtained also might be included.

Any of this information constitutes a "communication about the lawyer or the lawyer's services," and is therefore subject to the requirements of Model Rule 7.1 as well as the prohibitions against false and misleading statements in Rules 8.4(c) (generally) and 4.1(a) (when representing clients). ...

As applied to lawyer websites, these rules allow a lawyer to include accurate information that is not misleading about the lawyer and the lawyer's law firm, including contact information and information about the law practice. To avoid misleading readers, this information should be updated on a regular basis. ...

B. Information about the Law

Lawyers have long offered legal information to the public in a variety of ways, such as by writing books or articles, giving talks to groups, or staffing legal hotlines. Lawyer websites also can assist the public in understanding the law and in identifying when and how to obtain legal services. Legal information might include general information about the law applicable to a lawyer's area(s) of practice, as well as links to other websites, blogs, or forums with related information. Information may be presented in narrative form, in a "FAQ" (frequently asked questions) format, in a "Q & A" (question and answer) format, or in some other manner.

Legal information, like information about a lawyer or the lawyer's services, must meet the requirements of Rules 7.1, 8.4(c), and 4.1(a). Lawyers may offer accurate legal information that does not materially mislead reasonable readers. To avoid misleading readers, lawyers should make sure that legal information is accurate and current, and should include qualifying statements or disclaimers... .

... To avoid misunderstanding, our previous opinions have recommended that lawyers who provide general legal information include statements that characterize the information as general in nature and caution that it should not be understood as a substitute for personal legal advice.

Such a warning is especially useful for website visitors who may be inexperienced in using legal services, and may believe that they can rely on general legal information to solve their specific problem. ...

C. Website Visitor Inquiries

Inquiries from a website visitor about legal advice or representation may raise an issue concerning the application of Rule 1.18 (Duties to Prospective Clients). Rule 1.18 protects the confidentiality of prospective client communications. It also recognizes several ways that lawyers may limit subsequent disqualification based on these prospective client disclosures when they decide not to undertake a matter. ...

... [I]t may be difficult to predict when the overall message of a given website communicates a willingness by a lawyer to discuss a particular prospective client-lawyer relationship. Imprecision in a website message and failure to include a clarifying disclaimer may result in a website visitor reasonably viewing the website communication itself as the first step in a discussion. Lawyers are therefore well-advised to consider that a website-generated inquiry may have come from a prospective client, and should pay special attention to including the appropriate warnings mentioned in the next section. ...

III. Warnings or Cautionary Statements Intended to Limit, Condition, or Disclaim a Lawyer's Obligations to Website Visitors

Warnings or cautionary statements on a lawyer's website can be designed to and may effectively limit, condition, or disclaim a lawyer's obligation to a website reader. Such warnings or statements may be written so as to avoid a misunderstanding by the website visitor that (1) a client-lawyer relationship has been created; (2) the visitor's information will be kept confidential; (3) legal advice has been given; or (4) the lawyer will be prevented from representing an adverse party.

Limitations, conditions, or disclaimers of lawyer obligations will be effective only if reasonably understandable, properly placed, and not misleading. This requires a clear warning in a readable format whose meaning can be understood by a reasonable person. If the website uses a particular language, any waiver, disclaimer, limitation, or condition must be in the same language. The appropriate information should be conspicuously placed to assure that the reader is likely to see it before proceeding.

Finally, a limitation, condition, waiver, or disclaimer may be undercut if the lawyer acts or communicates contrary to its warning.

INQUIRY

Political Contributions. Conduct rules address one other form of marketing. Many states require judges to run for election, meaning that those judges must periodically campaign. Voters re-elect incumbent judges at an overwhelming rate, but not every judicial election offers an incumbent judge, and even incumbents sometimes feel the need to campaign. Campaigns cost money. Judges and their designates hold fundraising events to cover campaign costs. Trial lawyers who appear before those judges, including criminal-defense lawyers who depend on judges to appointment them, are sometimes the target of fundraising requests. Other elected government officials hold influence over the selection of lawyers and law firms to provide legal services to government. These circumstances create an opportunity for mischief for judges and other elected government officials to sell, and lawyers to purchase, influence over appointments and contracts for legal services. ABA Model Rule 7.6 prohibits a lawyer from making or soliciting a political contribution for that kind of influence. Model Rule 7.6 does not prohibit making or soliciting a political contribution in general. Lawyers do give to judicial campaigns and assist judges with their campaigns. Model Rule 7.6 establishes a fine line compliance with which depends on sensitivity. Model Rule 7.6 puts in big trouble the lawyer who suggests that a campaign contribution will result in influence. Consider an identical state version of Model Rule 7.6.

> **DELAWARE R. PROF. CONDUCT 7.6: Political Contributions to Obtain Government Legal Engagements or Appointments by Judges.**
> A lawyer or law firm shall not accept a government legal engagement or an appointment by a judge if the lawyer or law firm makes a political contribution or solicits political contributions for the purpose of obtaining or being considered for that type of legal engagement or appointment.

D. Specializing

Advertising Certification.   Lawyers specialize in many fields. Family law, worker's compensation, intellectual property, and taxation are common examples. Law is certainly complex enough to require and reward specialization. A specialist in a law field can provide more efficient and effective services. Given the potential client benefits to lawyer specialization, specialization can also be another form of marketing. While clients like their lawyer to be able to address any legal issue that they face, clients also like to feel that their lawyer is a specialist in the field in which the client needs service. National boards examine and certify specialists in medical fields. It is clear when a physician is or is not a specialist. The same is not always true for lawyers. Some national organizations offer specialty training and certification. Many more state continuing-legal-education providers offer specialty training and certification. Yet there are varying levels of training among those educational providers and thus less confidence that certification by one equals certification by another. Certification by just any provider when the providers themselves are not necessarily meeting standards does not ensure that certification protects the public from misrepresentation. ABA Model Rule 7.4 addresses this concern by prohibiting lawyers from advertising specialty certification unless the state bar or American Bar Association recognizes the certifying provider whose name the lawyer must identify in the advertisement. *See, e.g.,* In re Anonymous, 783 N.E.2d 1130 (Ind. 2003) (reprimand for advertising as elder-law specialist when not so specialized); *cf.* In re Hughes & Coleman, 60 S.W.3d 540 (Ky. 2001) (permissible to advertise as "injury lawyer" without claiming specialization or certification). As you read an identical state version of Model Rule 7.4 followed by an illustrative case involving a state rule that further requires a disclaimer, consider again how lawyer advertising affects the course and quality of a lawyer's practice. Know, too, that while the Supreme Court has upheld the regulation of lawyer advertising on specialization, the First Amendment does limit that regulation. *See* Peel v. Attorney Registration & Disciplinary Commn. of Illinois, 496 U.S. 91 (1990) (plurality).

UTAH R. PROF. CONDUCT 7.4: **Communication of Fields of Practice.**
(a) A lawyer may communicate the fact that the lawyer does or does not practice in particular fields of law.
(b) A lawyer admitted to engage in patent practice before the United States Patent and Trademark Office may use the designation "Patent Attorney" or a substantially similar designation.
(c) A lawyer engaged in Admiralty practice may use the designation "Admiralty," "Proctor in Admiralty" or substantially similar designation.

(d) A lawyer shall not state or imply that a lawyer is certified as a specialist in a particular field of law, unless:

(1) the lawyer has been certified as a specialist by an organization that has been approved by an appropriate state authority or that has been accredited by the American Bar Association; and

(2) the name of the certifying organization is clearly identified in the communication.

Walker v. Board of Professional Responsibility,
Tennessee Supreme Court
38 S.W.3d 540 (2001)

... In February 1995, [respondent attorney Ted] Walker placed an advertisement for divorce services in the *Chattanooga News Free Press TV Magazine.* The ad was published over the week of February 12 through 18, 1995 and states in its entirety: "DIVORCE, BOTH PARTIES SIGN, $125 + COST, NO EXTRA CHARGES, Ted Walker, [address & telephone number]." On March 29, 1995, the Board's Disciplinary Counsel filed a complaint against Walker alleging that this advertisement listed divorce as a specific area of practice but did not include the disclaimer required by DR 2-101(C) of the Code of Professional Responsibility. ... In his response to the complaint, Walker argued that his advertisement fully complied with the United States Supreme Court's decision in *Bates v. State Bar of Arizona,* 433 U.S. 350[] (1977), and that "the law, as set out by the United States Supreme Court, is governing over a conflicting law by the Tennessee Supreme Court." After an exchange of correspondence with the Disciplinary Counsel, Walker apparently agreed to change his advertisement to add the required disclaimer. ... [Discipline officials filed a petition after Walker requested a hearing on the alleged violation.]

... [A] supplemental petition alleged that a complaint file had been opened pertaining to two advertisements placed in *The Chattanooga Times* on February 9, 1997: one in the *Chattanooga TV Guide* and one in the Business Directory Section of the classified ads. The TV guide ad stated: "DIVORCE, BOTH PARTIES SIGN, $90.00 + COURT COSTS $89.50, No 'Extra' Charges, TED WALKER, [phone number], Not certified as a specialist by the TN Commission on Certification and Specialization." The ad in the Business Directory Section was similar but did not contain the "not certified" statement. The Board's supplemental petition alleged that the ad in the *Chattanooga TV Guide* did not use "the precise language required by the Tennessee Supreme Court in quotation marks within Tenn. R.S.Ct. 8, DR 2-101(C)(2)(3), with no variations or abbreviations, an interpretation adopted by the

Board in *Tennessee Formal Ethics Opinion* 95-F-137." The supplemental petition also alleged that the advertisement in the Business Directory Section "include[d] no mandatory disclosure of specialty certification whatsoever, as is required under DR 2-101(C)(3)." The petition further alleged that Walker did not comply with DR 2-101(F) (pertaining to filing copies of advertisements within three days of their publication) as to either of the ads. ...

[Walker appealed the discipline board's and trial and appellate courts' findings that he had violated the conduct rules and that they were constitutional as applied.]

... We now consider both the constitutionality of the disclaimer rule Walker was sanctioned for having violated and whether he can be held responsible for the costs of this disciplinary action.

ANALYSIS

... The validity of commercial speech regulations is subject to what has been termed intermediate—as opposed to strict—scrutiny, according to a test announced in *Central Hudson Gas & Elec. Corp. v. Public Serv. Comm'n,* 447 U.S. 557[] (1980). [C] The test is as follows: "For commercial speech to come within that provision [the First Amendment], it at least must concern lawful activity and not be misleading. Next, we must ask whether the asserted government interest is substantial. If both inquiries yield positive answers, we must determine whether the regulation directly advances the government interest asserted, and whether it is not more extensive than is necessary to serve that interest." *Central Hudson,* 447 U.S. at 566[]. ...

The regulation before us requires that whenever a lawyer advertises his services in a particular area of law for which certification is available in Tennessee, he must disclose in the ad whether he is certified. DR 2-101(C). Since Walker was not certified as a civil trial specialist (which then covered the area of divorce law) yet he specifically mentioned divorce law in his ads, the disciplinary rule mandates that his ads include the following language: "Not certified as a civil trial specialist by the Tennessee Commission on Continuing Legal Education and Specialization." DR 2-101(C)(3). This regulation does not prohibit or limit speech; instead it requires more speech by way of an explanatory disclaimer.

The fact that the regulation requires disclosure rather than prohibition tends to make it less objectionable under the First Amendment. ...

... [U]nder current law—as announced in *Zauderer*[*v. Office of Disciplinary Counsel of Supreme Court of Ohio,* 471 U.S. 626 (1985)]—as long as the disclosure requirement is reasonably related to the state's interest in preventing deception of consumers, and not unduly burdensome, it should be upheld. ...

The Constitutionality of DR 2-101(C)(3)

The Board argues that Tennessee's interest in requiring non-certified attorneys who advertise specialty services to include a disclaimer in their ads is substantial: protecting consumers of legal services by allowing them to make informed judgments about which attorney to hire to handle their legal needs. We agree that this interest is substantial. ... *See generally Florida Bar[v. Went for It, Inc.],* 515 U.S. [618,] 625[] ("States have a compelling interest in the practice of professions within their boundaries, and ... as part of their power to protect the public health, safety, and other valid interests they have broad power to establish standards for licensing practitioners and regulating the practice of professions.") (quoting *Goldfarb v. Virginia State Bar,* 421 U.S. 773, 792[] (1975)).

Since the state's interest is substantial, the question is whether DR 2-101(C)(3) is reasonably related to promoting that interest. [Cc] The record before this Court when the certification disclaimer rule was considered in 1993 reveals that the Commission on Continuing Legal Education ("Commission"), which petitioned this Court to adopt the rule, had the following concern: lawyers who were advertising specialties were actually obtaining far fewer Continuing Legal Education hours of training than leading practitioners in that specialty area who were not advertising. [C][fn] This was problematic because an American Bar Association survey indicated that the public expected a lawyer who advertised in a particular area of law to have greater education in that area than other lawyers. [Cc] The Commission thought the public would be better served if presented with a more accurate picture of an advertising lawyer's level of education.

The disclaimer rule the Commission advocated and this Court ultimately adopted promotes the Commission's legitimate goal by clearly and succinctly providing the public with information about the certification status of attorneys who advertise their services. This information will help a consumer identify which lawyers may have more experience and education in a particular area of law[fn]— knowledge which will help that consumer hire a lawyer to represent his interests. ... [T]he information required by DR 2-101(C)(3) is one piece of information that will assist consumers in making those choices. The required disclaimer is therefore reasonably related to promoting the substantial interest of helping consumers to make informed judgments about which attorneys they should entrust with their legal needs.

Next, we must determine whether DR 2-101(C)(3) is unduly burdensome. ... This statement does not require an attorney who advertises his skills to disclose anything more than the basic fact of his non-certification; no extraneous information or lengthy detail is required. We hold that the disclaimer here satisfies the constitutional standard.

Finally, Walker argues that even if the disclosure rule is constitutional, the State cannot require him to use the precise language listed in DR 2-101(C)(3). He argues that any statement that conveys the same meaning as the specific language in the disciplinary rule is sufficient. ...

[W]e think that deviations from the specific wording of DR 2-101(C)(3) could lead to public confusion. The required disclaimer statement was worded in the most simple, direct fashion so that the public would have no difficulty understanding its meaning or comparing different attorney advertisements. This goal might easily be thwarted if attorneys were allowed to write their own disclaimer statements. Rather than focus on the intended message—that an attorney is not certified—a consumer would be forced to parse the meaning of different disclaimer statements, attempting to understand without any guidance why one attorney's disclaimer was different than another's.

The Board's interest in requiring uniform language is significant for another reason. Just as the absence of uniformity would require a consumer to compare many different disclaimer statements, so would the Board, and subsequently the courts, be forced to examine advertisement after advertisement in an effort to determine which attorneys substantially complied with DR 2-101(C)(3) and which attorneys fell somewhat short. This costly and inefficient task seems entirely unnecessary in light of the ease of complying with a uniform rule—especially one which is as short and free of burdensome detail as possible. ...

CONCLUSION

For the reasons discussed above, we affirm the Chancery Court's ruling that the disclaimer requirement of DR 2-101(C)(3) is constitutional and that Walker is required to pay for the costs of this disciplinary action under Supreme Court Rule 9 section 24.3. We remand to the Board for a determination of the total costs for which Walker is responsible.

Career and Professional Development

Advertising may be the last thing that a new lawyer does—or the first. New lawyers who join law firms tend not to have much say in the way that the law firm markets it services. Those decisions are made by the firm's management. New lawyers do work generated by senior lawyers who are already skilled at client relationships and business development. It can take years for a new lawyer to develop the identity and experience to know how to market the lawyer's services effectively—to become what lawyers call a *rainmaker.* Early attempts at rainmaking can be awkward. Firms tend not to want new lawyers interfering with longstanding client relationships until those lawyers develop the sensitivity and acumen that reliable marketing can take. On the other hand, new lawyers in solo practice or very small law firms may need to market their services immediately simply to have something to do. There are reliable ways in which new lawyers do so, often through court appointments, local bar referral services, and informal lawyer networks, while the new lawyers develop practice experience and skill. Although advertising has a place somewhere in this marketing mix, many lawyers do little or no direct advertising. Develop a sense of how marketing works in your field of interest and preferred law firm role.

CHAPTER XII

ACCESS

Inclusion, Diversity, Sensitivity, Service

> *[W]e fail to appreciate the dignity of our profession if we look for it either in profundity of learning or in forensic triumphs. . . . [I]ts reason for being must be found in the effective aid it renders to justice, and in the sense it gives of public security through its steady support of public order. These are commonplaces, but the strength of the law lies in its commonplace character; and it becomes feeble and untrustworthy when it expresses something different from the common thoughts of men.*
>
> — *Justice Thomas M. Cooley*

OBJECTIVE: Given indigent individuals needing lawyer services and community organizations needing lawyer services to continue and expand service to indigent individuals, articulate the professional norms, rules, and expectations for your providing those legal services.

Applicable Rules

1.14 Client with Diminished Capacity

6.1 Voluntary Pro Bono Publico Services

6.2 Accepting Appointments

6.3 Membership in Legal Services Organization

6.4 Law Reform Activities Affecting Client Interests.

6.5 Nonprofit and Court-Annexed Limited Legal Services

There is no justice in a legal system that serves only the privileged and powerful. Only by ensuring that the poor and disadvantaged have access to the justice system can the law profession achieve its most noble goals of equality, fairness, dignity, and liberty. Lawyers promote access to justice in at least four ways, by (1) providing pro bono service to individual indigent clients, (2) accepting court appointments to represent the indigent, (3) supporting legal-services organizations in their access work, and (4) ensuring that they serve clients with diminished capacity. Six ABA Model Rules address those four kinds of access activities addressed in this chapter's four sections. Let this chapter stimulate your thought as to how you will promote access to justice. The best lawyers engage in these activities.

A. Pro Bono Service

Social Imperatives. ABA Model Rule 6.1 urges lawyers to perform pro bono service, beginning, "Every lawyer has a professional responsibility to provide legal services to those unable to pay." Lawyers have many reasons beyond a conduct rule to perform pro-bono service. Those reasons certainly include moral and social imperatives, and professional oaths and identity. Empirical analysis of why lawyers perform pro bono places personal satisfaction at the top of the list, followed by professional obligation, employer policy, employer encouragement, professional value, reputation, experience, client interaction, work control, politics, religion, and recognition. *See* DEBORAH L. RHODE, PRO BONO IN PRINCIPLE AND IN PRACTICE—PUBLIC SERVICE AND THE PROFESSIONS 131 (Stanford Univ. Press 2005). While the reasons lawyers give for performing pro bono are plainly interrelated and complex, note again that pro bono service correlates to lawyer career satisfaction. *See* NANCY LEVIT & DOUGLAS O. LINDER, THE HAPPY LAWYER: MAKING A GOOD LIFE IN THE LAW 197 (Oxford Univ. Press 2010). Pro bono service derives not only from motivations but from worldviews and experiences including lifelong practices of volunteering. *See* DEBORAH A. SCHMEDEMANN, THORNS AND ROSES: LAWYERS TELL THEIR PRO BONO STORIES (Carolina Academic Press 2010). Pro bono service stands a good likelihood of making you a happier lawyer, even as it makes the community in which you live a better place for your pro bono clients and those who depend on them to live.

Value of Pro Bono. Pro bono service clearly has tremendous value for the indigent individuals who are its direct beneficiaries. Pro bono also benefits communities. Yet there are also substantial benefits for the lawyers who provide pro bono services. New lawyers gain valuable experience by handling matters that involve issues of great importance to indigent clients. Veteran attorneys are often willing to mentor new lawyers who provide pro bono services. As they handle pro bono assignments, new lawyers are able, early in their careers, to meet and interact with judges and veteran opposing counsel who respect the new lawyer's pro bono participation. Experienced lawyers also benefit. Pro bono work brings variety. A conventional career path may not have led the veteran lawyer to advocacy of causes that first inspired the lawyer to choose law as a career. Pro bono provides the opportunity to pursue ideals by representing those who are most in need. For all attorneys, the conscientious practice of law demands a professional concern for those who do not have access to justice. Pro bono is one way in which individual lawyers can contribute to the public good by protecting the legal rights of the poor.

  Business Imperatives. Lawyers are increasingly recognizing that pro bono service promotes a law firm's natural business imperative. Pro bono can transform a law practice. Some evidence suggests that pro bono service correlates positively with a law firm's financial success. *See* RHODE, *supra*, at 21. Lawyers must constantly respond to new demands for which they need new skills. Lawyers see law practice as changing rapidly. Old clients, whether individual or corporate, disappear. Old networks no longer seem to produce as many new clients. Old skills seem not to serve current clients. The communities within which lawyers practice are also changing rapidly. Pro bono challenges lawyers to build new cross-cultural and consultation skills, use new tools, and form new relationships within new service communities. It does so with ready-made clients whom the lawyer obtains at no marketing cost—indeed with a converse free marketing benefit. The clients come to you, or others send them to you, rather than you pursuing them. Judges, bar leaders, and community leaders laud and respect you for accepting them. The lawyer makes no assurances in order to secure the professional relationship other than competence and diligence in the representation. With no fees earned or anticipated, the consideration is instead the meaningfulness of the professional relationship and service. What could be better? Consider now an identical state version of Model Rule 6.1 urging pro bono service.

> **MINNESOTA R. PROF. CONDUCT 6.1: Voluntary Pro Bono Publico Service.**
> Every lawyer has a professional responsibility to provide legal services to those unable to pay. A lawyer should aspire to render at least 50 hours of pro bono publico legal services per year. In fulfilling this responsibility, the lawyer should:
> (a) provide a substantial majority of the 50 hours of legal services without fee or expectation of fee to:
> (1) persons of limited means; or
> (2) charitable, religious, civic, community, governmental, and educational organizations in matters that are designed primarily to address the needs of persons of limited means; and
> (b) provide any additional services through:
> (1) delivery of legal services at no fee or substantially reduced fee to individuals, groups, or organizations seeking to secure or protect civil rights, civil liberties, or public rights, or charitable, religious, civic,

community, governmental, and educational organizations in matters in furtherance of their organizational purposes, where the payment of standard legal fees would significantly deplete the organization's economic resources or would be otherwise inappropriate;
(2) delivery of legal services at a substantially reduced fee to persons of limited means; or
(3) participation in activities for improving the law, the legal system, or the legal profession.
In addition, a lawyer should voluntarily contribute financial support to organizations that provide legal services to persons of limited means.

INQUIRY

Aspirational Goal. Model Rule 6.1 is clearly aspirational. Rather than setting a mandatory number of hours of pro bono, Model Rule 6.1 urges that a lawyer "should aspire to render" the requisite 50 hours. Thus, there is no discipline for the lawyer who ignores Model Rule 6.1, as the rule's Comment [12] makes clear: "The responsibility set forth in this Rule is not intended to be enforced through disciplinary process." Model Rule 6.1 Comment [5] acknowledges that government lawyers, for example, may not have the liberty to represent individual pro bono clients and may have to fulfill their responsibility by one of the alternative means, perhaps the $350 buyout option. Comment [8] gives as examples of activities for improving the law to serve on a bar committee, take part in Law Day activities, teach law to other practitioners, serve as a mediator or arbitrator, and lobby for law changes in the legislature. While Model Rule 6.1 is aspirational, Florida's Rule 4-6.1 requires lawyers to report to the bar whether they meet its 20-hour or $350 contribution pro bono responsibility, giving its rule a mandatory flavor. *See* Schwarz v. Kogan, 132 F.3d 1387 (11th Cir. 1998) (upholding Florida rule against constitutional challenge). Which do you think makes the most sense, aspirational goals or mandated requirements? Regardless of whether you believe that pro bono should remain aspirational or whether bars should take steps to make it mandatory, there is one other value to pro bono that we have not yet mentioned. Regular pro bono contribution may serve as a mitigating factor in discipline proceedings. Consider the following illustrative case.

In re Fischer,
Colorado Supreme Court
89 P.3d 817 (2004)

Mark J. Fischer, the respondent in the underlying attorney discipline proceeding, appealed from the order of the Hearing Board disbarring him. [C] Fischer admitted that he violated the Rules of Professional Conduct by disbursing funds to his dissolution-of-marriage client, and to himself in the amount of his attorney fees, in a manner not in accordance with the terms of the separation agreement adopted by the court. The hearing Board held that disbarment was the presumed sanction for the respondent's misappropriation of funds and his violation of the court's order, and it found the mitigating circumstances offered by him insufficient to alter that sanction.

Because the Board did not appropriately consider and balance the aggravating and mitigating circumstances established as a matter of fact, and because it imposed an unreasonably harsh sanction on the respondent, we reverse its order of disbarment. ...

According to the stipulated statement of facts, in September 2001, Ms. McKinney and her husband, Mr. Gerald Hallman, entered into a Separation and Property Settlement Agreement, which was made an order of the court by its dissolution decree. The agreement called for Ms. McKinney to sell a piece of real property owned by the couple and a mobile home located on it. From the proceeds she agreed to pay certain enumerated debts, including three liens secured by the land, personal debts owed by her and Mr. Hallman, a $10,000 tax obligation, and $36,000 due on the purchase price of the mobile home, as well as $10,000 to Mr. Hallman. Only after these payments were made did the agreement entitle Ms. McKinney to receive whatever proceeds remained from the sales. The agreement also provided for the payments to be made directly from the closing or from the proceeds deposited in the respondent's trust account. ...

... Ultimately, the respondent was able to arrange a sale of the real property (but not the mobile home), including payment of $70,000 of the purchase price in November 2001, to be followed in December with payment of $23,000, secured by a promissory note.

Neither Mr. Hallman nor his attorney attended the closings, but by correspondence with the respondent, Hallman's attorney confirmed her understanding that her client would receive his $10,000 from the proceeds of the sale held in the respondent's trust account. After the first closing, the respondent wrote to Hallman's attorney, indicating that the liens on the property had been paid from the $70,000 and that he had also paid certain of Ms. McKinney's personal debts, including his own claim of $4,000 for attorney fees. He indicated that the other debts his client was obliged to pay by the terms of the agreement would be handled when the additional $23,000 was paid but that he had been instructed by his client not to pay Mr. Hallman any money at that time, and perhaps not at all. As justification, he noted that Ms. McKinney had been forced to discount the property by at least $5,000 because of an inadequate and unapproved sewer system.

After not receiving any disbursement from the December payment of $23,000, Mr. Hallman filed a Motion for Release of Money Pursuant to the Settlement Agreement. The respondent's accounting, which he was ordered by the court to provide, indicated that Ms. McKinney had received a total of $53,108.30 and the respondent had received an additional $6,468 as attorney fees. The $10,000 tax obligation had not been paid, and Mr. Hallman had not been paid the $10,000 required by the separation agreement. The respondent offered, as justification for refusing to pay Hallman, that his client had directed him as her attorney to withhold payment from her former husband because of the losses incurred due to his failure to disclose significant issues regarding the mobile home.

The district court found that the funds from the sale of the property were not disbursed in accordance with the agreement of the parties and order of the court, apparently for the reason that Ms. McKinney instructed the respondent to disburse funds contrary to the agreement. The court entered a provisional judgment in favor of Mr. Hallman and against Ms. McKinney for $47,083.82, which was vacated by stipulation of the parties after the respondent personally satisfied all of the financial terms and conditions outlined in the separation agreement. This satisfaction by the respondent included payments of $10,000 to Mr. Hallman, $3,794.97 to Hallman's attorney for additional attorney fees incurred by the respondent's actions, the respondent's personal assumption of the $36,000 debt on the unsold mobile home, payment of an additional $400 debt listed in the agreement, and payment of $3,596.48 to the Colorado Department of Revenue, fully resolving the "$10,000 tax obligation" referred to in the agreement.

In the stipulated statement of facts, the respondent also acknowledged that he should not have deviated from the disbursement schedule of the agreement without first seeking court approval, and that his actions had damaged Mr. Hallman both by delaying receipt of his $10,000 share of the equity in the land and by leaving him temporarily liable on the $10,000 tax obligation. ... [T]he respondent also conceded that he should have seen his role as an officer of the court and should have followed the court's direction, as set out in its order... .

... Under the circumstances of his particular case, even if the respondent's conduct would have warranted disbarment in the absence of mitigation, sufficient facts in mitigation were established to make suspension, rather than disbarment, the appropriate sanction. Foremost among these were the respondent's recognition of his ethical violations and acceptance of responsibility for the injuries caused to others and the judicial system, evidenced by his cooperation with the Office of Attorney Regulation Counsel, his expressions of remorse, and his attempts to make whole the injured parties and clear up the problems caused by his behavior, at his own expense. *See* ABA Standard 9.32(a)-(m). ...

Of considerable significance was the respondent's attempt to repair the damage his conduct had caused to his client's former husband, creditors of the couple, and the judicial system by accepting personal responsibility for all debts that were the subject of the separation agreement and any additional expenses. The ABA Standards for Imposing Lawyer Sanctions recognize a timely good faith effort to make restitution or rectify the consequences of misconduct as a mitigating factor. *See Id.* at 9.32(d). While acknowledging that some courts have held otherwise, the Standards consider it the better policy to allow a good faith effort to make restitution to be considered in mitigation in order both to encourage lawyers to reduce the injuries they have caused and help insure recognition of the wrongfulness of their conduct. [C] As the comments also make clear, it is the fact that restitution is made voluntarily and of the lawyer's own initiative that is important, even if that occurs in response to a complaint filed with the appropriate regulatory agency. Restitution prior to the initiation of disciplinary proceedings therefore present the clearest case for mitigation, while restitution later in the proceedings present a weaker case. *See* ABA Standard 9.32 cmt. ...

Furthermore, as acknowledged by the Board, the respondent presented considerable evidence of other mitigation, including his excellent reputation in the profession, *see* ABA Standard 9.32(g) (character or reputation a factor in mitigation); his record of pro bono and community service, *see In re Fong,* 308 A.D.2d 19, 762 N.Y.S.2d 367 (2003) (considerable evidence in mitigation, including attorney's regular pro bono work on behalf of four community organizations); *In re Mason,* 1997 WL 275107 (Cal.Bar Ct.1997) (attorney's pro bono work is a mitigating factor); *Disciplinary Action Against Dvorak,* 554 N.W.2d 399 (Minn.1996) (mitigating factors included substantial pro bono work and volunteer work provided to community by attorney); and the opinion of others, including the judge who presided over the dissolution proceeding, that he was not a risk to the public. *See* Standard 9.32(g). ...

Because we have determined that the Board did not appropriately consider and balance the aggravating and mitigating circumstances established as a matter of fact, and that it imposed an unreasonably harsh sanction on the respondent, we reverse its order of disbarment. Because we also believe a proper application of the ABA Standards for Imposing Lawyer Sanctions leads to the conclusion that the respondent's conduct warrants suspension, for a period sufficient to require his reinstatement following suspension, [c], we now order the suspension of the respondent from the practice of law for a period of one year and one day beginning March 10, 2003, the effective date of the Board's order of disbarment.

INQUIRY

Low Bono. Notice that Model Rule 6.1(b)(2) urges not only free service to the indigent but also service at reduced fees. Reduced fees do not mean charging the going rate and then treating the non-paying client's account receivable as uncollectible. The American Bar Association Standing Committee on Pro Bono and Public Service's *Standards for Programs Providing Civil Pro Bono Legal Services to Persons of Limited Means* Standard 3.5-6 titled "Attorneys' Fees Policy" urges that "[a] pro bono program should establish and communicate to clients and volunteers a policy regarding the receipt of attorneys' fees by program volunteers." Your willingness to provide low-bono service means something to your client's dignity. Conventional wisdom is that a successful law practice requires just two ingredients: clients and the right kind of clients. Law practice does depend on having clients to serve. The "right" client can certainly mean a client who pays your top hourly rate. Yet it can also mean clients who while unable to afford your usual hourly rate can still pay some fee—what some have called *low bono*. *See* Leslie C. Levin, *Pro Bono and Low Bono in the Solo and Small Law Firm Context*, in ROBERT GRANFIELD & LYNN MATHER, EDS., PRIVATE LAWYERS & THE PUBLIC INTEREST 156, 159 (Oxford Univ. Press 2009). Another important reminder is that while Model Rule 7.1 prohibits solicitation of paying clients, presumably including low-paying clients, it does not prohibit soliciting pro-bono clients—meaning offering your free help to someone in need.

Defining Pro Bono. Confusion exists over what qualifies as pro bono service. The State Bar of Michigan's Pro Bono Reference Manual states, "The attention given to public interest legal service has not eliminated the confusion that exists about what services actually qualify as pro bono.... For example, some attorneys limit their focus to the 'no fee' aspect of pro bono service. As a consequence, they will make the error of assuming that the will they draft at no cost for Aunt Martha is a pro bono service, even though Aunt Martha is comfortably middle class. Pro bono contemplates services for low-income individuals and groups." Another lawyer may make the error of assuming that serving as a coach for a Little League team for disadvantaged children constitutes pro bono service. Yet pro bono must involve the use of lawyer skills. The profession designates as public service other good works for the community. As the State Bar of

Michigan's then-president Victoria Roberts observed in 1997, "Lawyers do a tremendous amount of public service which is not pro bono representation. It should also be recognized and valued. But the reason there is a distinction in our Voluntary Standard is to assure that lawyers use their legal skills to help those who need to navigate the justice system but who cannot navigate it without assistance from someone who has the necessary skills. It is important that lawyers understand this distinction and the paramount need to use their legal skills to represent indigent clients in civil matters."

Distinguishing Pro Bono. Pro bono service does not, in all cases, require direct client representation. A footnote to the State Bar of Michigan's Voluntary Standard explains that other acceptable pro bono activities include "serving on a local pro bono committee or the board of directors of a legal aid or legal services program, training other attorneys through a structured program, engaging in community legal education programs, or advising not-for-profit, low income, or public interest organizations or groups." Check your knowledge as to which of the following is pro bono and which public service: counseling an indigent consumer about the terms of a rent-to-own furniture contract (pro bono); coordinating a community drive to collect used furniture for the poor (public service); mentoring a new lawyer handling a first pro bono referral (pro bono); mentoring an underprivileged teenager (public service); membership on the board of directors of a poverty law program (pro bono); membership on the board of directors of a nonprofit opera company (public service).

Quality of Representation. Pro bono does not mean that the quality of the representation changes. Lawyers providing pro bono service owe clients the same duties that they would if the clients were compensating them. When you accept a pro bono case, promptly open and maintain a case file in the usual manner, including conflict-checking, calendaring, tracking of case expenses, and time keeping. Do not treat a pro-bono case with less formality and rigor than a contingency fee or hourly case. Although you will not bill the client for your legal services, you should contemporaneously record your time, services, and costs in the reliable manner you ordinarily do for other cases. Keeping track of your time is an important management tool. It may also be necessary for a fee request if law should allow for it at a later date. The point, though, is to give each client, whether pro bono or not, your competent and diligent service.

B. Appointments

Accepting Appointments. While lawyers ordinarily have the liberty to choose their own clients—a powerful force in shaping a law practice and community—you have just seen one limitation on that liberty that lawyers should aspire to provide pro bono service. This section addresses a second limitation on that liberty. Courts have traditionally held common law or statutory authority to appoint a lawyer to represent an indigent party. *See* Bothwell v. Republic Tobacco Co., 912 F. Supp. 1221 (D. Neb. 1995) (history of appointive power). *Appointment* means that a judge or judicial assistant will contact a lawyer who practices before the court and request that lawyer to represent the indigent party. Courts may have some authority to require rather than merely request a lawyer to represent an indigent party on appointment, *see, e.g.,* Scheehle v. Justice of Supreme Court of Arizona, 120 P.3d 1092 (2005), although the Supreme Court has declined to rule on the issue, *see* Mallard v. United States District Court, 490 U.S. 296 (1989), perhaps hoping that lawyers will not make it do so, and there is contrary authority that forced service can in certain circumstances be an unconstitutional taking, *see, e.g.,* Jewell v. Maynard, 383 S.E.2d 536 (Va. 1989). ABA Model Rule 6.2 captures that sense of obligation by providing that a lawyer must accept an appointment unless having good cause not to do so. Read an identical state version of Model Rule 6.2 for what may constitute good cause.

> **WEST VIRGINIA R. PROF. CONDUCT 6.2: Accepting Appointments.**
> A lawyer shall not seek to avoid appointment by a tribunal to represent a person except for good cause, such as:
> (a) representing the client is likely to result in violation of the Rules of Professional Conduct or other law;
> (b) representing the client is likely to result in an unreasonable financial burden on the lawyer; or
> (c) the client or the cause is so repugnant to the lawyer as to be likely to impair the client-lawyer relationship or the lawyer's ability to represent the client.

INQUIRY

Appointments in Criminal Cases. Given Sixth Amendment rights to counsel in certain criminal cases, courts hearing criminal cases maintain systems for appointing and compensating counsel in criminal cases where indigent defendants have that constitutional right. States and local government fund and maintain public-defender offices, and courts maintain appointed-counsel lists for those purposes. Yet while Model Rule 6.2 would apply just as much to a court's appointment of a lawyer in a criminal case, and courts do sometimes use their authority to appoint criminal-defense counsel without that counsel actually volunteering by placing counsel's name on the court's appointment list, Model Rule 6.2 instead addresses primarily those instances where the judge believes that a party in a civil case, where there is no constitutional right and are no funds for compensation, requires representation, or where the court has an extraordinary criminal case that requires specific counsel. Can you discern why courts would not routinely use Model Rule 6.2's obligation to appoint unwilling criminal-defense counsel? The Sixth Amendment right is to *effective* assistance of counsel. An appointment system must satisfy that constitutional obligation of providing qualified and earnest counsel, when frequent involuntary appointments might not. *See* Zarabia v. Bradshaw, 912 P.2d 5 (Ariz. 1996). Indeed, a criminal-defense appointment system probably must compensate counsel at least minimally in order to be constitutional, both as to the defendant's rights and the rights of the appointed lawyers. *See* Arnold v. Kemp, 813 S.W.2d 770 (Ark. 1991). Your chances of having the court tap you to represent a defendant in a homicide or other serious criminal case are small.

Appointment Lists. Many jurisdictions have lists of lawyers who are willing to serve as court-appointed attorneys for indigent people. As indicated above, these appointments are not just for criminal practice but include appointment to represent parents and children in abuse cases, the elderly in cases where a question regarding their legal capacity exists, the mentally ill over their commitment, and myriad other situations. Court-appointed lawyers are usually paid a very low hourly rate to represent such individuals but are willing to accept the low compensation in exchange for receiving regular appointments. Model Rule 6.2 prevents lawyers from *cherry picking* the best appointments. Can you articulate how? Why would a lawyer want to cherry pick, anyway? Consider an illustrative case in which three lawyers withdrew from an appointment and a fourth attempted to do so. Not every appointment is easy.

The Florida Bar v. Rubin,

Florida Supreme Court
549 So.2d 1000 (1989)

... Between April 1984 and February 1985, Russell Sanborn was represented on a first-degree murder charge by a series of three lawyers, each of whom eventually sought and was granted, for various reasons, permission to withdraw. In February 1985, the court granted respondent Rubin's request that he be allowed to represent Sanborn for no fee, based upon Rubin's assurance that he would be prepared for trial by the previously scheduled date of April 29, 1985. On that date, just prior to jury selection, Rubin also petitioned the court for permission to withdraw. Though he gave vague reasons for withdrawal, Rubin's message to the court was that his client was planning to testify untruthfully. The court denied the motion and ordered him to proceed to trial. ... When the case was restored to the trial calendar, Rubin again sought to withdraw on the same grounds. His motion again was denied. When he refused to proceed to trial, the court issued a contempt order, which was affirmed on appeal. [C] This Court denied review of the district court decision and denied Rubin's petition for a writ of habeas corpus. He served thirty days in jail for contempt. Sanborn subsequently was represented by a public defender and was convicted.

The question before us is not whether Rubin was legally obligated to obey the court order. That matter has been decided adversely to him by the courts and he has been properly sanctioned for his refusal. Rather, the question is whether he was ethically required to obey. We are concerned here with whether he violated the Code, not with whether he violated the law. The issue in this case is whether a lawyer may disobey a court order because he or she believes that order to be erroneous. ...

A grievance committee of the Bar recommended that Rubin be privately reprimanded for misconduct. Rubin rejected the recommendation and demanded a trial before a referee. ...

The Bar contends that Rubin had no right to refuse to obey a lawful court order and that such refusal, in effect, constitutes a per se ethics violation. Rubin, on the other hand, contends that the Code itself is the source of his trouble, that it *required* him to disobey the order.

... Undeniably, Rubin was placed in a difficult situation when it became clear to him that the client intended to commit perjury. The rules provided little guidance as to how to proceed, and indeed placed Rubin in the position where he would have to choose which rule to violate. However, Rubin initially followed the proper course by seeking to withdraw, and then appealing the denial of that motion. In this way he properly tested the validity of the trial court's order preventing him from withdrawing. ...

... Despite this, Rubin maintained that the district court's decision was erroneous and refused to proceed to trial, thereby flaunting the trial court's order and the mandate of the district court. For this he was held in contempt. In affirming the contempt order, the Third District Court stated:

> Rubin is certainly free to disagree and maintain his personal view of what the law is or should be, or indeed his personal view of what some higher law provides. It is, however, the decision of the

mortal judges in *Sanborn v. State,* having not been stayed, much less set aside, by some higher court with jurisdiction over the matter, which Rubin must obey. Thus, even if, arguendo, it might have been later determined that *Sanborn v. State* was wrongly decided, Rubin's contumacious refusal to follow the undisturbed order to proceed would be nonetheless punishable as a direct contempt.... [T]his rule of law is essential to the maintenance of our system of laws as a whole. [C]

We totally agree. An attorney is not permitted to ignore and refuse to follow a court order based upon his personal belief in the invalidity of that order. To countenance that course is to court pandemonium and a breakdown of the judicial system. ... To hold otherwise would be to give any attorney claiming a sincere belief in the invalidity of an order carte blanche to disregard that order. [C] Such a situation would be intolerable.

In this case, Rubin properly challenged the order and lost. It was then incumbent upon him to follow the dictates of the trial court. ... Rubin argues that if he had followed the procedure outlined by the district court he would then be open to discipline for violation of other provisions of the Code. However, if Rubin had been cited for violation of the Code for following the court-prescribed procedure, his good faith reliance on the trial court's order and the mandate of the district court would have been a good, and most likely a complete, defense. ...

For the foregoing reasons, we ... find Rubin guilty of the charged violations. The Florida Bar asks that a public reprimand be imposed, and we concur. Accordingly, it is the judgment of this Court that attorney Ellis S. Rubin is publicly reprimanded by publication of this opinion in the *Southern Second* reporter. Rubin is ordered to pay the costs of this proceeding. Judgment is entered against him for $817.40, for which sum let execution issue.

It is so ordered.

INQUIRY

Declining for Good Cause. Appointments can work much like other pro bono service in improving a law practice. One should accept appointments and must do so when the court orders that there is no good cause to decline. *See* In re Kleinsmith, 124 P.3d 579 (N.M. Ct. App. 2005) (affirming contempt penalty for disobeying appointment order); *see also* Hawkins v. Commn. for Lawyer Discipline, 988 S.W.2d 927 (Tex. Ct. App. 1999) (follow appointment order while challenging it). Yet there are times and cases to decline. Model Rule 6.2 lists three examples of good cause to decline an appointment: (1) rule violation; (2) unreasonable financial burden; or (3) a representation-impairing repugnant cause. Can you think of examples of each cause? For example, a lawyer must decline appointment if the lawyer has a non-consentable conflict of interest. *Cf.* Burke v. Lewis, 122 P.3d 533 (Utah 2005) (appointment creates safe harbor against arguable rule violations lawyer brings to court's attention). When deciding whether accepting an appointment would result in unreasonable financial burden, you might consider whether you can make yourself available on the scheduled trial date, how much discovery will be necessary to prepare the case for trial (keeping in mind that your firm is likely to bear case expenses), and how many hours will it take to prepare and how many days will it take to try the case. *See, e.g.,* Synergy Assocs., Inc. v. Sun Biotechnologies, Inc., 350 F.3d 681 (7th Cir. 2003) (could should not reappoint counsel who withdraws from case when owed $93,000). As to repugnant causes, Model Rule 6.2(c) sets a high bar that the repugnance must impair the representation—a standard that may depend on the lawyer's personal beliefs or experience. Is incompetence in the subject law field an excuse? Courts have great faith in a lawyer's ability to learn a field quickly to serve as appointed counsel, *see, e.g.,* Reese v. Owens-Corning Fiberglass, 962 F. Supp. 1418 (D. Kan. 1997); Stern v. Grand, 773 P.2d 1074 (Colo. 1989), particularly when the court also has the power to appoint experienced co-counsel, *see* Cunningham v. Sommerville, 388 S.E.2d 301 (W.Va. 1989). Whatever an appointed lawyer decides, the lawyer should timely communicate the decision to the court in writing.

C. Legal-Services Organizations

Legal Aid. Federal, state, and local funding supports legal-services organizations, or *legal aid*, in many communities. Do not confuse legal aid with public-defender services. Public-defender offices provide representation to indigent defendants in criminal cases. Legal aid provides representation to indigent parties in certain civil cases, typically family law matters involving domestic-abuse allegations or termination of parental rights, and landlord-tenant matters involving eviction. Legal-aid offices may also provide representation in Social Security proceedings and some bankruptcy cases. Legal-aid organizations may depend in part on compensated staff attorneys and in part on rosters of pro bono lawyers. They also depend on a board of directors comprised of volunteer local lawyers. Lawyers know the local legal needs and how to deliver legal services to satisfy them. A board of directors of a legal-aid organization can provide the organization with a range of important governance skills and administrative resources from assessing leadership and management to community assessment, systems development, public relations, court relations, pro bono recruitment, and fundraising. ABA Model Rule 6.3 addresses some of the concerns that a lawyer should have in volunteering to support a legal-aid organization. As you read an identical state version of Model Rule 6.3, see if you can articulate those concerns.

> **WEST VIRGINIA R. PROF. CONDUCT 6.3: Membership in Legal Services Organization.**
> A lawyer may serve as a director, officer or member of a legal services organization, apart from the law firm in which the lawyer practices, notwithstanding that the organization serves persons having interests adverse to a client of the lawyer. The lawyer shall not knowingly participate in a decision or action of the organization:
> (a) if participating in the decision or action would be incompatible with the lawyer's obligations to a client under Rule 1.7; or
> (b) where the decision or action could have a material adverse affect on the representation of a client of the organization whose interests are adverse to a client of the lawyer.

INQUIRY

Conflicts of Interest. Lawyers do not have multiple-representation conflicts solely out of being an officer, director, or member of a legal-services organization. Membership is not representation. Yet keep in mind that Model Rule 1.7(a)(2) also forbids conflicts of interests where the lawyer's interests materially limit the representation. Leadership or membership in a legal-services organization could in theory limit a lawyer's client representation. To address that concern, Model Rule 6.3 authorizes a degree of adversity between the interests of the organization's clients and the interests of the client of the lawyer who supports the organization. For example, a lawyer who represents property owners may support a legal-aid organization that represents tenants whose interests are adverse to the interests of the property owners. Can you see the potential benefit to both sides—property owners and tenants—from having the property owners' lawyer on the board of a legal-aid organization serving tenants? While Model Rule 6.3 encourages lawyers to support legal-aid organizations, it does not excuse nonconsentable conflicts. Model Rule 6.3(a) refers explicitly to Model Rule 1.7 on concurrent conflicts of interest. Model Rule 6.3(b) alerts a lawyer to watch for specific instances where an organization client may be harmed by the lawyer influencing a decision in favor of the lawyer's own private client. Consider an illustrative case in which a lawyer-director of a legal-services organization took the appropriate steps to extricate her from a potential conflict affecting her private practice.

E.E.O.C. v. Luby's Inc.,
United States District Court for the District of Arizona
347 F. Supp.2d 743 (2004)

Plaintiff-Intervenor Sally Case, represented by lawyers from the Arizona Center for Disability Law ("ACDL"), has filed a motion to disqualify attorney Kimberly Fatica and her law firm, Brockelman & Fatica, from representing Defendant Luby's in this case ([c]). ... For the reasons set forth below, the Court will deny the motion.

Background

The Equal Employment Opportunity Commission ("EEOC") filed this action on May 27, 2004, alleging that Defendant Luby's had discriminated against Ms. Case on the basis of her disability. On August 9, 2004, Ms. Case moved to intervene as a Plaintiff. The Court granted the motion on August 18, 2004 ([c]).

The ACDL is a non-profit public-interest law firm designated by the Governor of Arizona to provide protection and advocacy services for people with developmental disabilities. The ACDL implements federal programs and receives federal funds for the protection of the disabled. The ACDL's volunteer board of directors ("Board") includes individuals with disabilities, family members of individuals with disabilities, and others who have experience or interest in disability law. The Board includes several attorneys.

The facts relevant to this motion are not disputed. Ms. Fatica served on the ACDL Board from May 2000 to August 2004, including service as vice president of the Board from June 2004 to August 2004. Ms. Fatica also served on the ACDL Legal Committee, which reviews litigation proposals. Ms. Fatica's law firm generally represents management interests in employment disputes. When Ms. Fatica joined the ACDL Board in 2000, she inquired about possible conflicts that might arise if clients of her firm were adverse to ACDL clients. She was advised by ACDL Executive Director Leslie Cohen that the organization had a screening policy to deal with such situations. Under that policy, an attorney Board member representing a party adverse to an ACDL client would be screened from any information relating to the case and would not participate in deliberations or decisions about the case.

During 2004, Ms. Fatica and her firm were asked to represent Luby's. On June 17, 2004, Ms. Fatica received an email from the ACDL indicating that staff attorneys would seek Board approval to commence litigation against Luby's on behalf of an ACDL client. Ms. Fatica deleted the email without reading it and promptly contacted Ms. Cohen, informing Ms. Cohen of her representation of Luby's and requesting that she be screened from all communications and information relating to the ACDL's representation of a party adverse to Luby's. Ms. Cohen agreed that any potential conflict problems could be avoided through the ACDL screening process. On this basis, Ms. Fatica agreed to represent Luby's in this case and began working on the matter in late June. She thereafter received no confidential information from the ACDL relating to this case and took no part in any Board discussion concerning the representation of Sally Case.

Staff attorneys for the ACDL later concluded that Ms. Fatica's representation of Luby's presented a conflict of interest. They suggested to Ms. Cohen that Ms. Fatica should be asked to withdraw from representing Luby's and, if she chose not to do so, that a motion for disqualification should be filed. Ms. Cohen did not agree. Rather, on August 25, 2004, she informed Ms. Fatica of the staff attorneys' concern and asked her to take one of several steps [including to] resign from the Board, take a leave of absence from the Board, or withdraw from the representation of Luby's. After considering the matter for two days, Ms. Fatica decided to resign from the Board.

Her resignation did not satisfy the ACDL staff attorneys. After seeking counsel from outside lawyers, discussing the matter internally, and asking Ms. Fatica to stop representing Luby's-a step Ms. Fatica declined to take-the ACDL attorneys filed this motion.

Discussion

Several facts are key. They are not disputed by the parties.

First, Ms. Fatica has never had an attorney-client relationship with Sally Case. Ms. Case is represented by the ACDL staff attorneys, not by Ms. Fatica, her law firm, or other members of the Board. ...

Second, Ms. Fatica acquired no confidential information about Sally Case or her claims while serving on the ACDL Board. Although she was sent an email containing such information, she deleted the email and notified the ACDL that she should receive no such information. The ACDL does not claim that Ms. Fatica read the email or received other confidential information about Ms. Case.

Third, because she has resigned from the Board, Ms. Fatica will not receive any confidential information about Sally Case or her claim in the future. Ms. Fatica's resignation eliminates even the risk of inadvertent disclosure.

Fourth, the ACDL is not a party to this litigation. For purposes of this analysis, it must be remembered that Ms. Fatica's relationship was with the Plaintiff-Intervenor's law firm, not the Plaintiff-Intervenor herself. ...

... Because she has never represented Sally Case, Ms. Fatica's defense of Luby's does not present a concurrent conflict of interest as defined by ER 1.7, where the representation of one client is directly adverse to another client. ...

Nor does ER 1.9 apply. That rule prohibits a lawyer "who has formerly represented a client in a matter" from thereafter representing another person in the same or a substantially related matter if the person's interests would be materially adverse to the former client. Neither Sally Case nor the ACDL are Ms. Fatica's former clients.

... The ACDL asserts that Ms. Fatica had access to important information about attorneys' fees it has received in settlement of cases, information that might give Ms. Fatica insight into the ACDL's likely settlement position, including the extent of its willingness to compromise attorneys' fees. Similarly, the ACDL asserts that Ms. Fatica gained information about injunctive-type relief the ACDL often seeks in settlement as well as other information that might be relevant to the ACDL's litigation strategy. In other words, it is the information Ms. Fatica acquired about the ACDL, not about Sally Case or her claims, that forms the basis for this disqualification motion.

Although the Court does not doubt the sincerity of the ACDL attorneys in making this argument, the Court cannot agree that Ms. Fatica's access to this information requires her disqualification. The ethical rules specifically address a lawyer's service on the board of a legal services organization. ER 6.3 states that "[a] lawyer may serve as a director, officer or member of a legal services organization, apart from the law firm in which the lawyer practices, *notwithstanding that the organization serves persons having interests adverse to a client of the lawyer.*" (Emphasis added.) The ethical rule then specifically explains how such conflicts are to be handled: "The lawyer shall not knowingly participate in a decision or action of the organization: (a) if participating in the decision would be incompatible with the lawyer's obligations to a client under ER 1.7; or (b) where the decision could have a material adverse effect on the representation of a client of the organization whose interests are adverse to a client of the lawyer." Subpart (a) of this rule is designed to protect clients in the position of Luby's. Subpart (b) is designed to protect clients in the position of Sally Case, but does so by stating that the lawyer-director may not participate in decisions that could have a material adverse effect on Sally Case. The rule does not state that lawyers are prohibited from representing clients adverse to Sally Case. Rather, it requires that lawyers adopt the kind of screening policy that was explained to Ms. Fatica when she joined the Board in May of 2000—the lawyer representing an adverse client must be screened from any Board information or decisions that could adversely effect the ACDL's client.

... The only authority contained in the ethical rules that applies directly to this case is ER 6.3. That rule reflects a strong policy in favor of lawyers serving on the boards of legal service organizations. It is designed to encourage such service, assuring lawyers that they will not be disqualified from representing clients adverse to the legal services organization, provided they exercise care not to acquire confidential information concerning the organization's client.

The ACDL's fundamental argument—that Ms. Fatica's access to general information concerning ACDL attorneys' fees and litigation strategies should disqualify her from representing Luby's—would nullify ER 6.3. Directors virtually always acquire this kind of information from the organizations they serve. ... In short, the ACDL's position is fundamentally at odds with the provisions of ER 6.3, the ethical rule adopted by this Court to govern these situations.

Moreover, the ACDL's position would sweep more broadly than the rule that applies to law firms. If the ACDL was a traditional law firm, and if Ms. Fatica had been a partner in that firm rather than a director of a legal services organization, she could leave the law firm and represent Luby's in a case adverse to her former firm's client so long as she had obtained no confidential information about that client while at the firm. *See* ER 1.9(b). The fact that she might have substantial information about her former firm's finances or litigation strategies would not prohibit her representation of a client adverse to the firm's client. *Id.* If such general information does not disqualify a lawyer leaving a law firm, neither does it disqualify a lawyer leaving a director's position with a public service law firm like the ACDL. ...

Conclusion

ER 6.3 makes clear that a lawyer in Ms. Fatica's position is not disqualified from representing Luby's if she screens herself from information related to Sally Case, as she did in this situation. The cases described above would support disqualification of Ms. Fatica if she continued to be a member of the ACDL Board with access to such information, or if she acquired such information before her resignation, but neither has occurred here. Ms. Fatica has taken the steps necessary to preserve her ability to represent Luby's.

IT IS ORDERED:

... Plaintiff-Intervenor's Motion for Disqualification of Counsel ([c]) is **denied.** ...

INQUIRY

Legal-Services Programs. Legal-aid organizations are not the only source for clients of limited means to obtain limited legal services. Courts and nonprofit organizations may maintain programs through which a client can obtain limited specific services of a lawyer. ABA Model Rule 6.5, titled "Nonprofit and Court-Annexed Limited Legal Services Programs," in its Comment [1] identifies as examples legal-advice hotlines, advice-only clinics, and court-annexed form centers and counseling programs for unrepresented litigants, where lawyers may serve as volunteers. The large number and relative anonymity of those brief consultations reduce the risks associated with conflicts of interest. A lawyer is unlikely to shape such brief advice based on an adverse client representation or acquire confidential information to use in that other representation. Some matters lend themselves to unbundled services, where a lawyer might review a document and consult with a client without providing additional services. Family and estate matters where parties and interested persons have clear objectives and good factual knowledge but need review of a legal document are examples. What if a lawyer takes on the short-term consult-only representation of a legal-aid program client whose interests could potentially conflict with a current or future client of the lawyer? Read Model Rule 6.5 for how the conduct rules tend to encourage a lawyer to undertake such representations.

> **MARYLAND R. PROF. CONDUCT 6.5: Nonprofit and Court-Annexed Limited Legal Services Programs.**
> (a) A lawyer who, under the auspices of a program sponsored by a nonprofit organization or court, provides short-term limited legal services to a client without expectation by either the lawyer or the client that the lawyer will provide continuing representation in the matter:
> (1) is subject to Rules 1.7 and 1.9(a) only if the lawyer knows that the representation of the client involves a conflict of interest; and
> (2) is subject to Rule 1.10 only if the lawyer knows that another lawyer associated with the lawyer in a law firm is disqualified by Rule 1.7 or 1.9(a) with respect to the matter.
> (b) Except as provided in paragraph (a)(2), Rule 1.10 is inapplicable to a representation governed by this Rule.

INQUIRY

Ask-a-Lawyer Programs. Model Rule 6.5 has two key components. The first component defines Model Rule 6.5's narrow scope. Model Rule 6.5 applies only to lawyers who are participating in pro bono programs that are sponsored by non-profit legal entities (often bar associations) and courts. The structure of these programs tends to limit the scope of the lawyer-client relationship and the services that the lawyer provides to the pro bono client. For example, some bar associations operate a "Call a Lawyer" or "Meet a Lawyer" day where members of the public can have a free telephone call or meeting with a lawyer through which to receive legal advice. Those programs make clear that lawyer and client form no relationship beyond the consultation unless both lawyer and client specifically agree to extend their relationship beyond the consultation. Model Rule 6.5's second key component serves to facilitate and encourage lawyers to participate in these types of pro bono programs. Can you see how Model Rule 6.5 facilitates participation?

Turning a Blind Eye. Appreciate how generous Model Rule 6.5 is in encouraging lawyers to provide short-term limited legal services to program clients. In effect, Model Rule 6.5(a)(1) permits a lawyer to avoid conflict-checking, turning Model Rule 1.7's prohibition against concurrent conflicts of interest into a prohibition against *knowing* concurrent conflicts of interest. It does the same for conflicts of interest involving former clients, turning Model Rule 1.9(a)'s prohibition into a prohibition against knowing violations. Model Rule 6.5(a)(2) does the same for imputed disqualification, turning Model Rule 1.10's prohibition against conflicts imputed among lawyers in a firm into a prohibition against *known* imputed conflicts. In proverbial parlance, Model Rule 6.5 permits a lawyer to turn a blind eye toward conflicts—definitely *not* the approach of the conflicts rules in general.

Law-Reform Activities. When a lawyer wins or loses a client's case, especially one on appeal resulting in a published opinion, the lawyer is shaping the law. Yet lawyers also contribute to the development of the law outside of their private paying practices. They often do so by participating in organizations that advocate law reform. Law-reform organizations represent many different political and social views, ideologies, faiths, and belief systems, ethnicities, and specific interests. Americans act through private associations and organizations. Lawyers can have great influence within those organizations when those organizations address reform of the laws. ABA Model Rule 6.4 authorizes a lawyer to participate in an organization seeking a law reform that is adverse to the interests of the lawyer's client. Under Model Rule 6.4, the lawyer needs only disclose that the lawyer has a client (whose identity the lawyer needs not disclose) whose interests would benefit from a decision the organization is making. Read an identical state version of Model Rule 6.4 for these provisions.

MARYLAND R. PROF. CONDUCT 6.4: Law Reform Activities Affecting Client Interests.
A lawyer may serve as a director, officer or member of an organization involved in reform of the law or its administration notwithstanding that the reform may affect the interests of a client of the lawyer. When the lawyer knows that the interests of a client may be materially benefited by a decision in which the lawyer participates, the lawyer shall disclose that fact but need not identify the client.

D. Inclusive Representation

Diminished-Capacity Clients. Representing clients with different abilities signifies another access to justice issue. Lawyers represent the mentally impaired. They also represent individuals who had full capacity until their legal crisis brought on an emotional impairment. They also represent children and others who have less capacity than a fully capable adult has. Lawyers must adjust their conduct in those situations to the client's needs and capacities. A client's incapacity does not relieve a lawyer of obligations but, instead, adds the obligation that the lawyer must accommodate the diminished capacity. *See* In re Flack, 33 P.3d 1281 (Kan. 2001) (two years of probation for lawyer who among other violations failed to consult with terminally ill client); *see also* In re M.R., 638 A.2d 1274 (N.J. 1994) (lawyer must advocate Down's syndrome client's objectives unless absurd or harmful). ABA Model Rule 1.14 requires that the lawyer maintain a normal relationship with the client as reasonably far as the lawyer is able. Model Rule 1.14 then permits a lawyer to take reasonably necessary protective action when the client's impairment threatens substantial harm to the client against which the client cannot protect. Model Rule 1.14 even permits a lawyer to seek a guardian for the impaired client under those circumstances, authorizing necessary confidential disclosures. As you read an identical state version of Model Rule 1.14, try to discern what it means to keep the lawyer-client relationship as normal as reasonably possible, illustrated in part by the following case.

DELAWARE R. PROF. CONDUCT 1.14: Client with Diminished Capacity.
(a) When a client's capacity to make adequately considered decisions in connection with a representation is diminished, whether because of minority, mental impairment or for some other reason, the lawyer shall, as far as reasonably possible, maintain a normal client-lawyer relationship with the client.
(b) When the lawyer reasonably believes that the client has diminished capacity, is at risk of substantial physical, financial or other harm unless action is taken and cannot adequately act in the client's own interest, the

lawyer may take reasonably necessary protective action, including consulting with individuals or entities that have the ability to take action to protect the client and, in appropriate cases, seeking the appointment of a guardian ad litem, conservator or guardian.

(c) Information relating to the representation of a client with diminished capacity is protected by Rule 1.6. When taking protective action pursuant to paragraph (b), the lawyer is impliedly authorized under Rule 1.6(a) to reveal information about the client, but only to the extent reasonably necessary to protect the client's interests.

In the Matter of Disciplinary Action Against Kuhn,

North Dakota Supreme Court
785 N.W.2d 195 (2010)

PER CURIAM.

[¶1] ... Determining there is clear and convincing evidence Kuhn violated N.D.R. Prof. Conduct 1.14, we direct that Kuhn be suspended from the practice of law for ninety days and that he pay the costs of the disciplinary proceeding in the amount of $2,654.07.

I.

[¶2] Kuhn has been licensed to practice law in the courts of North Dakota since July 8, 1974. Shortly after he started his practice, he began to do tax work for Jake Leno. In 2005, Kuhn wrote a will for Jake Leno. In that will, Jake Leno devised his condominium to his daughter, Kathleen McKinley.

[¶3] In 2006, McKinley filed a petition for appointment of a guardian/conservator for Jake Leno. The district court appointed Guardian and Protective Services, Inc. ("GAPS"), as Jake Leno's temporary guardian/conservator. The district court also appointed a physician, guardian ad litem, and visitor to meet with Jake Leno and report back to the district court.

[¶4] The court-appointed physician reported Jake Leno suffered from "Parkinson's disease with concurrent adult onset diabetes" and "some short term memory loss," and indicated Jake Leno needed full-time care. The guardian ad litem reported she "firmly believe[d] that the proposed ward needs a guardian." Jake Leno's former home health care provider informed the guardian ad litem Jake Leno "has Parkinson's disease and dementia of the Alzheimer's type." The court-appointed visitor also recommended Jake Leno needed a guardian/conservator.

[¶5] At the hearing on the guardianship/conservatorship petition, Kuhn represented Jake Leno's sons, Ronald Leno and Randy Leno. Ronald Leno and Randy Leno testified they were willing to serve as Jake Leno's guardians/conservators. Jake Leno testified he did not think he needed a guardian/conservator. The district court found Jake Leno "has a current medical diagnosis of Parkinson's disease with adult onset diabetes and exhibits short term memory loss." The district court concluded Jake Leno was incapacitated and appointed GAPS full guardian and conservator, with full control over his place of residence, legal matters, financial matters, and medical treatment.

[¶6] In 2007, an unidentified person contacted Kuhn's office and told Kuhn's receptionist Jake Leno wanted his will changed. Kuhn testified at the disciplinary hearing that he thought an employee of GAPS had contacted his office to change the will. However, Kuhn acknowledged he did not contact GAPS to verify whether one of its employees had called his office. Kuhn learned later one of Jake Leno's caregivers had contacted his office. After speaking with Jake Leno, Kuhn drafted a new will that gave all of Jake Leno's property, including the condominium, to the three children equally, instead of devising the condominium solely to McKinley.

[¶7] Kuhn testified that at the time he wrote the will he "knew [Jake Leno] had been declared incompetent" and "there was allegations that he had dementia of the Alzheimer's type." Kuhn took two of his employees to Jake Leno's apartment to act as witnesses as Jake Leno executed the new will. Kuhn testified at the disciplinary hearing regarding his state of mind:

> I was a little uneasy because he was in—under a judicial order that said he was incompetent. So I questioned him, I questioned his caregiver to ask her if he's-how he's doing. And she said, "Oh, he's fine. He knows what's going on, and, Jake, he knows." And I questioned him in front of the witnesses-in front of the two witnesses about the will. Told him exactly what—what he was doing. And said, "Now, are you sure this is what you want to do? This is what's going to happen." And he said, "Yes." So, I mean, my impression that day was that he was fine.

[¶8] A year later, McKinley sent a letter to Kuhn protesting his actions regarding Jake Leno's new will. Kuhn, as preparer of the will, subsequently filed a petition seeking an order determining the validity of the will. The district court dismissed the petition, stating, "[T]he guardianship/conservatorship created for the Ward Jake Leno, granted to the appointed guardian/conservator full authority for all legal matters on behalf of Jake Leno, effective as of the date of appointment. The attempted execution of a Will thereafter by the Ward Jake Leno is therefore without legal authority and therefore invalid." Kuhn did not appeal the district court's order.

[¶9] In 2009, counsel for the Disciplinary Board filed a petition alleging Kuhn had violated N.D.R. Prof. Conduct 1.14, Client With

Limited   Capacity,   by   his   actions   regarding   Jake   Leno's
guardianship/conservatorship hearing and second will. ...

[¶10] The hearing panel found "Kuhn's testimony that he believed
that GAPS was aware of Jake Leno's desire to make a new will is not
credible." ...   The hearing panel also concluded Kuhn violated N.D.R.
Prof. Conduct 1.14, Client With Limited Capacity, when he "prepared a
new will for Jake without communicating with or securing decision-
making   authority   from   GAPS,   the   court-appointed   guardian   and
conservator with full authority over Jake's legal matters." ...

II.

... [¶16] Rule 1.14 of the North Dakota Rules of Professional
Conduct ... Comment 5 ... states, "If the client has an appointed
representative, the lawyer should ordinarily look to the representative
for decisions on behalf of the client. The lawyer should be cognizant of
the extent of the powers and duties conferred upon the client's
appointed representative." [C] The hearing panel concluded Kuhn
violated Rule 1.14 when he "prepared a new will for Jake without
communicating with or securing decision-making authority from
GAPS,   the   court-appointed   guardian   and   conservator   with   full
authority over Jake's legal matters."

[¶17] Kuhn argues he did not violate Rule 1.14 because he was
abiding by his client's wishes. Kuhn cites Comment 3 of Rule 1.14:
"The fact that a client is a minor or has limited capacity does not
diminish the lawyer's obligation to treat the client with attention and
respect. Even if the person has an appointed representative, the
lawyer should as far as possible accord the represented person the
status of client, particularly in maintaining communication. Appointed
representatives include guardians ad litem, conservators, guardians,
individuals appointed in a durable power of attorney or in an
advanced health care directive." Kuhn argues he was fulfilling his duty
to give Jake Leno attention and respect when he drafted the new will.

[¶18] Kuhn concedes he had a responsibility to communicate with
Jake Leno's guardian/conservator, but Kuhn testified he believed he
was acting with the consent of GAPS. The hearing panel found this
testimony was not credible. ...

[¶20] The record shows Kuhn knew Jake Leno had been declared
incapacitated and GAPS had been named his guardian with full
authority over his legal matters. Kuhn was present at the guardianship
hearing. He reviewed all the documents indicating Jake Leno suffered
from Parkinson's disease and short-term memory loss. He concedes it
was his responsibility to communicate with Jake Leno's guardian. He
failed to meet this responsibility, however. Kuhn's understandable
desire to give his client attention and respect does not overcome Jake
Leno's incapacity to make legal decisions on his own behalf. Kuhn did

not look to Jake Leno's appointed representative, as required by N.D.R. Prof. Conduct 1.14, comment 5. Kuhn persisted in executing a will that was invalid because of Jake Leno's incapacity. Furthermore, we do not ignore the fact the second will drafted by Kuhn benefitted Ronald Leno and Randy Leno, Kuhn's clients at the guardianship/conservatorship hearing. Clear and convincing evidence indicates Kuhn violated N.D.R. Prof. Conduct 1.14. ...

III.

[¶24] On the basis of the record, we ... accept the hearing panel's finding that Kuhn clearly and convincingly violated N.D.R. Prof. Conduct 1.14, Client With Limited Capacity. We order Kuhn be suspended from the practice of law for ninety days, effective August 1, 2010, and that he pay the costs of the disciplinary proceeding in the amount of $2,654.07.

INQUIRY

Practical and Strategic Issues. The above *Kuhn* case suggests not only the challenges of keeping the lawyer-client relationship normal but also some of the practical and strategic issues doing so can raise. A client who has diminished capacity may or may not have the state of mind necessary to make independent and binding decisions about the client's own affairs. Lawyers then have the challenge of deciding to what extent to indulge and side with the client over the question of capacity, when others challenge that capacity. It can be a Hobson's choice—a choice in which the lawyer may lose either way. In the above *Kuhn* case the lawyer clearly erred by accepting the client's conclusion that the client had capacity when a court had already adjudged the client not competent. Now consider a case in which the lawyer took the opposite tack. What would you have done in each of these cases? Is there a foolproof approach?

In re S.H.,
Alaska Supreme Court
987 P.2d 735 (1999)

EASTAUGH, Justice.
I. *INTRODUCTION*
S.H. sued his former employer and others. His attorneys in that action were Clapp, Peterson & Stowers (CPS). Asserting that they believed S.H. to be incapable of making rational decisions about settlement of that lawsuit, S.H.'s attorneys later petitioned the superior court to appoint a conservator for S.H. The court appointed a

conservator, who settled S.H.'s claims against his former employer. S.H. appeals from the decision to appoint a conservator. We conclude that it was not error to appoint a conservator under the circumstances of this case. ...

II. *FACTS AND PROCEEDINGS*

Anchorage Refuse, Inc. (ARI) employed S.H. from 1991 to 1993. In April 1995 S.H. sued ARI and individual ARI officers and employees alleging that his fellow employees sadistically and physically mistreated him. CPS represented S.H. on a contingent fee basis in that lawsuit.

From May 1995 to December 1996 CPS pursued the case, remaining in close and frequent contact with S.H. CPS attorneys Marcus Clapp and Thomas Van Flein grew increasingly uneasy, however, about S.H.'s growing obsession with the case. There was evidence S.H. displayed various indicia of instability, including irrational behavior,[fn] paranoia,[fn] inclinations toward gratuitous dismissal of his personal injury suit,[fn] a tendency to threaten his own witnesses,[fn] the desire to initiate direct and inappropriate dealings with opposition counsel and the judge,[fn] and a marked lack of confidentiality.[fn] In May 1996 Clapp wrote a letter to S.H. regarding S.H.'s behavior in the case. Van Flein arranged for S.H. to visit Dr. Marjorie Smith, a psychiatrist, for counseling in preparation for trial.

Psychiatric experts examined S.H. in 1996 and 1997, in connection with both the ARI litigation and the conservatorship proceeding. The perception among the majority of these experts... was that a mental impairment made S.H. unable to think rationally at times. ...

In December 1996 mediation began between S.H. and ARI. ARI offered to settle for $500,000. S.H. personally stated he thought he could get $2 million. According to the mediator, S.H. then made "accusations against lawyers and judges without any foundation for them." S.H. refused to accept ARI's offer.

Believing S.H. to be incapable of handling his own affairs, CPS commenced a new proceeding by filing a "Petition for Appointment of Limited Conservator/Guardian Ad Litem of a Person." On December 30 Superior Court Judge Karen L. Hunt appointed Ernest Schlereth to act as S.H.'s attorney in the conservatorship/ guardianship proceeding.

In January 1997, when it appeared a settlement with ARI might be reached, Schlereth and CPS agreed to dismiss the petition; when S.H. refused to agree to the settlement, CPS and Schlereth agreed to reinstate the petition. ...

The hearing lasted three days. The master ... recommended that the superior court appoint a special conservator to act on S.H.'s behalf for purposes of the ARI litigation... . The superior court adopted the master's report,[fn] and appointed Paul Cossman as the Special

Conservator. After reviewing the case, Cossman concluded: "I have no doubt that it is in the best interests of [S.H.] to accept the settlement offer of $500,000." Cossman expressed his opinion that "[S.H.'s] chances of recovering a judgment in excess of the settlement offer were basically nonexistent."

Cossman, CPS, and ARI then stipulated to interplead the settlement funds. The $500,000 settlement proceeds were deposited with the court registry and await distribution pending resolution of this dispute. ...

III. *Discussion*

... The final appointment question is whether there was sufficient factual basis ... to find S.H. unable to manage his property effectively. ...

S.H.'s doctors provided considerable evidence of his inability. Dr. Marjorie Smith opined that she did not believe S.H. could work with any attorney on the ARI case and come to a reasonable decision. Dr. Bruce Smith opined that S.H. was "functionally impaired" and disconnected from "others' reality." Dr. Aaron Wolf stated that he agreed with Dr. Marjorie Smith's diagnosis of S.H. "right down the line." And Betty Wells, the court visitor, recommended that a guardian be appointed to make litigation decisions for S.H.

The superior court did not commit clear error in accepting the evidence as clear and convincing proof of S.H.'s inability to manage his property and affairs effectively. ...

S.H. claims that CPS "ignored its fiduciary duty" to him, and its duty to use reasonable care[fn] and to exercise "the utmost good faith, integrity, fairness, and fidelity."[fn] He implies that CPS decided to settle not because it held S.H.'s interests to heart but because his case "required a lot of time, and after a certain period it was apparent that it would not bring in a large fee" for CPS.

Alaska Rule of Professional Conduct 1.14(b) permits a lawyer to "seek the appointment of a guardian or take other protective action with respect to a client only when the lawyer reasonably believes that the client cannot adequately act in the client's own interest." If the requirements of Rule 1.14 are met, a lawyer may seek a guardian to protect the client's interests despite the client's disapproval. Because we have concluded that the superior court did not err in appointing a conservator, we necessarily conclude that CPS acted reasonably in filing its petition. We accordingly reject S.H.'s argument that CPS acted disloyally or breached any duty by filing the petition. ...

IV. *CONCLUSION*

We AFFIRM the order appointing the conservator. We VACATE the order imposing the conservatorship costs on CPS, and REMAND with directions that these costs be imposed on S.H.

> **"What Were They Thinking?"**
>
> As you may have discerned from the above *In re S.H.* opinion, while a mentally impaired client has a strong interest in rational decision-making, so, too, may a lawyer have an interest in a more rational decision than the client is making. That tension can be particularly acute over settlement offers, at a time when the litigation and settlement negotiations may exacerbate a client's impairment. Were the lawyers in the above case acting out of self-interest or the client's interest? How would you be sure if you were the involved lawyer?

INQUIRY

Representing Children. When a lawyer represents a child, working with a parent or other guardian empowered, or conservator appointed, to make decisions for the child, the lawyer must under Model Rule 1.14(a) keep the lawyer-client relationship as normal as reasonably possible. That duty would ordinarily mean communicating with the child about the matter sufficient for the child to express preferences, even if ultimately the guardian or conservator will decide for the child. For example, in a personal-injury case, probate rules may require that the lawyer obtain a probate-court order appointing a parent or other guardian as a conservator to make litigation decisions for the minor plaintiff, but the lawyer will still communicate with the child unless the child is so young as not to be able to understand the proceeding. Family members may be present for and help in the communications, but the lawyer still represents the child, not the family members. The lawyer remains a lawyer and does not become a guardian merely by providing the child with legal services. The lawyer must ordinarily treat the child client's information as confidential if the child can make an informed decision as to the effects of withholding that information. *See* L.A. COUNTY ETHICS OP. 504 (2000) (confidentiality applies to informed and capable child's disclosure of sexual abuse); *cf.* N.C. ETHICS OP. 98-18 (1999) (lawyer's disclosure to parent, of child's crime, is authorized if parent must make informed decision for child).

Protective Actions. Comment [5] to Model Rule 1.14 lists protective actions that a lawyer may need to take to prevent substantial physical, financial, or other harm to the client. Those actions include "consulting with family members, using a reconsideration period to permit clarification or improvement of circumstances, [and] using voluntary surrogate decisionmaking tools such as durable powers of attorney or consulting with support groups, professional services, adult-protective agencies or other individuals or entities that have the ability to protect the client." For example, a lawyer may reveal a client's suicidal ideation to family members or other health officials for the client's physical safety. *See* ALASKA ETHICS OP. 2005-1 (2005). One challenge that a lawyer faces in consulting with others telling them of the client's diminished capacity is that the consultation may adversely affect the lawyer's relationship with the client, resulting in the client's termination of the lawyer's services. If the lawyer chooses to seek a guardian or conservator's appointment, then the lawyer better hope to prevail. see In re S.H., 987 P.2d 735 (Alaska 1999) (lawyer does not commit violation when succeeding in obtaining conservator's appointment against client's instructions). Model Rule 1.14 leaves these judgments to the lawyer's sensitivity, while explicitly indicating that the lawyer should make only those disclosures that the threat to the client requires. See In re Mullins, 649 N.E.2d 1024 (Ind. 1995) (reprimand of lawyer who disclosed confidential information to news media in emergency guardianship proceeding over vegetative ward whose parents authorized termination of life support). Consider the following case illustrating the hazard of a lawyer cooperating with a client's involuntary commitment.

In re Guardianship of Henderson,
New Hampshire Supreme Court
838 A.2d 1277 (2003)

BROCK, C.J.

MEMORANDUM OPINION

The ward, Jason Henderson, appeals the decision of the Hillsborough County Probate Court (*Cloutier*, J.), appointing a guardian over his person. We reverse and remand.

When Phyllis Henderson filed a petition for guardianship over her son, the probate court appointed an attorney to represent Jason's interests in the guardianship proceeding. During his interview with court-appointed counsel, Jason dismissed the accusations in the petition as defamatory, questioned why the issue of a psychiatric examination was being raised at that time and generally challenged the accuracy of the information in the guardianship petition. In her report to the probate court, however, counsel concluded that appointing Jason's mother as his guardian would be "reasonable."

Jason, now represented by other counsel, contends that he was deprived of the full assistance of legal counsel in his defense of the involuntary guardianship proceedings. Specifically, he maintains that his appointed counsel effectively assumed the role of guardian ad litem, rather than that of legal counsel.

The right to legal counsel for any person for whom a guardianship is sought "shall be absolute and unconditional." RSA 464-A:6, I (1992). Even when an attorney is appointed to represent an allegedly incapacitated person, "the lawyer shall, as far as reasonably possible, maintain a normal client-lawyer relationship with the client." *N.H. R. Prof. Conduct* 1.14(a). Accordingly, at a minimum, the lawyer must "develop a strategy, in collaboration with the client, for solving the legal problems of the client." *N.H. R. Prof. Conduct* 1.1(c)(3).

In addition to the appointment of legal counsel, the guardianship statute permits the trial court, in its discretion, to appoint a guardian ad litem when it appears that the rights of the allegedly incapacitated person are not fully represented. *See* RSA 464-A:41, I (Supp.2002). The guardian ad litem must act "in the best interest" of the proposed ward. *See System-Wide Guardian Ad Litem Application, Certification and Practice* Rule 2.4.1(b)(3).

In creating distinct provisions for legal counsel and a guardian ad litem, the legislature acknowledged that the two roles address different overarching concerns in a guardianship proceeding. Even when representing a client with a disability, legal counsel must, as far as reasonably possible, carry out the client's decisions. *See N.H. R. Prof. Conduct* 1.14(a). The guardian ad litem, on the other hand, should "reach an independent conclusion on what is in the best interest of [the proposed ward] but, in reaching such conclusion, may, in appropriate cases, consider the preferences of [the proposed ward]." *System-Wide Guardian Ad Litem Application, Certification and Practice* Rule 2.4.2(b).

Here, counsel blurred the boundaries of the two roles. In her seven-page report to the probate court, counsel—acting as legal counsel—presents certain facts that suggest that Jason was not incapacitated, including the explicit acknowledgment that, absent a complete evaluation, "it is impossible to know whether or not Jason is incompetent." After recitation of facts that portrayed Jason as a "troubled thirty-one year old young man," however, counsel—effectively acting as guardian ad litem—ultimately concluded that "since the mother seeks temporary guardianship for the purposes of seeking care for her son, it would appear reasonable that this Court appoint her guardian of the person of her son."

In a guardianship proceeding, the proposed ward is entitled to counsel who will undertake representation of his or her legal interests. [C] Because Jason did not have the full assistance of legal counsel to attack the guardianship petition, we reverse and remand.

Reversed and remanded.

INQUIRY

Cross-Cultural Representation. The nation's diversity continues to grow. The 2000 Census showed the nation's population to be one-third Hispanic American, African American, Asian American, Native American, and other ethnic minority. To provide access to justice for all persons, lawyers must have cultural competency, meaning skills that enable lawyers to serve clients who are diverse in worldviews, belief systems, personal values, and interpersonal practices and preferences. The Clinical Legal Education Association's 2007 *Best Practices for Legal Education* lists sensitivity to the needs of diverse clients as one of five professional values. Cultural competencies cover a wide range of areas, but communication is primary. It is important how we speak and listen. Communication varies. What one client understands and appreciates might offend another client. Cognitive practices, individual and family resources, cultural references, and relationship preferences also vary. Cultural competence implies a lawyer's willingness to recognize that the lawyer has the lawyer's own cultural lens and must modify that lens to appreciate and serve others.

Communication Registers. Take an example from the area of inter-cultural communication. Language has various registers from highly informal to highly formal with everything in between. Lawyers typically converse in a consultative language register that is in the middle of the formality spectrum (neither highly formal nor informal) but still assumes a sort of transactional or barter relationship. Using a lawyer's transactional register in a family situation would, for instance, be inappropriate. Family members in many cultures communicate less formally without assuming or requiring that there be a transaction between speakers. Effective lawyers intuitively employ a range of language registers depending on the client's own cultural competence. Those registers may be intimate as between parent and child, casual as between friends, consultative in the usual professional form, formal in a ceremonial fashion, or even frozen in scripted and memorialized language. The good lawyer adjusts to the client's register, not the other way around. Language register connect closely to hidden rules and cognitive preferences within various cultures.

Sound Inter-Cultural Practices. Lawyers can increase their cultural competency by following some basic practices. *Introduce yourself* in a manner that puts the client at ease, always saying your name so as not to make you appear aloof, insular, uncaring, or arrogant. *Match the client's language register* and communicate accordingly. Not all clients share your verbal skills and interests. They may speak in indirect and generalized fashion and using frequent non-verbal assists. Avoid power struggles over language. Appreciate the client's humor.   Recognize cultural references.   Accept and employ them to contextualize and communicate solutions. *Ask why the client needs assistance* before making any assumptions.   Ask open-ended questions like, "What worries you?" or "What do you want to happen?" Respect the client's freedom and personality.   Be wary of assuming that the client has purely legal goals.   Legal goals may be enmeshed in social, political, moral, financial, familial, ethical, personal, and spiritual goals, or legal goals may be absent. *Listen to the client* rather than to your own judgment about what is important.   Let the client decide. Develop context for the client's situation—whether personal, medical, legal, family, or social. *Watch the client* for reactions as you summarize the client's goals and your advice on how to achieve them. If the client does not share your confidence in the solution you proposed, you may not have understood the client properly, or you may have assumed that the client has capabilities and resources that the client does not have. *Describe steps* in manageable components.   Think of each step that a larger task requires, and then explain those steps for the client. Assign to the client only those tasks that the client believes are clearly manageable.   Be a coach, not a commander or judge. *Confirm the plan* that you have developed.   Help clients plan and prioritize.   Finally, *express optimism and hope* about the client's situation no matter how dire it may seem to you. Building and maintaining hope is essential for clients who have few resources.   Stress the client's internal assets— perhaps the client's perseverance and tenacity, or the client's knowledge of truth, or the client's ethics and faith.   Letting the client know that you value the relationship may contribute more to the client's situation than any legal service you are able to provide.

Access to the Profession.   A representative profession is an important part of inclusive representation. It was not until the 1970s that American law schools enrolled significant numbers of women and students of color.   Harvard Law School barred women until 1950. Washington and Lee Law School barred women until 1972.   Until 1971, women lawyers represented only about 3% of the law profession. By 1980, women were 34% of J.D. candidates and 8% of the profession.   By 2000, women were 27% of the profession and approaching one-half of J.D. candidates. Women have entered private law practice and corporate counsel offices in lower relative percentages but government and legal aid offices in higher relative percentages when compared to the apportionment of male lawyers between those same sectors.   Although the legal profession is now comprised of about 30% women, women represent significantly smaller percentages of corporate general counsel, law-firm partners, and law-firm managing partners. The entry of women into the legal profession continues to influence the law in such areas as disability rights, domestic violence prevention, and workplace sexual harassment. It also influences law practice in such areas as pregnancy and parental-care leave, flexible and part-time schedules, telecommuting and contract services, and alternative careers.

Lawyers of Color. Until the 1980s, most African-American lawyers had attended one of the nation's four predominanty black law schools, as a consequence and vestige of segregation. Minority J.D.-candidate enrollment increased in absolute numbers from 5,568 in 1971 to 29,489 in 2004, the latter representing 21% of J.D. candidates. African-American lawyers increased from 1% of the profession in 1970 to 4.2% in 2000, by which time minority lawyers constitued 12.9% of the profession. Despite advances, African Americans remain significantly underrepresented in the profession when compared to the general population, as do Latinos, Native Americans, and Asian Americans. Minority underrepresentation is particularly acute at higher levels within the profession, where (for instance) in 2000 minority lawyers still comprised only 3.3% of law-firm partners. Ethnic minorities are also underrepresented in the legal profession when compared to other professions. While only 9.7% of lawyers in the United States are ethnic minorities, minorities comprise 20.8% of accountants, 24.6% of physicians, and 18.2% of college professors. *See* ABA Commission on Racial and Ethnic Diversity in the Profession, *Goal IX Report 2005-2006: The Status of Racial and Ethnic Diversity in the American Bar Association.* (ABA Feb. 2006). Just as it has in the case of women, the presence of increasing numbers of minority lawyers has influenced the law and its practice in a variety of ways through committed and effective leadership, service, and scholarship.

Increasing Access. The high cost of legal education, law-school admission standards, and law-firm recruiting and retention practices influence these unacceptable statistics. School-based mentor, pipeline, and other qualifications programs now promote early identification and preparation of minority candidates for law careers. Scholarship programs address costs. A subcommittee of the ABA's Council on Legal Education and Admission to the Bar has proposed modifying law-school accreditation standards. Law firms and corporations employing them increasingly recognize the value of diverse viewpoints and experiences among the lawyers they employ, and give increasing attention to minority-recruitment and retention data and practices. There is a long way for the legal profession yet to go, even while there has been much progress. It remains the responsibility of all lawyers to ensure that there is equal access to the law and legal profession.

Career and Professional Development

Pro bono service can be an important credit in job searches and interviews. Reflecting pro bono service on a resume can look impressive. It can also create connections between you and the firm's representatives who interview you. Shared experiences can mean a lot when establishing new relationships. If your pro bono service experience happens to match an interest or experience of your interviewer, then you have a natural point for discussion and agreement. Pro bono service also reflects your commitment to the community and to your own professional obligations and development. Not all firms value pro bono service equally, even though ABA Model Rule 6.1 Comment [11] urges that firms enable and encourage all lawyers to provide pro bono services. You can learn from websites and in informational interviews the extent to which employers take seriously a lawyer's responsibility to provide pro bono service. Consider making that investigation a part of your career and professional development.

CHAPTER XIII

AUTHORITY

Judges, Judicial Campaigns, Elections

[W]hen [God] created man, and endued him with freewill to conduct himself in all parts of life, he laid down certain immutable laws of human nature, whereby that freewill is in some degree regulated and restrained, and gave him also the faculty of reason to discover the purport of those laws.
— *William Blackstone*

OBJECTIVE: Given professional interaction with judges in various circumstances, articulate the norms, rules, and conventions governing judicial conduct.

Applicable Rules

ABA Code of Judicial Conduct Canons 1, 2, 3, and 4

Lawyers have no distinct authority of their own but know how to draw on the authority of law and judges. The quality of a lawyer's relationship to authority does a lot to define the quality of the lawyer. Lawyers who believe that they have inherent authority are so badly mistaken that their belief will distort their character and presage their downfall. Any authority that a lawyer holds is delegated authority belonging to law, rule, and judges. Among the worst of offenses that a lawyer can commit is to exceed the authority delegated to a lawyer. For example, a lawyer in some jurisdictions has court-rule authority to issue subpoenas for specific purposes and no other purposes. The lawyer who abuses that delimited power by issuing a subpoena for unauthorized ulterior purposes commits a tort, court-rule violation, and conduct-rule violation, and may also have committed a crime. The moment that a lawyer exceeds the delegated authority that lawyers occasionally hold, the lawyer becomes a petty tyrant and law breaker, not long for the profession. The prior 12 chapters have shown many of the limits on the delegated authority that lawyers hold. Those chapters have shown that whatever delegated authority a lawyer holds, the lawyer must exercise in obedience, truth, and relationship, to provide access to justice, with respect, authenticity, loyalty, and integrity.

This chapter turns from the limitation on lawyers to the limitations on the judges who on occasion delegate their authority to lawyers, by their rulings, orders, and judgments, and the proceedings they countenance. The Multistate Professional Responsibility Exam tests examinees not only on the ABA Model Rules of Professional Conduct but also on the ABA Code of Judicial Conduct. The reason is that lawyers depend on judges. Lawyers interact with judges in various ways, through pleadings, motions, and other court papers, in correspondence, in court hearings and chamber conferences, and occasionally also on the telephone or outside of court. To interact productively with judges, lawyers must know the rules and conventions that constrain judges. Woe to the lawyer who induces or tempts a judge to violate the code of judicial conduct, whether intentionally or unintentionally. Successful lawyers know the legal and ethical duties judges and fellow lawyers must fulfill and strive to conduct their practices to help judges and colleagues fulfill their duties. They are remembered and appreciatedo for doing so. To accomplish that objective, this chapter has a different organization from the prior 12 chapters. It begins with an introduction on the regulation of judges generally. It then addresses each of the several specific rules within four successive canons included in the ABA Code of Judical Conduct and most state judicial conduct codes.

A. Regulating Judges

History of Regulation. The regulation of judges in the United States draws its history from the English common law system, where kings held powers of appointment and removal over judges. Those powers made judges relatively independent from the parties whose matters they decided and the communities within which they made their decisions but still held them accountable to the reigning authorities. That federal Article III judges have lifetime appointment with removal only by impeachment was the framers' attempt to remove that last vestige of authoritarian influence from the decisions of judges. Much of judicial regulation today retains that character of attempting to isolate and free judges from outside influence. Public disenchantment with the way in which judicial decisions protected property and corporate interests in the latter part of the 19th century and early part of the 20th century led the American Bar Association to adopt the ABA Canons of Judicial Ethics as a guide to salutary judicial behavior, urging judges to be learned and scientific rather than partial. The Canons were not a set of rules or regulations.

ABA Code of Judicial Conduct.   The American Bar Association adopted the ABA Model Code of Judicial Conduct in 1972 and made substantial amendments to it in 1990 before finally adopting the ABA Code of Judicial Conduct in 2007.   The current ABA Code of Judicial Conduct does regulate judicial conduct, meaning that judges who violate similar state versions may suffer discipline up to removal from office. *See, e.g.,* Moore v. Judicial Inquiry Commn., 891 So.2d 848 (Ala. 2004) (removal of state supreme court justice for disobeying federal order).   Some state versions, though, retain an aspirational "should" language rather than the mandatory "shall" used in the ABA Code. *See, e.g.,* DELAWARE CODE OF JUDICIAL CONDUCT.   Despite the ABA Code's mandatory language, as in the case of the ABA Model Rules of Professional Conduct for lawyers, the ABA Code of Judicial Conduct has no direct regulatory effect on any judges.   A jurisdiction must adopt its own judicial code regulating its own judges.   The great majority of states have adopted the ABA Code of Judicial Conduct with few changes.   In that respect, the ABA Code of Judicial Conduct is different from the ABA Model Rules of Professional Conduct, where quite a few states have retained portions of the earlier ABA Code of Professional Responsibility or modified more heavily the ABA Model Rules.   While subject to the code of judicial conduct adopted in their jurisdiction, judges may also be subject to state statutes, state court administrative rules, and state and local court rules. *See, e.g.,* 28 U.S.C. §144 (recusal for personal bias);   28 U.S.C. §455 (recusal for partiality);   MICH. CT. R. 2.003 (recusal for partiality).

Organization of the ABA Code.   The ABA Code of Judicial Conduct, like the ABA Model Rules of Professional Conduct, begins with a long, eloquent, and meaningful Preamble articulating the meaning and purpose of the professional role.   The Code then includes a Scope provision describing the organization of the Code.   The Code also includes introductory Terminology and Application provision.   As to the individual rules, like the Model Rules, the Code contains mandatory provisions ("a judge shall") the violation of which could result in discipline.   It also includes permissive statements ("a judge may") that authorize or condone certain conduct.   The Code also contains aspirational statements ("a judge should").   The Code groups these provisions into four Canons, each of a common theme. The text below reproduces similar state versions of each of the Code's provisions. First, though, read a similar state version of the ABA Code of Judicial Conduct's Preamble.   Judges occupy a special place in the justice system. See how the Preamble articulates that place while connecting it with the expectations we hold for a judge.

> **WYOMING CODE OF JUDICIAL CONDUCT: Preamble.**
> [1] An independent, fair and impartial judiciary is indispensable to our system of justice. The United States legal system is based upon the principle that an independent, impartial, and competent judiciary, composed of men and women of integrity, will interpret and apply the law that governs our society. Thus, the judiciary plays a central role in preserving the principles of justice and the rule of law. Inherent in all the Rules contained in this Code are the precepts that judges, individually and collectively, must respect and honor the judicial office as a public trust and strive to maintain and enhance confidence in the legal system.
> [2] Judges should maintain the dignity of judicial office at all times, and avoid both impropriety and the appearance of impropriety in their professional and personal lives. They should aspire at all times to conduct that ensures the greatest possible public confidence in their independence, impartiality, integrity, and competence.
> [3] The Wyoming Code of Judicial Conduct establishes standards for the ethical conduct of judges and judicial candidates. It is not intended as an exhaustive guide for the conduct of judges and judicial candidates, who are governed in their judicial and personal conduct by general ethical standards as well as by the Code. The Code is intended, however, to provide guidance and assist judges in maintaining the highest standards of judicial and personal conduct, and to provide a basis for regulating their conduct through disciplinary agencies.

Scope. Conduct rules are only one fixed place in a constellation of obligations professionals owe to others, the profession, the state and nation, and themselves. The ABA Code of Judicial Conduct's Scope provision helps judges understand what that place is. Read a similar state version for its outline of how the judicial conduct rules operate next to constitutions, statutes, the common law, and other law, rules, and regulations. Does it make you want to be a judge? Does it help you respect judges more than you did previously?

> **WYOMING CODE OF JUD. CONDUCT: Scope.**
> [1] The Wyoming Code of Judicial Conduct consists of four Canons, numbered Rules under each Canon, and Comments that generally follow and explain each Rule. Scope and Terminology sections provide additional guidance in interpreting and applying the Code. An Application section establishes when the various Rules apply to a judge or judicial candidate.
> [2] The Canons state overarching principles of judicial ethics that all judges must observe. Although a judge may be disciplined only for violating a Rule, the Canons provide important guidance in interpreting the Rules. Where a Rule contains a permissive term, such as "may" or "should," the conduct being addressed is committed to the personal and professional discretion of the judge or candidate in question, and no disciplinary action should be taken for action or inaction within the bounds of such discretion.

[3] The Comments that accompany the Rules serve two functions. First, they provide guidance regarding the purpose, meaning, and proper application of the Rules. They contain explanatory material and, in some instances, provide examples of permitted or prohibited conduct. Comments neither add to nor subtract from the binding obligations set forth in the Rules. Therefore, when a Comment contains the term "must," it does not mean that the Comment itself is binding or enforceable; it signifies that the Rule in question, properly understood, is obligatory as to the conduct at issue.

[4] Second, the Comments identify aspirational goals for judges. To implement fully the principles of this Code as articulated in the Canons, judges should strive to exceed the standards of conduct established by the Rules, holding themselves to the highest ethical standards and seeking to achieve those aspirational goals, thereby enhancing the dignity of the judicial office.

[5] The Rules of the Wyoming Code of Judicial Conduct are rules of reason that should be applied consistent with constitutional requirements, statutes, other court rules, and decisional law, and with due regard for all relevant circumstances. The Rules should not be interpreted to impinge upon the essential independence of judges in making judicial decisions.

[6] Although the black letter of the Rules is binding and enforceable, it is not contemplated that every transgression will result in the imposition of discipline. Whether discipline should be imposed should be determined through a reasonable and reasoned application of the Rules, and should depend upon factors such as the seriousness of the transgression, the facts and circumstances that existed at the time of the transgression, the extent of any pattern of improper activity, whether there have been previous violations, and the effect of the improper activity upon the judicial system or others.

[7] The Code is not designed or intended as a basis for civil or criminal liability. Neither is it intended to be the basis for litigants to seek collateral remedies against each other or to obtain tactical advantages in proceedings before a court.

Civil and Criminal Liability. Part [7] of the ABA Code's Scope provision makes clear that the judicial conduct rules are not standards for civil liability. In any case, judges have absolute judicial immunity from civil liability. *See, e.g.,* Sherman v. Almeida, 747 A.2d 470 (R.I. 2000). On the other hand, judges are subject to the criminal codes. Judges can and do commit crimes for which they receive punishment under criminal codes.

Terminology. Like any well-drafted code, the ABA Code of Judicial Conduct contains words and phrases that the reader should understand to be terms of art. The Terminology section of the Code defines those terms of art. Skim a state version of the Code's Terminology section for some of its more unusual terms of art fitted to a judicial rather than lawyer code. Can you anticipate from this key terminology some of the issues the Code's substantive provisions address? Can you guess from the terminology what challenges judges face?

WYOMING CODE OF JUD. CONDUCT: **Terminology.**
Each time any term listed below is used in a Rule in its defined sense, it is followed by an asterisk (*).
"Appropriate authority" means the authority having responsibility for initiation of disciplinary process in connection with the violation to be reported. See Rule 2.15.
"Contribution" means both financial and in-kind contributions, such as goods, professional or volunteer services, advertising, and other types of assistance, which, if obtained by the recipient otherwise, would require a financial expenditure. See Rules, 3.7, and 4.1.
"De minimis," in the context of interests pertaining to disqualification of a judge, means an insignificant interest that could not raise a reasonable question regarding the judge's impartiality. See Rule 2.11.
"Domestic partner" means a person with whom another person maintains a household and an intimate relationship, other than a person to whom he or she is legally married. See Rules 2.11, 3.13, and 3.14.
"Economic interest" means ownership of more than a de minimis legal or equitable interest. Except for situations in which the judge participates in the management of such a legal or equitable interest, or the interest could be substantially affected by the outcome of a proceeding before a judge, it does not include:
(1) an interest in the individual holdings within a mutual or common investment fund;
(2) an interest in securities held by an educational, religious, charitable, fraternal, or civic organization in which the judge or the judge's spouse, domestic partner, parent, or child serves as a director, an officer, an advisor, or other participant;
(3) a deposit in a financial institution or deposits or proprietary interests the judge may maintain as a member of a mutual savings association or credit union, or similar proprietary interests; or
(4) an interest in the issuer of government securities held by the judge.
See Rules 1.3, 2.11, and 3.2.
"Fiduciary" includes relationships such as executor, administrator, trustee, or guardian. See Rules 2.11, 3.2, and 3.8.
"Impartial," "impartiality," and "impartially" mean absence of bias or prejudice in favor of, or against, particular parties or classes of parties, as well as maintenance of an open mind in considering issues that may come before a judge. See Canons 1, 2, and 4, and Rules 1.2, 2.2, 2. 10, 2.11, 2.13, 3.1, 3.12, 3.13, and 4.2.
"Impending matter" is a matter that is imminent or expected to occur in the near future. See Rules 2.9, 2.10, 3.13, and 4.2.
"Impropriety" includes conduct that violates the law, court rules, or provisions of this Code, and conduct that undermines a judge's independence, integrity, or impartiality. See Canon 1 and Rule 1.2.
"Independence" means a judge's freedom from influence or controls other than those established by law. See Canons 1 and 4, and Rules 1.2, 3.1, 3.12, 3.13, and 4.2.
"Integrity" means probity, fairness, honesty, uprightness, and soundness of character. See Canons 1 and 4, and Rules 1.2, 3.1, 3.12, 3.13, and 4.2.

"Judicial candidate" means any person, including a sitting judge, who has expressed interest in or is seeking selection for or retention in a judicial office. A person becomes a judicial candidate when he or she submits an expression of interest or applies for a judicial office, or, where the process does not require an expression of interest or an application, when he or she engages in communications relating to his or her possible selection for a judicial office. See Rules 2.11, 4.1, and 4.2.

"Knowingly," "knowledge," "known," "knows," and "know" mean actual knowledge of the fact in question. A person's knowledge may be inferred from circumstances. See Rules 1.3, 2.11, 2.15, 2.16, 3.2, 3.6, and 4.2.

"Law" encompasses court rules as well as statutes, constitutional provisions, and decisional law. See Rules 1.1, 2.1, 2.2, 2.6, 2.7, 2.9, 3.1, 3.9, 3.12, 3.13, 3.14, 3.15, 4.1, and 4.4.

"Member of the judge's family" means a spouse, domestic partner, child, grandchild, parent, grandparent, or other relative or person with whom the judge maintains a close familial relationship. See Rules 3.7, 3.8, 3.10, and 3.11.

"Member of a judge's family residing in the judge's household" means any relative of a judge by blood or marriage, or a person treated by a judge as a member of the judge's family, who resides in the judge's household. See Rules 2.11 and 3.13.

"Nonjudicial candidate" means any person, including a sitting judge, who is seeking selection for nonjudicial office by election or appointment. A person becomes a candidate for nonjudicial office as soon as he or she makes a public announcement of candidacy, declares or files as a candidate with the election or appointment authority, authorizes or, where permitted, engages in solicitation or acceptance of contributions or support, or is nominated for election or appointment to office. See Rule 4.4.

"Nonpublic information" means information that is not available to the public. Nonpublic information may include, but is not limited to, information that is sealed by statute or court order or impounded or communicated in camera, and information offered in grand jury proceedings, presentencing reports, juvenile cases, psychiatric reports, or other confidential reports. See Rule 3.5.

"Pending matter" is a matter that has commenced. A matter continues to be pending through any appellate process until final disposition. See Rules 2.9, 2.10, 3.13, and 4.2.

"Political organization" means a political party or other group sponsored by or affiliated with a political party or candidate, the principal purpose of which is to further the election or appointment of candidates for political office. See Rule 4.1.

"Third degree of relationship" includes the following persons: great-grandparent, grandparent, parent, uncle, aunt, brother, sister, child, grandchild, great-grandchild, nephew, and niece. See Rule 2.11.

Application. There are judges, and then there are judges. To which judges—full-time judges, part-time judges, retired judges who serve on recall, candidates for judgeships, etc.—does the ABA Code of Judicial Conduct apply? Well, to no one, actually. The real question is to whom state judicial codes apply. State versions of the ABA Code's Application section describe to whom the state judicial code applies. Consider a state version below that addresses the most recognizable judicial roles, while appreciating that the ABA Code of Judicial Conduct addresses additional less-recognized judicial roles.

WYOMING CODE OF JUD. CONDUCT: Application.

The Application section establishes when the various Rules apply to a judge or judicial candidate.

I. Applicability of this Code

(A) The provisions of the Code apply to all full-time judges. Part II of this section identifies those provisions that apply to part-time judges. Canon 4 applies to judicial candidates.

(B) A judge, within the meaning of this Code, is anyone who is authorized to perform judicial functions, including but not limited to, justices of the supreme court, district court judges and commissioners, circuit court judges and magistrates, special masters, referees, municipal judges and alternate municipal judges, and a retired judge, commissioner or magistrate who has been given a general or special appointment to hear cases by the Wyoming Supreme Court, but shall not include administrative hearing officers or other members of the administrative law judiciary.

II. Part-Time Judge

A judge who serves on a part-time basis by retention election or under a continuing appointment, including a retired judge who has been given a general or special appointment to hear cases by the Wyoming Supreme Court,

(A) is not required to comply:

(1) with Rules 2.10(A) and 2.10(B) (Judicial Statements on Pending and Impending Cases), except for matters heard or pending before him or her while serving as a judge; or

(2) at any time with Rules 3.4 (Appointments to Governmental Positions), 3.8 (Appointments to Fiduciary Positions), 3.9 (Service as Arbitrator or Mediator), 3.10 (Practice of Law), 3.11 (Financial, Business, or Remunerative Activities), 3.14 (Reimbursement of Expenses and Waivers of Fees or Charges), 3.15 (Reporting Requirements), 4.1 (Political and Campaign Activities of Judges and Judicial Candidates in General), 4.2 (Political and Campaign Activities of Judicial Candidates in Public Retention Elections), 4. 3 (Activities of Candidates for Appointive Judicial Office), and 4.4 (Activities of Judges Who Become Nonjudicial Candidates); and

(B) shall not act as a lawyer in a proceeding in which the judge has served as a judge or in any other proceeding related thereto.

III. Time for Compliance

A person to whom this Code becomes applicable shall comply immediately with its provisions, except that those judges to whom Rules 3.8 (Appointments to Fiduciary Positions) and 3.11 (Financial, Business, or Remunerative Activities) apply shall comply with those Rules as soon as reasonably possible, but in no event later than one year after the Code becomes applicable to the judge.

B. Promoting Independence

Canon 1. Consistent with the history reflected above, the ABA Code of Judicial Conduct makes judicial independence the primary subject of its Canon 1. Promoting judicial independence first involves complying with the law rather than following judicial whim or submitting to party or non-party influence. Judicial independence also both depends on public confidence and promotes public confidence. If the public does not trust the judiciary, it cannot perform. Trust comes from a public sense that judges are making independent decisions based on law. As you read the following provisions from a similar state version of the ABA Code of Judicial Conduct's Canon 1, see if you can discern which provisions are specific enough that state officials might discipline a judge for violating them. See, too, if you can articulate ways in which a judge might violate those provisions—and ways in which a lawyer might intentionally or unintentionally induce a judge to do so. Remember, your challenge is to ensure that you help a judge comply at all times with the judge's judicial obligations and that you not be a witting or unwitting accomplice to judicial violations.

> **WYOMING CODE OF JUDICIAL CONDUCT: Canon 1. A Judge Shall Uphold and Promote Independence, Integrity, and Impartiality of the Judiciary, and Shall Avoid Impropriety and the Appearance of Impropriety.**
>
> **Rule 1.1: Compliance with the Law.**
> A judge shall comply with the law,* including the Code of Judicial Conduct.
>
> **Rule 1.2: Promoting Confidence in the Judiciary.**
> A judge shall act at all times in a manner that promotes public confidence in the independence,* integrity,* and impartiality* of the judiciary, and shall avoid impropriety* and the appearance of impropriety.*
>
> **Rule 1.3: Avoiding Abuse of the Prestige of Judicial Office.**
> A judge shall not abuse the prestige of judicial office to advance the personal or economic interests* of the judge or others, or knowingly* allow others to do so.

I N Q U I R Y

Evident Partiality. What do you think it might mean for a judge to exhibit partiality toward a party? Judges evaluate evidence and arguments as a matter of their judicial responsibilities. They are constantly making judgments that one party or another might perceive to reflect partiality when it is instead an evaluation, however accurate or inaccurate, of the arguments and evidence. Those evaluations are not partiality. *See, e.g.,* United States v. Hefferon, 314 F.3d 211 (5th Cir. 2002) (criticizing counsel as making unsupported assertions is not partiality). Judging requires taking sides at some point. Adverse rulings are not enough to show partiality. *See* State v. Stockert, 684 N.W.2d 605 (N.D. 2004). Judges may even question witnesses under FED. R. EVID. 614(b) and similar state rules, *see, e.g.,* Logue v. Dore, 103 F.3d 1040 (1st Cir. 1997), which is an act that parties might easily misconstrue to be adversarial and partial in nature. Judges, though, must take care not to so aggressively cross-examine a witness as to reflect partiality against the party who offers the witness. *See* United States v. Godwin, 272 F.3d 659 (4th Cir. 2001). They should also not comment in front of the jury on a witness's credibility when the jury has the prerogative to make credibility judgments. *Cf.* Navellier v. Sletten, 262 F.3d 923 (9th Cir. 2001) (curative instruction cures defect).

C. Upholding Law

Canon 2. A judge's primary obligation is to uphold the law. Upholding the law sounds like both an obvious and simple thing, except for vagaries in the law itself. Yet upholding the law can simultaneously take several subtle sensitivities and courageous commitments. Judge must maintain a certain decorum, for example. *See, e.g.,* In re Schapiro, 845 So.2d 170 (Fla. 2003) (public reprimand for bullying lawyers appearing before respondent judge); In re Barr, 13 S.W.2d 525 (Tex. Rev. Trib. 1998) (removal for referring to female lawyers as "babes" and making other sexist comments). Upholding the law also requires sound administration, dependent on sound judicial temperament. *See* Fletcher v. Commission on Judicial Performance, 968 P.2d 958 (Cal. 1998) (removal for lack of judicial temperament). Notice, for instance, how Rule 2.3 requires the judge not only to refrain from bias but also to require lawyers and court staff to do so. Upholding the law can also take refraining from specific behaviors, for example, unauthorized ex parte communications. Pay special attention to Rule 2.9, a provision easily offended. Also, note Rule 2.11 on judicial disqualification. The ABA Code of Judicial Conduct now includes additional detail on that subject, although states have not yet widely adopted those revisions. Rules 2.14 and 2.15 should also interest the practitioner. Just as you did while reading Canon 1 above, read a similar state version of Canon 2 below, identifying which rules are specific enough that a judge could violate them, what concern each rule addresses, and what conduct might constitute a rule violation. A significant recent Supreme Court decision addressing when the due process clause requires a judge's recusal follows, along with a state court case illustrating recusal for evident bias.

MINNESOTA CODE OF JUDICIAL CONDUCT: Canon 2. A Judge Shall Perform the Duties of Judicial Office Impartially, Competently, and Diligently.

Rule 2.1. Giving Precedence to the Duties of Judicial Office.
The duties of judicial office, as prescribed by law,* shall take precedence over all of a judge's personal and extrajudicial activities.

Rule 2.2. Impartiality and Fairness.
A judge shall uphold and apply the law,* and shall perform all duties of judicial office fairly and impartially.*

Rule 2.3. Bias, Prejudice, and Harassment.
(A) A judge shall perform the duties of judicial office, including administrative duties, without bias or prejudice.
(B) A judge shall not, in the performance of judicial duties, by words or conduct manifest bias or prejudice, or engage in harassment, including but not limited to bias, prejudice, or harassment based upon race, sex, gender, religion, national origin, ethnicity, disability, age, sexual orientation, marital status, socioeconomic status, or political affiliation, and shall not permit court staff, court officials, or others subject to the judge's direction and control to do so.
(C) A judge shall require lawyers in proceedings before the court to refrain from manifesting bias or prejudice, or engaging in harassment, based upon attributes including but not limited to race, sex, gender, religion, national origin, ethnicity, disability, age, sexual orientation, marital status, socioeconomic status, or political affiliation, against parties, witnesses, lawyers, or others.
(D) The restrictions of paragraphs (B) and (C) do not preclude judges or lawyers from making legitimate reference to the listed factors, or similar factors, when they are relevant to an issue in a proceeding.

Rule 2.4. External Influences on Judicial Conduct.
(A) A judge shall not be swayed by public clamor or fear of criticism.
(B) A judge shall not permit family, social, political, financial, or other interests or relationships to influence the judge's judicial conduct or judgment.
(C) A judge shall not convey or permit others to convey the impression that any person or organization is in a position to influence the judge.

Rule 2.5. Competence, Diligence, and Cooperation.
(A) A judge shall perform judicial and administrative duties competently, promptly, efficiently and diligently.
(B) A judge shall cooperate with other judges and court officials in the administration of court business.

Rule 2.6. Ensuring the Right to Be Heard.
(A) A judge shall accord to every person who has a legal interest in a proceeding, or that person's lawyer, the right to be heard according to law.*

(B) A judge may encourage parties to a proceeding and their lawyers to settle matters in dispute but shall not act in a manner that coerces any party into settlement.

Rule 2.7. Responsibility to Decide.

A judge shall hear and decide matters assigned to the judge, except when disqualification is required by Rule 2.11 or other law.*

Rule 2.8. Decorum, Demeanor, and Communication with Jurors.

(A) A judge shall require order and decorum in proceedings before the court.

(B) A judge shall be patient, dignified, and courteous to litigants, jurors, witnesses, lawyers, court staff, court officials, and others with whom the judge deals in an official capacity, and shall require similar conduct of lawyers, court staff, court officials, and others subject to the judge's direction and control.

© A judge shall not commend or criticize jurors for their verdict other than in a court order or opinion in a proceeding.

Rule 2.9. Ex Parte Communications.

(A) A judge shall not initiate, permit, or consider ex parte communications, or consider other communications made to the judge outside the presence of the parties or their lawyers, concerning a pending* or impending matter,* except as follows:

(1) When circumstances require it, ex parte communication for scheduling, administrative, or emergency purposes, which does not address substantive matters or issues on the merits, is permitted, provided:

(a) the judge reasonably believes that no party will gain a procedural, substantive, or tactical advantage as a result of the ex parte communication; and

(b) the judge makes provision promptly to notify all other parties of the substance of the ex parte communication, and gives the parties an opportunity to respond.

(2) A judge may obtain the written advice of a disinterested expert on the law* applicable to a proceeding before the judge, if the judge gives advance notice to the parties of the person to be consulted and the subject matter of the advice to be solicited, and affords the parties a reasonable opportunity to object and respond to the notice and to the advice received.

(3) A judge may consult with court staff and court officials whose functions are to aid the judge in carrying out the judge's adjudicative responsibilities, or with other judges, provided the judge makes reasonable efforts to avoid receiving factual information that is not part of the record, and does not abrogate the responsibility personally to decide the matter.

(4) A judge may, with the consent of the parties, confer separately with the parties and their lawyers in an effort to settle matters pending* before the judge.

(5) A judge may initiate, permit, or consider any ex parte communication when expressly authorized by law* to do so.

(B) If a judge inadvertently receives an unauthorized ex parte communication bearing upon the substance of a matter, the communication should be noted as received and returned to the sender without review by the judge. If a judge inadvertently reviews an unauthorized ex parte communication bearing upon the substance of a matter, the judge shall make provision to notify the parties promptly of the substance of the communication and provide the parties with an opportunity to respond.

(C) A judge shall not investigate facts in a matter independently, and shall consider only the evidence presented and any facts that may properly be judicially noticed.

(D) A judge shall make reasonable efforts, including providing appropriate supervision, to ensure that this Rule is not violated by court staff, court officials, and others subject to the judge's direction and control.

Rule 2.10. Judicial Statements on Pending and Impending Cases.

(A) A judge shall not make any public statement that might reasonably be expected to affect the outcome or impair the fairness of a matter pending* or impending* in any court, or make any nonpublic statement that might substantially interfere with a fair trial or hearing.

(B) A judge shall not, in connection with cases, controversies, or issues that are likely to come before the court, make pledges, promises, or commitments that are inconsistent with the impartial* performance of the adjudicative duties of judicial office.

© A judge shall require court staff, court officials, and others subject to the judge's direction and control to refrain from making statements that the judge would be prohibited from making by paragraphs (A) and (B).

(D) Notwithstanding the restrictions in paragraph (A), a judge may make public statements in the course of official duties, may explain court procedures, and may comment on any proceeding in which the judge is a litigant in a personal capacity.

(E) Subject to the requirements of paragraph (A), a judge may respond directly or through a third party to allegations in the media or elsewhere concerning the judge's conduct in a matter.

Rule 2.11. Disqualification.

(A) A judge shall disqualify himself or herself in any proceeding in which the judge's impartiality* might reasonably be questioned, including but not limited to the following circumstances:

(1) The judge has a personal bias or prejudice concerning a party or a party's lawyer, or personal knowledge of facts that are in dispute in the proceeding.

(2) The judge knows that the judge, the judge's spouse, a person with whom the judge has an intimate relationship, a member of the judge's household, or a person within the third degree of relationship to any of them, or the spouse or person in an intimate relationship with such a person is:

(a) a party to the proceeding, or an officer, director, general partner, managing member, or trustee of a party;

(b) acting as a lawyer in the proceeding;

© a person who has more than a de minimis interest that could be substantially affected by the proceeding; or

(d) likely to be a material witness in the proceeding.

(3) The judge knows that he or she, individually or as a fiduciary, or the judge's spouse, parent, child, or any other member of the judge's family residing in the judge's household, a person with whom the judge has an intimate relationship, or any other member of the judge's household, has an

economic interest in the subject matter in controversy or in a party to the proceeding.

(4) The judge, while a judge or a judicial candidate, has made a public statement, other than in a court proceeding, judicial decision, or opinion, that commits or appears to commit the judge to reach a particular result or rule in a particular way in the proceeding or controversy.

(5) The judge:

(a) served as a lawyer in the matter in controversy, or was associated with a lawyer who participated substantially as a lawyer in the matter during such association;

(b) served in governmental employment, and in such capacity participated personally and substantially as a lawyer or public official concerning the proceeding, or has publicly expressed in such capacity an opinion concerning the merits of the particular matter in controversy;

(c) was a material witness concerning the matter; or

(d) previously presided as a judge over the matter in another court.

(B) A judge shall keep informed about the judge's personal and fiduciary economic interests, and make a reasonable effort to keep informed about the personal economic interests of the judge's spouse, a person with whom the judge has an intimate relationship, and any member of the judge's household.

(C) A judge subject to disqualification under this Rule, other than for bias or prejudice under paragraph (A)(1), may disclose on the record the basis of the judge's disqualification and may ask the parties and their lawyers to consider, outside the presence of the judge and court personnel, whether to waive disqualification. If, following the disclosure, the parties and lawyers agree, without participation by the judge or court personnel, that the judge should not be disqualified, the judge may participate in the proceeding. The agreement shall be incorporated into the record of the proceeding.

Rule 2.12. Supervisory Duties.

(A) A judge shall require court staff, court officials, and others subject to the judge's direction and control to act in a manner consistent with the judge's obligations under this Code.

(B) A judge with supervisory authority for the performance of other judges shall take reasonable measures to ensure that those judges properly discharge their judicial responsibilities, including the prompt disposition of matters before them.

Rule 2.13. Administrative Appointments.

(A) In making administrative appointments, a judge:

(1) shall exercise the power of appointment impartially* and on the basis of merit; and

(2) shall avoid nepotism, favoritism, and unnecessary appointments.

(B) A judge shall not approve compensation of appointees beyond the fair value of services rendered.

Rule 2.14. Disability and Impairment.

A judge having a reasonable belief that the performance of a lawyer or another judge is impaired by drugs or alcohol, or by a mental, emotional, or physical condition, shall take appropriate action, which may include a confidential referral to a lawyer or judicial assistance program.

Rule 2.15. Responding to Judicial and Lawyer Misconduct.

(A) A judge having knowledge* that another judge has committed a violation of this Code that raises a substantial question regarding the judge's honesty, trustworthiness, or fitness as a judge in other respects shall inform the appropriate authority.*

(B) A judge having knowledge* that a lawyer has committed a violation of the Rules of Professional Conduct that raises a substantial question regarding the lawyer's honesty, trustworthiness, or fitness as a lawyer in other respects shall inform the appropriate authority.*

(C) A judge who receives credible information indicating a substantial likelihood that another judge has committed a violation of this Code shall take appropriate action.

(D) A judge who receives credible information indicating a substantial likelihood that a lawyer has committed a violation of the Rules of Professional Conduct shall take appropriate action.

Rule 2.16. Cooperation with Disciplinary Authorities.

(A) A judge shall cooperate and be candid and honest with judicial and lawyer disciplinary agencies.

(B) A judge shall not retaliate, directly or indirectly, against a person known* or suspected to have assisted or cooperated with an investigation of a judge or a lawyer.

_____

Caperton v. A.T. Massey Coal Co.,

United States Supreme Court
_ U.S. _, 129 S.Ct. 2252 (2009)

Justice KENNEDY delivered the opinion of the Court.

In this case the Supreme Court of Appeals of West Virginia reversed a trial court judgment, which had entered a jury verdict of $50 million. Five justices heard the case, and the vote to reverse was 3 to 2. The question presented is whether the Due Process Clause of the Fourteenth Amendment was violated when one of the justices in the majority denied a recusal motion. The basis for the motion was that the justice had received campaign contributions in an extraordinary amount from, and through the efforts of, the board chairman and principal officer of the corporation found liable for the damages.

Under our precedents there are objective standards that require recusal when "the probability of actual bias on the part of the judge or decisionmaker is too high to be constitutionally tolerable." Withrow v. Larkin, 421 U.S. 35, 47[] (1975). Applying those precedents, we find that, in all the circumstances of this case, due process requires recusal.

I

In August 2002 a West Virginia jury returned a verdict that found respondents A.T. Massey Coal Co. and its affiliates (hereinafter Massey) liable for fraudulent misrepresentation, concealment, and tortious interference with existing contractual relations. The jury awarded petitioners ... Caperton ... the sum of $50 million in compensatory and punitive damages. ...

Don Blankenship is Massey's chairman, chief executive officer, and president. After the verdict but before the appeal, West Virginia held its 2004 judicial elections. Knowing the Supreme Court of Appeals of West Virginia would consider the appeal in the case, Blankenship decided to support an attorney who sought to replace Justice McGraw. Justice McGraw was a candidate for reelection to that court. The attorney who sought to replace him was Brent Benjamin.

In addition to contributing the $1,000 statutory maximum to Benjamin's campaign committee, Blankenship donated almost $2.5 million to "And For The Sake Of The Kids," a political organization formed under 26 U.S.C. §527. The §527 organization opposed McGraw and supported Benjamin. [C] Blankenship's donations accounted for more than two-thirds of the total funds it raised. [C] This was not all. Blankenship spent, in addition, just over $500,000 on independent expenditures—for direct mailings and letters soliciting donations as well as television and newspaper advertisements—"'to support ... Brent Benjamin.'" [C]

To provide some perspective, Blankenship's $3 million in contributions were more than the total amount spent by all other Benjamin supporters and three times the amount spent by Benjamin's own committee. [C] Caperton contends that Blankenship spent $1 million more than the total amount spent by the campaign committees of both candidates combined. [C]

Benjamin won. ...

In October 2005, before Massey filed its petition for appeal in West Virginia's highest court, Caperton moved to disqualify now-Justice Benjamin under the Due Process Clause and the West Virginia Code of Judicial Conduct, based on the conflict caused by Blankenship's campaign involvement. Justice Benjamin denied the motion in April 2006. He indicated that he "carefully considered the bases and accompanying exhibits proffered by the movants." But he found "no objective information ... to show that this Justice has a bias for or against any litigant, that this Justice has prejudged the matters which comprise this litigation, or that this Justice will be anything but fair and impartial." [C] In December 2006 Massey filed its petition for appeal to challenge the adverse jury verdict. The West Virginia Supreme Court of Appeals granted review.

In November 2007 that court reversed the $50 million verdict against Massey. ...

Caperton sought rehearing, and the parties moved for disqualification of three of the five justices who decided the appeal.

Photos had surfaced of Justice Maynard vacationing with Blankenship in the French Riviera while the case was pending. [C] Justice Maynard granted Caperton's recusal motion. On the other side Justice Starcher granted Massey's recusal motion, apparently based on his public criticism of Blankenship's role in the 2004 elections. In his recusal memorandum Justice Starcher urged Justice Benjamin to recuse himself as well. He noted that "Blankenship's bestowal of his personal wealth, political tactics, and 'friendship' have created a cancer in the affairs of this Court." [C] Justice Benjamin declined Justice Starcher's suggestion and denied Caperton's recusal motion.

The court granted rehearing. Justice Benjamin, now in the capacity of acting chief justice, selected Judges Cookman and Fox to replace the recused justices. Caperton moved a third time for disqualification... . Caperton ... included the results of a public opinion poll, which indicated that over 67% of West Virginians doubted Justice Benjamin would be fair and impartial. Justice Benjamin again refused to withdraw... .

In April 2008 a divided court again reversed the jury verdict, and again it was a 3-to-2 decision. ...

We granted certiorari. [C]

II

... [T]he Court has recognized ... [that] "most matters relating to judicial disqualification [do] not rise to a constitutional level." FTC v. Cement Institute, 333 U.S. 683, 702[] (1948). The early and leading case on the subject is Tumey v. Ohio, 273 U.S. 510, [523] (1927). There, the Court stated that "matters of kinship, personal bias, state policy, remoteness of interest, would seem generally to be matters merely of legislative discretion." [C]

The *Tumey* Court concluded that the Due Process Clause incorporated the common-law rule that a judge must recuse himself when he has "a direct, personal, substantial, pecuniary interest" in a case. *Ibid.* This rule reflects the maxim that "[n]o man is allowed to be a judge in his own cause; because his interest would certainly bias his judgment, and, not improbably, corrupt his integrity." The Federalist No. 10, p. 59 (J. Cooke ed.1961) (J. Madison); [c]. ...

... [T]he Court has identified additional instances which, as an objective matter, require recusal. These are circumstances "in which experience teaches that the probability of actual bias on the part of the judge or decisionmaker is too high to be constitutionally tolerable." Withrow[v. Larkin], 421 U.S.[35,] 47[(1975)]. ...

The first involved the emergence of local tribunals where a judge had a financial interest in the outcome of a case, although the interest was less than what would have been considered personal or direct at common law. ...

This was the problem addressed in *Tumey*. There, the mayor of a village had the authority to sit as a judge (with no jury) to try those accused of violating a state law prohibiting the possession of alcoholic beverages. Inherent in this structure were two potential conflicts. First, the mayor received a salary supplement for performing judicial duties, and the funds for that compensation derived from the fines assessed in a case. No fines were assessed upon acquittal. The mayor-judge thus received a salary supplement only if he convicted the defendant. 273 U.S., at 520[]. Second, sums from the criminal fines were deposited to the village's general treasury fund for village improvements and repairs. *Id.* at 522[].

The Court held that the Due Process Clause required disqualification "both because of [the mayor-judge's] direct pecuniary interest in the outcome, and because of his official motive to convict and to graduate the fine to help the financial needs of the village." *Id.* at 535[]. ... The Court articulated the controlling principle: "Every procedure which would offer a possible temptation to the average man as a judge to forget the burden of proof required to convict the defendant, or which might lead him not to hold the balance nice, clear and true between the State and the accused, denies the latter due process of law." *Ibid.* The Court was thus concerned with more than the traditional common-law prohibition on direct pecuniary interest. It was also concerned with a more general concept of interests that tempt adjudicators to disregard neutrality.

This concern with conflicts resulting from financial incentives was elaborated in Ward v. Monroeville, 409 U.S. 57[] (1972), which invalidated a conviction in another mayor's court. In *Monroeville*, unlike in *Tumey*, the mayor received no money; instead, the fines the mayor assessed went to the town's general fisc. ... The principle, instead, turned on the "'possible temptation'" the mayor might face; the mayor's "executive responsibilities for village finances may make him partisan to maintain the high level of contribution [to those finances] from the mayor's court." *Ibid.* As the Court reiterated in another case that Term, "the [judge's] financial stake need not be as direct or positive as it appeared to be in *Tumey*." Gibson v. Berryhill, 411 U.S. 564, 579[] (1973).... .

The second instance requiring recusal that was not discussed at common law emerged in the criminal contempt context, where a judge had no pecuniary interest in the case but was challenged because of a conflict arising from his participation in an earlier proceeding. ...

III

Based on the principles described in these cases we turn to the issue before us. This problem arises in the context of judicial elections, a framework not presented in the precedents we have reviewed and discussed.

Caperton contends that Blankenship's pivotal role in getting Justice Benjamin elected created a constitutionally intolerable probability of actual bias. Though not a bribe or criminal influence, Justice Benjamin would nevertheless feel a debt of gratitude to Blankenship for his extraordinary efforts to get him elected. That temptation, Caperton claims, is as strong and inherent in human nature as was the conflict the Court confronted in *Tumey* and *Monroeville* when a mayor-judge (or the city) benefited financially from a defendant's conviction, as well as the conflict ... when a judge was the object of a defendant's contempt.

Justice Benjamin was careful to address the recusal motions and explain his reasons why, on his view of the controlling standard, disqualification was not in order. ... We do not question his subjective findings of impartiality and propriety. Nor do we determine whether there was actual bias.

Following accepted principles of our legal tradition respecting the proper performance of judicial functions, judges often inquire into their subjective motives and purposes in the ordinary course of deciding a case. This does not mean the inquiry is a simple one. ...

The difficulties of inquiring into actual bias, and the fact that the inquiry is often a private one, simply underscore the need for objective rules. Otherwise there may be no adequate protection against a judge who simply misreads or misapprehends the real motives at work in deciding the case. The judge's own inquiry into actual bias, then, is not one that the law can easily superintend or review, though actual bias, if disclosed, no doubt would be grounds for appropriate relief. In lieu of exclusive reliance on that personal inquiry, or on appellate review of the judge's determination respecting actual bias, the Due Process Clause has been implemented by objective standards that do not require proof of actual bias. See *Tumey*, 273 U.S. at 532[]; [cc]. In defining these standards the Court has asked whether, "under a realistic appraisal of psychological tendencies and human weakness," the interest "poses such a risk of actual bias or prejudgment that the practice must be forbidden if the guarantee of due process is to be adequately implemented." *Withrow*, 421 U.S. at 47[].

We turn to the influence at issue in this case. Not every campaign contribution by a litigant or attorney creates a probability of bias that requires a judge's recusal, but this is an exceptional case. [C] We conclude that there is a serious risk of actual bias—based on objective and reasonable perceptions—when a person with a personal stake in a particular case had a significant and disproportionate influence in placing the judge on the case by raising funds or directing the judge's election campaign when the case was pending or imminent. The inquiry centers on the contribution's relative size in comparison to the total amount of money contributed to the campaign, the total amount spent in the election, and the apparent effect such contribution had on the outcome of the election.

Applying this principle, we conclude that Blankenship's campaign efforts had a significant and disproportionate influence in placing Justice Benjamin on the case. ...

Massey responds that Blankenship's support, while significant, did not cause Benjamin's victory. In the end the people of West Virginia elected him, and they did so based on many reasons other than Blankenship's efforts. Massey points out that every major state newspaper, but one, endorsed Benjamin. [C] It also contends that then-Justice McGraw cost himself the election by giving a speech during the campaign, a speech the opposition seized upon for its own advantage. [C] ...

Whether Blankenship's campaign contributions were a necessary and sufficient cause of Benjamin's victory is not the proper inquiry. Much like determining whether a judge is actually biased, proving what ultimately drives the electorate to choose a particular candidate is a difficult endeavor, not likely to lend itself to a certain conclusion. ... Due process requires an objective inquiry into whether the contributor's influence on the election under all the circumstances "would offer a possible temptation to the average ... judge to ... lead him not to hold the balance nice, clear and true." *Tumey, supra,* at 532[]. In an election decided by fewer than 50,000 votes... , Blankenship's campaign contributions—in comparison to the total amount contributed to the campaign, as well as the total amount spent in the election—had a significant and disproportionate influence on the electoral outcome. And the risk that Blankenship's influence engendered actual bias is sufficiently substantial that it "must be forbidden if the guarantee of due process is to be adequately implemented." *Withrow, supra,* at 47[].

The temporal relationship between the campaign contributions, the justice's election, and the pendency of the case is also critical. It was reasonably foreseeable, when the campaign contributions were made, that the pending case would be before the newly elected justice. ...

IV

Our decision today addresses an extraordinary situation where the Constitution requires recusal. Massey and its *amici* predict that various adverse consequences will follow from recognizing a constitutional violation here—ranging from a flood of recusal motions to unnecessary interference with judicial elections. We disagree. The facts now before us are extreme by any measure. ...

The judgment of the Supreme Court of Appeals of West Virginia is reversed, and the case is remanded for further proceedings not inconsistent with this opinion.

It is so ordered.

Chief Justice ROBERTS, with whom Justice SCALIA, Justice THOMAS, and Justice ALITO join, dissenting[, omitted].

In re Blake,
Mississippi Supreme Court
912 So.2d 907 (2005)

JESS H. DICKINSON, Justice.

¶1. Before the Court are Petitions for Writ of Mandamus filed by attorney Stuart Robinson, Jr., and his clients (collectively Robinson), seeking recusal of Circuit Judge Tomie T. Green in seven pending cases and all future cases in which Robinson appears as counsel.[fn] Robinson claims that Judge Green "demonstrates probable bias (sic) and a lack of impartiality as regards [Robinson], such that her Honor should be recused from this case, and any other cases currently pending before her Honor, or subsequently assigned to her Honor, wherein [Robinson] is counsel." Although Judge Green sharply disputes Robinson's interpretation of events, the factual basis for Robinson's claim is essentially undisputed.

BACKGROUND FACTS

¶2. The controversy apparently began in a lawsuit filed by David Alexander Clein against Kendall Blake, M.D., et al., when Judge Green set the matter for trial. Robinson, who was employed as counsel to represent the defendants, requested time to confer with experts regarding potential conflicts. Judge Green denied the request.[fn] When Robinson later learned that all three of his retained experts would be unavailable due to "existing conflicts with the trial date, and the death of one (1) expert," he filed a motion for continuance, which was denied, followed by a renewal of the motion for continuance which also was denied. Robinson then applied for a writ of mandamus, asking this Court to intervene. His request was denied, and the case proceeded to trial on February 11, 2002.[fn]

Expert Controversy.

¶3. During trial, an issue surfaced involving Robinson's ability to produce one of his experts, Dr. Greer Richardson, for live testimony, rather than submitting his testimony by deposition. Having been informed long before trial that Dr. Richardson had a conflict[fn] with the trial date, Robinson had already deposed him for trial purposes. However, Dr. Richardson informed Robinson by letter dated August 29, 2001, that, if he was needed to appear live at trial, he would try to make arrangements to get there. In his response to Dr. Richardson the next day, Robinson said he would like for Dr. Richardson to appear live, and he asked Dr. Richardson to keep him advised of his availability. ...

¶6. The trial began, as scheduled, with Dr. Richardson still unsure about his ability to travel to Jackson for live testimony. During the week of trial, the subject apparently came up (although we aren't told how), and Robinson apparently informed Judge Green that Dr. Richardson might be able to testify live. Judge Green responded by saying, "So what I offered to you ahead of time,[fn] you now want to say if he doesn't come then you want to have the deposition by tape?" Robinson responded in the affirmative.

¶7. At this point, it appears to this Court that the issue had been clearly and respectfully presented by Robinson to Judge Green, and that she clearly understood. What is unclear is why the matter didn't simply drop until time for Dr. Richardson's testimony, at which time he would either walk to the witness stand, or Robinson would offer his deposition testimony. For whatever reason, Judge Green did not let the matter drop. The exchange that next took place cannot be reconciled with anything previously stated or anything elsewhere in the record. For clarity, we will recite the relevant portion of the record provided to us, verbatim:

> **THE COURT:** So, again, Mr. Robinson, Dr. Richardson will be here correct?
>
> **MR. ROBINSON:** He has booked a flight and we anticipate him being here. I would say 99.99 percent chance that he will be here.
>
> **THE COURT:** Mr. Robinson, why are you playing games with words. I knew whether my witnesses were going to be at trial when I was practicing law. Why is it that you don't know whether Dr. Richardson will be here or not?
>
> **MR. ROBINSON:** Because he previously advised us that he would not be able to be here for the trial and we've also had one witness die, one of our experts, so I'm a little-
>
> **THE COURT:** I didn't ask you about nobody else but Dr. Richardson. I'm saying why don't you know whether Dr. Richardson will be here or not. I'm well aware that tomorrow none of us may be here. But I want to know why you can't tell me that Dr. Richardson will be here. He's your expert.

MR. ROBINSON: Yes, ma'am. What I said a few minutes ago, he previously advised us that he could not make it.... We're going to call him by video in accordance with the rules.

MR. STEVENS: Dr. Leventen is the one that was indicated to this court was too old to travel.

THE COURT: Hold on. If you say in accordance with the rules one more time, counsel, I know the rules. I understand the rules very well. So from now on you don't have to put that editorial at the end of every statement because every time that you've said it have you noticed I hesitated. I'm counting. I understand very well what the rules are, but this morning you can't tell me whether Dr. Richardson will be here and you come up with this nice way of saying you can't guarantee, you're 99 percent sure that he'll be here, but if he doesn't, you want to use his deposition.

We have been arguing over this back and forth for a year now, Mr. Robinson, and I just cannot believe that you couldn't find you a couple of experts that would not be a problem that the plaintiff would have the benefit of their testimony and be able to rebut or cross-examine.... But it's their case. And if they don't want that doctor here live to testify to that jury, that's fine with me. That's what I told them when they decided to make the interlocutory appeal. But it doesn't bother me when people appeal. That's just the nature of the beast. But for some reason attorneys think they can threaten the judge by saying they want to take an interlocutory appeal. If I were a younger lawyer that might would work, but I been practicing too long. So, in terms of that, I'll just need to have the depositions so that when you do make your objections I'll know how I'm going to rule because I will have read the depositions. But I am not as dumb as you think. I know very well what Mr. Robinson and the other attorneys are doing when they are playing the game with Dr. Richardson, and it is a game.

MR. STEVENS: And I think you're a lot smarter than me by the way.

THE COURT: If he is going to be here, he's going to be here. If he isn't, he isn't. But they are taking a chance on me because they may not have Dr. Richardson either way. ...

MR. ROBINSON: If I may address, Your Honor. Your Honor called and spoke with Dr. Munn. If the court thinks that we're playing games I don't have any problem with you calling Dr. Richardson. We work with the facts we're given and end up doing the best we can.

THE COURT: I asked you whether Dr. Richardson on Monday was going to be here on Friday.

MR. ROBINSON: And I gave you an honest answer based upon the information available to me.

THE COURT: Counsel, I've never had anyone at any trial at any time I've been on this bench tell me in the terms that you told me Monday, that you may or may not have an expert. This is the first time anybody walked in an told me, well, we don't know because our expert is at a convention. You knew a year ago, a year ago, that Dr. Richardson was not going to be here. Is that correct?

MR. ROBINSON: Your Honor, I've given you the information as honestly as I can. If you want me to take the stand and give it to you that way or you can call Dr. Richardson. All I can do is give you-

THE COURT: I want you to answer my question. You knew a year ago that Dr. Richardson was not going to be here; am I correct?

MR. ROBINSON: When you set this case for trial, we checked and there was a conflict. These things were planned a year in advance. That's why we moved for a continuance, which you denied.

THE COURT: And you appealed it and the Supreme Court denied it.

MR. ROBINSON: That's my problem, yes, ma'am.

THE COURT: And evidently they looked at the fact that you knew a year ago that Dr. Richardson couldn't be here, didn't you?

MR. ROBINSON: One of them agreed with us. And, Judge, I can only do what I can do. And if there is something else you tell me to do, I'll do my best to accommodate the court.

THE COURT: Get Dr. Richardson here on Friday. You said you'd do what I wanted you to do, and we'll have him testify on Saturday morning.

MR. ROBINSON: I'll do the best I can. I cannot tell you that he'll definitely be here.

THE COURT: You couldn't tell me anything Monday.

MR. ROBINSON: I gave you an honest answer Monday, and I'm giving you an honest one today.

THE COURT: No, you did not give me an honest answer. You're not giving me an honest answer today. I asked you about the Supreme Court ruling and you told me one person agreed with you. Do you have an order from that one person?

MR. ROBINSON: No, I don't have an order from that one person.

THE COURT: So why did you say that?

MR. ROBINSON: Because it was the truth.

THE COURT: But why did you feel it was necessary to say that to me, Mr. Robinson?

MR. ROBINSON: Judge, I can see we're going to disagree. I respect Your Honor, and I will do whatever I can to accommodate the court and abide by the ruling of the court. There's nothing more than I can do.

THE COURT: I'll ask you again. Then why did you say to this court that one person agreed with you? What was the reason for you to say that to me, Mr. Robinson?

MR. ROBINSON: I can't remember the context it came up but that is an accurate fact.

THE COURT: And what's the significant of that?

MR. ROBINSON: None.

THE COURT: So why did you say it?

MR. ROBINSON: I cannot tell you, Judge.

THE COURT: I know you can.

MR. ROBINSON: I guess in responding to your questions.

THE COURT: I do understand, Mr. Robinson. You know something, there has not been a single questions that I've asked you that you have answered directly, not a single one. And we expect witnesses to get on the stand and answer the question that we direct to them. But how can we do that when I have not had you this entire case when I asked you a question to give me a direct answer.

MR. ROBINSON: Your Honor, I feel like I have. We'll just have to agree to disagree I guess.

THE COURT: I don't know whether we do or not. But I do expect integrity in the attorneys getting up here before me.

MR. ROBINSON: You have that.

THE COURT: No, sir, I do not, Mr. Robinson. Anytime I ask you a questions and you can't give me a direct answer, I'm not sure I got integrity or not. Now I knew when I said that I wouldn't be here Friday exactly what was going to happen and I could have written it down and it still would have been true that the moment I said I was not going to be here Friday, you-all would come in and tell me Dr. Richardson couldn't get here for Saturday.

MR. ROBINSON: Well, if you believe that you'll-

THE COURT: Can he get here for Monday?

MR. ROBINSON: Yes, And if Your Honor, if you want to put me on the stand or even Dr. Richardson to-

THE COURT: He can be here for Monday?

MR. ROBINSON: Yes, ma'am.

THE COURT: We'll have him here on Monday morning. Bring the jury in. I assume that that means then that I don't have to rule on any of these objections. We'll have Dr. Richardson live on Monday morning, and it's absolutely timely, simply because we are out of term....

¶8. After diligent search by the members of this Court, we are unable to locate within the transcript or other papers provided to us,[fn] the source of Judge Green's anger and vitriol toward Robinson concerning production of Dr. Richardson. ...

¶15. In support of his motion, Mr. Robinson cites from the trial transcript other examples of hostile statements by Judge Green.... .

¶16. The record provides no justification whatsoever for Judge Green's animosity and sarcasm toward Robinson. We recognize and endorse a trial judge's duty to control the courtroom, using reasonable measures to efficiently move matters along and keep over-zealous counsel in check. However, the professional obligations of dignity, respect and decorum is not limited to counsel. Canon 1 of the Code of Judicial Conduct states, "A judge should participate in establishing, maintaining, and enforcing high standards of conduct, and shall personally observe those standards so that the integrity and independence of the judiciary will be preserved." ...

Judge Green's Response to the Petition.

¶25. In addition to her response to the "show-cause" order, Judge Green filed a response to the Petition for Writ of Mandamus. Therein, she made the following statement:

> Trial judges of a not-traditional gender and/or hue are not always well received by attorneys who prefer more traditional jurists. Many attorneys take offense at having to appear before or be subjected to rulings or instructions of the cout (sic). However, I have never had a situation where an attorney intentionally misrepresented the court's conduct to an appellate court in an attempt to malign the court's character and integrity. Any and all responses by the court, the petitioning attorney, or any attorney for that matter, are directly responsible (sic) to the attorney's conduct, misconduct or failures.

¶26. Judge Green then implores us to read the "full transcript submitted by the petitioners in the context of pretrial hearings that petitioners chose not to request court reporters." She asks us to "consider the motives or lack of motive of the judge, as well as those of the Petitioners." She further characterizes Robinson's averments as "false allegations" and efforts at "intimidation, harassment and retaliation" against the court. She states that the claims "are without merit, are frivolous, and should be dismissed." She accuses Robinson of "evasiveness in response to the court's inquiry." She claims to be frustrated at Robinson's "tactics and misrepresentations to the court." She accuses him of using "questionable tactics" in "manufacturing a case for recusal by the court," and in "soliciting or entertaining unfounded allegations."

¶27. Other than these broad-brush, unsupported attacks on Robinson, Judge Green does not respond to the specific issues raised by Robinson. Nor does she direct us to a single instance of "false allegations," "intimidation," or "evasiveness." If such conduct occurred, there is no suggestion of it in the record presented to us.

ANALYSIS

¶28. For the sake of clarity, we point out that judges and lawyers are not required to like each other. They are, however, required to maintain a reasonable level of respect, decorum and professional courtesy. ...

¶29. Lawyers are expected, even required, to represent their clients with zeal and passion. This sometimes leads to particularly aggressive statements made on the spur of the moment, in an effort to attain for the client every permissible advantage and gain.

¶30. Judges are expected to control the courtrooms and move cases along, so that respect for the judiciary and the legal system is maintained. Sometimes, frustration and impatience are brought on by the judge's perception of how attorneys could better handle matters before their court. An attorney's attempt to properly represent his or her client can, on occasion, be viewed by a trial judge as an attempt to delay or obfuscate. When this happens, trial judges have little time to fully analyze the motives of lawyers. The natural reaction of all but the most disciplined judges will sometimes lead to displays of anger, frustration and surprising vocabulary. This often will result in the appearance of personal animosity which, in turn, can provoke fear of prejudice.

¶31. But demonstrating that a lawyer was overly aggressive, or that a judge was grouchy, irritated and less than circumspect in selection of vocabulary, has little to do with proving impartiality. Rarely do judges allow their frustration, anger, impatience and irritation to influence the dispensation of justice. However, recusal is required if a personal tension between a lawyer and judge would lead a reasonable person to question whether the judge would have a personal bias or prejudice concerning the lawyer's client. [C] ...

¶33. The oath of office taken by all trial judges, including Judge Green, requires that judges "administer justice without respect to persons," and that they "faithfully and impartially execute and perform" all of their duties.

¶34. The Code of Judicial Conduct which guides the behavior of judges requires recusal "in proceedings in which their impartiality might be questioned by a reasonable person knowing all the circumstances...." Canon 3(E)(1). This is so, even if none of the specific reasons for recusal cited in the Canon apply. Comment, Canon 3(E)(1). ...

¶38. ... [T]he record before us clearly demonstrates that Judge Green entertained a high degree of hostility toward Robinson and that her conduct during the exchange regarding Dr. Richardson's availability to testify was not an isolated loss of temper. Later, in proceedings regarding the misplaced exhibits and again when Robinson made a routine request for a court reporter, Judge Green's animosity continued and appeared to increase. While we do not know the reason for this demeanor on her part, nothing in the record, in the briefs of the plaintiff, or in Judge Green's responses indicate any actions on the part of either Robinson or his co-counsel suggesting that her actions were responsive to improper conduct on their part. When invited to explain the circumstances, Judge Green made conclusory allegations, including those of racial and gender prejudice, which are totally without support in the record.

¶39. In spite of the leeway given judges in the management of their courts, here we find nothing before us which would explain Judge Green's conduct. We further find that her continued hostility even beyond the trial to post-trial efforts to obtain an accurate record is such as to cause a reasonable person aware of all the circumstances to question whether Robinson's clients can get a fair hearing in her court. Additionally, her totally unsupported and reckless charges of gender and racial prejudice pulled from thin air were totally inappropriate and are further evidence of her hostility.

¶40. For reasons we need not discuss here, it has not been this Court's practice to grant prospective recusal, and we decline to do so now. We shall review any request for recusal in future cases on a case-by-case basis.

¶41. IT IS THEREFORE ORDERED that the petitions are granted to the extent that they seek the recusal of Circuit Judge Tomie T. Green in each of the seven pending cases in which Stuart Robinson, Jr. is attorney of record and Judge Green is recused in these seven cases... .

¶42. IT IS FURTHER ORDERED that the petitions are denied to the extent that they request Judge Green's recusal in all future cases in which Robinson appears as counsel.

¶43. SO ORDERED.

INQUIRY

Financial Influences. ABA Code of Judicial Conduct Rule 2.4 prohibits external influences on a judge's judgment including personal financial influences. If the judge or judge's immediate family member has a financial interest in a case's outcome, then the judge must not hear the case. A bribe is, of course, an impermissible external financial influence. *See* Bracy v. Gramley, 520 U.S. 899 (1997) (decisions by bribed judge violate due process). Sitting on the board of directors of an organization that has a case before the judge in which the outcome may affect the organization's financial interests is also an impermissible external financial influence. *See, e.g.,* Liljeberg v. Health Services Acquisition Corp., 486 US. 847 (1988). Resignation from the board or divestitute of the personal financial interest may cure the influence and permit a judge to continue. If a party seeks to manipulate a judicial assignment by retaining a law firm in which the judge has a family-member relationship that would disqualify the judge from serving, then the judge may instead disqualify the law firm. *See* In re Bell-South Corp., 334 F.3d 941 (11th Cir. 2003).

D. Personal Conduct

Canon 3. A judge's obligations to the office do not end when the judge steps off the bench or leaves the courthouse. The public also concerns itself with the personal conduct of judges. Personal conduct influences public duties and reflects public character. For example, as Rule 3.1 indicates, a judge who participates in personal activities that lead to the judge's frequent disqualification affects the judge's ability to perform judicial service. Personal activities that lead to disqualification may be financial, political, or even social in nature, as indicated by Rule 2.11 above. *See, e.g.,* In re Ellender, 889 So.2d 225 (La. 2004) (one-year suspension for judge who appeared at party in blackface and prison suit); In re Lowery, 999 S.W.2d 639 (Tex. Rev. Trib. 1998) (removal for, among other things, using racist profanities in parking-lot dispute). Crimes can also lead to removal from office. *See, e.g.,* In re Jones, 581 N.W.2d 876 (Neb. 1998) (death threat by judge). On the other hand, personal activities of a charitable nature may help a judge understand the community better while helping the public respect the court and judge. Read the following similar state versions of the rules in ABA Code of Judicial Conduct Canon 3 for the personal activities that the canon encourages and discourages. Can you articulate why the Code includes each provision? How might you interact with a judge to discourage the judicial prohibitions and encourage judicial aspirations? Judges will occasionally rely on leading practitioners in the bar for both purposes, to ensure that their conduct stays within the rules and to find suitable outlets to promote respect for the judiciary. Pay particular attention to Rule 3.7 on a judge's participation in outside organizations and Rule 3.13 on a judge accepting a gift. Can you anticipate when one of those situations those rules address might arise involving you and a judge acquaintance? *See, e.g.,* In re Luzzo, 756 So.2d 76 (Fla. 2000) (public reprimand of judge for accepting free baseball tickets from law firm). An illustrative case follows the similar state version of Canon 3.

INDIANA CODE OF JUDICIAL CONDUCT: **Canon 3. A Judge Shall Conduct the Judge's Personal and Extrajudicial Activities to Minimize the Risk of Conflict with the Obligations of Judicial Office.**

RULE 3.1: Extrajudicial Activities in General.
A judge may engage in extrajudicial activities, except as prohibited by law* or this Code. However, when engaging in extrajudicial activities, a judge shall not:
(A) participate in activities that will interfere with the proper performance of the judge's judicial duties;

(B) participate in activities that will lead to frequent disqualification of the judge;

(C) participate in activities that would appear to a reasonable person to undermine the judge's independence,* integrity,* or impartiality;*

(D) engage in conduct that would appear to a reasonable person to be coercive; or

(E) make use of court premises, staff, stationery, equipment, or other resources, except for incidental use or for activities that concern the law, the legal system, or the administration of justice.

RULE 3.2: Appearances before Governmental Bodies and Consultation with Government Officials.

A judge shall not appear voluntarily at a public hearing before, or otherwise consult with, an executive or a legislative body or official, except:

(A) in connection with matters concerning the law,* the legal system, or the administration of justice;

(B) in connection with matters about which the judge acquired knowledge or expertise in the course of the judge's judicial duties; or

(C) when the judge is acting pro se in a matter involving the judge's legal or economic interests or those of members of the judge's family residing in the judge's household, or when the judge is acting in a fiduciary* capacity.

RULE 3.3: Testifying as a Character Witness.

A judge shall not testify as a character witness in a judicial, administrative, or other adjudicatory proceeding or otherwise vouch for the character of a person in a legal proceeding, except when duly summoned.

RULE 3.4: Appointments to Governmental Positions.

A judge shall not accept appointment to a governmental committee, board, commission, or other governmental position except with prior approval of the Indiana Supreme Court, unless it is one that concerns the law,* the legal system, or the administration of justice.

RULE 3.5: Use of Nonpublic Information.

A judge shall not intentionally disclose or use nonpublic information* acquired in a judicial capacity for any purpose unrelated to the judge's judicial duties.

RULE 3.6: Affiliation with Discriminatory Organizations.

(A) A judge shall not hold membership in any organization that practices invidious discrimination on the basis of race, sex, gender, religion, national origin, ethnicity, or sexual orientation.

(B) A judge shall not use the benefits or facilities of an organization if the judge knows* or should know that the organization practices invidious discrimination on one or more of the bases identified in paragraph (A). A judge's attendance at an event in a facility of an organization that the judge is not permitted to join is not a violation of this Rule when the judge's attendance is an isolated event that could not reasonably be perceived as an endorsement of the organization's practices.

RULE 3.7: Participation in Educational, Religious, Charitable, Fraternal, or Civic Organizations and Activities.

(A) Except as provided by Rule 3.7(A)(2), a judge may not directly solicit funds for an organization. However, subject to the requirements of Rule 3.1, a judge may participate in activities sponsored by organizations or governmental entities concerned with the law, the legal system, or the administration of justice, and those sponsored by or on behalf of educational, religious, charitable, fraternal, or civic organizations not conducted for profit, including but not limited to the following activities:

(1) assisting such an organization or entity in planning related to fund-raising, volunteering services or goods at fund-raising events, and participating in the management and investment of the organization's or entity's funds;

(2) soliciting* contributions* for such an organization or entity, but only from members of the judge's family,* or from judges over whom the judge does not exercise supervisory or appellate authority;

(3) soliciting membership for such an organization or entity, even though the membership dues or fees generated may be used to support the objectives of the organization or entity, but only if the organization or entity is concerned with the law, the legal system, or the administration of justice;

(4) appearing or speaking at, receiving an award or other recognition at, being featured on the program of, and permitting his or her title to be used in connection with an event of such an organization or entity, but if the event serves a fund-raising purpose, the judge may not be a featured speaker or guest of honor;

(5) making recommendations to such a public or private fund-granting organization or entity in connection with its programs and activities, but only if the organization or entity is concerned with the law, the legal system, or the administration of justice; and

(6) serving as an officer, director, trustee, or nonlegal advisor of such an organization or entity, unless it is likely that the organization or entity:

(a) will be engaged in proceedings that would ordinarily come before the judge; or

(b) will frequently be engaged in adversary proceedings in the court of which the judge is a member, or in any court subject to the appellate jurisdiction of the court of which the judge is a member.

(B) A judge may encourage lawyers to provide pro bono publico legal services.

RULE 3.8: Appointments to Fiduciary Positions.

(A) A judge shall not accept appointment to serve in a fiduciary* position, such as executor, administrator, trustee, guardian, attorney in fact, or other personal representative, except for the estate, trust, or person of a member of the judge's family,* and then only if such service will not interfere with the proper performance of judicial duties.

(B) A judge shall not serve in a fiduciary position if the judge as fiduciary will likely be engaged in proceedings that would ordinarily come before the judge, or if the estate, trust, or ward becomes involved in adversary proceedings in the court on which the judge serves, or one under its appellate jurisdiction.

(C) A judge acting in a fiduciary capacity shall be subject to the same restrictions on engaging in financial activities that apply to a judge personally.

(D) If a person who is serving in a fiduciary position becomes a judge, he or she must comply with this Rule as soon as reasonably practicable, but in no event later than one year after becoming a judge.

RULE 3.9: Service as Arbitrator or Mediator.

A judge shall not act as an arbitrator or a mediator or perform other judicial functions apart from the judge's official duties unless expressly authorized by law.*

RULE 3.10: Practice of Law.

A judge shall not practice law. A judge may act pro se and may, without compensation, give legal advice to and draft or review documents for a member of the judge's family,* but is prohibited from serving as the family member's lawyer before a tribunal. This Rule does not prohibit the practice of law pursuant to military service.

RULE 3.11: Financial, Business, or Remunerative Activities.

(A) A judge shall not engage in any business, financial, or other remunerative activity if engaging in the activity would:

(1) interfere with the proper performance of judicial duties;

(2) lead to frequent disqualification of the judge;

(3) involve the judge in frequent transactions or continuing business relationships with lawyers or other persons likely to come before the court on which the judge serves; or

(4) result in violations of other provisions of this Code.

RULE 3.12: Compensation for Extrajudicial Activities.

A judge may accept reasonable compensation for extrajudicial activities permitted by this Code or other law* unless such acceptance would appear to a reasonable person to undermine the judge's independence,* integrity,* or impartiality.*

RULE 3.13: Acceptance and Reporting of Gifts, Loans, Bequests, Benefits, or Other Things of Value.

(A) A judge shall not accept any gifts, loans, bequests, benefits, or other things of value, if acceptance is prohibited by law* or would appear to a reasonable person to undermine the judge's independence,* integrity,* or impartiality.*

(B) Unless otherwise prohibited by law, or by paragraph (A), a judge may accept the following without publicly reporting such acceptance:

(1) items with little intrinsic value, such as plaques, certificates, trophies, and greeting cards;

(2) gifts, loans, bequests, benefits, or other things of value from friends, relatives, or other persons, including lawyers, whose appearance or interest in a proceeding pending* or impending* before the judge would in any event require disqualification of the judge under Rule 2.11;

(3) ordinary social hospitality;

(4) commercial or financial opportunities and benefits, including special pricing and discounts, and loans from lending institutions in their regular

course of business, if the same opportunities and benefits or loans are made available on the same terms to similarly situated persons who are not judges;

(5) rewards and prizes given to competitors or participants in random drawings, contests, or other events that are open to persons who are not judges;

(6) scholarships, fellowships, and similar benefits or awards, if they are available to similarly situated persons who are not judges, based upon the same terms and criteria;

(7) books, magazines, journals, audiovisual materials, and other resource materials supplied by publishers on a complimentary basis for official use; or

(8) gifts, awards, or benefits associated with the business, profession, or other separate activity of a spouse, a domestic partner,* or other family member of a judge residing in the judge's household,* but that incidentally benefit the judge;

(9) gifts incident to a public testimonial;

(10) invitations to the judge and the judge's spouse, domestic partner, or guest to attend without charge:

(a) an event associated with a bar-related function or other activity relating to the law, the legal system, or the administration of justice; or

(b) an event associated with any of the judge's educational, religious, charitable, fraternal or civic activities permitted by this Code, if the same invitation is offered to nonjudges who are engaged in similar ways in the activity as is the judge.

(C) Unless otherwise prohibited by law or by paragraph (A), a judge may accept any other gift, loan, bequest, benefit, or other thing of value but must report such acceptance to the extent required by Rule 3.15.

RULE 3.14:   Reimbursement of Expenses and Waivers of Fees or Charges.

(A) Unless otherwise prohibited by Rules 3.1 and 3.13(A) or other law,* a judge may accept reimbursement of necessary and reasonable expenses for travel, food, lodging, or other incidental expenses, or a waiver or partial waiver of fees or charges for registration, tuition, and similar items, from sources other than the judge's employing entity, if the expenses or charges are associated with the judge's participation in extrajudicial activities permitted by this Code.

(B) Reimbursement of expenses for necessary travel, food, lodging, or other incidental expenses shall be limited to the actual costs reasonably incurred by the judge and, when appropriate to the occasion, by the judge's spouse, domestic partner,* or guest.

(C) A judge who accepts reimbursement of expenses or waivers or partial waivers of fees or charges on behalf of the judge or the judge's spouse, domestic partner, or guest shall publicly report such acceptance as required by Rule 3.15.

RULE 3.15: Financial Reporting Requirements.

(A) A judge shall publicly report the amount or value of:

(1) compensation received for extrajudicial activities whether or not permitted by Rule 3.12;

(2) gifts and other things of value as permitted by Rule 3.13(C), unless the value of such items, alone or in the aggregate with other items received from the same source in the same calendar year, does not exceed $150.00; and

(3) reimbursement of expenses and waiver of fees or charges permitted by Rule 3.14(A), unless the amount of reimbursement or waiver, alone or in the aggregate with other reimbursements or waivers received from the same source in the same calendar year, does not exceed $150.00.

(B) When public reporting is required by paragraph (A), a judge shall report the date, place, and nature of the activity for which the judge received any compensation; the description of any gift, loan, bequest, benefit, or other thing of value accepted; and the source of reimbursement of expenses or waiver or partial waiver of fees or charges.

(C) The public report required by paragraph (A) shall be made annually on the Statement of Economic Interests.

In re Mosley,
Nevada Supreme Court
102 P.3d 555 (2004)

SHEARING, C.J.

On May 22, 2000, a special prosecutor for the Nevada Commission on Judicial Discipline (the Commission) filed charges against the Honorable Donald M. Mosley, District Judge for the Eighth Judicial District Court. The complaint contained the following allegations: Count I, that Judge Mosley violated Nevada Code of Judicial Conduct (NCJC) Canon 2B in August 1999 by writing a letter on official judicial letterhead to the principal at his son's school; Count II, that Judge Mosley violated NCJC Canon 2B in February 1998 by writing a letter on official judicial letterhead to the principal at his son's school.... .

From February 25, 2002, through February 28, 2002, the Commission conducted a formal evidentiary hearing. The Commission concluded that Judge Mosley had committed the violations alleged in Counts I[and] II[and other counts]... . The Commission also determined that the appropriate discipline was to require Judge Mosley to attend the first general ethics course at the National Judicial College at his own expense, to pay a $5,000 fine, and to receive strongly worded censures for violating ethics rules.

Judge Mosley appeals, alleging that there was insufficient evidence to support the Commission's findings and that the Commission erred in other respects. We conclude that clear and convincing evidence supports the Commission's findings on all counts but Counts III and IV and affirm the Commission's determination of the appropriate discipline for Judge Mosley.

DISCUSSION
... Counts I & II: Use of judicial letterhead

The evidence adduced at the hearing established that Judge Mosley and his ex-girlfriend, Terry Mosley, who is also referred to as Terry Figliuzzi, have a child named Michael. Judge Mosley and Figliuzzi have been involved in a bitter child custody dispute. In June 1998, Judge Mosley was awarded custody of Michael. After that custody order was issued, Judge Mosley sent two letters to Michael's school. Both of those letters were written on Eighth Judicial District Court letterhead. The letters explained that Judge Mosley had been awarded custody of his son, and asked that the school prohibit Figliuzzi from visiting Michael at school.

The letters were addressed to the principals of Michael's school, Diane Reitz and Frank Cooper. Reitz testified that it was part of the school's procedure to have a letter along with a custody order placed in the student's file. Reitz and Cooper testified that they were not influenced by the fact that Judge Mosley was a district court judge and that they knew, before receiving the letters, that he was a judge.

The Commission found that Judge Mosley violated NCJC Canon 2B. For Counts I and II, the Commission ordered Judge Mosley to attend the first available general ethics course at the National Judicial College at his own expense.

NCJC Canon 2B provides, in pertinent part:

> A judge shall not allow family, social, political or other relationships to influence the judge's judicial conduct or judgment. A judge shall not lend the prestige of judicial office to advance the private interests of the judge or others; nor shall a judge convey or permit others to convey the impression that they are in a special position to influence the judge.

Whether judicial letterhead may be used for personal reasons is an issue of first impression for this court. While NCJC Canon 2B does not specifically address the use of judicial letterhead for personal purposes, the commentary to NCJC Canon 2B provides some guidance:

> Judges should distinguish between proper and improper use of the prestige of office in all of their activities. For example, it would be improper for a judge to allude to his or her judgeship to gain a personal advantage such as deferential treatment when stopped by a police officer for a traffic offense. Similarly, judicial letterhead must not be used for conducting a judge's personal business.

> A judge must avoid lending the prestige of judicial office for the advancement of the private interests of others. For example, a judge must not use the judge's judicial position to gain advantage in a civil suit involving a member of the judge's family.

Judge Mosley asserts that he did not violate NCJC Canon 2B because both school principals knew that he was a district court judge before he sent letters to them on judicial letterhead. Judge Mosley also contends that because principals Cooper and Reitz did not provide special treatment to Judge Mosley, he was not advancing his position by using his judicial letterhead.

The United States Supreme Court, in interpreting a section of the federal judicial code, has held that a judge is not to be evaluated by a subjective standard, but by the standard of an objective reasonable person, because "people who have not served on the bench are often all too willing to indulge suspicions and doubts concerning the integrity of judges."[fn*Liljeberg v. Health Services Acquisition Corp.,* 486 U.S. 847, 864-65 (1988).] ...

In interpreting the judicial canons, we adopt the objective reasonable person standard. In applying that standard, we conclude that there was clear and convincing evidence produced at the evidentiary hearing that an objective reasonable person could conclude that Judge Mosley wrote letters on his judicial letterhead to his son's school in an attempt to gain a personal advantage in violation of NCJC Canon 2B.

E. Judicial Campaigns

Canon 4. Some states elect judges, while others appoint them, and still others appoint them but make them stand before the voters for retention elections. Candidates and incumbent judges running for judicial have a fine line to tread. The public needs and deserves information about judicial candidates to make informed decisions. Judicial campaigns contribute to that information and public evaluation. Campaigns also cost money for advertising, organization, travel, and other expenses. Candidates for judicial office in smaller districts may finance their campaign solely or primarily out of personal funds, without political-party support, eliminating or reducing many of the influence issues. Candidates in larger judicial districts, particularly in statewide appellate races, may raise substantial outside funds into the millions of dollars, with the support of political parties and organizations, raising prospects for influence. Judges run on non-partisan ballots, although there are states in which parties nominate candidates for the high court non-partisan race. Partisanship (political parties) play significant roles even in non-partisan races. Read a similar state version of ABA Code of Judicial

Conduct Canon 4 for the concerns it addresses. As you do so, imagine where you might need to know these rules as you interact with judges or candidates running for judicial office. A significant recent Supreme Court decision applying the First Amendment to judicial campaigns follows.

WYOMING CODE OF JUDICIAL CONDUCT: **Canon 4. A Judge or Candidate for Judicial Office Shall Not Engage in Political or Campaign Activity That is Inconsistent with the Independence, Integrity, or Impartiality of the Judiciary.**

Rule 4.1: Political and Campaign Activities of Judges and Judicial Candidates in General.
(A) Except as permitted by law,* or by Rules 4.2, 4.3, and 4.4, a judge or a judicial candidate* shall not:
(1) act as a leader in, or hold an office in, a political organization;*
(2) make speeches on behalf of a political organization;*
(3) publicly endorse or oppose a candidate for any public office;
(4) solicit funds for, pay an assessment to, or make a contribution* to a political organization* or a candidate for public office;
(5) attend or purchase tickets for dinners or other events sponsored by a political organization* or a candidate for public office;
(6) engage in any other political activity except on behalf of measures to improve the law, legal system or the administration of justice or except as permitted under the sections of this Canon.
(B) A judge or judicial candidate* shall take reasonable measures to ensure that other persons do not undertake, on behalf of the judge or judicial candidate,* any activities prohibited under paragraph (A).

Rule 4.2: Political and Campaign Activities of Judicial Candidates in Public Retention Elections.
(A) A judge who is a candidate* for retention in office shall:
(1) act at all times in a manner consistent with the independence,* integrity,* and impartiality* of the judiciary;
(2) comply with all applicable retention election, retention election campaign, and retention election campaign fund-raising laws and regulations of this jurisdiction;
(3) maintain the dignity appropriate to judicial office, and shall encourage members of his or her family to adhere to the same standards of political conduct that apply to the judge;
(4) prohibit public officials or employees subject to the judge's direction or control from doing for the judge what he or she is prohibited from doing under this Canon; and except to the extent authorized under subsection (B), the judge shall not allow any other person to do for the judge what he or she is prohibited from doing under this Canon;
(5) not make pledges or promises of conduct in office other than the faithful and impartial* performance of the duties of the office; announce how the judge would rule on any case or issue that might come before the judge; or misrepresent his or her identity, qualifications, present position, or other fact.

(B) A judge who is a candidate* for retention in office shall abstain from any campaign activity in connection with the judge's own candidacy unless there is active opposition to his or her retention in office. If there is active opposition to the retention of a candidate* judge:

(1) the judge may speak at public meetings;

(2) the judge may use advertising media, provided that the advertising media is within the bounds of proper judicial decorum;

(3) a nonpartisan citizens' committee or committees advocating the judge's retention in office may be organized by others, either on their own initiative or at the request of the judge;

(4) any committee organized pursuant to subsection (B)(3) may raise funds for the judge's retention election campaign, but the judge shall not solicit funds personally or accept any funds except those paid to the judge by a committee for reimbursement of the judge's retention election campaign expenses; and,

(5) the judge shall not be advised of the source of funds raised y the committees.

(6) the judge shall not knowingly,* or with reckless disregard for the truth, make any false or misleading statement;

(7) the judge shall not make any statement that would reasonably be expected to affect the outcome or impair the fairness of a matter pending* or impending* in any court; or

(8) the judge shall not in connection with cases, controversies, or issues that are likely to come before the court, make pledges, promises, or commitments that are inconsistent with the impartial* performance of the adjudicative duties of judicial office.

Rule 4.3: Activities of Candidates for Appointive Judicial Office.

A candidate for appointment to judicial office may:

(A) communicate with the appointing or confirming authority, including any selection, screening, or nominating commission or similar agency; and

(B) seek endorsements for the appointment from any individual.

Rule 4.4: Activities of Judges Who Become Nonjudicial Candidates.

(A) A judge shall resign his or her judicial office when the judge becomes a candidate for a nonjudicial* elective office, except the judge may continue to hold his or her judicial office while a candidate for election to or serving as a delegate in a state or federal constitutional convention, if otherwise permitted by law* to do so.

(B) Upon becoming a nonjudicial candidate* for an appointive office, a judge is not required to resign from judicial office, provided that the judge complies with the other provisions of this Code.

Republican Party of Minnesota v. White,
United States Supreme Court
536 U.S. 765 (2002)

Justice SCALIA delivered the opinion of the Court.

The question presented in this case is whether the First Amendment permits the Minnesota Supreme Court to prohibit candidates for judicial election in that State from announcing their views on disputed legal and political issues.

I

Since Minnesota's admission to the Union in 1858, the State's Constitution has provided for the selection of all state judges by popular election.   [C]   Since 1912, those elections have been nonpartisan.   [C]   Since 1974, they have been subject to a legal restriction which states that a "candidate for a judicial office, including an incumbent judge," shall not "announce his or her views on disputed legal or political issues."   Minn.Code of Judicial Conduct, Canon 5(A)(3)(d)(i) (2000). This prohibition, promulgated by the Minnesota Supreme Court and based on Canon 7(B) of the 1972 American Bar Association (ABA) Model Code of Judicial Conduct, is known as the "announce clause."   Incumbent judges who violate it are subject to discipline, including removal, censure, civil penalties, and suspension without pay. [C] Lawyers who run for judicial office also must comply with the announce clause.   Minn. Rule of Professional Conduct 8.2(b) (2002) ("A lawyer who is a candidate for judicial office shall comply with the applicable provisions of the Code of Judicial Conduct").   Those who violate it are subject to, *inter alia,* disbarment, suspension, and probation.   Rule 8.4(a); Minn. Rules on Lawyers Professional Responsibility 8-14, 15(a) (2002).

In 1996, one of the petitioners, Gregory Wersal, ran for associate justice of the Minnesota Supreme Court. In the course of the campaign, he distributed literature criticizing several Minnesota Supreme Court decisions on issues such as crime, welfare, and abortion. A complaint against Wersal challenging, among other things, the propriety of this literature was filed with the Office of Lawyers Professional Responsibility, the agency which, under the direction of the Minnesota Lawyers Professional Responsibility Board,[fn] investigates and prosecutes ethical violations of lawyer candidates for judicial office. The Lawyers Board dismissed the complaint; with regard to the charges that his campaign materials violated the announce clause, it expressed doubt whether the clause could constitutionally be enforced. Nonetheless, fearing that further ethical complaints would jeopardize his ability to practice law, Wersal withdrew from the election. In 1998, Wersal ran again for the same office. Early in that race, he sought an advisory opinion from the Lawyers Board with regard to whether it planned to enforce the announce clause.   The Lawyers Board responded equivocally, stating that, although it had significant doubts about the constitutionality of the provision, it was unable to answer his question because he had not submitted a list of the announcements he wished to make.[fn]

Shortly thereafter, Wersal filed this lawsuit in Federal District Court against respondents,[fn] seeking, *inter alia,* a declaration that the announce clause violates the First Amendment and an injunction against its enforcement. ... Other plaintiffs in the suit, including the Minnesota Republican Party, alleged that, because the clause kept Wersal from announcing his views, they were unable to learn those views and support or oppose his candidacy accordingly. ... [T]he District Court found in favor of respondents, holding that the announce clause did not violate the First Amendment. [C] Over a dissent by Judge Beam, the United States Court of Appeals for the Eighth Circuit affirmed. [C] We granted certiorari. [C]

II

... We know that "announc[ing] ... views" on an issue covers much more than *promising* to decide an issue a particular way. The prohibition extends to the candidate's mere statement of his current position, even if he does not bind himself to maintain that position after election. All the parties agree this is the case, because the Minnesota Code contains a so-called "pledges or promises" clause, which *separately* prohibits judicial candidates from making "pledges or promises of conduct in office other than the faithful and impartial performance of the duties of the office," [c]—a prohibition that is not challenged here and on which we express no view. ...

... [I]t is clear that the announce clause prohibits a judicial candidate from stating his views on any specific nonfanciful legal question within the province of the court for which he is running, except in the context of discussing past decisions—and in the latter context as well, if he expresses the view that he is not bound by *stare decisis.*[fn]

Respondents contend that this still leaves plenty of topics for discussion on the campaign trail. These include a candidate's "character," "education," "work habits," and "how [he] would handle administrative duties if elected." [C] Indeed, the Judicial Board has printed a list of preapproved questions which judicial candidates are allowed to answer. These include how the candidate feels about cameras in the courtroom, how he would go about reducing the caseload, how the costs of judicial administration can be reduced, and how he proposes to ensure that minorities and women are treated more fairly by the court system. [C] Whether this list of preapproved subjects, and other topics not prohibited by the announce clause, adequately fulfill the First Amendment's guarantee of freedom of speech is the question to which we now turn.

III

As the Court of Appeals recognized, the announce clause both prohibits speech on the basis of its content and burdens a category of speech that is "at the core of our First Amendment freedoms"—speech about the qualifications of candidates for public office. [C] The Court of Appeals concluded that the proper test to be applied to determine the constitutionality of such a restriction is what our cases have called strict scrutiny, [c]; the parties do not dispute that this is correct. Under the strict-scrutiny test, respondents have the burden to prove that the announce clause is (1) narrowly tailored, to serve (2) a compelling state interest. *E.g., Eu v. San Francisco County Democratic Central Comm.,* 489 U.S. 214, 222[] (1989). In order for respondents to show that the announce clause is narrowly tailored, they must demonstrate that it does not "unnecessarily circumscrib[e] protected expression." *Brown v. Hartlage,* 456 U.S. 45, 54[] (1982).

The Court of Appeals concluded that respondents had established two interests as sufficiently compelling to justify the announce clause: preserving the impartiality of the state judiciary and preserving the appearance of the impartiality of the state judiciary. [C] ...

A

One meaning of "impartiality" in the judicial context—and of course its root meaning—is the lack of bias for or against either *party* to the proceeding. Impartiality in this sense assures equal application of the law. That is, it guarantees a party that the judge who hears his case will apply the law to him in the same way he applies it to any other party. ...

We think it plain that the announce clause is not narrowly tailored to serve impartiality (or the appearance of impartiality) in this sense. Indeed, the clause is barely tailored to serve that interest *at all,* inasmuch as it does not restrict speech for or against particular *parties,* but rather speech for or against particular *issues.* ...

B

It is perhaps possible to use the term "impartiality" in the judicial context (though this is certainly not a common usage) to mean lack of preconception in favor of or against a particular *legal view.* This sort of impartiality would be concerned, not with guaranteeing litigants equal application of the law, but rather with guaranteeing them an equal chance to persuade the court on the legal points in their case. Impartiality in this sense may well be an interest served by the announce clause, but it is not a *compelling* state interest, as strict scrutiny requires. A judge's lack of predisposition regarding the relevant legal issues in a case has never been thought a necessary component of equal justice, and with good reason. For one thing, it is virtually impossible to find a judge who does not have preconceptions about the law. As then-Justice REHNQUIST observed of our own Court: "Since most Justices come to this bench no earlier than their middle years, it would be unusual if they had not by that time formulated at least some tentative notions that would influence them in their interpretation of the sweeping clauses of the Constitution and their interaction with one another. It would be not merely unusual, but extraordinary, if they had not at least given opinions as to constitutional issues in their previous legal careers." *Laird v. Tatum,* 409 U.S. 824, 835[] (1972) (memorandum opinion). Indeed, even if it were possible to select judges who did not have preconceived views on legal issues, it would hardly be desirable to do so. "Proof that a Justice's mind at the time he joined the Court was a complete *tabula rasa* in the area of constitutional adjudication would be evidence of lack of qualification, not lack of bias." *Ibid.* ...

C

A third possible meaning of "impartiality" (again not a common one) might be described as open-mindedness. This quality in a judge demands, not that he have no preconceptions on legal issues, but that he be willing to consider views that oppose his preconceptions, and remain open to persuasion, when the issues arise in a pending case. This sort of impartiality seeks to guarantee each litigant, not an *equal* chance to win the legal points in the case, but at least *some* chance of doing so. ...

Respondents argue that the announce clause serves the interest in open-mindedness, or at least in the appearance of openmindedness, because it relieves a judge from pressure to rule a certain way in order to maintain consistency with statements the judge has previously made. The problem is, however, that statements in election campaigns are such an infinitesimal portion of the public commitments to legal positions that judges (or judges-to-be) undertake, that this object of the prohibition is implausible. Before they arrive on the bench (whether by election or otherwise) judges have often committed themselves on legal issues that they must later rule upon. ...

IV

To sustain the announce clause, the Eighth Circuit relied heavily on the fact that a pervasive practice of prohibiting judicial candidates from discussing disputed legal and political issues developed during the last half of the 20th century. [C] It is true that a "universal and long-established" tradition of prohibiting certain conduct creates "a strong presumption" that the prohibition is constitutional: "Principles of liberty fundamental enough to have been embodied within constitutional guarantees are not readily erased from the Nation's consciousness." *McIntyre v. Ohio Elections Comm'n,* 514 U.S. 334, 375-377[] (1995) (SCALIA, J., dissenting). The practice of prohibiting speech by judicial candidates on disputed issues, however, is neither long nor universal. ...

There is an obvious tension between the article of Minnesota's popularly approved Constitution which provides that judges shall be elected, and the Minnesota Supreme Court's announce clause which places most subjects of interest to the voters off limits. ... The disparity is perhaps unsurprising, since the ABA, which originated the announce clause, has long been an opponent of judicial elections. See ABA Model Code of Judicial Conduct, Canon 5(C)(2), Comment (2000) ("[M]erit selection of judges is a preferable manner in which to select the judiciary"); An Independent Judiciary: Report of the ABA Commission on Separation of Powers and Judicial Independence 96 (1997) ("The American Bar Association strongly endorses the merit selection of judges, as opposed to their election..."). That opposition may be well taken (it certainly had the support of the Founders of the Federal Government), but the First Amendment does not permit it to achieve its goal by leaving the principle of elections in place while preventing candidates from discussing what the elections are about. ...

The Minnesota Supreme Court's canon of judicial conduct prohibiting candidates for judicial election from announcing their views on disputed legal and political issues violates the First Amendment. Accordingly, we reverse the grant of summary judgment to respondents and remand the case for proceedings consistent with this opinion.

It is so ordered.

Justice O'CONNOR, concurring[, omitted].
Justice KENNEDY, concurring[, omitted].

Justice STEVENS, dissenting[, omitted].
Justice GINSBURG, dissenting[, omitted].

Career and Professional Development

Your ability to conduct yourself responsibly within the profession, whether in interacting with judges or in other endeavors, is what makes you a lawyer. Your knowledge of conduct rules and professional norms and conventions is invaluable to employers, whether your law firm or clients. When lawyers are responsible, lawyers are producers. They make economies, communities, corporations, families, and individuals better. Employers of lawyers—both law firms and clients—want to hear that from you, that you appreciate that your value lies in your responsible action undertaken to add value to your clients' matters. Professional responsibility is productive, purposeful, and engaging. Focus your career and professional development around professional responsibility, and you will do well for you and others.

CONCLUSION

Personal and Professional Identity

We hope that you have seen that personal and professional responsibility begins (in Chapter 1) with your willingness and commitment to obey authority. You cannot be responsible without being responsible *to* something or someone. At the same time, obedience is a prerequisite to citizenship, as Chapter 2 shows. One cannot become a citizen of any nation without agreeing to obey its constitution and laws. Membership in any group requires the same commitment to uphold its defining norms. For you to be a lawyer, you must take an oath that requires you to commit publicly to obey the national and state constitutions, and the rules and fundamental norms of the law profession. Obedience and citizenship are the entry points to the law profession. For each of us to succeed and prosper individually, and for all of us to succeed and prosper collectively, we need obedience to the common morality reflected in constitutions, laws, conduct rules, and the commitments that underlie them.

Submitting to national and state constitution and laws, and to the profession's rules and norms, qualifies you for professional relationship with clients, which was the subject of Chapter 3. You define that client relationship by the mastery you show through your competence and diligence. Sound relationship, though, also requires authenticity marked by transparent, candid, and confidential communications, which was the subject of Chapter 4. To maintain client relationships, you must also be reasonable and productive in the fees that you charge, which was the subject of Chapter 5. To carry out the objectives of a client relationship, you must be respectful to judges, other lawyers, and the public, as Chapter 6 showed. Some representations, particularly those that involve clients with diminished capacity, communicating and dealing with unrepresented persons, and uninformed tribunals, require you to show candor and sensitivity, as Chapter 7 showed.

Honesty is then your hallmark as a professional, meaning as Chapter 8 showed that you would be truthful in all statements to others while maintaining only meritorious claims, expediting those claims, and preserving the tribunal's decorum. You will match your general honesty with specific loyalty to your clients, avoiding as Chapter 9 showed all conflicts involving clients, former clients, and prospective clients. Your honesty and loyalty will make your actions and intentions transparent in all roles whether as a law partner, government employee, arbitrator, mediator, or other third-party neutral. These actions will contribute to your reputation, keeping your marketing sound as you attract clients to you, as Chapter 11 showed. You will then have contributed to access to justice, as Chapter 12 showed, which is your fundamental reason for entering the law profession. Together, the attributes you acquire and conduct in which you engage will make you fit to appeal to and invoke the authority of law, even as you help judges comply with their judicial code of conduct, as Chapter 13 showed.

You should also have seen from your studies in this course that ethics is learned behavior. Many of us enter the study of personal and professional responsibility believing that we are innately ethical and responsible. These studies should have called into question your confidence in your own judgment independent of the profession's rules and norms. We need the rules because our own judgment often errs on the side of self-interest. We tend to reach and grasp what we should not and, conversely, to let go when we should reach out, grasp, hold on, and support. We tend to trust where we should not and to fail to trust where we should. We offer loyalty to whom we should not while eschewing loyalty to those whom we should. We fail to respect and fail to produce. We are less than honest and less than transparent.

The rules point out these faults while pointing us toward our goal, which is to have the integrity necessary to invoke authority properly and consistently on behalf of our clients. Lawyers are producers of economic and social goods. Lawyers do not simply divide the American pie. We are responsible for making the pie larger. We are each individually responsible for services of value, to help our clients produce goods and services of value. Beyond performing competent work within the rules of conduct, we each have an obligation to consider the ends of our work, meaning the uses to which our clients are putting our services. Our services should supplement, vitalize, and enlarge the economic and social goods our clients produce within their best yearnings. Lawyers have the responsibility to produce goods of value.

We also need the rules because law practice presents complex relationships and situations far beyond the experience of nonlawyer individuals. You are still learning what it means to be a lawyer. Law practice is complex. You must master and exercise simultaneously dozens of rich professional competencies. Good lawyers make law practice look easy. Yet like other masteries, whether a fine chef or a professional golfer or dancer, law practice is not easy to make look easy. Behind the apparent ease of professional performance are inevitable years of study, discipline, failure, assessment, and reform. No course does more to advance you along that path to mastery than the course in professional responsibility. Congratulations on having completed a large step toward that mastery.

Career and Professional Development

It is our privilege from time to time to see recent and not-so-recent graduates whom we taught as students. Understand how satisfying those visits are to us. You change so quickly. The confidence, skill, and accomplishment that we see in recent graduates are simply marvels to witness. Some people go years (maybe even decades) without changing much in understanding and outlook. They seem to be the same person, not having stretched and grown. What we see in you is that you are reaching, challenging yourselves, and maturing in such engaging ways. Continue to do so. Continue to explore professional responsibility. Take deliberate action to broaden your circle of professional contacts, however brief those contacts may be. Study shows that job opportunities, personal growth, professional development, and innovation come not from close and regular acquaintances but from encounters in ever-wider circles. Make yourself a student of other lawyers and then of other persons and professionals. Take an interest in the service and development of others, and you will find that you serve and develop yourself.

APPENDIX I

CALIFORNIA RULES OF PROFESSIONAL CONDUCT

CHAPTER 1: PROFESSIONAL INTEGRITY IN GENERAL
Rule 1-100. Rules of Professional Conduct, in General.
(A) Purpose and Function.

The following rules are intended to regulate professional conduct of members of the State Bar through discipline. They have been adopted by the Board of Governors of the State Bar of California and approved by the Supreme Court of California pursuant to Business and Professions Code sections 6076 and 6077 to protect the public and to promote respect and confidence in the legal profession. These rules together with any standards adopted by the Board of Governors pursuant to these rules shall be binding upon all members of the State Bar.

For a willful breach of any of these rules, the Board of Governors has the power to discipline members as provided by law.

The prohibition of certain conduct in these rules is not exclusive. Members are also bound by applicable law including the State Bar Act (Bus. & Prof. Code, 6000 et seq.) and opinions of California courts. Although not binding, opinions of ethics committees in California should be consulted by members for guidance on proper professional conduct. Ethics opinions and rules and standards promulgated by other jurisdictions and bar associations may also be considered.

These rules are not intended to create new civil causes of action. Nothing in these rules shall be deemed to create, augment, diminish, or eliminate any substantive legal duty of lawyers or the non-disciplinary consequences of violating such a duty.

(B) Definitions.

(1) "**Law Firm**" means:

(a) two or more lawyers whose activities constitute the practice of law, and who share its profits, expenses, and liabilities; or

(b) a law corporation which employs more than one lawyer; or

(c) a division, department, office, or group within a business entity, which includes more than one lawyer who performs legal services for the business entity; or

(d) a publicly funded entity which employs more than one lawyer to perform legal services.

(2) "**Member**" means a member of the State Bar of California.

(3) "**Lawyer**" means a member of the State Bar of California or a person who is admitted in good standing of and eligible to practice before the bar of any United States court or the highest court of the District of Columbia or any state, territory, or insular possession of the United States, or is licensed to practice law in, or is admitted in good standing and eligible to practice before the bar of the highest court of, a foreign country or any political subdivision thereof.

(4) "**Associate**" means an employee or fellow employee who is employed as a lawyer.

(5) "**Shareholder**" means a shareholder in a professional corporation pursuant to Business and Professions Code section 6160 et seq.

(C) Purpose of Discussions.

Because it is a practical impossibility to convey in black letter form all of the nuances of these disciplinary rules, the comments contained in the Discussions of the rules, while they do not add independent basis for imposing discipline, are intended to provide guidance for interpreting the rules and practicing in compliance with them.

(D) Geographic Scope of Rules.

(1) As to members:These rules shall govern the activities of members in and outside this state, except as members lawfully practicing outside this state may be specifically required by a jurisdiction in which they are practicing to follow rules of professional conduct different from these rules.

(2) As to lawyers from other jurisdictions who are not members:These rules shall also govern the activities of lawyers while engaged in the performance of lawyer functions in this state; but nothing contained in these rules shall be deemed to authorize the performance of such functions by such persons in this state except as otherwise permitted by law.

(E) These rules may be cited and referred to as "Rules of Professional Conduct of the State Bar of California."

Rule 1-110. Disciplinary Authority of the State Bar.

A member shall comply with conditions attached to public or private reprovals or other discipline administered by the State Bar pursuant to Business and Professions Code sections 6077 and 6078 and rule 956, California Rules of Court.

Rule 1-120. Assisting, Soliciting, or Inducing Violations.

A member shall not knowingly assist in, solicit, or induce any violation of these rules or the State Bar Act.

Rule 1-200. False Statement Regarding Admission to the State Bar.

(A) A member shall not knowingly make a false statement regarding a material fact or knowingly fail to disclose a material fact in connection with an application for admission to the State Bar.

(B) A member shall not further an application for admission to the State Bar of a person whom the member knows to be unqualified in respect to character, education, or other relevant attributes.

(C) This rule shall not prevent a member from serving as counsel of record for an applicant for admission to practice in proceedings related to such admission.

Rule 1-300. Unauthorized Practice of Law.

(A) A member shall not aid any person or entity in the unauthorized practice of law.

(B) A member shall not practice law in a jurisdiction where to do so would be in violation of regulations of the profession in that jurisdiction.

Rule 1-310. Forming a Partnership With a Non-Lawyer.

A member shall not form a partnership with a person who is not a lawyer if any of the activities of that partnership consist of the practice of law.

Rule 1-311. Employment of Disbarred, Suspended, Resigned, or Involuntarily Inactive Member.

(A) For purposes of this rule:

(1) "**Employ**" means to engage the services of another, including employees, agents, independent contractors and consultants, regardless of whether any compensation is paid;

(2) "**Involuntarily inactive member**" means a member who is ineligible to practice law as a result of action taken pursuant to Business and Professions Code sections 6007, 6203(c), or California Rule of Court 958(d); and

(3) "**Resigned member**" means a member who has resigned from the State Bar while disciplinary charges are pending.

(B) A member shall not employ, associate professionally with, or aid a person the member knows or reasonably should know is a disbarred, suspended, resigned, or involuntarily inactive member to perform the following on behalf of the member's client:

(1) Render legal consultation or advice to the client;

(2) Appear on behalf of a client in any hearing or proceeding or before any judicial officer, arbitrator, mediator, court, public agency, referee, magistrate, commissioner, or hearing officer;

(3) Appear as a representative of the client at a deposition or other discovery matter;

(4) Negotiate or transact any matter for or on behalf of the client with third parties;

(5) Receive, disburse or otherwise handle the client's funds; or

(6) Engage in activities which constitute the practice of law.

(C) A member may employ, associate professionally with, or aid a disbarred, suspended, resigned, or involuntarily inactive member to perform research, drafting or clerical activities, including but not limited to:

(1) Legal work of a preparatory nature, such as legal research, the assemblage of data and other necessary information, drafting of pleadings, briefs, and other similar documents;

(2) Direct communication with the client or third parties regarding matters such as scheduling, billing, updates, confirmation of receipt or sending of correspondence and messages; or

(3) Accompanying an active member in attending a deposition or other discovery matter for the limited purpose of providing clerical assistance to the active member who will appear as the representative of the client.

(D) Prior to or at the time of employing a person the member knows or reasonably should know is a disbarred, suspended, resigned, or involuntarily inactive member, the member shall serve upon the State Bar written notice of the employment, including a full description of such person's current bar status. The written notice shall also list the activities prohibited in paragraph (B) and state that the disbarred, suspended, resigned, or involuntarily inactive member will not perform such activities. The member shall serve similar written notice upon each client on whose specific matter such person will work, prior to or at the time of employing such person to work on the client's specific matter. The member shall obtain proof of service of the client's written notice and shall retain such proof and a true and correct copy of the client's written notice for two years following termination of the member's employment with the client.

(E) A member may, without client or State Bar notification, employ a disbarred, suspended, resigned or involuntarily inactive member whose sole function is to perform office physical plant or equipment maintenance, courier or delivery services, catering, reception, typing or transcription, or other similar support activities.

(F) Upon termination of the disbarred, suspended, resigned, or involuntarily inactive member, the member shall promptly serve upon the State Bar written notice of the termination.

Rule 1-320. Financial Arrangements With Non-Lawyers.

(A) Neither a member nor a law firm shall directly or indirectly share legal fees with a person who is not a lawyer, except that:

(1) An agreement between a member and a law firm, partner, or associate may provide for the payment of money after the member's death to the member's estate or to one or more specified persons over a reasonable period of time; or

(2) A member or law firm undertaking to complete unfinished legal business of a deceased member may pay to the estate of the deceased member or other person legally entitled thereto that proportion of the total compensation which fairly represents the services rendered by the deceased member; or

(3) A member or law firm may include non-member employees in a compensation, profit-sharing, or retirement plan even though the plan is based in whole or in part on a profit-sharing arrangement, if such plan does not circumvent these rules or Business and Professions Code section 6000 et seq.; or

(4) A member may pay a prescribed registration, referral, or participation fee to a lawyer referral service established, sponsored, and operated in

accordance with the State Bar of California's Minimum Standards for a Lawyer Referral Service in California.

(B) A member shall not compensate, give, or promise anything of value to any person or entity for the purpose of recommending or securing employment of the member or the member's law firm by a client, or as a reward for having made a recommendation resulting in employment of the member or the member's law firm by a client. A member's offering of or giving a gift or gratuity to any person or entity having made a recommendation resulting in the employment of the member or the member's law firm shall not of itself violate this rule, provided that the gift or gratuity was not offered or given in consideration of any promise, agreement, or understanding that such a gift or gratuity would be forthcoming or that referrals would be made or encouraged in the future.

(C) A member shall not compensate, give, or promise anything of value to any representative of the press, radio, television, or other communication medium in anticipation of or in return for publicity of the member, the law firm, or any other member as such in a news item, but the incidental provision of food or beverage shall not of itself violate this rule.

Rule 1-400. Advertising and Solicitation.

(A) For purposes of this rule, "**communication**" means any message or offer made by or on behalf of a member concerning the availability for professional employment of a member or a law firm directed to any former, present, or prospective client, including but not limited to the following:

(1) Any use of firm name, trade name, fictitious name, or other professional designation of such member or law firm; or

(2) Any stationery, letterhead, business card, sign, brochure, or other comparable written material describing such member, law firm, or lawyers; or

(3) Any advertisement (regardless of medium) of such member or law firm directed to the general public or any substantial portion thereof; or

(4) Any unsolicited correspondence from a member or law firm directed to any person or entity.

(B) For purposes of this rule, a "**solicitation**" means any communication:

(1) Concerning the availability for professional employment of a member or a law firm in which a significant motive is pecuniary gain; and

(2) Which is;

(a) delivered in person or by telephone, or

(b) directed by any means to a person known to the sender to be represented by counsel in a matter which is a subject of the communication.

(C) A solicitation shall not be made by or on behalf of a member or law firm to a prospective client with whom the member or law firm has no family or prior professional relationship, unless the solicitation is protected from abridgment by the Constitution of the United States or by the Constitution of the State of California. A solicitation to a former or present client in the discharge of a member's or law firm's professional duties is not prohibited.

(D) A communication or a solicitation (as defined herein) shall not:

(1) Contain any untrue statement; or

(2) Contain any matter, or present or arrange any matter in a manner or format which is false, deceptive, or which tends to confuse, deceive, or mislead the public; or

(3) Omit to state any fact necessary to make the statements made, in the light of circumstances under which they are made, not misleading to the public; or

(4) Fail to indicate clearly, expressly, or by context, that it is a communication or solicitation, as the case may be; or

(5) Be transmitted in any manner which involves intrusion, coercion, duress, compulsion, intimidation, threats, or vexatious or harassing conduct.

(6) State that a member is a "certified specialist" unless the member holds a current certificate as a specialist issued by the California Board of Legal Specialization pursuant to a plan for specialization approved by the Supreme Court.

(E) The Board of Governors of the State Bar shall formulate and adopt standards as to communications which will be presumed to violate this rule 1-400. The standards shall only be used as presumptions affecting the burden of proof in disciplinary proceedings involving alleged violations of these rules. "Presumption affecting the burden of proof" means that presumption defined in Evidence Code sections 605 and 606. Such standards formulated and adopted by the Board, as from time to time amended, shall be effective and binding on all members.

(F) A member shall retain for two years a true and correct copy or recording of any communication made by written or electronic media. Upon written request, the member shall make any such copy or recording available to the State Bar, and, if requested, shall provide to the State Bar evidence to support any factual or objective claim contained in the communication.

Rule 1-500. Agreements Restricting a Member's Practice.

(A) A member shall not be a party to or participate in offering or making an agreement, whether in connection with the settlement of a lawsuit or otherwise, if the agreement restricts the right of a member to practice law, except that this rule shall not prohibit such an agreement which:

(1) Is a part of an employment, shareholders', or partnership agreement among members provided the restrictive agreement does not survive the termination of the employment, shareholder, or partnership relationship; or

(2) Requires payments to a member upon the member's retirement from the practice of law.

(3) Is authorized by Business and Professions Code sections 6092.5, subdivision (i) or 6093.

(B) A member shall not be a party to or participate in offering or making an agreement which precludes the reporting of a violation of these rules.

Rule 1-600. Legal Service Programs.

(A) A member shall not participate in a nongovernmental program, activity, or organization furnishing, recommending, or paying for legal services, which allows any third person or organization to interfere with the member's independence of professional judgment, or with the client-lawyer relationship, or allows unlicensed persons to practice law, or allows any third person or organization to receive directly or indirectly any part of the consideration paid to the member except as permitted by these rules, or otherwise violates the State Bar Act or these rules.

(B) The Board of Governors of the State Bar shall formulate and adopt Minimum Standards for Lawyer Referral Services, which, as from time to time amended, shall be binding on members.

Rule 1-700. Member as Candidate for Judicial Office.

(A) A member who is a candidate for judicial office in California shall comply with Canon 5 of the Code of Judicial Ethics.

(B) For purposes of this rule, "candidate for judicial office" means a member seeking judicial office by election. The determination of when a member is a candidate for judicial office is defined in the terminology section of the California Code of Judicial Ethics. A member's duty to comply with paragraph (A) shall end when the member announces withdrawal of the member's candidacy or when the results of the election are final, whichever occurs first.

Rule 1-710. Member as Temporary Judge, Referee, or Court-Appointed Arbitrator.

A member who is serving as a temporary judge, referee, or court-appointed arbitrator, and is subject under the Code of Judicial Ethics to Canon 6D, shall comply with the terms of that canon.

CHAPTER 2: RELATIONSHIP AMONG MEMBERS
Rule 2-100. Communication With a Represented Party.

(A) While representing a client, a member shall not communicate directly or indirectly about the subject of the representation with a party the member knows to be represented by another lawyer in the matter, unless the member has the consent of the other lawyer.

(B) For purposes of this rule, a "**party**" includes:

(1) An officer, director, or managing agent of a corporation or association, and a partner or managing agent of a partnership; or

(2) An association member or an employee of an association, corporation, or partnership, if the subject of the communication is any act or omission of such person in connection with the matter which may be binding upon or imputed to the organization for purposes of civil or criminal liability or whose statement may constitute an admission on the part of the organization.

(C) This rule shall not prohibit:

(1) Communications with a public officer, board, committee, or body;

(2) Communications initiated by a party seeking advice or representation from an independent lawyer of the party's choice; or

(3) Communications otherwise authorized by law.

Rule 2-200. Financial Arrangements Among Lawyers.

(A) A member shall not divide a fee for legal services with a lawyer who is not a partner of, associate of, or shareholder with the member unless:

(1) The client has consented in writing thereto after a full disclosure has been made in writing that a division of fees will be made and the terms of such division; and

(2) The total fee charged by all lawyers is not increased solely by reason of the provision for division of fees and is not unconscionable as that term is defined in rule 4-200.

(B) Except as permitted in paragraph (A) of this rule or rule 2-300, a member shall not compensate, give, or promise anything of value to any lawyer for the purpose of recommending or securing employment of the member or the member's law firm by a client, or as a reward for having made a recommendation resulting in employment of the member or the member's law firm by a client. A member's offering of or giving a gift or gratuity to any lawyer who has made a recommendation resulting in the employment of the member or the member's law firm shall not of itself violate this rule, provided that the gift or gratuity was not offered in consideration of any promise, agreement, or understanding that such a gift or gratuity would be forthcoming or that referrals would be made or encouraged in the future.

Rule 2-300. Sale or Purchase of a Law Practice of a Member, Living or Deceased.

All or substantially all of the law practice of a member, living or deceased, including goodwill, may be sold to another member or law firm subject to all the following conditions:

(A) Fees charged to clients shall not be increased solely by reason of such sale.

(B) If the sale contemplates the transfer of responsibility for work not yet completed or responsibility for client files or information protected by Business and Professions Code section 6068, subdivision (e), then;

(1) if the seller is deceased, or has a conservator or other person acting in a representative capacity, and no member has been appointed to act for the seller pursuant to Business and Professions Code section 6180.5, then prior to the transfer;

(a) the purchaser shall cause a written notice to be given to the client stating that the interest in the law practice is being transferred to the purchaser; that the client has the right to retain other counsel; that the client may take possession of any client papers and property, as required by rule 3-700(D); and that if no response is received to the notification within 90 days of the sending of such notice, or in the event the client's rights would be prejudiced by a failure to act during that time, the purchaser may act on behalf of the client until otherwise notified by the client. Such notice shall comply with the requirements as set forth in rule 1-400(D) and any provisions relating to attorney-client fee arrangements, and

(b) the purchaser shall obtain the written consent of the client provided that such consent shall be presumed until otherwise notified by the client if no response is received to the notification specified in subparagraph (a) within 90 days of the date of the sending of such notification to the client's last address as shown on the records of the seller, or the client's rights would be prejudiced by a failure to act during such 90-day period.

(2) in all other circumstances, not less than 90 days prior to the transfer;

(a) the seller, or the member appointed to act for the seller pursuant to Business and Professions Code section 6180.5, shall cause a written notice to be given to the client stating that the interest in the law practice is being transferred to the purchaser; that the client has the right to retain other counsel; that the client may take possession of any client papers and property, as required by rule 3-700(D); and that if no response is received to the notification within 90 days of the sending of such notice, the purchaser may act on behalf of the client until otherwise notified by the client. Such notice shall comply with the requirements as set forth in rule 1-400(D) and any provisions relating to attorney-client fee arrangements, and

(b) the seller, or the member appointed to act for the seller pursuant to Business and Professions Code section 6180.5, shall obtain the written consent of the client prior to the transfer provided that such consent shall be presumed until otherwise notified by the client if no response is received to the notification specified in subparagraph (a) within 90 days of the date of the sending of such notification to the client's last address as shown on the records of the seller.

(C) If substitution is required by the rules of a tribunal in which a matter is pending, all steps necessary to substitute a member shall be taken.

(D) All activity of a purchaser or potential purchaser under this rule shall be subject to compliance with rules 3-300 and 3-310 where applicable.

(E) Confidential information shall not be disclosed to a non-member in connection with a sale under this rule.

(F) Admission to or retirement from a law partnership or law corporation, retirement plans and similar arrangements, or sale of tangible assets of a law practice shall not be deemed a sale or purchase under this rule.

Rule 2-400. Prohibited Discriminatory Conduct in a Law Practice.

(A) For purposes of this rule:

(1) "**law practice**" includes sole practices, law partnerships, law corporations, corporate and governmental legal departments, and other entities which employ members to practice law;

(2) "**knowingly permit**" means a failure to advocate corrective action where the member knows of a discriminatory policy or practice which results in the unlawful discrimination prohibited in paragraph (B); and

(3) "**unlawfully**" and "**unlawful**" shall be determined by reference to applicable state or federal statutes or decisions making unlawful discrimination in employment and in offering goods and services to the public.

(B) In the management or operation of a law practice, a member shall not unlawfully discriminate or knowingly permit unlawful discrimination on the basis of race, national origin, sex, sexual orientation, religion, age or disability in:

(1) hiring, promoting, discharging, or otherwise determining the conditions of employment of any person; or

(2) accepting or terminating representation of any client.

(C) No disciplinary investigation or proceeding may be initiated by the State Bar against a member under this rule unless and until a tribunal of competent jurisdiction, other than a disciplinary tribunal, shall have first adjudicated a complaint of alleged discrimination and found that unlawful conduct occurred. Upon such adjudication, the tribunal finding or verdict shall then be admissible evidence of the occurrence or non-occurrence of the alleged discrimination in any disciplinary proceeding initiated under this rule. In order for discipline to be imposed under this rule, however, the finding of unlawfulness must be upheld and final after appeal, the time for filing an appeal must have expired, or the appeal must have been dismissed.

CHAPTER 3: PROFESSIONAL RELATIONSHIP WITH CLIENTS
Rule 3-100. Confidential Information of a Client

(A) A member shall not reveal information protected from disclosure by Business and Professions Code section 6068, subdivision (e)(1) without the informed consent of the client, or as provided in paragraph (B) of this rule.

(B) A member may, but is not required to, reveal confidential information relating to the representation of a client to the extent that the member reasonably believes the disclosure is necessary to prevent a criminal act that the member reasonably believes is likely to result in death of, or substantial bodily harm to, an individual.

(C) Before revealing confidential information to prevent a criminal act as provided in paragraph (B), a member shall, if reasonable under the circumstances:

(1) make a good faith effort to persuade the client: (i) not to commit or to continue the criminal act or (ii) to pursue a course of conduct that will prevent the threatened death or substantial bodily harm; or do both (i) and (ii); and

(2) inform the client, at an appropriate time, of the member's ability or decision to reveal information as provided in paragraph (B).

(D) In revealing confidential information as provided in paragraph (B), the member's disclosure must be no more than is necessary to prevent the criminal act, given the information known to the member at the time of the disclosure.

(E) A member who does not reveal information permitted by paragraph (B) does not violate this rule.

Rule 3-110. Failing to Act Competently.

(A) A member shall not intentionally, recklessly, or repeatedly fail to perform legal services with competence.

(B) For purposes of this rule, "**competence**" in any legal service shall mean to apply the

1) diligence,

2) learning and skill, and

3) mental, emotional, and physical ability reasonably necessary for the performance of such service.

(C) If a member does not have sufficient learning and skill when the legal service is undertaken, the member may nonetheless perform such services competently by

1) associating with or, where appropriate, professionally consulting another lawyer reasonably believed to be competent, or

2) by acquiring sufficient learning and skill before performance is required.

Rule 3-120. Sexual Relations With Client.

(A) For purposes of this rule, "**sexual relations**" means sexual intercourse or the touching of an intimate part of another person for the purpose of sexual arousal, gratification, or abuse.

(B) A member shall not:

(1) Require or demand sexual relations with a client incident to or as a condition of any professional representation; or

(2) Employ coercion, intimidation, or undue influence in entering into sexual relations with a client; or

(3) Continue representation of a client with whom the member has sexual relations if such sexual relations cause the member to perform legal services incompetently in violation of rule 3-110.

(C) Paragraph (B) shall not apply to sexual relations between members and their spouses or to ongoing consensual sexual relationships which predate the initiation of the lawyer-client relationship.

(D) Where a lawyer in a firm has sexual relations with a client but does not participate in the representation of that client, the lawyers in the firm shall not be subject to discipline under this rule solely because of the occurrence of such sexual relations.

Rule 3-200. Prohibited Objectives of Employment.

A member shall not seek, accept, or continue employment if the member knows or should know that the objective of such employment is:

(A) To bring an action, conduct a defense, assert a position in litigation, or take an appeal, without probable cause and for the purpose of harassing or maliciously injuring any person; or

(B) To present a claim or defense in litigation that is not warranted under existing law, unless it can be supported by a good faith argument for an extension, modification, or reversal of such existing law.

Rule 3-210. Advising the Violation of Law.

A member shall not advise the violation of any law, rule, or ruling of a tribunal unless the member believes in good faith that such law, rule, or ruling is invalid. A member may take appropriate steps in good faith to test the validity of any law, rule, or ruling of a tribunal.

Rule 3-300. Avoiding Interests Adverse to a Client.

A member shall not enter into a business transaction with a client; or knowingly acquire an ownership, possessory, security, or other pecuniary interest adverse to a client, unless each of the following requirements has been satisfied:

(A) The transaction or acquisition and its terms are fair and reasonable to the client and are fully disclosed and transmitted in writing to the client in a manner which should reasonably have been understood by the client; and

(B) The client is advised in writing that the client may seek the advice of an independent lawyer of the client's choice and is given a reasonable opportunity to seek that advice; and

(C) The client thereafter consents in writing to the terms of the transaction or the terms of the acquisition.

Rule 3-310. Avoiding the Representation of Adverse Interests.

(A) For purposes of this rule:

(1) **"Disclosure"** means informing the client or former client of the relevant circumstances and of the actual and reasonably foreseeable adverse consequences to the client or former client;

(2) **"Informed written consent"** means the client's or former client's written agreement to the representation following written disclosure;

(3) **"Written"** means any writing as defined in Evidence Code section 250.

(B) A member shall not accept or continue representation of a client without providing written disclosure to the client where:

(1) The member has a legal, business, financial, professional, or personal relationship with a party or witness in the same matter; or

(2) The member knows or reasonably should know that:

(a) the member previously had a legal, business, financial, professional, or personal relationship with a party or witness in the same matter; and

(b) the previous relationship would substantially affect the member's representation; or

(3) The member has or had a legal, business, financial, professional, or personal relationship with another person or entity the member knows or reasonably should know would be affected substantially by the resolution of the matter; or

(4) The member has or had a legal, business, financial, or professional interest in the subject matter of the representation.

(C) A member shall not, without the informed written consent of each client:

(1) Accept representation of more than one client in a matter in which the interests of the clients potentially conflict; or

(2) Accept or continue representation of more than one client in a matter in which the interests of the clients actually conflict; or

(3) Represent a client in a matter and at the same time in a separate matter accept as a client a person or entity whose interest in the first matter is adverse to the client in the first matter.

(D) A member who represents two or more clients shall not enter into an aggregate settlement of the claims of or against the clients, without the informed written consent of each client.

(E) A member shall not, without the informed written consent of the client or former client, accept employment adverse to the client or former client where, by reason of the representation of the client or former client, the member has obtained confidential information material to the employment.

(F) A member shall not accept compensation for representing a client from one other than the client unless:

(1) There is no interference with the member's independence of professional judgment or with the client-lawyer relationship; and

(2) Information relating to representation of the client is protected as required by Business and Professions Code section 6068, subdivision (e); and

(3) The member obtains the client's informed written consent, provided that no disclosure or consent is required if:

(a) such nondisclosure is otherwise authorized by law, or

(b) the member is rendering legal services on behalf of any public agency which provides legal services to other public agencies or the public.

Rule 3-320. Relationship With Other Party's Lawyer.

A member shall not represent a client in a matter in which another party's lawyer is a spouse, parent, child, or sibling of the member, lives with the member, is a client of the member, or has an intimate personal relationship with the member, unless the member informs the client in writing of the relationship.

Rule 3-400. Limiting Liability to Client.

A member shall not:

(A) Contract with a client prospectively limiting the member's liability to the client for the member's professional malpractice; or

(B) Settle a claim or potential claim for the member's liability to the client for the member's professional malpractice, unless the client is informed in writing that the client may seek the advice of an independent lawyer of the client's choice regarding the settlement and is given a reasonable opportunity to seek that advice.

Rule 3-500. Communication.

A member shall keep a client reasonably informed about significant developments relating to the employment or representation, including promptly complying with reasonable requests for information and copies of significant documents when necessary to keep the client so informed.

Rule 3-510. Communication of Settlement Offer.

(A) A member shall promptly communicate to the member's client:

(1) All terms and conditions of any offer made to the client in a criminal matter; and

(2) All amounts, terms, and conditions of any written offer of settlement made to the client in all other matters.

(B) As used in this rule, "**client**" includes a person who possesses the authority to accept an offer of settlement or plea, or, in a class action, all the named representatives of the class.

Rule 3-600. Organization as Client.

(A) In representing an organization, a member shall conform his or her representation to the concept that the client is the organization itself, acting through its highest authorized officer, employee, body, or constituent overseeing the particular engagement.

(B) If a member acting on behalf of an organization knows that an actual or apparent agent of the organization acts or intends or refuses to act in a manner that is or may be a violation of law reasonably imputable to the organization, or in a manner which is likely to result in substantial injury to the organization, the member shall not violate his or her duty of protecting all confidential information as provided in Business and Professions Code section 6068, subdivision (e). Subject to Business and Professions Code section 6068, subdivision (e), the member may take such actions as appear to the member to be in the best lawful interest of the organization. Such actions may include among others:

(1) Urging reconsideration of the matter while explaining its likely consequences to the organization; or

(2) Referring the matter to the next higher authority in the organization, including, if warranted by the seriousness of the matter, referral to the highest internal authority that can act on behalf of the organization.

(C) If, despite the member's actions in accordance with paragraph (B), the highest authority that can act on behalf of the organization insists upon action or a refusal to act that is a violation of law and is likely to result in substantial injury to the organization, the member's response is limited to the member's right, and, where appropriate, duty to resign in accordance with rule 3-700.

(D) In dealing with an organization's directors, officers, employees, members, shareholders, or other constituents, a member shall explain the identity of the client for whom the member acts, whenever it is or becomes apparent that the organization's interests are or may become adverse to those of the constituent(s) with whom the member is dealing. The member shall not mislead such a constituent into believing that the constituent may communicate confidential information to the member in a way that will not be used in the organization's interest if that is or becomes adverse to the constituent.

(E) A member representing an organization may also represent any of its directors, officers, employees, members, shareholders, or other constituents, subject to the provisions of rule 3-310. If the organization's consent to the dual representation is required by rule 3-310, the consent shall be given by an appropriate constituent of the organization other than the individual or constituent who is to be represented, or by the shareholder(s) or organization members.

Rule 3-700. Termination of Employment.

(A) In General.

(1) If permission for termination of employment is required by the rules of a tribunal, a member shall not withdraw from employment in a proceeding before that tribunal without its permission.

(2) A member shall not withdraw from employment until the member has taken reasonable steps to avoid reasonably foreseeable prejudice to the rights of the client, including giving due notice to the client, allowing time for employment of other counsel, complying with rule 3-700(D), and complying with applicable laws and rules.

(B) Mandatory Withdrawal.

A member representing a client before a tribunal shall withdraw from employment with the permission of the tribunal, if required by its rules, and a member representing a client in other matters shall withdraw from employment, if:

(1) The member knows or should know that the client is bringing an action, conducting a defense, asserting a position in litigation, or taking an appeal, without probable cause and for the purpose of harassing or maliciously injuring any person; or

(2) The member knows or should know that continued employment will result in violation of these rules or of the State Bar Act; or

(3) The member's mental or physical condition renders it unreasonably difficult to carry out the employment effectively.

(C) Permissive Withdrawal.

If rule 3-700(B) is not applicable, a member may not request permission to withdraw in matters pending before a tribunal, and may not withdraw in other matters, unless such request or such withdrawal is because:

(1) The client

(a) insists upon presenting a claim or defense that is not warranted under existing law and cannot be supported by good faith argument for an extension, modification, or reversal of existing law, or

(b) seeks to pursue an illegal course of conduct, or

(c) insists that the member pursue a course of conduct that is illegal or that is prohibited under these rules or the State Bar Act, or

(d) by other conduct renders it unreasonably difficult for the member to carry out the employment effectively, or

(e) insists, in a matter not pending before a tribunal, that the member engage in conduct that is contrary to the judgment and advice of the member but not prohibited under these rules or the State Bar Act, or

(f) breaches an agreement or obligation to the member as to expenses or fees.

(2) The continued employment is likely to result in a violation of these rules or of the State Bar Act; or

(3) The inability to work with co-counsel indicates that the best interests of the client likely will be served by withdrawal; or

(4) The member's mental or physical condition renders it difficult for the member to carry out the employment effectively; or

(5) The client knowingly and freely assents to termination of the employment; or

(6) The member believes in good faith, in a proceeding pending before a tribunal, that the tribunal will find the existence of other good cause for withdrawal.

(D) Papers, Property, and Fees.

A member whose employment has terminated shall:

(1) Subject to any protective order or non-disclosure agreement, promptly release to the client, at the request of the client, all the client papers and property. "Client papers and property" includes correspondence, pleadings, deposition transcripts, exhibits, physical evidence, expert's reports, and other items reasonably necessary to the client's representation, whether the client has paid for them or not; and

(2) Promptly refund any part of a fee paid in advance that has not been earned. This provision is not applicable to a true retainer fee which is paid solely for the purpose of ensuring the availability of the member for the matter.

CHAPTER 4: FINANCIAL RELATIONSHIP WITH CLIENTS
Rule 4-100. Preserving Identity of Funds and Property of a Client.

(A) All funds received or held for the benefit of clients by a member or law firm, including advances for costs and expenses, shall be deposited in one or more identifiable bank accounts labelled "Trust Account," "Client's Funds Account" or words of similar import, maintained in the State of California, or, with written consent of the client, in any other jurisdiction where there is a substantial relationship between the client or the client's business and the other jurisdiction. No funds belonging to the member or the law firm shall be deposited therein or otherwise commingled therewith except as follows:

(1) Funds reasonably sufficient to pay bank charges.

(2) In the case of funds belonging in part to a client and in part presently or potentially to the member or the law firm, the portion belonging to the member or law firm must be withdrawn at the earliest reasonable time after the member's interest in that portion becomes fixed. However, when the right of the member or law firm to receive a portion of trust funds is disputed by the client, the disputed portion shall not be withdrawn until the dispute is finally resolved.

(B) A member shall:

(1) Promptly notify a client of the receipt of the client's funds, securities, or other properties.

(2) Identify and label securities and properties of a client promptly upon receipt and place them in a safe deposit box or other place of safekeeping as soon as practicable.

(3) Maintain complete records of all funds, securities, and other properties of a client coming into the possession of the member or law firm and render appropriate accounts to the client regarding them; preserve such records for a period of no less than five years after final appropriate distribution of such funds or properties; and comply with any order for an

audit of such records issued pursuant to the Rules of Procedure of the State Bar.

(4) Promptly pay or deliver, as requested by the client, any funds, securities, or other properties in the possession of the member which the client is entitled to receive.

(C) The Board of Governors of the State Bar shall have the authority to formulate and adopt standards as to what "records" shall be maintained by members and law firms in accordance with subparagraph (B)(3). The standards formulated and adopted by the Board, as from time to time amended, shall be effective and binding on all members.

Rule 4-200. Fees for Legal Services.

(A) A member shall not enter into an agreement for, charge, or collect an illegal or unconscionable fee.

(B) Unconscionability of a fee shall be determined on the basis of all the facts and circumstances existing at the time the agreement is entered into except where the parties contemplate that the fee will be affected by later events. Among the factors to be considered, where appropriate, in determining the conscionability of a fee are the following:

(1) The amount of the fee in proportion to the value of the services performed.

(2) The relative sophistication of the member and the client.

(3) The novelty and difficulty of the questions involved and the skill requisite to perform the legal service properly.

(4) The likelihood, if apparent to the client, that the acceptance of the particular employment will preclude other employment by the member.

(5) The amount involved and the results obtained.

(6) The time limitations imposed by the client or by the circumstances.

(7) The nature and length of the professional relationship with the client.

(8) The experience, reputation, and ability of the member or members performing the services.

(9) Whether the fee is fixed or contingent.

(10) The time and labor required.

(11) The informed consent of the client to the fee.

Rule 4-210. Payment of Personal or Business Expenses Incurred by or for a Client.

(A) A member shall not directly or indirectly pay or agree to pay, guarantee, represent, or sanction a representation that the member or member's law firm will pay the personal or business expenses of a prospective or existing client, except that this rule shall not prohibit a member:

(1) With the consent of the client, from paying or agreeing to pay such expenses to third persons from funds collected or to be collected for the client as a result of the representation; or

(2) After employment, from lending money to the client upon the client's promise in writing to repay such loan; or

(3) From advancing the costs of prosecuting or defending a claim or action or otherwise protecting or promoting the client's interests, the repayment of which may be contingent on the outcome of the matter. Such costs within the meaning of this subparagraph (3) shall be limited to all reasonable expenses of litigation or reasonable expenses in preparation for litigation or in providing any legal services to the client.

(B) Nothing in rule 4-210 shall be deemed to limit rules 3-300, 3-310, and 4-300.

Rule 4-300. Purchasing Property at a Foreclosure or a Sale Subject to Judicial Review.

(A) A member shall not directly or indirectly purchase property at a probate, foreclosure, receiver's, trustee's, or judicial sale in an action or proceeding in which such member or any lawyer affiliated by reason of personal, business, or professional relationship with that member or with that member's law firm is acting as a lawyer for a party or as executor, receiver, trustee, administrator, guardian, or conservator.

(B) A member shall not represent the seller at a probate, foreclosure, receiver, trustee, or judicial sale in an action or proceeding in which the purchaser is a spouse or relative of the member or another lawyer in the member's law firm or is an employee of the member or the member's law firm.

Rule 4-400. Gifts From Client.

A member shall not induce a client to make a substantial gift, including a testamentary gift, to the member or to the member's parent, child, sibling, or spouse, except where the client is related to the member.

CHAPTER 5: ADVOCACY AND REPRESENTATION
Rule 5-100. Threatening Criminal, Administrative, or Disciplinary Charges.

(A) A member shall not threaten to present criminal, administrative, or disciplinary charges to obtain an advantage in a civil dispute.

(B) As used in paragraph (A) of this rule, the term "**administrative charges**" means the filing or lodging of a complaint with a federal, state, or local governmental entity which may order or recommend the loss or suspension of a license, or may impose or recommend the imposition of a fine, pecuniary sanction, or other sanction of a quasi-criminal nature but does not include filing charges with an administrative entity required by law as a condition precedent to maintaining a civil action.

(C) As used in paragraph (A) of this rule, the term "**civil dispute**" means a controversy or potential controversy over the rights and duties of two or more parties under civil law, whether or not an action has been commenced, and includes an administrative proceeding of a quasi-civil nature pending before a federal, state, or local governmental entity.

Rule 5-110. Performing the Duty of Member in Government Service.

A member in government service shall not institute or cause to be instituted criminal charges when the member knows or should know that the charges are not supported by probable cause. If, after the institution of criminal charges, the member in government service having responsibility for prosecuting the charges becomes aware that those charges are not supported by probable cause, the member shall promptly so advise the court in which the criminal matter is pending.

Rule 5-120. Trial Publicity.

(A) A member who is participating or has participated in the investigation or litigation of a matter shall not make an extrajudicial statement that a reasonable person would expect to be disseminated by means of public communication if the member knows or reasonably should know that it will have a substantial likelihood of materially prejudicing an adjudicative proceeding in the matter.

(B) Notwithstanding paragraph (A), a member may state:

(1) the claim, offense or defense involved and, except when prohibited by law, the identity of the persons involved;

(2) the information contained in a public record;

(3) that an investigation of the matter is in progress;

(4) the scheduling or result of any step in litigation;

(5) a request for assistance in obtaining evidence and information necessary thereto;

(6) a warning of danger concerning the behavior of a person involved, when there is reason to believe that there exists the likelihood of substantial harm to an individual or the public interest; and

(7) in a criminal case, in addition to subparagraphs (1) through (6):

(a) the identity, residence, occupation, and family status of the accused;

(b) if the accused has not been apprehended, information necessary to aid in apprehension of that person;

(c) the fact, time, and place of arrest; and

(d) the identity of investigating and arresting officers or agencies and the length of the investigation.

(C) Notwithstanding paragraph (A), a member may make a statement that a reasonable member would believe is required to protect a client from the substantial undue prejudicial effect of recent publicity not initiated by the member or the member's client. A statement made pursuant to this paragraph shall be limited to such information as is necessary to mitigate the recent adverse publicity.

Rule 5-200. Trial Conduct.

In presenting a matter to a tribunal, a member:

(A) Shall employ, for the purpose of maintaining the causes confided to the member such means only as are consistent with truth;

(B) Shall not seek to mislead the judge, judicial officer, or jury by an artifice or false statement of fact or law;

(C) Shall not intentionally misquote to a tribunal the language of a book, statute, or decision;

(D) Shall not, knowing its invalidity, cite as authority a decision that has been overruled or a statute that has been repealed or declared unconstitutional; and

(E) Shall not assert personal knowledge of the facts at issue, except when testifying as a witness.

Rule 5-210. Member as Witness.

A member shall not act as an advocate before a jury which will hear testimony from the member unless:

(A) The testimony relates to an uncontested matter; or

(B) The testimony relates to the nature and value of legal services rendered in the case; or

(C) The member has the informed, written consent of the client. If the member represents the People or a governmental entity, the consent shall be obtained from the head of the office or a designee of the head of the office by which the member is employed and shall be consistent with principles of recusal.

Rule 5-220. Suppression of Evidence.

A member shall not suppress any evidence that the member or the member's client has a legal obligation to reveal or to produce.

Rule 5-300. Contact With Officials.

(A) A member shall not directly or indirectly give or lend anything of value to a judge, official, or employee of a tribunal unless the personal or family relationship between the member and the judge, official, or employee is such that gifts are customarily given and exchanged. Nothing contained in this rule shall prohibit a member from contributing to the campaign fund of a judge running for election or confirmation pursuant to applicable law pertaining to such contributions.

(B) A member shall not directly or indirectly communicate with or argue to a judge or judicial officer upon the merits of a contested matter pending before such judge or judicial officer, except:

(1) In open court; or

(2) With the consent of all other counsel in such matter; or

(3) In the presence of all other counsel in such matter; or

(4) In writing with a copy thereof furnished to such other counsel; or

(5) In ex parte matters.

(C) As used in this rule, **"judge"** and **"judicial officer"** shall include law clerks, research attorneys, or other court personnel who participate in the decision-making process.

Rule 5-310. Prohibited Contact With Witnesses.

A member shall not:

(A) Advise or directly or indirectly cause a person to secrete himself or herself or to leave the jurisdiction of a tribunal for the purpose of making that person unavailable as a witness therein.

(B) Directly or indirectly pay, offer to pay, or acquiesce in the payment of compensation to a witness contingent upon the content of the witness's testimony or the outcome of the case. Except where prohibited by law, a member may advance, guarantee, or acquiesce in the payment of:

(1) Expenses reasonably incurred by a witness in attending or testifying.

(2) Reasonable compensation to a witness for loss of time in attending or testifying.

(3) A reasonable fee for the professional services of an expert witness.

Rule 5-320. Contact With Jurors.

(A) A member connected with a case shall not communicate directly or indirectly with anyone the member knows to be a member of the venire from which the jury will be selected for trial of that case.

(B) During trial a member connected with the case shall not communicate directly or indirectly with any juror.

(C) During trial a member who is not connected with the case shall not communicate directly or indirectly concerning the case with anyone a member knows is a juror in the case.

(D) After discharge of the jury from further consideration of a case a member shall not ask questions of or make comments to a member of that jury that are intended to harass or embarrass the juror or to influence the juror's actions in future jury service.

(E) A member shall not directly or indirectly conduct an out of court investigation of a person who is either a member of the venire or a juror in a manner likely to influence the state of mind of such person in connection with present or future jury service.

(F) All restrictions imposed by this rule also apply to communications with or investigations of members of the family of a person who is either a member of a venire or a juror.

(G) A member shall reveal promptly to the court improper conduct by a person who is either a member of a venire or a juror, or by another toward a person who is either a member of a venire or a juror or a member of his or her family, of which the member has knowledge.

(H) This rule does not prohibit a member from communicating with persons who are members of a venire or jurors as a part of the official proceedings.

(I) For purposes of this rule, "**juror**" means any empaneled, discharged, or excused juror.

APPENDIX II

DELAWARE RULES OF PROFESSIONAL CONDUCT

Preamble: A lawyer's responsibilities

[1] A lawyer, as a member of the legal profession, is a representative of clients, an officer of the legal system and a public citizen having special responsibility for the quality of justice.

[2] As a representative of clients, a lawyer performs various functions. As advisor, a lawyer provides a client with an informed understanding of the client's legal rights and obligations and explains their practical implications. As advo-cate, a lawyer zealously asserts the client's position under the rules of the adversary system. As negotiator, a lawyer seeks a result advantageous to the client but consistent with requirements of honest dealings with others. As an evalua-tor, a lawyer acts by examining a client's legal affairs and reporting about them to the client or to others.

[3] In addition to these representational functions, a lawyer may serve as a third-party neutral, a nonrepresenta-tional role helping the parties to resolve a dispute or other matter. Some of these Rules apply directly to lawyers who are or have served as third-party neutrals. See, e.g., Rules 1.12 and 2.4. In addition, there are Rules that apply to law-yers who are not active in the practice of law or to practicing lawyers even when they are acting in a nonprofessional capacity. For example, a lawyer who commits fraud in the conduct of a business is subject to discipline for engaging in conduct involving dishonesty, fraud, deceit or misrepresentation. See Rule 8.4.

[4] In all professional functions a lawyer should be competent, prompt and diligent. A lawyer should maintain communication with a client concerning the representation. A lawyer should keep in confidence information relating to representation of a client except so far as disclosure is required or permitted by the Rules of Professional Conduct or other law.

[5] A lawyer's conduct should conform to the requirements of the law, both in professional service to clients and in the lawyer's business and personal affairs. A lawyer should use the law's procedures only for

legitimate purposes and not to harass or intimidate others. A lawyer should demonstrate respect for the legal system and for those who serve it, including judges, other lawyers and public officials. While it is a lawyer's duty, when necessary, to challenge the recti-tude of official action, it is also a lawyer's duty to uphold legal process.

[6] As a public citizen, a lawyer should seek improvement of the law, access to the legal system, the administration of justice and the quality of service rendered by the legal profession. As a member of a learned profession, a lawyer should cultivate knowledge of the law beyond its use for clients, employ that knowledge in reform of the law and work to strengthen legal education. In addition, a lawyer should further the public's understanding of and confidence in the rule of law and the justice system because legal institutions in a constitutional democracy depend on popular participa-tion and support to maintain their authority. A lawyer should be mindful of deficiencies in the administration of justice and of the fact that the poor, and sometimes persons who are not poor, cannot afford adequate legal assistance. There-fore, all lawyers should devote professional time and resources and use civic influence to ensure equal access to our system of justice for all those who because of economic or social barriers cannot afford or secure adequate legal coun-sel. A lawyer should aid the legal profession in pursuing these objectives and should help the bar regulate itself in the public interest.

[7] Many of a lawyer's professional responsibilities are prescribed in the Rules of Professional Conduct, as well as substantive and procedural law. However, a lawyer is also guided by personal conscience and the approbation of pro-fessional peers. A lawyer should strive to attain the highest level of skill, to improve the law and the legal profession and to exemplify the legal profession's ideals of public service.

[8] A lawyer's responsibilities as a representative of clients, an officer of the legal system and a public citizen are usually harmonious. Thus, when an opposing party is well represented, a lawyer can be a zealous advocate on behalf of a client and at the same time assume that justice is being done. So also, a lawyer can be sure that preserving client con-fidences ordinarily serves the public interest because people are more likely to seek legal advice, and thereby heed their legal obligations, when they know their communications will be private.

[9] In the nature of law practice, however, conflicting responsibilities are encountered. Virtually all difficult ethical problems arise from conflict between a lawyer's responsibilities to clients, to the legal system and to the lawyer's own interest in remaining an ethical person while earning a satisfactory living. The Rules of Professional

conduct often pre-scribe terms for resolving such conflicts. Within the framework of these Rules, however, many difficult issues of professional discretion can arise. Such issues must be resolved through the exercise of sensitive professional and moral judgment guided by the basic principles underlying the Rules. These principles include the lawyer's obligation zeal-ously to protect and pursue a client's legitimate interests, within the bounds of the law, while maintaining a profes-sional, courteous and civil attitude toward all persons involved in the legal system.

[10] The legal profession is largely self-governing. Although other professions also have been granted powers of self-government, the legal profession is unique in this respect because of the close relationship between the profession and the processes of government and law enforcement. This connection is manifested in the fact that ultimate authority over the legal profession is vested largely in the courts.

[11] To the extent that lawyers meet the obligations of their professional calling, the occasion for government regu-lation is obviated. Self-regulation also helps maintain the legal profession's independence from government domination. An independent legal profession is an important force in preserving government under law, for abuse of legal authority is more readily challenged by a profession whose members are not dependent on government for the right to practice.

[12] The legal profession's relative autonomy carries with it special responsibilities of self-government. The profes-sion has a responsibility to assure that its regulations are conceived in the public interest and not in furtherance of paro-chial or self interested concerns of the bar. Every lawyer is responsible for observance of the Rules of Professional Conduct. A lawyer should also aid in securing their observance by other lawyers. Neglect of these responsibilities com-promises the independence of the profession and the public interest which it serves.

[13] Lawyers play a vital role in the preservation of society. The fulfillment of this role requires an understanding by lawyers of their relationship to our legal system. The Rules of Professional Conduct, when properly applied, serve to define that relationship.

SCOPE

[14] The Rules of Professional Conduct are rules of reason. They should be interpreted with reference to the pur-poses of legal representation and of the law itself. Some of the Rules are imperatives, cast in the terms "shall" or "shall not." These define proper conduct for purposes of professional discipline. Others, generally cast in the term

"may," are permissive and define areas under the Rules in which the lawyer has discretion to exercise professional judgment. No disciplinary action should be taken when the lawyer chooses not to act or acts within the bounds of such discretion. Other Rules define the nature of relationships between the lawyer and others. The Rules are thus partly obligatory and disciplinary and partly constitutive and descriptive in that they define a lawyer's professional role. Many of the Com-ments use the term "should." Comments do not add obligations to the Rules but provide guidance for practicing in com-pliance with the Rules.

[15] The Rules presuppose a larger legal context shaping the lawyer's role. That context includes court rules and statutes relating to matters of licensure, laws defining specific obligations of lawyers and substantive and procedural law in general. The Comments are sometimes used to alert lawyers to their responsibilities under such other law.

[16] Compliance with the Rules, as with all law in an open society, depends primarily upon understanding and vol-untary compliance, secondarily upon reenforcement by peer and public opinion and finally, when necessary, upon en-forcement through disciplinary proceedings. The Rules do not, however, exhaust the moral and ethical considerations that should inform a lawyer, for no worthwhile human activity can be completely defined by legal rules. The Rules sim-ply provide a framework for the ethical practice of law.

[17] Furthermore, for purposes of determining the lawyer's authority and responsibility, principles of substantive law external to these Rules determine whether a client-lawyer relationship exists. Most of the duties flowing from the client-lawyer relationship attach only after the client has requested the lawyer to render legal services and the lawyer has agreed to do so. But there are some duties, such as that of confidentiality under Rule 1.6, that attach when the law-yer agrees to consider whether a client-lawyer relationship shall be established. See Rule 1.18. Whether a client-lawyer relationship exists for any specific purpose can depend on the circumstances and may be a question of fact.

[18] Under various legal provisions, including constitutional, statutory and common law, the responsibilities of government lawyers may include authority concerning legal matters that ordinarily reposes in the client in private cli-ent-lawyer relationships. For example, a lawyer for a government agency may have authority on behalf of the govern-ment to decide upon settlement or whether to appeal from an adverse judgment. Such authority in various respects is generally vested in the attorney general and the state's attorney in state

government, and their federal counterparts, and the same may be true of other government law officers. Also, lawyers under the supervision of these officers may be authorized to represent several government agencies in intragovernmental legal controversies in circumstances where a private lawyer could not represent multiple private clients. These Rules do not abrogate any such authority.

[19] Failure to comply with an obligation or prohibition imposed by a Rule is a basis for invoking the disciplinary process. The Rules presuppose that disciplinary assessment of a lawyer's conduct will be made on the basis of the facts and circumstances as they existed at the time of the conduct in question and in recognition of the fact that a lawyer of-ten has to act upon uncertain or incomplete evidence of the situation. Moreover, the Rules presuppose that whether or not discipline should be imposed for a violation, and the severity of a sanction, depend on all the circumstances, such as the willfulness and seriousness of the violation, extenuating factors and whether there have been previous violations.

[20] Violation of a Rule should not itself give rise to a cause of action against a lawyer nor should it create any pre-sumption in such a case that a legal duty has been breached. In addition, violation of a Rule does not necessarily war-rant any other nondisciplinary remedy, such as disqualification of a lawyer in pending litigation. The rules are designed to provide guidance to lawyers and to provide a structure for regulating conduct through disciplinary agencies. They are not designed to be a basis for civil liability. Furthermore, the purpose of the Rules can be subverted when they are in-voked by opposing parties as procedural weapons. The fact that a Rule is a just basis for a lawyer's self-assessment, or for sanctioning a lawyer under the administration of a disciplinary authority, does not imply that an antagonist in a col-lateral proceeding or transaction has standing to seek enforcement of the Rule.

[21] The Comment accompanying each Rule explains and illustrates the meaning and purpose of the Rule. The Pre-amble and this note on Scope provide general orientation. The Comments are intended as guides to interpretation, but the text of each rule is authoritative.

Rule 1.0. Terminology

(a) "Belief" or "believes" denotes that the person involved actually supposed the fact in question to be true. A person's belief may be inferred from circumstances.

(b) "Confirmed in writing," when used in reference to the informed consent of a person, denotes informed consent that is given in writing by the person or a writing that a lawyer promptly transmits to the person confirming an oral in-formed consent. See paragraph (e) for the definition of "informed consent." If it is not feasible to obtain or transmit the writing at the time the person gives informed consent, then the lawyer must obtain or transmit it within a reasonable time thereafter.

(c) "Firm" or "law firm" denotes a lawyer or lawyers in a law partnership, professional corporation, sole proprietor-ship or other association authorized to practice law; or lawyers employed in a legal services organization or the legal department of a corporation or other organization.

(d) "Fraud" or "fraudulent" denotes conduct that is fraudulent under the substantive or procedural law of the appli-cable jurisdiction and has a purpose to deceive.

(e) "Informed consent" denotes the agreement by a person to a proposed course of conduct after the lawyer has communicated adequate information and explanation about the material risks of and reasonably available alternatives to the proposed course of conduct.

(f) "Knowingly," "known," or "knows" denotes actual knowledge of the fact in question. A person's knowledge may be inferred from circumstances.

(g) "Partner" denotes a member of a partnership, a shareholder in a law firm organized as a professional corpora-tion, or a member of an association authorized to practice law.

(h) "Reasonable" or "reasonably" when used in relation to conduct by a lawyer denotes the conduct of a reasonably prudent and competent lawyer.

(i) "Reasonable belief" or "reasonably believes" when used in reference to a lawyer denotes that the lawyer be-lieves the matter in question and that the circumstances are such that the belief is reasonable.

(j) "Reasonably should know" when used in reference to a lawyer denotes that a lawyer of reasonable prudence and competence would ascertain the matter in question.

(k) "Screened" denotes the isolation of a lawyer from any participation in a matter through the timely imposition of procedures within a firm that are reasonably adequate under the circumstances to protect information that the isolated lawyer is obligated to protect under these Rules or other law.

(l) "Substantial" when used in reference to degree or extent denotes a material matter of clear and weighty impor-tance.

(m) "Tribunal" denotes a court, an arbitrator in a binding arbitration proceeding or a legislative body, administra-tive agency or other body acting in an adjudicative capacity. A legislative body, administrative agency or other body acts in an adjudicative capacity when a neutral official, after the presentation of evidence or legal argument by a party or parties, will render a binding legal judgment directly affecting a party's interests in a particular matter.

(n) "Writing" or "written" denotes a tangible or electronic record of a communication or representation, including handwriting, typewriting, printing, photostating, photography, audio or video recording and e-mail. A "signed" writing includes an electronic sound, symbol or process attached to or logically associated with a writing and executed or adopted by a person with the intent to sign the writing.

Rule 1.1. Competence

A lawyer shall provide competent representation to a client. Competent representation requires the legal knowledge, skill, thoroughness and preparation reasonably necessary for the representation.

Rule 1.2. Scope of representation

(a) Subject to paragraphs (c) and (d), a lawyer shall abide by a client's decisions concerning the objectives of repre-sentation and, as required by Rule 1.4, shall consult with the client as to the means by which they are to be pursued. A lawyer may take such action on behalf of the client as is impliedly authorized to carry out the representation. A lawyer shall abide by a client's decision whether to settle a matter. In a criminal case, the lawyer shall abide by the client's deci-sion, after consultation with the lawyer, as to a plea to be entered, whether to waive jury trial and whether the client will testify.

(b) A lawyer's representation of a client, including representation by appointment, does not constitute an endorse-ment of the client's political, economic, social or moral views or activities.

(c) A lawyer may limit the scope of the representation if the limitation is reasonable under the circumstances and the client gives informed consent.

(d) A lawyer shall not counsel a client to engage, or assist a client, in conduct that the lawyer knows is criminal or fraudulent, but a lawyer may discuss the legal consequences of any proposed course of conduct with a client and may counsel or assist a client to make a good faith effort to determine the validity, scope, meaning or application of the law.

Rule 1.3. Diligence

A lawyer shall act with reasonable diligence and promptness in representing a client.

Rule 1.4. Communication

(a) A lawyer shall:

(1) promptly inform the client of any decision or circumstance with respect to which the client's informed consent, as defined in Rule 1.0(e), is required by these Rules;

(2) reasonably consult with the client about the means by which the client's objectives are to be accomplished;

(3) keep the client reasonably informed about the status of the matter;

(4) promptly comply with reasonable requests for information; and

(5) consult with the client about any relevant limitation on the lawyer's conduct when the lawyer knows that the cli-ent expects assistance not permitted by the Rules of Professional Conduct or other law.

(b) A lawyer shall explain a matter to the extent reasonably necessary to permit the client to make informed deci-sions regarding the representation.

Rule 1.5. Fees

(a) A lawyer shall not make an agreement for, charge, or collect an unreasonable fee or an unreasonable amount for expenses. The factors to be considered in determining the reasonableness of a fee include the following:

(1) the time and labor required, the novelty and difficulty of the questions involved, and the skill requisite to per-form the legal service properly;

(2) the likelihood, if apparent to the client, that the acceptance of the particular employment will preclude other employment by the lawyer;

(3) the fee customarily charged in the locality for similar legal services;

(4) the amount involved and the results obtained;

(5) the time limitations imposed by the client or by the circumstances;

(6) the nature and length of the professional relationship with the client;

(7) the experience, reputation, and ability of the lawyer or lawyers performing the services; and

(8) whether the fee is fixed or contingent.

(b) The scope of the representation and the basis or rate of the fee and expenses for which the client will be respon-sible shall be communicated to the client, preferably in writing, before or within a reasonable time after commencing the representation, except when the lawyer will charge a regularly represented client on the same basis or rate. Any changes in the basis or rate of the fee or expenses shall also be communicated to the client.

(c) A fee may be contingent on the outcome of the matter for which the service is rendered, except in a matter in which a contingent fee is prohibited by paragraph (d) or other law. A contingent fee agreement shall be in a writing signed by the client and shall state the method by which the fee is to be determined, including the percentage or percentages that shall accrue to the lawyer in the event of settlement, trial or appeal; litigation and other expenses to be deducted from the recovery; and whether such expenses are to be deducted before or after the contingent fee is calculated. The agreement must clearly notify the client of any expenses for which the client will be liable whether or not the client is the prevailing party. Upon conclusion of a contingent fee matter, the lawyer shall provide the client with a written statement stating the outcome of the matter and, if there is a recovery, showing the remittance to the client and the method of its determination.

(d) A lawyer shall not enter into an arrangement for, charge, or collect:

(1) any fee in a domestic relations matter, the payment or amount of which is contingent upon the securing of a di-vorce or upon the amount of alimony or support, or property settlement in lieu thereof; or

(2) a contingent fee for representing a defendant in a criminal case.

(e) A division of fee between lawyers who are not in the same firm may be made only if:

(1) the client is advised in writing of and does not object to the participation of all the lawyers involved; and

(2) the total fee is reasonable.

(f) A lawyer may require the client to pay some or all of the fee in advance of the lawyer undertaking the represen-tation, provided that:

(1) The lawyer shall provide the client with a written statement that the fee is refundable if it is not earned,

(2) The written statement shall state the basis under which the fees shall be considered to have been earned, whether in whole or in part, and

(3) All unearned fees shall be retained in the lawyer's trust account, with statement of the fees earned provided to the client at the time such funds are withdrawn from the trust account.

Rule 1.6. Confidentiality of information

(a) A lawyer shall not reveal information relating to the representation of a client unless the client gives informed consent, the disclosure is impliedly authorized in order to carry out the representation, or the disclosure is permitted by paragraph (b).

(b) A lawyer may reveal information relating to the representation of a client to the extent the lawyer reasonably believes necessary:

(1) to prevent reasonably certain death or substantial bodily harm;

(2) to prevent the client from committing a crime or fraud that is reasonably certain to result in substantial injury to the financial interests or property of another and in furtherance of which the client has used or is using the lawyer's ser-vices;

(3) to prevent, mitigate, or rectify substantial injury to the financial interests or property of another that is reasona-bly certain to result or has resulted from the client's commission of a crime or fraud in furtherance of which the client has used the lawyer's services;

(4) to secure legal advice about the lawyer's compliance with these Rules;

(5) to establish a claim or defense on behalf of the lawyer in a controversy between the lawyer and the client, to es-tablish a defense to a criminal charge or civil claim against the lawyer based upon conduct in which the client was in-volved, or to respond to allegations in any proceeding concerning the lawyer's representation of the client; or

(6) to comply with other law or a court order.

Rule 1.7. Conflict of interest: Current clients

(a) Except as provided in paragraph (b), a lawyer shall not represent a client if the representation involves a concur-rent conflict of interest. A concurrent conflict of interest exists if:

(1) the representation of one client will be directly adverse to another client; or

(2) there is a significant risk that the representation of one or more clients will be materially limited by the lawyer's responsibilities to another client, a former client or a third person or by a personal interest of the lawyer.

(b) Notwithstanding the existence of a concurrent conflict of interest under paragraph (a), a lawyer may represent a client if:

(1) the lawyer reasonably believes that the lawyer will be able to provide competent and diligent representation to each affected client;

(2) the representation is not prohibited by law;

(3) the representation does not involve the assertion of a claim by one client against another client represented by the lawyer in the same litigation or other proceeding before a tribunal; and

(4) each affected client gives informed consent, confirmed in writing.

Rule 1.8. Conflict of interest: Current clients: Specific rules

(a) A lawyer shall not enter into a business transaction with a client or knowingly acquire an ownership, possessory, security or other pecuniary interest adverse to a client unless:

(1) the transaction and terms on which the lawyer acquires the interest are fair and reasonable to the client and are fully disclosed and transmitted in writing to the client in a manner that can be reasonably understood by the client;

(2) the client is advised in writing of the desirability of seeking and is given a reasonable opportunity to seek the advice of independent legal counsel on the transaction; and

(3) the client gives informed consent, in a writing signed by the client, to the essential terms of the transaction and the lawyer's role in the transaction, including whether the lawyer is representing the client in the transaction.

(b) A lawyer shall not use information relating to representation of a client to the disadvantage of the client unless the client gives informed consent, except as permitted or required by these Rules.

(c) A lawyer shall not solicit any substantial gift from a client, including a testamentary gift, or prepare on behalf of a client an instrument giving the lawyer or a person related to the lawyer any substantial gift unless the lawyer or other recipient of the gift is related to the client. For purposes of this paragraph, related persons include a spouse, child, grandchild, parent, grandparent or other relative or individual with whom the lawyer or the client maintains a close, familial relationship.

(d) Prior to the conclusion of representation of a client, a lawyer shall not make or negotiate an agreement giving the lawyer literary or media rights to a portrayal or account based in substantial part on information relating to the rep-resentation.

(e) A lawyer shall not provide financial assistance to a client in connection with pending or contemplated litigation, except that:

(1) a lawyer may advance court costs and expenses of litigations, the repayment of which may be contingent on the outcome of the matter; and

(2) a lawyer representing an indigent client may pay court costs and expenses of litigation on behalf of the client.

(f) A lawyer shall not accept compensation for representing a client from one other than the client unless:

(1) the client gives informed consent;

(2) there is no interference with the lawyer's independence of professional judgment or with the client-lawyer rela-tionship; and

(3) information relating to representation of a client is protected as required by Rule 1.6.

(g) A lawyer who represents two or more clients shall not participate in making an aggregate settlement of the claims of or against the clients, or in a criminal case an aggregated agreement as to guilty or nolo contendere pleas, unless each client gives informed consent, in a writing signed by the client. The lawyer's disclosure shall include the existence and nature of all the claims or pleas involved and of the participation of each person in the settlement.

(h) A lawyer shall not:

(1) make an agreement prospectively limiting the lawyer's liability to a client for malpractice unless the client is in-dependently represented in making the agreement; or

(2) settle a claim or potential claim for such liability with an unrepresented client or former client unless that per-son is advised in writing of the desirability of seeking and is given a reasonable opportunity to seek the advice of inde-pendent legal counsel in connection therewith.

(i) A lawyer shall not acquire a proprietary interest in the cause of action or subject matter of litigation the lawyer is conducting for a client, except that the lawyer may:

(1) acquire a lien authorized by law to secure the lawyer's fee or expenses; and

(2) contract with a client for a reasonable contingent fee in a civil case.

(j) A lawyer shall not have sexual relations with a client unless a consensual sexual relationship existed between them when the client-lawyer relationship commenced.

(k) While lawyers are associated in a firm, a prohibition in the foregoing paragraphs (a) through (i) that applies to any one of them shall apply to all of them.

Rule 1.9. Duties to former clients

(a) A lawyer who has formerly represented a client in a matter shall not thereafter represent another person in the same or a substantially related matter in which that person's interests are materially adverse to the interests of the former client unless the former client gives informed consent, confirmed in writing.

(b) A lawyer shall not knowingly represent a person in the same or a substantially related matter in which a firm with which the lawyer formerly was associated had previously represented a client:

(1) whose interests are materially adverse to that person; and

(2) about whom the lawyer had acquired information protected by Rules 1.6 and 1.9(c) that is material to the mat-ter;

unless the former client gives informed consent, confirmed in writing.

(c) A lawyer who has formerly represented a client in a matter or whose present or former firm has formerly repre-sented a client in a matter shall not thereafter:

(1) use information relating to the representation to the disadvantage of the former client except as these Rules would permit or require with respect to a client, or when the information has become generally known; or

(2) reveal information relating to the representation except as these Rules would permit or require with respect to a client.

Rule 1.10. Imputation of conflicts of interest: General rule

(a) Except as otherwise provided in this rule, while lawyers are associated in a firm, none of them shall knowingly represent a client when any one of them practicing alone would be prohibited from doing so by Rules 1.7 or 1.9, unless the prohibition is based on a personal interest of the prohibited lawyer and does not present a significant risk of materi-ally limiting the representation of the client by the remaining lawyers in the firm.

(b) When a lawyer has terminated an association with a firm, the firm is not prohibited from thereafter representing a person with interests materially adverse to those of a client represented by the formerly associated lawyer and not currently represented by the firm, unless:

(1) the matter is the same or substantially related to that in which the formerly associated lawyer represented the client; and

(2) any lawyer remaining in the firm has information protected by Rules 1.6 and 1.9(c) that is material to the mat-ter.

(c) When a lawyer becomes associated with a firm, no lawyer associated in the firm shall knowingly represent a client in a matter in which that lawyer is disqualified under Rule 1.9 unless:

(1) the personally disqualified lawyer is timely screened from any participation in the matter and is apportioned no part of the fee therefrom; and

(2) written notice is promptly given to the affected former client.

(d) A disqualification prescribed by this rule may be waived by the affected client under the conditions stated in Rule 1.7.

(e) The disqualification of lawyers associated in a firm with former or current government lawyers is governed by Rule 1.11.

Rule 1.11. Special conflicts of interest for former and current government officers and employees

(a) Except as law may otherwise expressly permit, a lawyer who has formerly served as a public officer or employee of the government:

(1) is subject to Rule 1.9(c); and

(2) shall not otherwise represent a client in connection with a matter in which the lawyer participated personally and substantially as a public officer or employee, unless the appropriate government agency gives its informed consent, confirmed in writing, to the representation.

(b) When a lawyer is disqualified from representation under paragraph (a), no lawyer in a firm with which that law-yer is associated may knowingly undertake or continue representation in such a matter unless:

(1) the disqualified lawyer is timely screened from any participation in the matter and is apportioned no part of the fee therefrom; and

(2) written notice is promptly given to the appropriate government agency to enable it to ascertain compliance with the provisions of this rule.

(c) Except as law may otherwise expressly permit, a lawyer having information that the lawyer knows is confiden-tial government information about a person acquired when the lawyer was a public officer or employee, may not repre-sent a private client whose interests are adverse to that person in a matter in which the information could be used to the material disadvantage of that person. As used in this Rule, the term "confidential government information" means in-formation that has been obtained under governmental authority and which, at the time this Rule is applied, the govern-ment is prohibited by law from disclosing to the public or has a legal privilege not to disclose and which is not other-wise available to the public. A firm with which that lawyer is associated may undertake or continue representation in the matter only if the disqualified lawyer is timely screened from any participation in the matter and is apportioned no part of the fee therefrom.

(d) Except as law may otherwise expressly permit, a lawyer currently serving as a public officer or employee:

(1) is subject to Rules 1.7 and 1.9; and

(2) shall not:

(i) participate in a matter in which the lawyer participated personally and substantially while in private practice or nongovernmental employment, unless the appropriate government agency gives its informed consent, confirmed in writing; or

(ii) negotiate for private employment with any person who is involved as a party or as lawyer for a party in a matter in which the lawyer is participating personally and substantially, except that a lawyer serving as a law clerk to a judge, other adjudicative officer or arbitrator may negotiate for private employment as permitted by Rule 1.12(b) and subject to the conditions stated in Rule 1.12(b).

(e) As used in this Rule, the term "matter" includes:

(1) any judicial or other proceeding, application, request for a ruling or other determination, contract, claim, con-troversy, investigation, charge, accusation, arrest or other particular matter involving a specific party or parties, and

(2) any other matter covered by the conflict of interest rules of the appropriate government agency.

Rule 1.12. Former judge, arbitrator, mediator or other third-party neutral

(a) Except as stated in paragraph (d), a lawyer shall not represent anyone in connection with a matter in which the lawyer participated personally and substantially as a judge or other adjudicative officer or law clerk to such a person or as an arbitrator, mediator or other third-party neutral, unless all parties to the proceeding give informed consent, con-firmed in writing.

(b) A lawyer shall not negotiate for employment with any person who is involved as a party or as lawyer for a party in a matter in which the lawyer is participating personally and substantially as a judge or other adjudicative officer or as an arbitrator, mediator or other third-party neutral. A lawyer serving as a law clerk to a judge or other adjudicative offi-cer may negotiate for employment with a party or lawyer involved in a matter in which the clerk is participating per-sonally and substantially, but only after the lawyer has notified the judge or other adjudicative officer.

(c) If a lawyer is disqualified by paragraph (a), no lawyer in a firm with which that lawyer is associated may know-ingly undertake or continue representation in the matter unless:

(1) the disqualified lawyer is timely screened from any participation in the matter and is apportioned no part of the fee therefrom; and

(2) written notice is promptly given to the parties and any appropriate tribunal to enable them to ascertain compli-ance with the provisions of this rule.

(d) An arbitrator selected as a partisan of a party in a multimember arbitration panel is not prohibited from subse-quently representing that party.

Rule 1.13. Organization as client

(a) A lawyer employed or retained by an organization represents the organization acting through its duly authorized constituents.

(b) If a lawyer for an organization knows that an officer, employee or other person associated with the organization is engaged in action, intends to act or refuses to act in a matter related to the representation that is a violation of a legal obligation to the organization, or a violation of law which reasonably might be imputed to the organization, and is likely to result in substantial injury to the organization, the lawyer shall proceed as is reasonably necessary in the best interest of the organization. In determining how to proceed, the lawyer shall give due consideration to the seriousness of the violation and its consequences, the scope and nature of the lawyer's representation, the responsibility in the or-ganization and the apparent motivation of the person involved, the policies of the organization concerning such matters and any other relevant considerations. Any measures taken shall be designed to minimize disruption of the organization and the risk of revealing information relating to the representation to persons outside the organization. Such measures may include among others:

(1) asking for reconsideration of the matter;

(2) advising that a separate legal opinion on the matter be sought for presentation to appropriate authority in the or-ganization; and

(3) referring the matter to higher authority in the organization, including, if warranted by the seriousness of the matter, referral to the highest authority that can act on behalf of the organization as determined by applicable law.

(c) If, despite the lawyer's efforts in accordance with paragraph (b), the highest authority that can act on behalf of the organization insists upon action, or a refusal to act, that is clearly a violation of law and is likely to result in substan-tial injury to the organization, the lawyer may resign in accordance with Rule 1.16.

(d) In dealing with an organization's directors, officers, employees, members, shareholders or other constituents, a lawyer shall explain the identity of the client when the lawyer knows or reasonably should know that the organization's interests are adverse to those of the constituents with whom the lawyer is dealing.

(e) A lawyer representing an organization may also represent any of its directors, officers, employees, members, shareholders or other constituents, subject to the provisions of Rule 1.7. If the organization's consent to the dual repre-sentation is required by Rule 1.7, the consent shall be given by an appropriate official of the organization other than the individual who is to be represented, or by the shareholders.

Rule 1.14. Client with diminished capacity

(a) When a client's capacity to make adequately considered decisions in connection with a representation is dimin-ished, whether because of minority, mental impairment or for some other reason, the lawyer shall, as far as reasonably possible, maintain a normal client-lawyer relationship with the client.

(b) When the lawyer reasonably believes that the client has diminished capacity, is at risk of substantial physical, financial or other harm unless action is taken and cannot adequately act in the client's own interest, the lawyer may take reasonably necessary protective action, including consulting with individuals or entities that have the ability to take action to protect the client and, in appropriate cases, seeking the appointment of a guardian ad litem, conservator or guardian.

(c) Information relating to the representation of a client with diminished capacity is protected by Rule 1.6. When taking protective action pursuant to paragraph (b), the lawyer is impliedly authorized under Rule 1.6(a) to reveal infor-mation about the client, but only to the extent reasonably necessary to protect the client's interests.

Rule 1.15. Safekeeping property

(a) A lawyer shall hold property of clients or third persons that is in a lawyer's possession in connection with a repre-sentation separate from the lawyer's own property. Funds shall be kept in a separate account designated solely for funds held in connection with the practice of law in this jurisdiction. Such funds shall be maintained in the state in which the lawyer's office is situated, or elsewhere with the consent of the client or third person. Funds of the lawyer that are rea-sonably sufficient to pay bank charges may be deposited therein; however, such amount may not exceed $1,000 and must be separately stated and accounted for in the same manner as clients' funds deposited therein. Other property shall be identified as such and appropriately safeguarded. Complete records of such account funds and other property shall be kept by the lawyer and shall be preserved for a period of five years after the completion of the events that they re-cord.

(b) Upon receiving funds or other property in which a client or third person has an interest, a lawyer shall promptly notify the client or third person. Except as stated in this Rule or otherwise permitted by law or by agreement with the client, a lawyer shall promptly deliver to the client or third person any funds or other property that the client or third person is entitled to receive and, upon request by the client or third person, shall promptly render a full accounting re-garding such property.

(c) When in the course of representation a lawyer is in possession of property in which both the lawyer and another person claim interests, the property shall be kept separate by the lawyer until there is an accounting and severance of their interests. If a dispute arises concerning their respective interests, the portion in dispute shall be kept separate by the lawyer until the dispute is resolved.

(d) A lawyer engaged in the private practice of law must maintain financial books and records on a current basis, and shall preserve the books and records for at least five years following the completion of the year to which they re-late, or, as to fiduciary books and records, five years following the completion of that fiduciary obligation. The mainte-nance of books and records must conform with the following provisions:

(1) All bank statements, cancelled checks (or images and/or copies thereof as provided by the bank), records of electronic transfers, and duplicate deposit slips relating to fiduciary and non-fiduciary accounts must be preserved. Records of all electronic transfers from fiduciary accounts shall include the name of the person authorizing transfer, the date of transfer, the name of recipient and confirmation from the banking institution confirming the number of the fiduciary account from which the funds are withdrawn and the date and time the request for transfer was completed.

(2) Bank accounts maintained for fiduciary funds must be specifically designated as "Rule 1.15A Attorney Trust Account" or "1.15A Trust Account" or "Rule 1.15A Attorney Escrow Account" or "1.15A Escrow Account," and must be used only for funds held in a fiduciary capacity. A designation of the account as a "Rule 1.15A Attorney Trust Ac-count" or "1.15A Trust Account" or "Rule 1.15A Attorney Escrow Account" or "1.15A Escrow Account," must appear in the account title on the bank statement. Other related statements, checks, deposit slips, and other documents main-tained for fiduciary funds, must contain, at a minimum, a designation of the account as "Attorney Trust Account" or "Attorney Escrow Account."

(3) Bank accounts and related statements, checks, deposit slips, and other documents maintained for non-fiduciary funds must be specifically designated as "Attorney Business Account" or "Attorney Operating Account," and must be used only for funds held in a non-fiduciary capacity. A lawyer in the private practice of law shall maintain a non-fiduciary account for general operating purposes, and the account shall be separate from any of the lawyer's personal or other accounts.

(4) All records relating to property other than cash received by a lawyer in a fiduciary capacity shall be maintained and preserved. The

records must describe with specificity the identity and location of such property.

(5) All billing records reflecting fees charged and other billings to clients or other parties must be maintained and preserved.

(6) Cash receipts and cash disbursement journals must be maintained and preserved for each bank account for the purpose of recording fiduciary and non-fiduciary transactions. A lawyer using a manual system for such purposes must total and balance the transaction columns on a monthly basis.

(7) A monthly reconciliation for each bank account, matching totals from the cash receipts and cash disbursement journals with the ending check register balance, must be performed. The reconciliation procedures, however, shall not be required for lawyers using a computer accounting system or a general ledger.

(8) The check register balance for each bank account must be reconciled monthly to the bank statement balance.

(9) With respect to all fiduciary accounts:

(A) A subsidiary ledger must be maintained and preserved with a separate account for each client or third party in which cash receipts and cash disbursement transactions and monthly balances are recorded.

(B) Monthly listings of client or third party balances must be prepared showing the name and balance of each client or third party, and the total of all balances.

(C) No funds disbursed for a client or third party must be in excess of funds received from that client or third party. If, however, through error funds disbursed for a client or third party exceed funds received from that client or third party, the lawyer shall transfer funds from the non-fiduciary account in a timely manner to cover the excess disbursement.

(D) The reconciled total cash balance must agree with the total of the client or third party balance listing. There shall be no unidentified client or third party funds. The bank reconciliation for a fiduciary account is not complete unless there is agreement with the total of client or third party accounts.

(E) If a check has been issued in an attempt to disburse funds, but remains outstanding (that is, the check has not cleared the trust or escrow bank account) six months or more from the date it was issued, a lawyer shall promptly take steps to contact the payee to determine the reason the check was not deposited by the payee, and shall issue a replace-ment check, as necessary and appropriate. With regard to abandoned or unclaimed trust funds, a lawyer shall comply with requirements of Supreme Court Rule 73.

(F) No funds of the lawyer shall be placed in or left in the account except as provided in Rule 1.15(a).

(G) No funds which should have been disbursed shall remain in the account, including, but not limited to, earned legal fees, which must be transferred to the lawyer's non-fiduciary account on a prompt and timely basis when earned.

(H) When a separate real estate bank account is maintained for settlement transactions, and when client or third party funds are received but not yet disbursed, a listing must be prepared on a monthly basis showing the name of the client or third party, the balance due to each client or third party, and the total of all such balances. The total must agree with the reconciled cash balance.

(10) If a lawyer maintains financial books and records using a computer system, the lawyer must cause to be printed each month a hard copy of all monthly journals, ledgers, reports, and reconciliations, and/or cause to be created each month an electronic backup of these documents to be stored in such a manner as to make them accessible for re-view by the lawyer and/or the auditor for the Lawyers' Fund for Client Protection.

(e) A lawyer's financial books and records must be subject to examination by the auditor for the Lawyers' Fund for Client Protection, for the purpose of verifying the accuracy of a certificate of compliance filed each year by the lawyer pursuant to Supreme Court Rule 69. The examination must be conducted so as to preserve, insofar as is consistent with these Rules, the confidential nature of the lawyer's books and records. If the lawyer's books and records are not located in Delaware, the lawyer may have the option either to produce the books and records at the lawyer's office in Delaware or to produce the books and records at the location outside of Delaware where they are ordinarily located. If the produc-tion occurs outside of Delaware, the lawyer shall pay any additional expenses incurred by the auditor for the purposes of an examination.

(f) A lawyer holding client funds must initially and reasonably determine whether the funds should or should not be placed in an interest-bearing depository account for the benefit of the client. In making such a determination, the lawyer must consider the financial interests of the client, the costs of establishing and maintaining the account, any tax reporting procedures or requirements, the nature of the transaction involved, the likelihood of delay in the relevant pro-ceedings, whether the funds are of a nominal amount, and whether the funds are expected to be held by the lawyer for a short period of time. A lawyer must at reasonable intervals consider whether changed circumstances would warrant a different determination with respect to the deposit of client funds. Except as provided in these Rules, interest earned on client funds placed into an interest-bearing depository account for the benefit of the client (less any deductions for service charges or other fees of the depository institution) shall belong to the client whose funds are deposited, and the lawyer shall have no right or claim to such interest.

(g) A lawyer holding client funds who has reasonably determined, pursuant to subsection (f) of this Rule, that such funds need not be deposited into an interest-bearing depository account for the benefit of the client must maintain a pooled interest-bearing depository account for the deposit of the funds; provided, however, that this requirement shall not apply to a lawyer who either has obtained inactive status pursuant to Supreme Court Rule 69(d), or has obtained a Certificate of Retirement pursuant to Supreme Court Rule 69(f), or has formally elected to opt out of this requirement in accordance with the procedure set forth below in subparagraph (k).

(h) A lawyer who maintains such a pooled account shall comply with the following:

(1) The account shall include only client's funds which are nominal amount or are expected to be held for a short period of time.

(2) No interest from such an account shall be made available to a lawyer or law firm.

(3) Lawyers or law firms depositing client funds in a pooled interest-bearing account under this paragraph (h) [(g)] shall direct the depository institution:

(a) To remit interest, net any service charges or fees, as computed in accordance with the institution's standard ac-counting practice, at least quarterly, to the Delaware Bar Foundation; and

(b) To transmit with each remittance to the Delaware Bar Foundation a statement showing the name of the lawyer or law firm on whose accounting remittance is sent and the rate of interest applied; with a copy of statement to be transmitted to the lawyer or law firm by the Delaware Bar Foundation.

(i) The funds transmitted to the Delaware Bar Foundation shall be available for distribution for the following pur-poses:

(1) To improve the administration of justice;

(2) To provide and to enhance the delivery of legal services to the poor;

(3) To support law related education;

(4) For each other purposes that serve the public interest.

The Delaware Bar Foundation shall recommend for the approval of the Supreme Court of the State of Delaware, such distributions as it may deem appropriate. Distributions shall be made only upon the Court's approval.

(j) Lawyers or law firms, depositing client funds in a pooled interest-bearing depository account under this para-graph shall not be required to advise the client of such deposit or of the purposes to which the interest accumulated by reason of such deposits is to be directed.

(k) The procedure available for opting out of the requirement to maintain pooled interest-bearing accounts are as follows:

(1) Prior to December 15, 1983, a lawyer wishing to decline to maintain a pooled interest-bearing account[s] de-scribed in this paragraph for any calendar year may do so by submitting a Notice of Declination in writing to the Clerk of the Supreme Court *ab initio* or before December 15 of the preceding calendar year. Any such submission shall re-main effective, unless revoked and need not be renewed for any ensuing year.

(2) Any lawyer who has not filed a Notice of Declination on or before December 15, 1983, may elect not to main-tain a pooled interest-bearing depository account for client funds as required and instead to maintain a pooled deposi-tory account for such funds that does not bear interest or that bears interest solely for the benefit of the clients who de-posited the funds by certifying that the lawyer or law firm opts out of the obligation to comply with the requirements by timely submission of the Annual Registration Statement required by Supreme Court Rule 69(b)(i). Any such certifica-tion shall release the lawyer or law firm submitting it from participation effective as of the date that the certification is submitted and it shall remain effective until revoked as set forth below without need for renewal for any ensuing year.

(3) Notwithstanding the foregoing provisions of this subparagraph, any lawyer or law firm may petition the Court at any time and, for good cause shown, may be granted leave to opt out of the obligation to comply with the mandatory requirements of this paragraph.

(l) An election to opt out of the obligation to comply with paragraph (h) hereof may be revoked at any time upon the opening by a non-participating lawyer or law firm of a pooled interest-bearing account as previously described and due notification thereof to the Court Administrator of the Supreme Court pursuant to Supreme Court Rule 69(g).

(m) A lawyer shall not disburse fiduciary funds from a bank account unless the funds deposited in the lawyer's fi-duciary account to be disbursed, or the funds which are in the lawyer's unrestricted possession and control and are or will be timely deposited, are good funds as hereinafter defined. "Good funds" shall mean:

(1) cash;

(2) electronic fund ("wire") transfer;

(3) certified check;

(4) bank cashier's check or treasurer's check;

(5) U.S. Treasury or State of Delaware Treasury check;

(6) Check drawn on a separate trust or escrow account of an attorney engaged in the private practice of law in the State of Delaware held in a fiduciary capacity, including his or her client's funds;

(7) Check of an insurance company that is authorized by the Insurance Commissioner of Delaware to transact in-surance business in Delaware;

(8) Check in an amount no greater than $10,000.00;

(9) Check greater than $10,000.00, which has been actually and finally collected and may be drawn against under federal or state banking regulations then in effect;

(10) Check drawn on an escrow account of a real estate broker licensed by the state of Delaware up to the limit of guarantee provided per transaction by statute.

Rule 1.15A. Trust account overdraft notification

(a) Every attorney practicing or admitted to practice in this jurisdiction shall designate every account into which at-torney trust or escrow funds are deposited either as 'Rule 1.15A Attorney Trust Account' or '1.15A Trust Account' or 'Rule 1.15A Attorney Escrow Account' or '1.15A Escrow Account,' pursuant to Rule 1.15(d)(2).

(b) Bank accounts designated as 'Rule 1.15A Attorney Trust Account' or '1.15A Trust Account' or 'Rule 1.15A At-torney Escrow Account' or '1.15A Escrow Account,' pursuant to Rule 1.15(d)(2) shall be maintained only in financial institutions approved by the Lawyers' Fund for Client Protection (the "Fund").

(c) The Supreme Court may establish rules governing approval and termination of approved status for financial insti-tutions and the Fund shall annually publish a list of approved financial institutions. No trust or escrow account shall be maintained in any financial institution that does not agree to make such reports. Any such agreement shall apply to all branches of the financial institution and shall not be canceled except upon thirty (30) days notice in writing to the Fund.

(d) The overdraft notification agreement shall provide that all reports made by the financial institution shall be in the following format:

(1) In the case of a dishonored instrument, the report shall be identical to the overdraft notice customarily for-warded to the depositor, and shall include a copy of the dishonored instrument to the ODC no later than seven (7) calendar days following a request for the copy by the ODC.

(2) In the case of instruments that are presented against insufficient funds, but which instruments are honored, the report shall identify the financial institution, the attorney or law firm, the account number, the date of presentation for payment, and the date paid, as well as the amount of the overdraft created thereby.

(e) Reports shall be made simultaneously with, and within the time provided by law for, notice of dishonor. If an instrument presented against insufficient funds is honored, then the report shall be made within seven (7) calendar days of the date of presentation for payment against insufficient funds.

(f) Every attorney practicing or admitted to practice in this jurisdiction shall, as a condition thereof, be conclusively deemed to have consented to the reporting and production requirements mandated by this rule.

(g) Nothing herein shall preclude a financial institution from charging a particular attorney or law firm for the rea-sonable costs of producing the reports and records required by this rule.

(h) The terms used in this section are defined as follows:

(1) "Financial institution" includes banks, savings and loan associations, credit unions, savings banks and any other business or persons which accept for deposit funds held in trust by attorneys.

(2) "Properly payable" refers to an instrument which, if presented in the normal course of business, is in a form re-quiring payment under the laws of Delaware.

(3) "Notice of dishonor" refers to the notice which a financial institution is required to give, under the laws of Delaware, upon presentation of an instrument which the institution dishonors.

Rule 1.16. Declining or terminating representation

(a) Except as stated in paragraph (c), a lawyer shall not represent a client or, where representation has commenced, shall withdraw from the representation of a client if:

(1) the representation will result in violation of the rules of professional conduct or other law;

(2) the lawyer's physical or mental condition materially impairs the lawyer's ability to represent the client; or

(3) the lawyer is discharged.

(b) Except as stated in paragraph (c), a lawyer may withdraw from representing a client if:

(1) withdrawal can be accomplished without material adverse effect on the interests of the client;

(2) the client persists in a course of action involving the lawyer's services that the lawyer reasonably believes is criminal or fraudulent;

(3) the client has used the lawyer's service to perpetrate a crime or fraud;

(4) a client insists upon taking action that the lawyer considers repugnant or with which the lawyer has a funda-mental disagreement;

(5) the client fails substantially to fulfill an obligation to the lawyer regarding the lawyer's services and has been given reasonable warning that the lawyer will withdraw unless the obligation is fulfilled;

(6) the representation will result in an unreasonable financial burden on the lawyer or has been rendered unrea-sonably difficult by the client; or

(7) other good cause for withdrawal exists.

(c) A lawyer must comply with applicable law requiring notice to or permission of a tribunal when terminating a representation. When ordered to do so by a tribunal, a lawyer shall continue representation notwithstanding good cause for terminating the representation.

(d) Upon termination of representation, a lawyer shall take steps to the extent reasonably practicable to protect a client's interests, such as giving reasonable notice to the client, allowing time for employment of other counsel, surrendering papers and property to which the client is entitled and refunding any advance payment of fee or expense that has not been earned or incurred. The lawyer may retain papers relating to the client to the extent permitted by other law.

Rule 1.17. Sale of law practice

A lawyer or a law firm may sell or purchase a law practice, or an area of law practice, including good will, if the fol-lowing conditions are satisfied:

(a) The seller ceases to engage in the private practice of law, or in the area of practice that has been sold in the ju-risdiction in which the practice has been conducted;

(b) The entire practice, or the entire area of practice, is sold to one or more lawyers or law firms;

(c) The seller gives written notice to each of the seller's clients regarding:

(1) the proposed sale;

(2) the client's right to retain other counsel or to take possession of the file; and

(3) the client's consent to the transfer of the client's files will be presumed if the client does not take any action or does not otherwise object within ninety (90) days of receipt of the notice.

In a matter of pending litigation, if a client cannot be given notice, the representation of that client may be trans-ferred to the purchaser only upon entry of an order so authorizing by a court having jurisdiction. The seller may dis-close to the court in camera information relating to the representation only to the extent necessary to obtain an order authorizing the transfer of a file. If approval of the substitution of the purchasing lawyer for the selling lawyer is required by the rules of any tribunal in which a matter is pending, such approval must be obtained before the matter can be included in the sale.

(d) The fees charged clients shall not be increased by reason of the sale.

Rule 1.18. Duties to prospective client

(a) A person who discusses with a lawyer the possibility of forming a client-lawyer relationship with respect to a mat-ter is a prospective client.

(b) Even when no client-lawyer relationship ensues, a lawyer who has had discussions with a prospective client shall not use or reveal information learned in the consultation, except as Rule 1.9 would permit with respect to informa-tion of a former client.

(c) A lawyer subject to paragraph (b) shall not represent a client with interests materially adverse to those of a pro-spective client in the same or a substantially related matter if the lawyer received information from the prospective cli-ent that could be significantly harmful to that person in the matter, except as provided in paragraph (d). If a lawyer is disqualified from representation under this paragraph, no lawyer in a firm with which that lawyer is associated may knowingly undertake or continue representation in such a matter, except as provided in paragraph (d).

(d) When the lawyer has received disqualifying information as defined in paragraph (c), representation is permissi-ble if:

(1) both the affected client and the prospective client have given informed consent, confirmed in writing, or:

(2) the lawyer who received the information took reasonable measures to avoid exposure to more disqualifying in-formation than was reasonably necessary to determine whether to represent the prospective client; and

(i) the disqualified lawyer is timely screened from any participation in the matter and is apportioned no part of the fee therefrom; and

(ii) written notice is promptly given to the prospective client.

Rule 2.1. Advisor

In representing a client, a lawyer shall exercise independent professional judgment and render candid advice. In ren-dering advice, a lawyer may refer not only to law but to other considerations, such as moral, economic, social and po-litical factors, that may be relevant to the client's situation.

Rule 2.2. Intermediary (Deleted)

Rule 2.3. Evaluation for use by third persons

(a) A lawyer may provide an evaluation of a matter affecting a client for the use of someone other than the client if the lawyer reasonably believes that making the evaluation is compatible with other aspects of the lawyer's relationship with the client.

(b) When the lawyer knows or reasonably should know that the evaluation is likely to affect the client's interests materially and adversely, the lawyer shall not provide the evaluation unless the client gives informed consent.

(c) Except as disclosure is authorized in connection with a report of an evaluation, information relating to the evaluation is otherwise protected by Rule 1.6.

Rule 2.4. Lawyer serving as third-party neutral

(a) A lawyer serves as a third-party neutral when the lawyer assists two or more persons who are not clients of the lawyer to reach a resolution of a dispute or other matter that has arisen between them. Service as a third-party neutral may include service as an arbitrator, a mediator or in such other capacity as will enable the lawyer to assist the parties to resolve the matter.

(b) A lawyer serving as a third-party neutral shall inform unrepresented parties that the lawyer is not representing them. When the lawyer knows or reasonably should know that a party does not understand the lawyer's role in the mat-ter, the lawyer shall explain the difference between the lawyer's role as a third-party neutral and a lawyer's role as one who represents a client.

Rule 3.1. Meritorious claims and contentions

A lawyer shall not bring or defend a proceeding, or assert or controvert an issue therein, unless there is a basis in law and fact for doing so that is not frivolous, which includes a good faith argument for an extension, modification or rever-sal of existing law. A lawyer for the defendant in a criminal proceeding, or the respondent in a proceeding that could result in incarceration, may nevertheless so defend the proceeding as to require that every element of the case be estab-lished.

Rule 3.2. Expediting litigation

A lawyer shall make reasonable efforts to expedite litigation consistent with the interests of the client.

Rule 3.3. Candor toward the tribunal

(a) A lawyer shall not knowingly:

(1) make a false statement of fact or law to a tribunal or fail to correct a false statement of material fact or law pre-viously made to the tribunal by the lawyer;

(2) fail to disclose to the tribunal legal authority in the controlling jurisdiction known to the lawyer to be directly adverse to the position of the client and not disclosed by opposing counsel; or

(3) offer evidence that the lawyer knows to be false. If a lawyer, the lawyer's client, or a witness called by the law-yer, has offered material evidence and the lawyer comes to know of its falsity, the lawyer shall take reasonable remedial measures, including, if necessary, disclosure to the tribunal. A lawyer may refuse to offer evidence, other than the tes-timony of a defendant in a criminal matter, that the lawyer reasonably believes is false.

(b) A lawyer who represents a client in an adjudicative proceeding and who knows that a person intends to engage, is engaging or has engaged in criminal or fraudulent conduct related to the proceeding shall take reasonable remedial measures, including, if necessary, disclosure to the tribunal.

(c) The duties stated in paragraph (a) and (b) continue to the conclusion of the proceeding, and apply even if com-pliance requires disclosure of information otherwise protected by Rule 1.6.

(d) In an ex parte proceeding, a lawyer shall inform the tribunal of all material facts known to the lawyer which will enable the tribunal to make an informed decision, whether or not the facts are adverse.

Rule 3.4. Fairness to opposing party and counsel

A lawyer shall not:

(a) unlawfully obstruct another party's access to evidence or unlawfully alter, destroy or conceal a document or other material having potential evidentiary value. A lawyer shall not counsel or assist another person to do any such act;

(b) falsify evidence, counsel or assist a witness to testify falsely, or offer an inducement to a witness that is prohib-ited by law.

(c) knowingly disobey an obligation under the rules of a tribunal, except for an open refusal based on an assertion that no valid obligation exists;

(d) in pretrial procedure, make a frivolous discovery request or fail to make reasonably diligent efforts to comply with a legally proper discovery request by an opposing party;

(e) in trial, allude to any matter that the lawyer does not reasonably believe is relevant or that will not be supported by admissible evidence, assert personal knowledge of facts in issue except when testifying as a witness, or state a per-sonal opinion as to the justness of a cause, the credibility of a witness, the culpability of a civil litigant or the guilt or innocence of an accused; or

(f) request a person other than a client to refrain from voluntarily giving relevant information to another party unless:

(1) the person is a relative or an employee or other agent of a client; and

(2) the lawyer reasonably believes that the person's interests will not be adversely affected by refraining from giv-ing such information.

Rule 3.5. Impartiality and decorum of the tribunal

A lawyer shall not:

(a) seek to influence a judge, juror, prospective juror or other official by means prohibited by law;

(b) communicate or cause another to communicate ex parte with such a person or members of such person's family during the proceeding unless authorized to do so by law or court order; or

(c) communicate with a juror or prospective juror after discharge of the jury unless the communication is permitted by court rule;

(d) engage in conduct intended to disrupt a tribunal or engage in undignified or discourteous conduct that is de-grading to a tribunal.

Rule 3.6. Trial publicity

(a) A lawyer who is participating or has participated in the investigation or litigation of a matter shall not make an extrajudicial statement that the lawyer knows or reasonably should know will be disseminated by means of public communication and will have a substantial likelihood of materially prejudicing an adjudicative proceeding in the mat-ter.

(b) Notwithstanding paragraph (a), a lawyer may state:

(1) the claim, offense or defense involved and, except when prohibited by law, the identity of the persons involved;

(2) information contained in a public record;

(3) that an investigation of a matter is in progress;

(4) the scheduling or result of any step in litigation;

(5) a request for assistance in obtaining evidence and information necessary thereto;

(6) a warning of danger concerning the behavior of a person involved, when there is reason to believe that there ex-ists the likelihood of substantial harm to an individual or to the public interest; and

(7) in a criminal case, in addition to subparagraphs (1) through (6):

(i) the identity, residence, occupation and family status of the accused;

(ii) if the accused has not been apprehended, information necessary to aid in apprehension of that person;

(iii) the fact, time and place of arrest; and

(iv) the identity of investigating and arresting officers or agencies and the length of the investigation.

(c) Notwithstanding paragraph (a), a lawyer may make a statement that a reasonable lawyer would believe is re-quired to protect a client from the substantial undue prejudicial effect of recent publicity not initiated by the lawyer or the lawyer's client. A statement made pursuant to this paragraph shall be limited to such information as is necessary to mitigate the recent adverse publicity.

(d) No lawyer associated in a firm or government agency with a lawyer subject to paragraph (a) shall make a state-ment prohibited by paragraph (a).

Rule 3.7. Lawyer as witness

(a) A lawyer shall not act as advocate at a trial in which the lawyer is likely to be a necessary witness unless:

(1) the testimony relates to an uncontested issue;

(2) the testimony relates to the nature and value of legal services rendered in the case; or

(3) disqualification of the lawyer would work substantial hardship on the client.

(b) A lawyer may act as advocate in a trial in which another lawyer in the lawyer's firm is likely to be called as a witness unless precluded from doing so by Rule 1.7 or Rule 1.9.

Rule 3.8. Special responsibilities of a prosecutor

The prosecutor in a criminal case shall:

(a) refrain from prosecuting a charge that the prosecutor knows is not supported by probable cause;

(b) make reasonable efforts to assure that the accused has been advised of the right to, and the procedure for ob-taining, counsel and has been given reasonable opportunity to obtain counsel;

(c) not seek to obtain from an unrepresented accused a waiver of important pretrial rights, such as the right to a pre-liminary hearing;

(d)(1) make timely disclosure to the defense of all evidence or information known to the prosecutor that tends to negate the guilt of the accused or mitigates the offense, and, in connection with sentencing, disclose to the defense and to the tribunal all unprivileged mitigating information known to the prosecutor, except when the prosecutor is relieved of this responsibility by a protective order of the tribunal;

(2) when the prosecutor comes to know of new, credible and material evidence establishing that a convicted de-fendant did not commit the offense for which the defendant was convicted, the prosecutor shall, unless a court author-izes delay, make timely disclosure of that evidence to the convicted defendant and any appropriate court, or, where the conviction was obtained outside the prosecutor's jurisdiction, to the chief prosecutor of the jurisdiction where the con-viction occurred;

(e) not subpoena a lawyer in a grand jury or other criminal proceeding to present evidence about a past or present client unless the prosecutor reasonably believes:

(1) the information sought is not protected from disclosure by any applicable privilege;

(2) the evidence sought is essential to the successful completion of an ongoing investigation or prosecution; and

(3) there is no other feasible alternative to obtain the information;

(f) except for statements that are necessary to inform the public of the nature and extent of the prosecutor's action and that serve a legitimate law enforcement purpose, refrain from making extrajudicial comments that have a substan-tial likelihood of heightening public condemnation of the accused and exercise reasonable care to prevent investigators, law enforcement personnel, employees or other persons assisting or associated with the prosecutor in a criminal case from making an extrajudicial statement that the prosecutor would be prohibited from making under Rule 3.6 or this Rule.

Rule 3.9. Advocate in nonadjudicative proceedings

A lawyer representing a client before a legislative body or administrative agency in a nonadjudicative proceeding shall disclose that the appearance is in a representative capacity and shall conform to the provisions of Rules 3.3(a) through (c), 3.4(a) through(c) and 3.5(a) and (c).

Rule 3.10. Communication with or investigation of jurors (Deleted)

Rule 4.1. Truthfulness in statements to others

In the course of representing a client a lawyer shall not knowingly:

(a) make a false statement of material fact or law to a third person; or

(b) fail to disclose a material fact when disclosure is necessary to avoid assisting a criminal or fraudulent act by a client, unless disclosure is prohibited by Rule 1.6.

Rule 4.2. Communication with person represented by counsel

In representing a client, a lawyer shall not communicate about the subject of the representation with a person the law-yer knows to be represented by another lawyer in the matter, unless the lawyer has the consent of the other lawyer or is authorized to do so by law or a court order.

Rule 4.3. Dealing with unrepresented person

In dealing on behalf of a client with a person who is not represented by counsel, a lawyer shall not state or imply that the lawyer is disinterested. When the lawyer knows or reasonably should know that the unrepresented person misunder-stands the lawyer's role in the matter, the lawyer shall make reasonable efforts to correct the misunderstanding. The lawyer shall not give legal advice to an unrepresented person, other than the advice to secure counsel, if the lawyer knows or reasonably should know that the interests of such a person are or have a reasonable possibility of being in conflict with the interests of the client.

Rule 4.4. Respect for rights of third persons

(a) In representing a client, a lawyer shall not use means that have no substantial purpose other than to embarrass, delay or burden a third person, or use methods of obtaining evidence that violate the legal rights of such a person.

(b) A lawyer who receives a document relating to the representation of the lawyer's client and knows or reasonably should know that the document was inadvertently sent shall promptly notify the sender.

Rule 5.1. Responsibilities of partners, managers, and supervisory lawyers

(a) A partner in a law firm, and a lawyer who individually or together with other lawyers possesses comparable mana-gerial authority in a law firm, shall make reasonable efforts to ensure that the firm has in effect measures giving reason-able assurance that all lawyers in the firm conform to the Rules of Professional Conduct.

(b) A lawyer having direct supervisory authority over another lawyer shall make reasonable efforts to ensure that the other lawyer conforms to the Rules of Professional Conduct.

(c) A lawyer shall be responsible for another lawyer's violation of the Rules of Professional Conduct if:

(1) the lawyer orders or, with knowledge of the specific conduct, ratifies the conduct involved; or

(2) the lawyer is a partner or has comparable managerial authority in the law firm in which the other lawyer prac-tices, or has direct supervisory authority over the other lawyer, and knows of the conduct at a time when its conse-quences can be avoided or mitigated but fails to take reasonable remedial action.

Rule 5.2. Responsibilities of a subordinate lawyer

(a) A lawyer is bound by the Rules of Professional Conduct notwithstanding that the lawyer acted at the direction of another person.

(b) A subordinate lawyer does not violate the Rules of Professional Conduct if that lawyer acts in accordance with a supervisory lawyer's reasonable resolution of an arguable question of professional duty.

Rule 5.3. Responsibilities regarding non-lawyer assistants

With respect to a nonlawyer employed or retained by or associated with a lawyer:

(a) a partner in a law firm, and a lawyer who individually or together with other lawyers possesses comparable managerial authority in a law firm, shall make reasonable efforts to ensure that the firm has in effect measures giving reasonable assurance that the person's conduct is compatible with the professional obligations of the lawyer;

(b) a lawyer having direct supervisory authority over the nonlawyer shall make reasonable efforts to ensure that the person's conduct is compatible with the professional obligations of the lawyer; and

(c) a lawyer shall be responsible for conduct of such a person that would be a violation of the Rules of Professional Conduct if engaged in by a lawyer if:

(1) the lawyer orders or, with the knowledge of the specific conduct, ratifies the conduct involved; or

(2) the lawyer is a partner or has comparable managerial authority in the law firm in which the person is employed, or has direct supervisory authority over the person, and knows of the conduct at a time when its consequences can be avoided or mitigated but fails to take reasonable remedial action.

Rule 5.4. Professional independence of a lawyer

(a) A lawyer or law firm shall not share legal fees with a nonlawyer, except that:

(1) an agreement by a lawyer with the lawyer's firm, partner, or associate may provide for the payment of money, over a reasonable period of time after the lawyer's death, to the lawyer's estate or to one or more specified persons;

(2) a lawyer who undertakes to complete unfinished legal business of a deceased lawyer may pay to the estate of the deceased lawyer that proportion of the total compensation which fairly represents the services rendered by the de-ceased lawyer;

(3) a lawyer who purchases the practice of a deceased, disabled, or disappeared lawyer may, pursuant to the provi-sions of Rule 1.17, pay to the estate or other representative of that lawyer the agreed-upon purchase price;

(4) a lawyer or law firm may include nonlawyer employees in a compensation or retirement plan, even though the plan is based in whole or in part on a profit-sharing arrangement; and

(5) a lawyer may share court-awarded legal fees with a nonprofit organization that employed, retained or recom-mended employment of the lawyer in the matter.

(b) A lawyer shall not form a partnership with a nonlawyer if any of the activities of the partnership consist of the practice of law.

(c) A lawyer shall not permit a person who recommends, employs, or pays the lawyer to render legal services for another to direct or regulate the lawyer's professional judgment in rendering such legal services.

(d) A lawyer shall not practice with or in the form of a professional corporation or association authorized to prac-tice law for a profit, if:

(1) a nonlawyer owns any interest therein, except that a fiduciary representative of the estate of a lawyer may hold the stock or interest of the lawyer for a reasonable time during administration;

(2) a nonlawyer is a corporate director or officer thereof or occupies the position of similar responsibility in any form of association other than a corporation; or

(3) a nonlawyer has the right to direct or control the professional judgment of a lawyer.

Rule 5.5. Unauthorized practice of law; multijurisdictional practice of law

(a) A lawyer shall not practice law in a jurisdiction in violation of the regulation of the legal profession in that juris-diction, or assist another in doing so.

(b) A lawyer who is not admitted to practice in this jurisdiction shall not:

(1) except as authorized by these Rules or other law, establish an office or other systematic and continuous pres-ence in this jurisdiction for the practice of law; or

(2) hold out to the public or otherwise represent that the lawyer is admitted to practice law in this jurisdiction.

(c) A lawyer admitted in another United States jurisdiction or in a foreign jurisdiction, and not disbarred or sus-pended from practice in any jurisdiction, may provide legal services on a temporary basis in this jurisdiction that:

(1) are undertaken in association with a lawyer who is admitted to practice in this jurisdiction and who actively par-ticipates in the matter;

(2) are in or reasonably related to a pending or potential proceeding before a tribunal in this or another jurisdiction, if the lawyer, or a person the lawyer is assisting, is authorized by law or order to appear in such proceeding or reasona-bly expects to be so authorized;

(3) are in or reasonably related to a pending or potential arbitration, mediation, or other alternative dispute resolu-tion proceeding in this or another jurisdiction, if the services arise out of or are reasonably related to the lawyer's prac-tice in a jurisdiction in which the lawyer is admitted to practice and are not services for which the forum requires pro hac vice admission; or

(4) are not within paragraphs (c)(2) or (c)(3) and arise out of or are reasonably related to the lawyer's practice in a jurisdiction in which the lawyer is admitted to practice.

(d) A lawyer admitted in another United States jurisdiction, or in a foreign jurisdiction, and not disbarred or sus-pended from practice in any jurisdiction, may provide legal services in this jurisdiction that:

(1) are provided to the lawyer's employer or its organizational affiliates after compliance with Supreme Court Rule 55.1(a)(1) and are not services for which the forum requires pro hac vice admission; or

(2) are services that the lawyer is authorized to provide by federal law or other law of this jurisdiction.

Rule 5.6. Restrictions on right to practice

A lawyer shall not participate in offering or making:

(a) a partnership, shareholders, operating, employment, or other similar type of agreement that restricts the rights of a lawyer to practice after termination of the relationship, except an agreement concerning benefits upon retirement; or

(b) an agreement in which a restriction on the lawyer's right to practice is part of the settlement of a client contro-versy.

Rule 5.7. Responsibilities regarding law-related services

(a) A lawyer shall be subject to the Rules of Professional Conduct with respect to the provision of law-related ser-vices, as defined in paragraph (b), if the law-related services are provided:

(1) by the lawyer in circumstances that are not distinct from the lawyer's provision of legal services to clients; or

(2) in other circumstances by an entity controlled by the lawyer individually or with others if the lawyer fails to take reasonable measures to assure that a person obtaining the law-related services knows that the services are not legal services and that the protections of the client-lawyer relationship do not exist.

(b) The term "law-related services" denotes services that might reasonably be performed in conjunction with and in substance are related to the provision of legal services, and that are not prohibited as unauthorized practice of law when provided by a nonlawyer.

Rule 6.1. Voluntary pro bono publico service

A lawyer should render public interest legal service. A lawyer may discharge this responsibility by providing profes-sional services at no fee or a reduced fee to persons of limited means or to public service or charitable groups or organizations, by service in activities for improving the law, the legal system or the legal profession, and by financial support for organizations that provide legal services to persons of limited means.

Rule 6.2. Accepting appointments

A lawyer shall not seek to avoid appointment by a tribunal to represent a person except for good cause, such as:

(a) representing the client is likely to result in violation of the Rules of Professional Conduct or other law;

(b) representing the client is likely to result in an unreasonable financial burden on the lawyer; or

(c) the client or the cause is so repugnant to the lawyer as to be likely to impair the client-lawyer relationship or the lawyer's ability to represent the client.

Rule 6.3. Membership in legal services organization

A lawyer may serve as a director, officer or member of a legal services organization, apart from the law firm in which the lawyer practices, notwithstanding that the organization serves persons having interests adverse to a client of the lawyer. The lawyer shall not knowingly participate in a decision or action of the organization:

(a) if participating in the decision or action would be incompatible with the lawyer's obligations to a client under Rule 1.7; or

(b) where the decision or action could have a material adverse effect on the representation of a client of the organi-zation whose interests are adverse to a client of the lawyer.

Rule 6.4. Law reform activities affecting client interests

A lawyer may serve as a director, officer or member of an organization involved in reform of the law or its admini-stration notwithstanding that the reform may affect the interests of a client of the lawyer. When the lawyer knows that the interests of a client may be materially benefitted by a decision in which the lawyer participates, the lawyer shall disclose that fact but need not identify the client.

Rule 6.5. Non-profit and court-annexed limited legal-service programs

(a) A lawyer who, under the auspices of a program sponsored by a nonprofit organization or court, provides short-term limited legal services to a client without expectation by either the lawyer or the client that the lawyer will provide continuing representation in the matter:

(1) is subject to Rules 1.7 and 1.9(a) only if the lawyer knows that the representation of the client involves a con-flict of interest; and

(2) is subject to Rule 1.10 only if the lawyer knows that another lawyer associated with the lawyer in a law firm is disqualified by Rule 1.7 or 1.9(a) with respect to the matter.

(b) Except as provided in paragraph (a)(2), Rule 1.10 is inapplicable to a representation governed by this Rule.

Rule 7.1. Communications concerning a lawyer's services

A lawyer shall not make a false or misleading communication about the lawyer or the lawyer's services. A communi-cation is false or misleading if it contains a material misrepresentation of fact or law, or omits a fact necessary to make the statement considered as a whole not materially misleading.

Rule 7.2. Advertising

(a) Subject to the requirements of Rules 7.1 and 7.3, a lawyer may advertise services through written, recorded or electronic communication, including public media.

(b) Except as permitted by Rule 1.5(e), a lawyer shall not give anything of value to a person for recommending the lawyer's services except that a lawyer may

(1) pay the reasonable costs of advertisements or communications permitted by this Rule;

(2) pay the usual charges of a legal service plan or a not-for-profit or qualified lawyer referral service. A qualified lawyer referral service is a lawyer referral service that has been approved by an appropriate regulatory authority; and

(3) pay for a law practice in accordance with Rule 1.17.

(c) Any communication made pursuant to this rule shall include the name and office address of at least one lawyer or law firm responsible for its content.

Rule 7.3. Direct contact with prospective clients

(a) A lawyer shall not by in-person, live telephone or real-time electronic contact solicit professional employment from a prospective client when a significant motive for the lawyer's doing so is the lawyer's pecuniary gain, unless the person contacted:

(1) is a lawyer; or

(2) has a family, close personal, or prior professional relationship with the lawyer.

(b) A lawyer shall not solicit professional employment from a prospective client by written, recorded or electronic communication or by in-person, telephone or real-time electronic contact even when not otherwise prohibited by para-graph (a), if:

(1) the prospective client has made known to the lawyer a desire not to be solicited by the lawyer; or

(2) the solicitation involves coercion, duress or harassment.

(c) Every written, recorded or electronic communication from a lawyer soliciting professional employment from a prospective client known to be in need of legal services in a particular matter shall include the words "Advertising Ma-terial" on the outside envelope, if any, and at the beginning and ending of any recorded or electronic communication, unless the recipient of the communication is a person specified in paragraphs (a)(1) or (a)(2).

(d) Notwithstanding the prohibitions in paragraph (a), a lawyer may participate with a prepaid or group legal ser-vice plan operated by an organization not owned or directed by the lawyer that uses in-person or telephone contact to solicit memberships or subscriptions for the plan from persons who are not known to need legal services in a particular matter covered by the plan.

Rule 7.4. Communication of fields of practice and specialization

(a) A lawyer may communicate the fact that the lawyer does or does not practice in particular fields of law.

(b) A lawyer admitted to engage in patent practice before the United States Patent and Trademark Office may use the designation "Patent Attorney" or a substantially similar designation;

(c) A lawyer engaged in Admiralty practice may use the designation "Admiralty," "Proctor in Admiralty" or a sub-stantially similar designation.

(d) A lawyer shall not state or imply that a lawyer is certified as a specialist in a particular field of law, unless:

(1) the lawyer has been certified as a specialist by an organization that has been approved by an appropriate state authority or that has been accredited by the American Bar Association; and

(2) the name of the certifying organization is clearly identified in the communication.

Rule 7.5. Firm names and letterheads

(a) A lawyer shall not use a firm name, letterhead or other professional designation that violates Rule 7.1. A trade name may be used by a lawyer in private practice if it does not imply a connection with a government agency or with a public or charitable legal services organization and is not otherwise in violation of Rule 7.1.

(b) A law firm with offices in more than one jurisdiction may use the same name or other professional designation in each jurisdiction, but identification of the lawyers in an office of the firm shall indicate the jurisdictional limitations on those not licensed to practice in the jurisdiction where the office is located.

(c) The name of a lawyer holding a public office shall not be used in the name of a law firm, or in communications on its behalf, during any substantial period in which the lawyer is not actively and regularly practicing with the firm.

(d) Lawyers may state or imply that they practice in a partnership or other organization only when that is the fact.

Rule 7.6. Political contributions to obtain government legal engagements or appointments by judges

A lawyer or law firm shall not accept a government legal engagement or an appointment by a judge if the lawyer or law firm makes a political contribution or solicits political contributions for the purpose of obtaining or being consid-ered for that type of legal engagement or appointment.

Rule 8.1. Bar admission and disciplinary matters

An applicant for admission to the bar, or a lawyer in connection with a bar admission application or in connection with a disciplinary matter, shall not:

(a) knowingly make a false statement of material fact; or

(b) fail to disclose a fact necessary to correct a misapprehension known by the person to have arisen in the matter, or knowingly fail to respond to a lawful demand for information from an admission or disciplinary authority, except that this rule does not require disclosure of information otherwise protected by Rule 1.6.

Rule 8.2. Judicial and legal officials

(a) A lawyer shall not make a statement that the lawyer knows to be false or with reckless disregard as to its truth or falsity concerning the qualifications or integrity of a judge, adjudicatory officer or public legal officer, or a candidate for election or appointment to judicial or legal office.

(b) A lawyer who is a candidate for judicial office shall comply with the applicable provisions of the Code of Judi-cial Conduct.

Rule 8.3. Reporting professional misconduct

(a) A lawyer who knows that another lawyer has committed a violation of the rules of Professional Conduct that raises a substantial question as to that lawyer's honesty, trustworthiness or fitness as a lawyer in other respects, shall inform the appropriate professional authority.

(b) A lawyer who knows that a judge has committed a violation of applicable rules of judicial conduct that raises a substantial question as to the judge's fitness for office shall inform the appropriate authority.

(c) This Rule does not require disclosure of information otherwise protected by rule 1.6.

(d) Notwithstanding anything in this or other of the rules to the contrary, the relationship between members of ei-ther (i) the Lawyers Assistance Committee of the Delaware State Bar Association and counselors retained by the Bar Association, or (ii) the Professional Ethics Committee of the Delaware State Bar Association, or (iii) the Fee dispute Conciliation and Mediation Committee of the Delaware State Bar Association, or (iv) the Professional Guidance Com-mittee of the Delaware State Bar Association, and a lawyer or a judge shall be the same as that of attorney and client.

Rule 8.4. Misconduct

It is professional misconduct for a lawyer to:

(a) violate or attempt to violate the Rules of Professional Conduct, knowingly assist or induce another to do so or do so through the acts of another;

(b) commit a criminal act that reflects adversely on the lawyer's honesty, trustworthiness or fitness as a lawyer in other respects;

(c) engage in conduct involving dishonesty, fraud, deceit or misrepresentation;

(d) engage in conduct that is prejudicial to the administration of justice;

(e) state or imply an ability to influence improperly a government agency or official or to achieve results by means that violate the Rules of Professional Conduct or other law; or

(f) knowingly assist a judge or judicial officer in conduct that is a violation of applicable rules of judicial conduct or other law.

Rule 8.5. Disciplinary authority; choice of law

(a) Disciplinary Authority. A lawyer admitted to practice in this jurisdiction is subject to the disciplinary authority of this jurisdiction, regardless of where the lawyer's conduct occurs. A lawyer not admitted in this jurisdiction is also sub-ject to the disciplinary authority of this jurisdiction if the lawyer provides or offers to provide any legal services in this jurisdiction. A lawyer may be subject to the disciplinary authority of both this jurisdiction and another jurisdiction for the same conduct.

(b) Choice of Law. In any exercise of the disciplinary authority of this jurisdiction, the rules of professional con-duct to be applied shall be as follows:

(1) for conduct in connection with a matter pending before a tribunal, the rules of the jurisdiction in which the tri-bunal sits, unless the rules of the tribunal provide otherwise; and

(2) for any other conduct, the rules of the jurisdiction in which the lawyer's conduct occurred, or, if the predomi-nant effect of the conduct is in a different jurisdiction, the rules of that jurisdiction shall be applied to the conduct. A lawyer shall not be subject to discipline if the lawyer's conduct conforms to the rules of a jurisdiction in which the law-yer reasonably believes the predominant effect of the lawyer's conduct will occur.

CURRENT THROUGH: February 16, 2010.

APPENDIX III

MICHIGAN RULES OF PROFESSIONAL CONDUCT

RULE 1.0 SCOPE AND APPLICABILITY OF RULES AND COMMENTARY

(a) These are the Michigan Rules of Professional Conduct. The form of citation for this rule is MRPC 1.0.

(b) Failure to comply with an obligation or prohibition imposed by a rule is a basis for invoking the disciplinary process. The rules do not, however, give rise to a cause of action for enforcement of a rule or for damages caused by failure to comply with an obligation or prohibition imposed by a rule. In a civil or criminal action, the admissibility of the Rules of Professional Conduct is governed by the Michigan Rules of Evidence and other provisions of law.

(c) The text of each rule is authoritative. The comment that accompanies each rule does not expand or limit the scope of the obligations, prohibitions, and counsel found in the text of the rule.

PREAMBLE, SCOPE AND TERMINOLOGY
PREAMBLE: A LAWYER'S RESPONSIBILITIES

This preamble is part of the comment to Rule 1.0, and provides a general introduction to the Rules of Professional Conduct.

[1] A lawyer is a representative of clients, an officer of the legal system and a public citizen having special responsibility for the quality of justice.

[2] As a representative of clients, a lawyer performs various functions. As advisor, a lawyer provides a client with an informed understanding of the client's legal rights and obligations and explains their practical implications. As advocate, a lawyer zealously asserts the client's position under the rules of the adversary system. As negotiator, a lawyer seeks a result advantageous to the client but consistent with requirements of honest dealing with others. As intermediary between clients, a lawyer seeks to reconcile their divergent interests as an advisor and, to a limited extent, as a spokesperson for each client. A

lawyer acts as evaluator by examining a client's legal affairs and reporting about them to the client or to others.

[3] In all professional functions a lawyer should be competent, prompt and diligent. A lawyer should maintain communication with a client concerning the representation. A lawyer should keep in confidence information relating to representation of a client except so far as disclosure is required or permitted by the Rules of Professional Conduct or other law.

[4] A lawyer's conduct should conform to the requirements of the law, both in professional service to clients and in the lawyer's business and personal affairs. A lawyer should use the law's procedures only for legitimate purposes and not to harass or intimidate others. A lawyer should demonstrate respect for the legal system and for those who serve it, including judges, other lawyers and public officials. While it is a lawyer's duty, when necessary, to challenge the rectitude of official action, it is also a lawyer's duty to uphold legal process.

[5] As a public citizen, a lawyer should seek improvement of the law, the administration of justice and the quality of service rendered by the legal profession. As a member of a learned profession, a lawyer should cultivate knowledge of the law beyond its use for clients, employ that knowledge in reform of the law and work to strengthen legal education. A lawyer should be mindful of deficiencies in the administration of justice and of the fact that the poor, and sometimes persons who are not poor, cannot afford adequate legal assistance, and should therefore devote professional time and civic influence in their behalf. A lawyer should aid the legal profession in pursuing these objectives and should help the bar regulate itself in the public interest.

[6] Many of a lawyer's professional responsibilities are prescribed in the Rules of Professional Conduct, as well as substantive and procedural law. However, a lawyer is also guided by personal conscience and the approbation of professional peers. A lawyer should strive to attain the highest level of skill, to improve the law and the legal profession and to exemplify the legal profession's ideals of public service.

[7] A lawyer's responsibilities as a representative of clients, an officer of the legal system, and a public citizen are usually harmonious. Thus, when an opposing party is well represented, a lawyer can be a zealous advocate on behalf of a client and at the same time assume that justice is being done. So also, a lawyer can be sure that preserving client confidences ordinarily serves the public interest because people are more likely to seek legal advice, and thereby heed their legal obligations, when they know their communications will be private.

[8] In the nature of law practice, however, conflicting responsibilities are encountered. Virtually all difficult ethical problems

arise from conflict between a lawyer's responsibilities to clients, to the legal system, and to the lawyer's own interest in remaining an upright person while earning a satisfactory living. The Rules of Professional Conduct prescribe terms for resolving such conflicts. Within the framework of these rules many difficult issues of professional discretion can arise. Such issues must be resolved through the exercise of sensitive professional and moral judgment guided by the basic principles underlying the rules.

[9] The legal profession is largely self-governing. Although other professions also have been granted powers of self-government, the legal profession is unique in this respect because of the close relationship between the profession and the processes of government and law enforcement. This connection is manifested in the fact that ultimate authority over the legal profession is vested largely in the courts.

[10] To the extent that lawyers meet the obligations of their professional calling, the occasion for government regulation is obviated. Self-regulation also helps maintain the legal profession's independence from government domination. An independent legal profession is an important force in preserving government under law, for abuse of legal authority is more readily challenged by a profession whose members are not dependent on government for the right to practice.

[11] The legal profession's relative autonomy carries with it special responsibilities of self-government. The profession has a responsibility to assure that its regulations are conceived in the public interest and not in furtherance of parochial or self-interested concerns of the bar. Every lawyer is responsible for observance of the Rules of Professional Conduct. A lawyer should also aid in securing their observance by other lawyers. Neglect of these responsibilities compromises the independence of the profession and the public interest which it serves.

[12] Lawyers play a vital role in the preservation of society. The fulfillment of this role requires an understanding by lawyers of their relationship to our legal system. The Rules of Professional Conduct, when properly applied, serve to define that relationship.

SCOPE

[13] The Rules of Professional Conduct are rules of reason. They should be interpreted with reference to the purposes of legal representation and of the law itself. Some of the rules are imperatives, cast in the terms "shall" or "shall not." These define proper conduct for purposes of professional discipline. Others, generally cast in the term "may," are permissive and define areas under the rules in which the

lawyer has professional discretion. No disciplinary action should be taken when the lawyer acts or chooses not to act within the bounds of such discretion. Other rules define the nature of relationships between the lawyer and others. The rules are thus partly obligatory and disciplinary and partly constitutive and descriptive in that they define a lawyer's professional role. Many of the comments use the term "should." Comments do not add obligations to the rules, but provide guidance for practicing in compliance with the rules.

[14] The rules presuppose a larger legal context shaping the lawyer's role. That context includes court rules and statutes relating to matters of licensure, laws defining specific obligations of lawyers, and substantive and procedural law in general. Compliance with the rules, as with all law in an open society, depends primarily upon understanding and voluntary compliance, secondarily upon reinforcement by peer and public opinion, and finally, when necessary, upon enforcement through disciplinary proceedings. The rules do not, however, exhaust the moral and ethical considerations that should inform a lawyer for no worthwhile human activity can be completely defined by legal rules. The rules simply provide a framework for the ethical practice of law.

[15] Furthermore, for purposes of determining the lawyer's authority and responsibility, principles of substantive law external to these rules determine whether a client-lawyer relationship exists. Most of the duties flowing from the client-lawyer relationship attach only after the client has requested the lawyer to render legal services and the lawyer has agreed to do so. But there are some duties, such as that of confidentiality under Rule 1.6, that may attach when the lawyer agrees to consider whether a client- lawyer relationship shall be established. Whether a client-lawyer relationship exists for any specific purpose can depend on the circumstances and may be a question of fact.

[16] Under various legal provisions, including constitutional, statutory and common-law, the responsibilities of government lawyers may include authority concerning legal matters that ordinarily reposes in the client in private client-lawyer relationships. For example, a lawyer for a government agency may have authority on behalf of the government to decide upon settlement or whether to appeal from an adverse judgment. Such authority in various respects is generally vested in the attorney general and the prosecuting attorney in state government, and their federal counterparts, and the same may be true of other government law officers. Also, lawyers under the supervision of these officers may be authorized to represent several government agencies in intragovernmental legal controversies in circumstances where a private lawyer could not represent multiple private clients.

They also may have authority to represent the "public interest" in circumstances where a private lawyer would not be authorized to do so. These rules do not abrogate any such authority.

[17] As indicated earlier in this comment, a failure to comply with an obligation or prohibition imposed by a rule is a basis for invoking the disciplinary process. The rules presuppose that disciplinary assessment of a lawyer's conduct will be made on the basis of the facts and circumstances as they existed at the time of the conduct in question and in recognition of the fact that a lawyer often has to act upon uncertain or incomplete evidence of the situation. Moreover, the rules presuppose that whether or not discipline should be imposed for a violation, and the severity of a sanction, depend on all the circumstances, such as the willfulness and seriousness of the violation, extenuating factors and whether there have been previous violations.

[18] As also indicated earlier in this comment, a violation of a rule does not give rise to a cause of action, nor does it create any presumption that a legal duty has been breached. The rules are designed to provide guidance to lawyers and to provide a structure for regulating conduct through disciplinary agencies. They are not designed to be a basis for civil liability. Furthermore, the purposes of the rules can be subverted when they are invoked by opposing parties as procedural weapons. The fact that a rule is a just basis for a lawyer's self-assessment, or for sanctioning a lawyer under the administration of a disciplinary authority, does not imply that an antagonist in a collateral proceeding or transaction has standing to seek enforcement of the rule. Accordingly, nothing in the rules should be deemed to augment any substantive legal duty of lawyers or the extradisciplinary consequences of violating such a duty.

[19] Moreover, these rules are not intended to govern or affect judicial application of either the client-lawyer or work-product privilege. Those privileges were developed to promote compliance with law and fairness in litigation. In reliance on the client-lawyer privilege, clients are entitled to expect that communications within the scope of the privilege will be protected against compelled disclosure. The client-lawyer privilege is that of the client and not of the lawyer. The fact that in exceptional situations the lawyer under the rules has a limited discretion to disclose a client confidence does not vitiate the proposition that, as a general matter, the client has a reasonable expectation that information relating to the client will not be voluntarily disclosed and that disclosure of such information may be judicially compelled only in accordance with recognized exceptions to the client-lawyer and work-product privileges.

[20] The lawyer's exercise of discretion not to disclose information under Rule 1.6 should not be subject to reexamination. Permitting such reexamination would be incompatible with the general policy of promoting compliance with law through assurances that communications will be protected against disclosure.

[21] The comment accompanying each rule explains and illustrates the meaning and purpose of the rule. The Preamble and this note on scope provide general orientation. The Comments are intended as guides to interpretation, but the text of each Rule is authoritative. The comments are intended as guides to interpretation, but the text of each rule is authoritative.

TERMINOLOGY

"**Belief**" or "**believes**" denotes that the person involved actually supposed the fact in question to be true. A person's belief may be inferred from circumstances.

"**Consult**" or "**consultation**" denotes communication of information reasonably sufficient to permit the client to appreciate the significance of the matter in question.

"**Firm**" or "**law firm**" denotes a lawyer or lawyers in a private firm, lawyers employed in the legal department of a corporation or other organization and lawyers employed in a legal services organization. See Comment, Rule 1.10.

"**Fraud**" or "**fraudulent**" denotes conduct having a purpose to deceive and not merely negligent misrepresentation or failure to apprise another of relevant information.

"**Knowingly**," "**known**," or "**knows**" denotes actual knowledge of the fact in question. A person's knowledge may be inferred from circumstances.

"**Partner**" denotes a member of a partnership and a shareholder in a law firm organized as a professional corporation.

"**Reasonable**" or "**reasonably**" when used in relation to conduct by a lawyer denotes the conduct of a reasonably prudent and competent lawyer.

"**Reasonable belief**" or "**reasonably believes**" when used in reference to a lawyer denotes that the lawyer believes the matter in question and that the circumstances are such that the belief is reasonable.

Reasonably should know" when used in reference to a lawyer denotes that a lawyer of reasonable prudence and competence would ascertain the matter in question.

"**Substantial**" when used in reference to degree or extent denotes a material matter of clear and weighty importance.

CLIENT-LAWYER RELATIONSHIP
Rule 1.1 Competence

A lawyer shall provide competent representation to a client. A lawyer shall not:

(a) handle a legal matter which the lawyer <u>knows</u> or should know that the lawyer is not competent to handle, without associating with a lawyer who is competent to handle it;

(b) handle a legal matter without preparation adequate in the circumstances; or

(c) neglect a legal matter entrusted to the lawyer.

Rule 1.2 Scope of Representation

(a) A lawyer shall seek the lawful objectives of a client through <u>reasonably</u> available means permitted by law and these rules. A lawyer does not violate this rule by acceding to reasonable requests of opposing counsel that do not prejudice the rights of the client, by being punctual in fulfilling all professional commitments, or by avoiding offensive tactics. A lawyer shall abide by a client's decision whether to accept an offer of settlement or mediation evaluation of a matter. In a criminal case, the lawyer shall abide by the client's decision, after consultation with the lawyer, with respect to a plea to be entered, whether to waive jury trial, and whether the client will testify. In representing a client, a lawyer may, where permissible, exercise professional judgment to waive or fail to assert a right or position of the client.

(b) A lawyer may limit the objectives of the representation if the client consents after <u>consultation</u>.

(c) A lawyer shall not counsel a client to engage, or assist a client, in conduct that the lawyer knows is illegal or fraudulent, but a lawyer may discuss the legal consequences of any proposed course of conduct with a client and may counsel or assist a client to make a good-faith effort to determine the validity, scope, meaning, or application of the law.

(d) A lawyer shall not counsel a client to engage, or assist a client, in conduct that the lawyer <u>knows</u> is criminal or <u>fraudulent</u>, but a lawyer may discuss the legal consequences of any proposed course of conduct with a client and may counsel or assist a client to make a good faith effort to determine the validity, scope, meaning or application of the law.

(e) When a lawyer <u>knows</u> that a client expects assistance not permitted by the Rules of Professional Conduct or other law, the lawyer shall <u>consult</u> with the client regarding the relevant limitations on the lawyer's conduct.

Rule 1.3 Diligence

A lawyer shall act with <u>reasonable</u> diligence and promptness in representing a client.

Rule 1.4 Communication

(a) A lawyer shall keep a client <u>reasonably</u> informed about the status of a matter and promptly comply with reasonable requests for information. A lawyer shall notify the client promptly of all settlement offers, mediation evaluations, and proposed plea bargains.

(b) A lawyer shall explain a matter to the extent <u>reasonably</u> necessary to permit the client to make informed decisions regarding the representation.

Rule 1.5 Fees

(a) A lawyer shall not enter into an agreement for, charge, or collect an illegal or clearly excessive fee. A fee is clearly excessive when, after a review of the facts, a lawyer of ordinary prudence would be left with a definite and <u>firm</u> conviction that the fee is in excess of a reasonable fee. The factors to be considered in determining the reasonableness of a fee include the following:

(1) the time and labor required, the novelty and difficulty of the questions involved, and the skill requisite to perform the legal service properly;

(2) the likelihood, if apparent to the client, that the acceptance of the particular employment will preclude other employment by the lawyer;

(3) the fee customarily charged in the locality for similar legal services;

(4) the amount involved and the result obtained;

(5) the time limitations imposed by the client or by the circumstances;

(6) the nature and length of the professional relationship with the client;

(7) the experience, reputation, and ability of the lawyer or lawyers performing the services; and

(8) whether the fee is fixed or contingent.

(b) When the lawyer has not regularly represented the client, the basis or rate of the fee shall be communicated to the client, preferably in writing, before or within a <u>reasonable</u> time after commencing the representation.

(c) A fee may be contingent on the outcome of the matter for which the service is rendered, except in a matter in which a contingent fee is prohibited by paragraph (d) or by other law. A contingent-fee agreement shall be in writing and shall state the method by which the fee is to be determined, including the percentage or percentages that shall accrue to the lawyer in the event of settlement, trial or appeal, litigation and other expenses to be deduced from the recovery, and whether such expenses are to be deduced before or after the contingent fee is calculated. Upon conclusion of a contingent-fee matter, the lawyer shall provide the client with a written statement stating the outcome of the matter and, if there is a recovery, showing the remittance to the client and the method of its determination.

(d) A lawyer shall not enter into an arrangement for, charge, or collect a contingent fee in a domestic relations matter or in a criminal matter.

(e) A division of a fee between lawyers who are not in the same firm may be made only if:

(1) the client is advised of and does not object to the participation of all the lawyers involved; and

(2) the total fee is reasonable.

Rule 1.6 Confidentiality of Information

(a) "**Confidence**" refers to information protected by the client-lawyer privilege under applicable law, and "**secret**" refers to other information gained in the professional relationship that the client has requested be held inviolate or the disclosure of which would be embarrassing or would be likely to be detrimental to the client.

(b) Except when permitted under paragraph (c), a lawyer shall not knowingly:

(1) reveal a confidence or secret of a client;

(2) use a confidence or secret of a client to the disadvantage of the client; or

(3) use a confidence or secret of a client for the advantage of the lawyer or of a third person, unless the client consents after full disclosure.

(c) A lawyer may reveal:

(1) confidences or secrets with the consent of the client or clients affected, but only after full disclosure to them;

(2) confidences or secrets when permitted or required by these rules, or when required by law or by court order;

(3) confidences and secrets to the extent reasonably necessary to rectify the consequences of a client's illegal or fraudulent act in the furtherance of which the lawyer's services have been used;

(4) the intention of a client to commit a crime and the information necessary to prevent the crime; and

(5) confidences or secrets necessary to establish or collect a fee, or to defend the lawyer or the lawyer's employees or associates against an accusation of wrongful conduct.

(d) A lawyer shall exercise <u>reasonable</u> care to prevent employees, associates, and others whose services are utilized by the lawyer from disclosing or using <u>confidences</u> or <u>secrets</u> of a client, except that a lawyer may reveal the information allowed by paragraph (c) through an employee.

Rule 1.7 Conflict of Interest: General rule

(a) A lawyer shall not represent a client if the representation of that client will be directly adverse to another client, unless:

(1) the lawyer <u>reasonably believes</u> the representation will not adversely affect the relationship with the other client; and

(2) each client consents after <u>consultation</u>.

(b) A lawyer shall not represent a client if the representation of that client may be materially limited by the lawyer's responsibilities to another client or to a third person, or by the lawyer's own interests, unless:

(1) the lawyer <u>reasonably believes</u> the representation will not be adversely affected; and

(2) the client consents after <u>consultation</u>. When representation of multiple clients in a single matter is undertaken, the consultation shall include explanation of the implications of the common representation and the advantages and risks involved.

Rule 1.8 Conflict of Interest: Prohibited Transactions

(a) A lawyer shall not enter into a business transaction with a client or <u>knowingly</u> acquire an ownership, possessory, security or other pecuniary interest adverse to a client unless:

(1) the transaction and terms on which the lawyer acquires the interest are fair and <u>reasonable</u> to the client and are fully disclosed and transmitted in writing to the client in a manner which can be reasonably understood by the client;

(2) the client is given a <u>reasonable</u> opportunity to seek the advice of independent counsel in the transaction; and

(3) the client consents in writing thereto.

(b) A lawyer shall not use information relating to representation of a client to the disadvantage of the client unless the client consents after <u>consultation,</u> except as permitted or required by <u>Rule 1.6</u> or <u>Rule 3.3</u>.

(c) A lawyer shall not prepare an instrument giving the lawyer or a person related to the lawyer as parent, child, sibling, or spouse any substantial gift from a client, including a testamentary gift, except where the client is related to the donee.

(d) Prior to the conclusion of representation of a client, a lawyer shall not make or negotiate an agreement giving the lawyer literary or media rights to a portrayal or account based in substantial part on information relating to the representation.

(e) A lawyer shall not provide financial assistance to a client in connection with pending or contemplated litigation, except that:

(1) a lawyer may advance court costs and expenses of litigation, the repayment of which may be contingent on the outcome of the matter; and

(2) a lawyer representing an indigent client may pay court costs and expenses of litigation on behalf of the client.

(f) A lawyer shall not accept compensation for representing a client from one other than the client unless:

(1) the client consents after consultation;

(2) there is no interference with the lawyer's independence of professional judgement or with the client-lawyer relationship; and

(3) information relating to representation of a client is protected as required by Rule 1.6.

(g) A lawyer who represents two or more clients shall not participate in making an aggregate settlement of the claims of or against the clients, or in a criminal case an aggregated agreement as to guilty or nolo contendere pleas, unless each client consents after consultation, including disclosure of the existence and nature of all the claims or pleas involved and of the participation of each person in the settlement.

(h) A lawyer shall not:

(1) make an agreement prospectively limiting the lawyer's liability to a client for malpractice unless permitted by law and the client is independently represented in making the agreement; or

(2) settle a claim for such liability with an unrepresented client or former client without first advising that person in writing that independent representation is appropriate in connection therewith.

(i) A lawyer related to another lawyer as parent, child, sibling or spouse shall not represent a client in a representation directly adverse to a person who the lawyer knows is represented by the other lawyer except upon consent by the client after consultation regarding the relationship.

(j) A lawyer shall not acquire a proprietary interest in a cause of action or subject matter of litigation the lawyer is conducting for a client, except that the lawyer may:

(1) acquire a lien granted by law to secure the lawyer's fee or expenses; and

(2) contract with a client for a <u>reasonable</u> contingent fee in a civil case, as permitted by <u>Rule 1.5</u> and MCR 8.121.

Rule 1.9 Conflict of Interest: Former Client

(a) A lawyer who has formerly represented a client in a matter shall not thereafter represent another person in the same or substantially related matter in which that person's interests are materially adverse to the interests of the former client unless the former client consents after <u>consultation</u>.

(b) Unless the former client consents after consultation, a lawyer shall not <u>knowingly</u> represent a person in the same or substantially related matter in which a <u>firm</u> with which the lawyer formerly was associated had previously represented a client,

(1) whose interests are materially adverse to that person; and

(2) about whom the lawyer has acquired information protected by <u>Rule 1.6</u> and <u>1.9(c)</u> that is material to the matter.

(c) A lawyer who has formerly represented a client in a matter or whose present or former <u>firm</u> has formerly represented a client in a matter shall not thereafter:

(1) use information relating to the representation to the disadvantage of the former client except as <u>Rule 1.6</u> or <u>3.3</u> would permit or require with respect to a client, or when the information has become generally <u>known</u>; or

(2) reveal information relating to the representation except as <u>Rule 1.6</u> or <u>3.3</u> would permit or require with respect to a client.

Rule 1.10 Imputed Disqualification: General Rule

(a) While lawyers are associated in a <u>firm</u>, none of them shall <u>knowingly</u> represent a client when any one of them practicing alone would be prohibited from doing so by <u>Rule 1.7</u>, <u>1.8(c)</u>, <u>1.9</u> or <u>2.2</u>.

(b) When a lawyer becomes associated with a <u>firm</u>, the firm may not knowingly represent a person in the same or a substantially related matter in which that lawyer, or a firm with which the lawyer was associated, is disqualified under <u>Rule 1.9(b)</u>, unless:

(1) the disqualified lawyer is screened from any participation in the matter and is apportioned no part of the fee therefrom; and

(2) written notice is promptly given to the appropriate tribunal to enable it to ascertain compliance with the provisions of this rule.

(c) When a lawyer has terminated an association with a <u>firm</u>, the firm is not prohibited from thereafter representing a person with interests materially adverse to those of a client represented by the formerly associated lawyer, and not currently represented by the firm, unless:

(1) the matter is the same or substantially related to that in which the formerly associated lawyer represented the client; and

(2) any lawyer remaining in the firm has information protected by Rules 1.6 and 1.9(c) that is material to the matter.

(d) A disqualification prescribed by this Rule may be waived by the affected client under the conditions stated in Rule 1.7.

Rule 1.11 Successive Government and Private Employment

(a) Except as law may otherwise expressly permit, a lawyer shall not represent a private client in connection with a matter in which the lawyer participated personally or substantially as a public officer or employee, unless the appropriate government agency consents after consultation. No lawyer in a firm with which that lawyer is associated may knowingly undertake or continue representation in such a matter unless:

(1) the disqualified lawyer is screened from any participation in the matter and is apportioned no part of the fee therefrom; and

(2) written notice is promptly given to the appropriate government agency to enable it to ascertain compliance with the provisions of this rule.

(b) Except as law may otherwise expressly permit, a lawyer having information that the lawyer knows is confidential government information about a person acquired when the lawyer was a public officer or employee, may not represent a private client whose interests are adverse to that person in a matter in which the information could be used to the material disadvantage of that person. A firm with which that lawyer is associated may undertake or continue representation in the matter only if the disqualified lawyer is screened from any participation in the matter and is apportioned no part of the fee therefrom.

(c) Except as law may otherwise expressly permit, a lawyer serving as a public officer or employee shall not:

(1) participate in a matter in which the lawyer participated personally and substantially while in private practice or nongovernmental employment, unless under applicable law no one is, or by lawful delegation may be, authorized to act in the lawyer's stead in the matter; or

(2) negotiate for private employment with any person who is involved as a party or as lawyer for a party in a matter in which the lawyer is participating personally or substantially, except that a lawyer serving as a law clerk to a judge, other adjudicative officer or arbitrator

may negotiate for private employment in accordance with <u>Rule 1.12(b)</u>.

(d) As used in this Rule, the term **"matter"** includes:

(1) any judicial or other proceeding, application, request for a ruling or other determination, contract, claim, controversy, investigation, charge, accusation, arrest or other particular matter involving a specific party or parties; and

(2) any other matter covered by the conflict of interest rules of the appropriate government agency.

(e) As used in this Rule, the term **"confidential government information"** means information which has been obtained under governmental authority and which, at the time this rule is applied, the government is prohibited by law from disclosing to the public or has a legal privilege not to disclose, and which is not otherwise available to the public.

Rule 1.12 Former Judge or Arbitrator

(a) Except as stated in paragraph (d), a lawyer shall not represent anyone in connection with a matter in which the lawyer participated personally and substantially as a judge or other adjudicative officer, arbitrator, or law clerk to such a person, unless all parties to the proceeding consent after <u>consultation</u>.

(b) A lawyer shall not negotiate for employment with any person who is involved as a party, or as an attorney for a party, in a matter in which the lawyer is participating personally and substantially as a judge or other adjudicative officer or arbitrator. A lawyer serving as a law clerk to a judge, other adjudicative officer, or arbitrator may negotiate for employment with a party or attorney involved in a matter in which the clerk is participating personally and substantially, but only after the lawyer has notified the judge, other adjudicative officer, or arbitrator.

(c) If a lawyer is disqualified by paragraph (a), no lawyer in a <u>firm</u> with which that lawyer is associated may <u>knowingly</u> undertake or continue representation in the matter unless:

(1) the disqualified lawyer is screened from any participation in the matter and is apportioned no part of the fee therefrom; and

(2) written notice is promptly given to the appropriate tribunal to enable it to ascertain compliance with the provisions of this rule.

(d) An arbitrator selected as a partisan of a party in a multimember arbitration panel is not prohibited from subsequently representing that party.

Rule 1.13 Organization as Client

(a) A lawyer employed or retained to represent an organization represents the organization as distinct from its directors, officers, employees, members, shareholders, or other constituents.

(b)If a lawyer for an organization knows that an officer, employee, or other person associated with the organization is engaged in action, intends to act, or refuses to act in a matter related to the representation that is a violation of a legal obligation to the organization, or a violation of law which <u>reasonably</u> might be imputed to the organization, and that is likely to result in substantial injury to the organization, the lawyer shall proceed as is reasonably necessary in the best interest of the organization. In determining how to proceed, the lawyer shall give due consideration to the seriousness of the violation and its consequences, the scope and nature of the lawyer's representation, the responsibility in the organization, and the apparent motivation of the person involved, the policies of the organization concerning such matters, and any other relevant considerations. Any measures taken shall be designed to minimize disruption of the organization and the risk of revealing information relating to the representation to persons outside the organization. Such measures may include among others:

(1) asking reconsideration of the matter

(2) advising that a separate legal opinion on the matter be sought for presentation to appropriate authority in the organization; and

(3) referring the matter to higher authority in the organization, including, if warranted by the seriousness of the matter, referral to the highest authority that can act in behalf of the organization as determined by applicable law.

(c) When the organization's highest authority insists upon action, or refuses to take action, that is clearly a violation of a legal obligation to the organization or a violation of law which reasonably might be imputed to the organization, and that is likely to result in <u>substantial</u> injury to the organization, the lawyer may take further remedial action that the lawyer reasonably believes to be in the best interest of the organization. Such action may include revealing information otherwise protected by <u>Rule 1.6</u> only if the lawyer reasonably <u>believes</u> that

(1) the highest authority in the organization has acted to further the personal or financial interests of members of that authority which are in conflict with the interests of the organization; and

(2) revealing the information is necessary in the best interest of the organization.

(d) In dealing with an organization's directors, officers, employees, members, shareholders or other constituents, a lawyer shall explain the identity of the client when the lawyer <u>believes</u> that such explanation is necessary to avoid misunderstandings on their part.

(e) A lawyer representing an organization may also represent any of its directors, officers, employees, members, shareholders or other constituents, subject to the provisions of <u>Rule 1.7</u>. If the organization's consent to the dual representation is required by <u>Rule 1.7</u>, the consent shall be given by an appropriate official of the organization other than the individual who is to be represented, or by the shareholders.

Rule 1.14 Client Under a Disability

(a) When a client's ability to make adequately considered decisions in connection with the representation is impaired, whether because of minority, mental disability or for some other reason, the lawyer shall, as far as <u>reasonably</u> possible, maintain a normal client-lawyer relationship with the client.

(b) A lawyer may seek the appointment of a guardian or take other protective action with respect to a client only when the lawyer <u>reasonably believes</u> that the client cannot adequately act in the client's own interest.

Rule 1.15 Safekeeping Property

(a) A lawyer shall hold property of clients or third persons that is in a lawyer's possession in connection with a representation separate from the lawyer's own property. All funds of the client paid to a lawyer or <u>law firm</u>, other than advances for costs and expenses, shall be deposited in an interest- bearing account in one or more identifiable banks, savings and loan associations, or credit unions maintained in the state in which the law office is situated, and no funds belonging to the lawyer or the law firm shall be deposited therein except as provided in this rule. Other property shall be identified as such and appropriately safeguarded. Complete records of such account funds and other property shall be kept by the lawyer and shall be preserved for a period of five years after termination of the representation.

(b) Upon receiving funds or other property in which a client or third person has an interest, a lawyer shall promptly notify the client or third person. Except as stated in this rule or otherwise permitted by law or by agreement with the client, a lawyer shall promptly deliver to the client or third person any funds or other property that the client or third person is entitled to receive and, upon request by the client or third person, shall promptly render a full accounting regarding such property.

(c) When in the course of representation a lawyer is in possession of property in which both the lawyer and another person claim interests, the property shall be kept separate by the lawyer until there is an accounting and severance of their interests. If a dispute arises concerning their respective interests, the portion in dispute shall be kept separate by the lawyer until the dispute is resolved.

(d)(1) Except as set forth in paragraph (d)(2), a lawyer who or a law firm which receives client funds shall maintain a pooled interest-bearing trust account for deposit of client funds, other than advances for costs and expenses, which at the time of receipt and deposit the lawyer or law firm reasonably anticipates will generate $50 or less in interest during the period for which it is anticipated such funds are to be held. Such an account shall comply with the following:

(A) No interest from the account shall be made available to the lawyer or law firm.

(B) The account shall include all client funds which are not expected to earn more than $50 in interest during the period it is anticipated such funds are to be held unless such funds are deposited in an interest-bearing account specified in paragraph (d)(2). The good-faith decision by the lawyer as to whether funds are expected to earn this amount is not reviewable by a disciplinary body.

(C) Funds deposited with a bank, savings and loan association, or credit union shall be subject to withdrawal upon request and without delay, and the account shall be insured by an agency of the federal government.

(D) The interest paid on the account shall not be less than the rate paid by the bank, savings and loan association, or credit union to any other nonlawyer customers on accounts of the same class within the institution.

(E) The lawyer or law firm shall direct the bank, savings and loan association, or credit union to:

(i) remit the interest, less reasonable service charges, at least quarterly to the Michigan State Bar Foundation.

(ii) transmit, with each remittance to the Michigan State Bar Foundation, a report which shall identify each lawyer or law firm and the amount of the remittance attributable to each account maintained by each lawyer or law firm; and

(iii) transmit to the depositing lawyer or law firm, in accordance with normal procedures for reporting to depositors, a report which shall indicate account balances, the rate of interest applied, interest earned, service charges, and the amount remitted to the Michigan State Bar Foundation.

(2) All client funds shall be deposited in the account specified in paragraph (d)(1) unless they are deposited in:

(A) a separate interest-bearing trust account for the particular client or client's matter on which the interest will be paid to the client; or

(B) a pooled interest-bearing trust account with subaccounting by the financial institution or by the lawyer or <u>law firm</u> that will provide for computation of interest earned by each client's funds and the payment thereof to the client.

Rule 1.16 Declining or Terminating Representation

(a) Except as stated in paragraph (c), a lawyer shall not represent a client or, where representation has commenced, shall withdraw from the representation of a client if:

(1) the representation will result in violation of the Rules of Professional Conduct or other law;

(2) the lawyer's physical or mental condition materially impairs the lawyer's ability to represent the client; or

(3) the lawyer is discharged.

(b) except as stated in paragraph (c), a lawyer may withdraw from representing a client if withdrawal can be accomplished without material adverse effect on the interests of the client, or if:

(1) the client persists in a course of action involving the lawyer's services that the lawyer <u>reasonably believes</u> is criminal or <u>fraudulent</u>;

(2) the client has used the lawyer's services to perpetrate a crime or <u>fraud</u>;

(3) a client insists upon pursuing an objective that the lawyer considers repugnant or imprudent;

(4) the client fails substantially to fulfill an obligation to the lawyer regarding the lawyer's services and has been given <u>reasonable</u> warning that the lawyer will withdraw unless the obligation is fulfilled;

(5) the representation will result in an unreasonable financial burden on the lawyer or has been rendered unreasonably difficult by the client; or

(6) other good cause for withdrawal exists.

(c) When ordered to do so by a tribunal, a lawyer shall continue representation notwithstanding good cause for terminating the representation.

(d) Upon termination of representation, a lawyer shall take reasonable steps to protect a client's interests, such as giving reasonable notice to the client, allowing time for employment of other counsel, surrendering papers and property to which the client is entitled, and refunding any advance payment of fee that has not been earned. The lawyer may retain papers relating to the client to the extent permitted by law.

Rule 1.17 Sale of Law Practice

(a) A lawyer or a <u>law firm</u> may sell or purchase a private law practice, including good will, pursuant to this rule.

(b) The fees charged clients shall not be increased by reason of the sale, and a purchaser shall not pass on the cost of good will to a client. The purchaser may, however, refuse to undertake the representation unless the client consents to pay fees regularly charged by the purchaser for rendering substantially similar services to other clients prior to the initiation of the purchase negotiations.

(c) Actual written notice of a pending sale shall be given at least 91 days prior to the date of the sale to each of the seller's clients, and the notice shall include:

(1) notice of the fact of the proposed sale;

(2) identity of the purchaser;

(3) the terms of any proposed change in the fee agreement permitted under paragraph (b);

(4) notice of the client's right to retain other counsel or to take possession of the file; and

(5) notice that the client's consent to the transfer of the client's file to the purchaser will be presumed if the client does not retain other counsel or otherwise object within 90 days of receipt of the notice.

If the purchaser has identified a conflict of interest that the client cannot waive and that prohibits the purchaser from undertaking the client's matter, the notice shall advise that the client should retain substitute counsel to assume the representation and arrange to have the substitute counsel contact the seller.

(d) If a client cannot be given actual notice as required in paragraph (c), the representation of that client may be transferred to the purchaser only upon entry of an order so authorizing by a judge of the judicial circuit in which the seller maintains the practice. The seller or the purchaser may disclose to the judge in camera information relating to the representation only to the extent necessary to obtain an order authorizing the transfer of a file.

(e) The sale of the good will of a law practice may be conditioned upon the seller ceasing to engage in the private practice of law for a reasonable period of time within the geographical area in which the practice had been conducted.

COUNSELOR
Rule 2.1 Advisor

In representing a client, a lawyer shall exercise independent professional judgment and render candid advice. In rendering advice, a lawyer may refer not only to law but to other considerations such as moral, economic, social and political factors, that may be relevant to the client's situation.

Rule 2.2 Intermediary

(a) A lawyer may act as intermediary between clients if:

(1) the lawyer <u>consults</u> with each client concerning the implications of the common representation, including the advantages and risks involved and the effect on the client-lawyer privileges, and obtains each client's consent to the common representation;

(2) the lawyer <u>reasonably believes</u> that the matter can be resolved on terms compatible with the clients' best interests, that each client will be able to make adequately informed decisions in the matter and that there is little risk of material prejudice to the interests of any of the clients if the contemplated resolution is unsuccessful; and

(3) the lawyer <u>reasonably believes</u> that the common representation can be undertaken impartially and without improper effect on other responsibilities the lawyer has to any of the clients.

(b) While acting as intermediary, the lawyer shall <u>consult</u> with each client concerning the decisions to be made and the considerations relevant in making them, so that each client can make adequately informed decisions.

(c) A lawyer shall withdraw as intermediary if any of the clients so requests, or if any of the conditions stated in paragraph (a) is no longer satisfied. Upon withdrawal, the lawyer shall not continue to represent any of the clients in the matter that was the subject of the intermediation.

Rule 2.3 Evaluation for Use by Third Persons

(a) A lawyer may undertake an evaluation of a matter affecting a client for the use of someone other than the client if:

(1) the lawyer <u>reasonably believes</u> that making the evaluation is compatible with other aspects of the lawyer's relationship with the client; and

(2) the client consents after <u>consultation</u>.

(b) Except as disclosure is required in connection with a report of an evaluation, information relating to the evaluation is otherwise protected by <u>Rule 1.6</u>.

ADVOCATE
Rule 3.1 Meritorious Claims and Contentions

A lawyer shall not bring or defend a proceeding, or assert or controvert an issue therein, unless there is a basis for doing so that is not frivolous. A lawyer may offer a good-faith argument for an extension, modification, or reversal of existing law. A lawyer for the defendant in a criminal proceeding, or the respondent in a proceeding that could result in incarceration, may so defend the proceeding as to require that every element of the case be established.

Rule 3.2 Expediting Litigation

A lawyer shall make <u>reasonable</u> efforts to expedite litigation consistent with the interests of the client.

Rule 3.3 Candor Toward the Tribunal

(a) A lawyer shall not <u>knowingly</u>:

(1) make a false statement of material fact or law to a tribunal;

(2) fail to disclose a material fact to a tribunal when disclosure is necessary to avoid assisting a criminal or <u>fraudulent</u> act by the client;

(3) fail to disclose to the tribunal legal authority in the controlling jurisdiction <u>known</u> to the lawyer to be directly adverse to the position of the client and not disclosed by opposing counsel; or

(4) offer evidence that the lawyer <u>knows</u> to be false. If a lawyer has offered material evidence and comes to know of its falsity, the lawyer shall take <u>reasonable</u> remedial measures.

(b) The duties stated in paragraph (a) continue to the conclusion of the proceeding, and apply even if compliance requires disclosure of information otherwise protected by <u>Rule 1.6</u>.

(c) A lawyer may refuse to offer evidence that the lawyer <u>reasonably believes</u> is false.

(d) In an ex parte proceeding, a lawyer shall inform the tribunal of all material facts <u>known</u> to the lawyer which will enable the tribunal to make an informed decision, whether or not the facts are adverse.

Rule 3.4 Fairness to Opposing Party and Counsel

A lawyer shall not:

(a) unlawfully obstruct another party's access to evidence or unlawfully alter, destroy or conceal a document or other material having potential evidentiary value. A lawyer shall not counsel or assist another person to do any such act;

(b) falsify evidence, counsel or assist a witness to testify falsely, or offer an inducement to a witness that is prohibited by law;

(c) <u>knowingly</u> disobey an obligation under the rules of a tribunal except for an open refusal based on an assertion that no valid obligation exists;

(d) in pretrial procedure, make a frivolous discovery request or fail to make <u>reasonably</u> diligent effort to comply with a legally proper discovery request by an opposing party;

(e) during trial, allude to any matter that the lawyer does not <u>reasonably believe</u> is relevant or that will not be supported by admissible evidence, assert personal knowledge of facts in issue except when testifying as a witness, or state a personal opinion as to the justness of a cause, the credibility of a witness, the culpability of a civil litigant or the guilt or innocence of an accused; or

(f) request a person other than a client to refrain from voluntarily giving relevant information to another party unless:

(1) the person is a relative or an employee or other agent of a client; and

(2) the lawyer <u>reasonably believes</u> that the person's interests will not be adversely affected by refraining from giving such information.

Rule 3.5 Impartiality and Decorum of the Tribunal

A lawyer shall not:

(a) seek to influence a judge, juror, prospective juror or other official by means prohibited by law;

(b) communicate ex parte with such a person except as permitted by law; or

(c) engage in conduct intended to disrupt a tribunal.

Rule 3.6 Trial Publicity

A lawyer shall not make an extrajudicial statement that a reasonable person would expect to be disseminated by means of public communication if the lawyer <u>knows</u> or reasonably should know that it will have a <u>substantial</u> likelihood of materially prejudicing an adjudicative proceeding.

Rule 3.7 Lawyer as Witness

(a) A lawyer shall not act as advocate at a trial in which the lawyer is likely to be a necessary witness except where:

(1) the testimony relates to an uncontested issue;

(2) the testimony relates to the nature and value of legal services rendered in the case; or

(3) disqualification of the lawyer would work <u>substantial</u> hardship on the client.

(b) A lawyer may act as advocate in a trial in which another lawyer in the lawyer's <u>firm</u> is likely to be called as a witness unless precluded from doing so by <u>Rule 1.7</u> or <u>Rule 1.9</u>.

Rule 3.8 Special Responsibilities of a Prosecutor

The prosecutor in a criminal case shall:

(a) refrain from prosecuting a charge that the prosecutor <u>knows</u> is not supported by probable cause;

(b) make <u>reasonable</u> efforts to assure that the accused has been advised of the right to, and the procedure for obtaining, counsel and has been given reasonable opportunity to obtain counsel;

(c) not seek to obtain from an unrepresented accused a waiver of important pretrial rights, such as the right to a preliminary hearing;

(d) make timely disclosure to the defense of all evidence or information <u>known</u> to the prosecutor that tends to negate the guilt of the accused or mitigates the offense, and in connection with sentencing, disclose to the defense and to the tribunal all unprivileged mitigating information known to the prosecutor, except when the prosecutor is relieved of this responsibility by a protective order of the tribunal;

(e) exercise <u>reasonable</u> care to prevent investigators, law enforcement personnel, employees or other persons assisting or associated with the prosecutor in a criminal case from making an extrajudicial statement that the prosecutor would be prohibited from making under <u>Rule 3.6</u>.

Rule 3.9 Advocate in Nonadjudicative Proceedings

A lawyer representing a client before a legislative or administrative tribunal in a nonadjudicative proceeding shall disclose that the appearance is in a representative capacity and shall conform to the provisions of <u>Rules 3.3(a) through (c)</u>, <u>3.4(a) through (c)</u>, and <u>3.5</u>.

TRANSACTIONS WITH PERSONS OTHER THAN CLIENTS
Rule 4.1 Truthfulness in Statements to Others

In the course of representing a client, a lawyer shall not <u>knowingly</u> make a false statement of material fact or law to a third person.

Rule 4.2 Communication with Person Represented by Counsel

In representing a client, a lawyer shall not communicate about the subject of the representation with a party whom the lawyer <u>knows</u> to be represented in the matter by another lawyer, unless the lawyer has the consent of the other lawyer or is authorized by law to do so.

Rule 4.3 Dealing with Unrepresented Person

In dealing on behalf of a client with a person who is not represented by counsel, a lawyer shall not state or imply that the lawyer is disinterested. When the lawyer knows or <u>reasonably should know</u> that the unrepresented person misunderstands the lawyer's role in the matter, the lawyer shall make reasonable efforts to correct the misunderstanding.

Rule 4.4 Respect for Rights of Third Persons

In representing a client, a lawyer shall not use means that have no substantial purpose other than to embarrass, delay, or burden a third person, or use methods of obtaining evidence that violate the legal rights of such a person.

LAW FIRMS AND ASSOCIATIONS
Rule 5.1 Responsibilities of a Partner or Supervisory Lawyer

(a) A partner in a law firm shall make reasonable efforts to ensure that the firm has in effect measures giving reasonable assurance that all lawyers in the firm conform to the Rules of Professional Conduct.

(b) A lawyer having direct supervisory authority over another lawyer shall make reasonable efforts to ensure that the other lawyer conforms to the Rules of Professional Conduct.

(c) A lawyer shall be responsible for another lawyer's violation of the Rules of Professional Conduct if:

(1) the lawyer orders or, with knowledge of the specific conduct, ratifies the conduct involved; or

(2) the lawyer is a partner in the law firm in which the other lawyer practices, or has direct supervisory authority over the other lawyer, and knows of the conduct at a time when its consequences can be avoided or mitigated but fails to take reasonable remedial action.

Rule 5.2 Responsibilities of a Subordinate Lawyer

(a) A lawyer is bound by the Rules of Professional Conduct notwithstanding that the lawyer acted at the direction of another person.

(b) A subordinate lawyer does not violate the Rules of Professional Conduct if that lawyer acts in accordance with a supervisory lawyer's reasonable resolution of an arguable question of professional duty.

Rule 5.3 Responsibilities Regarding Nonlawyer Assistants

With respect to a nonlawyer employed by or retained by or associated with a lawyer:

(a) a partner in a law firm shall make reasonable efforts to ensure that the firm has in effect measures giving reasonable assurance that the person's conduct is compatible with the professional obligations of the lawyer;

(b) a lawyer having direct supervisory authority over the nonlawyer shall make reasonable efforts to ensure that the person's conduct is compatible with the professional obligations of the lawyer; and

(c) a lawyer shall be responsible for conduct of such a person that would be a violation of the Rules of Professional Conduct if engaged in by a lawyer if:

(1) the lawyer orders or, with the knowledge of the specific conduct, ratifies the conduct involved; or

(2) the lawyer is a _partner_ in the _law firm_ in which the person is employed, or has direct supervisory authority over the person, and _knows_ of the conduct at a time when its consequences can be avoided or mitigated but fails to take _reasonable_ remedial action.

Rule 5.4 Professional Independence of a Lawyer

(a) A lawyer or _law firm_ shall not share legal fees with a nonlawyer, except that:

(1) an agreement by a lawyer with the lawyer's _firm_, _partner_ or associate may provide for the payment of money, over a _reasonable_ period of time after the lawyer's death, to the lawyer's estate or to one or more specified persons;

(2) a lawyer who purchases the practice of a deceased, disabled, or disappeared lawyer may, pursuant to the provisions of _Rule 1.17_, pay to the estate or other representative of that lawyer the agreed-upon purchase price; and

(3) a lawyer or _law firm_ may include nonlawyer employees in a compensation or retirement plan, even though the plan is based in whole or in part on a profit-sharing arrangement.

(b) A lawyer shall not form a partnership with a nonlawyer if any of the activities of the partnership consist of the practice of law.

(c) A lawyer shall not permit a person who recommends, employs, or pays the lawyer to render legal services for another to direct or regulate the lawyer's professional judgment in rendering such legal services.

(d) A lawyer shall not practice with or in the form of a professional corporation or association authorized to practice law for a profit, if:

(1) a nonlawyer owns any interest therein, except that a fiduciary representative of the estate of a lawyer may hold the stock or interest of the lawyer for a reasonable time during administration;

(2) a nonlawyer is a corporate director or officer thereof; or

(3) a nonlawyer has the right to direct or control the professional judgment of a lawyer.

Rule 5.5 Unauthorized Practice of Law

A lawyer shall not:

(a) practice law in a jurisdiction where doing so violates the regulation of the legal profession in that jurisdiction; or

(b) assist a person who is not a member of the bar in the performance of activity that constitutes the unauthorized practice of law.

Rule 5.6 Restrictions on Right to Practice

A lawyer shall not participate in offering or making:

(a) a partnership or employment agreement that restricts the right of a lawyer to practice after termination of the relationship, except an agreement concerning benefits upon retirement or as permitted in Rule 1.17; or

(b) an agreement in which a restriction on the lawyer's right to practice is part of the settlement of a controversy between private parties.

PUBLIC SERVICE

Rule 6.1 Voluntary Pro Bono Publico Service

A lawyer should render public interest legal service. A lawyer may discharge this responsibility by providing professional services at no fee or a reduced fee to persons of limited means, or to public service or charitable groups or organizations. A lawyer may also discharge this responsibility by service in activities for improving the law, the legal system, or the legal profession, and by financial support for organizations that provide legal services to persons of limited means.

Rule 6.2 Accepting Appointments

A lawyer shall not seek to avoid appointment by a tribunal to represent a person except for good cause, such as:

(a) representing the client is likely to result in violation of the Rules of Professional Conduct or other law;

(b) representing the client is likely to result in an unreasonable financial burden on the lawyer; or

(c) the client or the cause is so repugnant to the lawyer as to be likely to impair the client-lawyer relationship or the lawyer's ability to represent the client.

Rule 6.3 Membership in Legal Services Organization

(a) A lawyer may serve as a director, officer, or member of a legal services organization, apart from the law firm in which the lawyer practices, notwithstanding that the organization serves persons having interests adverse to a client of the lawyer. The lawyer shall not knowingly participate in a decision or action of the organization:

(1) if participating in the decision or action would be incompatible with the lawyer's obligations to a client under Rule 1.7; or

(2) where the decision or action could have a material adverse effect on the representation of a client of the organization whose interests are adverse to a client of the lawyer.

(b) A lawyer may participate in and pay the usual charges of a not-for-profit lawyer referral service that recommends legal services to the public if that service:

(1) maintains registration as a qualified service with the State Bar, under such rules as may be adopted by the State Bar, consistent with these rules;

(2) is operated in the public interest for the purpose of referring prospective clients to lawyers; pro bono and public service legal programs; and government, consumer or other agencies that can best provide the assistance needed by clients, in light of their financial circumstances, spoken language, any disability, geographical convenience, and the nature and complexity of their problems;

(3) is open to all lawyers licensed and eligible to practice in this state who maintain an office within the geographical area served, and who:

(i) meet reasonable and objective requirements of experience, as established by the service;

(ii) pay reasonable registration and membership fees not to exceed an amount established by the State Bar to encourage widespread lawyer participation; and

(iii) maintain a policy of errors and omissions insurance, or provide proof of financial responsibility, in an amount at least equal to the minimum established by the State Bar;

(4) ensures that the combined fees and expenses charge a prospective client by a qualified service and a lawyer to whom the client is referred not exceed the total charges the client would have incurred had no referral service been involved; and

(5) makes no fee-generating referral to any lawyer who has an ownership interest in, or who operates or is employed by, the qualified service, or who is associated with a <u>law firm</u> that has an ownership interest in, or operates or is employed by, a qualified service.

(c) The requirements of subrule (b) do no apply to

(1) a plan of prepaid legal services insurance authorized to operate in the state, or a group or prepaid legal plan, whether operated by a union, trust, mutual benefit or aid association, corporation or other entity or person, which provides unlimited or a specified amount of telephone advice or personal communications at no charge to the members or beneficiaries, other than a periodic membership or beneficiary fee, and furnishes to or pays for legal services for its members or beneficiaries;

(2) individual lawyer-to-lawyer referrals;

(3) lawyers jointly advertising their services in a manner that discloses that such advertising is solely to solicit clients for themselves; or

(4) any pro bono legal assistance program that does not accept fees from lawyers or clients for referrals.

(d) The State Bar or any aggrieved person may seek an injunction in the circuit court to enjoin violations of subrule (b). In the event the injunction is granted, the petitioner shall be entitled to reasonable costs and attorney fees.

(e) A lawyer may participate in and pay the usual charges of a plan or organization defined in subrule (c)(1), if that plan or organization:

(1) has filed with the State Bar of Michigan a written plan disclosing the name under which it operates; the name, address, and telephone number of its chief operating officer; and the plan terms, conditions of eligibility, schedule of benefits, subscription charges and agreements with counsel;

(2) updates its filings within 30 days of any material change;

(3) in January of each year following its inception files a statement representing that it continues to do business under the terms and conditions reflected in its filings as amended to date.

These filing requirements shall not apply to not-for-profit legal aid associations.

Rule 6.4 Law Reform Activities Affecting Client Interests

A lawyer may serve as a director, officer or member of an organization involved in reform of the law or its administration notwithstanding that the reform may affect the interests of a client of the lawyer. When the lawyer knows that the interests of a client may be materially benefitted by a decision in which the lawyer participates, the lawyer shall disclose that fact but need not identify the client.

Rule 6.5 Professional Conduct

(a) A lawyer shall treat with courtesy and respect all persons involved in the legal process. A lawyer shall take particular care to avoid treating such a person discourteously or disrespectfully because of the person's race, gender, or other protected personal characteristic. To the extent possible, a lawyer shall require subordinate lawyers and nonlawyer assistants to provide such courteous and respectful treatment.

(b) A lawyer serving as an adjudicative officer shall, without regard to a person's race, gender, or other protected personal characteristic, treat every person fairly, with courtesy and respect. To the extent possible, the lawyer shall require staff and others who are subject to the adjudicative officer's direction and control to provide such fair, courteous, and respectful treatment to persons who have contact with the adjudicative tribunal.

INFORMATION ABOUT LEGAL SERVICES
Rule 7.1 Communications Concerning a Lawyer's Services

A lawyer may, on the lawyer's own behalf, on behalf of a <u>partner</u> or associate, or on behalf of any other lawyer affiliated with the lawyer or the lawyer's <u>law firm</u>, use or participate in the use of any form of public communication that is not false, <u>fraudulent</u>, misleading, or deceptive. A communication shall not:

(a) contains a material misrepresentation of fact or law, or omits a fact necessary to make the statement considered as a whole not materially misleading;

(b) be likely to create an unjustified expectation about results the lawyer can achieve, or state or imply that the lawyer can achieve results by means that violate the Rules of Professional Conduct or other law; or

(c) compares the lawyer's services with other lawyers' services, unless the comparison can be factually substantiated.

Rule 7.2 Advertising

(a) Subject to the provisions of these rules, a lawyer may advertise.

(b) A copy or recording of an advertisement or communication shall be kept for two years after its last dissemination along with a record of when and where it was used.

(c) A lawyer shall not give anything of value to a person for recommending the lawyer's services except that a lawyer may:

(i) pay the <u>reasonable</u> costs of advertisements or communications permitted by this rule;

(ii) participate in, and pay the usual charges of, a not-for-profit lawyer referral service or other legal service organization that satisfies the requirements of <u>Rule 6.3(b)</u>; and

(iii) pay for a law practice in accordance with <u>Rule 1.17</u>.

Rule 7.3 Direct Contact with Prospective Clients

(a) A lawyer shall not solicit professional employment from a prospective client with whom the lawyer has no family or prior professional relationship when a significant motive for the lawyer's doing so is the lawyer's pecuniary gain. The term "solicit" includes contact in person, by telephone or telegraph, by letter or other writing, or by other communication directed to a specific recipient, but does not include letters addressed or advertising circulars distributed generally to persons not <u>known</u> to need legal services of the kind provided by the lawyer in a particular matter, but who are so situated that they might in general find such services useful, nor does the term "solicit" include "sending truthful and nondeceptive letters to potential clients known to face particular legal problems" as elucidated in Shapero v Kentucky Bar Ass'n, 486 US 466; 108 SCt 1916; 100 LEd2d 475 (1988).

(b) A lawyer shall not solicit professional employment from a prospective client by written or recorded communication or by in-person or telephone contact even when not otherwise prohibited by paragraph (a), if:

(1) the prospective client has made <u>known</u> to the lawyer a desire not to be solicited by the lawyer; or

(2) the solicitation involves coercion, duress or harassment.

Rule 7.4 Communication of Fields of Practice and Certification

A lawyer may communicate the fact that the lawyer does or does not practice in particular fields of law.

Rule 7.5 Firm Names and Letterheads

(a) A lawyer shall not use a <u>firm</u> name, letterhead or other professional designation that violates <u>Rule 7.1</u>. A trade name may be used by a lawyer in private practice if it does not imply a connection with a government agency or with a public or charitable legal services organization and is not otherwise in violation of <u>Rule 7.1</u>.

(b) A <u>law firm</u> with offices in more than one jurisdiction may use the same name in each jurisdiction, but identification of the lawyers in an office of the firm shall indicate the jurisdictional limitations on those not licensed to practice in the jurisdiction where the office is located.

(c) The name of a lawyer holding a public office shall not be used in the name of the <u>law firm</u>, or in communications on its behalf, during any <u>substantial</u> period in which the lawyer is not actively and regularly practicing with the firm.

(d) Lawyers may state or imply that they practice in a partnership or other organization only when that is the fact.

MAINTAINING THE INTEGRITY OF THE PROFESSION
Rule 8.1 Bar Admission and Disciplinary Matters

(a) An applicant for admission to the bar, or a lawyer in connection with a bar admission application or in connection with a disciplinary matter, shall not:

(1) <u>knowingly</u> make a false statement of material fact; or

(2) fail to disclose a fact necessary to correct a misapprehension known by the person to have arisen in the matter, or knowingly fail to respond to a lawful demand for information from an admissions or disciplinary authority, except that this rule does not require disclosure of information otherwise protected by Rule 1.6.

(b) An applicant for admission to the bar

(1) shall not engage in the unauthorized practice of law (this does not apply to activities permitted under MCR 8.120), and

(2) has a continuing obligation, until the date of admission, to inform the standing committee on character and fitness, in writing if any answers in the applicant's affidavit of personal history change or cease to be true.

Rule 8.2 Judicial and Legal Officials

(a) A lawyer shall not make a statement that the lawyer knows to be false or with reckless disregard as to its truth or falsity concerning the qualifications or integrity of a judge, adjudicatory officer or public legal officer, or of a candidate for election or appointment to judicial or legal office.

(b) A lawyer who is a candidate for judicial office shall comply with the applicable provisions of the Code of Judicial Conduct.

Rule 8.3 Reporting Professional Misconduct

(a) A lawyer having knowledge that another lawyer has committed a violation of the Rules of Professional Conduct that raises a substantial question as to that lawyer's honesty, trustworthiness or fitness as a lawyer in other respects, shall inform the Attorney Grievance Commission.

(b) A lawyer having knowledge that a judge has committed a significant violation of the Code of Judicial Conduct that raises a substantial question as to the judge's honesty, trustworthiness or fitness for office shall inform the Judicial Tenure Commission.

(c) This rule does not require disclosure of:

(1) information otherwise protected by Rule 1.6; or

(2) information gained by a lawyer while serving as an employee or volunteer of the substance abuse counseling program of the State Bar of Michigan, to the extent the information would be protected under Rule 1.6 from disclosure if it were a communication between lawyer and client.

Rule 8.4 Misconduct

It is professional misconduct for a lawyer to:

(a) violate or attempt to violate the Rules of Professional Conduct, <u>knowingly</u> assist or induce another to do so, or do so through the acts of another;

(b) engage in conduct involving dishonesty, <u>fraud</u>, deceit, misrepresentation, or violation of the criminal law, where such conduct reflects adversely on the lawyer's honesty, trustworthiness, or fitness as a lawyer;

(c) engage in conduct that is prejudicial to the administration of justice;

(d) state or imply an ability to influence improperly a government agency or official; or;

(e) knowingly assist a judge or judicial officer in conduct that is a violation of the Code of Judicial Conduct or other law.

Rule 8.5 Disciplinary Authority; Choice of Law

A lawyer licensed to practice in this jurisdiction is subject to the disciplinary authority of this jurisdiction, regardless of whether the lawyer is engaged in practice elsewhere. A lawyer who is licensed to practice in another jurisdiction and who is admitted to practice in this jurisdiction is subject to the disciplinary authority of this jurisdiction.

INDEX

ABA Code of Judicial Conduct, 535
 application of, 539
 organization of, 535
 preamble, 536
 scope, 536
 terminology, 537
Accepting representation, 96
Access to legal services, 469,497
 appointments, 506
  accepting, 506
  criminal cases, in, 506
  declining, 509
  lists, 507
 ask-a-lawyer programs, 517
 business imperative, 499
 children, representing, 525
 cross-cultural representation, 528
  communication registers, 528
  sound inter-cultural practices, 528
 diminished-capacity clients, 518
  practical and strategic issues, 522
  representing children, 525
  protective actions for, 525
 inclusive representation, 518
 law-reform activities, 517
 legal-services organizations, 510
  conflicts of interest and, 511
  legal aid, 510
  legal services programs, 516
 pro bono service, 498
  aspirational goal, 500
  business imperative, 499
  defining, 504
  distinguishing, 505
  low bono, 504
  quality of representation, 505
  social imperative, 498
  value of, 498
 social imperative of, 498

Access to the profession, 529
 increasing access, 530
 lawyers of color, 530
Admission, 50
 character, 52
 finances and, 60
 Multi-State Professional Responsibility Exam, 51
 personal behavior and, 61
 pro hac vice, 88
 reciprocity, 51
 representations to bar, 60
 temporary, 88
Adversaries, respect for, 243
Advertising, 454,470
 certifications, 491
 disclosing licensure, 458
 false or misleading, 454
 First Amendment protection of, 472
  specific advertisements, 482
 law-firm names, 457
 law-firm websites, 486
 lawyer referral services, 471
  lawyer-to-lawyer referrals, 472
  paying for referrals, 472
 political contributions, 490
 specialties, 491
 unjustified expectations, 455
 unsubstantiated comparisons, 456
 websites, 486
Advising agents, 263
Advisor, 149
Aggregate settlements, 398
Allocation of authority, 101
 decisions to settle, 102
Ambulance chasing, 465
American Bar Association, 17,48
Appointments, 506
 accepting, 506

criminal cases, in, 506
declining, 509
lists, 507
Armani, Frank, 421
Associations of lawyers, 48
affinity bar associations, 49
integrated bars, 50
local bar associations, 49
Attorney-client privilege, waiver, 242
Authority, relationship to, 534

Bar admission, 50
character, 52
finances and, 60
Multi-State Professional Responsibility
Exam, 51
personal behavior and, 61
pro hac vice, 88
reciprocity, 51
representations to bar, 60
temporary, 88
Bar application, 53
Bar associations, 48
Berry, John, 53
Billing practices, 200
Business transactions with a client, 392

Cahill, Kimberly, 200
Candid advice, 158
Candor toward tribunals, 300
beyond representation, 307
correcting false statements, 309
definition of tribunal, 306
disclosing legal authority, 310
false statements, 301
misleading silence, 305
offering false evidence, 314
temptation against, 305
Catch-all, 3
Certification, advertising, 491
Character, 52
definition of good, 53
Charges, 33
Charging liens, 203
Client autonomy and sale of a law
practice, 232
Client directives, frivolous, 339
Client property, 214
lawyer trust accounts, 218
interest on, 218
rule against commingling, 217
safekeeping, 215
Client-protection funds, 219

Commingling, rule against, 217
Communication, 142,454
advertising, 454
advice and counsel, 149
authorized by law, 292
between clients, 292
broader advice, 160
candid advice, 158
employees of represented corporation,
with, 299
false or misleading, 454
independent professional judgment, 149
informed consent, 142
registers, 528
unrepresented person, with, 291
authorized by law, 292
subject matter of representation, 294
Communication registers, 528
Compensation, collateral, 398
Competence, 18,114
acquiring proficiency, 116
conduct rule, 114
dimensions of, 115
incompetence, consequences of, 116
excusable neglect, 117
Completing representation, 97
Concurrent conflicts of interest, 374
Conduct rules, generally, 18
Confidentiality, 168
attorney-client privilege, 187
evaluations for third persons, 450
implied authorization to disclose, 173
mitigating crime, 177
organization clients, and, 187
preventing bodily harm, 174
preventing crime or fraud, 186,285
self-protective measures, 186
Conflict-of-interest rules, 372
aggregate settlements, 398
business transactions with a client, 392
client consent to conflicts, 373
client expense, and, 374
client relations, and, 374
collateral compensation, 398
concurrent conflicts of interest, 374
conflict-recognition techniques, 372
current-client conflicts, 374
difficulty of, 372
evaluations for third persons, 446
financial assistance to a client, 397
former-client conflicts, 400
gifts from a client, 393
government service, in, 422

confidential information from, 429
current government lawyer, 432
former government lawyer, 424
    imputed disqualification, and, 426
    negotiating for employment, 426
imputed disqualification, 406,411,414
    associated in a firm, 415
    changing firms, 406
    joining a firm, 422
    leaving firms, 422
    screening, 415
informed consent, 383
malpractice claims, limiting, 399
malpractice claims, settling, 399
multiple adverse representations, 383
nonconsentable conflicts, 382
opinion letters and, 446
positional conflicts, 378
prospective clients, and, 407
    intake procedures, 411
sexual relations with a client, 399
specific conflicts, 388
specificity of, 372
third-party neutrals and, 432,442
    imputed disqualification of, 438
    negotiating for employment, 438
    screening of, 438
transactional conflicts, 387
Consent to conflicts, 373
Constitutional right to testify, 319
Contingency fees, 204
    agreement for, 205
    reasonableness of, 208
Contributions, political, 490
Crime, 177
    mitigating, 177
    preventing, 182
Crimes, by lawyer, 54
Cross-cultural representation, 528
    communication registers, 528
Cross-examination, 271

Decisions to settle, 102
Declining representation, 95-97,113
    grounds, 97
Decorum of the tribunal, 343
    ex-parte communications, 356
    improper communications, 343
    improper influence, 343
    interviewing jurors, 351
    means prohibited by law, 355
    trial publicity, 356
        gag orders, 360

permitted extrajudicial statements, 361
    prejudicing a proceeding, 357
Defending criminal cases, 340
Dilatory actions to impede, 341
    causes and motives for delay, 342
    types of delay, 343
Diligence, 131
    extraordinary circumstances, 134
Diminished-capacity clients, 518
    practical and strategic issues, 522
    representing children, 525
    protective actions for, 525
Disciplinary authority, 22
Discipline procedures, 27
Disclosing legal authority, 310
Disclosure, 33
    inadvertent document, 241
    licensure, of, 457
    metadata, 242
    necessity of, 33
    preventing crime or fraud, 285
Discovery abuses, 251
Disqualification, hardship, 364
Distinguishing current from former clients, 401
Divided representation, 165
Division of fees, 213
Dual representation, 165
Due process, 11
Duty to report misconduct, 37
    time and place of report, 44

Endorsing client's cause, 106
Enforcement, other forms of, 34
Engagement fees, 203
Escusable neglect, 117
Ethics opinions, 20
Ex parte proceedings, 320
Exoneration, 270
Expediting litigation, 340
    causes and motives for delay, 342
    types of delay, 343
Expenses, reasonable, 201

Fairness to opposing party, 243
    discipline for unfairness, 259
    discovery abuses, 251
    economics of unfairness, 252
    interfering with witnesses, 262
    threatening opposing counsel, 252
    zealous advocacy and, 245
Faith, 9

False evidence, offering, 313
    constitutional right to testify, 319
    criminal or fraudulent conduct, 320
    ex-parte proceedings, 320
    knowledge of falsity, 318
    refusal to offer false evidence, 319
Falsehoods, immaterial, 285
Federal and foreign lawyers, 90
Federal prosecutors, 272
Fee sharing with nonlawyers, 12-17
Fees, 190
    attitude toward, 193
    billing practices, 200
    charging liens, 203
    collateral compensation, conflict, 398
    commingling, rule against, 217
    contingency fees, 204
        agreement for, 205
        reasonableness of, 208
    division of, 213
    documenting, 201
    engagement, 203
    lawyer trust accounts, 218
        interest on, 218
    money laundering, 214
    non-refundable, 202
    quantum meruit, 211
    reasonable expenses, 201
    reasonableness of, 195
        determining reasonableness, 200
    regulation of, 194
    retainer, 202
    retaining liens, 203
    types, 190
Fiduciary practice, 214
Finances and bar admission, 60
Financial assistance to a client, 397
Financing practice, 11
Finch, Atticus, 456
First Amendment protection, 472,570
    advertising, 472
    judicial campaigns, 570
    specific advertisements, 482
Fitness, 67
    disability, and, 67
    question of, 43
    substance abuse and, 68
Former clients, distinguishing from current clients, 401
Fraud, preventing, 182
Frivolous claims and contentions, 331
    client directives, 339
    defending criminal cases, 340
    extending or modifying law, 336
    reasonable investigation of, 332
    reversing law, 336

Gag orders, 360
Ghostwriting, 111
Gifts from a client, 393
Goals of discipline, 23
Good character, 53
Government service, lawyers in, 422
    confidential information from, 429
    current government lawyer, 432
    former government lawyer, 424
        imputed disqualification, and, 426
        negotiating for employment, 426
Group legal services, 469

Hearing on discipline charges, 34
Honesty, 279
    representation, course of, 280
Humanism, 9

Imputed disqualification, 406,411,414
    associated in a firm, 415
    changing firms, 406
    joining a firm, 422
    leaving firms, 422
    screening, 415
Inadvertent document disclosure, 241
Independent professional judgment, 149
Independence, of lawyers, 10-11
Inducing others to commit wrongs, 293
Inferring knowledge, 43
Initial review for discipline, 28
Instrumentalism, 7
Intake procedures, 411
Interfering with witnesses, 262
Investigation, request for, 28
Informed consent, 143
Insurance counsel, 154

Judges, 273
    campaigns, judicial, 568
        First Amendment, and, 570
    criticizing, 275
    disqualification, 547
    financial influences, 560
    independence of, 541
    judicial campaigns, 276
    knowing false statements about, 274
    partiality, 541
    personal conduct, 561
    regulating, 534

ABA Code of Judicial Conduct, 535
application of, 539
organization of, 535
preamble, 536
scope, 536
terminology, 537
campaigns, judicial, 568
independence of, 541
partiality, 541
personal conduct, 561
upholding law, 542
upholding law, 542
respect for, 273
Judicial campaigns, 276

Keller, 50
Knowledge, inferring, 43

Law-firm departures, 100
Law-firm letterhead, 458
Law-firm names, 457
Law school admission, 52
Law-related services, 35
Lawyer as witness, 361
advocate nonadjudicative matters, 368
advocate as witness, 361
disqualification as hardship, 364
tactical abuse, 368
permissible dual roles, 364
Lawyer discipline, 22
Lawyer referral services, 471
lawyer-to-lawyer referrals, 472
paying for referrals, 472
Lawyer trust accounts, 218
interest on, 218
Legal aid, 510
Legal officials, respect for, 273
Legal-services organizations, 510
conflicts of interest and, 511
legal aid, 510
legal services programs, 516
Letterhead, law-firm, 458
Levels of discipline, 23
Licensure, 50
disclosure of, 457
other jurisdictions, in, 83
temporary admission, 88
Liens, 203
charging, 203
retaining, 203
Limited-scope representation, 107
appeals, 112
ghostwriting, 111

Limiting liability, 135
Litigation, withdrawing from, 98
grounds for, 99
retaining liens, 99
Lobbying by integrated bar, 50
Loyalty, 371
persistent, 400
value of, 371
Low bono service, 504

Magna Carta, 10
Malpractice, 122
causation, 126
challenges to claim for, 129
defenses to claim of, 130
errors in judgment, 124
ineffective assistance of counsel, 135
insurance for, 130
policy, types of, 130
limiting liability for, 135,399
non-client liability, 125
settling liability for, 135,399
Malpractice insurance, 130
policies, types of, 130
Managerial authority, 219
Mandatory rules, 19
Marketing, 470
Mental health, 72
compensating tools, 72
service to others, 74
Meritorious contentions, 326
bringing & defending proceedings, 326
client directives, 339
defending criminal cases, 340
extending or modifying law, 336
frivolousness, determining, 331
reasonable investigation of, 332
reversing law, 336
Metadata, 242
Misconduct, 3
Mitigating crime, 182
Mixed legal services, 35
Morality, 8
Money laundering, 214
Multi-State Professional
Responsibility Exam, 51
timing, 51
Multi-jurisdictional practice, 88
federal and foreign lawyers, 90
Muth, Jon, 8

Nifong, Michael, 266
Non-lawyer assistants, supervision of,

228
Non-refundable fees, 202
Nuremberg defense, 223

O'Connor, Sandra Day, 339
Obtaining evidence, 241
Opinion letters, conflicts, 446
Opinions, ethics, 20
Organization as client, 161
    authorized constituents, 162
    confidentiality, 187
    reporting up, 163
    reporting out, 163
    Sarbanes-Oxley Act, 163
Organization of the bar, 47
Overreaching, preventing, 291

Parallel sanctions, 327
Personal behavior and bar admission, 61
Perspectives, 2
    choices, 6
    complexity, 3
    faith, 9
    guidance, 5
    humanism, 9
    identity, 5
    instrumentalism, 7
    legacy, 4
    morality, 8
    necessity, 2
    pragmatism, 6
    realism, 8
    reflexivity, 4
    reputation, 5
    significance, 2
    worldviews, 6
Plea negotiation, 272
Political contributions, 490
Pragmatism, 6
Preventing crime or fraud, 182
Privileged information, 44
    waiver of privilege, 242
Pro bono service, 498
    aspirational goal, 500
    business imperative, 499
    defining, 504
    distinguishing, 505
    low bono, 504
    quality of representation, 505
    social imperative, 498
    value of, 498
Pro hac vice admission, 88
Procedures for discipline, 27

Professionalism, 35
    beyond the minimum, 36
    significance of, 35
    styles of, 36
Profit sharing with nonlawyers, 12-17
Prosecutor, 264
    cross-examination, 272
    federal, 272
    plea negotiation, 272
    special duties, 264
    suppressing evidence, 265
Prospective client, defined, 95
    conflicts and, 407
        intake procedures, 411
Public statements, 270

Quantum meruit, 211

Reading rules, 19
Realism, 8
Reasonable investigation, 332
Reciprocity, 51
Referral services, 471
    lawyer-to-lawyer referrals, 472
    paying for referrals, 472
Regulations governing lawyers, 21
Reporting misconduct, 37
    duty to report, 37
    time and place for, 44
Representation, 94
    accepting, 96
    completing, 97
    course of, honesty during, 280
    declining, 95-96, 113
        grounds, 97
    definition of, 94-95
    divided, 165
    dual, 165
    limited scope, 107
        appeals, 112
        ghostwriting, 111
    scope of, 100
    terminating, 95, 98
    unbundled services, 107
    withdrawal from, 113
Representation of respondent lawyers, 33
Representations to bar, 60
Represented corporations, 298
    managerial employees of, 298
    other employees of, 299
Represented persons, 291
    communication with, 292
    overreaching, preventing, 291

respect for, 291
Request for investigation, 28-29
Respect for adversaries, 243
Respect for judges, 273
knowing false statements, 273
Respect toward others, 236
Responsibility for nonlawyer assistants, 229
Responsibility of partners, 220
Responsibility of subordinate, 224
mitigating factors, 228
Restrictions on practice, 90
Retainer fees, 202
non-refundable fees, 202
Retaining liens, 203
Roberts, Victoria A., 293
Role consistency, 361
advocate nonadjudicative matters, 368
advocate as witness, 361
disqualification as hardship, 364
tactical abuse, 368
permissible dual roles, 364
Rule of law, 10
Ruses, 284

Safekeeping property, 215
Sale of a law practice, 232
client autonomy and, 232
conditions of, 233
Sarbanes-Oxley Act, 163,450
regulations under, 164
Scope of representation, 100
Second opinions, 298
Self-representation, 80
Service to others, 74
Settle, decisions to, 102
Settling malpractice liability, 135
Sexual relations with a client, 399
Sources, 10
Solicitation, 459
access to legal services and, 469
ambulance chasing, 465
educational information and, 470
group legal services, 469
real-time communication, 465
Solovy, Jerold 4
Specialties, advertising, 491
Standards for imposing discipline, 23
Statutes governing lawyers, 21
Subordinate lawyers, 223
mitigating factors, 228
Substance abuse and fitness, 68,72
Substantial question of fitness, 43

Supervising trust accounts, 232
Supervision of lawyers, 219
mitigating factors, 228
subordinate lawyers, 223
Supervision of nonlawyers, 228
delegating responsibly, 228
Supervisory lawyers, 220
Suppressing evidence, 266

Temporary admission, 88
Terminating representation, 95,98
Terminology, 45
Third-party neutrals, conflicts, 432,442
imputed disqualification of, 438
negotiating for employment, 438
screening of, 438
Third persons, respect for, 237
obtaining evidence, 241
Threatening opposing counsel, 252
Trial procedures, violating, 264
Trial publicity, 356
gag orders, 360
permitted extrajudicial statements, 361
prejudicing a proceeding, 357
Tribunal decorum, 343
ex-parte communications, 356
improper communications, 343
improper influence, 343
interviewing jurors, 351
means prohibited by law, 355
trial publicity, 356
gag orders, 360
permitted extrajudicial statements, 361
prejudicing a proceeding, 357
Truthfulness, 279
candor toward tribunals, 300
immaterial falsehoods, 285
in statements to others, 281
knowledge of falsity, 283
offering false evidence, 313
ruses, 284

Unauthorized practice, 74
administrative proceedings, 80
definition of practice, 75
ghostwriting, 111
licensure in other jurisdictions, 83
self-representation and, 81
Unbundling services, 107
Unrepresented persons, 286
advising, 290
communication between clients, 292

dealing with, 287
disclosing interests to, 286

Veasey, Norman, 121
Violating court rules, 263
    trial procedures, 264

Waiver of privilege, 242
Websites, advertising using, 486
    interactive websites, 486
Withdrawing from litigation, 98,113
    grounds for, 99
    retaining liens, 99
Witness, lawyer as, 361
    advocate nonadjudicative matters, 368
    advocate as witness, 361
    disqualification as hardship, 364
        tactical abuse, 368
    permissible dual roles, 364
Witnesses, 262
    cross-examination, 271
    interfering with, 262
Worldviews, 6

Zealous advocacy, 245

CPSIA information can be obtained at www.ICGtesting.com
Printed in the USA
BVOW060042111111

275484BV00004B/2/P